GRECO-ROMAN WATERS

The first of its kind, this book presents a wide range of passages exploring many aspects of the Greco-Roman watery world: physics, philosophy, weather, medicine, marine biology, religion and mythology, infrastructure, sailing, mercantile activities, and waterways that have been politicized.

Offering a deep look at the many ways that water culture impacted the ancient world, both abstractly and tangibly, this collection provides a glimpse into the ancient mind and lived experience. It includes passages from literary, documentary, and visual evidence, organized along seven over-arching themes: "The Science of Water," "Water and Living Creatures," "Water in Religion and Myth," "Water and Society," "Humans on the Water," "Mercantile Waters," and "Conquering the Waters." Each selection is introduced by a contextualizing, exegetical paragraph. Explanatory notes assist with unfamiliar concepts; additional readings (both modern and ancient) are suggested; and cross references show the links between sections and topics.

Greco-Roman Waters: A Sourcebook is suitable for students and scholars of ancient science and technology, the ancient environment, and the history of science, as well as those interested in the philosophy, intellectual culture, and environmental attitudes of the ancient Greco-Roman Mediterranean world.

Georgia L. Irby is Professor of Classical Studies at William and Mary, USA. Her publications include *Conceptions of the Watery World*, *Using and Conquering the Watery World*, *A Companion to Science, Technology, and Medicine in Ancient Greece and Rome*, and *Encyclopedia of Ancient Natural Scientists* (with Paul T. Keyser).

Routledge Sourcebooks for the Ancient World

Recent titles include:

Pagans and Christians in Late Antiquity
A Sourcebook, 2nd edition
A.D. Lee

Greek and Roman Technology
A Sourcebook of Translated Greek and Roman Texts, 2nd edition
Andrew N. Sherwood, Milorad Nikolic, John W. Humphrey, and John P. Oleson

Italy Before Rome
A Sourcebook
Katherine McDonald

Sexuality in Greek and Roman Society and Literature
A Sourcebook, 2nd edition
Marguerite Johnson

Ancient Women Writers of Greece and Rome
Bartolo A. Natoli, Angela Pitts, Judith P. Hallett

Greco-Roman Waters
A Sourcebook
Georgia L. Irby

For a full list of titles in this series, please visit https://www.routledge.com/Routledge-Sourcebooks-for-the-Ancient-World/book-series/RSAW

GRECO-ROMAN WATERS

A Sourcebook

Georgia L. Irby

LONDON AND NEW YORK

First published 2025
by Routledge
4 Park Square, Milton Park, Abingdon, Oxon OX14 4RN

and by Routledge
605 Third Avenue, New York, NY 10158

Routledge is an imprint of the Taylor & Francis Group, an informa business

British Library Cataloguing-in-Publication Data
A catalogue record for this book is available from the British Library

Library of Congress Cataloging-in-Publication Data
Names: Irby, Georgia L. (Georgia Lynette), 1965– author
Title: Greco-Roman waters : a sourcebook / Georgia L. Irby.
Description: Abingdon, Oxon ; New York, NY : Routledge, 2025. | Series: Routledge sourcebooks for the ancient world | Includes bibliographical references and index.
Identifiers: LCCN 2024058800 (print) | LCCN 2024058801 (ebook) | ISBN 9781032569314 cloth | ISBN 9781032569307 paperback | ISBN 9781003437741 ebook
Subjects: LCSH: Water and civilization—Greece | Water and civilization—Rome | Hydrology—Greece | Hydrology—Rome
Classification: LCC DF78 .I73 2025 (print) | LCC DF78 (ebook) | DDC 938—dc23/eng/20250325
LC record available at https://lccn.loc.gov/2024058800
LC ebook record available at https://lccn.loc.gov/2024058801

ISBN: 978-1-032-56931-4 (hbk)
ISBN: 978-1-032-56930-7 (pbk)
ISBN: 978-1-003-43774-1 (ebk)

DOI: 10.4324/9781003437741

Typeset in Times New Roman
by Apex CoVantage, LLC

CONTENTS

IMAGE AND MAP CREDITS

ANCIENT WEIGHTS AND MEASUREMENTS

amphora: Roman, 48 sextarii, c. 27.84 liters (7.36 gallons)
congius: Roman, 1/8 of an amphora, c. 3.6 liters (c. 6.4 pints)
digit: Roman, 1/16 Roman foot, 18.5 millimeters (0.73 inch)
hippicon (c. 2,300 feet = c. 710 meters)
hydria: Greek, c. 20 liters (5 gallons)
iugerum: 240 by 120 Roman paces (about 1/4 of a hectare or about 0.6 acres)
orguia: c. 6 feet (1.8 meters)
pace (Roman foot): 11.65 inches = 29.6 centimeters
parasang: Persian, 30 *stadia*
pechus/pecheis: Greek, "cubit," the distance from the elbow to the tip of the middle finger (c. half a meter or 18 inches)
quinaria: Roman, c. 4.2 square centimeters (0.65 square inches)
Roman mile = 1,000 double paces (c. 4,854 feet or 1,480 meters): slightly shorter than the English mile (5,280 feet = 1,609.3 meters)
sextarius: Roman, about a pint
stadium: 600 Greek feet (not standardized) based on the length of the local stadium

Olympian: c. 630 feet/192.8 meters
Athenian: c. 607 feet/185 meters
Egyptian c. 516 feet/157.5 meters

GREEK AND ROMAN COINS

denarius: standard Roman silver coin, worth 10 *asses*

drachma: standard Greek coin, usually silver (sometimes gold), minted by each city-state with variable weight (Attic = c. 4.3 grams [0.15 ounces])

mina: Near Eastern, Attic mina was c. 436.6 grams (15.40 ounces), worth about 10 sheep

quadrans: Roman: a very low-value bronze coin (a fourth part of some larger coin) worth one-quarter of an *as*

as: aes grave: a large early Roman coin, bronze, 272, 327, or 341 grams (0.6, 0.72, 0.75 ounces)

sesterces: Roman, 1/4 of a *denarius*

talent: a weight of gold or silver, standardized as 100 Roman pounds

ABBREVIATIONS

AE	*L'Année épigraphique*
AWP	Hippocratic *Airs, Waters, Places*
BC	Caesar, *Civil Wars*
BG	Caesar, *Gallic Wars*
CIL	*Corpus Inscriptionum Latinarum* (17 vols.: Berlin: https://cil.bbaw.de/en/homenavigation/the-cil/volumes)
DK	Hermann Diels and Walther Kranz. 1906–1922. *Die Fragmente der Vorsokratiker.* 3 vols. (Berlin)
FGrHist	Felix Jacoby. 1923–. *Die Fragmente der griechischen Historiker* (Berlin)
HA	Aristotle, *Inquiry into Animals*
HP	Theophrastus, *Inquiry into Plants*
IG	*Inscriptiones Graecae* (15 vols.: Berlin-Brandenburg Academy of Sciences and Humanities: http://telota.bbaw.de/ig/)
ILS	Hermann Dessau. 1892–1916. *Inscriptiones Latinae Selectae.* 3 vols. (Berlin)
NA	Aelian, *Characteristics of Animals*
NH	Pliny, *Natural History*
NQ	= Seneca, *Natural Questions*
PA	Aristotle, *Parts of Animals*
RIB	R.G. Collingwood and R.P. Wright. 1955–. *Roman Inscriptions of Britain.* (Oxford): https://romaninscriptionsofbritain.org/
TEGP	Daniel W. Graham. 2010. *The Texts of Early Greek Philosophy: The Complete Fragments and Selected Testimonies of the Major Presocratics.* 2 vols. Cambridge.

ACKNOWLEDGMENTS

This collection has its genesis in a course that I have the privilege of teaching to first year students at William and Mary, "Why Water Matters," where students learn about the fluidity of critical inquiry and the scholarly process as an interplay between primary sources, scholarly training, and the scholar's own cultural biases or even political prejudices. Together we investigate critical questions regarding human engagement with the natural world; our sources of information; the advantages and disadvantages of those sources (often fragmentary, poorly preserved, inadequately contextualized, and insufficiently curated); and our understanding, perception, and interpretation of those sources: that is to say, how social, cultural, and political factors influence our perception of the environment; and how our own attitudes to the natural world shape our culture, art, literature, and politics. This sourcebook is very much the product of that conversation, as are my two water volumes with Bloomsbury (2021).

I am, as ever, grateful to the Inter-Library Loan Staff at Swem Library at William and Mary, who sometimes even seem to anticipate the needs of their patrons, as well as the cheerful, knowledgeable, and efficient staff in Information Technology who keep my digital resources in good working order.

I am profoundly grateful to the Loeb Classical Library Foundation whose generous grant subsidized a year-long research leave that allowed me the space and time to concentrate on two book-length projects, including this one, with minimal distraction. I am also deeply indebted to Thorsten Fögen, William H. Hutton, Duane W. Roller, and Richard J.A. Talbert for their consistent support and encouragement over the years. Professor Roller, in addition, read the entire draft. As always, his eagle-eye caught many infelicities, and his encyclopedic comments have improved

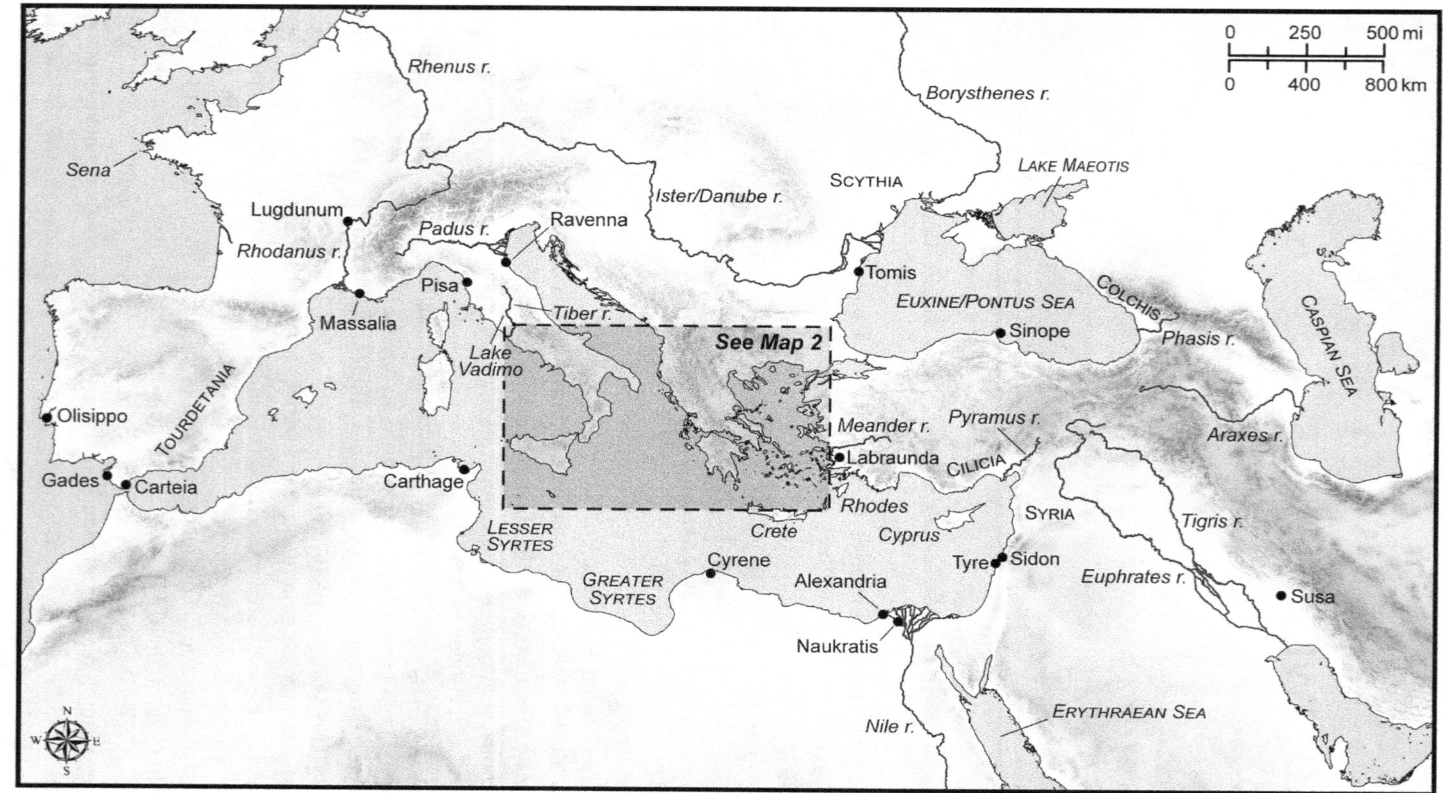

MAP 1 The Mediterranean and Middle East (*Ancient World Mapping Center*)

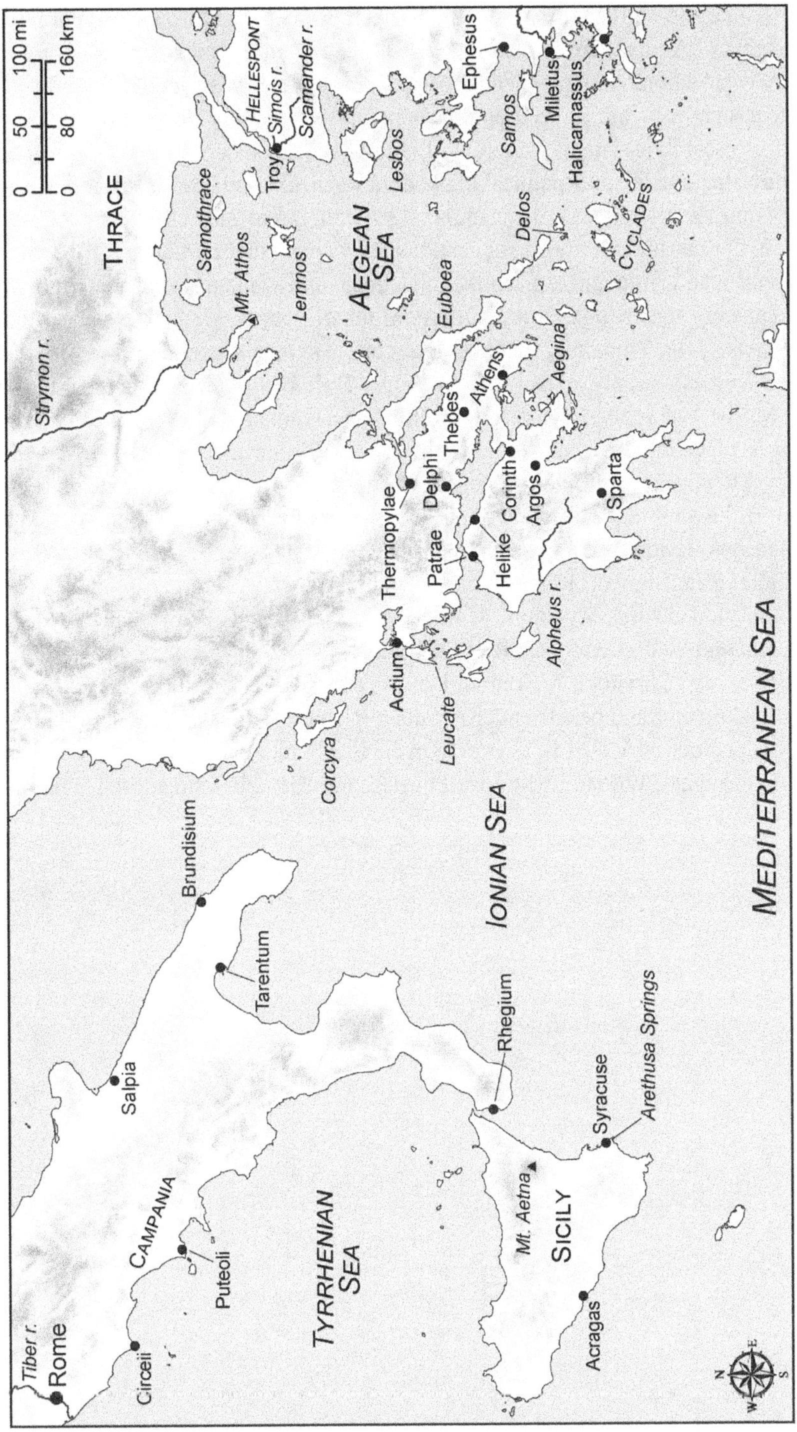

MAP 2 Italy and Greece (*Ancient World Mapping Center*)

the substance and spirit of the text. This project also benefited from the comments and insights of Andrea Brock who likewise read the entire manuscript, pointing to me to new questions and new scholarship. I am, beyond description, grateful for their generosity of time as well as their encouragement. My deepest thanks also go to my research assistant, Angélique Lemarchand, who scrupulously examined the entire manuscript and painstakingly double-checked all the translations and primary-source references. She caught slips both great and small and offered countless thoughtful and useful suggestions. Any errors that remain are my own.

I should also to recognize friends, colleagues, and students whose encouragement keeps my spirits high: Tejas Aralere, Mitchell Brown, Michael Bryant, Mike Crookshank, John Donahue, Andrew Francois, Michael Gaynes, Joyce Holmes with her endless supply of smiles and hugs, Bob Holschuh Simmons, Martha Jones, Molly Ayn Jones-Lewis, Jeanne and Toby Kinnett, Jake Kirchner (*sit tibi terra levis*), Justin Jones, Gayle and Butch Kubala, Steve Link, Robin McCall, Phaedra McNorton, Antoinette Marold, Elizabeth Mead, Robin McCall, Pete Moxon, Bill Napolitano, Jasmane Ormand, Rebecca Paynter, Lily Panoussi, Huntley Polanshek, Linda Reilly, Jessamyn Rising, Jennifer Roberts, Letty Roller, Russ Sage, Sibel Zandi-Sayak, Rebecca and Marshall Scheetz, Georgia Scotts Renck, Byron Stayskal, Jessica Stephens, Molly Swetnam-Burland, Yumi Suzuki, Joseph Valles, Jim and Wendy Waldeck, Rich Watkins, Ben Zhang, and my mentors James C. Anderson and Christoph F. Konrad. I am, as ever, indebted to John L. Robinson, my nautical mentor and best friend. My father, Richard E. Irby, from whom I inherited my capacious curiosity, is, as ever, woven deeply into the fabric of these pages, as are my brothers, William, who loved turtles, and Richard, who adored William.

INTRODUCTION

Water is an essential resource for life on earth, and water access and purity remains a perennial, global concern, considering, for example, infrastructure failures in Flint, MI, and Jackson, MS, which left many residents of a "first-world country" without access to clean, reliable water. More seriously are the cascading effects of poverty, war, and pandemic on the water supplies in less wealthy global regions. Water is perhaps the clearest metric of climate change, manifested through the binary extremes of drought and super-storms. Seventy-one percent of the earth is covered in water, and water—the earth's only self-renewing vital resource—exists in the air as vapor and as moisture in the soil. The human body (over 50% water) cannot survive without water for more than a few days. Finally, as the world's population grows, access to clean, safe water becomes increasingly politicized, and the next great war, so political theorists speculate, will likely be over water.

Water is also the most visible natural resource in Mediterranean antiquity. The sea was the lifeline of Greek communities, the great equalizer that separated island-*poleis* and helped develop the strong Greek sense of independence. Water connected communities and provided sustenance through fishing as well as wealth. Water caused disease and promoted healing. Water was the playground of maritime deities and the abode of terrifying sea monsters. Ancient Mediterranean peoples conquered water with ships, and they aimed to ameliorate maritime gods with rituals.

Thus, it only follows that the ancients, curious about every aspect of their environment, would also think deeply about water in all its aspects and attempt to harness its powers (through agriculture, sailing, ritual purity, and hydraulic engineering which could convey water into even the thirstiest deserts) and mitigate its threats (flooding, storms, water-borne diseases). Understanding and controlling water thus puts an Anthropocene stamp on the natural world and increases the divide between the human animal and the environment.

DOI: 10.4324/9781003437741-1

The passages in this sourcebook present how Greco-Roman thinkers, authors, and statesmen understood, appreciated, and manipulated water in all its aspects from theoretical, magical, mythological to practical, legal, political.

Water as a Bounding Principle

The Mediterranean Sea dominates Greco-Roman antiquity, and its very name suggests the significance of water to Greco-Roman culture. The Greeks called it *Thalassa* ("the Sea," "this Sea," or "our Sea").[1] The Romans called it *Mare Nostrum* ("Our Sea").[2] While *Mare Nostrum* may have been the cartographic center. From the time of Homer, the map was framed by the circumambient Ocean (Homer, *Iliad* 18.483–490, *Odyssey* 5.275). Moreover, the early cartographers Anaximander and Hekataeus proposed that prominent rivers separate major landmasses: the Nile River flows between Libya (Africa) and Asia, the Tanais River and the Pontus separates Asia from Europe, the Mediterranean Sea delimits Europe from Libya. This paradigm would endure. Plato, moreover, would describe the peoples dwelling between the Phasis River and Pillars of Herakles as "living around the sea like ants or frogs around a marsh" (*Phaedo* 109b). These rivers and seas were teeming with fish and traffic; they demarked and connected places and people, and they served conveniently as lines on theoretical maps.

Water was also central to Greco-Roman cultural identity. The sea dominates both the landscape and mythscape: Herakles, Jason, and Odysseus traveled by sea. Fanciful sea monsters were envisaged in both myth and zoology. Sea-faring accounts in Greco-Roman literature, moreover, are vivid, technical, and detailed, owing to deep thoughtfulness about the sea in all its moods: Odysseus employed celestial navigation (#5.1.11A), and Aeneas' helmsman Palinurus was a master of the art (#5.1.3C). Storms at sea are realistically interpreted (#1.9.11B; Lucan, *Pharsalia* 1.498–503). The sea was the *lingua franca* of the ancient world: literature and popular culture were misted with nautical references, analogies, and metaphors, most notably Plato's ship of state (#7.2.3).

Water was also a focus of ritual and myth. In the Greek pantheon, two powerful Olympian gods represented binary aspects of the sea: Poseidon, the Earth-Shaker and cause of storms at sea, embodied the wild, unpredictable nature of the sea (#3.11.1); Athena subjugated Poseidon's roiling sea with the technology of sailing

1 ἡ θάλασσα: the Sea (e.g., *Iliad* 2.294, *Odyssey* 5.413); ἡ μεγάλη θάλασσα: the Great Sea (Arrian, *Indika* 2.7); ἡ ἡμέτερα θάλασσα: Our Sea (Plato, *Phaedo* 113a; Aelian, *NA* 12.25; Strabo 1.2.29); ἥδε ἡ θάλασσα: this sea (Herodotus 1.1, 185, 4.39); τῆς νῦν ἑλληνικῆς θαλάσσης: the Hellenic Sea (Herodotus 5.54, Thucydides 1.5; Plutarch, *Cimon* 13); ἡ θάλαττα ἡ καθ' ημάς: the sea around us (Polybius 1.3.9); ἡ παρ' ἡμῖν θάλασσα: the Sea near us (Plato, *Phaedo* 113a; Strabo 2.5.18); πέλαγός τε θαλάσσης: the deep sea of salt-water (Apollonius, *Argonautica* 4.608).

2 "Mediterranean" did not come into common use until the 6th century CE, recorded as such by Isidore of Seville (*Etymologies or Origins* 9.1.8). This represents a paradigm shift as emphasis was transferred from sea (*mare*) to land *(terra)*.

(boats and navigation) that enabled humanity's maritime conquest (#7.2.4). Rituals also accompanied sailing expeditions (#3.11). Water, moreover, was an agent of cultic purification and absolute destruction which could punish humans for hubris against the gods (#3.6).

Gods explored water, and natural philosophers theorized about it. The Titan Atlas is said to have seen the "depths" of the entire sea (*Odyssey* 1.52–53), and Plato's *Phaedo* imagines the deep-water realm (#1.3.3E), an analog to his famous allegory of the cave (109b–13d). According to *The Alexander Romance* (3rd century CE, five centuries after Alexander's death), Alexander descended in a spherical glass submarine in order to discover what was on the seabed. This charming but apocryphal tale speaks to humanity's intense curiosity about the watery realm, the dominant geographical feature of the Mediterranean world, the sea.

Ancient Sources

Theoretical knowledge about water was seamlessly aligned with geography, astronomy, meteorology, biology, and much else, all of which was informed by philosophical prejudice. Despite the fragmentary nature of the evidence, it is possible to tease out Greco-Roman knowledge, understanding, interpretation, and use of water (including oceans and seas) from a long scholarly tradition. Knowledge of rivers, lakes, and the sea was systematically gathered on a global scale. Alexander's admiral, Nearchus (360–300 BCE), for example, collected important hydrological data in India, and Arrian's *Periplus of the Euxine Sea* is invaluable for hydrology of the Black Sea in the 1st century CE. Pytheas of Massalia (Alexander's contemporary) and Posidonius of Apamea (135–51 BCE), moreover, each composed books entitled *On Ocean,* neither of which survives aside from a few scant fragments.

Other authors wrote more broadly on water. Thales (6th century BCE) was the first Greek natural philosopher, and his rational explanations of the world begin with water, whether as a generative element or catalyst, we cannot know. What is clear is that Thales understood that life simply cannot exist without water. In Empedocles' (b. c. 480 BCE) four-element theory, water is one of the four essential building blocks of the material world. Aristotle (384–322 BCE) also thought deeply and wrote about the nature of water (*Meteorology* 1.12–2.3), as did his student Theophrastus (c. 371–287 BCE), whose *On Waters* survives partly, but only in Arabic (Sharples and Gutas 1998: 190–219). Theophrastus also wrote *On Fish* (extant in Greek: Diogenes Laërtius, *Life of Theophrastus* 47; Sharples 1992: 347–385) and *On the Sea* (lost). Finally, Plutarch (c. 40–120 CE) debated the relative merits of water and fire and in his short *Whether Fire or Water Is More Useful* (#1.1.2). Also invaluable for watery matters in particular is Seneca the Younger's (4 BCE to CE 65) *Natural Questions*, which probably opened with his account of terrestrial waters (the order of the books is disputed) and includes lengthy considerations of meteorological phenomena. Other essential sources include geographical authors

(Eratosthenes, Strabo), travelers' accounts and coasting guides (*Periploi*), Pliny the Elder's (23/24–79 CE) encyclopedic *Natural History*, and poets in Greek (Homer, Aeschylus, Pindar) and Latin (Vergil, Ovid, among others). In addition, marine animals receive dedicated attention in Oppian of Anazarbus' (2nd century CE) *On Fishing*, a versified account of the fauna of the deep sea; and Aelian of Praeneste's (3rd century CE) *On the Nature of Animals*, relying heavily on earlier sources (including Pliny, *NH* books 9, 32).

Understanding and explaining the nature of water enables control over it. Technology—control over nature—was Prometheus' gift to humanity, which, together with the art of sailing, enabled human beings to expand influence and access to resources, not just along coastal waters, but beyond the Pillars of Herakles.[3] These *technai* ("skills") facilitate human control over the natural world, and Plutarch was one of many ancient thinkers who would argue that the natural world thus becomes all the more valuable when it has been "improved" by human intervention (#1.1.2). Water, consequently, affects every aspect of daily and civic life, and water-concerns include access, collection and storage, and private and public comfort and health. Hydraulic installations (aqueducts, dams, canals, harbors, fountains, baths) proved indispensable to daily life, but their function as symbols of authority and munificence was just as important. Julius Frontinus' (40–103 CE) *Aqueducts* is indisputably the most important literary source for Roman hydraulic engineering. Moreover, seas and rivers fed consumers with tuna and other delicacies, including garum (#6.4.3), a byproduct of the salt-fishing industry and widely-used culinary relish. Trade was conducted along the roads of the Mediterranean (quicker, cheaper, and more comfortable by water than by land).

Modern Studies

Modern scholars have considered both theoretical and practical engagement with ancient waters. Albin Lesky (1947) focused on the evolution of the ancient Greek relationship with the sea, including mythology, as a process of adaptation from landlocked peoples to coastal settlers. Wachsmuth (1967) has marshalled evidence for nautical cults. Corvisier (2008) viewed the Greek attitude to the sea as ambivalent: while inhospitable, the sea also fosters commerce and inspires mythology. Horden and Purcell (2000) investigated the complex links between people and the micro-ecologies of the Mediterranean region. Broodbank's magisterial volume (2013) treats geological, topographical, and ecological changes in the Mediterranean's basin at length. Beaulieu (2016) focused on the symbolic resonance of aquatic mythology. Hydraulic infrastructure, moreover, has been a particularly fertile node of scrutiny (see in particular Wikander 2000). Other studies focus on aspects of the ancient world as they relate to the sea, including marine resources (Marzano 2013),

3 Cf. Aeschylus, *Prometheus Bound* 437–471; Irby-Massie 2008.

piracy (de Souza 1999), naval warfare (Mason 2003; DeSantis 2017; Rees 2019; Bradford 2019), navigation (Arnaud 2005; Kowalski 2012; Beresford 2013), and ships (Morrison 1968; Casson 1995; McGrail 2001; Pitassi 2011).

Methodology

The collection of passages here is curated broadly (both geographically and temporally) from Greek and Roman literary and documentary sources on watery matters in the ancient world. While our focus is on Greece (Athens, in particular, where the evidence is particularly rich) and Rome (which likewise has a robust archive), Greco-Roman culture permeated the Mediterranean Basin and beyond. The evidence takes us from the Black Sea to the Erythraean Sea to Britain to Ultima Thule. Our earliest written source is the Greek epic poet Homer (8th century BCE); our latest sources include Justinian's *Digest* (6th century CE). While the vast quantity of evidence militates against comprehensiveness, my hope is that this sourcebook is a lively, informative, and representative selection that sheds insight into the Greco-Roman experience of their watery world: how they understood it, imagined it, employed it, abused it, manipulated it to conquer the natural environment and improve their own existence.

The material falls into seven broad categories, each introduced with brief explanatory paragraphs. In the "The Science of Water," the focus is on the physics and nature of water: What is the world made of and how does it come into being? How do lakes differ from seas? How do we explain density, salinity, tidal activity? What is the relationship between land and water? How do we account for seemingly paradoxical watery phenomena: underground rivers, floating islands, and waters that, for example, change the color of cattle who drink from them or induce intoxication? How do we explain weather events: clouds, rain, thunder, snow?

In "Water and Living Creatures," we focus on the effects of water on human health: water-borne illnesses (e.g., typhoid) and healing springs. We also survey ancient understandings of aquatic and amphibious flora and fauna. Aristotle studied many marine fauna (cephalopods, dolphins, octopods, etc.), comprehending some of what he observed, missing the mark on other aspects (e.g., the function of the blowhole [#2.2.11C] or baleen [#2.2.12A]). Theophrastus, likewise, examined and classified marine flora, including "seaweed of a marvelous size" (#2.3.2B).

In "Water In Religion and Myths," we turn to the spiritual and unobservable aspects of water culture. We consider water gods (#3.1) including Ocean who was thought to be the source of all gods, the hybrid Triton, the metamorphic Thetis. Objects in water are shaped by the watery environment and are able to transform into other shapes, thus giving rise to watery hybrids (#3.2–3.5): seahorses, capricorns, and sea monsters. Water, moreover, was a powerful focus of ritual, as a force of purification and symbol of death (#3.10). Finally, sailors have always been superstitious (#3.11), cultivating marine gods with simple and complex rites and praying to gods who could avert storms, mitigate seasickness, or generally aid those who travel by sea.

In "WATER AND SOCIETY," our focus is on water management and infrastructure. We investigate water access (#4.1) and quality (#4.2), urban planning (#4.4), and hydraulic infrastructure as it enhances human life within communities (#4.5–7): aqueducts, sewers, irrigation, water clocks, hydraulic machines. There were, moreover, attempts to reclaim land from marshes (#4.8) and even create artificial waters (#4.9). The Romans, moreover, engaged in destructive hydraulic mining (#4.10).

In "HUMANS ON THE WATER," we explore the rich culture of sailing in the Mediterranean, including the history of Mediterranean sailing and long-distance sails, the military sailing season, technical aspects of sailing, knowledge of the winds and navigating by bearings and signs from nature (#5.1). Our passages also delve into how "ordinary" folk were able to travel by sea and what obstacles they may have faced (#5.2: ferries, seasickness). Also of importance is the infrastructure that facilitated sailing: harbors were constructed and dredged, canals shortened the distance of journeys, bridges allowed traffic across rivers, and lighthouses guided sailors safely to harbor (#5.3). Sailors also left messages on stone recording the gods they worshipped, gifts made to fellow sailors, honors paid to deceased companions (#5.4).

In "MERCANTILE WATERS," we consider commercial concerns: trade routes, hubs, the mercantile sailing season (#6.1); threats to trade (piracy: #6.2). In addition, many luxury goods were harvested from the sea, and we explore methods of collecting and processing marine commodities, both practical (fish, salt, sponges, garum: #6.3–4) and luxury (murex purple, pearls, coral: #6.5).

In the last part, "CONQUERING THE WATERS," we consider how powerful men politicized waterways and how waterways and maritime activities created and bolstered local identity and contributed to "national" identity and empire-building. Athens forefronted their naval victory against the invading Persians at Salamis (#7.2). The Tiber River was central to Rome's development and identity (#7.4.1). Augustan propaganda emphasized the naval victory at Actium (#7.4.3). *Naumachia* at Rome underscored the city's far reach of authority (#7.4.4). And Britain, beyond Ocean (the Atlantic), served as a vanity project for Roman emperors, again and again, as proof of *Oceanus Domitus* (#7.4.5).

This material complements my two water monographs (*Conceptions of the Watery World in Greco-Roman Antiquity* and *Using and Conquering the Watery World in Greco-Roman Antiquity*, 2021): the genesis of those two volumes came from a first-year course that I offer at William and Mary (*Why Water Matters*). It is my hope that the contextualizing sentences will make this exciting body of work approachable and comprehensible even to those who lack nuanced experience with classical antiquity. Interest in the environment is not new. Greco-Roman thinkers and writers were well aware of environmental effects, and they aimed to understand, mitigate, or control them. The environment, then as now, affects every aspect of life on earth, and this sourcebook offers a glimpse into Greco-Roman daily, civic, ritual, and political life as the ancients engaged with what was arguably their most abundant and important resource, water.

While the topic is image-rich, practical considerations limit how many illustrations can be included, and I have necessarily been selective in creating figures and choosing images that depict unusual and less accessible concepts.

Translations and Transliterations

All translations are my own unless otherwise specified. By its very nature, translation is an act of interpretation. I have, nonetheless, aimed (within the parameters of English idiom) to be as faithful as possible to the original texts in order to represent the ancient voices as closely as possible and preserve their charming idiosyncrasies, which should then give the reader a better taste of how ancient Greek and Roman writers viewed the watery world.

The transliteration of Greek is contentious, as scholars debate whether to retain the Anglicized spellings or to Hellenize them for greater fidelity with the original language. In the interest of accessibility, "traditional" Anglicized orthography of most familiar Greek names is used (though some Hellenized spellings are also employed for less familiar names). Although Sokrates (Socrates) and Empedokles (Empedocles) or Theophrastos (Theophrastus) should cause no confusion, Aristoteles (Aristotle), Epikouros (Epicurus), and Dioskourides (Dioscorides) may raise eyebrows, and Herakleitos (Heraclitus) may seem like a mystifying string of unpronounceable letters. Despite existing conventions and every effort at consistency, T.E. Lawrence's thoughts on the transliteration of Arabic names remain applicable to any effort at transliteration:

> Arabic names won't go into English, exactly, for their consonants are not the same as ours, and their vowels, like ours, vary from district to district. There are some "scientific systems" of transliteration, helpful to people who know enough Arabic not to need helping, but a wash-out for the world.
>
> (Seven Pillars of Wisdom. *New York: Doubleday reprint 1991, 21)*

PART I

The Science of Water

Here we investigate how ancient thinkers understood and interpreted watery phenomena, that is to say, the science of water. The first rational Greek thinker, Thales of Miletus, viewed the world as shaped by water: whether water was the formative material of the world or a catalyst for physical change in Thales' system remains unclear. Nonetheless, water remained an essential component of Greek physics (#1.2), as one of the four material elements (together with earth, air, and fire). Water, changed by salt, filled the much-scrutinized sea and ocean which dominated Greek mythology, commerce, warfare, and cartography. This salt-sea, furthermore, invited many questions about its nature and differences from fresh water (#1.3), and it interacted with earth, shaping coastlines and cycling between wet and dry (#1.4). The salt-sea was also fed by rivers that coursed through the lands: we consider just a very few of the more remarkable rivers (#1.5) together with the seemingly remarkable phenomenon of underground rivers (#1.6). Some waters also defied expectation, behaving in contradictory or paradoxical ways (#1.7) and supporting floating islands (#1.8).

1.1 Introduction

1.1.1 Best Is Water

Pindar (c. 518–438 BCE) was a Greek lyric poet from Thebes who penned odes praising the winners of panhellenic Games (Olympian, Pythian, Isthmian, and Nemean) and was widely admired for his eloquence and subtlety of thought. Pindar refers frequently to water as an important feature of ordinary life: necessary

DOI: 10.4324/9781003437741-2

for washing, sailing, fishing, therapeutics, and even drinking. Just as water is the preeminent element, the Olympics are the preeminent games.

> Best is water, but gold appears like shining fire, man-exalting in the night standing out with wealth. But if you long to sing athletic contests, Dear heart, seek no further than the sun, another radiant star warming daily through the solitary aether, nor let us sing contests better than the Olympian Games.
>
> *(Pindar,* Olympian *1.1–8)*

1.1.2 Whether Fire or Water Is More Useful

Plutarch (c. 40–120 CE*) was a Greek philosopher, born at Chaeronea in Boeotia (Greece). He studied mathematics and Platonic philosophy at Athens and lived most of his life in Chaeronea. He served as a priest of Apollo at Delphi (near his hometown) and was awarded with Roman citizenship. While he probably never visited Rome, Plutarch did serve as an administrator in Greece under the Roman emperor Hadrian (r. 117–138). Plutarch is most famous for his biographies of prominent Greeks and Romans, and he remains an important source for many aspects of ancient thought.*

Here we have a brief treatise from Plutarch's Moralia ("Table Talk")*, a loose collection of some 80 or so essays and speeches on various topics in ethics, customs, and philosophy. This essay,* Whether Fire or Water Is More Useful*, falls into two contradictory parts, dealing first with the advantages of water and the perils of fire, before exploring the benefits of fire and the shortcomings of water (most Greek thinkers believed in four elements: earth, air, water, and fire). For Plutarch, while water is essential to human life, it is merely inert and ungenerating without the agency of fire. Fire, however, is the catalyst that enables all life and even human reasoning. Consequently, fire is the lynchpin of technology, which is how humanity can control and tame nature. Plutarch's anthropocentric conclusion is syllogistic: fire is an element; fire enables technology; technology enables vision; through fire human beings can improve their souls by observing the heavens. Plutarch's analysis of two elements thus transitions into a morality lesson.*

> 1. Best is water, but gold is shining fire, says Pindar (*Olympian* 1.1). Inasmuch as he has openly granted second place to fire, Hesiod aligns with Pindar saying: "surely in the first place chaos came into being" (*Theogony* 116). For most people, then, it seems that water is called in this fashion from its flowing. But there are equal witnesses for each: some declaiming that fire is the *arche* (beginning) of everything, and, like a seed, that it makes everything from itself and that to itself it receives everything from a conflagration. Dismissing the authorities, let us scrutinize rather where the theories lead us with respect to each other.
>
> 2. And yet, is not that one more useful which we need everywhere and continuously and most of all, accordingly as an instrument and an implement

and—by god—as a friend who at every time and at each crisis is ready at hand? Indeed fire is not always useful. It happens that we are weighed down by it and are removed from it. But there is a need of water in both winter and summer, both for the ailing and for the healthy, both night and day, and there is not a time when a person does not need water. At any rate, they call the deceased *alibantes* since they lack moisture (*libas*), that is to say, wateriness, and for this reason they are deprived of life. And humankind has often existed without fire, but never without water. But what is known from the beginning and at the same time as the first foundation of humanity is more useful than that which is discovered later. For it is clear that *physis* (nature) gave the one as indispensable. But for an overabundance of utility, some skill and contrivance found the other. Therefore, it is not possible to say when water was not known to people, nor can any of the gods or heroes be called its discoverer. For nearby, when humans came into being, it was straightaway already in existence, and it provided for our creation. But they say that the use of fire was discovered yesterday and early in the morning by Prometheus.[1] Our life was without fire, but not without water. And they demonstrate that this is not a poetic forgery owing to our lifestyle. For some races of folk exist apart from fire, living their lives without houses and without hearths and under the sky. And even Diogenes the Cynic ("Dog") employed fire least of all, so that—gulping down a raw polypod (octopus or squid)—he said, "for you I do not throw my life aside." Neither did anyone think it good or possible to live apart from water.

3. And why do I trivially examine the nature of folks I've come across? While there are many creatures, or rather infinite types, perhaps only the race of people knows the use of fire. The rest live fireless lifestyles and use fireless nourishment, and this is their livelihood. For grazers, flyers, creepers feed on roots and fruit and flesh without fire. But without water, neither creatures of the sea nor of dry land nor of the air can exist. And also those, some of which Aristotle says do not drink, employing internal water, live off the flesh of living creatures as food (*HA* 601b). More useful therefore is that element without which not even one living type stands or endures.

4. Let us depart from those employing fire and water to the things that we use, plants and fruits. Some of these do not altogether have any share of heat, but others have the least amount, and inscrutably so. For a watery nature provides all sprouts, making them strong and fruit-bearing. And why is it necessary that I recount both wine and oil and all the remaining things which we gather, and also milk and things cut from honeycombs, lying visibly and wherever, and even wheat, seemingly a dry foodstuff, but with change and fermentation[2] and melting, it becomes watery in nature?

1 The Titan who gifted humankind with reliable access to fire. For Prometheus' gift of technology: Irby-Massie 2008.
2 Before 3500 BCE, the Egyptians had been fermenting grain to produce beer.

5. And that which harms is never the more useful. Fire, therefore, is especially destructive as a stream, but the nature of water is never damaging. And, further, the more beneficial of the two elements is the one which is cheaper and offers its assistance separate from any preparation. But a supply of wood is needed for fire. On account of this, the wealthy share in fire more than the poor, kings more than private individuals. But water extends even this human-loving benevolence, equality, homogeneity. For it requires neither tools nor instruments, without needing anything, and is complete of itself, good.

6. Still, that which utterly destroys its utility by increasing is more unprofitable. Such is fire which, like an all-consuming wild beast, also devours everything nearby, and fire is helpful with investigation and skill and with moderation rather than by its own nature. But water never causes fear. And also of the two, the one is more useful with the other. Fire does not allow moisture, nor in association with water is fire at all serviceable. But water is useful with fire. At any rate, the heat of water is beneficial and healing for medical treatments and easily perceived. Not anyone would find a watery fire, but water, thus even both cold and warm, is beneficial to humanity.

7. And, while there are four elements, water of itself provides a fifth: thus some might say, it makes the element "sea." None of these is less beneficial than the other elements, especially on account of trade. Therefore, when our livelihood was wild and lacking social interaction, this element joined us together and made us complete, establishing aid and commerce with each other, working out partnerships and friendships. Heraclitus (*TEGP* 93) therefore says "if there were not a sun, then it would be night." It is consequently possible to say, likewise, that if there were no sea, then of all creatures humankind would be the most fierce and deficient. But the vine came to the Hellenes from India; from Hellas, the Greeks gave the use of grain to those beyond the sea; from Phoenicia, they conveyed letters as a monument against forgetfulness. Thus, most of humanity was prevented from becoming wineless and grainless and uneducated. How, therefore, is water not more beneficial than another element, and even more beneficial?

8. What consequently could someone have to say on the opposite point of view? Because, therefore, the craftsman god (Hephaestus/Vulcan) had four elements for the construction underlying the whole world. Of these again there is a difference: that earth and water are placed underneath, providing customary raw material, and molding and sharing in the cosmos and its arrangement and its nature, they say, and its birth, and whatever might be partaken from the other elements. Wind and fire make and craft and rouse supine things—lifeless until that point—to genesis. Of these two, fire is straightaway the first and leads the way. This is clear from reasoning: earth without heat is sterile and fruitless, but fire, possessing and scattering, disposes the earth, as it grows ripe, to genesis. One could find no reason why rocks and mountain-tops become like skeletons except that they partake in fire either very little or not at all.

9. On the whole, water exists far from the preservation or generation of other things and, being complete of itself, to the extent that the lack of fire is the destruction of water. Therefore, heat holds together each thing in its proper formation and keeps watch on its particular essence and accordingly on everything else and also water. When fire desists and falls short, things become rotten and there is death for water. And the deficiency of heat is ruin. For instance, marshes and stagnated waters and some waters settled within hollows with no outlet are wretched and, in the end, become putrid, partaking in the least amount of movement, which in turn preserves the heat within each thing by fanning. Thus, on account of the motion of the heat existing within, we especially call waters that are carried along and flowing "living." How, accordingly, should that not be the more beneficial of the two, that which has offered a cause of existence to the other, just as fire does for water? And indeed, that which destroys life, when altogether removed, is clearly more beneficial. For, how something deprived is able to exist, this offers a cause when it did exist. Moisture, therefore, is at hand even in corpses; and it is not removed altogether since the corpses of bodies would then not putrefy: putrefaction is not a change to moistness from dryness, but rather a destruction of moisture in the flesh. Death is nothing other than the absolute cessation of heat. Coldest thus are the dead, and, if someone would attack a corpse, they would blunt the edge of their razor on account of the excessive coldness. And in a living creature itself, those parts sharing in the least amount of fire are those most lacking in sensitivity, like bones and hair and those parts furthest away from the heart. For, in general, the difference becomes greater with the presence of fire than with the absence of moisture: for moisture does not produce plants and fruits, but warm moisture produces living things; the coldness of water is weaker and not altogether productive. And, furthermore, if water were fruitful by its own nature, it would necessarily always bear fruit by itself; but, on the contrary, it is even harmful.

10. But, from the beginning, regarding the use of fire as fire, we do not require the use of water. But, to the contrary, water would become an impediment: for it quenches, and it destroys fire. And, for the most part, the use of water is not possible without fire: heated, water is more beneficial, but otherwise harmful. And heat has made the sea more beneficial, since it differs from other waters in no other respect. Thus, of the two, better is that which offers an advantage of itself, not attached to the other. Still, water is uniquely serviceable to the touch for those bathing or washing, but fire benefits every sense: observed close at hand and from a distance, consequently, its sumptuousness is also added to its other uses.

11. For to say that a human ever existed without fire is ridiculous, nor is humanity altogether able to exist without fire. But there are differences in type as in other things. And some do not require external fire: they do not need external heat, but they have an abundance and sufficiency of heat in themselves. This must be said also about other living creatures, whichever ones do not need fire,

so that, in this respect, the need of fire outstrips the need of water, as is probable. Water is never such that it is not required externally; but fire is independent on account of its great excellence. Thus, therefore, as a general is better who prepares the city so that it does not need external allies, thus also the element which offers external aid very often does not prevail in what is needed. This must be mentioned even concerning other living beings which lack fire. Further, someone might take an opposite point of view, that this, fire, is the most useful, which we alone use, because we are able to select the better part from reasoning: for what is more serviceable to humanity than reason? But it is not present in those creatures without reason. What then? On account of this, is what has been discovered by the foresight of our better part less serviceable for this reason?

12. And since we have come to this point of our reasoning, what is more advantageous for life than skill? Fire has discovered and preserves all the arts. Consequently, they make Hephaestus the founder of these technologies. And the life of humans is of a short time, as Ariston[3] says (F 403): sleep, like a tax-collector steals half of this. But I would rather say that it rouses the darkness in the night. But there is no advantage to wakefulness if fire does not offer us the benefits of daytime and eliminate the difference of day and night. If then, there is nothing more profitable for humanity than living, and fire multiplies this living, how then could fire not be the most useful of all?

13. And, to be sure, would not the most advantageous element be that in which the senses partake in the greatest ratio? Do you not then see, therefore, that none of the senses employ watery nature by itself separately, apart from breath or fire mixed in, and every sense partakes in fire, such as providing a life-force, especially sight, which is the sharpest of those senses in the body, being a mass of fire, and that which offers trust in the gods? But in addition, Plato (*Timaeus* 471-b) has said that we are able to conform our souls to the movements of those things in the sky on account of our faculty of sight.

(Plutarch, Whether Fire or Water Is More Useful *955d–958e;*
for ancient theories of vision: Ierodiakonou 2015)

1.2 Physics

1.2.1 From Water Come All Things

From Miletus, an important Greek port in Asia Minor (western Turkey), Thales (b. c. 625 BCE) was widely regarded as the first Greek thinker to consider the natural world in a rational way, suggesting physical, rather than divine or mythical, causes of natural phenomena, and sparking perhaps the most exciting intellectual revolution. Among other things, Thales is credited with predicting a solar eclipse

3 Possibly the physician from Aigina (c. 450–400 BCE: see Galen 15.45 [5.15Kühn]).

in 585 and using geometry to measure the height of pyramids in Egypt and the distance of ships at sea. Thales may also have proposed a system of material monism, positing one element or idea as the arche *(origin or beginning) of the cosmos. But he left no writings, and his thoughts were incompletely redacted by later commentators. What Thales really proposed we shall never know, but Thales' theory seems to have derived from his own critical observations of the natural world. He was, nonetheless, the first to ask, "What is the stuff of the world?"*

A. *Aëtius was a 1st-/2nd century-CE doxographer whose* Opinions of the Philosophers *and* Physical and Moral Extracts *are valuable sources for early thought.*

> Thales the Milesian asserted that the beginning of all things was water. For, from water, he says, all things exist and into water all things dissolve. He conjectures it first from this, that for all living things the generative beginning is a watery existence. Thus, it is likely also that all things have their beginning from water. Secondly, that all plants are nourished in water and bear fruit, but when deprived of water they become parched. Third, that the very fire of the sun and stars is nourished by the exhalations of waters, as is even the cosmos.
>
> *(Thales,* TEGP *16 = Aëtius,* Opinions of the Philosophers *1.3.1, S1.10.12; cf. Vitruvius,* On Architecture *8.1.1)*

B. *Hippolytus (c. 170–c. 235 CE) was a bishop of Rome and may have been the author of* Refutation of All Heresies, *a Christian polemic cataloguing heretical beliefs including traditional Greco-Roman practices and gnostic beliefs. For water and weather: #1.9.*

> Thales the Milesian, one of the Seven Wise Men, is said to have been the first to put his hand to natural philosophy. This one said that the beginning and end of all things is water. All things are created from water that is congealed and again dissolved, and all things are carried on it. From water are earthquakes and the twistings of winds and movements of the stars.
>
> *(Thales,* TEGP *20 = Hippolytus,* Refutation of All Heresies *1.1.1–4)*

1.2.2 Elemental Change

A. *Like Thales, Anaximenes (fl. c. 555–535 BCE), who had studied under Thales' student Anaximander (#1.4.1A), was a material monist, positing air as the source of the natural world, adding that the process of condensation and rarefaction gave different compositional densities to physical objects. Anaximenes was the first to ask, "How does stuff change?"*

> The Milesian Anaximenes, son of Eurystratus, being a companion of Anaximander, himself says that underlying *physis* (nature) is singular and

boundless—just like that one, Anaximander, believed—but not undefined, like Anaximander believed, but defined, calling it air. With respect to thinness or congealment it differs in essence: thinning, it becomes fire; thickening, it becomes wind, and then cloud, and still more thick, water, then earth, then stones. Other things come from these. Anaximenes also makes motion everlasting, on account of which change happens.

(Anaximenes, TEGP *3 = Simplicius,* Physics *24.26–25.1)*

B. *Anaximenes' theory is proved with a simple experiment.*

Just as ol' Anaximenes thought, let us not omit either coldness in a substance or warmth, but let us approach them as a common occurrence of material undergoing changes. For Anaximenes says that coldness is the constricting and congealment of matter, but warmth is thinning and languid: *chalaron*: for thus calling it even with the word. Consequently, it is not unreasonable to say that a person releases both warmth and coldness from the mouth. For the breath, squeezed and congealed by the lips, becomes cold, but—the mouth at ease—the released breath becomes warm by rarefaction. But Aristotle therefore takes this argument as Anaximenes' mistake (*Physics* 187a12–16): for with a relaxed mouth we release heat from our very selves, but when we puff—contracting the lips—it is not from us, but the air in front of the mouth is pushed and falls in front, becoming cold.

(Anaximenes, TEGP *7 = Plutarch,* On the Principle of Cold *947f–948a; cf. Plutarch,* Life of Aemilius Paullus *14.2–11)*

1.2.3 Two Elements

*Xenophanes of Colophon, just north of Miletus (b. c. 570 BCE), was the first natural philosopher to write in verse. He traveled widely (perhaps he also earned a living as an itinerant minstrel), and was one of the first to question the reliability of the senses: although a true reality exists—he thought—human beings are unable to know it. Xenophanes is particularly well-known for the epigram about horses and cows designing gods in their own images (*TEGP *32 = Clement of Alexandria,* Miscellanies *5.110). Xenophanes rejected material monism, instead suggesting a two-element theory, perhaps inspired by Menelaus' curse on his fellow Achaean warriors who feared to meet Hector, the Trojan champion, in battle, "may you all become earth and water" (Homer,* Iliad *7.99). Sextus Empiricus (2nd century CE) was a practicing physician who wrote on Pyrrhonistic philosophy, rejecting dogma and advocating for suspension of judgment with the goal of achieving* ataraxia *("freedom from anxiety") by means of neither denying or affirming anything.*

For all things are born from earth and also water.

(Xenophanes, TEGP *51 = Sextus Empiricus,* Against the Professors *10.314)*

1.2.4 Water and Change

From Ephesus, a port town between Miletus and Colophon, Heraclitus (535–475 BCE) devised a contentious philosophy that reflected contemporary politics as stress mounted between the expanding Persian Empire and the Greek city-states in Ionia. For Heraclitus, fire was the source of the physical world, and Strife was the organizing principle. Heraclitus is particularly well-known for surmising that the world is in a state of constant flux and that opposites in balance impose order on the sensible world. His thought, refined by Aristotle, was the basis of Stoicism, a widely accepted philosophical, ethical, and physical system in the ancient Greek world (see #1.3.5B note).

A. At any rate, Heraclitus says that all things give way and nothing stays put, and likening all existing things to a river's stream he says how you could not step twice into the same river.

(Heraclitus, TEGP *63 = Plato,* Cratylus *402a8–10)*

B. According to Homer and Heraclitus and all such people, they think that all things, like currents, are set in motion.

(Heraclitus, TEGP *64 = Plato,* Theaetetus *160d6–8)*

C. For it is not possible to step twice in the same river, according to Heraclitus, nor to engage twice with a dying (mortal) creature in a static state. But by sharpness and celerity of change, it scatters and brings waters together again. Neither again nor later but at the same time, it combines and relinquishes and accretes and departs.

(Heraclitus, TEGP *66 = Plutarch,* On the E at Delphi *392b–c)*

1.2.5 Four Elements

Empedocles of Acragas (in Sicily), born c. 480 BCE, was a scientific poet with wide-ranging interests. Despite critical gaps, sizable fragments of his poems On Nature *and* On Purification *survive. In brief, Empedocles believed in a cosmic system wherein four "elements" cycled between a state of total separation and total mixture, governed by the forces of Love (total mixture) and Hate (total separation). Empedocles was building on a mythic elemental paradigm that posited three building blocks of the material world: Gaia (earth), Ouranos (sky/air), and Okeanos (water): "underworld" (Tartarus) was occasionally added as a fourth (Homer,* Iliad *3.278, 15.187–188; Hesiod,* Theogony *678–683, 736–745). These divine beings were among the deities who first came into existence, providing the armature of the cosmos (Homer,* Iliad *18.483;* Odyssey *1.52–54, 5.293–296; Irby-Massie 2008: 144–145). The theory was embraced by Aristotle and thus endured as nearly unimpeachable in the ancient world. Here Empedocles connects his own elemental roots to three Olympian deities. Nestis seems to be a Sicilian deity whose cult resembled Persephone's (Hades' bride in the Greek tradition: see Kingsley 1995: 348).*

> Zeus is fire, Hera the life-bringer is earth who produces fruits for the purpose of life, Aedoneus (Hades) is air, because, while seeing all things through air, we do not see it (air) alone, Nestis is water. For only this (water) is the vehicle of food for all things to be nourished. But of its own accord water itself is unable to feed those being fed. For if water could nourish, Empedocles says, then living things would never be caught by hunger: water is always abundant in the cosmos. On account of this, Empedocles calls this Nestis "water," since, being the cause of nourishment, it does not have the means to feed those things to be fed.
>
> *(Empedocles,* TEGP *27 = Hippolytus,* Refutation *7.29.5–6)*

1.2.6 Geometry of the Elements

Socrates (d. 399 BCE, who wrote nothing) and his student Plato (428/7–348/7 BCE) further developed Presocratic natural philosophy, synthesizing their thought and treating foundational questions with greater nuance, including the reliability of sensory perception and how change is possible (since change and stability belong to separate realms of reality). Regarding perception, Plato posited two planes of existence: unchanging, incorporeal reality, wherein dwell the Ideal Forms, and the mutable, corporeal world of "seeming" or "becoming," the world of human existence. True reality is defined by the unchanging Forms in whose Ideal mutable objects partake: ships in the realm of "becoming," for example, share in the essential characteristics of the Ideal Ship (the ability to float and move across water under sail or oar), but other features are secondary (hull shape, deck length, number of masts or rowers, prow decoration). For Plato, a benevolent, rational Demiurge (Craftsman) guides the cosmos and imposes order externally.

*Plato also scrutinized the intrinsic nature of water, one of his three interchangeable elements, explaining a geometrical atomic theory that ultimately derives from Pythagorean, Democritean, and Empedoclean physics (*Timaeus *53c–57c). Two-dimensional right-angled isosceles triangles and half-equilateral triangles combine and dissolve to form the five three-dimensional building blocks of sensible objects, and elements can consequently transform from one into the others. Four of these solids are connected to Empedocles' elements.*

> Therefore, assigning this figure (cube) to earth, we preserve the likely account. In turn, of the remaining elements, to water is assigned the least movable shape (icosahedron), the most moveable is assigned to fire (tetrahedron), the middle one to air (octahedron). Moreover, we assign the smallest body to fire, the largest to water, the middle one to air. And still, the sharpest is assigned to fire, the second sharpest to air, and the third to water. Regarding all these, the one having the fewest

faces (tetrahedron) necessarily becomes the most mobile, and, being the sharpest of all, and even the lightest, combined from the fewest parts of the same type . . .

From all that we have already said about these types, the elements would probably behave thusly. Falling in with fire and broken up by its sharpness, whether it happens to be dissolved in fire itself or in a body of air or even water, earth would be carried on until a portion of earth meeting up with it and itself combined together again with portions of earth, it would again become earth, for its shape would not ever go into another shape. But water, cleft by fire, or even by air, makes space to combine into one body of fire and two of air. And fragments of air dissolved from one part could become two bodies of fire. And then, when a little bit of fire, embraced in air, or a lot of water or even some earth, moving within them as they are carried along, two bodies of fire—as they fight and are conquered with its crushing—combine into one unit of air. And when air is prevailed over and cut into pieces, one entire shape of water is joined together from two entire and one half portions of air.

(Plato, Timaeus *56a, d-e)*

1.2.7 Aristotelian Properties of Water

A. *Rejecting abstract thought, Aristotle (384–322 BCE) was Plato's student and Alexander the Great's teacher, and a polymath whose body of work includes nearly every topic of human thought (physics, metaphysics, astronomy, meteorology, zoology, ethics, etc.). Aristotle preferred empirical observation and axiomatic deduction, and he categorized physical objects according to purpose or function, all reducible to Four Causes (Formal, Material, Efficient, Final). The Final Cause overrules the other causes: a ship's purpose determines its form (boat-shaped), material (wood), and method of creation (efficient cause: carpentry). Aristotle also considered the four-element theory too confining and thus defined the elements according to four interchangeable properties (hot, cold, dry, wet).*

Since an earlier discussion (*On the Heavens* 304b23–305a13) has established that for some bodies creation appears to occur from another body, at the same time and according to sense-perception: for there would not be change: change is the accident of touching. This must be explained: what is the method of change into other objects and whether each can come-to-be from another or some can and others cannot. That all the elements, therefore, have been produced to change into each other is clear. For coming-to-be is a process into and out of opposite qualities, and all the elements have properties opposite to each other on account of innate differences. For some, both qualities are opposite, such as for fire and water: fire is dry and hot; but water is wet and cold. For others, only one quality differs, such as for air and water: air is wet and hot, water is wet and cold. Consequently, it is clear that each thing is created to come from each thing, and it is not difficult to see how this happens according to each element. For all elements exist from all elements, but there is a distinction according to relative speed and slowness and ease and difficulty. For elements that have correspondences with each other, the change will be quick; for elements that do not have an affinity, their changes will be slow owing to the fact that it is easier that one thing change than many, such as air from fire, with one quality being changed: for the one is hot and dry, the other is hot and wet, so that if dryness is conquered by moistness, then there is air. And from air, there is water if the heat is conquered by coldness: the one is hot and moist, the other is cold and moist, so that if the heat is changed, then there is water. With respect to the same method, from water there is earth, from earth, fire. For both have correspondences with both: for water is wet and cold, and earth is cold and dry, so that when the wateriness is conquered, there is earth. And again, since fire is dry and hot, and earth is cold and dry, if the coldness is destroyed, then there is fire from earth.

(Aristotle, On Coming-to-be and Passing-away *331a8–b2; cf. Aristotle,* Meteorology *378b11–26)*

B. *Thus, Aristotle could account for transmutations and changes of state (solid, liquid, gas), with endless possibilities as one element neatly transformed into another in a proto-chemical reaction: #1.4.4B§10.*

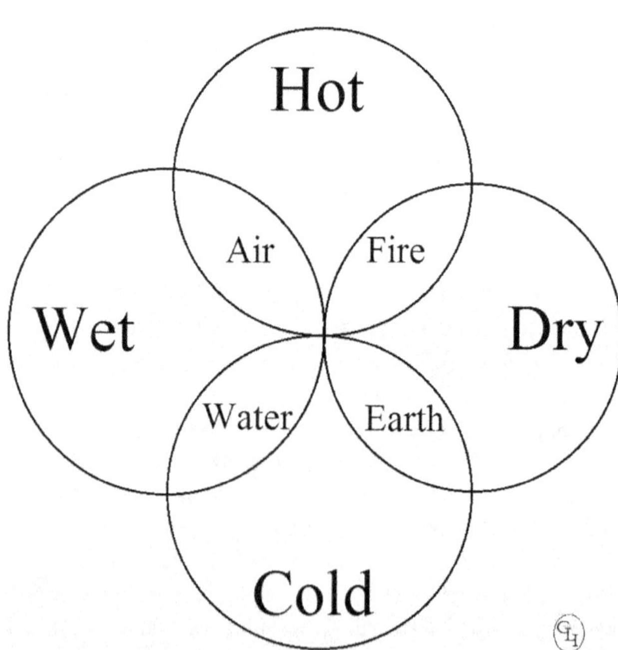

FIGURE 1.2.7B Transformations of properties: diagram by Georgia L. Irby.

C. *Within the cosmos, spheres of individual elements take their proper place from lightest (fire) to heaviest (earth).*

> Water stretches around the earth, just as the sphere of air stretches around water and around air is what is called the sphere of fire.
>
> *(Aristotle,* Meteorology *354b24–26)*

D. *Aristotle's theory was the dominant explanation of change in the corporeal world and found wide expression, including in the Roman poet Ovid of Sulmo near Rome (b. 43 BCE), best known for his* Metamorphoses, *a collection of mythological transformations. But he also penned love poetry (including the* Ars Amatoria *["Art of Love"], with advice on where and how to hook up, for both men and women), a versified account of the Roman religious calendar (*Fasti, *surviving only for the first half of the year), two collections of verses from his exile in Tomis on the Black Sea (*Tristia *and* Letters from Pontus*), a brief treatise on makeup (*Medicaments for the Female Face*), and another on fishing (*Halieutica *[Salt-Fishing]). Here we have an extract from Pythagoras' speech concerning transformation in the natural world as proof of the existence of immortal souls.*

> These things, which we call elements, which transformations drive about, are not constant. Apply your minds: I will teach. The eternal world holds four generative bodies. From these, two are heavy and born below by their own weight: earth and water. And just as many lack weight and, with nothing pressing them down, they seek the upper regions: air and fire, more pure than air. Although these are distant in space, nonetheless, they all are made from themselves and fall into themselves: loosened earth rarefies into liquid waters; attenuated moisture goes away into breezes and air; and with its weight removed the slenderest air flickers into the loftiest fires. Then they come back, and the same order is rewoven: for thickened fire comes across into dense air, this into waters, and rolled-up swells are compressed into earth.
>
> *(Ovid,* Metamorphoses *15.238–251)*

1.2.8 Microvoids

While the four-element theory was widely embraced, especially owing to Aristotle's imprimatur, *some theories blurred the distinctions between pluralism (four elements) and atomism (the theory of atoms and void, first posited by Leucippus and his famous student Democritus of Abdera, b. c. 460 BCE). Despite his Aristotelian/Peripatetic education, Strato of Lampsakos (d. 268 BCE)—tutor of Ptolemy II Philadelphus ("sister-loving," r. 285–246 BCE) in Alexandria, and the third* scholarch *("headmaster") of the Peripatetic school in Athens—proffered a hybrid theory of "microvoids," as preserved by Simplicius of Cilicia (c. 480–560 CE), a Neoplatonic doxographer and commentator who aimed to harmonize Platonic and Aristotelian thought.*

Strato from Lampsakos, nevertheless, tries to demonstrate that there is a hollow distributed through each body, such that it is not continuous, saying that "in water or air or any other body neither is light nor warmth nor any other corporeal power able to slip through altogether. For how could rays of the sun descend to the bottom of a jar? For if water does not have voids, but the rays disperse the water by force, then full jars would happen to overflow, and some of the rays would not bend back towards the space above, and others would fall down to the bottom."

(Simplicius, On Aristotle's Physics *217b27 11–18)*

1.2.9 Water Proves the Atomic Theory

The atomists believed that all sensible objects were formed with uncuttable atoms and void, a theory rejected by Aristotle but embraced by the Epicurean school of philosophy. The Roman poet Lucretius (c. 55 BCE), who penned the fullest description of the theory in his six-book epic On the Nature of Things, *both described the nature of water (with its soft, round atoms, facilitating fluidity and not dislodging other atoms) and employed water to prove the existence of otherwise tiny, unobservable atoms of water.*

A. Indeed those things, which correspond in body as liquids, ought to be from elements lighter and rounder. For a drink of poppy seeds is as easy as one of water, and the little globes are not viscous among themselves and likewise, when struck, a poppy seed is rolled downwards just as easily as water.

(Lucretius, On the Nature of Things *2.451–455)*

B. Finally, clothes hung on a wave-broken shore grow moist, and the same clothes grow dry when stretched out in the sun. But neither how the water's moisture settles in nor again how it escapes from the heat is observed. Therefore, moisture is scattered into small parts which the eyes are by no means able to observe.

(Lucretius, On the Nature of Things *1.305–10)*

C. Moreover, although things seem to be solid, you would nonetheless perhaps see that they are characterized with an attenuated body: in rocks and caves the liquid moisture of waters trickles through, and they all weep with abundant tears.

(Lucretius, On the Nature of Things *1.346–349)*

1.2.10 Water Is Essential to All Living Things

The Roman architect and engineer Vitruvius (b. c. 85 BCE) composed On Architecture, *a ten-book compendium, written during a period of intense rebuilding* *in the 20s BCE after decades of destructive civil war. Vitruvius believed that all human learning was relevant to architecture, and that architecture (like medicine and other avenues of human inquiry) must harmonize with climate and topography (*On Architecture *6.1.2). Here the particular importance of water is explained in an especially moralizing and Romanizing way (cf. #1.1.2).*

If there were truly animals without the power of blood, bloodless and deprived of the fluid of their beginnings, they would become dry. Therefore, the divine mind has not established the things which are particularly necessary for people as difficult and expensive like pearls, gold, silver, and other things which neither the body nor nature requires. But the things without which the life of mortal folk is not able to be secure, these things the divine mind has poured out, prepared for distribution through the entire world. And so, from these, if by chance something of the breath is lacking in the body, air then—designated for restoring the breath—performs that restoration. The force of the sun is ready for the aid of warmth, and the discovery of fire makes life more secure. Likewise, terrestrial fruit, offering superfluous abundances of foods to satisfy desires, continuously feeds and nourishes pasturing animals. Truly, water, not only by the utility of a drink but also by furnishing countless necessities, supplies benefits, pleasing because they are free.

(Vitruvius, On Architecture *8 preface 3)*

Consequently, (water is) especially necessary for life and pleasures and for daily use.

(Vitruvius, On Architecture *8.1.1; cf. #4.3A)*

1.3 Oceans and Seas

1.3.1 How Do Seas and Lakes Differ?

Polyclitus of Larissa (fl. 360–300 BCE) was a Greek historian who wrote about Persia, Mesopotamia, and India (Athenaeus, Learned Banqueters *539a), and was an important geographical source for Strabo and Pliny.*

Polyclitus (F 7) proffers the belief concerning the Caspian Sea, that this sea is a lake: for it produces serpents and the water is sweet.

(Strabo, Geography *11.7.4)*

1.3.2 Circumambient Ocean

A. *The theory that Ocean surrounds the world dates back to Homer (fl. 750–700 BCE), an early Greek poet ascribed with composing the* Iliad *and* Odyssey, *which provide valuable information on the early Greek view of how the world works. In Homer, the cosmos represented on Achilles' shield, made by Hephaestus/Vulcan, god of fire and technology, is framed by an encircling Ocean.*

> On the shield, Hephaestus placed the great strength of the river Ocean along the outermost edge of the strongly made shield.
>
> *(Homer,* Iliad *18.607–608)*

B. *Herodotus (b. c. 485 BCE) of Halicarnassus is best known for his nine-book account of the wars between the allied Greeks* poleis *and Persian Empire (499–480 BCE) with its fascinating ethnographic digressions on the Egyptian and Scythian peoples. Here he categorically rejects the circumambient Ocean, owing to the lack of empirical evidence.*

> They say that Ocean flows around everything, beginning at the rising of the sun, but they do not prove it.
>
> *(Herodotus,* Histories *4.8.2; cf.* Histories *4.36.2)*

C. *The polymath Strabo (b. c. 65 BCE) of Amaseia on the Pontus (Black Sea) is best known for his 17-book* Geography, *a description of the entire Greco-Roman world in the early 1st century CE, extracting data from his geographical predecessors, including Homer whom he called the "Father of Geography." Here Strabo's proof of the circumambient ocean (or at least not disproof).*

> That the *oikoumene* (inhabited world) is an island is to be accepted first from sense-perception and then from experience. For in every place that is accessible for humanity to advance to the extremes of the earth, the sea which we call "Ocean" is discovered. And where, by sense-perception, it is not allowed to grasp this, reason indicates it. For, regarding the eastern side, the one along the Indians, and the western side, the one along the Iberians and Maurousians, one can sail altogether for a long distance towards the regions of the South Wind and the North Wind. But, regarding the remaining portion—unsailed by us up to now—where no travelers sailing in opposite directions meet up with each other, the length is not extensive if someone would add up the parallel intervals accessible to us. It is not likely that the Atlantic is divided into two seas, cleft by such narrow straits that prevent circumnavigation, but it is rather more likely that the Atlantic is flowing together and continuous. For, those undertaking a circumnavigation, and then turning back, say that they were pushed back not by some land in their way and hindering them from sailing beyond, but rather by difficulty and desolation: the sea offered no less passage than before.
>
> *(Strabo,* Geography *1.1.8–9)*

1.3.3 Nature of Ocean

A. *River Ocean (#3.1.1) is the source of all, according to personified Sleep, whom Hera/Juno has asked to lull Zeus to sleep after she seduces him: Hera and the pro-Greek gods hope to meddle in the battle at Troy, against Zeus' express command that the gods not interfere.*

> Then, answering, delightful Sleep addressed her, "Hera, honored goddess, daughter of great Kronos, I would easily put to sleep any of the everlasting gods, even River Ocean, who as the source created all."
>
> *(Homer,* Iliad *14.242–246)*

B. *Mighty Ocean is the source of all rivers, but still would not dare defy Zeus, according to Achilles as he slays Asteropaeos, the grandson of the Axius River. Zeus was Achilles' great-grandfather.*

> Just as Zeus is stronger than rivers flowing to the sea, again the descendant of Zeus is stronger than the children of a river. And next to you is a great river, if he is able to defend you at all. But it is not possible to battle Zeus the son of Kronos. Nor does Lord Achelous vie with Zeus, nor the great strength of deep-flowing Ocean, from whom all the rivers and the entire sea and all the springs and the deep wells flow. But even Ocean dreads the lightning of great Zeus and his terrible thunder, when it crashes from the sky.
>
> *(Homer,* Iliad *21.190–199)*

C. *Hesiod (fl. c. 750–650 BCE) of Askra (an inland town near Mt. Helikon) was a didactic poet whose* Theogony *recounts the creation of the Greek cosmos. For Hesiod Ocean is a river (Greek:* potamos*) implying a circumambient Ocean.*

> Passing lovely among the goddesses, children were born in the unharvested sea of Nereus and Doris, the lovely-haired daughter of Ocean, the perfect river.
>
> *(Hesiod,* Theogony *240–242)*

D. *Evoking Homer (#1.3.3C), Xenophanes noted the symbiosis of the sea with water and wind.*

> The source of water is the sea, and the source of wind. For without the great sea there would not be wind nor the currents of rivers nor the rainy water of the air, but the great sea is the generator of both clouds and rivers.
>
> *(Xenophanes,* TEGP *55 = Geneva scholium on* Iliad *21.196)*

E. *Plato explored the nature of the soul in his* Phaedo, *a dialogue set in Socrates' jail cell on the day he was executed. Here, contemplating his pending death,*

Socrates explains his theoretical hydrology as a katabasis (descent) into the Underworld wherein all bodies of water, including Ocean, are interlinked beneath the earth.

> 111c. But as to places within the earth, along the hollows, in a circle around the whole *oikoumene* ("inhabited world"), some are deeper and more spread out than the one in which we dwell, but others, being deeper, have less expanse than the hollows near us. There are some which are shallower in depth than here and also wider. And under the earth all the hollows are channeled to each other in many places along both narrower and broader channels, and they have outlets where much water flows from one to the others just like into mixing bowls. And there is an inexplicable magnitude of ever-flowing rivers under the earth, of both hot waters and cold. And there is much fire and great rivers of fire and many rivers of moist mud, both more pure and more turbid, just like those rivers in Sicily in front of the torrent of flowing mud and the lava-stream itself.[4] And, as if by chance, each of these hollows is filled each time that even a flowing occurs. All these waters move downward and up just like a swing existing in the earth. And this very swinging exists on account of some such nature.
>
> 112a. One of the hollows of the earth happens to be huge and pierced right through the entire earth, this is the same one which Homer mentions, saying, "at a distance where the lowest gulf is under the earth" (*Iliad* 8.14), which both he and also many other poets have elsewhere called Tartarus. For the rivers, all of them, flow together towards this chasm, and out of it they flow back again. Each becomes such as they are on account of the earth through which they flow. And the cause of the outflowing, consequently, and the inflowing is with respect to the streamings because they do not have a bottom nor a watery base. The water is lifted and swells up and down, and the air and wind around it do this same thing. And the wind and air follow the water along both when it rushes headlong to that side of the earth and when it rushes to this side here. And, just like the flowing breath of breathing creatures, it both breathes out and breathes in. And there the breath, swayed together with water, furnishes terrible and inexplicable winds, both coming in and going out. But, when therefore the water withdraws to the so-called below-place, then along those streams through the earth it flows, and it also fills these same hollows just like people irrigating fields. When in turn the streams leave away from there and speed back a second time, they again fill the hollows here. Being full, through the channels and through the earth, arriving at the places where a path has been made for each one, they make seas and marshes and rivers and springs. From

4 Possibly a reference to the eruption of Aetna in 389/8 BCE. Plato had visited Sicily twice.

there, sinking again down in the earth, some going around longer places and more fulsomely, others going around places smaller and shallower, again they fall towards Tartarus, some further down by far than where they flowed off, others less so. Then they all flow lower than their efflux. Some fall out straight down from where they flow in, but others flow along the same place. There are those which—altogether coming around in a circle, twisting either once or also many times around the earth just like serpents—falling as far down as possible, fall up again. But it is possible to fall on each side as far as the middle but not further. For uphill is the portion for both streams on each side. But, regarding the other streams, they are many and large, and they flow in every direction. Among these many, there happen to be four streams in particular, of which the greatest and outermost, flowing around in a circle, is the one called Ocean.

113a. Flowing straight down and opposite is Acheron ("woe") which flows through other deserts and indeed, flowing under the earth, arrives at the Acherousian Marsh where the souls of many deceased people arrive: some remain for allotted times, some for a longer time, others for a shorter time, and they are sent back for the births of living creatures. The third river of these falls from the middle, and near its mouth it falls towards a large space burning with much fire and it makes a marsh larger than the sea around us, boiling with water and mire. From there it goes in a circle, turbid and muddy, rolled within the earth. At another time it even reaches the edges of the Acherousian Marsh, but is not mixed with its water. Twisted many times under the earth, it falls down lower than Tartarus. For this is what they call Pyriphlegethon ("Fiery") whose lava flows, as it tears off earth where the lava happens upon it. Straight down from this one, the fourth river falls out to a place at first frightful and savage, which—having a color altogether very blue—they call Stygian ("Hateful"), and they say that the marsh which the falling river creates is the Styx River. But falling in from there and grasping frightful powers in the water, having plunged down in the earth and rolling around, the river passes opposite the Pyriphlegethon and moves away into the Acherousian Marsh from the opposite side. The water of this river is not mixed, but, going around in a circle, it also falls towards Tartarus opposite the Pyriphlegethon. The name for this one, as the poets say, is the Cocytus River ("Wailing").

(Plato, Phaedo *111c–13c; cf. Aristotle,* Meteorology *355b34–356a34 where Aristotle debunks Plato's hydrology as "impossible")*

1.3.4 Salinity

A. *Xenophanes was the first to hypothesize why some waters (seawater) are salty while others are not.*

Xenophanes said that the sea is salty because of the many mixtures that flow in it. But Metrodoros[5] thinks that on account of the act of spreading in the earth, thanks to this, the sea becomes salty.

(Xenophanes, TEGP *59 = Hippolytus,* Refutations *1.14.4)*

B. *For Empedocles the sea is a product of a sweating earth.*

Empedocles (thinks that the sea is) the sweat of the earth burnt by the sun on account of being compressed all the more.

(Empedocles, TEGP *100 = Aëtius,* Placita *3.16.3)*

C. *For Aristotle the sea is salty because of the mixture of moist (watery) and dry exhalations (earthy, containing residues that result from the natural process of generation).*

We must try to offer a reason also for the sea's saltiness. It is clear by many signs that fluid becomes such through the mixing of something . . . some say that the sea is born from burnt earth.[6] But this declaration is absurd. However, the truth is from some such reason. For, just as in those matters already expressed (that saltiness in the body is a factor of a lack of digestion), thus, in the whole world, concerning things that are produced and come-into-being according to nature, it is necessary to consider how this same earth is the residue of combusted things, as indeed there is regarding every exhalation on dry land. For this very same process furnishes much and the bulk of it. While the essence is mixed in, just as we said, and the dry exhalation is turned into vapor, when it combines into cloud and water, it must necessarily take along some of the mass and the property of that material, and be carried down again in rain. And these things always occur according to some arranged order so that it is proved that the process consequently partakes of an arranged orderliness. This, therefore, is the genesis of saltiness in water . . . For it therefore happens that the sea becomes saltier for this, the following reason: a portion of salty water is always drawn up with the sweet. But the drawn-up water is proportionately less salty and bitter than the sweet water in rain. Consequently, it is possible to say that the whole is equalized. Proving it, let us say that seawater is boiled and the vapor is not separated, when it is again combined.

(Aristotle, Meteorology *358a4–5, 15–28, 358b12–19)*

D. *Among the works apocryphally ascribed to Aristotle is* Problems, *a compilation of 38 short "tell me why" books, seeking explanations for nearly 900 phenomena from human anatomy to music, and incorporating passages from both Aristotle*

5 The atomist Metrodoros of Chios (400–350 BCE) was a student of Democritus of Abdera.

6 Aristotle's source here is unclear.

himself and his students. In Book 23, the Aristotelian author asks 41 questions about saltwater, sometimes giving different explanations for the same phenomenon: here, why is the top layer of the sea saltier?

> Why are the upper parts of the sea saltier than the lower parts and also warmer? Likewise, also in wells of potable water the surface is saltier than the depths. And yet it should be saltier lower down. For the salty is heavier. Consequently, do the sun and air always draw up the lightest substances from water? For fresher water is always lighter, and sun and air draw up substances from the closer spots, so that from the surface of the sea and also from drinkable waters, the remainder of what has been drawn up is necessarily lighter than that from which no water—or less sweet water—has been drawn up. On account of this, the upper layers are warmer. For salty water is warmer than drinkable water. And this is why some Heraclitian philosophers say that from drinkable water, drying out and compressing, come stones and also earth, but the sun produces vapor from the sea.
>
> *(Aristotelian* Problems *23.30 = 934b24–36)*

1.3.5 Density

A. *Salt (and other admixtures) determines water density.*

> The fact that saltiness occurs from a mixture is clear not only from what we've already said, but also if someone forming a wax jar would place it into the sea, binding its mouth in such ways that the sea is not poured in. For what enters through the wax is drinkable water,[7] just as earthiness is separated out through a strainer, as well as what made the water salty through mixing. This is the cause of its weight—salt-water weighs more than drinkable water—and its thickness. For thickness (density) differs such that boats with cargoes of the same weight dip down a little in rivers, but in the sea they carry their cargoes conveniently and favorably. Therefore, some of those loading their ships in rivers have suffered because of this ignorance. There is proof that the mass of something mixed in becomes thicker: if someone would make water very salty, mixing in salt, then eggs will float. Water consequently becomes nearly just like mud: the sea has such a quantity of earthy bodies. This same thing occurs regarding salted fish.
>
> But if there exists such a marsh (the Dead Sea) in Palestine, as they mythologize—if someone, binding a person or a yoked animal, would toss them—that they would float and not sink under the water, this would be witness to the things being said. For they say that the marsh is so bitter and salty that there are no fish

7 While water can pass through wax, so too can salt.

in it, and that you would clean your cloaks, if you shake them out after wetting them. All such things are tokens of the things being said, that some substance makes water salty and that the essence therein is earthy.

(Aristotle, Meteorology *358b36–359a25)*

B. *The Stoic philosopher Seneca the Younger (d. 65 CE) served as Nero's tutor and speech writer. Seneca was also a prolific writer whose output included works on Stoic ethics,*[8] *several tragedies, and* Natural Questions (NQ), *querying meteorology (things in the "middle of the air": including earthquakes, volcanoes, comets, as well as winds and weather phenomena). Here is his explanation of buoyancy: why things float in some bodies of water but sink in others.*

It is well known that there are certain lakes which support people unskilled at swimming. There was one in Sicily, and in Syria there still is a stagnant lake (Dead Sea) in which bricks float and things tossed in are unable to sink, although they might be heavy. The cause of this phenomenon is abundantly clear. Weigh anything you like and set it against the water, provided the measure for each is equal. If the water is heavier, it holds up anything lighter than itself and it lifts the lighter object above its surface by as much as the object is lighter. Heavier objects will sink. But if the weight of the water and the object against which you have measured the water will be equal, the object will neither go down nor stand up, but it will be equaled with the water and it will indeed float, but nearly submerged and sticking up in no part. This is why certain logs are carried above water almost entirely, and why others are submerged to the middle, and why still others sink to the level of the water.

(Seneca, NQ *3.25.5–6)*

1.3.6 Tides

A. *Tidal activity was long recognized, intimated by Homer who described Ocean as "backflowing" (*Iliad *18.399;* Odyssey *20.65), and, from the 4th century BCE, understood as connected with the moon. There is a vague awareness of the link*

8 In brief, Stoicism was the synthesis of Aristotelian physics with Heraclitus' ethical physics, a coherent ethical and physical philosophy that was governed by a single first principle: i.e., everything is in contact with the divine fiery soul. Transmutative elements derive from and return to fire as the ratios of heat, cold, wet, and dry cycle back and forth (Alexander of Aphrodisias, *On the Soul*, 26, 16; *On Mixtures* 224, 15. Sambursky 1959: 1–20; Sandbach 1975: 82–85; see #1.2.7). Change and movement are possible because *pneuma* (breath) binds the cosmos through *tonike kinesis* (kinetic tension), a simultaneous motion in opposite directions that results in cohesion and equilibrium, analogous to oscillating waves that occur when a stone is tossed into a confined pool (seemingly anticipating theories of wave expansion and force field vibrations of modern physics: see Aëtius 1.7.33. Sambursky 1959: 1–7). The ultimate goal was the eradication of irrational fears by understanding and correctly interpreting the causes of natural phenomena.

between the moon and tides in this text (3rd century BCE–2nd century CE) spuriously attributed to Aristotle.

> Many tides and tidal waves are said always to come around together with the moon at some ordained times.
>
> *(Aristotelian* On the Universe *396a26–28)*

B. *Seleukos of Seleukia on the Tigris (fl. 165–135 BCE) was an astronomer who advocated for heliocentrism (most Greek thinkers believed that the earth was stationary at the center of the cosmos) and penned the first study of tidal activity, partially preserved in Strabo's extract of Posidonius' redaction (for Posidonius: #1.9.2C).*

> But he (Posidonius: F 18) says that Seleukos from the Erythraean Sea[9] says that there is some inconsistency in these matters and also regularity according to the variations of the zodiac constellations. If the moon is in the equinoctial zodiac constellation, then the effects are uniform, but if the moon is in the solstitial constellations, the effects are uneven both in fullness and speed, but, for each, the irregularity is according to the proximity of the moon.
>
> *(Strabo,* Geography *3.5.9)*

C. *Pliny the Elder (d. 79 CE) was a Roman military leader, administrator, and polymath who traveled widely (serving in Germany, Hispania Tarraconensis, Africa, and probably both Gallia Narbonensis and Belgica). Among other things he wrote on Rome's wars with Germany and the art of throwing javelins from horseback, but he is best known for his 36-book compendium of Roman knowledge, the encyclopedic* Natural History. *Pliny was the first to record the eight-year tidal cycle of recurring lunar phases. Note also that, since daylight was divided into twelve equal hours, the length of an hour varied from season to season. See Eckenrode 1975.*

> The many-folded differential of the moon is still even clear, and the first differential of all is within seven days. To be sure, the tides, being moderate from the new moon to the half-moon, overflow more fully and especially froth up at the full moon. And then they grow soft at the seventh day, equal to the first tides, and again they increase when the moon is divided at its other side. In union with the sun, tides are equal to the tides of the full moon. When the moon is northward and receding far from the lands, the tides are gentler than when the moon, departing to southern regions, exerts her force with a closer effort. Through years by eights, tides are called back to the beginnings of their motion

9 Red Sea, Persian Gulf, Indian Ocean.

and to increments equal to the hundredth circuit of the moon. All these increase owing to the annual effects of the sun, swelling most of all at the two equinoxes and even more at the autumnal equinox than the vernal one, but they are empty in winter and more so at the summer solstice. Nevertheless, they do not occur at those particular moments of time that I have said, but instead after a few days, just as neither in conjunction with a full moon or a very new moon, but afterwards, and not immediately when the earth shows or hides the moon or bends it in the middle phase, but about two equinoctial hours later, since the effect of all things which are done in the sky falls more slowly than the sight of them, just as with lightning, thunder, and thunder-bolts.

Moreover, all tides in the ocean cover and lay bare more space than in the rest of the sea, whether because it is more energetic over the whole rather than a part, or because the open magnitude experiences the force of the star (i.e., moon), efficaciously advancing over a wide area, as the narrows confine the same power. For this reason, neither lakes nor rivers are moved in a similar way. Pytheas of Massalia is the authority that tides swell to 80 cubits above Britain.

(Pliny, NH *2.215–17; cf. Seneca,* NQ *3.28.6; lightning: #1.9.4; Pytheas: #5.1.2C)*

D. *While tides in the Mediterranean are mild, the greater amplitude of Oceanic tides were perplexing and concerning. The* Periplus of the Erythraean Sea *(mid-1st century CE, author unknown) provides a vivid glimpse of sailing and commercial conditions in the Erythraean Sea. Particularly dramatic were the tides near Barygaza.*

But about Barygaza, it is much greater. Suddenly the depth is visible, and some portion of the land is just now dry but was sailed over just a short time ago; under the attack of the entire sea, very violently and forcibly compressed, the rivers are carried up against the nature of the flow for many *stadia*.

(Anonymous, Erythraean Sea *45)*

E. *In 325 BCE, Alexander of Macedon encountered drastic oceanic tides as his fleet lay at anchor off the island of Cilluta beyond the Indus' mouth. The ships suffered a great deal of damage. Arrian of Nicomedia was a Greek historian, soldier, and public servant whose* Anabasis *on Alexander the Great's campaigns (including an ethnography of India) survives. He also wrote a* Periplus of the Euxine Sea, *as an administrative report for the emperor Trajan (r. 98–117 CE).*

After they anchored in that place, a misfortune occurred: the sucking back (ebbtide) of the great sea so that their ships were cut off on dry land. And this, thus unknown beforehand to those around Alexander, itself furnished no little consternation, and even greater anxiety when, after some time passed, the water was again at hand and the ships were lifted up. Whichever of the ships the tide overtook, holding steady in the mud, these were raised unharmed to a height and, suffering nothing severe, sailed back again. But whichever ships were left behind on rather dry ground and did not have a firm standing, some fell against each other as the crowded wave came against them; others, shattered, were dashed together on the ground. Alexander therefore repaired these ships from the supplies at hand.

(Arrian, Anabasis *6.19.1–2)*

F. *Julius Caesar was a Roman statesman, general, and dictator who also thought deeply about geography and weather (essential knowledge for military success) and even commissioned a world-map that was eventually completed by his heir, Augustus (r. 27 BCE–14 CE). Caesar recounted the particularly high tide that frustrated his crossing of the English Channel and invasion of invade Britain in 55 BCE.*

That same night it happened that the moon was full, a day which is accustomed to bring about the highest tides in Ocean, and this was unknown to us. At that time, the tide completely filled up the long boats, in which Caesar took care to transport the army, and which he had beached on dry land; and a storm damaged the freighters, which were made fast at anchor. Nor was any opportunity of managing or helping them given to us. After many ships were broken to pieces, and—since the rest were useless with their lines, anchors, and remaining tack lost—a great disturbance fell over the entire army, a thing which necessarily happened: for there were not any other ships by which the troops could be conveyed back. And all things were lacking which were useful for refurbishing the ships, and, because it was agreed that it was suitable to winter in Gaul, grain had not been provided for in these places against the winter.

(Caesar, BG *4.29; cf.* BG *4.23.4, 28.3, 5.9.1)*

1.3.7 Surface of Sea/Water

A. *A geometrical explanation that water at rest is spherical.*

But because the surface of the water appears this way (spherical), they take as a principle the fact that water is always naturally disposed to stream together. The hollower spot is closer to the center. Therefore, let the lines AB and AΓ be drawn from the center, and let the line BΓ be joined. Therefore, the line at the base, from which is drawn AD, is shorter than those from the center. Now that place is hollower, so that water will flow around until there is a balance. But now, AE is equal to those lines from the center, such that it is necessary that there be water near those lines from the center. For then it (the water) will be at rest. For the line binding the lines from the center is circular. Therefore, the surface of water from which BEΓ (is drawn) is spherical.

(Aristotle, On the Heavens *287b4–14)*

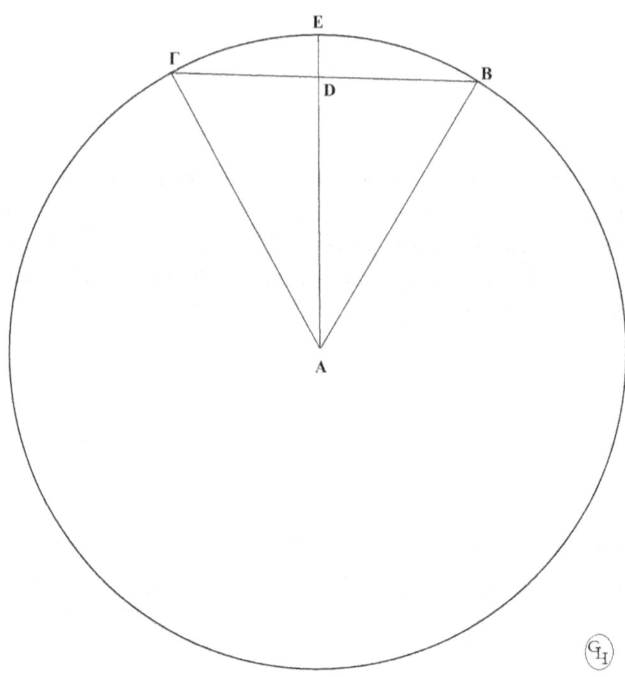

FIGURE 1.3.7A Water at rest is spherical: diagram by Georgia L. Irby.

B. *Several proofs of ocean's (and the earth's) sphericity.*

Nothing else in the nature of things is more obvious to observe. For hanging droplets of water are balled up everywhere in small spheres and—trickled on dust or positioned on the wooly surface of leaves—they are discerned as with complete roundness. And in full cups, the middle especially swells up, which things are more easily comprehended by reasoning than by sight, on account of the minuteness of the moisture and its softness settling into itself. And this is even more remarkable: that in full cups, with a very little bit of liquid added, what is extra overflows. But to the contrary, when heavy objects are added, often up to 20 silver *denarii*, probably because, received within, they lift the liquid into a peak. But liquids poured on the projecting body of water glide down. This is the same reason on account of which land, visible from the masts, is not seen from ships' decks, and, on account of which, as a vessel recedes from a distance, if something that shines is fastened on the top of the mast, little by little it seems to descend and is eventually obscured. Finally, by what other shape could the ocean, which we acknowledge is furthest out, cohere and not fall away without a confining edge? That very question returns us to the realm of the marvelous as to how, even though it is spherical, the sea does not fall away at its edge.

(Pliny, NH *2.163–165)*

C. *The polymath Eratosthenes of Cyrene (b. 276/272 BCE) wrote widely on mathematics, harmonic theory, chronology, grammar, and literary criticism, but is best known for his three-book* Geography *(staunchly criticized by Hipparchus*[10] *but excerpted by Strabo and others) and for deducing the most accurate ancient estimate of the earth's circumference (252,000* stadia*, about 24,662 miles [c. 39,700 kilometers]; the modern figure is 24,901 miles [c. 40,070 kilometers]). Eratosthenes suggested that, while the Mediterranean may be a single sea, it does not have a single surface.*

Thus, Eratosthenes is naïve, so that, although being a mathematician, he does not endorse the opinion that Archimedes articulated in his *On Floating Bodies*, that, when water settles and remains at rest, its appearance is spherical, the sphere having the same center as the earth. All those engaging in mathematics to any degree accept this opinion. But he (Eratosthenes) does not think that the inner sea (Mediterranean), although being a single sea, as he says, is arrayed under a single surface, not even in waterscapes near each other. And he makes engineers the witnesses of such stupidity, although mathematicians consider engineering a subset of mathematics. For Eratosthenes (F 16) says that Demetrius[11] tried to cut through the Peloponnesian Isthmus (in 302–301 BCE) to prepare a sailing passage for his expedition. But he was prevented by engineers taking measurements and reporting that in the Corinthian basin the sea was down over Cenchreae, so that if he should cut through the spot in its middle, then the whole strait around Aegina and even Aegina itself and the nearby islands would become submerged. Nor would the canal be useful.

(Strabo, Geography *1.3.11; for Archimedes: #5.1.15D; canals: #5.3.5)*

1.3.8 Currents

A. *Generated by many factors including the variable densities of contiguous bodies of water that differ in salinity or temperature (e.g., the warm Gulf Stream), currents are complex hydrological phenomena. But ancient authors would have been*

10 Fl. 160–130 BCE, Hipparchus of Nicaea was an astronomer and mathematician, best known for discovering the precession of the equinoxes, the time wherein the equinoxes make a complete circuit around the ecliptic (c. 25,800 years, that is to say, how long it takes for the vernal equinox (which shifts westward about one degree every 72 years) to make a complete circuit through the zodiac (cf. Ptolemy, *Almagest* 3.4).

11 I of Macedon "Poliorcetes": "Besieger of Cities": see #5.1.15C, #7.3D.

able to study only surface currents which are largely created by the Coriolis force (inertial force resulting from the earth's rotation) together with winds and their interplay with coastal geography.

> There the Southwest Wind thrusts the great wave towards the leftward headland of Crete.
>
> *(Homer,* Odyssey *3.295)*

B. *The currents in the strait near the mountains on Diodoros Island in the Erythraean Sea are especially strong.*

> There is a channel, not long, driving the sea and blocking it into a strait where the island of Diodoros cuts the 60-stadia passage in the middle. Therefore, a violent current along that same passage blows down from mountains lying alongside.
>
> *(Anonymous,* Erythraean Sea *25)*

C. *Most dramatic and easiest to scrutinize were the currents within straits. For Aristotle, refluent currents in Mediterranean Straits result from the contraction of water within the narrows.*

> The sea seems to flow in the narrowest places where, through the framing coastline, the open sea contracts from a large to a small space, because it (the water) often sways back and forth. In a large quantity of sea, this is unobserved. But in the narrows between land masses, a scant passage restrains the water, and there the shores constrict the swaying waters, a compression that seemed slight in the open sea but now seem great.
>
> *(Aristotle,* Meteorology *354a5–10)*

1.3.9 Whirlpools

A. *Occurring naturally where contrary currents meet or where tides affect fast currents in narrow straits, whirlpools are another sailing hazard. The most famous Mediterranean whirlpool is the notoriously treacherous Charybdis, spewing water and flames whenever Typhon, whom the gods buried under Mt. Aetna, moved (Homer,* Odyssey *12.104–105; Vergil,* Aeneid *3.420–423). One of the most harrowing descriptions comes from Strabo.*

> Charybdis is pointed out a little way from the city (Messana) and in the strait, extraordinarily deep, into which the flowing backwaters naturally pull down boats, which are swept away with a twisting around and great whirling. Gulped down and torn asunder, shards of wreckage are carried off towards the shore of Tauromenium, which, from this mischance, they call Kopria ("Refuse Heap").
>
> *(Strabo,* Geography *6.2.3)*

B. *Here the phenomenon is explained.*

Why, sometimes, are ships in the sea in fair weather altogether swallowed down and become unseen, so that no shards of wreckage float up? Is it when a cave-like place in the earth beneath the sea fissures open at the same time as a ship follows the wind to the sea and within the depth? Likewise, the sea, carried in a complete circle, is born downward. This is a whirlpool, and, in the strait around Messana, ships suffer this on account of the current—since whirlpools occur because of this current—and they are swallowed down to the depth on account of these things and also because the sea is deep and the earth below is cavernous to a great distance. Therefore whirlpools, forcing ships towards these caverns, carry them. Consequently, wreckage does not float up from there. But a current happens when—once the previous wind has ceased—the wind blows in the opposite direction over the sea still flowing under the first wind, especially when a South Wind is blowing in the opposite direction. Blowing at each other in opposite directions, currents thus jostle each other just as in rivers, and they become whirlpools. Twisted around, the beginning of the motion, strong, is carried upward. Since, therefore, it is not possible that the currents rush towards the side—for they are pushed in opposite directions from each other—it is necessary that they be thrust to the deep, so that the whirlpool necessarily carries down with it whatever has been grasped. Consequently, ships are turned up on end. It is also already recalled that a ship has fallen straight down (i.e., prow first).

(Aristotelian Problems *23.5 = 932a1–21)*

C. *A particularly dangerous stretch of water that includes whirlpools in the Erythraean Sea.*

Beyond the Sinthus River (Indus), there is another bay, unobservable, along the north. It is called Eirinon, in addition it is called "the Small" on one part and "the Big" on the other. Both seas are shallow, having whirlpools, nimble and continuous and a long way from land, as ships often run aground and are wrecked, left upon the shoals: the mainland is not even visible. A promontory stands out from this bay, bending from Eirinon at the east and south and to the west, itself encompassing the bay called Baraca, enclosing seven islands. There, those coming around the opening fall off a little backwards, and, running back, they escape to the open sea. But ships that are enclosed within that Baraca Bay are lost: for the waves are great and very deep, and the sea is tumultuous and murky and full of whirlpools and roiling eddies. The depth ("bottom") in some places is greatly severed, in other places rocky and sheer so that some anchors dropped there are quickly cut off, but others are crushed on the bottom. For those approaching from the deep sea, there is a sign of these dangers: overly large and dark serpents. In other places around these coasts and those around Barygaza, the serpents, smaller and with a bright greenish color and golden, encounter travelers.

(Anonymous, Periplus of the Erythraean Sea *40)*

1.3.10 Reefs

Like whirlpools, reefs pose another hazard to mythical and historical sailors, and many had names, such as the "Ass of Antron" below Antron in the Euboean Strait (Strabo, Geography *9.5.14). See #5.1.16§150 for a ship race in which one over-enthusiastic competitor runs afoul of a reef.*

A. *Returning from Troy, Agamemnon's ship is caught on the treacherous Caphereus Reef, south-east of Euboea.*

> Another greater pestilence calls to us shipwrecked men. There the swell is slight, mendacious with jagged shoals where the deceitful Caphereus covers its confined rocks with whirlpools. The strait rages with crags, and the surge always ferments with an alternating interchange.
>
> *(Seneca,* Agamemnon *557–560)*

B. *In 480 BCE, three Persian ships went aground in eastern Greece, and a stone beacon was later erected to mark the hazard.*

> Three of ten barbarian (Persian) ships drove on the "herm" (reef), the one between Scione and Magnesia, called the "Ant." Here the Barbarians[12] then placed a pillar of stone on the reef. Driving through from Therme when the obstacle became clear to them, they sailed through in all their ships.
>
> *(Herodotus,* Histories *7.183)*

C. *Born c. 110 CE, Pausanias traveled widely through Greece, penning a travelogue,* The Description of Greece, *describing significant geographical sites with their landmarks and sacred spaces, a valuable source for mythology, religion, art history, and much else. Pausanias includes the account of a human-built reef installed for security at Aegina, an island in the gulf between Attica and the Peloponnese. British admiralty charts and underwater surveys bear out Pausanias' claim, but the manufactured reef at Aegina seems to be a unique ancient hydraulic infrastructure.*

> Of the Hellenic islands, Aegina is the most difficult to sail towards. For rocks rise up from under the salt-sea around all of it and like a hog's back. They say that Aeacus[13] engineered these things because of a fear of piracy from the sea and so that the coastline would not be without danger for enemy men.
>
> *(Pausanias,* Description of Greece *2.29.6)*

12 #5.3.5D and note.

13 A son of Zeus, mythical king of Aegina, and one of the three judges in the Underworld.

1.3.11 Sea Depth

A. *The ancients asked many questions about the nature of water, including ocean depth (the Titan Atlas presumably knew the "depths of all the seas": Homer,* Odyssey *1.52–54). Water depths, which sailors tried to measure, are important data (to avoid shoals). While archaeological evidence suggests that sailors have been taking soundings from before 2000 BCE, Herodotus provides the earliest Greek literary evidence (#1.6A).*

> The springs of the Nile, being bottomless, flow from the middle of these hills. And half of the water flows to Egypt and to the north, but the other half flows to Aethiopia and the south. The scribe of Athena's treasury in Sais said that King Psammetichus of Egypt (7th century BCE) arrived at an experiment: Psammetichus sent a woven rope of many thousand *orguiae* down in the spring, but it did not arrive at the bottom.[14]
>
> *(Herodotus,* Histories *2.28.3–4)*

B. *According to Aristotle, very heavy seawater flows to its natural deepest place (*Meteorology *355a33–b5), but seas and oceans are not equally deep.*

> Indeed everything within the Pillars of Herakles flows according to the earth's hollows and the size of rivers: the Maeotis flows into the Pontus, and this one into the Aegean. But the seas beyond these do these things less clearly. This happens in those seas (Maeotis, Pontus, Aegean), on account of the size of their rivers—for more rivers flow into the Pontus and the Maeotis than a place many times larger—and owing to the shallowness of the depth. The sea consequently seems to become even deeper: the Pontus more than the Maeotis, the Aegean more than the Pontus, and the Sicilian deeper than the Aegean. But the Sardonian and Tyrrhenic Seas are the deepest of all. The waters beyond the Pillars, however, are shallow on account of the mud, and they are without wind since the sea is in a hollow.
>
> *(Aristotle,* Meteorology *354a13–23)*

> For, just as we say, this is the place of water (the bottom). Consequently, all rivers flow to it and all waters and everything generated from water. For there is a flow to the hollowest place and the sea holds this part of the earth.
>
> *(Aristotle,* Meteorology *355b15–19)*

C. *Aelian of Praeneste in southern Italy (b. 170 BCE) penned a monumental* On the Nature of Animals (NA) *in 17 books, a summary in Greek of earlier zoological*

14 See Pausanias, *Description of Greece* 2.37.5 where Nero's (r. 54–68) attempt to plumb the Alcyonian Lake in the southern Argolid, in the hydraulically active region around the springs of Lerna, also failed.

knowledge, whose sources included Aristotle and Pliny the Elder, and an important source for Medieval Bestiaries wherein animal behavior is viewed according to the moralizing tenets of Christianity. While many have speculated on the depths of Ocean, Aelian emphasizes that such knowledge remains theoretical.

They say that humans have examined the sea to a depth of 300 *orguiae*, but no further beyond that. But if fishes and even still if wild animals swim underneath that level, or if those waters are impassable for them—while the sea gods and spirits of saltwater and, to be sure, the ruler of the watery essence (Poseidon/Neptune) have all obtained their place—neither do I inquire closely nor has anyone else said.

(Aelian, NA *9.35; cf. Pliny,* NH *2.102; Oppian,* Fishing *1.82–89)*

1.3.12 Exploring Deep Water

A. *Dedicating his work to M. Aurelius and Commodus (co-r. 176–180* CE*), Oppian of Cilicia penned a five-book collection of hexameter verses,* On Fishing, *in which he explored the characteristics, habitats, reproduction, and survival tactics of marine fauna, the art of fishing, and how fishes deceive fishermen. While the ancients lacked the means to explore deep seafloors and measure salinity, temperature, or other hydrological data, Oppian implies that fisherman could map the seabed through autopsy. See #6.3.1 (Sponge cutters) and #6.5.2 (Pearl divers).*

Fishermen sail above the obscured sea with a bold heart, and they have looked down into the depths not visible, and with their skills they have divided the salty sea through measuring it.

(Oppian, Fishing *1.9–12)*

B. *Even though sophisticated diving equipment was unknown, some divers developed snorkel-like gear which helped them prolong their dives.*

Some divers are thus furnished with equipment for breathing, in order that, remaining in the sea for a long time, they draw air from above through an implement.

(Aristotle, PA *659a9–11)*

C. *And some divers employed diving helmets for deeper underwater expeditions (cf. Frost 1968).*

Similarly, lowering a cauldron, they facilitate breathing for divers. This cauldron does not fill with water, but it keeps the air in. The cauldron is plunged down forcefully. Thusly, it is immersed straight down; for water flows within anything immersed at an inclined angle.

(Aristotelian Problems *32.5 = 960b32–35)*

1.4 Land and Water

1.4.1 Cycling Between Land and Water

A. *Anaximander of Miletus (b. c. 610), Thales' student, viewed the natural world as a rational system, hypothesizing the existence of a seed-like substance from which emerged the material world. Anaximander's interests included astronomy and meteorology, and he is credited with drawing the first map of the Greek world. Like other early thinkers, his writings survive in extracts and later redactions. Here we have Anaximander's theory of the origin of the sea.*

For some say that the sea is the remainder of primal wetness. For the space around the earth was moist, and then some of the wetness was vaporized by the sun, and wind was born from it. And the turnings of the sun and moon move and make their turnings around these same things on account of those same vapors and exhalations where there is an abundance of it. And the remainder of the primordial moisture in the hollow places of the earth is the sea. Consequently, constantly desiccated by the sun, it diminishes, and in the end it will be altogether dry. Of this opinion, as Theophrastus observes (*On Waters*?), were Anaximander and Diogenes.

(*Anaximander,* TEGP *35* = *Alexander,* Commentary on Aristotle's Meteorology *67.3–12*)

B. *It was widely believed that the world cycles through periods of wetness and desiccation.*

For the same portions of the earth are neither always under water or dry, but they change according to the birth and loss of rivers. Consequently, the areas around both firm land and the sea change: the one does not always endure as earth and the other not always as sea for all time. But sea occurs where there was dry land, and then again land where there was sea. According to some orderly arrangement and cycle, to be sure, it is necessary that these things are thought to occur. The beginning of these things and the reason is that the regions inside the earth, just like the bodies of plants and animals, experience prime and old age. Except for them (plants and animals), such things do not happen to occur according to a part, but the whole body necessarily blooms and perishes. For the earth, this occurs according to each section on account of coldness and warmth. These things increase and perish because of the sun and its revolution.[15] Because

15 For most Greco-Roman thinkers the earth was stationary and celestial bodies, including the sun, revolved around it. Heliocentrism contradicted Aristotelian physics (motion ceases when natural place is reached; therefore, the earth, the heaviest element, is motionless: #1.2.7C). Some ancient thinkers considered the merits of heliocentrism, including Anaximander, Seleukos of Seleukia (Plutarch, *Platonic Questions* 8.1), and possibly Pliny (*NH* 2.116).

of these things and their power, parts of earth receive a different power, so that moistness is able to remain in some parts up to a point, and then they dry out and become old again. But other places keep coming to life and become moistened according to place. It is necessary that, as some places grow dry, springs disappear. While these things happen, rivers become small with respect to their former large size, then finally they become dry. And it is necessary that, while rivers change and vanish in some places from there, the sea also changes analogously. For wherever those portions encroach, driven back from the rivers, it necessarily makes the squeezed-out land dry. And where there are parts filled up by flowing rivers, silted up, they dry out, and from there they again become marshy. But because the entire nature of the earth's birth occurs gradually and in prolonged spans of time in contrast with our own lifespan, these occurrences escape our notice, as the perdition and loss of entire peoples occurs before the transition of these processes is remembered from beginning to end.

(Aristotle, Meteorology *351a19–b14)*

1.4.2 *Inland Fossilized Marine Fauna*

The presence of fossilized marine fauna at inland sites strongly indicates that the cosmos cycles between periods of wetness and dryness.

Xenophanes thinks that a mixture of earth with sea occurs, and in time earth is loosed by wateriness, saying that he has such proofs: that inland and in mountains mussel-shells are found; and in Syracusan stone quarries he says that the impression of fishes and seaweed have been discovered, and in Paros the impression of coral (or bay) in a rock's depth, and in Melite (Malta) shards of absolutely all sea creatures. These things, he says, occurred when all things were muddied over long ago, and the impressions in that mud had dried out. Xenophanes says that all humans will be destroyed when earth, conveyed down to sea, becomes mud; then there will be a beginning of genesis anew, and this transformation occurs in all cosmoi.

(Xenophanes, TEGP *59 = Hippolytus,* Refutations *1.14.5–6; cf. Eratosthenes* F *15; Ovid,* Metamorphoses *15.262–269; Strabo,* Geography *1.3.4)*

1.4.3 *Siltation*

A. *Siltation is usually a gradual, nearly imperceptible process that often changes the nature of bodies of water, including their salinity and navigability (#5.1.12). Rapid sedimentation over a short time, however, is also known at Rome in the Tiber (Brock et al. 2021) and is particularly pronounced at harbors at Ephesus (#5.3.3I; for Ostia: #5.3.3G–H; Lisé-Pronovost et al. 2019). Polybius of Megalopolis (215–133 BCE) was a Greek general and diplomat, deported to Rome in 168, where he became friends with the Roman statesman Publius Cornelius Scipio Aemilianus. Polybius traveled widely, even venturing beyond the Pillars of*

Herakles, and he penned a History of Rome *to explain Rome's swift rise to power to a Greek readership. Two of his books (4–5) focus on geography (surviving in extracts in Strabo). Here Polybius outlines the process of siltation as it occurs in the Pontus (Black Sea) and Maeotis (Sea of Azov).*

> Indeed, we say that the Pontus is silting up both now and long ago, and that in time the Maeotis will be entirely silted up, assuming the same disposition remains around those places and the causes of siltation remain continuously active. Since time is boundless, and all the hollows are altogether bounded, it is clear that even if a fig[16] of siltation were brought in, in time the hollows would become full. According to nature in boundless time, accretion reaches some limit or it perishes, even if it happens according to the least amount (for I perceive this now), it is necessarily completed according to this proposition. But when the accretion is not tiny but exceedingly great and some soil is brought in, it is clear that at some time siltation will not occur, but quickly and now, as has truly been said by me. Indeed it appears to happen. For the Maeotis is already silted up. For the greater part of it has a depth of seven and five *orguiae*: accordingly, it is no longer navigable by large ships without a pilot. In the beginning, the Maeotis was a sea confluent around the Pontus, as the ancients agree, but it is now a sweet-water lake after the sea was squeezed out by the poured-in silt and the prevailing incursion of rivers. And around the Pontus something similar will happen, and it is occurring now, but it is not very much evident to many observers because of the size of the hollow basin. But to be sure, to those watching the shallows attentively, this occurrence is clear.
>
> *(Polybius,* Histories *4.40.4–10, cf. 4.42.3–5)*

B. *The dramatic effects of siltation in the Pyramus River (Ceyhan, in Turkey).*

> Stepping down from the mountains, the Pyramus River brings so much soil down to the sea, some from Cataonia and some from the Cilician plains, that this oracle is reported regarding it: "for those folk yet to be, the silver eddying Pyramus, coming down to Cyprus, would arrive at the sacred shore." For something similar occurs also in Egypt, where the Nile is always turning still more space into dry land by silting up the sea. And so Herodotus says that Egypt is the gift of the Nile (*Histories* 2.5). But the poet (Homer) had the Pharos first as sea-borne (*Odyssey* 4.353) but not, as now, close to land in Egypt.
>
> *(Strabo,* Geography *12.2.4)*

C. *Siltation also offers crude evidence for the site of Troy, observed by Hestiaia of Alexandria (3rd century BCE?, a woman who wrote a commentary on Homer's* Iliad, *now lost), repeated by Demetrius of Skepsis (early 2nd century BCE, whose*

16 I.e., very tiny bit.

historical and geographical commentary on the Iliad *was at least 26 books long, also fragmentary), and finally extracted by Strabo here.*

> Demetrius also provides Hestiaia the Alexandrian as a witness, she who wrote about Homer's *Iliad*, and inquired if the war occurred around the current city of Troy and the Trojan Plain, which the poet (Homer) understands as between the city and the sea: for the plain in front of the current city seems to be a later creation, silted from the rivers.
>
> *(Strabo,* Geography *13.1.36)*

D. *There is also a tradition that Tiber Island, in the Tiber River flowing through Rome, was built up by silt and detritus thrown into the river in 509 BCE. Livy (59 BCE–17 CE) wrote a monumental history of Rome,* From the Foundation of the City, *beginning with its establishment by Romulus in 753 BCE down to Augustus' principate, of which only books 1–10 (753–292 BCE) and 21–45 (218–167 BCE) survive.*

> By chance, it is said that there was a crop of spelt, ripe for harvest. But because this consecrated produce of the field (the Campus Martius) was unlucky for eating, a great force of men—sent in at the same time after the harvest had been cut back—poured the crop with its chaff together with baskets into the Tiber flowing with its weak current, as is customary in the midsummer heat. And thus the grain's accumulations, smeared with mud, settled in the hesitating shoals. Little by little, from that grain and the other conveyed materials, which a river randomly brings to that place, an island was made. I believe that afterwards piers were added by hand and also infrastructure so that the land was projecting above the river and stable for supporting temples and also porticos.
>
> *(Livy,* From the Foundation of the City *2.5.3–4)*

1.4.4 Sources of Terrestrial Waters

A. *Anaxagoras of Clazomenae (b. c. 500 BCE) envisioned a cosmos wherein generative, boundless material was infinitely divisible, thus accounting for even microscopic change. Anaxagoras' cosmos was overseen deistically by* Nous, *"Mind," who set cosmic material into a whirling vortex, creating the sensible world and governing the motion of celestial bodies around the earth. Anaxagoras was probably also the first Greek thinker to explain lunar and solar eclipses correctly. Here, the genesis of rivers.*

> Of those waters on the earth Anaxagoras says that sea arose from waters within the earth—from which settled waters became thus as they are while they evaporate—and also from rivers flowing down. Rivers also take their foundation from rains and from those waters in the earth. For the earth is hollow and has

water in its cavities. Anaxagoras says that the Nile is increased in the summer as waters are conveyed to it from snows from southerly regions.

(Anaxagoras, TEGP *38 = Hippolytus,* Refutation *1.8.4–5; Nile: #1.5.1A)*

B. *While there is a great deal of disagreement over the order of the books in Seneca's* Natural Questions, *the book on terrestrial waters was the first one (Hines 2000). Here, Seneca explores the nature and origins of rivers, debunking earlier theories, including those of Anaxagoras. Seneca is probably citing from Theophrastus' lost* On Waters.

4. First let us seek in what manner the earth supplies continuous courses of rivers, whence such a great supply of water comes forth. We marvel that the seas do not feel the increase of rivers. The fact that the land does not feel the loss of exiting waters is equally to be wondered at. For what is it that thus either has filled the earth so that it is able to furnish so great a supply from a hidden reserve, or repeatedly supplies it? Whatever rationale we offer regarding a river, the same will be the explanation of streams and springs.

5. Certain people think that the earth accepts whatever water it has emitted, and on account of this, the seas do not grow because they do not return back to themselves whatever has flowed in, but straightaway they give those waters back to the earth. For, along an obscured route, water approaches the land, and it comes openly, and it is then returned along a hidden path. The sea is nourished in this transit because it sets aside its bitterness, assailed through many windings of lands, and its deformity. In such a great variety of soil, water doffs off its taste and crosses over to pure water.

6. Certain folk think that, whatever the land takes up from rain, it returns it again, and in the place of proof they posit that there are very few rivers in these places where rain is infrequent. Consequently, they say that the deserts of Aethiopia are dry and that very few springs are found in inner Africa, because the nature of the sky there is seething and nearly always summery. And so the sands lie rough without trees, without cultivation, sprinkled with rare rains, which they immediately drink up. But, to the contrary, it is agreed that Germany and Gaul and Italy, close to those places, abound in streams and rivers because they utilize a moist sky, and the summertime does not even lack rains.

7. You will see that many things are able to be said against this theory. First of all, I, an attentive gardener of my own vines, affirm that no rain is so great that it can make the ground moist beyond a depth of ten paces. All the moistness is consumed within the first crust, and the moisture does not descend to the lower levels. How then is rain, which tinges only the topsoil, able to supply strength to rivers? The greater part of it is carried away through riverbeds into the sea. Scant is that which the earth swallows, nor does the earth hold onto that rain. For either the ground is dry and takes into itself whatever is poured in. Or the earth, overfull if anything has fallen beyond natural desire, shuts it out. And so

rivers are not augmented by the first rains because a thirsty ground draws all the rain into itself. But what about the fact that certain rivers break through rocks and mountains? What do rains confer on these rivers which are carried down through bare crags and do not have land on which to settle? Add the fact that, in the driest places, wells are driven down to a deep span of 200 or 300 paces and those wells come upon rich veins of waters at a level to which rain does not penetrate so that you might know that celestial moisture has not been collected there, but instead that water at those depths is accustomed to be called "living" water. And also, on that same argument, this opinion is refuted: that certain springs on the highest summit of a mountain overflow. It appears that those springs are driven up from below or are conceived there, because all rainwater runs downward.

8. Certain folk think that somehow in the exterior part of the lands there lie vast marshes and great navigable lakes; they think that somehow the seas, stretched out in a huge span, are poured within valleys, and thus the inner regions of the lands abound in sweet waters no less widely than Ocean and its bays pool up around us, indeed even more widely because the earth extends more deeply there. Therefore, those rivers are carried out from that deep abundance of water. Why should you wonder if the earth does not feel rivers withdrawn when the seas do not feel rivers added?

9. For certain folk, this cause is pleasing: they say that the land has hollow recesses within itself and a lot of air. This air, necessarily pressed down by heavy darkness, becomes cold. Then the air, sluggish and unmoved, is converted into water when it ceases to carry itself. Just as above us the change of air makes rain, so below the lands this change makes a river or a stream. Above us, sluggish and heavy air is unable to stand firm. For at times it is attenuated by the sun, at some times it is expanded by the winds, so there are long intervals between rains. But underground, whatever there is that converts air into water, it is always the same, perpetual shadow, eternal frigidity, inert density. Therefore, this will always provide the causes for a spring or river. It pleases us Stoics that the earth is mutable. This also, whatever it breathes out, because it is not conceived in a free atmosphere, straightaway becomes thick and is turned into moisture. You thus have the first cause of waters being born under the earth.

10. Perhaps also add the fact that all things are made from all things: from water, air; from air, fire; from fire, air.[17] Therefore, why should water not be made from earth? If earth is mutable into other elements, it is even mutable into water, especially into this. For each is a related thing, each is heavy, each is dense, each is collected at the edge of the world. From water, earth is created; why is water then not made from earth?

17 See #1.2.7.

"But rivers are huge!" When you see how large they are, look again at from how much they derive. Are you amazed when they constantly slip, and some are even snatched up violently, that there is always a new supply at hand for them? But why, if you marvel at this, when the winds drive all the air onward, does the air not fail, but flows equally through days and nights? Air, however, is not conveyed in a bed, like rivers, but it wanders through the vast span of sky with a broad stroke. Why are you amazed if any wave is left which comes up after so many waves have been broken? . . .

11. "But, therefore," someone says, "if the causes whereby rivers and also springs arise are perpetual, why are they sometimes dried out, and why do they sometimes come out from places where they had not been before?" Their paths are often disturbed by an earthquake, and the down-rush cuts off the course of waters which then, held back, seek new outlets. In some places, they make an attack, or they are transferred from one place to another by the shaking of the earth itself.

For us, it is customary that rivers overflow when their channels are lost, then, because they have lost their way, they make a new one. Theophrastus (*On Waters*?) said that this happened on Mt. Corcyrus, on which a new supply of springs emerged after an earth tremor. But it is also thought that there are other causes, which otherwise call waters out or cast them down or turn them aside. Once upon a time, Mt. Haemus (in Thrace) was water-poor. When a tribe of Gauls, besieged by Cassander (r. Macedon 305–297), conveyed themselves onto that mountain and cut down the trees, a huge abundance of water appeared, which evidently the groves were drawing down towards their own nourishment. Because these trees were overturned, the moisture, which ceased being consumed by the vegetation, overflowed. Theophrastus says that the same thing also happened around Magnesia. But—may it be permitted to speak peacefully with Theophrastus—this is not likely, because the most watery areas are those which are the shadiest. This would not occur if the vegetation, whose nourishment is close at hand, dried out the waters. The supply of rivers truly drips from the inmost earth and is conceived further than it can wander away from its roots. Then trees that have been cut desire more moisture: for they draw up moisture, not only that they might live but also that they might grow.

Theophrastus says that the same thing occurred around Arcadia, which was a city on the island of Crete: the springs and rivers stopped, because the earth stopped being cultivated when the city was demolished. But after the place received back its farmers, it also received back its waters. Theophrastus posited this as the cause for the dryness: the fact that the compressed earth became hard and, unagitated, it was not able to send up rainwaters. How therefore do we see many springs in deserted places? Finally, we discover more places that begin to be cultivated on account of their waters than places which began to have water because they were being cultivated. For perhaps you understand that it is not rainwater which conveys the most enormous rivers, suitable for large ships from their source, because through winter and summer the flow from the headwaters is equal. Rainfall is able to make a torrent, but it is not able to create a river slipping between its banks with an equal course. Rains do not do this, but they do urge the rivers on.

(Seneca, NQ *3.4–11, cf. Aristotle,* Meteorology *349b3–355b25; Lucretius,* On the Nature of Things *2.471–476, 5.261–272, 6.631–638; Pliny,* NH *2.166)*

1.5 Rivers[18]

1.5.1 Nile

A. *One source of fascination was the Nile's seemingly unusual behavior, its summertime flooding: Greek (and other European) rivers swell during the wet winter season. Among the early theories were Etesian Winds blowing from the northwest Mediterranean in the summertime (Thales,* TEGP *21), melting snow (Anaxagoras: #1.4.4A), summer rains (Callisthenes* F *12b). Here, Herodotus details and debunks early theories.*

20. But some Greeks wishing to be notable for cleverness uttered three ideas about this river: two of which I do not deem worthy to recall except for wanting to indicate what they are. One of these says that Etesian Winds are why the river floods, hindering the Nile from flowing out to the sea. But the Etesians at any rate do not often blow, and the Nile does this same thing. In addition, if the Etesians were the cause, then it would be necessary that other rivers, which flow in directions opposite the Etesians, would behave similarly and according to the behavior of the Nile, and even more so, being smaller and supplying a weaker flow. But there are many rivers in Syria and also in Libya which in no way behave such as the Nile does.

21. The other explanation is even more ignorant than the one already mentioned, but more marvelous to express: this opinion says that the same river, the Nile, contrives these things, its summer flooding, flowing from Ocean which flows around the entire earth.

22. The third of these opinions, although the most reasonable, is especially false: for it says nothing but this, declaring that the Nile flows from melting snow. But the Nile flows from Libya through the middle of Aethiopia, and empties into Egypt. How can it flow from snow, for the most part flowing from the hottest regions to cooler ones? For someone thinking through such things concerning how there is in no way any truth to the notion that the river flows from

18 For the Tiber, #7.4.1.

snow, as the first and greatest proof, winds blowing from these places supply warmth. The second proof is that the place continues being rainless and iceless. But with falling snow there is every necessity of raining within five days so that if it did snow it would then rain in these places. The third proof is that the people are dark-skinned from the burning heat. Moreover, kites and swallows, being there through the year, do not leave, and cranes, fleeing the winter in the Scythian region, go back and forth to winter in these places (Egypt). And, accordingly, if it snowed and such a thing happened with respect to the country in which the Nile flows and from which it rises, then none of these things would happen, as necessity has assigned.

23. But the opinion about Ocean that is offered according to the secrets of mythology does not require disproof. For I do not know any river Ocean, and I think that Homer or someone of the earlier poets came upon the name and introduced it to their poetry.

24. But if it is necessary to recall the opinions that were set forth, then I will explain the one that I do accept about these unseen matters: why it seems to me that the Nile swells in the summer. During the wintertime, the sun, driven away from its original through-way, goes over Libya inward from the coast. But now, with the briefest clarification, all to be said is the following: for whichever land this deity (Helios/the sun) is closest to and whichever he is over, this region seems especially thirsty, and the inland flows of these rivers are withered.

25. But to clarify in a more fulsome recap, it happens thusly. For, passing over Libya inward from the coast—just as the air through the whole region is bright and along these regions the place is warm and the winds are cool—the sun does just the sort of thing he accustomed to do in summer, crossing through the middle of the sky. For he draws water up to himself, and, having drawn it up, he pushes it back to the inland regions; and then the winds, catching up the water and scattering it, melt it. And as is reasonable, those winds blowing from this same region, the South Wind and the Lips (southwest) are the rainiest of all the winds by far. For it seems to me that the sun does not send back all the water of the Nile annually each time, but some waters are kept back around himself (the sun). Then, as the winter grows milder, the sun departs back to the mid-sky, and from there he draws similarly from all the rivers. In the meantime, those other rivers flow more abundantly when much rainy water mingles in them, just as the country is rained on and becomes full of gullies. But in summer, as the rains slack off, the rivers are weak, drawn up by the sun. But the Nile, being rainless—the only river drawn up by the sun at this time (winter)—reasonably flows lower than its level in the summer by far. For during summer, together with all other waters, this one (the Nile) is drawn up equally, but in winter he alone, the Nile, is squeezed out.

26. Thus the sun is acknowledged as the cause of these things (summer flooding). But, according to my opinion, this same sun is the reason for the dry air, burning the very through-way. For thus, summer always occupies the inland of

Libya. But, if the timing of the seasons were changed, so that now the North Wind and winter arose in the part of the sky where the setting of the South Wind and midday winds are, then the South Wind would now set in this place and the North Wind in that place. If these things were so, the sun, driven out from mid-heaven by the winter and the North Wind, would pass over the inland of Europe as now he passes over Libya, and I expect that traversing through all of Europe he (the sun) would do the same to the Ister as he does to the Nile.

27. And I have this opinion about the wind, that it does blow from the Nile: it is extremely unreasonable that from warm places any wind would blow: a breeze enjoys blowing from some cool place.

(Herodotus, Histories *2.20–27; winds: #5.1.9)*

B. *The Nile was also a source of fascination for its unknown source* (*eventually discovered and confirmed by John Hanning Speke [1862] and Henry Morton Stanley [1875]*)*, and several theories were posited: Aeschylus (c. 525/4 BCE–456/4 BCE) ascribed the headwaters to the otherwise unknown Papyrus Mountains* (Prometheus Bound *810–12). Alexander the Great (d. 323 BCE) believed that the Nile emerged from the Indus. Like Herodotus (2.34), Pliny believed that the origin simply could not be ascertained because the river flows through scorching desert (uninhabitable and thus un-investigable). Here is the Nile's complex course as Pliny envisioned it. Note the anthropomorphism, the notion that some places are too hot for human habitation, and the prejudice that nature exists in service to humankind.*

51. The Nile, rising from uncertain springs, traveling through deserted and blazing places with an immense span of length—investigated only by unarmed reputation without the battles that have discovered all the rest of the lands—has its origin, as King Juba[19] was able to scrutinize, in a mountain of lower Mauretania, not far from Ocean, straightaway in an overflowing lake which they call Nilides ("child of the Nile"). There the *alabatae* fish are found, as well as *coracini*, and *siluri*.[20] Also from there a crocodile, dedicated in the Iseum at Caesarea,[21] is seen today as proof. Moreover, it has been noted that the Nile increases proportionately as snows or rains in Mauretania saturate the region.

52. Poured out from this lake, the river deems it unworthy to flow through sandy and filthy places, and it hides itself along a journey of several days. But soon it breaks out in another, larger lake in the territory of the Masaeylians of Caesarea Mauretania. And just as it surveys communities of people, with proofs of having the same animals. Received again in the sands, it is hidden again in

19 Juba II (c. 48 BCE–23 CE), raised and educated in Rome, returned to Mauretania as king in 25 BCE. His wife was Cleopatra Selene, daughter of Cleopatra VII and Marc Antony. Juba was a considerable scholar who wrote extensively on many topics including an *On Arabia* and books on history and geography (Roller 2003).

20 Modern equivalencies of these fishes are uncertain.

21 *Iseum*: temple of Isis. *Caesarea* (Mauretania): the Mediterranean coast of Algeria.

the deserts for (a journey of) 20 days up to the closest Aethiopians,[22] and when again it senses a human being, it shoots up from a spring, probably the one which they call "Black."

53. There, separating Africa from Aethiopia, even if not immediately peopled, nonetheless crowded with wild animals and beasts, the Nile is an artisan of forests. The river cuts through the middle of Aethiopia, and there it is called Astapus, which in the language of those folk means "water flowing from the darkness." It thus sprinkles countless islands, some so vast in size that, although with its fierce speed, nonetheless in a course of five days, not shorter, it flies across. Around its most famous island, Meroe, it is called Astorbes on the left channel: this is the branch of water coming from the darkness.

54. On the right it is called Astusapes, which adds the indication of a "side-branch." It is not called "Nile" before it joins itself whole again in concordant waters. Thus, even as yet, it is still called Giris for some miles as before. And for Homer it is called "the Aegyptian River" over its entire course (*Odyssey* 4.477), and for others, "Triton." Immediately dashed against the islands, it is urged on by so many obstructions, finally shut in by mountains, elsewhere not more violent, conveyed over hastening waters to the Aethiopian place which are called *Catadupi* ("Downward Crash"). At the last cataract between obstructing rocks, it is believed not to flow but to rush with a huge din. Afterwards it is gentle—the ferocity tamed in shattered waves and for some time exhausted by its span—although it spews itself out in many throats into the Egyptian Sea, and on certain days, spread over all Egypt, it floats fertilely over the land.

(Pliny, NH *5.51–54)*

C. *Marcus Tullius Cicero (106–43 BCE) was a Roman statesman, orator, and politician (who staunchly defended the rights of wealthy, land-holding senators against the rights of less fortunate Romans). He was also a Stoic philosopher who wrote on ethics, the ideal state, and human nature. Here he observes the effects of the Nile's din on those dwelling near Catadupa: this anecdote about the Nile helps (explain why human beings cannot hear the constantly playing "music of the spheres" produced by the motions of celestial bodies).*

The ears of men filled with this sound grow deaf. For no sense is more dull in you. Just like at those places called Catadupa where the Nile rushes headlong from the loftiest mountains: the tribe which inhabits that place, on account of the loudness of the sound, lack the sense of hearing.

(Cicero, On the Republic *6.19)*

22 The western Aethiopians near Egypt: the ancients imagined two Aethiopian races divided between the setting and rising of Hyperion (the sun: *Odyssey* 1.22–25). The eastern Aethiopians, however, had straight hair and spoke a different language (Herodotus 7.70.2; cf. Diodorus Siculus, *Library of History* 3.8; Strabo, *Geography* 2.3.8).

D. *Seneca devoted a full book of his* Natural Questions *to the Nile River (on which, no doubt, Pliny relied heavily). Here, the extreme sport of riding the rapids.*

> Among the wonders of this river, I have learned about the unbelievable audacity of the inhabitants. By twos they settle into tiny boats: one guides the boat, the other bales. Then, much jostled about between the swift frenzy of the Nile and its waves dashing back and forth, at length they hold the slenderest channels, through which they escape the narrows of the crags. And, when poured out over the whole wave, they control the rushing boat by hand and—the spectators greatly afraid—they are thrown head-long. Although you would lament and might believe that they were already submerged and overwhelmed by so great a mass of water, sent like a catapult a long way from the spot into which they had fallen, they sail. The falling wave does not submerge them but instead hands them over to flat waters.
>
> *(Seneca,* NQ *4A2.6)*

1.5.2 Ister/Hister/Danube

A. *The Ister, as the eastern portion of the river was called, was attested as early as Hesiod (*Theogony *339) and long viewed as analogous with the Nile, as implied by Herodotus (*Histories *1.5.1). Like the Nile, its headwaters were a source of mystery and its seven mouths (actually far more) a source of fascination. According to legend, it was through the Ister that Jason and his Argonauts made their escape from the Euxine, believing that the river would provide passage to the Adriatic and facilitate a circumnavigation of the world. Jason's story is most fulsomely recorded by Apollonius of Rhodes (3rd century BCE), whose subtle* Argonautica *served as a model for Vergil and Ovid and also sketched a complex mythical geography.*

> There is some river, the highest horn of Ocean, wide and deep even for a towing ship to pass through. Calling it the Ister, they have marked out its farthest point. For a while it cuts through untried regions as this single river. For, beyond the blast of the North Wind in the Riphaean Mountains,[23] its springs roar and boil far away. But when it reaches the boundaries of the Thracian Scythians,[24] there it is divided in two, and it casts this water with the eastern salt-sea (Euxine), but

23 The "gusty" mountains near the Scythian Ocean at the northern extent of Europe and Asia, beyond which dwelled the Hyperboreans, first mentioned by Alcman of Sparta F 58 (seventh century BCE), and quickly becoming a symbol of the distant edges of the earth (Aeschylus F 183; Sophocles, *Oedipus at Colonus* 1248).

24 The ancients distinguished the "Asiatic Scythians" (Saca: inhabiting the northern and eastern Eurasian Steppe) from "European Scythians" (Cimmerians, and peoples dwelling along the Pontus and Crimea).

the hinder part goes cleaving through a deep basin of the Trinakrion Sea[25] which bends towards your land, if the Achelous River truly emerges from your land.[26]

(Apollonius, Argonautica *4.282–293)*

B. *Here Strabo takes his predecessors to task for perpetuating the falsehood that the Ister debouches into the Adriatic.*

For this reason, Hipparchus argues that the Pontus would be joined with the Adriatic in some places, just as the Ister does, splitting off from regions along the Pontus and flowing into each sea (Pontus and Adriatic) on account of the situation of the terrain. But the Ister does not have its origins from the regions along the Pontus. But, to the contrary, it rises from the mountains above the Adriatic, nor does it flow into each sea, but only into the Pontus, and it is split only in those mouths along the Pontus. Hipparchus did not recognize this common mistake of those before him. His predecessors supported the idea that there was some river having the same name as the Ister but debouching into the Adriatic, after dividing from it (the Ister proper), from which a race of Istrians, through whose territory the river was born, took their name, and along which Jason made his return sail from Colchis along it.

(Strabo, Geography *1.3.15; cf. 1.2.39; Diodorus Siculus,* Library of History *4.56.7; for Hipparchus: #1.3.7C note)*

C. *The Romans called the western portion of the river the Danube, first cited by Caesar, BG 6.25.2 (cf. Seneca,* NQ *3.27.9). Together with the Rhine, the Danube marked Rome's northern imperial frontier. Here Pliny laid out the river's course, including correctly situating its source in the Abnoua mountain range in Germany.*

Thence to the mouths of the Hister: its source is in Germany on the yoke of Mt. Abnouae, facing the Gallic town Rauricum (Augst, near Basel), and it slips many miles beyond the Alps and through countless tribes under the name of the Danube. With an immense increase of waters, it is called the Hister where it first washes Illyricum, with 60 tributaries flowing in, nearly half being navigable, and it rolls out into the Pontus in six rivers. The first mouth is the Peuces, and next Peuce island, itself on the closest bed and called "Sacred," is swallowed up by a great swamp, 19 Roman miles long. From this same bed above Histropolis is a lake, 63 paces in circumference: they call it Halmyris ("Salty"). The second mouth is called Naracustoma, the third is the "Lovely" Mouth, next to the island Sarmatica, the fourth is the "False Mouth." Next is the island "Mosquito Crossing," afterwards is the "Northern Mouth" and the "Barren

25 Sicilian Sea, south of the Adriatic.

26 While the Achelous does emerge in the western Peloponnese, the Ister does not debouch into the Adriatic or Sicilian Seas.

Mouth." The individual mouths are so large that to a length of 40 miles, the sea is conquered by them, and a draught of water is perceived as sweet.

(Pliny, NH *4.79)*

1.5.3 Scamander and Simois

Rivers were protected by eponymous deities, and it was often impossible to distinguish river from god (see #3.1). During one battle of the Trojan War, the Greek hero Achilles slaughtered countless Trojans whose corpses were piled up into the rivers Scamander/Xanthus ("Tawny") and Simois. The rivers reacted dramatically. In the end, the gods sent Hephaestus, god of fire and technology, to dry out the plains with fire.

Nor did Scamander cease from his rage, but he was all the more furious at the son of Peleus (Achilles), and raising up the swell of his flow as a crest, he exhorted Simois, shouting out, "Dear brother, let us both check his strength, since quickly he will utterly destroy the great city of King Priam, and the Trojans will not stand fast in battle. But, with all haste come help and fill your waters from your springs, and urge on your streambed. Make a great wave stand, stirring up a clangor of logs and stones, so we might stop this savage man who is strong now, eager to be equal to the gods. For I say that neither will his strength defend him, nor his beauty, nor that lovely armor which will lay stretched out somewhere at the bottom covered under slime. And I will wrap him in sand, pouring over him infinite silt. Nor will the Achaeans know where to gather his bones. I will cover him with so much slime from above. Here also his tombstone will be fashioned, nor will he have need of a burial cairn when the Achaeans honor him with funeral rites."

(Homer, Iliad *21.305–327; cf. Strabo 13.1.34; for Achilles' armor: #3.1.6C introduction)*

1.5.4 Araxes

Pomponius Mela, working under Claudius (r. 41–54 CE), wrote the earliest Latin-language account of the geography of the Roman Empire in the 1st century CE, providing a selective survey of important or interesting cities, towns, monuments, religious sites, and natural landmarks. Here we have a lively description of the Araxes River (Aras), which debouches into the Caspian), and its waterfall.

Sent down from the side of the Taurus massif, until it cuts the fields of Armenia, the Araxes slips along placidly and silently. Nor is it clear into which part it goes, although you might be watching. When it comes down into harsher terrain, pressed here and there by crags, the narrower it is, all the more swiftly it shatters itself repeatedly against the opposite banks of crags. And, on account of this, it is rolled stridently down with a great rumble so quickly that, where it is about to fall from a precipice into low-lying areas, it does not immediately deflect a wave, but conveys it beyond the channel which it holds, uplifted with a span of more than a *iugerum* and itself carrying itself without a bed—its waters hanging. Then where it descends, curved and along a bow-shaped bed, it becomes peaceful and again silent and, scarcely flowing into it, it washes the shore.

(Mela, On the Circuit of the World *3.40; cf. Strabo,* Geography *11.14.3; Pliny,* NH *6.2)*

1.5.5 Phasis

The unusual properties of the Phasis River (Rioni), debouching into the Black Sea.

From there we sailed to the Phasis River, 90 *stadia* distant from Mogros. Of all the rivers I know, the Phasis furnishes the lightest water and is most especially changeable in color. One might judge its lightness with a weight and by this, the fact that it floats on the sea and is not mixed in, just as Homer says that the Titaresius River (in Thessaly) floats above the Peneius River like oil (*Iliad* 2.754), and if skimming along the floating river, sweet water is drawn up. But if someone would plunge a pitcher to a depth, the water would be briny. Indeed, the entire Pontus is composed somewhat of much sweeter water than the sea beyond (i.e., the Aegean). And the reason for this is that the rivers are measurable neither in number nor size. There is proof of its sweetness, if it is necessary for perceptible phenomena, that those folks dwelling near the sea lead their hoof-stock down to the sea and water their animals along it: the cattle seem to drink there gladly. And the thought prevails that this drink is more beneficial for them than sweet water. The color of the Phasis is similar to water dipped from lead or tin. But, standing, it becomes very clear. Moreover, it is the established practice that those sailing into the Phasis do not bring other water in. But when they enter the Phasis' flow, there is a command that they pour out all the water that is in their ships. If they don't, the prevailing thought is that those neglectful of this mandate will not have a good voyage. The water of the Phasis is not moldered, but it remains pure for more than ten years, except for this, that it changes to the sweeter.

(Arrian, Periplus *8; cf. Apollonius,* Argonautica *2.1261; Strabo,* Geography *11.3.4; Pliny,* NH *6.13)*

1.5.6 Tigris

The 2nd-century-CE On the Names of Rivers and Mountains *is a short work in Greek ascribed to Plutarch, but recognized as pseudepigraphal in the scholium* *to the 9th c. manuscript (*Palatinus Graecus Heidelbergensis *398). In 25 sections the author chronicled the back stories of rivers from Gaul to India including how the rivers received their names and the unusual plants and stones, with mystical properties, found in them. The work may have been intended as parody, and the sources cited by the author may be fabrications. Here we have a selection from the chapter on the Tigris River.*

The Tigris River is from Armenia, carrying its flow down to the Araxes and the Arsacidan lake. It was earlier called Sollax which translates as "carrying downward." But it was called Tigris for this reason: Dionysus, insane because of Hera's intentions,[27] wandered over land and sea, wishing to be released from his suffering. Coming upon places in Armenia and not able to cross the aforementioned river, he called out to Zeus. Happening to listen, the god sent him a tiger on which Dionysus was conveyed across without danger. For the honor of the happenstances, Dionysus renamed the river Tigris, as Theophilus tells in book one of his *On Stones* . . .

In this same river is born a stone called *myndan*, altogether white: if someone has one, that person would never be injured by a wild beast, as Leon of Byzantium narrates in book 3 of his *On Rivers*.

(Pseudo-Plutarch, The Names of Rivers and Mountains *24.1–2)*

1.6 Underground Rivers

A. *Aristotle's explanation for rivers that flow partly underground.*

The swallowing down of rivers makes it clear that there are these chasms and clefts under the earth. This often happens on the earth. As in the Peloponnese, there are many such occurrences around Arcadia. The reason is owing to the land being mountainous: it does not have outlets from the hollows to the sea. For, filled and not having an efflux, rivers find a way through to the deep, as the waters therein are forced below. Therefore, such events most certainly occur around Hellas, but they are small in scope. But under the Caucasus there is a lake which the residents call a sea (Caspian). This lake—into which many and large rivers throw themselves—not having an obvious outflow, runs out under the land along the Coraxi, around the regions called the Deeps of the Pontus. This deep part of the sea is boundless. No one at any rate, after dropping a lead-line, has ever been able to find its bottom. In this spot, about 300 *stadia* away from land, the water delivers a river over a large area, but not continuously, but in three parts.

27 Hera, queen of the gods, was very jealous of her husband's (Zeus) illegitimate children, including Dionysus and Herakles, and did what she could to make their lives miserable. There is a long-standing tradition that she drove Herakles insane (Apollodorus, *Library* 2.4.12), but not Dionysus, whom instead she attacked with pirates. Hera did, however, drive Dionysus' aunt Ino (Leukothea) mad: the author may be conflating the Ino and Herakles stories.

And around Liguria some river, not smaller than the Rhodanus, is swallowed down and emerges again in another place: the Rhodanus is able to be navigated.

(Aristotle, Meteorology *351a1–18)*

B. *Ascribing emotion to bodies of water, Pliny has provided a few more examples.*

Because of a real hatred of the sea, certain rivers go under their bottoms, just like the Arethusa, a Syracusean spring into which things thrown into the Alpheus River appear. The Alpheus in turn, flowing through Olympia, is poured upon the Peloponnesian shoreline. These rivers go under the lands and are again returned: the Lycus in Asia, the Erasinus in Argolica, the Tigris in Mesopotamia. And whatever is dipped in a spring of Asclepius at Athens, these things are returned in the Phalericon Harbor (Athens). And a river plunged within the Atinatian Field comes out after 20 miles, as does the Timavus in Aquileia.[28]

(Pliny, NH *2.225; for the Alpheus: #3.8C)*

C. *The most famous underground river was the Alpheus, mythologized and celebrated by the poets (e.g.,* Greek Anthology *9.362, 683). Lucian of Samosata in Syria (c. 125 to after 180 CE) was a prolific satirist and keen observer of human nature, ridiculing superstition, religious practices, and belief in the paranormal. In his* Dialogues of the Sea Gods, *Lucian crafts gossipy conversations between mythical sea dwellers (including dolphins and the winds). Here Poseidon asks why Alpheus has gone underground.*

Poseidon: What now, Alpheus? You alone of the rivers falling into the sea do not mix with the salt, as is the custom for all rivers. Dispersing, you do not stop yourself, but you press on through the sea, altogether and protecting your sweet flow, and still unmixed and pure, plunging down in the deep—I don't know where—like cormorants and herons. You are likely to lift your head up somewhere and again show yourself.

Alpheus: It's a matter of love, Poseidon, so don't cross-examine me. You yourself have often been in love.

Poseidon: So, it's a woman, do you love a nymph or Nereids of the salt-sea?

Alpheus: Nope, it's a spring, Poseidon.

Poseidon: And where in the world does she flow?

Alpheus: She is a Sicilian islander. They call her Arethusa.

Poseidon: Alpheus, I know Arethusa, not at all hard on the eyes, but transparent, and she spouts up through a clear path, and she is conspicuous with her pebbles, altogether appearing like silver above them.

28 At the head of the Adriatic in the northeastern corner of Italy; Timavus (Timao).

Alpheus: How truly you know my fountain, Poseidon! So, I'm hurrying towards her.

Poseidon: Go on then and good luck with the love affair. But tell me this, where do you yourself see your Arethusa, you being Arcadian and she in the Sicilian regions?

Alpheus: You're holding me back, I'm in a hurry, Poseidon, asking all your picky little questions.

Poseidon: Well said. Go off to your beloved and, coming up from the sea, mingle with your fountain and become one water.

(Lucian, Dialogues of the Sea Gods 3)

D. *Here, Ovid gives Arethusa's much darker side of the story.*

Nurturing Ceres, untroubled after her daughter was received back,[29] which was the cause of her flight, asks, "Why, Arethusa, are you a sacred fountain?" The waves fell silent: their goddess lifted her head up from the deep spring, and drying her green locks with her hand, she narrated the ancient love affair of the Elean River. "I was one part of the nymph-band, who are in Achaea (western Greece)," she said, "and no other one more eagerly wandered through the groves, nor did any other nymph more diligently set the snares. But although a reputation for beauty was never sought out by me, however much I was strong, I had the name of beauty, nor did my loveliness, too much praised, please me, the thing in which others were accustomed to rejoice. A country girl, I blushed at my dowry of body, and I thought it a crime to be pleasing. Exhausted, I returned from the Stymphalian Woods—as I recall—the heat was great, and my labor doubled it greatly. I came upon waters without an eddy, going along without a murmur, transparent to the ground, through which every pebble in the deep was countable: you would think it was scarcely moving. White willow-groves and a poplar nurtured by the water were giving off a natural shade of their own free will to the sloping banks. I approached and first dipped a trace of a foot, then up to the knee. Nor content with this, I ungirt and placed my soft clothing on a bent willow and, naked, I plunged in the waters. While I splashed and drew the waters, gliding them in a thousand ways,[30] and I tossed my arms, shaken, I do not know what murmur I perceived under the eddy, and frightened I stood at the edge of the closer bank. 'Where do you hurry, Arethusa?' spoke a voice from under the waves. Alpheus again with his deep voice said, 'Where do you hurry?' Just as I was, I fled without my clothes: the other bank held them. So much he

29 Wanting a bride, Hades received permission from his brother Zeus to wed his own niece Persephone, daughter of Demeter/Ceres and Zeus/Jupiter. Hades kidnapped the girl, and her mother mournfully searched, finally brokering a deal for Persephone's partial return to the world of the living: *Homeric Hymn 2 to Demeter.*

30 Note Arethusa's joy, simply playing in water after a day of intense exertion.

was pressing on and burning. And, because I was naked, I seemed readier to him. So I was running, and he was wildly pressing on: like doves on a trembling wing flee a raptor, so the raptor is accustomed to press upon the doves. All the way under Orchomenos and Psophis and Cyllene and the Maenalian groves and the icy Erymanthus and Elis I endured running.[31] Nor was he swifter than I. But, unequal to his strength, I was unable to suffer the course, but he endured the long labor. Nonetheless through fields, through mountains covered with forest, rocks also and crags and, where there was no path, I ran. The sun was at my back. I saw that his long shadow stretched out before my feet, unless fear was seeing those things. But the din of his feet certainly frightened me, and the deep puffing of his mouth was blowing on my hair ribbons. Exhausted from the labor of flight, I said, 'Bring help—I am seized—Diana,[32] to your weapon-bearer, to whom you have often given your bows to carry and the arrows, shut within your quiver!' The goddess was moved, and she tossed over me alone something she was carrying from the thick clouds. The river encircled me, covered with mist. And, ignorant, he queried about the hollow cloud. And twice, unaware, he walked around the place where the goddess had covered me, and twice 'Oh, Arethusa!' he called out, 'Oh, Arethusa!' What then of my wretched soul? Was I not similar to a lamb, if anywhere she hears wolves howling around lofty stables, or to a rabbit, who, hiding in a thornbush, discerns the hostile faces of dogs and dares to give no movement with his body? Nonetheless, he did not withdraw: for he did not observe any traces of my feet further on; he watched the cloud and the place. Icy sweat seizes my confined joints, and blue drops fall from my entire body, and where I move my foot, a pool trickles out, and dew falls from my hair. And very quickly I am changed into fluids, as I now retell the events to you. But the river recognizes the beloved waters and—the face of a man, which he had taken on, put aside—he is turned into his earlier waves, and he mixes himself with me. The Delian goddess clefts open the ground. And, submerged, I am conveyed in vast hollows to Ortygia, which, pleasing because of the cognomen of my goddess,[33] first led me out underneath upper breezes."

(Ovid, Metamorphoses *5.572–641)*

1.7 Paradoxical Waters

A. *Greek and Roman writers were fascinated with waterscapes that exhibited unusual and often paradoxical properties, found at the distant edges, and authors*

31 Arethusa's flight takes her past several towns in the Peloponnese.

32 A virginal goddess of the hunt, transitions for girls, and childbirth. Arethusa was among Diana's nymphs and thus was also expected to be virginal in order to remain in the goddess' company and favor.

33 Diana is "Ortygian," because she was born on the island of Ortygia. As "Delian," she enjoyed robust worship at Delos, where she assisted her mother in giving birth to Apollo: *Homeric Hymn to Artemis* 3.14–18.

listed their effects without explanation. Here, a warning posted on Cia (Chios, in the eastern Aegean, south of Lesbos).

> Likewise on the island of Cia there is a spring, from which those who drink unknowingly become foolish, and there is an epigram carved with this sentiment: "pleasant is a drink of this spring, but anyone who drinks it will have rocky perceptions." There are, moreover, these verses in Greek: "pleasant is a stream from a chilly river, but whoever drinking this is stony in the mind."
>
> *(Vitruvius,* On Architecture *8.3.22)*

B. *Water can affect the coat colors of sheep and horses.*

> In certain rivers there is a marvelous force: there are some which, when drunk, tinge flocks of sheep; and within a certain time the sheep which were black now sport white wool; those which came in as white walk out as black. In Boeotia two rivers accomplish this: the name of one of them is Melas ("black"), from its effect. Both rivers emerge from the same lake, accomplishing different things. In Macedonia also, as Theophrastus says (*On Waters*?), those who want to make their sheep white lead them to the Haliacmon River:[34] when the sheep have drunk this water for any length of time, they are changed not otherwise than if they had been dyed. But if they have a need for dark wool, at the ready there is a dyer for free: to the Peneius River[35] they drive that same flock. I have it from good sources that there is a river in Galatia (central Anatolia) which does the same thing for all animals, and that in Cappadocia (southeast of Galatia), when a horse, but no other animal, drinks from a particular river, the horse's coat is changed and dappled with white.
>
> *(Seneca,* NQ *3.25.3–4)*

C. *The "Fountain of the Sun" in northern Africa exhibits unusual properties that are probably a factor of ambient heat remaining constant: the spring simply appears to be warmer or cooler at certain times of the day.*

> Then towards Catabathmos is the province Cyrenaica, and in it are the oracle of Hammon of renowned trustworthiness, and the fountain which they call "of the Sun," and a certain cliff sacred to Auster (South Wind). When the cliff is touched by the hand of a person, the Auster rises up excessively and, driving the sands like the sea, thus rages as with waves. The fountain boils in the middle of the night, soon and gradually becoming lukewarm, it becomes cold with the

34 The longest river flowing entirely in Greece, emerging in the Gramos mountains in northern Greece and debouching into the Aegean.

35 Emerging in the Pindus mountains and flowing through the vale of Tempe in Thessaly between Mts. Olympus and Ossa.

sunlight. Then, as the sun rises, the fountain thus grows colder immediately, (and is) especially stiff by noon. Then again it takes on warmth, and is hot at the beginning of the night, and as the night proceeds, thus it becomes warmer again, and the fountain boils thoroughly when it is midnight.

(Mela, On the Circuit of the World *1.39)*

D. *And a few more examples from Pliny. Note how Pliny credits his sources: such citations are often the only attestations of these thinkers.*

15. In Boeotia at the temple of the god Trophonius,[36] next to the Hercynian River, there are two springs, one conveys memory, the other forgetfulness, thence they have acquired these names.

In Cilicia[37] near the town Cescus, the Nuus River flows: Marcus Varro[38] says that the senses of those drinking from it become more acute, and on the island of Cea there is a spring from which senses become blunted, at Zama in Africa, from which voices become melodious.

16. Eudoxus says that wine will come as a bore to those who drink from Lake Clitorius, but Theopompus says that people will become inebriated drinking from that same spring which we've just mentioned. Mucianus says that at Andros,[39] from the spring of Liber (Dionysus) on the seven established days of his festival, wine flows, but if the liquid is carried away from the sight of the temple, it changes back to water.

17. Polyclitus says that people are anointed from the Liparis ("Shiny") River near Soloi in Cilicia. Theophrastus (*On Waters*?) says this same thing about a spring of the same name in Aethiopia. And Lycos says that among the Oratae of India there is a spring whose waters light lamps. The same thing is said about a fountain in Ecbatana.[40] Theopompus says that there is a lake in Scotussa (in central Thessaly) which heals wounds.

18. Juba II[41] says that, in the Trogodyte regions,[42] there is a Lake Insanus ("of madness") so-called because of its wicked force: three times a day, the water becomes bitter and salty and then again sweet, as often again at night, bubbling

36 A minor oracular deity credited with building Apollo's temple at Delphi (*Homeric Hymn 8 to Apollo*).

37 The strip of coast in the eastern Mediterranean north of Cyprus.

38 #2.1.1E.

39 *Gaius Licinius Mucianus*: an energetic general, statesman, and writer, who helped elevate Vespasian (r. 69–70 CE). *Andros*: the northernmost of the Cyclades islands.

40 The ancient capital of the Medes (Iran).

41 #1.5.1B§51 and note.

42 "Nibblers," inhabiting eastern Africa, the "source of the sun" (Pliny 5.34; cf. Diodorus Siculus, *Library of History* 3.32.3; Strabo, *Geography* 16.4.17, 17.3.7, Mela, *On the Circuit of the World* 1.44). In Herodotus they were swift, cave-dwellers (hole-dwellers) whose language sounded like screeching bats (4.183.4). Not to be confused with the cave-dwelling Troglodytes (#5.1.2B§7: there are no caves in eastern Africa).

up with white serpents 20 cubits in length. The same man says that a spring in Arabia spurts out with such a force that it spits back every weight dashed in.

(Pliny, NH *31.15–18)*

E. *Some waters cause tooth loss.*

Moreover, at Susa,[43] in which city is the kingdom of the Persians, there is a little spring, and those who drink from it lose their teeth. Likewise, there is an epigram written on the spring, which indicates this sentiment: that the water is excellent for washing, but, if it is drunk, it shakes the teeth from the roots. Here are the verses of this epigram in Greek: "the rocky waters you see, friend, people can wash their hands in these. But should you take the shining water of this leafy hollow, on the same day as your drink, your grinding saws will fall out and render your jaw orphaned."

(Vitruvius, On Architecture *8.3.23; cf.* Paradox. Florentinus Mirabilia de aquis *26.1)*

F. *Further examples plus a remedy for the loss of teeth owing to bad waters.*

Not only do the crimes of beasts injure, but sometimes also the characteristics of waters and places. In Germany across the Rhenus, when the military camp was moved forward by Germanicus Caesar (11 CE), in this maritime region there was only one spring of sweet water. Drinking from it, within two years the teeth fall out and the joints in the knees become unhinged. Physicians called these evils *stomacae* ("scurvy of the gums") and *scelotyrben* ("paralysis of the legs"). As a remedy, a plant which is called *britannica*[44] was found, health-bringing not only for the sinews and evils of the mouth, but also a remedy against throat infection as well as against serpents. It has dark, oblong leaves, a dark root. Its sap is pressed out even from the root. They call the flower *vibones*, which—if gathered before thunder is heard and then devoured—keeps folks safe from fear of sore-throat for an entire year. The tribe of the Frisi—at that time in faith with Rome[45]—in which the camp was situated, instructed the Romans about that plant, and I wonder about the reason of the name (*britannica*), unless by chance, bordering on Ocean, they have proclaimed it as if for neighboring Britain. The plant, consequently, was not so-called because it flourished there (in Britain). This is also certain: at that time Britain was a free island.

(Pliny, NH *25.20–21; for Germanicus: #1.9.1D introduction)*

43 In the lower Zagros Mountains, about 250 kilometers (160 miles) east of the Tigris River, became a political center under Darius I (r. 522–486 BCE) who built a palace, among other things there.

44 The antiscorbutic *radix britannica* whose properties were likely learned by Germanicus' army doctors from the local Frisians (Davies 1970: 92).

45 The Frisians had participated in a revolt against Roman authority in 28 CE (Tacitus, *Annals* 4.72).

1.8 Floating Islands

"Floating islands" are natural phenomena in marshes and other wetlands, comprised of aquatic plants and mud, and ranging in size from a few inches to several feet. Since some such masses were large enough to support trees and animals, ancient sources seem to understand them as unanchored "proper" islands. We must distinguish between the "floating" islands of mythology and aggregated floating vegetation that resembled islands. See also #2.3.5D for aquatic flora on floating islands.

A. *There were two particularly famous floating islands in Greek mythology. Here we have Aeolia the home of Aeolus, king of the winds, which Odysseus visited as he made his way across the Mediterranean from Troy to Ithaca after the Trojan War.*

> Then we arrived at the island Aeolia. There dwelled Aeolus, son of Hippotes, dear to the deathless gods, on a floating island. All around it is an unbroken bronze wall, and a cliff runs up smoothly.
>
> *(Homer,* Odyssey *10.1–4)*

B. *The other floating island was Delos, which was anchored after allowing Leto/ Latona to give birth to her son there. Vergil (b. 70 BCE), whose verses are infused with an awareness of both the environment and world geography, composed several major works:* Eclogues, *a collection of ten lyric poems*; *the* Georgics *in four books, a versified account of agricultural matters; and the* Aeneid *in 12 books, narrating the travails of Venus' son Aeneas, the Trojan hero, as he led survivors across the Mediterranean to a new homeland in Italy, culminating eventually in the founding of the Roman race.*

> We are conveyed from port, and lands and cities recede. In the middle of the sea, a sacred land is cultivated, very much pleasing to the mother of the Nereids (Doris) and Aegean Neptune. The dutiful bow-stretching god (Apollo) bound this little island, wandering around from Myconus and lofty Gyaros,[46] and he gave it over to be cultivated, unmoved, and to despise the winds.
>
> *(Vergil,* Aeneid *3.73–77)*

C. *Observing a floating island at Cutiliae (central Italy), Seneca's explanation.*

> I myself saw a floating island at Cutiliae, and another that is conveyed in the lake of Vadimo: the lake is in the Statonian region, near Rome. The island at Cytilae both has trees and nurtures plants. Nonetheless, the island is supported on the water and is driven to this and that part not only by wind but even by a breeze. And never, day and night, is its standing position in a single place: to

46 Both islands are in the Cyclades.

such an extent it is moved even by a light puff. The reason for this is two-fold: the weight of its healing water, and for this reason the water is heavy. And the material of the island itself is conveyable: it is not of a solid body although it does nourish trees. Perhaps the thick water clung to and restrained the light trunks and leaves that were sprinkled in the lake. And so, even if there are rocks on that island, you will find them eaten out and tubular, such as those which hardened moisture forms, especially around the streams of medicinal springs where deposits of waters join together and the foam is made solid. By necessity that which is thickened from a windy and empty substance is light.

(Seneca, NQ *3.25.8–10; cf. Macrobius 1.7.28; for medicinal springs: #2.1.6)*

D. *Pliny the Younger (Gaius Plinius Caecilius Secundus: 61–c. 113 CE) was the nephew and student of Pliny the Elder. The younger Pliny was a lawyer and civil servant, holding the various magistracies at Rome, culminating with a governorship in Bithynia-Pontus (c. 110 CE). He was also a prolific letter-writer, polishing private correspondence for publication: book ten of his* Letters, *addressed to the emperor Trajan (r. 98–117), provides unique insight into the administrative methodology of imperial Rome (see #4.5.4A). Here the younger Pliny recounts islands floating in Lake Vadimo with wide-eyed wonder.*

As I was walking around these places—my wife's grandfather's property in Amorica—someone pointed out to me an adjoining lake by the name of Vadimo. At the same time certain incredible things were narrated. I went up to it. The lake is enclosed, resembling a wheel lying flat and equal everywhere. There is no bend, no obliquity, all measurements equal, and as if hollowed and dug out by the hand of an artisan. The color is white-blue, a little green and a little subdued. There is a scent of sulfur and a medicating taste. There is a power whereby fractures are made solid. The size is moderate, but nonetheless it feels the winds, and it swells with waves. There is no boat in this lake: for it is sacred. But islands float on it, all grassy with reed and rush, and whatever other plants the rather fertile marsh and that very edge of the lake support. Each island has its own form and size. And the edge on all of them is scraped smooth, because they are dashed either on the shore or they often rub and are rubbed against themselves. For all, the height is equal, all are equally light. To be sure, the islands dip with a low bottom in the appearance of a keel. And this is seen from each side, uplifted and submerged equally in the same water. Sometimes joined and connected, they are similar to a continent; sometimes they are born apart by quarrelling winds. Sometimes, left alone with serenity, they float individually. Often the smaller islands cling to the larger ones, just like little skiffs to freighters. Often the larger and smaller islands undertake among themselves a path as if like a racecourse and a contest. Again, all are driven to the same place, they advance to the shore where they stand, and now in this direction and that, they return and remove portions of the lake. Then at length, they do not come together when they hold the middle of the lake. It is agreed that hoof-stock, pursuing grasses, are thus accustomed to step forth onto those islands as onto the edge of the lake. Nor do they—snatched away from the shore as if carried off and placed (on a ship)—understand in advance that the ground is mobile: they are terrified at the water on all sides. Soon, stepping off where the wind has born them, they no more understand that they have disembarked than they had perceived that they had embarked. The same lake is discharged into a river which—when it has given itself to the eyes for a little while[47]—is plunged in a cave and, hidden, it courses deeply below. And if it accepts anything that was drawn down, it keeps that object and brings it out. I have written these things to you because I believed them to be no less unknown than pleasing. For works of nature delight you also, like myself, equal to none.

(Pliny the Younger, Epistle *8.20.4–10; cf. Pliny,* NH *2.209)*

1.9 Weather

1.9.1 Predicting Weather from Signs

A. *Ascribed to the polymath Democritus is a calendar that generalizes annual weather patterns as they are portended by celestial bodies, an ancient methodology known to farmers and versified by Hesiod (*Works and Days*) and Vergil (*Georgics*). Geminus of Rhodes (1st century BCE) was an astronomer, mathematician, and philosopher. His* Introduction to the Phaenomena, *an astronomical primer, survives, but other works are redacted by later authors.*

(Scorpio): according to Democritus, on the fourth day when the Pleiades set at dawn: wintery winds like to blow a great deal, thickly and coldly; trees especially begin to drop their leaves. On the thirteenth day, according to Democritus, the Lyre rises together with the rising sun; and the air becomes wintery for the most part.

(Sagittarius): on the 16th day, according to Democritus, the Eagle rises together with the sun. And it likes to indicate thunder and lightning and water or wind or both, for the most part.

(Capricorn): on the 12th day, according to Democritus, the South Wind blows for the most part.

(Aquarius): on the third day, according to Euctemon, the Lyre sets in the evening. Rainy. According to Democritus, unlucky. Stormy. On the 16th day, according to Democritus, the west wind begins to blow, and 43 days remain until the tropics (solstices).

(Pisces): on the fourth day, according to Democritus, the variable days, called "halcyon,"[48] occur. On the 14th day, according to Democritus, the cold winds, called "bird-migrational winds," blow for about nine days.

47 I.e., visible for a short space.

48 Halcyons, tropical kingfishers, would breed during the calm weather of the winter solstice, inspiring the phrase "halcyon days," the seven days preceding and following the winter solstice: Aristotle, *HA* 542b1–6.

(Aries): according to Democritus, the Pleiades are hidden (i.e., they set) together with the setting sun, and they are unseen for 40 nights.
(Gemini): on the 10th day, according to Democritus, water occurs (i.e., it rains).
On the 29th day, according to Democritus, Orion begins to rise and likes to indicate weather according to himself.

(Democritus, TEGP *145 = Geminus,* Calendar *101.25)*

B. *The anonymous, peripatetic author of* On Weather Signs, *ascribed to Theophrastus (c. 371–287 BCE), collected several methods of forecasting weather, including signs from the moon and sun as well as animal behavior. Here we may have the first version of the familiar adage, "red skies at night, sailor's delight; red skies at morning, sailors take warning."*

These signs, therefore, seem to indicate rain: the clearest is thus at dawn when—just before the sun rises—the sky appears all red. For it signifies rain either on the same day or within three days more or less. There are other clear signs: if not beforehand, then to be sure within the third day a reddened sky at sunset signifies (rain), but less so than at dawn.

(Theophrastean On Weather Signs *10; cf. Matthew 16.2–3; Vegetius,* Epitome of Military Science *4.41)*

C. *The author of* On Weather Signs *is aware of the localized nature of weather and its indicators.*

When at night a cloud, white and long, will cut through Mt. Hymettus (near Athens) down from the peaks, water (rain) will occur for the most part in a few days. And if a cloud settles on Aegina in the temple of Zeus Hellanius,[49] water will often occur. If there is a lot of watery weather in winter, the springtime will usually be dry. If the winter has been dry, then spring will be watery. When there has been much snow in winter, then there will generally be a good harvest.

(Theophrastean On Weather Signs *24)*

D. *Aratus of Soloi in Cilicia (b. c. 300 BCE) composed a didactic poem,* Phaenomena *("Appearances"), in which he surveyed weather signs from celestial bodies (moon, sun, star, constellations), weather phenomena, and the behavior of animals. The work was widely admired in antiquity, translated into Latin several times, including by Cicero and Germanicus (15 BCE–19 CE: a member of the Roman imperial family who campaigned in Germany and was favored by the emperor*

49 Zeus Panhellanius, "of all the Hellenes."

Augustus), and inspired Vergil's weather account in the Georgics. *Here we have Aratus' account of how the moon forecasts weather for the month.*

778. First, examine carefully the horns on each side of the moon. At one time the evening inscribes her with one light, at another time her horns are with other shapes as the moon waxes: with one shape on the third day, another on the fourth. And from them you can learn about the coming month. For the moon, being slender and clear around the third day, indicates calm weather; but if slender and especially ruddy, windy weather; but if thick and with blunted horns, she has a fleeting light on the third and fourth night since she is blunted by the South Wind or impending rain. But if, bringing in the third day, the moon appears neither leaning forward or leaning back from both horns, but, straight, the horns curve on each side, then winds will blow from the west that night. But if she leads the fourth day straight in this manner, she indicates a gathering storm. But if the upper horn nods forward, she indicates the North Wind. But if she nods back, the South Wind. But when on the third day a ring surrounds her all around, altogether ruddy, a storm is indicated: the ruddier she is, the more intense the storm.

799. Look at the moon, full and half-full, both waxing and returning again to her horn, and from her color she ordains the weather for each month. Altogether spotless, she indicates fair weather. All stained with red, she expects paths of winds. Elsewhere, blackened, she expects rainy weather. Signs, however, are not prepared for you for all the individual days. Whatever happens on the third and fourth day indicates weather conditions until the half-moon; those of half-moon up to the full moon, and again from the full moon to the waning half-moon, and straightaway again from the fourth day of the new moon, and the third day of the new month. If rings encircle the moon all around, lying around either in threes or twos or even in a single halo: with a single halo the moon expects wind or calm; with a broken ring, wind; with a fading ring, calm. If there are two rings round the moon, there will be stormy weather. A triple ring would bring greater storms, and even more if blackened, and even still more if broken. Thus, you might learn these signs of the moon for the month.

(Aratus, Phaenomena *778–818)*

E. *Vergil explored the agricultural calendar in hexameter verses in his* Georgics. *Weather, of course, is very concerning to the farmer, and here, within a longer passage on various weather signs (*Georgics *1.351–463), Vergil here describes how animals read the weather.*

Never does rain harm folks unaware. For either, aloft from the deep valleys, cranes flee the rising storm, or young cows, looking up, catch the breezes with their noses spreading open, or a reproving swallow flies around her pond, and in the mud, frogs sing an ancient lament. Rather often an ant carries out her eggs from her inmost roofs, rubbing away a narrow path, and a huge rainbow takes a drink, and an army of crows, withdrawing from their fodder in a long battle-line, is rattled with thick wings.

(Vergil, Georgics *1.373–382)*

F. *Signs of impending storms and safe havens off Egypt's eastern coast.*

Beyond this place—the land already gently advancing to the south—there is the emporium of Aromatics (Spices) and a steep promontory at the edge of the barbarian land towards the east. The anchorage on the saltwater is rough and dangerous at the right time on account of the place facing the north. The sign of a storm about to occur in this place is that the deep water becomes more turbid and changes color. When this occurs, all sailors flee to the large promontory, a place and a shelter which is called Taba. Merchandise comes into this market similar to aforementioned imports. The exports in this place are cassia and gizer and asypha and magla and moto (varieties of cinnamon) and frankincense.

(Anonymous, Erythraean Sea *12)*

G. *Weather signs from the sea, within a lengthier discussion of weather prognostication (Pliny,* NH *18.340–365).*

And there is a sign from the waters. If a calm sea will race about in port and roar within itself, it predicts wind. If it does the same thing in winter, it also indicates rain. If the shores and banks resound in calm weather, it indicates a rough storm, likewise a noise from the sea in calm weather or scattered foam or bubbling waters indicate rough storms. Marine lungs (jellyfish) on the sea-surface portend a storm of several days. Often and in silence the sea rises, and—swelled up and higher than usual—it now confesses that there are winds within it.

(Pliny, NH *18.359)*

Animals also presage weather: dolphins cavorting in a tranquil sea indicate a breeze from where they come; likewise, splashing water in an agitated sea, dolphins presage calm weather. A cuttlefish flitting about, mussel-fishes clinging to objects, and sea-urchins fixing themselves to another object or ballasting themselves with sand, all these are signs of a storm.

(Pliny, NH *18.361; cf. 9.100)*

H. *We know practically nothing about Vegetius (c. 400 CE), who intimated that he was Christian. Publius Flavius Vegetius Renatus authored an* Epitome of Military Science *in which he described a rich array of military concerns, including recruitment and training, equipment and camps, legionary organization and administration and the duties of various officers, tactics and strategy (e.g., how to resist war elephants and scythed chariots), and the tenets of naval warfare.*

Needless to say, forecasting and dealing with weather is essential to military success. Here we have Vegetius' generalizing precis of weather signs. Note his admiration of Vergil and Varro (whose Naval Books *are lost).*

With many signs also both from a calm sky and also from storms, gales and calm weather are indicated, which the circle of the moon reveals as if in a mirror: a red color indicates wind, blue indicates rain, a mixture of each indicates rainstorms and raging gales. A happy and shining lunar orb promises serenity for sailors, which it wears on its face, especially if, during its fourth rising, it was not red along its blunt horns nor darkened with moisture poured in. The sun, rising or hiding the day, is also of interest, whether it rejoices with equal rays or is variegated with an obscuring cloud, whether bright with its customary luster or fiery with pressing winds, or not pale or spotted with threatening rain. Truly the air and the very sea and the size of clouds or their appearance prepare anxious sailors. From birds, and sometimes from fish, weather signs are indicated, which Vergil treated in the *Georgics* with nearly divine talent and Varro attended to scrupulously in his *Naval Books*. Helmsmen confess that they know these things, but they know them as far as the advantage of experience has instructed them, and no deeper training has shaped their knowledge.

(Vegetius, Epitome of Military Science *4.41)*

1.9.2 Clouds

A. *The earliest Greek explanation of clouds.*

Anaximenes says that clouds come into being from air thickened a bit more, and, that when air is gathered up together, rains are pressed out, and snow is pressed out when water, carried downward, congeals, and hail when windy material is gathered together with the moisture.

(Anaximenes, TEGP *26 = Aëtius,* Placita *3.4.1, S 1.31.1)*

B. *Some ancient texts survive only in translation, such as Theophrastus'* Meteorology, *which was translated into Arabic and Syriac (the Greek has been lost). Concurring with Anaximenes' account of the formation of clouds, here Theophrastus asks a new question: why do clouds float?*

Clouds come into existence for two reasons: because of the accumulation and thickness of air and its transformation into the nature of water or because of much vapor which ascends and with which the ascending vapors of the seas as well as the remaining fluids become mixed.

Air comes together and becomes thick for two reasons: because of coldness or because of contrary winds that squeeze it and bring it together. We can observe something similar among ourselves: when ascending vapor in the bath reaches the roof and cannot penetrate this roof because of its thickness, it accumulates and becomes water.

Although they are heavier than air, clouds float above the air for three reasons: firstly, because the quantity of air beneath the clouds is great and therefore heavy clouds cannot impose force on it. We can observe something similar among ourselves: when a man dips his hand in water and oil, then afterwards in sand and suspends it—the lower side turned up—no water or sand descends to the earth. The only reason is that water and sand, both because of their smallness and because they are heavy, cannot rise above the air or descend. When therefore their quantity is a little greater, they descend. So too in the same way dust sometimes remains hanging in the air for a long time and does not descend for precisely this reason. Furthermore, wood floats on water if there is much water; but if there is little water, the wood touches the bottom. We do not say that this happens on account of the air which penetrates the wood. For if you put a full vessel into water and submerge it up to its top, you will find exactly the same thing happening. The second reason is because clouds are constantly going and moving; and just as an arrow flies sideways without falling on the earth, so too clouds do not fall on the earth if they move sideways. The third reason: clouds cannot descend because of the vapor and wind which ascend from the earth.

(Theophrastus, Meteorology *7; trans. Daiber 1992: 266, slightly altered)*

C. *Posidonius of Apameia in Syria (c. 135–51 BCE) was a Stoic thinker who wrote broadly on history, geography, meteorology, cosmology, psychology, and mathematics and is considered the "most scientific" of the Stoics (Galen,* On the Opinions of Hippocrates and Plato *8.1.14:* Corpus Medicorum Graecorum *5.4.1.2, p. 482). Posidonius founded a school at Rhodes, came to Rome as the Rhodian ambassador in 87–86 BCE, and became friends with Cicero, Pompey the Great, and other influential Romans. Here, Posidonius' estimates for cloud heights.*

Posidonius (F 129) thinks that rainclouds and winds and mists reach an altitude of no less than 40 *stadia* from the earth. At that point there, the air is clean and flowing and with an undisturbed brightness. But from the windy air to the moon there are two million *stadia*, from there to the sun 500,000 *stadia*. With this span it happens that the sun's huge magnitude does not burn up the earth.

(Pliny, NH *2.85)*

1.9.3 Rainbows

A. *In Anaximenes, we have an early explanation of rainbows and moonbows, and an implication that the moon generates its own light.*

Anaximenes says that a rainbow occurs whenever the rays of the sun fall into thick, compressed air. Therefore, the first part of it shines crimson, burnt by the rays of the sun, partly dark, overwhelmed by moisture. And Anaximenes says that there is a rainbow at night around the moon, but not very often because the full moon is not always present, and its own light is weaker than the sun.

(Anaximenes, TEGP *33 = Scholium on Aratus 515.27; cf. Aristotle,* Meteorology *372a17–28)*

B. *Anaxagoras was the first to explain rainbows as optical phenomena.*

Anaxagoras says that what we call Iris (rainbow) in these clouds is a reflection of light back to the sun. It is thus the sign of a storm. For water scattered about a cloud will make wind or pour out rain.

(Anaxagoras, TEGP *47 = Scholium BT on Homer,* Iliad *15.547)*

C. *Aristotle explained rainbows as occurring when sunlight is reflected at fixed angles from clouds, thus generating an arc (*Meteorology *373a33–377a27). Here, double rainbows and the colors therein.*

Never is there a full circle of a rainbow nor a section larger than a semicircle. At the setting and rising of the sun, the circle is the smallest, largest at setting: in the sun's uppermost arc, the circle is uplifted and larger, but the rainbow-arc is smaller. After the autumnal equinox, during shorter days, a rainbow occurs every hour of the day. But in the warm seasons, it does not occur around midday. Nor do rainbows occur together more than by twos. Of such double rainbows, each is three-colored, and they have the same colors and equal in number to each other, but dimmer in the outer bow and lying opposite according to placement. For the inner bow has the first arc, the largest, scarlet; the outer bow has the smallest arc nearest this inner scarlet arc. And, with respect to the others, they are proportionate. The colors are almost only the ones which painters are not able to make. For they mix some colors, but scarlet and green and purplish-blue do not occur by mixing. The rainbow has these colors, but between scarlet and green, there is often a tawny, yellowish arc.

(Aristotle, Meteorology *371b28–372a12)*

1.9.4 Thunder and Lightning

Precipitation is often accompanied by thunder and lightning, which were understood as caused by clouds.

A. *Anaximander's preferred explanation for how the world works was wind, causing many phenomena, including thunder and lightning.*

Anaximander ascribed all things to wind. Thunderclaps, he said, are the sounds of a cloud being stricken. Why are thunderclaps uneven? Because the blow is itself uneven. Why is there thunder in clear weather? Because a blast springs through air, thick and split-open. And why does it sometimes not lightning but it does thunder? Because rather weak wind does not have the strength for a flame, but it does have the strength for a sound. What then is the lightning flash? The jostling of air sundered apart and dashing against itself bringing forth a gentle fire not about to get out. What is a thunderbolt? The course of sharper and thicker wind.

(Anaximander, TEGP *31 = Seneca,* NQ *2.18)*

B. *Thunder and lightning as violent events within the clouds.*

Empedocles says that when lightning falls into a cloud, expelling the air standing therein, its hissing and destruction create a crash, a lightning flash. Thunder is the pitch of the lightning.

(Empedocles, TEGP *104 = Aëtius,* Placita *3.3.7; for Empedocles: #1.2.5)*

C. *Anaxagoras and Empedocles correctly surmised that lightning occurs before thunder.*

Some, however, say that in the clouds there is fire. Empedocles says that what is enclosed in the clouds are rays of the sun. Anaxagoras believes that what is enclosed in the clouds is the material of the upper air which he calls fire, brought down below. They think that lightning is the flashing of this fire in the clouds, and that thunder is the noise and hissing of it being quenched, so that accordingly it seems thus that lightning occurs before thunder.

(Aristotle, Meteorology *369b13–19)*

D. *Aristotle erroneously argued that thunder occurs first.*

Lightning happens after the strike and later than the thunder, but it appears to advance on the sense of sight before the sense of hearing. The reasons are clear, on analogy with the rowers of triremes. For the first sound of the oars striking the water is heard as the oarsmen are already drawing back their oars.

(Aristotle, Meteorology *369b7–10)*

E. *While it was recognized that lightning is observed before thunder is heard (#1.9.4D), noting the delay between the observation of lightning and thunder, the Aristotelian author countered that we see the lightning flash before we hear the thunder that sparked it.*

Lightning, although it happens later, falls upon our senses before thunder since what is heard is outstripped by what is seen. For something seen can be noted from further away, but sound is detectable only when brought close, and especially when the one is the swiftest of all things—fire, I say—but the other is less swift, being airy in nature, and thus hearing occurs on contact.

(Aristotelian On the Universe *395a16–21; cf. Pliny,* NH *2.142)*

F. *Theophrastus corrected Aristotle's error, suggesting two possibilities: either lightning occurs first or both phenomena occur simultaneously (the latter is the case).*

> Lightning precedes thunder for two reasons: because the fire leaves the cloud very quickly; or because lightning and thunder occur at the same time, but we see the lightning more quickly than we can hear the thunder. Similarly, when we see a man from afar splitting firewood, we can first see his blow but later we hear the noise, whereas we do know that there must be a noise simultaneous with the blow. This is because the perception arrives at the eyes quicker than the noise reaches the ears. This is our report on thunder and lightning.
> *(Theophrastus,* Meteorology *5; trans. Daiber 1992: 263; cf. Pliny,* NH *2.142)*

1.9.5 Dew

A. *Dew occurs less frequently than other watery weather phenomena.*

> But dew is scant with respect to quantity; for its composition is of a day and its area is small, as its quick formation and meager magnitude make clear.
> *(Aristotle,* Meteorology *347b21–23)*

B. *Dew is formed as a factor of relative temperatures, especially in the colder Pontic regions of the Black Sea.*

> Everywhere dew comes into being because of south winds, not north winds, except in the Pontus. There the opposite occurs. For dew occurs there owing to north winds, and it does not happen during south winds. The reason is the same as why it occurs in mild weather, but not in wintry weather. For the South Wind effects mild weather, but the North Wind—for it is icy—makes wintry conditions by which it quenches the heat of vapor. But in the Pontus, the South Wind does not create mild weather thusly so that vapor occurs. But the North Wind, because of its iciness, standing all around, collects the warmth so that it does not steam any more. Very often it is possible to observe this phenomenon also in regions beyond the Pontus. For reservoirs steam because of northerly rather than southerly winds. But north winds quench warmth before any amount of it can coalesce. In southerly winds vapors are allowed to gather.
> *(Aristotle,* Meteorology *347a36–b12)*

C. *Theophrastus agreed with his teacher that, while some watery phenomena are created in the upper regions (troposphere), dew is formed closer to earth.*

> Dew comes about when, in the lower portion of the air, there exists that which also exists in the upper portion when clouds and rain occur. Namely, if the air becomes thick in the lower portions and compacts itself, or if vapors ascend and

> become thick in the air on account of coldness, then the thick part descends as a result of its heaviness, since there is not much air beneath it which could prevent it from descending, as the air above prevents the large quantity of clouds from going down and from letting small drops fall.
>
> *(Theophrastus,* Meteorology *11; trans. Daiber 1992: 267)*

1.9.6 Rain

For the Presocratics, the process of evaporation and condensation accounts for rain: fresh water is separated from the sea and drawn up as mist into clouds, then felted into raindrops, which finally return to the earth when clouds exhale their winds (see #1.9.2A, #1.9.8).

A. *Aristotle explained the rain cycle according to a hydrological cycle governed by the sun's heat.*

> Therefore, the efficient, primary, and first of the principles is the circle, along which the orbit of the sun—as it approaches and recedes—is obviously the cause of generation and destruction by which condensation and dissipation occur. While earth remains, the steaming moisture around it is carried away by the rays of the sun and the other sources of warmth up above. But while the heat lifting it up dissipates and scatters to the upper region, and while it is then quenched on account of being raised up further into the air above the earth, the vapor—cooled on account of the region and the removal of the heat—then condenses, and it again becomes water from air. Having become so, it is carried back to the earth.
>
> *(Aristotle,* Meteorology *346b22–33)*

B. *Aristotle also explained that this cycle occurs as heat is added or removed: the exhalation of water is vapor, and air condenses into water to form clouds. Aristotle's poetic analogy is a largely accurate account of convective rains that occur through the vertical process of evaporation, condensation, and precipitation, but he did not query the effects of topography or air masses on precipitation.*

> It is necessary to consider the rain cycle just like a river flowing up and down in a circle, composed of air and water. For when the sun is near, the river of vapor flows up, when the sun stands away, the stream of moisture flows down.
>
> *(Aristotle,* Meteorology *347a3–5)*

C. *Here we have Vergil's lovely description of the sky after a rainfall.*

> No less after a rain are you able to see and recognize suns and clear open skies with particular signs. For the edge of the stars seems sharp, and the moon rises, not liable to her brother's rays, and slender fleeces of wool (cirrus clouds) are

not carried through the sky, and the halcyons, beloved of Thetis, do not spread their wings towards the warm sun, nor do the filthy pigs remember to toss their bundles of straw, unbound with their snout. But, all the more, mists seek the depths and recline on the plain, and the night-owl, watching the sunset from her lofty summit, labors over her evening songs to no purpose.

(Vergil, Georgics *1.397–403; halcyons: #1.9.1A note)*

1.9.7 Frost and Snow

A. *Formation of frost and snow.*

Snow comes into existence when coldness freezes the clouds before they turn into water and—<after they have changed>—before one part of the water is connected with the other, as long as the water is scattered and dispersed in the form of very small drops which are separated by the air. For we can see with our own eyes that a lot of air is contained in snow. A proof of this is its softness; when it is pressed by the hand, snow is diminished in quantity, and, when it melts it becomes water; from its large quantity only a small quantity of water comes out. The reason for snow's whiteness is the abundance of air in it. A proof of this is the fact that we find all those bodies white in which much air is contained, as for example foam, oil—which is beaten with water—and semen.

(Theophrastus, Meteorology *9; trans. Daiber 1992: 267, slightly altered; cf. Aristotelian On the Universe 394a33–35; #1.9.2A)*

B. *While intellectual and cultural centers shifted over the two millennia that Greek and Roman powers dominated the Mediterranean, those centers (Athens, Alexandria, Rhodes, and Rome, among others) enjoyed fairly temperate weather. Snow, especially heavy snow, usually fell only well beyond the center, as experienced by Greek mercenaries in Armenia in 399 BCE and recounted by Xenophon of Athens (b. c. 430/425 BCE). Among Socrates' students but exiled from Athens, Xenophon wrote dialogues like his fellow student Plato, as well as treatises on horsemanship, hunting with dogs, and the Spartan constitution. Xenophon's wide experience as a general in the field informed his seven-book* Hellenika *treating events from 411 to 362, and his* Anabasis, *a first-hand account of his trek back to Greece with Greek mercenaries who had supported Cyrus the Younger against Artaxerxes II in a Persian civil war.*

From there they marched in three stages through a plain, 15 *parasangs*. And Tribazius followed, leading his command about ten *stadia* behind. And they arrived at a kingdom and many unwalled villages all around, full of many supplies. While they encamped, a great snowfall occurred during the night, and in the morning it seemed best to disperse the companies and their generals through the villages: for nothing of the enemy was visible and it appeared safe to stay there on account of the heavy snowfall. There they had supplies, whatever was good: sacrificial animals, grain, fragrant old wines, dried grapes, all sorts of beans and pulses. But some of the men, dispersing away from the encampment, said that they saw many fires burning in the night. It looked to the generals that their scattered billets were not safe, and it seemed best to bring the army back together. Hence, they came back together again, and the weather seemed to become clear again. But such an immense amount of snow fell on them during the night that it covered the weapons and the men lying there. And the snow hindered the draught animals. And there was a great deal of hesitation about getting up: for the snow, covering them as they were lying down, was warming for any man from whom it did not fall away. But when Xenophon took courage, standing up naked[50] to split wood, someone else, standing up quickly and taking the axe away from him, started splitting wood. After this, the rest of the men, getting up, kindled the fire and anointed themselves. For they discovered there a great deal of oil,[51] which they used instead of olive oil: suet and sesame and bitter almond and terebinth oil. And they found an unguent of these same ingredients.

(Xenophon, Anabasis *4.4.7–13)*

C. *The harrowing physical effects of extremely cold weather, including frostbite.*

Meanwhile, some of the collected enemy were in pursuit, and they snatched the weakening draught animals, and they were fighting with each other over them. Some of the soldiers were left behind: some were distressed in their eyes by the snow ("blinded"); others, by rot, lost the fingers from their feet (toes) because of the cold. For the eyes there was protection from the snow if someone marched holding something dark in front of his eyes; for the feet there was protection if someone kept moving and never took any rest and if he took off his sandals for the night. But many slept with their shoes on, and the straps dug into their feet, and the sandals froze all around. When the old sandals wore out, rough soles were fashioned from newly stripped-off ox-hides.

(Xenophon, Anabasis *4.5.12–14)*

D. *Winter conditions in the Caucasus and the summertime sport (or labor) of sledding down snow-covered mountains.*

Therefore the loftiest portions of the Caucasus are the most southerly, those next to Albania and Iberia and the territories of the Colchians and Heniochoi.[52]

50 Probably in his "shirtsleeves."

51 Slathering the body with oil would help retain warmth.

52 "Charioteers" inhabiting the northwestern region of Colchis on the eastern Pontus Dioscourias, whose settlements included Dioscourias.

Those whom they say assemble at Dioskourias dwell there. They come together, for the most part, for the sake of salt. Of these peoples, some inhabit the ridges, others lodge in valleys and live mostly on the flesh of wild animals and wild fruits and milk.[53] In the wintertime the peaks are pathless, but during the summer months they climb up the mountains, shod with untanned ox-hides, broad like drums, spiky on account of the snow and ice floes. They come down the mountains, sitting on skins with their merchandise and slipping down, just as happens in Atropian Media and on Mt. Masius in Armenia. There also, spiky wooden discs are fitted underneath their soles.

(Strabo, Geography *11.5.6)*

E. *Exiled to Tomis on the Black Sea, Ovid experienced several brutal winters first-hand.*

When sorrowful winter has shown his rough expression, and the earth becomes white with marble-like ice, and while Boreas (North Wind), as well as the snow, does not allow dwelling under the Bear (Ursa Major), then it is clear that these folk are pressed under the shivering pole. The snow lies, and—lest the sun and rain melt it—Boreas hardens the fallen snow and makes it perpetual. Therefore when an earlier snow has not yet dissolved, another one comes, and snowfall customarily remains in many places for two winters. So great is the force of Aquilo (North) when he is stirred, that he levels lofty turrets to the ground and carries away snatched-up roofs. With skins and trousers[54] stitched together, the people there ward off the icy evils and, of their entire bodies, only their faces are exposed. Often their hairs chime, moved by the hanging ice, and a white beard glistens with overspread ice. And wine stands naked, preserving the shape of its storage jar. They do not drink sips of pure wine, but instead they drink chunks of (frozen) wine.

(Ovid, Tristia *3.9–24)*

1.9.8 Hail

A. *Paradoxically falling during the warmer months, icy hail provoked curiosity and demanded explanation. See #1.9.2A.*

Hail therefore is ice, the water of congealed snow. Hail occurs especially in spring and autumn, less in summer, least of all in winter but only when it is not so cold. And, for the most part, hailstorms occur in more temperate

53 Milk was a common drink for folks dwelling on the edges of the world known to Greeks and Romans: such people lacked the climate, infrastructure, or knowledge to produce wine.

54 Worn widely by both men and women, trousers were considered "suitable for cold and northerly regions but by no means in southerly regions" (Strabo, *Geography* 11.13.9).

regions, snowstorms in more frigid areas. And it is not possible for water to congeal in the upper atmosphere. Nor is it possible for hail to congeal before becoming water; nor can water remain in mid-air for any period of time. Nor does hail behave thusly, just like raindrops that are carried upward on account of their smallness, lingering in air, like bits of earth and gold on account of their tiny size, floating on water in the air, with many small drops coming together, and large drops are conveyed down. It is not possible for this to occur in the case of hail: for congealed drops do not grow together like watery drops. It is clear therefore that waterdrops of such a size would remain aloft, but when congealed the drop could not be of such a size.

Some (Anaxagoras) think that the cause and genesis of this phenomenon (hail) is when a cloud has been pushed up towards the upper region of the air, being rather frigid because there the reflection of the sun's rays comes to the end of the earth, and the water coming there is congealed. Consequently, hail occurs in the summer and also particularly in warm regions, because for the most part heat lifts clouds away from the earth. But in very high places, hail occurs very infrequently, but it seems contrary, just as we see snow occurring especially in lofty places. Still very often a cloud has been seen carried along with a great noise near the earth so that there is fear among those who hear and see it, as if of something worse about to happen. And when—without the noise of such clouds having been seen—much hail occurs, and the size is unbelievable and in shape not rounded because the fall did not last long and their congealing occurred close to earth, and not, as those thinkers say, well above the earth. It is, moreover, necessary, especially for this reason, that the largest hailstones are formed. For hail is ice, and this is clear to each person. But large hailstones are not round in shape: this is proof of their congealment near the earth. For those carried a further distance, on account of being conveyed a long distance, become eroded in shape and smaller, as they are carried about. Therefore, that the congealing does not occur by forcing moisture up to a higher region is evident. But since we see that there is a reciprocal interchange between warmth and cold between each: on account of this, regions beneath the earth are cold during hot conditions here and warm during frigid conditions here. It seems necessary to think that this occurs in the upper latitudes, so that in warmer times the cold is reciprocally interchanged with the warmth in a cycle when it quickly makes water from clouds. Consequently, on warm days, raindrops are much larger than on a cold day, and rainfall is more furious. It is said that rain is more violent when heavier, and heavier rainfall occurs on account of the speed of condensing. For this is the very opposite of what Anaxagoras says: he declares that hail occurs when air is lifted up to the cold region; we say that it occurs when air falls to the warm region.

(Aristotle, Meteorology *347b35–348b16; cf. Seneca,* NQ *4.3.6)*

B. *Disagreeing with his teacher, Theophrastus offered three incompatible explanations (reliant on conflicting theories of cause and formation) as he forced the meteorological phenomenon to fit his theory. (Nonetheless, hailstones are not uniformly spherical and even small hailstones can be jagged).*

> Hail comes into existence when big drops of water are transformed and hardened by coldness. The hailstone is round because its edges are broken off during its descent, and therefore it is smooth; or because it consists of an element which by nature has a round shape, i.e., water; or because the coldness has hardened and compacted it from all sides in an equal manner.
>
> *(Theophrastus,* Meteorology *10; trans. Daiber 1992: 267)*

1.9.9 Earthquakes

A. *While most thinkers attributed the cause of earthquakes to wind (Aristotle,* Meteorology *368a27–34; Seneca,* NQ *6; Pliny,* NH *2.191–195), Anaximenes suggested water or its lack. (There may be here some confusion between earthquakes and landslides.)*

> Anaximenes says that the earth, moist or dry, breaks into pieces, and that it is shaken by hills breaking apart. Consequently, quakes occur during droughts and again during heavy rains. For during droughts, as was just said, the dried earth breaks up, and during rainy periods the hyper-saturated ground falls apart.
>
> *(Anaximenes,* TEGP *34 = Aristotle,* Meteorology *365b6–12)*

B. *Democritus proposed the same theory, reported by Aristotle with a little more detail.*

> Democritus says that the earth is full of water, and when it receives a large amount of rainwater, the earth is moved by this event. For, with more water than the hollows are able to receive, the water, violently forcing its way out, creates a quake. Likewise, falling water, with respect to its change of place, moves the dried-out earth as it draws water to its empty places from the fuller ones.
>
> *(Democritus,* TEGP *78 = Aristotle,* Meteorology *365b1–6)*

1.9.10 Tsunamis

*Tsunamis occur when earthquakes shift the seabed, displacing several hundred kilometers of water. The earliest description of a tsunami appears in Homer (see #1.5.3), but several historical examples are attested. Seismic sea waves are not uncommon in the Mediterranean owing to a major fracture-zone through the Aegean, into Turkey, the Black Sea, and the Crimea (Smid 1970), which in part helps explain Plato's account of Atlantis (*Timaeus *20d–27d;* Critias *113b–120d), the wandering rocks in Homer (*Odyssey *12.59–72), and Jason's Symplegades (Apollonius,* Argonautica *2.565–571, 574–581).*

A. *Tsunamis and earthquakes.*

When a wave occurs with a quake, the reason is that opposite winds are blowing. This happens when the wind creating the earthquake is not altogether able to drive away the sea borne by another wind. But, thrusting it forth and piling it up, it gathers the water into such a mass. It is then necessary that as this first wind is growing smaller, the gathered water, forced by the opposite wind, crashes and makes an inundation. This happened in Achaea (373 BCE, western Greece) where there was a south wind and a north wind beyond. Then there was a calm. And—wind flowing towards the land—a tidal wave and earthquake occurred there at the same time. And, on account of the sea not giving a passage to the wind that was urged on from the land, the sea blocked the wind. Forcing each other back, the winds created the quake. The substance of the wave caused the flood.

(Aristotle, Meteorology *368a35–b13)*

B. *The tsunami of 479 BCE was caused by an earthquake in the Aegean, creating an extreme ebbtide that resulted in an unusually shallow sea. Persian invaders tried to take advantage of this natural disaster but were instead vanquished by it.*

When it happened that Artabazus[55] was besieging Potidaea for three months, there was a great sucking back of the sea and for a long time. Seeing that the sea became a shoal, the Barbarians went over it back to Pallene. But when they had crossed two parts of it, and there were three parts remaining, through which it was necessary to cross to go to Pallene, a great swell of the sea came upon them, such as none of the many swells that usually occurred there, as residents report. Some folk, therefore, not knowing how to swim, drowned, and the Potidaeans then utterly destroyed those Barbarians who knew how to swim and those who sailed over in boats. The Potidaeans say that the cause of the floodtide and the sea-rise and the Persian suffering is this: that those of the Persians who were destroyed by the sea had committed a sacrilege against a temple of Poseidon and his image in front of that temple. The Potidaeans declaring this as the reason seem to me to speak well.

(Herodotus, Histories *8.129)*

C. *The Athenian historian and general, Thucydides, recounted the Peloponnesian War (431–404 BCE) between Athens and Sparta in nine books, detailing causes, significant events (including the plague that affected Athens (#2.1.4) and Athens' ill-fated invasion of Syracuse), and the psychology of the major players. Thucydides*

55 *Artabazus*: one of Xerxes' generals. *Potidaea*: on the narrow join between the Pallene promontory (#5.3.5D and note) and the Chalcidian mainland in northeastern Greece.

was able to connect the floodtide with seismic activity during the tsunami of 426 BCE in the Malian Gulf, north of Thermopylae.

> The following summer the Peloponnesians and their allies came as far as the Isthmus[56] in order to invade Attica under the command of Agis, son of Archidamus, king of the Lacedaemonians; but because of a number of earthquakes, they turned back again, and the invasion did not occur. At about the same time as these earthquakes were rife, the sea at Orobiae in Euboea withdrew from the coastline, and then returned and inundated some portion of the city, then it withdrew again, and yet again what was once land is now sea; and those inhabitants who were unable to reach higher ground as they ran back, they perished. . . The cause of this, I think, is insofar as a very strong earthquake happened. Accordingly, the earthquake withdrew the sea and, suddenly recoiling, it rather brutally created a flood. It does not seem possible to me that so great a natural disaster could occur without the earthquake.
>
> *(Thucydides,* Peloponnesian War *3.89.1–2, 5)*

D. *In 373 BCE, a devastating tsunami occurred at Helike in the Peloponnese in two stages: an intense night quake, causing devastation, chaos, and fear (the darkness impeded escape, creating even more fear), followed by a morning tidal wave which killed those who survived the night quake. This natural disaster (like many others) was presaged by animal behavior.*

> They say that this is what happened in Helike. For when the Helikeans committed sacrileges against the Ionians who had approached them, and the Helikeans cut the throats of the Ionians at an altar,[57] then perhaps, as in Homer's phrase, "the gods made marvels appear to them" (*Odyssey* 12.394). For five days before Helike disappeared, as many mice as there were in that place and weasels and snakes and millipedes and beetles and the rest of the creatures which were there, they all withdrew in crowds along the road leading out to Keryneia. Seeing these events, the Helenikeans were amazed, nor were they able to come upon a reason. When the aforementioned creatures withdrew, a quake occurred in the night, and the city was sunk. And Helike was hidden by a great overflowing tidal wave, and by chance ten ships of the Lacedaemonians were overwhelmed with the aforementioned city.
>
> *(Aelian,* NA *11.19; cf. Diodorus Siculus,* Library of History *15.48; Strabo,* Geography *8.7.2; Pausanias,* Description of Greece *7.24.5–6)*

56 The narrow strip of land between the Peloponnese and Attica, at Corinth.

57 Thus, the Ionians were under the protection of the god to whom the altar was dedicated, and the violence against them was thus an act of hubris.

E. *In 126 BCE, Posidonius witnessed a tidal wave caused by the eruption of a volcano between Vulcano (Hiera) and Panarea (Euonymus), a small island north of Sicily.*

> Posidonius (F 227) says that according to his own memory, at about the summer solstice at dawn, between Hiera and Euonymus, the sea was seen raised up to an extraordinary height, and for some time it stood fast, heaped up in a mound, and then it stopped. And those daring to sail up to it fled after seeing dead fish driven out under the flow: for some of them were stricken with terror both by the heat and the foul smell. Sailing a little closer, one of the boats cast off some of those men on board, and with difficulty they saved themselves by swimming towards Lipara: these men became senseless like epileptics, but later returned to their customary mindset. And for many days afterwards, mud was seen blooming on the sea, and in many places flame hissed out and smoke and murky fire, but later it became a rock, hardened, similar to millstones. The governor of Sicily, Titus Flaminius, reported the situation to the Senate, and the Senate sent a deputation to offer burnt sacrifices to the gods of the Underworld and the gods of the sea both on the little island and on Lipara.
>
> *(Strabo,* Geography *6.2.11)*

F. *Strabo himself had witnessed the aftermath of a tsunami on Egypt's eastern coast (the year is uncertain).*

> While I was dwelling in Alexandria in Egypt, around Pelusium and Mt. Kasion, the sea rose and flooded over the land and made an island of the mountain so that the road along Kasion to Phoenicia became navigable.
>
> *(Strabo,* Geography *1.3.17)*

1.9.11 Super Storms

A. *Massive storms pelted both literary and historical landscapes and waterscapes of the ancient Greco-Roman world. Such storms were and are a very real danger to sea-faring cultures. Mythology preserves the memory of a destructive flood, sent by Jupiter/Zeus to punish the hubris of mankind who refused to worship the gods properly. Here we have Ovid's version, a return to the primal chaos from which the world emerged, as envisioned by Hesiod, Empedocles, and others.*

> 262. Immediately Jupiter locks the Aquilo (North Wind) in Aeolian caves and whatever blasts might put the clouds to flight. And he sends out the Notus (South Wind). The Notus flies with moist wings, covered with a pitch-pine fog over his frightful face. His beard is heavy with rains, water flows from his white hair. Clouds settle on his forehead, his feathers and folds drip with dew. And, when he presses the hanging clouds with his broad hand, a thunderous din

occurs. From here thick clouds are poured out from the aether. Dressed in varied colors, Iris[58] collects waters and brings nourishment to the clouds. Grainfields are spread horizontally, and the bitterly lamented vows of the farmer lie flat, and the futile labor of a long year vanishes.

274. Nor is Jove's anger content with his own sky, but his blue-green brother helps him with aiding winds. Neptune calls together his rivers and, after they have entered the halls of their sovereign, he says, "Now is not the time to engage in a long argument. Pour out your strengths: there is a need! Open your doors and—your mole removed—send out all the reins to your fonts." He orders. The rivers return and loosen their mouths from their fonts, and they roll into the sea in an unrestrained course.

283. Neptune himself strikes the earth with his trident, but she, the earth, quakes and opens up the paths of the waters because of the motion. Enlarged rivers rush through open fields, and they tear away not only orchards and at the same time cattle and also people and their homes but even the innermost objects in sacred places. If any home remains and, not overturned, is able to resist so great an evil, nonetheless, a higher wave covers its top, and its towers lie pressed down under the abyss. And now the sea and land have no distinction: all things are sea, and the shores lack a sea.

293. This man takes possession of a hill; another sits in his curved skiff and leads his oars there where he was recently plowing. That man navigates over grainfields and the roof of his submerged house. This one grasps a fish in a lofty elm tree. An anchor is fixed in a green meadow, if luck allows, or curved keels rub over vineyards cast underneath. And, where slender goats once plucked grass, now deformed seals place their bodies there. The Nereids (daughters of Nereus) are amazed at groves and cities and homes underwater. Dolphins hold the forests and strike against lofty branches and batter the agitated oaks. The wolf swims among the sheep, a wave conveys tawny lions, a wave conveys tigers. Nor do the forces of his crushing power benefit the boar, nor do swift legs benefit the stag from being carried off. The lands quake for a long time. When it is possible to stop, a wandering bird falls into the sea with exhausted wings. The immense liberty of the sea overwhelms the hills, and new floods strike mountain peaks. The greatest part is snatched up by the water. Those whom the wave has spared, long hungers break them with empty nourishment.

(Ovid, Metamorphoses *1.262–312; Triton: #3.1.2; Nereids: #3.1.5–6)*

B. *Juno, aiming to prevent Aeneas from reaching Italy, his destined new homeland (she supported the Greeks during the Trojan War), has commissioned a storm to*

58 "Rainbow," Juno's messenger.

scatter the Trojan fleet off the coast of Carthage. Vergil's account of this legendary storm is harrowing, histrionic, and technical.

> The winds, as if marshalled in a battle line, rush out where openings are given and blow over the lands with a whirlpool. They press upon the sea, and the Eurus (East Wind) and Notus (South Wind) together cast up the whole sea from its deepest foundations, and the Southwest Wind is thick with storms. The winds roll huge waves towards the shores. There the shouts of men follow and also the creaks of the rigging. Suddenly clouds snatch away both the sky and day from the eyes of the Teucrian (Trojan) refugees. Black night lies over the sea. The poles thunder and aether flashes with thick fires, and all things threaten the men with imminent death.
>
> *(Vergil,* Aeneid *1.82–91; cf. Homer,* Odyssey *5.283–296)*

C. *Seneca also imagines the course and effects of colossal storms. This selection introduces a longer account of the great flood which closes his book on terrestrial waters (* NQ 3.27*).*

> But this locus reminds me to ask: when will the deadly day of a deluge come? And to what degree will a great part of the earth be overwhelmed by waves? Whether it will happen owing to the strengths of the ocean and the external sea will rise against us, or thick rains without interruption and—summer expelled—stubborn winter will cast out the huge force of waters from broken clouds, or the earth will more bountifully pour out rivers and open up new sources, or there may not be one cause for such evil. But every method might act in concert; and rains might fall at the same time; rivers might grow; seas, roused from their foundations, might rush forth; and all things might join in a single battleline for the destruction of the human race. Thus it is. Nothing is difficult for Nature when she is hastening to her own end.
>
> *(Seneca,* NQ *3.27.1)*

D. *Sudden storms are a perennial threat, and historical accounts preserve many examples. One of the worst disasters at sea occurred during summer of 255 BCE (the first Carthaginian War) when the Roman admiralty disregarded the warnings of local pilots* (#5.1.13) *and lost nearly 80% of the fleet.*

> Crossing the strait of Messina safely and reaching the lands of Camarina, they fell upon such a large storm and such terrible misfortunes that it is not possible to describe worthily the magnitude of the event. For, of 364 vessels, only 80 managed to survive. Of the rest, some were submerged; others, shattered by the floodtide on sea-rocks and promontories, rendered the sea full of bodies and pieces of wreckage. No worse single disaster by sea happens to be known. The cause must not be blamed thus on chance as on the leaders. For the pilots

warned them many times not to sail along the outer coast of Sicily, which turns towards the Libyan coast, on account of its jaggedness and lacking in ports. At the same time the pilots also warned that the change in weather was not yet slackening, but was impending. For the sail occurred between the rising of Orion and the Dog (late summer). Paying attention to none of the pilots saying these things, the Romans sailed on the outer sea, eager to seize some cities in this *periplus*, since they were astounded at their good luck in battle. Except, on account of their slim hopes, they happened upon great misfortunes, but they then had recognized their ignorance.

(Polybius, Histories *1.37.1–6)*

E. *In 16 CE, the fleet of Tiberius' nephew Germanicus (#1.9.1D introduction) was campaigning in Germany and caught in the powerful southerly winds on the Amisia River (Ems). Two accounts survive. Here is the account by the Roman poet Albinovanus Pedo, known to Ovid (*Letters from Pontus *4.10) and thus contemporary with Germanicus.*

Now they see that Ocean—who bears huge monsters everywhere beneath its sluggish waves as well as savage whales and watery dogs—rises up and snatches the ships: the very din increases the sailors' fears. Now they believe that ships sink in the mire and the fleet is deserted by the breeze, and that they themselves are abandoned by helpless fate to be pulled to pieces by the sea-beasts. Unlucky lot!

(Seneca the Elder, Suasoria *1.15)*

F. *And here is the more "technical" version by Tacitus (c. 55 CE-c. 120 CE), a Roman statesman and historian, whose works include a two-part history of Rome (*Annals, *from the death of Augustus to Nero; and* Histories, *picking up with the civil war of 69 CE), a panegyric biography of his father-in-law (*Agricola*) and an ethnography of the German people (*Germany*).*

When the summer was nearly over, some of the legions were sent back to winter quarters by a land route. Germanicus Caesar conveyed most of the troops settled in the fleet along the river Amisia. At first the calm sea hummed with sails and was stricken by the oars of a hundred ships. Soon hail was poured from a black sphere of clouds, and at the same time from all sides, with varied blasts of winds, uncertain waves deprived the sight and hindered the steering of the Roman mariners. Quaking and ignorant of the hazards of the sea, while they confused the sailors or helped inconveniently, the soldiery interfered with the duties of the knowledgeable sailors. Then the whole sky and the entire sea withdrew to the Auster (South Wind), which—strong from the swollen lands of Germany, from its deep rivers, from its huge expanse of clouds and all the rougher owing to the rigidity of the nearby northern territory—snatched and scattered the ships into the open tracts of Ocean or against islands molested by steep crags or through hidden shoals. These things were avoided little by little and with difficulty. After that the tide was changing and carrying the fleet in the same direction as the wind. They were not able to cling with anchors, nor were they able to bale out the waves crashing on the decks. Horses, draught animals, packs, and even weapons were hurled overboard to lighten the hulls as they were flooding through their sides because of waves crashing over the deck.

(Tacitus, Annals *2.23)*

1.9.12 Seasonal Floods

A. *Caused either by excessive rain, seasonal weather, or erosion (or the wrath of a river god), flooding was a benefit (as with Nile's annual flooding) or concern. Here we have Plato's thoughts on the effects of cataclysmic flooding.*

Therefore, since many immense floods have occurred in 9,000 years—for such were the years from that time to our own—in all that time and in all those occurrences, soil washed down from higher ground does not pile up any amount of sediment worthy of mention, as in other regions. But, flowing around in a circle, the soil always disappears into the deep. Indeed, just as on small islands, what is left now with regard to what existed at one time is like the bones of a sick body, the soft and rich parts of the earth have flowed away, there remains only the stripped body of the land.

(Plato, Critias *111a–b; cf. Lucretius,* On the Nature of Things *1.277–287; Seneca,* NQ *6.17.2)*

B. *At Rome, the Tiber was prone to flooding, particularly after winter rainstorms. The earliest attempts to mitigate the flooding were overseen by Tarquinius Priscus, Rome's legendary fifth king (r. 616–578 BCE).*

And, with sewers directed into the Tiber at a slope, Tarquinius dried out the lowest places of the city around the Forum and the valleys interspersed between the hills, because they could not easily convey water from the flat places.

(Livy, From the Foundation of the City *1.38.6)*

C. *The destructive flood of 54 BCE.*

You would be amazed at the storms at Rome, and particularly along the Appian Way up to the Temple of Mars. The promenade of Crassipes[59] was carried away, as were gardens and many shops. A great force of water came all the way up to the public fishpond.

(Cicero, To Quintus *#25.8 [3.5])*

59 M. Furius Crassipes: Cicero's son-on-law, from a politically unremarkable family.

D. *Here is a more fulsome account of that same storm. Dio Cassius of Nicaea in Bithynia (c. 165 CE–235 CE) served as a senator, governor of Smyrna, and proconsul of Africa and later Pannonia. He composed an 80-book* Roman History *in Greek, surviving in part.*

> Meanwhile, either because excessive rains had occurred somewhere upstream above the city, or because a powerful sea-wind had driven back its outgoing tide, or still more likely, as assumed, by the act of some god, the Tiber suddenly rose so high as to inundate all the lower levels of the city and to overwhelm even many of the more elevated regions. The houses, therefore, constructed of brick, were soaked through, and they collapsed, while all the animals perished in the flood. Of those who did not find refuge in time, all of them were either caught in their dwellings or in the streets, and they lost their lives. The remaining houses, furthermore, became weakened since the disaster lasted for several days, causing injuries to many, either then or later.
>
> *(Dio Cassius,* Roman History *39.61.1–2; for the flood of 60 BCE:* Roman History *37.58.2–4)*

E. *There were attempts to control the Tiber's flooding with infrastructure, including efforts to raise the ground level by means of platforms (as at the Sant'Omobono Sanctuary in the early 5th century), but core surveys show a great level of siltation in the area around Rome in the 1st millennium BCE, and it remains an open question if land around Rome accrued by means of siltation or anthropic reclamation (Andrea Brock, personal correspondence; cf. Ammerman 1990, 1998) and periodic dredging (Wilson 2013: 270–271). Here Augustus aimed to mitigate flooding by keeping the Tiber free of debris (#5.3.4A)*

> For restraining floods, Augustus expanded and cleared away the Tiber's bed, once filled up with lumps of bronze and confined by the enlargement of buildings.
>
> *(Suetonius,* Augustus *30; cf. Tacitus,* Annals *1.76)*

F. *Bureaucracy and conflicting interests interfered with attempts to control flooding at Rome.*

> Then there was a motion in the senate introduced by Arruntius and Ateius, whether rivers and lakes—through which the Tiber swelled—should be altered for the sake of regulating the river's flooding. Envoys of townships and settlements were heard: those from Florentia (Florence) begged that the Clanis River, moved from its accustomed bed, should not be transferred into the stream of the Arno and bring disaster to them. The Interamnates discussed points corresponding to the Florentine objections: the most fertile fields of Italy would go to ruin if the Nar River (Nera), diverted into streams, were to become stagnant: for this was being planned. Nor were the Reatini silent: objecting that the

Veline lake (Lago di Piè-di-Lugo), where it was poured into the Nar, would be obstructed: to be sure it would burst out into nearby lands. For, in the best way, Nature had looked out for the affairs of mortal people, she who had given rivers their own sources, their own courses, as their origin, so their end. Also to be observed were the obligations of the ancestors, those who had consecrated rites and groves and altars for their ancestral streams. Moreover, they were not willing that Tiber himself, entirely deprived of his neighboring streams, would flow with less glory. Whether the prayers of the settlers prevailed, or the difficulty of the work, or irrational religiosity, it was conceded to the opinion of Piso who believed that nothing should be changed.

(Tacitus, Annals *1.79)*

G. *Claudius (r. 41–54 CE) had also tried to mitigate flooding with relief channels at Portus (Rome's port), but not altogether successfully. See also #5.3.3G.*

Titus Claudius Caesar, son of Drusus, Caesar Augustus Germanicus, Pontifex Maximus,[60] Tribune of the Plebs six times, consul-designate three times, imperator, father of his country, freed the city from the danger of flooding with channels led from the Tiber into the sea for the sake of the work of the port.

*(*CIL *14.85 [*ILS *207])*

H. *Claudius' efforts were merely a stopgap, and Trajan's (r. 98–117 CE) efforts to mitigate the Tiber's flooding were similarly unsuccessful, especially against severe storms. Trajan's drainage canal seems to be confirmed by an inscription from Ostia (*ILS *5797).*

Pliny to his friend Macrinus.

1. Is the sky also sour and troubled over there? Here there are constant storms and frequent floods. The Tiber has exceeded its bed and is poured deeply over lower banks. Although our emperor, as discerning as is possible, has drained the river with a ditch, the Tiber presses the valleys, it floats over the fields, and wherever there is flat ground, the river is seen instead of soil. From there, the Tiber forces back those streams which it is accustomed to receive and convey, mixed together, just as it comes to meet them, and so it covers the fields with foreign waters which the Tiber itself does not touch.

3. Furthermore, that most charming of rivers, and consequently as if invited and held back by the villas bordering its banks, the Anio has broken and snatched

60 Among imperial prerogatives were the office of *Pontifex Maximus* (the chief priest at Rome who had ultimate responsibility for all religious acts) and tribunician power which was held by the tribunes of the plebs during the Republic (including the authority to act on behalf of the interests of the plebeians against the Senate and the right to veto legislation, a powerful check against the senate and patrician politicians).

up the woods for the most part. It has undermined the hills. And, shut off in many places by a mole of fallen debris, while it seeks out its lost path, the Anio strikes and lifts itself against roofs and casts itself above the ruin.

4. They see what that storm has seized away from higher grounds: the furniture of the wealthy and heavy household stuff from one place, from another place equipment of the countryside, over there, cows, plows, plowmen, over here herds unfettered and free, and among these things are the trunks of trees or rafters of villas and gables floating variously and widely. And even those places to which the river did not rise are not free from evil. For, instead of the river, there is constant rain as well as whirlwinds cast down from the clouds, by which overturned works, priceless estates, shaken and even cleft public monuments are surrounded. Many people have been maimed, buried, crushed by falling debris of this kind, and the losses are increased by sorrow.

6. I fear that something similar is commensurate with the danger over there, and I ask you—if there is nothing such as these storms—that you console my apprehension as quickly as possible, but if there is such that you also let me know. For the difference is slight whether you suffer adversities or expect them, except nonetheless that there is a limit of suffering but not of fearing. For may you grieve with regard to as much as you know has happened and fear with regard to as much as it is able to occur. Be well.

(Pliny the Younger, Epistle *8.17; cf. Tacitus,* History *1.86)*

I. *The elder Pliny recognized the correlation between deforestation and worsening floods.*

Generally destructive floods are drawn down when forested land, accustomed to contain rainclouds and dissipate them, is pulled down from the hills.

(Pliny, NH *31.53)*

PART II

Water and Living Creatures

Here we investigate the connections between living beings (humans, animals, plants) and water. Greek and Roman thinkers recognized the connection between water and health (#2.1): clean water could foster good health, and tainted water could generate disease, from tooth loss to typhoid. Marine fauna were also much studied (#2.2): they were important commercially (fishing: #6.3), they were featured in mythology (#3.4), and they sparked the curiosity of observers like Aristotle who sought to understand how they were constructed and how they behaved, often providing a mirror of good and bad human conduct. Just as Aristotle categorized the animal world, his student Theophrastus categorized the plant world, providing remarkable descriptions of seaweed, reeds, lotus flowers, and other aquatic flora (#2.3).

2.1 Health and Disease

2.1.1 Good and Bad Waters

A. *Living in southern Italy, the Greek philosopher Alcmaeon of Croton (fl. c. 470 BCE) believed that health derives from the harmonious blending of elemental qualities (heat, cold, moist, dry). He was perhaps the first to discuss the effects of water quality on community health.*

Disease may also sometimes come about from external causes, from the quality of water, local environment, overwork, hardship, or something similar.

(Alcmaeon of Croton, DK 24B4 = Aëtius, Placita *5.30.1)*

DOI: 10.4324/9781003437741-3

B. *Waters have different effects depending on the consumer.*

> Seawater is the cleanest and dirtiest, for fishes it is drinkable and healthy, for people unpotable and ruinous.
>
> *(Heraclitus,* TEGP *79 = Hippolytus,* Refutations *9.10.5)*

C. *The effects of water on the health of an individual and even a region were well-noted in antiquity. Ancient medical thinkers, however, lacked a clear understanding of pathogens and pollutants, and they conceived of disease as occurring because of interactions with the environment (Nutton 2013: 26). Infectious disease was thus usually attributed to poor food or unusual airs and waters. Here we have the opening paragraph of a Hippocratic text entitled* Airs, Waters, Places (c. 430–400 *BCE: many works ascribed to the legendary physician, Hippocrates of Cos, were produced by his students or later followers), in which the author interrogated various environmental factors (position with respect to the sun and prevailing winds), water quality, and even ethnic traits. This short treatise's purpose was to help traveling physicians treat patients in a wide variety of environments. Note that* iatrike *is the "the art of healing," developed separately from popular religious and magical healing treatments.*

> To whoever wants to pursue the medical art correctly, it is necessary to do these things. First to think about the seasons of the year, whatever each is able to cause. For they do not altogether resemble each other, but they each differ a great deal among themselves and in the changes of season. Then consider warm and cold winds, especially the ones common to all folks, but then also those that are regional in each place. For it is necessary to ponder the capacities of the waters. For just as people differ in language and weight, so also each water differs a great deal in flavor and strength. Thus, when someone arrives at a city with which he is unacquainted, it is necessary to regard its position: how it lies towards the winds and towards the rising of the sun. For whatever place lies towards the north does not have the same effect as whatever place lies towards the south or towards the rising sun (east) or towards the setting sun (west). It is necessary to notice these things as thoroughly as possible: the waters which they have around them and whether they have marshy and soft waters, or stiff waters and those from high and rocky places, or salty and hard waters, and the earth, whether it is bare and waterless, or bushy and well-watered, or if it is stiflingly hot in a hollow, or elevated and cold. Also think about the lifestyle of the people, what sort they enjoy, or if they like to drink and take breakfast and if they are not given to hard work, or if they are fond of exercise and eating, or if they are abstemious.
>
> *(Hippocratic* Airs, Waters, Places *1; cf. #4.2.1B)*

D. *The link between environment and health was born out in 232* CE, *when Alexander Severus' (r. 222–235 CE) Illyrian troops fell ill because of the "stifling air" near the Euphrates in northern Syria, but recuperating at Antioch they found the air cooler and water "better," resembling the nippier, moister environment of their homeland. The episode is recorded by Herodian of Antioch (170–240* CE*), who was perhaps ethnically Syrian. Herodian wrote an eight-book contemporary history of Rome, treating events from the death of Marcus Aurelius (180 CE) to the beginning of Gordian III's reign (238).*

> Since these things were reported to Alexander Severus, who was severely ill either on account of despondency or because he was unused to the air, and so he became depressed. The rest of the army became discontented with Alexander and violently angry because the invading army had been betrayed by Alexander's equivocating and not keeping to his promises. All the more, Alexander was not enduring his illness or the stifling air. And his entire army was also sick, especially the Illyrian soldiers who were perishing. The Illyrians were accustomed to better and wintry water and air and, accordingly, more food, and they endured their illnesses with difficulty. Alexander decided to return to Antioch and, sending word to his army in Media,[1] he ordered them to return. But, as that army returned, most men perished in the mountains, and not a few were mutilated at their extremities in this ill-wintered place; from many very few returned. Alexander led his own crowd of soldiers with him, but many even from that division perished, so that it brought on the greatest depression and disrepute for the army and for Alexander, who failed in judgement and luck and lost most of the three divisions of the army which he had controlled in different disasters: disease, war, frost. But in Antioch, Alexander himself easily became strengthened by the pleasant chill and plentiful water of the city after the dry dirt in Mesopotamia.
>
> *(Herodian,* History of the Empire from the Death of Marcus *6.6.1–4)*

E. *Marcus Terentius Varro (81–27 BCE) of Raete, north of Rome, was a polymath and a public servant. He served on a land redistribution commission, organized Rome's first public library, and composed many works of scholarship, of which only two survive in part:* On the Latin Language *and* On Agriculture. *Here, advice for property buyers regarding on-site waters.*

> Care must be given insofar as possible to place a villa at the forested foot of a mountain where pastures are spacious, or likewise to place it against the winds which blow most wholesomely in the area. Most suitable is a villa which is positioned towards the rising equinoxes (east), since it has shade in the summer, sun in the winter. But if you are compelled to build next to a river, care should be taken that you not place your villa facing the river; for in winter it will be

1 Northwestern Iran.

excessively cold, and in summer not healthy. It also must be avoided if there will be any swampy places for these reasons, and because certain tiny animals[2] grow there which the eyes are not able to follow and which come through the air within the body through the mouth and nostrils, and they bring about troublesome diseases. Fundanius[3] says, "What am I able to do, if an estate of that sort should come to me as an inheritance, so that the pestilence is less harmful?" Agrius[4] says, "I can certainly respond to that question. You should sell it for as many coins as you are able, or if you are unable, you should abandon it!"

(Varro, On Agriculture *1.12.1–2)*

2.1.2 Typhoid

A. *Caused by* Salmonella typhi *in contaminated food or water, typhoid enters the blood stream through the intestines, multiplying within leukocytes and incubating for about two weeks, deposited in the bile, entering the intestinal tract, and then returning to the bloodstream for re-infection. This case study (c. 430–350 BCE) shows the disease's course in great detail and focuses on diagnostic signs that physicians still observe, including the color of the stool.*

For the wife of Hermoptolemus in the winter, there was a fever and a pain in the head. And whenever she drank, swallowing with difficulty, she sat up, and she said that her heart was weak. Her tongue was bluish-grey from the beginning. The cause seemed to be from a chill after a bath. She was sleepless night and day. After the first days, when asked, she said that her head was no longer still distressed, but instead her entire body was in pain. Thirst was sometimes excessive, sometimes moderate. On the fifth and sixth and up to the ninth day, she was nearly delirious, and in the middle of her coma she babbled half-understandable things to herself again and again. With her hand she sometimes reached for the stuccoed wall and some cold bandage for her head, and she would hold her hands towards her chest and sometimes would toss off her shawl. And on the surface of her eye, the right one, there was blood and a tear. The urine was always bad, as in children. From the beginning she passed somewhat yellowish stool, later exceedingly watery and of the same color. On the 11th day, her temperature seemed to be more moderate, and she was sometimes not thirsty to the point that if someone did not give her something to drink, she did not ask. After the first period, sleep usually occurred during the day, but at night she was sleepless, and she suffered

2 A rare reference to microscopic disease-spreading, water-dwelling creatures; cf. Lucretius' reference to "foreign" (*alienum*) pathogens infecting water, crops, food-supply, or air: *On the Nature of Things* 6.1119–1130; Retief and Cilliers 2000; see #2.1.3E; #4.4§1.

3 Caius Fundanius Varro's scholarly father-in-law (*On Agriculture* 1.2.1) and a friend of Cicero (*To Quintus* 1.3.8) whom the orator defended in 58 BCE.

4 Gaius Agrius, a Roman *eques* who followed Socratic philosophical teachings (Varro, *On Agriculture* 1.2.1).

more at night. On the ninth day her belly was agitated, watery, also on the 10th day. On the following days her stool was generally greater and the same. On earlier days there were fits of anger and weeping, as of a child, and shouting and fear and looking around whenever she awoke from her coma. On the 14th day, it was work to hold her down as she leapt up in fear and shouted suddenly and loudly, as if from a blow and terrible pain and fear when someone grasping her held her down for some brief time. Then again she rested, and then she would become calm again and remained sleepy, not seeing, and sometimes not hearing. She changed back and forth between both confusion and deep rest nearly the whole day. Towards the following night she passed something bloody, like mucus, and again muddy, and then very green and dark. On the 15th day, violent thrashing, and her fears and shouting became gentle, but the fierce behavior and angry tantrums and shouting persisted if what she wanted was not quickly done. Then she recognized everyone and everything straightaway after the first days, and the issue with the eye was resolved. But the anger and immoderate behavior and the shouting and the changing I described persisted through her coma. She heard unevenly, some things clearly even if someone spoke quietly, but it was necessary that things be said a little more loudly by others. Her feet were always as warm as the rest of her body to the final days. But on the 16th day, her feet were less warm. On the 17th day she was better than on the others, but into the night, drawing herself together with trembling she became rather feverish. And there was much thirst. But everything else persisted in the same way. But there was trembling around her hands, and she was tossing her head. The area under her eyes and the appearance of the eyes were bad, and her thirst was strong. After drinking, she asked again, and she snatched and drank furiously. Nor were they able to tear the cup away. Her tongue was dry, very red, and her entire mouth and lips bristled dry. Raising both hands to her mouth, she chewed them, and if anyone offered something else to be chewed or sipped, violently and angrily she drank it down and gulped it. And the area around her eye was still bad. Three or four days before the end, shivers fell upon her so that she drew her body in and covered herself up completely and panted. There were cramps in her legs, and coldness of the feet. Her thirst was the same, and the matters concerning her attitude were the same. Regarding her stool, it was either nothing or small and weak with some brief straining. On the last day, the 23rd, the eye was large in the morning, and her gaze was short. She took rest sometimes and without being covered and comatose. Towards evening, the movement of her right eye was similar to seeing or considering something, from the corner of the eye to the nose. She recognized people, and she answered what was asked, and her voice was lisping after a lot of talking, and broken and rough from the shouting.

(Hippocratic Epidemics *2.7.11)*

B. *The usual treatment for typhoid fever was the application of cold packs (intimated by the Hippocratic physician above and still used when the Prince of Wales, the future King Edward VII, became ill with typhoid fever in 1871). The symptoms suffered by Alexander of Macedon in 323 BCE seem to align with typhoid, including the nine-day incubation period from the onset of the fever until death. Alexander was accustomed to daily baths and may have thus exposed himself to water-borne vectors both through drinking and bathing. Here we have a clinical account of Alexander's illness. Nearchus was one of Alexander's chief naval officers and Medius was a Thessalian noble and military leader in Alexander's retinue. Note Plutarch's use of documentary sources, including daily journals ("newspapers").*

After entertaining Nearchus and his retinue brightly, then bathing, as he was accustomed, when about to go to sleep, Alexander continued partying with him, as Medius wanted. And here, drinking all the next day, Alexander began to be feverish. He did not become feverish after gulping down a "bowl of Hercules"[5] nor afterwards. But he was suddenly in pain in his back as though stricken with a spear, as some think is necessary to record just as if shaping a tragic and passionate exit of a great drama. But Aristoboulus[6] says that Alexander had a high fever, and, very thirsty, he drank a lot of wine. From this he became delirious, and he died on the 13th day of month Daesius.

In the *Journals* it is thus written about the disease. On the 18th day of the month Daesius (May/June), Alexander slept in the bathing room because of his fever. On the next day, after bathing, he went to his bedroom and spent the day playing dice with Medius. Then, bathing late and performing sacred rites to the gods and eating, he was feverish through the night. On the 20th day, bathing again, he burnt his usual sacrifice. And lying down in the bathing room, he spent his leisure with Nearchus, listening to the events of Nearchus' voyage and anecdotes about the great sea. On the 21st day, doing the same things, Alexander was more feverish, and he spent the night with difficulty, and on the next day he was excessively feverish. Transferred from the bathing room, he lay down in the great bath house, where he chatted with his officers about vacant army posts and how tested men might fill them. On the 24th day, excessively feverish, he was carried to perform his sacrifices. He then ordered the highest-ranking of his officers to stay in the courtyard, and the division commanders and company commanders to spend the night outside. Carried over to the further palace on the 25th day, Alexander slept. But the fever did not break. When his commanders approached, he was voiceless, and he was in a similar state the next day. Therefore, it seemed to the Macedonians that he was dead, and they came to the doors shouting, and they threatened their companions until they (the companions at Alexander's bedside) were overpowered. After the doors were opened to them, they all passed by the bed in their tunics by ones.

5 Mineral water? Hercules oversaw medical mineral springs: #2.1.6B.

6 *Aristobulus of Cassandreia*, an historian who accompanied Alexander on his campaigns.

During the day, those around Python and Seleucus sent word to the temple of Sarpedon to ask if they should care for Alexander there. The god ordained that they should leave him alone where he was. On the 28th day, in the afternoon, Alexander was dead (June 10/11 323 BCE).

(Plutarch, Alexander *75–76; cf. Oldach et al. 1998; Pope et al. 2012: 49)*

2.1.3 Malaria

Difficult to distinguish from typhoid, malaria was caused by parasite-infected mosquitoes, and it was widespread especially in swampy terrain where stagnant waters foster pathogens that cause fevers, vomiting, diarrhea, earaches, ulcers, gangrene, and heat spots.

A. *Ancient physicians observed symptomatic periodic fevers abating and recurring on a cycle of three or four days (tertian and quartan fevers, respectively), as recorded in Hippocratic* Affections *17–19. Celsus' description of malaria, nonetheless, has been praised as "the clearest and most exact description of the two clinical types of tertian fevers" (Marchiafava and Bignami 1894: 231–232). Aulus Cornelius Celsus (c. 25 BCE–50 CE) was an encyclopedist, like Pliny, but only his eight books on medicine survive. Although there is debate over whether Celsus was a practicing physician, his attention to detail in the medical books strongly suggests practical experience with complex operations, including cataract surgery (*On Medicine *7.7.14).*

There are two kinds of tertian fever. One begins and ends in the same way as quartan fevers, but with the distinction that there is complete recovery for one day, but the fever returns on the third. More dangerous by far is the other type which also recurs on the third day. In 48 hours, the paroxysm lasts for nearly 36 hours, sometimes a little less, sometimes a little more. Nor is there ever a complete cessation during the remission, but it is a little lighter, but only a little bit so. Most physicians call this type *hemitritaion* (half-tertian).

(Celsus, On Medicine *3.3.2; see Sallares et al. 2004: 311–328; Oerlemans and Tacoma 2014: 213–241)*

B. *Cures included diet and bloodletting but also magic. One magical cure is recorded in the medical poem of Quintus Serenus Sammonicus, court physician to Caracalla (r. 198–217 CE).*

On driving away half-tertian fevers: That which in Greek words is called half-tertian fever is more destructive. You will inscribe "*Abracadabra*" on a piece of paper, and underneath, you will repeat the word, but take out the last letter, and again and again let the elements fall away one by one in succeeding lines, until the letter is reduced into the end of the cone. Be mindful to encircle the neck (of the patient) with this amulet bound up with linen. Some recall that lion fat is useful. If you wish to bind coral, you should not hesitate to mix in pure emeralds; a smooth and costly gem should have a snowy color. Such fetters on the neck will benefit sluggish patients, and its marvelous power will remove death-bringing diseases.

ABRACADABRA
ABRACADABR
ABRACADAB
ABRACADA
ABRACAD
ABRACA
ABRAC
ABRA
ABR
AB
A

(Quintus Serenus Sammonicus, Liber Medicinalis
*(*De Medicina Praecepta Saluberrima*) 51)*

C. *Most Greco-Roman thinkers believed that the disease was caused by bad air from swampy regions (thus, in Latin, eponymously called the disease of "bad air":* malum aer, *coming into English through Medieval Italian as* mala aria, *"malaria"). Here, Empedocles (from Acragas, Sicily) is reported to have prevented a malarial outbreak at Selinus in south-western Sicily. The episode is attested numismatically in a* tetradrachma *issue (c. 435–417 BCE, Selinute) that shows the muscled, nude, horned river-god (Achelous) with a lustral branch and bowl making sacrifices at an altar. Behind the river god, a small bull stands on a pedestal, possibly representing "the previously untamed river" (Sear* GC *907*; BMC *2, 31; Russell 1955: figure 15). Diogenes Laertius (c. 150–250 CE) composed* Lives and Opinions of Eminent Philosophers, *an important synthesis of earlier evidence, now largely lost.*

When a pestilence befell the Selinites on account of the disgusting smell from the nearby river, so that they, the men, were dying, and the women were miscarrying, Empedocles thought to draw together two nearby rivers at his own expense. And mixing together the waters, he made them sweet. When the pestilence was abated thusly and the Selinites were then feasting along the river, Empedocles appeared, and, rising, the Selinites worshipped him and they offered prayers as if to a god. Wanting to confirm this belief, he leapt into the fire.

(Diogenes Laertius 8.2.70)

D. *In 413 BCE, Syracusan fighters succeeded in hedging Athenian invaders in the malarial coastlands, thus contributing to the Athenian defeat there (see Grmek*

1979: 141–163; Sallares 2002: 36). Here, the Athenians debated whether to leave or persist in the siege while the soldiers grew more ill with the delay.

> Meanwhile, the Athenian generals were deliberating on their situation both regarding the disaster and the weakness prevailing within the army. For they saw that they were not successful in their attempts and that the soldiers were overwhelmed in tarrying. They were oppressed by disease for two reasons: the season of the year in which men were especially sickly, and at the same time the place in which they were camped was marshy and dangerous. To them the conditions seemed hopeless.
>
> *(Thucydides,* Peloponnesian War *7.47.1–2)*

E. *While the ancients may not have known that mosquitoes were vectors of the disease, both Varro (#2.1.1E) and Columella hinted at swarms of contagion-bearing pathogens. Lucius Junius Moderatus Columella (c. 4–70 CE), born at Gades (Cadiz), penned a systematic treatment of agricultural concerns in 12 books in Latin, including one book in hexameter verse on horticulture, a tribute to Vergil whom he greatly admired.*

> For it is beneficial to have escaped some longer distance from the sea rather than a shorter one, because the middle spaces are full of rather heavy vapor. Nor indeed is it fitting that there be a swamp near buildings nor an adjoining military road, because swamps emit noxious stenches and produce animals armed with hostile barbs which fly against us in very thick swarms, and then it also sends out pests of swimming and creeping things destitute of their wintery moisture and poisoned with mire and fermented muck from which blind diseases are often drawn together, whose causes not even physicians are able to observe. But at every time of the year, rust and moisture ruin farm and domestic equipment and unstored and stored fruits.
>
> *(Columella,* On Agriculture *1.5.6)*

2.1.4 *Epidemics/"Plagues"*

Not to be confused with the Bubonic plague at the root of the "Black Death" in the 14th c., epidemics were believed to be caused by extreme conditions of temperature (cold or heat) or humidity (moisture or dryness), as, most famously, the "plague" in Athens at the beginning of the Peloponnesian War, noted also at Potidaea (Thucydides, Peloponnesian War *2.58): the disease took the life of the Athenian statesman Pericles and recurred in Athens in 427 (*Peloponnesian War *3.87). Thucydides, who survived infection, recorded its symptoms and course with a clinician's eye. Early speculation was that the malady was caused by a tainted water supply, quickly dismissed. But the water supply was nonetheless improved and secured soon thereafter (Scholium on Aristophanes,* Birds *997 quoting Phrynicus Monotropos,* F *376k). Finally, many of Thucydides' indications are symptomatic* *of typhoid, and some scholars suggest that—while the epidemic may have been caused by multiple pathogens—the principal illness may have been typhoid stemming from a sewage-contaminated water-supply (Rose and Masago 2007: 41–48; Pope et al. 2012: 56).*

47. When the Spartans were in Attica for not many days, a disease first began to occur among the Athenians, said to have broken out beforehand in many other places, both around Lemnos and in other regions. But to be sure neither such a plague nor any such ruin of human beings is remembered to have occurred. Neither at first did the physicians ward off the disease, not being of service because of their ignorance, but they themselves in particular were dying insofar as they were especially exposed to it. Nor did any human skill help. When folk approached the temples and proclaimed oracular responses, all such things were futile, and ceasing from these efforts, they went away, overcome by this evil.

48. It first began, so it is said, in Aethiopia beyond Egypt, then it went on towards Egypt and Libya and to much of the king's land. Then suddenly it fell onto the city of the Athenians and fastened first upon those people in the Piraeus,[7] so that it was said by them that the Peloponnesians threw *pharmaka* ("deadly drugs") into the wells. For there were not yet any fountains there. Later, the ailment reached the upper city, and folk then died in greater numbers. May each one, both physician and private individual, therefore, speak according to his own opinion, how and from where the disease likely arose, and what he thinks were the causes sufficient of so great a change. But I will speak about what sort of disease it is and from what things someone looking out for it should perceive, if it might occur once and again, especially if there might be some foreknowledge. I myself will tell these things clearly, having been sick with it, and myself having seen others suffering from it.

49. For that year, as was agreed by all, happened to be especially disease-free with regard to other sicknesses. But if someone was previously ill with some malady, all maladies would end in this one. With regard to others, for no ostensible reason, but suddenly, it first seized healthy folk with an intense heat of the head and redness and burning of the eyes and those things within—both the throat and the tongue—were immediately bloodlike and discharged a breath both unusual and foul-smelling. Next after these symptoms came sneezing and hoarseness, and not much later the distress went down to the chest with a severe cough. When it fixed into the heart, it turned it upside down. And purgings of bile, however many are named by physicians, came out, and these with great suffering. In most cases empty retching fell upon the patient resulting in violent spasms, for some ceasing with the retching, for others much later. Externally,

7 Port of Athens: #5.3.3F.

the body was not very much warm to the touch nor green, but excessively red, bruised, and bursting with small blisters and wounds. Internally thus the body burned so that the patients could endure neither the coverings of altogether light shawls and fine blankets nor anything other than nudity. The most pleasant thing would be to throw themselves into frigid water—and many of the neglected patients even jumped into the wells—collapsing with unsatiable thirst. A fulsome drink or smaller gulp went down the same. Moreover, the difficulty of not resting and sleeplessness was constantly pressing. And the body, for how long the disease was in full bloom, was not withered but, beyond expectation, held up against the hardship so that either most died on the seventh and ninth day from the internal fiery temperature, still having some strength, or, if they escaped thus far, the disease went down to the intestines, and painful skin-sores appeared, and at the same time acute diarrhea occurred. Many died later owing to weakness: for the evil coursed through the entire body beginning above first in the head, and if someone prevailed from most of the disease, the evil later marked the extremities.

(Thucydides, Peloponnesian War *2.47–49)*

2.1.5 Hydrophobia ("Rabies")

A. *While typhoid caused extreme, unquenchable thirst in its victims, victims bitten by animals infected with rabies might suffer from* hydrophobia *("fear of water"). Here, we have various treatments for dog bites, including a dramatic plunge-bath to restore the humors. How successful the plunge-pool remedy might have been is unknown.*

Moreover, if the dog was *rabiosus* ("frenzied"), its poison must be extracted with a cupping glass. Then if the spot is neither sinewy nor muscular, the wound must be singed. If it cannot be burnt, it is not an unworthy treatment for the patient's blood to be released. Then, when the wound has been cauterized, the medicaments which are beneficial for other wounds must be applied. But with respect to a wound that has not endured cauterization, there are medicaments which furiously consume the poison. After this, the wound should be filled by no new method, but by the one established above (5.26.30–36), and would be brought to healing. After the bite of a frenzied dog, some send their patients straightaway to the bath. And there the patients suffer to sweat, while the strengths of the body allow it, with the wound open so that poison might drip out from it all the more. Then the patients take in much and undiluted wine,[8] which is the antidote to all poisons. When this has happened over three days, the patient seems to be safe from danger.

8 In antiquity wine was usually consumed mixed (not "pure"): two parts wine to three parts water, or one part wine to three parts water for better varieties, yielding an alcohol by volume of 3% to 6%. Drinking unmixed wine was considered a sign of vulgar behavior.

Moreover, when too little has been done, a fear of water customarily arises—the Greeks call it hydrophobia—a very miserable type of disease, in which the patient is at the same time tormented by thirst and a fear of water, by which hope for the oppressed is slim. But nonetheless there is one remedy: to toss the unsuspecting patient into a pool not seen beforehand. If the patient does not have knowledge of swimming, allow him to drink the pool water after sinking, and now lift the victim up. If the patient does know how to swim, press him down, now and then, so that—although unwilling—he will be sated by water. For thus at the same time thirst and fear of water are simultaneously removed. But this cure raises another danger, lest stretching out the sinews exhausts a weak body jostled in frigid water. So that this not occur, the patient, straightaway from the pool, must be submerged in warm oil. Moreover, this is the particular antidote which I posited in an earlier passage (5.23.1b). When that one is not possible, there is another, if the patient does not yet shudder at water: a drink of water must be given, and if it displeases because of bitterness, honey should be added. But if this malady has already taken possession, it is possible for the antidote to be taken through pills.

(Celsus, On Medicine *5.27.2; cf. Pliny,* NH *34.151)*

B. *Dioscorides of Anazarbus in Cilicia (fl. c. 40–80 CE) traveled widely and collected the medicinal uses of many botanical, zoological, and mineral products in his five-book* On Medical Material, *in Greek. Here, we have the use of an amulet to treat hydrophobia, the "hair of the dog," so to speak.*

The liver of a rabid dog, eaten roasted by those bitten by it, is believed to keep the patient safe from rabies. As a precaution, they also use the canine tooth of the dog that bit them, tied in a little pouch, and fastened onto their arm.

(Dioscorides, Medical Material *2.47, trans. Beck)*

C. *Etymologically conspicuous is Dioscorides' prescription of madwort (*ἄλυσσον*: "lacking rage") whose name suggests the desired outcome.*

Madwort: it is a small undershrub, somewhat rough, single stalked, having round leaves. Adjacent to them is the fruit, resembling small double shields and containing a somewhat wide seed. It grows in mountainous and rough places.

When drunk, its decoction stops feverless retchings: it does the same also when held in the mouth or when smelled. Ground up with honey, this undershrub removes birthmarks and freckles. It is thought that it also treats rabies when chopped together with food and served. They say that it is good for the health of humans and beasts when hung in the home. Suspended with a purple strip of cloth, it cures young, domesticated animals.

(Dioscorides, Medical Material *3.91, trans. Beck)*

D. *Precautions against hydrophobia.*

Frenzy of dogs, when Sirius[9] blazes, is disease-bringing to people, as we have said. Thus from bites, there is a deadly fear of water. Therefore, it is resisted for 30 days when chicken excrement is mixed with dogs' fodder or, if the malady has already befallen, with hellebore. After a bite, the only remedy of any efficacy is discovered in a recent oracle: the root of a forest-rose which is called "dogrose." Columella is the source of this remedy (*On Agriculture* 7.12.14): if on the 40th day after it has been born, a puppy's tail is docked with a bite and its uppermost joint is removed—the sinew of the tail extracted—neither will the tail grow, nor will the dogs become frenzied.

(Pliny, NH *8.152–153; cf.* NH *32.53–55)*

2.1.6 Healing Waters

A. *Attached to a public bathhouse at Sabratha, Libya, is an inscribed mosaic featuring a pair of sandals and three strigils, commonly used for scraping oils from the skin. (Consider also the statues of Apollo, god of healing, Hygieia, health personified, and human anatomical votives unearthed in 2019 at the 2nd century BCE healing/bathing shrine at San Casciano dei Bagni.)*

It is a healthful thing to have bathed.

(Reynolds and Ward-Perkins 1952: #171 [Africa Proconsularis])

B. *The medicinal properties of hot and cold mineral springs were recognized and widely enjoyed. Herodotus merely hints at the curative properties of the hot springs at Thermopylae, the "hot gates" created by Athena for Herakles who presided over medicinal thermal springs at Thermopylae and Trachiniae (Scholiast on Aristophanes,* Clouds*; Croon 1952, 1956: 210–217; Malkin 2003: 228), as well as at spas in Italy, Sicily, and Dacia (cf. Dvorjetski 2007: 93–94).*

To the west of Thermopylae, an untrodden and precipitous mountain, lofty, was lifting up towards Oeta. To the east of the road, the sea comes next and then the shallows. Along this path there are warm bathing springs which the inhabitants call the "Pots." And an altar of Herakles has been established by the locals.

(Herodotus, Histories *7.176.3)*

9 The "Dog Star," a bright star in Canis Major whose heliacal rising is in the hot summer season and also marks the flooding of the Nile (#1.5.1A).

C. *The powers of medicinal warm springs vary with their characteristics.*

Now let us pursue common waters, both icy and hot. Regarding hot waters it must be asked whether the waters are born or become hot. We will also explain about certain other waters, which either a taste or some other utility render remarkable. For certain waters heal the eyes, certain ones the sinews. Certain waters completely cure long-standing faults and those despaired of by physicians. Certain waters heal sores. By means of a drink, certain waters nurture internal issues and lighten complaints of the entrails; certain waters suppress bleeding. The use of each one is as varied as its taste.

(Seneca, NQ *3.1.2; for the tastes and medicinal powers of mineral waters:* NQ *3.20–21)*

D. *There are many hot springs in Campania, including around the Acherusian Lake which people avoided because the springs were thought to rise from the River Styx in the Underworld (#1.3.3E) and were thus considered deadly. Baiae, however, was a popular resort town, in part for its medicinal springs.*

For one rounding the bend at Cape Misenum straightaway there is a harbor under the cape. And on it, after this harbor, forming a deep running bay, are Baiae and warm waters suitable for the luxuriant lifestyle and for the healing of diseases.

(Strabo, Geography *5.4.5; cf. Seneca,* NQ *3.24; Pliny,* NH *3.60, 31.5)*

E. *Medicinal waters at Pithecussae (an island in the bay of Naples: see Dvorjetski 2007: 84–85 and note 6).*

The warm waters there seem to treat those suffering from (kidney?) stones.

(Strabo, Geography *5.4.9; cf. Aristotelian* On Marvelous Things Heard *37b.)*

F. *Some waters were thought to cure skin ailments, and the Alpheus' ability to cure leprosy in particular may be etymological (ἀλφός:* alphos *["dull white leprosy"]).*

Near the cave of the Anigriadian nymphs is a spring by which the underlying region becomes boggy and marshy. The Anigros River[10] receives most of the water, deep and lazy, so that it forms stagnant pools. Muddy, for 20 *stadia*, the place emits a heavy odor and renders the fish inedible. Some relate a myth: here some of the centaurs washed off the poison from the Hydra.[11] Others relate a

10 In the western Peloponnese, emerging from Mt. Lapithos and debouching in the Ionian Sea.

11 Herakles tipped the points of his arrows with poisonous hydra blood (his second labor: Euripides, *Herakles* 419–424) and was frequently battling the centaurs, human-equine hybrids who symbolized raw nature in contrast with idealized, "orderly" Greek behavior.

different myth: Melampus used these waters as a cleansing remedy for purifying the daughters of Proteus.[12] A bath therein heals leprosy and white splotches and lichen-like scabs. They say that the Alpheus River is named for being a remedy of leprosy.

(Strabo, Geography *8.3.19; cf. Callimachus,* Marvels *F 1 = Antigonus,* Collection of Marvelous Stories *138 (Giannini 1966: 92); Pausanias,* Description of Greece *5.5.5)*

G. *Some people abused medicinal springs.*

I am amazed that Homer did not make mention of warm springs, and although he frequently observes otherwise that there are hot baths, evidently because the medical approach at that time was not this one which now employs the protection of healing waters. Moreover, sulfurated waters are useful for the sinews, alum-waters for paralysis or situations of a similar kind, bituminated waters (with asphalt) or those full of sodium carbonate, such as at Cutila (Thrace), are useful for drinking and purging. Many folk consider it a mark of glory to endure the heat of these springs for many hours, which is very harmful. For it is fitting to use the springs only a little longer than the baths, and afterwards dipping in icy, sweet water, not departing without an oil-rub, a practice which the common folk consider time-consumingly irksome. Consequently, no other practice poses greater dangers to bodies, since their heads are filled with the immensity of the stench and, sweating, people are weakened by the cold, while the remaining parts of their bodies are submerged. There is a similar mistake: how people boast in drinking a great deal of the mineral waters. I have seen some folk swollen from drinking to such an extent that the rings on their fingers were covered over by their skin, since the amount of the water quaffed down was not able to be returned (i.e., evacuated). Therefore, it is not fitting that drinking this water happen without a repeated taste of salt.

(Pliny, NH *31.59–60)*

H. *The science underlying the efficacy of mineral springs.*

Moreover, every warm spring is medicinal, precisely for this reason: because, cooked in distorted things like channels, it receives some strength for a benefit. For sulfurous springs refresh the breakdown of the sinews by thoroughly warming and burning out faulty humors from the bodies. Moreover, when the limbs of bodies—dissolved by paralysis or some other force of disease—receive alum springs, which refresh by warming the coolness with a contrary force of warmth

12 Melampus ("Black-Foot") was a healer who reputedly introduced the worship of Dionysus to Argos and then cured the daughters of Proteus of their madness caused by drunkenness and hangovers after they had indulged in too much wine (Apollodorus, *Library* 1.9.13).

through veins as they open, and by this method patients' limbs are continuously restored to their previous curative state. Furthermore, draughts of bitumen-rich waters are accustomed to heal weaknesses of the internal body by purging them.

(Vitruvius, On Architecture *8.3.4; cf. Strabo,* Geography *16.1.15; Pliny,* NH *35.178)*

I. *What are the therapeutic benefits of bathing in warm and cold potable waters? Galen of Pergamon in Turkey (129–215 CE) was a practicing physician with a philosophical outlook who wrote broadly on the medical arts (nearly 150 titles from short tracts to multi-book studies). He served as physician to the gladiatorial school in Pergamon, where he was able to make a scrupulous study of human anatomy, and also as court physician to Marcus Aurelius (r. 161–180 CE). Probably owing to his close work with gladiators, therapeutic bathing for athletes became a complex art form for Galen.*

Let the young man set forth in this thought-exercise arrive at the healthy advantage (of a bath) after exercising, as we've said earlier. In this case there is little advantage from it. For, from moderate exercise and the regular afore-mentioned post-workout therapy, he has already gained everything. Similarly, therefore, if the baths are well-prepared, they should also become part of the post-workout therapy, if indeed they truly soften both the inflexible and stretched body-parts and distribute anything extra and any waste being held in by the skin. But our athlete, as proposed in this thought experiment, seems to need neither of these things. For it does not seem likely that the waste products of soft flesh or fat arise at all during exercise. For these things follow from unrhythmic and violent movements. But all the waste products have been emptied from him and his stiff parts have been softened during the time of his post-workout therapy, so that the sweat and sand have been washed away. And if our athlete should use this at any time, he needs the dirt to be scraped off more than he needs to be warmed in a bath. And, therefore, it is accordingly necessary only to walk up to the water tank, but it is not necessary to spend time in the bath just like those who soften themselves up apart from exercise. Nor is it necessary to spend any time in the swimming bath. After washing, as I've said, let him hurry to the cold-water bath. Let this also be moderate and with respect to the moderate character of the body. On how great a need there is of cold water and even lukewarm water and even water heated by the sun, it will be described again. But, as has been said elsewhere before, it is not necessary to wash the best body naturally in cold water, until it grows up, in order that we don't stunt its growing. When the body has grown sufficiently, it is already accustomed to such a cold bath. For it, the cold bath, strengthens the entire body and renders the skin thick and hard. The cold bath is best for damage from external forces.

(Galen, On Preserving Health *3.4 [6.184–185Kühn])*

J. *Under Hadrian (r. 117–138 CE), at least, times were reserved for the ill to use public baths. The source, the* "Augustan Histories" *(*SHA*), is a messy collection of imperial biographies dating to the 4th/5th centuries CE, sparking robust debate regarding authorship (one or many?), authenticity, and accuracy. The* SHA *nonetheless is a valuable resource for the second CE emperors of Rome.*

Before the eighth hour, Hadrian allowed no one to bathe except the ill.

(SHA, Hadrian: *22.8)*

2.2 Marine Fauna

2.2.1 Giants of the Deep

The largest animals dwell in deep water, and these large biological marine animals would inspire the tales of mythical sea monsters (#3.5).

4. Moreover, most, and especially the largest, animals are in the Indian Sea, of which the baleen whales are *jugera* by fours long, *pristes* sharks 200 cubits, to be sure lobsters fill out four cubits, also in the Ganges River eels are 30 paces.

5. But in the deep waters, sea monsters appear especially around the solstices. Then whirlwinds rush out from there, then rains, then blasts, cast down from the yokes of mountains, overturn the seas from the deep and tumble sea monsters from the depths, agitated with waves in such a great crowd, like the schools of tuna elsewhere, so that Alexander the Great's fleet directed its course against their front in no other way than as if meeting a battle-line of the enemy.[13] It was not otherwise possible to evade them: they are terrified neither by a voice nor a sound nor a crash, but only by a blow, nor are they thrown into disorder except by a down-rush.

6. A huge peninsula of the Red Sea is called Cadara; with its projection, a capacious bay is formed, traversed by Ptolemy the king (II Philadelphus, r. 284–246) by rowing 12 days and nights since it receives no blast of a breeze.[14] In the quiet of this place, sea monsters grow to a numberless magnitude.

7. The admirals of Alexander the Great's fleets reported that the Gedrosi who inhabit the Arabis River make the doorjambs in their homes with jawbones of sea monsters, and that they joist their roofs with the bones, of which many—40 cubits in length—have been found. Sea monsters similar to cattle (dugong?)

13 See Arrian, *Indica* 21–42; see also #5.1.6C, #5.1.10C.

14 Ancient ships were powered by a combination of sails and rowing when the winds failed or there was a particular need for haste: see #3.2G.581, #5.1.9A–D. For the sustained program of the exploration of the Erythraean Sea (Red Sea, Persian Gulf, Indian Ocean) under the Ptolemies: Burstein 1996.

come out from there onto the land and, after feeding on the roots of fruit-bearing plants, they return to the sea. Certain ones there—with the heads of horses, donkeys, and bulls—feed on sown crops.

8. The largest animal in the Indian Sea are the *pristis* shark and baleen whale. In the Gallic Ocean (Bay of Biscay), there is the *physeter* whale, lifting itself like a very tall column and taller than the rigged sails of a ship, exhaling a flood. In the Gaditanean Ocean (Gulf of Cadiz), there is a tree (octopus) stretched out with vast branches over so great a distance that, for this reason (its size), it is believed never to have entered the Strait. There also appear those things that are called "wheels" from their similarity to wheels: these are distinguished by four spikes and two tiny eyes close on each side.

(Pliny, NH *9.4–8; cf. Oppian,* Fishing *5.46–49)*

2.2.2 *Animal Life Emerges from Water*

A. *Animal life, including people, was first generated in moisture.*

Anaximander says that the first living creatures were born in moisture, encompassed in thorny bark-casings, and stepping forth from the salt-sea, they alighted onto dry land and, cracking out from their bark-casing, they survived for a short time.

(Anaximander, TEGP *37 = Aëtius,* Placita *5.19.4)*

B. *Anaximander also suggested that humans arose as the spawn of fish-like creatures. Censorinus was a Roman grammarian who composed his* On the Birthday *in honor of his patron in 238 CE, treating many topics including natural history, astronomy, religion, and Greek philosophical doxography.*

Anaximander the Milesian said that either fishes or animals very similar to fishes seemed to him to arise from land and water after they grew warm. In these animals, humans grew and were retained in them as fetuses until puberty. Then at length when they broke out, they advanced as men and women who were able to nurture themselves.

(Anaximander, TEGP *38 = Censorinus,* On the Birthday *4.7)*

C. *Early humans were engendered like viviparous sharks.*

Those descendants of old Hellenus[15] also sacrifice to Poseidon Patrogenius ("Paternal-begetting"), believing, like the Syrians, that humankind was formed from the watery substance. Consequently, the Syrians honor the fish as of the

15 The son of Deucalion and Pyrrha, Hellenus survived a cataclysmic flood that killed most people (#1.9.11A). Hellenus was considered the founder of the race of Hellenes (Greeks).

same kind and with the same rearing, but more reasonably than the philosophizing of Anaximander. For Anaximander believed that fish and humans were not engendered in the same environment, but that people were first developed in fishes, appearing and being nourished just like dog-fishes and, when sufficiently formed to help themselves, at that time they emerged and grasped the land.

(Anaximander, TEGP *39 = Plutarch,* Table Talk *8.4 730e)*

2.2.3 Shellfish That Resemble Ships

A. *The nautilus (*Argonauta argo*) is so-called because it behaves like a ship and seems to have inspired the construction of ships. The nautilus does have 60–90 rigging-like tentacles.*

There is some fish covered up with a hollow shell, resembling polypods in shape, and which they call the nautilus, renowned for its very seamanship. It dwells in sand, and face-downward it rises towards the water's the surface, so that the sea might not fill it up. But when it swims above Amphitrite's[16] rushing waves, suddenly turned about, it sails just like a man experienced with a skiff. It advances two feet up just as along rigging. In its middle flows something like a fine sail which is stretched by the wind. But, touching the salt-sea up from below for two feet, these tiller-like appendages keep house and ship and fish on a straight course as guides. But when the nautilus might dread some evil at hand, no longer turned towards the winds, it flees, and it drags along all the rigging, sails, and tillers. And, within its shell, the nautilus receives the flood in a mass. Weighed down, it is submerged by the onrush of the water. Oh my! Whoever first discovered those chariots of the salt-sea, ships, whether some immortal devised them or some intrepid man first of all bragged to have passed through the wave, indeed observing a sailing fish, he turned out on his lathe a similar work of compacted wooden beams, spreading out the ships' rigging from the stern.

(Oppian, Fishing *1.338–359; cf. Aristotle,* HA *525a20–27; Pliny,* NH *9.88; Aelian,* NA *9.34)*

B. *The symbiotic relationship between a crustacean and its shell: for Pliny, the shell is a separate living creature.*

Mucianus[17] has described another creature (nautilus), seen by him in the Propontis (Sea of Marmara), similar to a sailing ship: its shell is keeled like a skiff,

16 A daughter of Nereus, the Old Man of the Sea. As the wife of Poseidon/Neptune, god of the sea, *Amphitrite* is a significant goddess of the sea in her own right and was proclaimed to be the mother of fish, seals, dolphins (Homer, *Odyssey* 4.404).

17 Pliny frequently relied on the authority of his contemporary Mucianus: #1.7D note.

with a curved stern and a beaked prow. Into this shell is buried a nauplius, an animal similar to a cuttlefish, only to have a companion playing at sailing. This happens in two ways: in tranquil water the carrying shell strikes out with little palms sent out like oars; but, if a breeze entertains, these same little palms are stretched out into the service of a rudder, and the folds of the shell are stretched out to the breeze. It is the pleasure of the one to carry, of the other to steer, and at the same time this pleasure alights onto two creatures lacking sense-perception, unless by chance—for it is agreed that this sight is a sad omen for navigators—human misfortune is the cause.

(Pliny, NH *9.94)*

2.2.4 Fishes and Crustaceans Anthropomorphized

A. *Many animals were thought to love music: stingrays (Aelian,* NA *1.39; see also #3.9B); crabs (*NA *6.31); dolphins (#2.2.11H).*

I have also heard this peculiarity of the sea-dove (stingray). When it is seen swimming underneath, someone dances on his salt-water boat and to be sure heckles some badinage. If there happens to be an aulos-player,[18] and he plays the aulos as an allurement and plays a tune, then the sea-dove is delighted beyond measure: for indeed they even have ears taking in the music, so they say, and eyes observing the dancing. Then, beguiled, the sea-dove rests and somehow floats up. One boater energetically waves on the aforementioned spells, someone else places out a creel and draws in the sea-dove, and—perhaps this is the strangest thing—thus charmed by the music, it escapes the dove's notice that it has been caught.

(Aelian, NA *17.18)*

B. *The whelk king.*

Round whelks even have a king, and they are obediently governed. This king is the largest in size, the most handsome in beauty. If it is desirable to sink, he is the first to do this. If it is expedient to rise, he also leads in this, and the rest follow him as he moves his place. Whoever might grasp this king knows well that he will fare better. Even more, if someone sees the king whelk being hunted, he goes away cheerfully, himself anticipating something auspicious. In Byzantium, a prize is even set before the one hunting and catching the aforementioned whelk-king. Members of the fishing guild each give an Attic *drachma* to the one who catches a whelk king, and this is the prize.

(Aelian, NA *7.32)*

18 A wind instrument, similar to a recorder, usually played two at a time.

C. *The military-like formation of schools of migrating fish.*

Fish then ramble and wander, some as crowds, like herds of cattle or a unit of hoplites marching according to squadron or phalanx, others proceed in an order according to a battleline, while others—you might say—are themselves companies of soldiers. Some are counted by tens and travel in such a formation. Some swim as couples. Others stay at home in their dens, and there they spend their lives.

(Aelian, NA *9.53)*

D. *Alliances between mackerel and fishermen (mackerel migrations: #6.3.6B).*

In the Ionian Sea near Epidaurus[19] where the Taulantii dwell is an island called "Athena's" and the sea-folk also dwell there. In addition a lagoon is also nearby. And a school of mackerel, accustomed to people and tame, feed here. Fishermen toss out food for them, and they have a truce with each other. The fish are thus free, and they have obtained an immunity from being hunted, and they advance to a full age, and even elderly mackerel live there. But they do not graze for free, nor are they ungracious over what they feed on. But taking their breakfast from the fishermen in the morning, then straightaway they themselves, the mackerel, go towards the hunt, as if consequently making payment for their breakfast. Going beyond the harbor, they set out towards the foreign mackerel. Coming upon them like some battle line or phalanx, since the domestic mackerel are in the same phylum and with the same nature, they swim up to the foreign mackerel. Those wild fish do not flee them nor do the tame fish chase them off, but they go off together. Then, coming around the newcomers and forming a circle and packing the wild mackerel closely together, the domesticated mackerel take up the middle—a great abundance of fish—and they do not allow the wild mackerel to escape. But they wait for their benefactors, and they reciprocate the fishermen with fish on which they are satiated. Arriving, therefore, the fishermen catch the wild mackerel and work up a great slaughter. But the tame fish return, hurrying to their lagoon, and, coming within their dens, they wait for their afternoon lunch. The fishermen arrive, taking care of lunch if they want to keep the fish as hunting accomplices and friends. To be sure, this occurs on as many days as there are.

(Aelian, NA *14.1)*

E. *Fishes treat their own wounds.*

The bass fish is braver than the elephant: he draws out a barb not from another fish but from himself when he falls upon a hook. He swings his head, first to the

19 On the eastern coast of the Peloponnese, the site on an important healing sanctuary to Asclepius, the Greek god of healing.

right and then to the other side, enduring the wound in his sinews and the pain from the ripped flesh, until he can eject the barb.

(Plutarch, On Whether Land or Sea Animals Are Cleverer *977b)*

F. *Other clever sea creatures, one with a nasty sense of humor.*

Scolopendrae are similar to the land animals which they call centipedes: when a hook has been swallowed, they vomit all their guts out until they disgorge the hook, and then they swallow back their guts. In similar danger, sea-foxes gulp down more, all the way to weak parts of the line which they easily nibble off. That which is called a *glanis* (shad) more cautiously bites at the hook and does not devour it but strips it of its morsels. The sea-ram (orca) gambols about like a thief, and, now hidden in the shade of rather large vessels, floating in the salt-water, it waits in case a desire of swimming lures anyone in. Now—its head lifted above the water—it watches for the skiffs of fishermen and, secretly swimming up to them, it sinks the fishing boats.

(Pliny, NH *9.145)*

2.2.5 Starfish and Seahorses

A. *For Pliny, the natural world was a source of wonder, including the starfish which Aristotle depicted as "sucking its food dry" (*PA *4.681b9–13) and whose shell Aelian described as soft (*NA *9.22). Their numbers were apparently so large in the Pyrrhic Bay (cutting from the west into Lesbos) that they were considered pests (Aristotle,* HA *5.548a7–9).*

In addition to these things, I see that authors famous for wisdom wonder at a star in the sea. This is its shape: in measure a small amount of flesh within, on the outside with a rather hard skin. They say that there is a fiery heat in the creature such that it burns up everything it touches in the sea. It finishes off all its food immediately. By what experiments this has been learned, I can by no means say easily, and I would consider it all the more remarkable that there is a daily opportunity of testing this observation.

(Pliny, NH *9.183; cf. Plutarch,* On Whether Land or Sea Animals Are Cleverer *27 978b)*

B. *Aside from Dioscorides, who simply described the seahorse as a "small marine animal" (*Medical Material *2.3), no other ancient author provides an account of the biological hippocamp, creatures more of myth and art in antiquity. In Pliny, however, we have a few medicinal recipes that include seahorse flesh.*

i. Hippocamps as drinks quench poison from the sea-hare.

(Pliny, NH *32.58)*

ii. Hippocamp ash replenishes hair lost from fox-mange, mixed with soda and pig-fat or straight-up in vinegar.

(Pliny, NH *32.67; cf. Dioscorides,* Medical Material *2.3)*

iii. The fat of a marine bull (seal), ash of small sea-fish with three *obols* of honey, the liver of a stingray cooked with oil, the ash of a hippocamp or dolphin smeared with water, these things remove skin splotches and psoriasis.

(Pliny, NH *32.83)*

iv. Roasted hippocamps, consumed, relieved pains of the side.

(Pliny, NH 32.93)

v. Roasted and rather often taken in food, hippocamps repair intemperance of the urine.

(Pliny, NH *32.109)*

vi. Hippocamps are killed in rose-oil so that those ill with chilly fevers might be rubbed down, and the seahorses are themselves attached (as amulets) to the sick.

(Pliny, NH *32.113)*

2.2.6 Glanis (Shad)

T*he diligent parenting practices of male shadfish.*

Of the river fish, the male *glanis* directs great care towards his spawn. For, after giving birth, the female leaves, but the male, remaining, would therefore guard wherever most of the clutch has settled, offering no other help than hindering the small fishes from snatching his roe. He does this for both 40 and 50 days until the roe—having grown larger—are able to escape from other fishes. The *glanis* is recognized by fishermen wherever he happens to be guarding the clutch: for in keeping the little fishes back, he dashes at the fishermen and makes a cry and a whimpering. Thus, he stays so affectionately by the eggs that, if the roe should cling on deep roots, each and every time, the fishermen draw the clutch to the shallowest place they can. But all the same the father *glanis* does not leave his clutch. But if he happens to be caught quickly by the hook on account of grasping at the approach of the little fishes, if he is accustomed to bite the hook, he does not leave the roe. But biting down with very hard teeth he destroys the hooks.

(Aristotle, HA *621a21–b23)*

2.2.7 Sea Turtles

A. *While loggerheads and green sea turtles are indigenous to the Mediterranean, they are little discussed. But one myth preserves the memory of a sea turtle that hunted in the waters off Sciron's steep cliff—a dangerous, narrow passage near Athens—waiting for the bandit to fling his victims into the sea and then eating them. The "turtle" is still visible at low tide. For Sciron: Ovid,* Metamorphoses *7.445; Pseudo-Apollodorus,* Epitome *1.2; Hyginus,* Fables *38.*

> They think that the Molouridan Rock is sacred to Leucothea and Palaemon.[20] But beyond them, they consider the cliff cursed because, dwelling there, whatever strangers he happened to meet, Sciron[21] threw them into the sea. A sea-turtle swam under those rocks to snatch up the bandit's victims. Sea turtles are the same as land turtles except for their size and feet: they have feet similar to seals.
>
> *(Pausanias,* Description of Greece *1.44.8; cf. Aristotle,* On Respiration *475b27–30;* HA *540a27–30)*

B. *Huge sea turtles are found in the Erythraean Sea. To be sure, Aelian, or his sources, exaggerated.*

> Also born in this sea are very large turtles whose shells become roofs: for one sea-turtle is 15 *pecheis* long, so that not a few people can live under it. It keeps out the most flamelike sun, and it offers shade to pleased folk. It is resistant against downpours of rain, and the shell is stronger than every terracotta tile, and it shakes off the collision of rainstorms, and those dwelling under the turtle shell hear it rattling in the storm, as if of waters falling on some roof. Yet there is no need to exchange a broken tile: for the tortoise shell is hard, and it is like hollowed-out rocks and the roofs over naturally vaulted caves.
>
> *(Aelian,* NA *16.17; cf. Pliny,* NH *9.35)*

2.2.8 Cephalopods: Cuttlefish and Octopods

A. *The cephalopod's defensive use of its ink sac.*

> Cuttlefish employ such deceits. For fixed in their heads there is dark-blue mud, darker than pitch, an obscure medicament of watery mist, which for them brings on a safeguard against destruction. When fear has grasped them, straightaway cephalopods eject their murky drops. And the ink stains everything all around the sea and, nebulous, obscures the sea-roads, and turns every eye about. Then, straightaway through this mud, the cephalopods easily flee both a person and a braver fish anywhere.
>
> *(Oppian,* Fishing *3.156–165; cf. Aristotle* HA *621b30–22a14; Pliny,* NH *9.86; Plutarch,* On Whether Land or Sea Animals Are Cleverer *978a–b)*

20 #3.11.5D introduction.

21 For Sciron: Ovid, *Metamorphoses* 7.445; Pseudo-Apollodorus, *Epitome* 1.2; Hyginus, *Fables* 38.

B. T*he octopod's lair, defensive use of camouflage, and regrowing tentacles.*

Alone of the soft creatures, octopods go out onto dry land, provided that the terrain is rough, for they hate softness. They eat the flesh of purple shellfish whose shells they break with an embrace of their "hairs" (tentacles), and so their den is discovered by the shards of shells lying about in front. Although the octopus is otherwise considered a stupid animal, in so far that it will swim to a person's hand, it is clever to some degree in its domestic affairs: it carries everything into its home, then it throws out the waste particles—gnawed away from the flesh—and it hunts the little fishes swimming up to the waste heap. The octopod changes color similar to its setting, especially out of fear. False is the notion that the octopod gnaws its own arms: for this happens to it by eels. But that the tentacles regrow like the tails of lizards is by no means false.

(Pliny, NH *9.86–87; cf. Aristotle,* HA *622a4–11)*

C. *The octopod's ability to change color was notoriously recorded in the literary record. Here we have two examples. Theognis of Megara (570–485 BCE) was an early Greek elegiac poet.*

Pindar (F 43) has made the polypods' change of color famous, saying, "harmonize in all the cities, turning your mind especially to the color of the sea-beast." And Theognis (F 215) similarly, "turn your mind to the many-colored polypod, who harmonizes with any rock, appearing to look as such."

(Plutarch, On Whether Land or Sea Animals Are Cleverer *978e)*

D. H*ow the octopod uses its tentacles.*

The polypod uses its coiling appendages like feet and hands. Food is therefore brought in with the two tentacles above the mouth. The last of the tentacles, very sharp and the only one that is partly white and double-hued at the tip, is uncoiled on the thorny side: for the smooth side is called the *rhachis*, where the hollow suckers are: octopods employ this tentacle in impregnating females. In the front cavity and above the tentacles, they have another cavity, through which they expel seawater that has been taken into this hollow body-part when they were grasping something with their mouth. The octopod turns this cavity about sometimes to the right, sometimes to the left. It also emits its mud (ink) from this hollow. The octopus swims sideways towards what is called the head, stretching out its feet. By swimming thusly, it happens to see forwards: for its eyes are on top and the mouth is behind.

(Aristotle, HA *524a3–16; cf.* PA *685a14–b16)*

E. *The octopus' reproductive process.*

After joining and impregnating, soft sea creatures have white eggs. In time, they become crumbly, just like the eggs of hard animals, and the polypod gives birth into its dens or into a terracotta pot or some other hollow receptacle, similar to the blooms on wild vine-tendrils or the fruit of the white poplar, as was mentioned earlier (*HA* 544a9). The eggs then hang on the receptacle when they have been ejected. The clutch has so many eggs that, being removed, they would fill a vessel larger by much than the mother's head, where she held the eggs.

Therefore, the polypods' eggs are formed after about 50 days, and tiny polypods crawl out from some eggs breaking open, just like spiders, but a large number of them. Not entirely clear yet is the nature of the limbs, according to each detail, but the overall shape is evident. On account of their minuteness and weakness, most of them perish. Some have been seen altogether so small that they are unjointed, but they move in response to where they are touched.

(Aristotle, HA *549b30–550a9)*

F. *A clever, larcenous octopod, and how it was finally defeated. Octopods can come onto land and climb trees!*

In the fishponds at Carteia,[22] a polypod was accustomed to emerge from the sea into the open lagoons and there plunder the salted fish—even the odor of salted fish is marvelous to all marine animals seeking it, for which reason salted fishes are smeared on fish-traps—this polypod turned the enormous wrath of the guards against itself owing to the frequency of the theft. Fences were put up, but the octopus crossed these by a tree. Nor was it able to be caught by the sharp skill of the dogs. From every side, the dogs attacked it returning at night, and the guards, roused up, were afraid of the animal's strangeness: first of all, its size was unheard of, then its color, smeared with brine, awful in its stench. Who would expect a polypod there or thus recognize it? As far as the guards were concerned, they seemed to be contending with a supernatural monster, for, with its terrible breath, it vexed the dogs, now lashed by the octopod's outermost "hairs" (tentacles), now stricken with the beast's rather strong, club-like arms. With difficulty it was able to be finished off with several tridents. The salt-fishermen showed Lucullus the octopus' head, the size of a jar, spacious enough to hold 15 amphoras, and so I might use the words of Trebius himself,[23] "the beards (tentacles) which they could scarcely reach round with both arms, knotty like clubs, 30 paces long, with cups or half-amphora basin-like vessels

22 At the head of the Bay of Gibraltar and an important center of the salt-fishing industry (#6.4.2).

23 Lucius Licinius Lucullus was consul in 151 BCE, later traveling to Spain when Trebius Niger served as governor of Hispania Baetica. Trebius' treatise on natural history was an important source for Pliny.

(suckers), and teeth commensurate in size. Its remains, preserved as a curiosity, weighed about 700 pounds.

(Pliny, NH *9.92–93; cf. Aelian,* NA *13.6)*

G. *This Red-Figure Fish Plate (Binningen Painter, third quarter of the 4th century BCE) from Paestum in southern Italy shows a bountiful sea-harvest scene: an animated octopus, a bream whose belly faces the center, gurnard whose belly faces the rim, scallop, starfish, mussel, and cockle.*

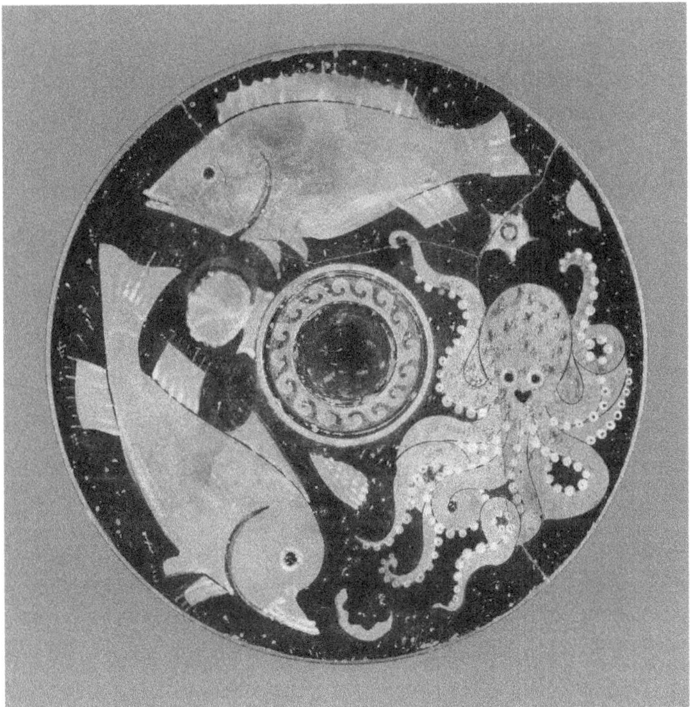

FIGURE 2.2.8G Paestan red-figure fish plate: attributed to the Binningen Painter, third quarter of 4th century BC, J. Paul Getty Museum 96.AE.240 (public domain).

2.2.9 Sharks

A. *Three categories of shark were recognized from the 50 or so species of the carnivorous cartilaginous fish that hunt in packs in the Mediterranean.*

There are three types of sea dogs. There are the largest of these in size, and they should be counted among the most daring of sea monsters.[24] The remaining

24 Great white sharks? which are found in Mediterranean waters.

two types, mud-dwelling in nature, extend to the length of a *pechus*. Of these, the spotted and stained sharks might be called *galeoi*. Calling the rest "spiny" sharks, you would not altogether miss the mark.[25] Dappled sharks, therefore, are softer with respect to their skin and flatter in the head. But, hard with respect to their hides and having heads coming to a sharp point, the others are distinguished with a white color. Moreover, sharp spines grow on them, one on the back fin, you might say, the other on the tail. Their spines are hard and rigid, and they emit something of a poison. Each type of small dogfish is caught in the mud and mire. And regarding the hunt, we may as well describe it. For bait, the fishermen let fall a white fish whose backbone has been cut out. When one shark is caught and falls on the hook, all the onlooking sharks jump on him and follow him as he is dragged from below, and they do not stop until they arrive at the boat. Sharks seem to do these things from rivalry, just as if the baited shark had robbed a pursuing shark of some small morsel somewhere for himself alone. Some sharks even often leap onto the ship and are readily caught.

(Aelian, NA *1.55; cf. Oppian,* Fishing *1.373–382)*

B. *Here we have Aristotle's remarkable description of the female shark's reproductive system, including the placenta-like membrane, long forgotten until Guillaume Rondelet quoted the passage in 1554 (*"Books about marine Fish in which the true Images of Fish are expressed"*). The shark placenta was confirmed by the Danish anatomist Nicolas Steno in 1673, but not widely known until Johannes Müller's 1842 paper,* "Regarding Aristotle's Smooth Shark."

Those sharks called "smooth" have their eggs between the uterus like dogfishes: these eggs descend to each forked part of the uterus. The zygotes are produced having an umbilical cord at the uterus, so that—as the eggs are consumed—the embryos appear similar to quadrupeds. The umbilical cord, being long, grows from the uterus on the lower part, each one joined—as if on a cotyledon[26] in a plant seed—to an embryo in the middle where the liver is. The nourishment of the cut-open embryo, even if it no longer has the egg, is egg-like. A chorion[27] and individual membranes grow around each of the embryos, just as in quadrupeds. The young embryos have their heads upwards, but maturing and becoming complete, their heads face down. On the left side, males are produced, and on the right, females, and on the same side at the same time, females and males. The embryos, cut open, have internal organs similar to those in quadrupeds, large, such as the liver, and supplied with blood.

(Aristotle, HA *565b2–17)*

25 I.e., hitting the center of a bull's-eye, a commonly used archery term implying success (Homer, *Odyssey* 2.251; Plato, *Republic* 423a; Achilles Tatius, *Leucippe and Clitophon* 18.6).
26 An embryonic leaf in a seed-bearing plant.
27 The outermost membrane of an embryo.

C. *Sharks were, and still are, a legitimate source of concern for sailors and swimmers who invade shark habitats. Shivers of sharks might attack divers, and here are methods of fighting them off. For pilot-fish (guide fish):* #3.11.13.

Combat with little dog-fish sharks is fierce. The sharks attack the groins and heels and every white part of the bodies. There is one safety: to go after them and, moreover, terrify them. For the shark is equally afraid of the person and frightened, and thus their lot is equal in the waters. When the shark comes to the surface of the water, there the danger is two-fold, since a diver's reasoning ability to go after the shark has been compromised while trying to emerge from the water. Every safety is in his companions. They drag a rope tied to the diver around his shoulders. Struggling against the shark, the diver shakes his left hand as a sign of danger. His right hand is in the fight with a seized knife. The dragging is moderate most of the time: but when the diver comes near the skiff, unless with a very quick force, the companions suddenly snatch the diver out, and the sharks see that the diver is taken away. But, removed from the hands of their companions, divers are often carried away, unless the diver can help his companions who are drawing him out of the water by rolling his body up like a ball. The other crewmen on the boat indeed stretch out their tridents. But the monster is clever in going under the ships and battling in safety. Therefore, every care for keeping watch against this evil is employed. The most certain security is to have seen flat-fish, because there are never flat-fish where there are nefarious beasts, wherefore divers call the flat-fish sacred.

(Pliny, NH *9.152–153)*

D. *The epigrammist and lyric poet Leonidas of Tarentum (3rd century BCE) imagined the last moments of the diver Tharsys, who died from a shark attack.*

I am buried both on land and at sea. This is the extraordinary end of Tharsys, son of Charmides. For plunging into the salt-sea for the sake of the stuck weight of the anchor, going down into the watery Ionian swell, I saved the anchor, but I myself returning from the deep came to harm even as I was reaching out my hands to the sailors. I was eaten. So great and savage a monster came upon me, he gulped me down all the way up to my belly button. The sailors raised half of me, an icy weight, from the salt-sea. But the other half, the *pristis* saw-fish shark had broken off. On this same shore, my good man, they buried the evil remains of Tharsys, and I did not return back to my homeland.

(Leonidas of Tarentum, Greek Anthology *7.506; cf.* Greek Anthology *9.269; for a shark attack off the beach at Athens: Plutarch,* Phocion *28.1–3)*

E. *This geometric krater shows six shipwrecked sailors hunted by a horde of predatory fishes: one victim has lost an arm, another is swallowed head-first, and others try to escape.*

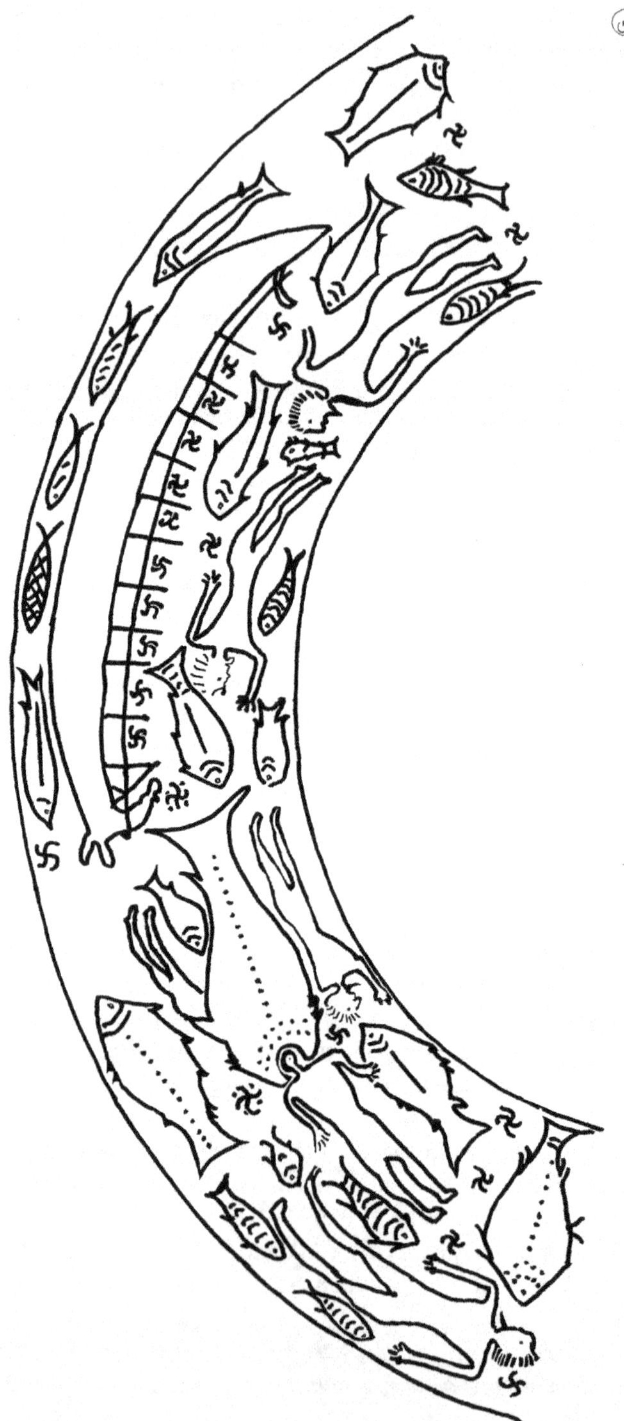

FIGURE 2.2.9E Shark attack: Ischia: Museo Archeologico, Pithekoussai 618813; drawing by Georgia L. Irby.

F. *Shark meat was (and remains) a culinary delicacy. Here we have Archestratus' recipe for saw-toothed shark, as preserved by Athenaeus of Naucratis (on the Nile, 2nd/3rd century CE), a rhetorician and grammarian whose 15-book* Deipnosophistae *(*Learned Banqueters*) is a valuable compendium of Greek social practices, including food, music, and dance. Athenaeus cited nearly 800 writers and 2,500 separate titles. Archestratus of Gela or Syracuse (in Sicily) composed* Hedypatheia *("Life of Luxury"), a hexameter guide for foodies in the 4th/3rd century BCE.*

> In those lovely *Counsels* Archestratus (F 24.1–17) recommends the following preparation: "In the city of the Toronaeans,[28] it is necessary to purchase the hollow bellies of a saw-tooth shark. Then with cumin and salt, not much, roast them. Apply nothing else, my dear person, except some early-harvest olive oil. When they are roasted, bring a sauce and the bellies with it.
>
> *(Athenaeus,* Learned Banqueters *7.310c)*

2.2.10 Seals

A. *Seals were ambiguously amphibious, occupying both land and sea, basking on rocks and coming to shore to give birth. But they were reviled, and Menelaus, king of Sparta, husband of Helen, complains about their stench when he is advised to hide among Proteus' seals on Pharos island (Egypt) to discover how to safely make his voyage homeward. See also #3.1.4.*

> All around Proteus, his seals, the children of the lovely deep salt-sea, sleep in heaps, emerging from the dark-blue water, and they breathe out the bitter stench of the very deep salt-sea.
>
> Proteus' daughter, Eidothea,[29] plunging beneath the broad bay of the sea, brought up from the sea four hides of seals, all were newly flayed. She contrived a trick against her father. Scooping out beds in the sandy beach, she sat waiting, and we came very close to her. She laid us down one after another, and cast a hide over each of us. And the ambush would have been very grim: for the stench of the sea-reared seals was deadly. Who could be lulled to sleep next to a sea monster? But she herself saved us and planned an advantage. Bringing it, she placed ambrosia[30] under the nose of each of us, very sweet to breathe. It made an end of the monster's stench. For the entire morning, we waited with suffering courage. The seals then came from the salt-sea in crowds. Next, they laid themselves down in a row along the breaking edge of the sea.
>
> *(Homer,* Odyssey *4.404–406, 435–449)*

28 Torone, in Macedonia on the Sithonia peninsula.

29 The "shapely/knowing goddess."

30 The food consumed by the gods (*Homeric Hymn 2 To Demeter* 49), as an ointment with the power to heal (Vergil, *Aeneid* 12.419), to preserve dead bodies (Homer, *Iliad* 16.670), to render a mortal immortal (Theocritus, *Idyll* 15.108), and apparently counter unpleasantly redolent scents.

B. T*he seal's ambivalently amphibious nature.*

The seal is among the intermediate living things. The seal does not take in water, but it breathes and sleeps and gives birth on land, near the beach, as if among the footed animals. It feeds and spends most of its time in the ocean, and consequently there must be discussion about it among the watery animals. The seal is born live, and it brings forth living progeny, and it produces a chorion[31] just like hoof-stock do. It gives birth to one or two pups, three at the most. It has two teats, and it suckles its little ones like quadrupeds. Like a person, the seal gives birth every season of the year, but especially at the same time as the first goats. The mother seal leads her pups, from when they are about 12 days old, to the sea, for many days, accustoming them to the sea in small stages. Stretching downward, the seal is carried, but it does not walk, because it is not able to support itself on its feet. It gathers and contracts itself. For it is fleshy and soft and has cartilaginous bones. It is difficult to kill a seal forcefully, unless someone strikes it on the temple, for its body is fleshy. It utters a sound like a cow. The female has genitalia like a ray, but in all other regards seal genitalia are similar to human sex organs.

(Aristotle, HA *566b27–567a14; cf. Aelian,* NA *9.9; Oppian,* Fishing *5.376–391)*

C. *Seals are trainable, and their hides, it was thought, retain a sensitivity to the rhythms of the sea.*

Seals take to discipline, and they greet the people at an exhibition with a voice or a nod, and they respond when called by name with a raucous growl. No animal is pressed by a deeper sleep. On land they also creep on their "wings" (fins), which they use in the sea, like feet. They say that seal pelts, even flayed from the body, retain a perception of the sea and they always tremble when the sea's tide is receding. Moreover, there is a sleep-inducing force in the right fin and, put under the head, it entices sleep.

(Pliny, NH *9.41–42)*

D. *Augustus (r. 27 BCE–14 CE) kept a sealskin as an amulet.*

About superstitions, we've heard such a thing. Rather a little weakly, Augustus grew frightened at thunder and lightning, so that he always and everywhere carried the pelt of a sea-cow (seal) as a remedy, and at every suspicion of a rather large storm, he took himself to a hidden and vaulted place, after he was once alarmed on a night-journey by a lightning strike, as we have said.

(Suetonius, Augustus *90)*

31 #2.2.9note.

E. *Seals were also observed grieving over deceased little ones. One instance was observed by the Pythagorean philosopher, Apollonius of Tyana (in Turkey, c. 15–100 CE), whose biography was penned in Greek by the philosopher Philostratus the Younger of Athens (c. 170–240 CE).*

> In Aegeae, I saw a seal caged for the beast-hunt so lamenting her dead pup, which she had given birth to in the cage, that she did not take food for three days, even though they are the most gluttonous of wild animals.
>
> *(Philostratus of Athens,* Apollonios of Tyana *2.14.4)*

F. *The seal who fell in love with a very ugly sponge diver.*

> Eudemus[32] says that a seal fell in love with a man who customarily dived for sponges, and the seal would advance from the sea and associate with the diver there where there was a cavernous rock. This man was the ugliest of his fellow sponge divers, but to the seal he seemed to be the most beautiful. Possibly this is not a marvel, when people have often fallen in love with less beautiful folk, having no feelings towards the handsomest folk and paying them no attention.
>
> *(Aelian,* NA *4.56)*

2.2.11 Dolphins

A. *Dolphins are well-represented in Greco-Roman art and literature, deeply anthropomorphized for their friendliness to humankind, featured on coinage, and lauded in verse. The omni-present dolphin was beloved by Poseidon, god of the sea. For dolphin metamorphoses: #3.2B–C.*

> Dolphins are glad on the far-sounding headlands, and they inhabit the seas, and there is no sea apart from dolphins. For Poseidon is excessively fond of them, because, as he was pursuing the dark-eyed daughter of Nereus, Amphitrite, who shrank from his bed, the dolphins showed him where to find her hiding in the homes of Ocean.
>
> *(Oppian,* Fishing *1.383–389)*

B. *Some characteristics of dolphins and porpoises and their differences.*

> The dolphin and the whale and other cetaceans, which do not have gills but blowholes, give live birth, as do the *pristis* shark and the ox-fish. None of these is seen to have eggs, but straightaway there is an embryo from which, when it is

32 Eudemus of Rhodes (?) (c. 370–c. 300 BCE), Aristotle's student who edited his teacher's writings. Eudemus wrote *History of Arithmetic*, *History of Geometry*, *History of Astronomy*, surviving in scant fragments.

articulated, comes a living creature, just as a human does and also four-footed animals. The dolphin generally produces one calf, occasionally two. The whale produces either two calves for the most part, or one. Similar to the dolphin is the porpoise. The porpoise is like a small dolphin, and it is generated in the Pontus Sea. The porpoise differs from the dolphin with respect to its smaller size, and it is broader across the back. The porpoise has a gray-blue color. Many people, moreover, say that the porpoise is a type of dolphin.

All animals which have a blowhole breathe, and they take in air: for they have lungs. A dolphin, when it was sleeping, has been observed lifting up its muzzle, and it snores while sleeping. The dolphin and porpoise have milk, and they suckle their calves, and they take the calves, still small, inside their bodies. Dolphin offspring attain their full growth quickly. For in ten years, they have obtained their final size. Dolphins are pregnant for ten months. The dolphin gives birth in the summer, and in no other season. It also happens that the dolphin disappears for about 30 days around the time of the Dog-Star.[33] The offspring follow their mothers for a long time, and it is an animal who loves its children. Dolphins live for many years. Some clearly have lived more than 25 years, others have even lived for 30 years. Nicking the tails of some, fishermen let them go so that in this way they might know their lifespans.

(Aristotle, HA *566b2–26)*

C. *According to Aristotle, blowholes served to expire ingested water. To the contrary, blowholes allow cetaceans to breathe. Over time, the organ moved to the top of the head, which is more frequently exposed to air than the snout. The spray (or blow) results from the forceful expulsion of air into the lower-pressure, colder atmosphere, where water vapor condenses, giving the appearance of a watery spray.*

Strangest of all living creatures are the dolphin and any other such animals dwelling in water and other cetaceans having this characteristic, such as whales and whichever of those animals has a blowpipe. For it is not easy to place each of these animals as only water-dwelling or land-dwelling, if one must classify those taking in air as land-dwelling and those taking in water as water-dwelling by nature. For cetaceans participate in both conditions: they take in seawater and discharge it through their pipe; and they discharge air with their two lungs. For they have this organ, and they breathe through it. Consequently, being caught in nets, a dolphin suffocates quickly on account of not breathing. Out of water, the dolphin can live for a long time, gasping and moaning, just like other breathing animals.

(Aristotle, HA *589a31–b11)*

33 #2.1.5D note.

D. *Further details about dolphin behavior, adapted from Aristotle and enhanced.*

The swiftest of all animals, not only marine animals, is the dolphin: swifter than a bird, sharper than a spear, and, if its mouth were not much lower than its muzzle, nearly in the middle of its belly, none of the fishes would escape its quickness. But the providence of nature brings on this delay, because, unless supine and turned over, dolphins do not seize their prey. This reason in particular displays their velocity: for, when roused by hunger, pursuing a fish fleeing into the deepest depths, dolphins have held their breath for a rather long time. Shot as if from a bow, they spring up to breathe, and they leap up with such force that they commonly fly over the sails of ships. They generally wander about in pairs. They bear pups after the tenth month in the summertime, sometimes by twos. They feed the pups from breasts, just like whales do, and they even carry their little ones, weak from infancy. To be sure, they accompany their progeny for a long time, even as adults, with great affection towards their offspring. They grow quickly; they are thought to reach their greatest size in ten years. They also live for 30 years, a thing that is known from a tail nicked as an experiment. Dolphins withdraw for 30 days around the rising of the Dog-Star[34] and are hidden in an unknown way, which is all the more marvelous if they are not able to breathe in water. They are accustomed to break out onto land for some uncertain reason, nor do they die immediately once land has been touched, but they die much more quickly if their blowpipe has been shut. The tongue, contrary to the nature of other aquatic animals, is mobile, short, and broad, differing by no means from a pig's tongue. For a voice, their groan is similar to a human moan, their back is turned up, their beak is flat-nosed: for this reason, amazingly, all of them recognize the name "Simo" ("snub nose") and prefer to be called thusly.

(Pliny, NH *9.20–23)*

E. *There are many examples of dolphins showing kindness or gratitude to human beings. Here we have the poignant tale of a dolphin who befriended a boy at Puteoli (Pozzuoli) on the northern shore of the Lago di Lucrino, west of Naples.*

The dolphin is not only friendly to humankind but also fond of musical skill. He is delighted by the singing of harmony but especially by the sound of a water-organ.[35] The dolphin does not dread a human as strange, but comes to meet ships. Rejoicing it cavorts and even competes as if outstripping ships under full sail, however fast they might be. Under the divine emperor Augustus, a dolphin, brought to the Lucrine Lake, with a marvelous love, esteemed the son of a certain poor man, a boy going from Baiae to Puteoli for school in

34 #2.1.5D.
35 #4.6.2.

literature, while tarrying at noon and calling the dolphin by the name of "Simo," the boy enticed the dolphin with morsels of bread which he carried on his journey: it would be grievous to report the event if it had not been handed down in the writings of Maecenas and Fabianus and Flavius Alfius and many others.[36] Called by the boy at whatever time of day, although hidden and concealed, the dolphin flew up from the depth, and eating from the boy's hand, offered its back to the boy to climb onto, burying the stingers of his fin as if within a sheath. The dolphin would carry the boy, thus received, through the great flat sea to Puteoli, conveying him back home in a similar fashion for several years until, when the boy died from disease, thereupon coming again and again to the customary place, sad and himself also like a mourner, a thing which no one could doubt: the dolphin gave out from grief.

(Pliny, NH *9.24–25)*

F. *Perhaps the most famous act of dolphin kindness was bestowed on Arion, told here by Lucian from the point of view of the dolphins.*

Poseidon: It is very well for you, Dolphins, that you are always such people-lovers, and long ago you conveyed Ino's son to the Isthmus receiving him from the Scironian cliffs after he fell with his mother.[37] And now after collecting this cithara player from Methymna (Lesbos), you have swum to Taenarum (Sicily) with his attire and cithara, nor did you overlook him about to be evilly murdered by those sailors.

Dolphins: Don't marvel, Poseidon, if we do something kindly for people, after we ourselves were changed from people to fishes. I blame Dionysus because, after vanquishing us in a sea-fight, he changed us.[38] By rights, he should only have subdued us, just as does to the others.

Poseidon: But what happened with this Arion, Dolphin?

Dolphin: Periander,[39] I suppose, was in love with him and often sent for him for his art. But, becoming wealthy from the tyrant, Arion desired to sail homeward to Methymna to show off his riches, and he embarked on some ferry boat of evil men. When, having a lot of gold and silver,

36 A friend and cultural advisor to Augustus, Gaius Clinius Maecenas (68–8 BCE) supported several important poets, including Vergil and Horace. A rhetorician and philosopher at Rome under Tiberius (r. 14–37) and Caligula (r. 37–41), Papirius Fabianus had an interest in natural history (Pliny refers to Fabianus' titles *On Animals* and *Books of Natural Causes*). Pliny consulted Flavius Alfius as an authority on dolphins.

37 Ino: #3.11.5D. In Lucian's version, Ino's son Melicertes also jumped and, like his mother, was saved. The Scironian Cliffs: #2.2.7A.

38 See #3.2B–C.

39 A tyrant of Corinth (d. 585 BCE). In ancient Greece, a tyrant was a leader who seized power unconstitutionally, but was not necessarily oppressive.

he showed it to them, then—it happened that they were in the middle of the Aegean—the sailors laid a plot against Arion. Swimming next to the ship, I heard the whole sordid affair. Then Arion said, "Since this seems best to you, let me take my stuff with me and sing my own funeral dirge and then toss myself in." The sailors agreed, and Arion collected his stuff, and he sang exceedingly clearly, and he fell into the sea so that straightaway he would be altogether dead. But catching him up and situating him, I swam away carrying him to Taenarum.

Poseidon: I commend your love of music. You gave back a worthy price for hearing his song.

(Lucian, Dialogue of the Sea Gods *5 (8))*

G. *Dolphins never forget a kindness, and they dutifully show their gratitude, as here in the waters around the Cyclades.*

When some dolphins in Byzantium fell and were caught in a fishing net, a local man, Coeranus by name, from a family from Paros, gave silver as a ransom to the fishermen and sent the dolphins away free, for which he received their gratitude. At any rate, so the story goes, once Coeranus was sailing, obtaining a penteconter (with 50 oars): he was in command of some Milesian men. When the ship turned over in the strait between Naxos and Paros and the others perished, the dolphins saved Coeranus, repaying him equally for the aforementioned good deeds: holding him fast, they swam out where a summit and the cavernous rock is indicated, and the place is called Coeraneian. At a later time, after Coraenus died, they cremated this same man near the shore. Then, to be sure, perceiving this from some place, the dolphins gathered, as if therefore attending his funeral rites, and for the whole time that the pyre burned, they remained as one friend faithful to another. When, however, the pyre was quenched, they swam away.

(Aelian, NA *8.3)*

H. *Dolphins are also faithful to each other.*

An animal who loves his fellows, the dolphin is steadfast. As witness, there is Ainos, a city in Thrace. It happened thus that a dolphin was caught and wounded, not to the point of death, but there was still life in the one taken by enemy hands. Therefore, his blood flowed out, and the other dolphins perceived this, and they arrived at the harbor as a pod, and, porpoising, they were clearly intending something not good. Accordingly, the Aeneans were alarmed and they discharged their captive. Those uncaptured dolphins, receiving the released prisoner like one of their own relatives, vanished as they left.

(Aelian, NA *5.6)*

I. *Some dolphins, however, are too clever for their own good and try to take advantage of human generosity.*

> A trapped dolphin, perceiving that he is in the bend of a net, patiently waits, not agitated but giddy. For without effort he feasts sumptuously on plentifully offered fish. But when he approaches near the shore, biting through the net, he flits away. But if he does not get away in time, escaping, the first time he suffers nothing terrible, but, stitching rushes to his dorsal fin, the fishermen send the dolphin away. But with blows the fishermen chastise the same dolphin, caught again, recognizing the miscreant from the seam. Rarely does this happen. Most dolphins have good sense regarding their pardon in the first place, and they keep a watch out not to commit another crime in future.
>
> *(Plutarch,* On Whether Land or Sea Animals Are Cleverer *978a)*

J. *Some dolphins who washed ashore were mourned with poignant funerary epigrams or even burial. The highly acclaimed epigrammist Aulus Licinius Archias of Antioch (fl. 120–161 BCE) traveled widely and was defended by Cicero against a charge of acquiring Roman citizenship illegally (*Pro Archias*). It is uncertain how many of the 35 epigrams attributed to Archias were composed by the Cicero's friend.*

> No longer darting through the deep roiling salt-sea, Dolphin, will you frighten the herds of the seas; nor, dancing to the strain of a reed-pipe full of holes, will you splash up your watery leaping next to the skiffs. Nor, creator of sea-foam, lifting up Nereids as before, will you convey them on your back to Tethys' boundaries. For when the sea was stirred, equal in height to the headland of Malea,[40] the waves thrust you on the sandy sands of the shore.
>
> *(Archias,* Greek Anthology *7.214; cf. 7.215, 216)*

2.2.12 Whales

A. *Several species of whales are found in Mediterranean waters, including sperm whales, fin whales, and common minke whales. Here Aristotle's description of baleen, which characterizes true "whales," but seems unaware of its function: that is, filtering krill from seawater.*

> In addition, *moustakia* ("mustache") whales do not have teeth in their mouth but whiskers like pigs'.
>
> *(Aristotle,* HA *519a23–25)*

40 The Malian Gulf, north of Thermopylae.

B. *Ancient taxonomy was hardly precise, and Greeks and Romans would have considered any very large marine a "whale" (or sea monster: #3.5), especially those hostile to people. Aelian here seems to be describing an orca (lacking baleen, and so technically not a whale).*

Sea-rams—whose names thus flow through to many peoples, but with respect to the facts that are not altogether clear, except for whatever the arts show—spend their winters between the Cyrnean (Corsican) and Sardinian Straits. They appear from out of the salt-sea. Dolphins swim around them, very large in size. Accordingly, the male sea-ram has a white band running between his eyes: you might call this band the diadem of Lysimachus or Antigonus or some other of the kings in Macedon.[41] The female sea-rams have crests like roosters, in this way they have locks attached below the neck. Each type of sea-ram, male and female, carries off dead bodies and they make meals out of them. They also even snatch away living people. And by means of the wave created from their swimming—since they are large and with excessive size—they even overturn ships, working up such a storm against the ships of their own accord. They even snatch away those standing on nearby land. Those inhabiting Cyrnos (Corsica) say that, when a ship was destroyed in a storm, a man who was an especially strong swimmer, managing a great deal of sea, reached some cape of their land, and emerging from the water he stood very bravely, since he was already free of all dangers and in safety and had agency of his own life. Then a sea-ram, swimming along, saw him standing there and, burning with hunger, rolled himself and arched up. And with his tail-part he thrashed a great deal of sea, and then he raised himself, lifted up from the swollen surge, and he came to the cape, and, elevated like a squall or a whirlwind, he snatched the man. Thus regarding Cyrnos, these are the prey and spoils of the sea-ram.

Those dwelling along the Ocean tell tales that the kings of ancient Athens, those from the seed of Poseidon,[42] wore on their heads the bands of the male sea-rams, tokens of their rule. And their wives, the queens, wore the locks of the others (female sea-rams) as proof of their authority. This fearful and very strong creature (the sea-ram) then has nostrils and breathes out a great deal of air and also draws in a great deal of air. It hunts seals in this way: when seals perceive that a sea-ram is somewhere nearby and is bringing destruction to them, they

41 In reference to Alexander's successor generals who carved up his empire: Lysimachus of Thessaly became king of Thrace (r. 306–281 BCE); Antigonus: #4.1.1E. Decorated ribbons and diadems were worn as symbols of royal authority.

42 Poseidon contested Athena for hegemony over the *polis* of Athens. While he lost his bid in the mythscape, and subsequently sent a devastating flood, in ritual, he remained a major civic god. After losing the contest, he created the salt-sea *Erecthēis* ("Sea of Erechtheus") and his cult on the acropolis was aligned with an ancient cult of Erechtheus, one of the chthonic founders of Athens: see Herodotus, *Histories* 8.55; Apollodorus, *Library* 3.14.1; Pausanias, *Description of Greece* 2.1.6, 2.15.5, 2.22.5.

swim as quickly as possible and pass over to land and they slink away and steal themselves within rocky out-croppings. But the sea-rams, perceiving the escape, pursue the seals and, standing face to face with the cave, from the stench of the seal-hide, they know that their prey is within. By some very strong stench, with their nostrils they draw in the air between themselves and the seal. Like a dart or the point of a spear, the seal shuns the assault of the ram's breath, and at first gradually withdraws, but in the end, the seal is drawn out from the cave by the forcible pull, and the seal follows unwillingly, as if therefore stretched tight with straps or reed-cords, and the seal shrieks and becomes lunch for the sea-ram.

(Aelian, NA *15.2)*

C. *Off the coast of Cyzicus in the Erythraean Sea in 325 BCE, Alexander's admiral Nearchus (#2.1.2B) encountered a pod of large marine animals, perhaps blue whales (*Balaenoptera musculus, *c. 80 feet [25 meters]) or toothed sperm whales (*Physeter macrocephalus*: c. 65 feet [20 meters]): both species are native to the Erythraean Sea.*

It is reasonable to assume that sailors prattle many things to the point of hyperbole. Nonetheless their tales intimate clearly both what happened and at the same time what suffering came to them, because expected—rather than real—danger underscores true peril. With respect to its amplitude, the stream of the spouting whales especially troubled them, producing a great mass of water and mist from their eruptions, so that the sailors could see not a thing in front of their feet. But then the local pilots—since Nearchus' men feared such things and were not observing the cause—explained that the whales were wild creatures, and one could drive them away after they heard a salpinx[43] and rattling. Because of this explanation Nearchus led his ships towards the tumult, to where the whales hindered his progress, and at the same time he terrified them with the salpinxes. The beasts then plunged into the sea, and then they appeared again at the stern as if offering naval combat. But straightaway they withdrew.

Those sailing even now to India describe the great size of these wild beasts and their appearance, but neither in crowds nor often attacking, but they, the whales, are driven away, scared by screaming and the salpinx. They say that these animals do not come near land, but that the stripped-bare bones of broken-up carcasses are easily cast up by the waves, and their bones furnish gathered material to the Ichthyphagoi[44] for building their huts. Nearchus (F 1b) says that the size of the whales is 23 *orguiae*.

(Strabo, Geography *15.2.12–13)*

43 A war-trumpet, comprised of a long, straight, narrow, bronze (or bone) tube with a bone mouthpiece and bronze conical finial, 0.8–1.2 meters (2.6–4 feet) in length.

44 "Fish-Eaters," dwelling along the east coast of Africa: Herodotus 1.200; Strabo 2.3; Pliny, *NH* 6.95.

D. *Pliny observed first-hand the excitement of an orca trapped in the harbor at Ostia during Claudius' reign (r. 41–54 CE). Note the contrast that Pliny has made between true whales (with baleen) and the aggressive orca.*

12. Baleen whales even enter into our seas. In the Gaditean Ocean, they say that whales are not seen before the winter solstice, and, moreover, that in the summer times they are hidden in a certain calm and spacious bay, and, rejoicing marvelously, they give birth there. They know that this is the orca, a beast hostile to other aquatic animals and whose image is able to be expressed by no description other than huge with flesh, ferocious with teeth.

13. Therefore, orcas burst into the secret lairs of other sea-beasts, and with a bite they mangle either their calves or newborns or sometimes even the pregnant sows, and with an attack they pierce their prey as with the beaks of Libernian warships. The larger sea-beasts are immobile for bending, sluggish in defending themselves and burdened by their own weight. Then, even heavy in the belly and weak from giving birth or suffering, the only assistance they know is to escape into the deep and defend themselves in the safe, deep ocean. To the contrary, orcas strive to attack them and oppose them and massacre them holed up in the narrows to drive them into the shoals, and to strike them on the rocks. These battles look as if the very sea is angry with itself when there are no winds in the bay but truly in reaction to the orcas' puffing and strikes because of surges as large as no whirlwinds ever whirl themselves up.

14. An orca was even seen in the Ostian harbor[45] besieged by the emperor Claudius. The orca came at that time when Claudius was completing construction of the port harbor and was lured by shipwrecks of hides conveyed from Gaul. Sating herself for several days, the orca ploughed a den in the shoal. Then, entombed in waves so high that in no way was she able to maneuver around, and, while she hunted for food, she was propelled onto the shore by the waves, and she projected a great deal of her back above the waters, like an inverted keeled-boat.

15. Caesar[46] ordered woven hunting nets to be stretched between the mouths of the harbor, and, setting out with the praetorian cohorts,[47] he offered the Roman people a beast-hunt-like spectacle as the soldiery tossed their spears from pitching ships, one of which we saw submerged after it was completely filled with water owing to the beast's blow-back.

(Pliny, NH *9.12–15; cf. Oppian,* Fishing *5.62–349)*

45 #5.3.3G–H.

46 Caesar came to be a title of respect for the sitting emperor. Claudius was not a blood relative of Julius Caesar, but his uncle was Tiberius, the son of Augustus' wife, Livia (Augustus was the grand-nephew of Julius Caesar.

47 The praetorian guard was an elite Roman citizen military corps serving as escorts and bodyguards for high-ranking Romans, especially the emperor.

E. *Whales were not usually deliberately hunted for food (despite the lengthy, detailed, harrowing description in Oppian: #2.2.12F), but they were consumed opportunistically, as in 548 CE, when Justinian (r. 527–565 CE) at long last decided to eliminate a large marine creature, called Porphyrios (probably an orca), after decades of maritime malfeasance likely committed by several whales over the years. The event is recorded by Procopius, a member of Justinian's retinue, who wrote contemporary histories in Greek.*

> At that time even, a sea-beast, whom the Byzantians called "Porphyrios," was conquered. This beast was troubling Byzantium (Constantinople) and the places around it for more than 50 years, not however continuously, but at an interval of a long time between attacks, as it thus might happen. And the whale sank many boats, and threw into confusion the passengers of many others, and overpowering them, he carried the boats very far away from their courses. Therefore it became a concern for the emperor Justinian to subdue the wild beast. But he had no means to accomplish this aim with any device. How it happened that he vanquished the beast, I shall make clear. It happened that while a great stillness held the sea, some huge crowd of dolphins flowed together at the mouth of the Euxine Sea. Suddenly seeing the sea-beast, they fled wherever each was able to be, but most came around the mouth of the Sagaris River.[48] The beast seized some of them, and straightaway he prevailed in gulping them down. Then, either out of hunger or belligerence, he hunted no less than before, until it escaped the beast's notice that he fell very close to land. From there, happening upon some deep mud, although he struggled and even moved all things so as to set himself free as quickly as possible, in no way was he able to escape the shoal, but he went deeper under the mud. When this news came to all those dwelling there, immediately they went to the place, striking him continuously from all sides with axes. They did not kill Porphyrios, but dragged the beast out with some thick reed-ropes. And placing him on wagons, they found him to be about 30 *pecheis* in length and about ten in breadth. Then some tasted the flesh, divided according to groups, in the moment. Others decided to preserve the portion that fell to them.
>
> *(Procopius,* History of the Wars *7.29.9–16)*

F. *Oppian's spectacular description of a whale-hunt. The hunt works on many registers. The whalers are courageous soldiers fighting a savage enemy who at the same time is also a worthy foe, eliciting pity from Oppian. The epic similes have been stripped from this lengthy passage in the interest of space.*

> 62. For all the huge beasts of the sea, apart from dog-fish sharks, the paths are heavy on their limbs and not at all well-shaped. For neither do the beasts see far

48 Sakyra, the third longest river in Turkey, emerging in the Bayat Plateau, winding towards the Black Sea into which it debouches.

in front of themselves nor do they travel the entire sea, weighed down by huge limbs, but rolling they are carried to and fro. Consequently, a fish goes with them everywhere as a companion, grey to look at, long in body, it has a slender tail. The fish leads in front, indicating the salt-sea. And they call the fish "the Guide."[49] But to the cetacean it is marvelously a companion, pilot, and guard. For it brings the whale easily where he wants to go, and the whale follows only that fish, always having a trusting mind for his confidante. The pilot-fish constantly twists near the whale and stretches his tail near the whale's eyes, which clarifies each detail, whether there is some prey to grasp, or therefore if calamity bristles nearby, or if there is some shallow stream which would be better to avoid. Speaking as if with a voice, the tail points out everything and precisely: the burden of the water obeys. For that one, the fish is champion and ears and light for the beast. Indeed, the whale hears by the fish, sees by the fish, entrusting to the fish the reigns of his life to guard. . . So that fish embraces the dangerous beast of the salt-sea with affection, as if steering a ship with a guiding steering-oar. . . The cetacean, untouchable with his unapproachable limbs, befriends a tiny fish. Therefore, one should grasp that scouting guide-fish, ensnaring him with the force of a hook and a tidbit. For while he lives, the sea-beast, pressed down, will never be overpowered. But when the guide-fish has gone, the whale's destruction will be swifter. For he no longer precisely knows the roads of the purple salt-sea, nor how to avoid the calamity at hand. But, like a merchant ship with a deceased helmsman, the whale wanders without precaution, without device, wherever the dark-blue water drives him, and he is carried along shadowy and incomprehensible paths, lacking his helpful pilot. Very often on a rock or a beach he drives on, wandering. Such a mist has fallen on his eyes.

111. Then the fish-piercers with nimble minds hasten to the work of the hunt, praying to the blessed whale-killing gods that they may catch the grievous monster of Amphitrite[50]. . . Then the daring soldiery of the sea hurry after the unguarded beast, his fishy guard now slain. First, in their minds, they estimate the whale's weight and how large he is. These are the signs of his limbs: for if rolling in the sea among the eddies, his dorsal fin is raised a little, appearing above the shining water, then that beast is large and excellent, and the heaving sea itself does not easily bear him. But if some of his back also appears, this announces that his weight is not so great. Paths are nimbler for weaker creatures. For these smaller monsters, a line, joined one after another with supporting windings of cord, is made ready, as thick as the forestays of the ship, neither thick nor small. Its length stretches out suitably to the prey. The well-worked hook is sharp with projecting barbs shifting to and fro. A twisted chain is tossed about the tip of the dark hook, strong, forged from brass, which can hold out against the baneful force of the whale's teeth and the spears of his cavernous

49 #3.11.13.
50 #2.2.3A note.

mouth. In the middle join, circular rings are fashioned, close-set to each other to restrain the beast's distraught thrashings and so that, bloody, he cannot break the iron chain straightaway, much angered by his destructive pain, but the fishermen let him roll through his wandering course here and there.

147. They then offer an ill-pleasing meal on a fishhook, a choice black bull-liver or a bull-shoulder suitable for the banqueter's jaws. Accompanying the hunters, just as with Ares (war), are many rather strong, sturdy, sharpened edges, tridents, hooks, heavy axes, whatever destructive implements are forged on shrieking anvils. Eagerly boarding their well-benched skiffs, in silence nodding to each other what is necessary, the warriors make ready. With their silent oar handles they whiten the untrembling sea, they guard against any noise, lest the great cetacean learn something and swim the depth of the sea under water, and their salty toil be undertaken in vain. But when they approach and fight together against their prize, then courageously from the prow they set out the destructive bait. When the whale sees the grievous banquet, he leaps and does not disregard it, obeying the shamelessness of his belly. Then, rushing eagerly at his curved fate, he takes hold. And straightaway the sharp hook sinks within the whale's broad throat, and on the points he is broken. And roused in his soul by the wound, vexed, he brandishes his destructive jaw against the sailors, earnestly desiring to dash to pieces the bronze cord. But his labor is empty. From there then, hastening with burning pain and groaning, the whale dives within the underwater hollows of the sea. Quickly the anglers let out all the line. For there is not strength in the men such as to drag the whale up and overpower the heavy, resisting monster, when he himself hastens to be carried downward, since he could easily drag them to the depths with their decked ship.

176. Straightaway they send down broad skins—filled with human breath, fitted to a line[51]—to the whale plunging into the water. But sorely angered by his pain, he has no care for the air-filled skins, but he drags them down, not willing and readily desiring the surface of the foamy sea. When he approaches the flat bottom, with a wretched heart he stops, foaming greatly, full of sorrow . . . Like an overworked horse, huffing, the whale stops. But the skins do not allow him to stay below, eager as he is, but immediately the skins hurry upwards and they dart out from the salt-sea, raised up into the air. Then another contest is set for the whale. To be sure, he first rushes at the thoughtless skins with his jaws, striving eagerly to ward them off as they drag him up. But the skins do not allow him to stay and flee like living creatures bolting for their lives. But, in his distress, the whale darts back again through the saltwater, and he roils up many eddies, once by necessity, another time willingly, dragging and being dragged

51 The practice of attaching inflated skins to harpoons, so they are easier to retrieve, is also attested in resource-poor 18th c. Greenland: *Relation of a Voyage in the North Sea, . . . made in the years 1767 and 1768 by M. de Kerguelen Tremarec* (*Pinkerton's Voyages*, vol. I. p. 790). See also #6.6.3D.

backwards . . . Then, first of all, a skin runs back to the surface, announcing victory, uplifting the spirits of the fisherfolk . . .

236. Immediately other skins rise up and emerge from the sea, dragging the heavy beast. And the accursed monster is dragged up, unwillingly, agitated in his spirit because of the exertion and the wound. Then the courage of the fisherfolk is awakened. Near the ships, they drive their well-oared vessels with oar blades. Resounding along the sea there is much splashing, much shouting of men in confusion urging and commanding each other to the contest . . . Then unquenchable watery Ares rouses them. One brandishes in his hand the long-tongued trident, another the spear with a sharp point, others wield a well-bent hook, and another a two-edged axe. There is work for all. For all, the whale's strong jaw prepares to attack their hands wielding an iron blade. Nearby they strike the beast and wound him, overtaking him violently. But the whale forgets his overbearing prowess, nor is he able to attack or restrain the hastening ship with his jaws. But with an overburdened swing of his wings (flippers) and with his topmost tail he digs through the deep wave and pushes the ships back towards their sterns, and he curves back the works and prowess of the oarsmen, like an opposing wind rolling back opposite waves against the prow. Resounding are the shouts of those throwing themselves into the work, and the entire swell is defiled with blood gushing from the whale's deadly wounds. The immense water seethes with cetacean blood, and the dark-blue salt-sea is reddened . . . But when the whale is overpowered by many gashed wounds, fate already carries him to the door of baneful death. The joyful whaling-folk, making fast, haul him to dry land, and, although unwilling, the beast is dragged, pierced with many barbs like bolts, nodding at his deadly fate as if heavy with wine. Then raising a paean of joy for their great victory, hastening with oars, singing their sharp refrain to their speeding oar blades, the whalers make the sea resound . . . But when the whale is brought near land, then his imminent, ultimate ruin rouses him: he struggles and thrashes at the sea with his fearful wings . . . He very much longs to reach the swells, but the strength of his prowess is destroyed, and his limbs obey him not at all, and snorting terribly he is dragged to dry land . . .

316. But even dead and stretched out on the beach, it is possible to fear approaching the grim corpse, with alarm at the beast who is no longer alive, shuddering at the teeth in those jaws. Taking courage after some time, the whalers gather round in a crowd, glancing in amazement at the ruins of the brutal creature. Then some stare at the deadly rows of teeth in his jaws, even the fearful tusks, like javelins springing up in three rows,[52] one after the other. Others handle the bronze-pierced wounds of the much-battling monster. Another one glances at the sharp thorn raising up with terrible blades (dorsal fin). Others

52 While Oppian classified the animal as a *ketos* (whale, cetacean), here we have an oblique reference to the multiple rows of teeth that characterize sharks (two to three rows for the spotted dogfish. ancient sources are surprisingly silent on this matter): #3.3B and note.

gazing at him marvel at his strength, others at his capacious belly and immeasurable head.

331. Looking at Amphitrite's bristly, dangerous beast, someone who customarily tarries more on dry lands than in ships, speaks to his companions who are nearby: "Gaia (Earth), dear nurturing one, you bore me and preserved me with terrestrial food, may I die in your bosom when my appointed day comes. May the labors of the sea be well-disposed and let me worship Poseidon from dry land. May no tiny dory send me along in troublesome waves, and may I not scan for winds or clouds in the air. For not so great for men is the terror of the rushing waves of the salt-sea nor of grievous sailing nor even of the distress which they—who always ride along with the shrieking, stormy winds—suffer, nor enough for those who perish in the watery fate of the salt-sea. But even more, sailors await such banqueting guests, coming upon un-tombed funeral rites, they strike the inner chambers of a wild beast's throat. I fear the nurse of such distresses. O, Sea, greetings from solid earth, may you be kind to me from a distance.

(Oppian, Fishing *5.62–349; cf. #6.3.1)*

2.2.13 Amphibious Creatures

A. *Ancient thinkers recognized that some marine animals breathed air (seals, dolphins, whales), and some, remarkably, dwelled simultaneously in water and on land (octopods [#2.2.8F], seals [#2.2.10]).*

Consequently, many creatures—inhaling air and giving birth to their children on land—take their nourishment from places in the water and spend most of their time in water. But these, alone of the animals, seem to tend to both sides. For someone could consider them "on-foot" (i.e., land) or in-water creatures. But of those taking in water, neither on-foot nor on-the-wing do they take their nourishment from the earth, in contrast with many of those creatures on-foot who take in air, and some such that they are not able to live apart from the nature of water: such as the so-called sea-turtles and crocodiles and river horses (hippopotami) and seals and some of the smaller animals such as the fresh water tortoise and the race of frogs. For all these choke unless they breathe at times. And they give birth and raise their young on dry land, sometimes near dry land, and they spend their time in the water.

(Aristotle, HA *589a18–31; cf. Aristotle,* Fragments *281 = Aelian,* NA *11.37; Athenaeus,* The Learned Banqueters *535f)*

B. *Frogs are true amphibians according to modern taxonomy, requiring water for breeding. Ancient sources cite their colorful hides and raucous croaking. Emphasizing the extent of the inhabited world, Plato compared people dwelling* *the imagery of frogs between the Phasis River and Pillars of Herakles as "living around the sea like ants or frogs around a marsh" (*Phaedo *109b). See also #4.1.1A where Latona turns the surly Laconians, who tried to prevent her from drinking their water, into frogs.*

i. *Here, the god Dionysus encounters a chorus of marsh frogs as he rows across the Acheron lake to reach the Underworld. The frogs try to throw Dionysus/Liber off his stroke, but they are vanquished as Dionysus outshouts them. Aristophanes (446–386 BCE) was an Athenian comic playwright whose works are both snapshots of daily life in Athens and scathing commentary on contemporary politicians and dignitaries (including Socrates whom Aristophanes caricatured in the* Clouds*). The following is a snippet of their longer exchange where the frogs introduce themselves (*Frogs *205–268).*

> Brekekekex-koax-koax, brekekekex-koax-koax, marshy children of the springs, let us croak a shout of hymns in harmony with the aulos,[53] our own sweet-sounding song, koax-koax, which we shouted about Nysean Dionysus son of Zeus in the marshes when a crowd of men, in drunken revelry on the holy festival of the Pots,[54] traipsed through our *temenos*.[55] Brekekekex-koax-koax.
>
> *(Aristophanes,* Frogs *209–220)*

ii. *Varieties of frogs. A richly illustrated manuscript dating to c. 1200 CE, the Aberdeen Bestiary (Aberdeen University Library MS 24) draws from classical sources and employs animals (real and imaginary) as Christianizing metaphors to explore human society and foibles. Pliny had described the "bramble frog" as the largest variety and poisonous (*NH *32.50).*

> And from these (frogs), certain ones are called "aquatic," certain ones "marshy," some "of the bramble bush" on account of the fact that they live in the brambles; "larger" than the rest. Some are called "very green frogs" because they live among the reeds and bushes, they are the smallest of all and the most green, mute and without a voice.
>
> *(*Aberdeen Bestiary *77v; cf. Pliny,* NH *8.110, 32.122)*

53 #2.2.4A and note.

54 Dionysus was born on the legendary mountain of Nysa. The festival of the Pots (*chutroi*) occurred annually on the third day of the Anthesteria (observed February/March), when Dionysus and deceased family members were honored: the second day, the day of the Pitchers, featured heavy drinking. The pitchers were dedicated to the god on the third day. Dionysus' Athenian sanctuary was located in the marshes southwest of the acropolis.

55 Sanctified land that is "cut off" (Greek *temno*: "I cut") from the ordinary, profane world.

iii. *Some frogs were indeed mute, as on the north African coast near modern Shahhat, Libya.*

> At Cyrene, the frogs were mute. Even though the croaking frogs have been imported from the continent, the race of mute frogs endures. They are also mute on the island of Seriphus (Cyclades), but these same creatures sing when transferred elsewhere, a thing which they say happens also in Siccanean Lake in Thessaly.
>
> *(Pliny,* NH *8.227; cf. Aelian,* NA *3.37; Ps-Aristotle,* On Marvelous Things Heard *70; Antigonus,* Collection of marvelous stories *4)*

iv. *Some frogs were known to be poisonous. Spleens and livers of such frogs were suggested as antidotes: Pliny,* NH *32.52.*

> There, frogs also have poisons, especially the bramble-dwelling frogs. And I have seen the Psylli[56] admitting them into a contest from glowing hot pans, and their deadliness quicker than even the bite of asps. A remedy is phrynion drunk in wine. Some call the plant *neurada* ("a nerve aggravator"), some call it *poterion* ("drinking cup"), with small flowers, many roots, sinewy, pleasant-smelling.
>
> *(Pliny,* NH *25.123; cf. Juvenal,* Satire *1.69–72)*

v. *A traveler dedicated a votive frog to the Nymphs in thanksgiving. Votive frogs are not uncommon, including one inscribed "Anion, son of Sonoos, to Boason" (probably a local god: see Lewis and Llewellyn-Jones 2018: 571).*

> This rain-loving attendant of the Nymphs, a watery minstrel, a frog delighting in nimble dripping waters, in bronze, some wayfarer placed this as an offering, after quenching his thirst hateful from the burning heat. For the frog pointed out water to the traveler as he turned aside, croaking a timely song from her dewy hollow with her amphibious mouth. Not leaving off the guiding tone, the wayfarer came upon a drink of sweet running springs for which he yearned.
>
> *(Plato,* Greek Anthology *6.43, one of 18 epigrams spuriously attributed to Plato)*

vi. *A unique reference to the unlikely practice of divination by examining the entrails of frogs in a satire treating the tensions between old Roman virtue and self-sufficiency against the influx of fancy (and weird) ideas imported from the east*

56 Native to northwestern Africa, renowned for curing serpent bites with their bodies: Pliny, *NH* 7.14; cf. Horace, *Epode* 17.30.

by immigrants and slaves. The Roman satirist Juvenal (Decimus Junius Juvenalis: c. 55 CE to after 127) composed biting commentary on the extravagance of contemporary Rome.

I have never examined the entrails of frogs.

(*Juvenal,* Satire *3.44)*

C. *Crocodiles. The ancients were familiar with crocodiles inhabiting both the Nile and Indus Rivers, and the lizards became a resonant symbol in Augustan public art to evoke Egypt and Augustus' defeat of Cleopatra, figuring into the* Ara Pacis, *Augustus' "Altar of Peace."*

i. *Herodotus, who visited Egypt, saw crocodiles first-hand, providing our first Greek description of these fascinating lizards.*

68. The nature of crocodiles is this. Over the four wintry months it eats nothing. Four-footed, it is both a dry-land and marshy animal. For it lays eggs and hatches them in the ground. And it spends most of the day on dry ground, but all night in the river: for the water is warmer than air and dew. Of all the dying creatures, we know that this one alone becomes very large from the smallest origin. For it lays eggs not much bigger than goose eggs, and the nestling is according to the egg's size, but growing it becomes up to 17 *pecheis* long and even more still. It has eyes like a pig and very large teeth and tusks in accord with the size of the body. Alone of wild animals, it has no tongue, nor does it move its lower jaw. But this creature, unique of wild animals, brings its upper jaw down to the lower one. It has very strong talons and scaly, unbreakable skin on its back. It is blind in water, but in clear air very sharp-sighted. Since it spends its time in the water, its mouth within is full of leeches. All birds and wild beasts flee from it, except the plover with whom it is peaceful because it is of service to the lizard: whenever the crocodile steps onto the ground from the water and then gapes—for it is accustomed to do this in general in the direction of the west wind—then the plover enters into its mouth and eats up the leeches. Assisted in this way, the crocodile is glad, and it does not harm the plover.

69. For some Egyptians, crocodiles are sacred. For others, not, but they treat them like enemies. Those dwelling around Thebes and the Moeris Marsh[57] consider them extremely holy. Among the crocodiles, each place nurtures one, taught to be tame, placing stone and golden earrings on its ears and bracelets

57 *Thebes* (Luxor) was an ancient capital of Egypt on the Nile about 800 kilometers south of the Mediterranean. *Lake Moeris* (Qarun) in the Faiyum Oasis about 80 kilometers (c. 50 miles) southwest of the Nile Delta.

around its forefeet,[58] and giving them special titbits and offerings, and treating them as best as they can as long as the crocodiles live. Embalming them, they bury the dead crocodiles in sacred tombs. But those dwelling around the *polis* Elephantine[59] even eat crocodiles and do not consider them sacred. They are not called crocodiles (by the Egyptians) but *champsai.* The Ionians called them crocodiles, likening their appearance to those lizards[60] (*krokodeiloi*) on their walls.

70. Many ways of hunting them are practiced, and of all sorts. I will write down this one which seems to me to be the worthiest of mention. Whenever a hunter has baited a chine of pig on a fishhook and sets it loose at the middle of the river, keeping a live pig at the edge of the river, he himself strikes the pig. Hearing the sound of the pig, the crocodile goes after the noise. Happening on the chine, he gulps it down. The hunters drag the fishing line. When the crocodile is dragged to the shore, first of all the hunter plasters its eyes over with mud. Doing this, he overcomes the remainder very favorably; not doing this, he vanquishes the crocodile with difficulty.

(Herodotus, Histories *2.68–70; cf. Diodorus Siculus,* Library of History *1.35)*

ii. *More on crocodile eggs.*

Both lizards and crocodiles, land and river varieties, give birth on land. Lizard eggs hatch on their own on land: for the lizard does not live into the next year. But the lizard's life is said not to be six months. The river crocodile lays many eggs, around 60 at most, white in color, and it sits over them for 60 days: for the length of its life is long. This creature becomes the largest living thing from the smallest eggs: for its egg is no larger than a goose egg, and its hatchling is according to the egg's size, but growing it becomes 17 *pecheis* in length. Some say that it grows as long as it lives.

(Aristotle, HA *558a14–30)*

iii. *Crocodiles are also found in India, a factor—to the ancient mindset—of the supposed symmetry between the Nile and Indian rivers.*

It is not beyond the realm of possibility that it rains (on the Nile) just as in India, since in other regards the land of the Indians is not unlike Aethiopia, and the Indian rivers, similar to the Aethiopian and Egyptian Nile, bear crocodiles, and some of them have both fishes and other sea monsters such as the Nile produces,

58 #3.8A.

59 A Nile island, Elephantine (Aswan) is so-called because it resembles an elephant tusk or for the rocks that resemble elephants, some 200 kilometers (c. 125 miles) south of Thebes.

60 An Ionian Greek word, *krokodeiloi*, instead of the more commonly used *sauros* (as in dino<u>saur</u>).

except for the water horse. But Onesicritus[61] says that Indian rivers also support hippopotamuses.

(Arrian, Indika *6.8)*

iv. *Like other predators, crocodiles were made to fight in the Roman arena, and they were very popular (Symmachus,* Letter *9.141) because of their rarity: exhibited in 58 BCE (Pliny,* NH *8.96), 2 BCE (Strabo 17.1.44; Dio Cassius 53.27.6), and again shortly after 130 CE (*SHA, Antoninus Pius *10.9). Here we also have a stark account of the wild animals in captivity. In the late 4th century CE, Quintus Aurelius Symmachus served as a proconsular governor of Africa in 373 CE, urban prefect of Rome in 384 and 385, and consul in 391. To support his son's political career, he also imported many wild animals and organized gladiatorial games and beast hunts.*

Symmachus to the sons of Nichomachus: I tried to keep crocodiles exhibited in a theatrical show for your visit. But their fasting was persistent and, prolonged for 50 days, it vexed them. In the second spate of games, they were killed off in the habit of fighting. But we hold back two of them, still breathing, for your arrival, although their abstinence from food promises that they are not able to live much longer.

(Quintus Aurelius Symmachus, Letter *6.43)*

D. *The river horse.*

i. *Here we have Herodotus' description of the hippopotamus, the earliest in Greek. Aristotle's description derives from Herodotus plus the claim that the internal organs resemble those of a horse (*HA *502a10–15: this may be an interpolated addition, according to Aristotle's German editors, Schneider [1811] and Dittmeyer [1907]). Arrian cites and debunks Onesicritus' observation that the hippopotamus is also found in India (*Indika *6.9).*

For river horses are sacred in the *nome*[62] of Papremis, but not elsewhere among the Egyptians. They display such a nature of form: they are four-footed, cloven-hoofed, hoofed like oxen, snub-nosed. They have the mane of a horse, they display tusks, and the tail and voice of a horse. They have the stature as large as the largest ox. Their skin is indeed so thick that, when dried, shaved javelins are made of it.

(Herodotus, Histories *2.71)*

61 Onesicritus of Asupulaia, a Cynic philosopher, was among Alexander's coterie in India, composing an account of the expedition with particular attention to the philosophical aspects of Indian culture and Indika as the paradigm of an ideal society. Onesicritus is wrong, of course, assuming that Arrian has correctly interpreted (or even consulted) the source.

62 *Nome*: a province or region of Egypt, called after the Greek word *nomos*: law, custom. *Papremis* perhaps modern Tell el-Afrin.

ii. *A hippopotamus on display at Rome.*

95. In that same Nile River, the hippopotamus is brought forth, a beast rather great in height, with cloven hoofs like an ox, with the back and mane and whinny of a horse, a tail and the curved teeth of boars, but less harmful, and unpierceable hides suitable for shields and helmets, unless they drip with moisture. The river horse feeds on grain, as they say, by an allotment prescribed daily in advance, and its tracks lead out of the field lest any traps be evident as it returns.

96. Marcus Scaurus[63] first displayed a hippopotamus and five crocodiles at Rome during the games of his aedileship: a temporary channel was created for them. The hippopotamus also stands out as a master in a certain type of cure: for, with its constant gluttony, plump, it goes out onto the shore to look for fresh cuttings of reeds. And where it sees a very sharp stalk, pressing its body, it wounds a certain vein in the leg and thus with a flow of blood it unburdens its diseased body and covers the wound again with mud.

(Pliny, NH *8.95–96)*

iii. *The hippopotamus evades angry farmers by seeking refuge in the River. Aelian had elsewhere described the river horse as the "most ungodly animal" for eating its own father (*NA *7.19).*

River horses are nurslings of the Nile. When the crops are ripe and the ears of grain are golden, they do not begin to crop them off and eat them right away, but passing alongside outside the cultivated crop, they make a guess as to which measured space will fill them up. Then, after calculating their sufficiency, they fall on the crop and, quite full, withdraw back on their hoofs, keeping the flow of the River at their back. They have ingeniously contrived that, if any farmers make an attack, warding off the hippos, they could scurry into the water with the greatest ease, facing their enemies, but the horses not keeping watch behind.

(Aelian, NA *5.53)*

2.3 Water Plants

2.3.1 Introduction

Theophrastus is rightly called the "Father of Botany," and his two multi-book studies, Enquiry into Plants *(*HP: *nine books) and* Causes of Plants *(*CP: *six books)*

63 Marcus Aemilius Scaurus (b. 92 BCE) was charged with extortion after his governorship of Syria (65–62 BCE), then later served as curule aedile in 58 BCE when he organized the games with exotic animals, failed to win the consulship in 53, and was exiled after a bribery conviction in 52. He had supported Pompey but later fell out of favor, perhaps because of his marriage to Pompey's former wife, Mucia.

*are a trove of information on Greek plant taxonomy. Following his teacher's methodology for animals (Aristotle, the "Father of Zoology"), Theophrastus recognized four broad classifications: trees (*HP *3–5), shrubs and undershrubs (*HP *6), and herbs (*HP *7). And he queried their forms, functions, parts, growing conditions, and cultivation. Theophrastus' account of aquatic plants (*HP *4.6–12) is remarkable for its vivid detail. Note the link of familiar land plants to aquatic analogues. Note also that it is often challenging, and sometimes impossible, to correlate an ancient plant (or animal) with a modern designation.*

It remains simply to discuss the greatest difference in the nature of trees and woody plants, which we mentioned above, that some happen to be land plants and others are water plants, just as the nature of living animals, so also of plants. Not only in marshes and lakes and rivers, but also in the sea (i.e., Mediterranean) several woody plants grow, and there are even trees beyond (i.e., Ocean). For in the water around us, all the water plants are small, and nothing rises above the sea. But in that water, Ocean, there are such plants even rising above the water level, and also other larger trees.

The aquatic plants around us are these: the most conspicuous and common are *phykos* seaweed and oyster-green moss and other such things. The most conspicuous and idiomatic according to regions are pine, fig, oak, vine, date. Of these some are close to land, others close to the deep sea, others are common to both. And some are many-shaped, like *phykos* seaweed, others have only one form. Of seaweed there is the broad-leafed, banded-formed type, having a green color, which some call a sea-leek, others call "sea-belts." It has a root, shaggy on the outside, layered within, reasonably long and compact, closely resembling *kromyogeteian* onions.

(*Theophrastus,* HP *4.6.1–2)*

2.3.2 Seaweed

A. *The Greco-Roman world was dominated by water, and there was a keen awareness of both coastal and oceanic seaweed.*

The hairy-leafed type, like fennel, not green but very pale, does not have a stem but is somehow straight of itself. This one grows on oysters and stones, not on the solid sea bottom like the other type. Both are near land, and hairy-leafed seaweed is close to land: sometimes it is only splashed over by the sea. The other type is further out.

(*Theophrastus,* HP *4.6.3)*

B. *Huge seaweed plants grow beyond the Pillars of Herakles.*

Seaweed outside the Pillars of Herakles is astonishing in size, so they say, and in breadth is as large as a palm. This seaweed is carried into the inner sea together with the flow from the external sea, and they call it "sea-leek." In this ocean in some regions, it comes up as if above a belly button. It is said to be annual and to grow at the end of spring. It flourishes in the summer and withers in the winter. In the winter times, it perishes and is cast out onto shore. All other seaweeds become weaker and gloomier in winter.

(Theophrastus, HP *4.6.5)*

C. *Seaweed for dying cloth.*

In Crete, abundant and beautiful seaweed grows on the rocks near land, with which they tinge not only ribbons but even wool and garments. Provided that the dye is new, the color is much more beautiful than murex purple.[64] This seaweed grows on the northern coast both more plentifully and more lovely, just like sponges and other such things.

(Theophrastus, HP *4.6.6)*

D. *Aquatic animals naturally feed on seaweed.*

Herding together, the murex purple snails make a honeycomb for their common use, just like bees, in which, it is said, they mate. They harvest edible bits of oyster-greens and seaweed, clinging to the shells, and they offer each other a sort of banquet in rounds, each one grazing on the next in turns.

(Plutarch, On Whether Land or Sea Animals Are Cleverer *980d)*

E. *Seaweed was not, however, considered ideal fodder for land creatures, but when Caesar was low on provisions in Africa in 47 BCE, seaweed was collected for the troops' animals.*

Compelled by necessity, veteran soldiers and cavalry—who had accomplished many campaigns on land and sea and had often been tormented by dangers and such a lack of provisions—collected seaweed on the shore and washed it in sweet water and gave to the hungry beasts, prolonging their life.

(Caesar, African War *24)*

F. *Some aquatic animals also employ seaweed for their nests.*

Wrasses, peculiarly, forming a nest as it were from seaweed, enfolds its spawn and shelters them from the waves.

(Plutarch, On Whether Land or Sea Animals Are Cleverer *981f)*

G. *After slaying the Medusa, whose snake-haired head, alive or deceased, changed everything that gazed on it to stone, Perseus vanquished a sea monster to save*

64 #6.5.1.

Andromeda, whom the gods demanded as atonement for her mother's (Cassiopeia) insult to the Nereids. By petrifying the sea monster, Perseus also turned seaweed into coral: #3.5B–C, #6.5.3.

Perseus washes his victorious hands in water drawn for him, and lest the harsh sand damage the snake-bearing head, he softens the ground with foliage and strews twigs (seaweed) born under the water and then places on them the head of Medusa, daughter of Phorcys.[65] A fresh sprout, just recently alive with moist sap, seizes the power of the monster and grows stiff by a touch and takes on a new stiffness in its branches and foliage. The nymphs of the deep sea then test this marvelous deed on more branches of seaweed, and they rejoice to touch these same things, and they repeat this. The seeds from petrified seaweed are scattered through the waves. The same nature even now remains in corals: corals take on hardness from a touch when a plant that was once in water is now in the air: it becomes stony above the waters.

(Ovid, Metamorphoses *4.740–752)*

2.3.3 Sea Trees and Reeds

Oceans also produce trees, and, as was the usual practice, Theophrastus compared the unfamiliar (aquatic flora) with more familiar terrestrial analogues.

In the sea there grows a plant which they call bay-laurel and olive. The sea-laurel is like the *aria* (holm-oak), but the sea-olive is like the land olive in foliage. The sea-olive has fruit very similar to olives, and it emits tears from which physicians compound a drug for staunching bleeding, which is very good.

(Theophrastus, HP *4.7.2)*

2.3.4 Reeds

A. *Papyrus is a common reed along the Nile and elsewhere with many uses, not the least of which is as writing material (on which a great deal of documentary texts, including private letters, survive). Here, the plant's growth-cycle and uses.*

The papyrus does not grow in a depth of water, but in water about two *pecheis* deep, sometimes in shallower water. The thickness of the root is as large as the wrist of a strong man, its length about four *pecheis*. It grows above the very ground, establishing slanting roots, fine ones and thick ones, into the mud, above the three-cornered reeds called papyrus, in size about ten *pecheis*, having

65 A son of Gaia and Pontus (Ocean), Phorcys ("Seal") was a primordial sea god, depicted with a brace of piscine tails and crab claws emanating from his belly: see Hesiod, *Theogony* 237–239. Medusa's mother was Keto (*Theogony* 270–276), in other words, a sea monster.

foliage, weak, insignificant, and altogether no fruit. The plants send up the reeds in many parts. The Egyptians use their roots instead of wood not only to burn but also to make many tools and all sorts of other things from papyrus roots. For the "wood" is plentiful and good. The papyrus itself is useful for many things. For they make boats from it, and from the bark they weave sails and mats for sleeping and some sorts of clothing and bedding and ropes and many more things. Best known to folk from the outside are the *biblia* ("book" rolls). But papyrus also especially provides food: for everyone chews papyrus on the spot and unprocessed and boiled and roasted, and they drink down the sap, and spit out the cud. Such is the papyrus and the advantages it offers. Papyrus also grows in Syria around a lake in which a sweet-scented reed grows, from which Antigonus[66] made lines for his ships.

(Theophrastus, HP *4.8.3)*

B. There were several varieties of reed, and some were suitable for making the musical pipes played in pairs (diaulos) *and commonly depicted in Greek art. The chapters following our selection describe cutting, curing, and manufacturing reed pipes.*

Concerning pipe playing, that the reeds grow in a nine-year cycle, as some say, and that this is its disposition, this is not true. But, on the whole, the pipe-reed grows in a full lake. Because in earlier times this seemed to happen especially every nine years, they made this as the growth of the reed, taking coincidence as the regular growth cycle. The pipe-reed grows when, after rainy weather, the water remains for at least two years, and all the better if the water remains longer. They recall this happening in earlier times when the affairs around Chaeronea occurred.[67] Before the battle they say that the lake was deep for several years. A little after the battle, when a virulent epidemic occurred, the lake filled, but the water did not remain but instead drained out in the winter and the reed did not grow. They say, and it seems reasonable, that the reed grows to a height in a deepening lake and, remaining for the next year, it matures. The matured reed is suitable for the mouthpieces of double flutes, while the reed for which the water did not persist is suitable for the cocoon.[68] Such is the growth of the reed.

(Theophrastus, HP *4.11.2–3)*

C. *Theophrastus also knew that some plants had "male" and "female" varieties, including bamboo in India. Bamboo was attested before Theophrastus, by Ctesias*

66 #4.1.1E.

67 The Battle of Chaeronea (338 BCE) resulted in a decisive victory of Macedonians under Philip II over resisting Greek city-states, paving the way for the even larger empire forged by Philip's son Alexander.

68 Some reed pipes were played by blowing into a "cap" or cocoon containing the reed.

*of Cnidus (a Greek physician in the entourage of Artaxerxes II campaigning against his brother Cyrus II in 401 BCE), who authored an early account of India and a history of Assyria and Persia (*FGrHist *688* F *1b = Diodorus Siculus,* Library of History *2.17.5 and* F *45 = Photius 72.14).*

The Indian reed is greatly different and as if altogether another kind. For the male bamboo is solid and the female is hollow: for they distinguish Indian reeds by male and female. Many reeds grow from a single foundation but not in clumps. The leaf is not long but is similar to the willow. Bamboo are large in size and compact, so that they are used for spears. These reeds grow along the Akesines River.[69] Every reed is full of life, both cut and burnt, it grows back more beautifully. It is also thick- and many-rooted, on account of which it is hard to destroy. The root is jointed, like the root of dog's-tooth grass, except not similar in every respect.

(Theophrastus, HP *4.11.13)*

2.3.5 Aquatic Flowers

A. *Odysseus' travails included a sojourn among the Lotus-Eaters in Northern Africa. The blue lotus (*Nymphaea caerulea*) was employed in ancient Egyptian ritual to achieve ritual euphoria, and anecdotal evidence suggests that the flower does have a psychoactive effect (Schimpf et al. 2023). Here, Odysseus is speaking.*

"For nine days I was conveyed by destructive winds over the fishy sea, but on the tenth we set foot on the land of the Lotus-Eaters, who nibble a flowery food. There we stepped on solid land and we drew fresh water. Straightaway my companions took their dinner by the swift ships. But after eating we drank a drink, then I sent out companions, two chosen men, a third following as a herald at the same time, to go out to understand what sort of men were in that land and if they eat grain.[70] Setting out straightaway they mingled with the Lotus-Eating folk. Nor did the Lotus-Eaters intend destruction on our companions, but they gave our men the lotus to eat. Whoever of them ate the honey-sweet fruit, no longer did he want to report back or return home, but, nibbling on the lotus, they wanted to stay with the Lotus-Eating people and to forget their homecoming. I myself led these men, wailing, back to the ships with force. Pulling them on the hollow ships, I bound them by pairs on the rowing benches. Then I commanded our other companions, making haste, to climb aboard on the swift ships, lest in any way someone else, eating the lotus flower, might forget his homecoming.

69 Chenab River, a major river, formed by the confluence of the Chandra and Bhaga Rivers, flowing through India and Pakistan.

70 Grain-eating, like wine-drinking, indicates civilization, i.e., agriculture and baking technology.

Straightaway they embarked and sat on their benches, seating themselves in order, they struck the dark-blue salt-sea with their oars."

(Homer, Odyssey *9.82–104)*

B. *The lotus is a flowering plant that thrives in marshlands. Here, the growing conditions, properties, and uses of the lotus flower.*

The plant called the lotus for the most part grows in plains when the region has been flooded. The nature of its stalk is similar to the Egyptian bean, and the leaves accordingly, except they are smaller and more delicate. Like the Egyptian bean, the stalk produces the fruit. Its flower is very white, resembling, in its slenderness, the leaves (petals) of the lily, but it produces many more leaves, thickly packed on each other. When the sun sets, these flowers close and cover up their heads. At the same time with the rising sun, they open up and appear above the water. The plant does this until the head is completely formed and the flowers have fallen off. The size of the head is about as large as the largest poppy, and it is girt round with grooves in the same way as the poppy. But the fruit is more closely packed in lotus flowers. This is nearly like millet. In the Euphrates, they say that the head and flowers dip and go under water in the evening until the middle of the night and to quite a depth. For it is not possible for a hand extending down to grasp one. After these things, when dawn is again at hand and facing the day, the plants appear above the water at the same time as the rising sun. And the flower opens, and opened-up it still rises, and a large part of it rises above the water.

The Egyptians, placing the lotus heads together, leave them to themselves to rot. When the pod decays, washing it in the river, they take out the fruit. Drying it and pounding it, they make bread and use it as food. The root of the lotus is chorion,[71] it is round, and its size is similar to a Cydonean apple.[72] Bark lies around it, black like a chestnut. The inside is white: boiled or roasted it becomes yolk-colored, sweet in taste. The root is also consumed raw but is best boiled in water and also roasted.

(Theophrastus, HP *4.8.9)*

C. *Like most botanicals, lotus also has medicinal applications, including as a treatment for mange. Pliny's organization of medicinal remedies follows the standard*

71 Referring to the lotus' egg-like membrane-like rhizomes or rootstalks (#2.2.9B and note).

72 Quinces, cultivated in the Hyrcanian Forest south of the Caspian.

"from head to foot" (a capite ad calcem) *organization. Like many of Pliny's remedies, this one etymological.*

> But by kind and individually we will weave together remedies for individual diseases of the body, beginning at the head. The root of the Heraclian waterlily improves fox-mange, whether ground with pitch or smeared on alone. *Polythrix* ("much-hair") differs from *callithrix* ("pretty-hair") because it has white reeds and more leaves and larger ones. It is also larger on the stem: it strengthens hair flowing down and makes it thick.
>
> *(Pliny,* NH *25.132)*

D. *Some other aquatic flowers. In antiquity, plants had local and regional names, adding an extra layer of challenge in harmonizing ancient and modern taxonomy.*

> Of these some are familiar: goat's-willow and waterlily and moonflower and duckweed and mare's-tail likely also grow elsewhere, but they are called by different names. There must be discussion about these. The goat's-willow is bushy by nature and like chaste tree; in form its leaf is similar but soft, like apples, and foamy. The flower is similar to that of the white poplar, smaller. It produces no fruit. For the most part, it grows on floating islands:[73] for there are some floating islands even here, as in Egypt around the marshes and in Thesprotian[74] and other lakes. It is smaller in water. Such is the goat's-willow.
>
> *(Theophrastus,* HP *4.10.2)*

73 #1.8.

74 A region in northwestern Greece.

PART III

Water in Religion and Myth

Here we consider the spiritual and unobservable aspects of water culture, especially the animistic connection between water and divinity where bodies of water (and other natural phenomena) were thought to be imbued with a spiritual essence. Water dominates Greek geography, society, and mythology, and there are many dedicated gods of water: Okeanos/Oceanus (the source of all gods) and his 6,000 children with Tethys, Nereus and his 50 daughters with Doris, as well as Triton, and others (#3.1), many of whom are metamorphic with the ability to change their own shapes or those of others (#3.2). Some mythical sea creatures are endearing (#3.4.2); others, sea monsters, provide a quest for heroes whereby they conquer the natural world (#3.5). Water was also a powerful focus of ritual, an indicator of purity or contamination (#3.6), and a medium for reading the will of the gods (#3.7), producing some creatures that were favored by some gods (#3.8) and others who were sympathetically aligned with natural and supernatural processes (#3.9). Water was also a symbol of death and a bounding principle between the worlds of the living and the dead (#3.10). Finally, those who traveled by water propitiated a variety of major and minor water gods with prayers, offerings, festivals, and superstitious rituals to avert storms, mitigate seasickness, or generally seek protection while they sail (#3.11).

3.1 Water Gods

3.1.1 Okeanos

A. *Okeanos (Ocean) is both the river that encircles the world (#1.3.2) and the anthropomorphized father of other waterways. Here, a catalogue of some of his watery children with Tethys.*

DOI: 10.4324/9781003437741-4

Tethys bore to Okeanos whirling rivers, Nile and Alpheus and Eridanus, deep eddying, Strymon, and Meander, and Ister, flowing beautifully, and Phasis, and Rhesus, and Achelous, silver-eddying, and Nessos and Rhodius and Haliacmon and Heptaporus and Grenicus and Aesepus and shining Simois and Peneius and Hermus, flowing well, and Caecus and Sangarius and great Ladon and Parthenius and Evenus and Aldescus, divine, and Scamander.[1] She gave birth to a holy race of daughters, who, with lord Apollo and the rivers, rear humanfolk on the earth—for they have this fate from Zeus—Peitho and Admete and Ianthe and shining Electra and Doris and Prymno and godlike Ourania, and Hippo and Clymene and Rhodeia and Callirhoe and Zeuxis and Clytie and Iduia and Pasithoe and Plexaure and Galaxaure and lovely Dione and Melobosis and Thoe and shapely Polydore and Cerceis, beautiful in form, and Plouto, cow-eyed, Perseis and Ianeira and Acaste and blonde Xanthe and Petraie and charming Menestho and Europa and Metis and Eurunome and Telesto with the saffron dress and Chryseis and Asia and lovely Calypso and Eudore and Tyche and Amphiro and swift flowing Ochyrhoe and Styx, who is the best of them all.[2] These were born from Okeanos and Tethys, the oldest maiden-gods. But there are many others. For there are 3,000 slender-ankled Okeanids,[3] who—spread wide and everywhere all the same—ply the earth and the depths of water, glorious children of goddesses. In turn there are as many other rivers, flowing with a crashing din, sons of Okeanos, whom queenly Tethys bore. It is troublesome for a mortal person to say the names of all, but each who dwell around them knows them.

(Hesiod, Theogony *337–370)*

1 *Nile*: #1.5.1; *Alpheus*: #1.6C; *Eridanus*: #3.1.5B and note; *Strymon*: #5.3.5F§24; *Meander*: Büyük Menderes, a switch-backing river in western Turkey; *Ister*: #1.5.2; *Phasis*: #1.5.5; *Rhesus, Heptaporus, Rhodius, Grenicus, Aesepus, Simois*, and *Scamander* (#1.5.3): seven of the eight rivers which Poseidon employed to topple the walls of Troy (Homer, *Iliad* 12.19–21); *Achelous*: #1.5.2A note; *Nessos* (Evenos River): #5.2.1A; *Haliacmon*: #1.7B note; *Heptaporus, Grenicus, Aesepus, Simois*: flowing along or from Mt. Ida (Homer, *Iliad* 12.17–22); *Peneius*: #1.7B note; *Hermus*: Gediz, flowing from Mt. Murat into the Gulf of İzmir; *Caecus*: Bakir Çay, a "Blind" river; *Sangarius*: Sakarya debouching into the southeastern section of the Black Sea; *Ladon*: a tributary of the Alpheus River; *Parthenius*: Bartin, a small "Maidenly" river emerging from Mt. Olgassys, flowing northward, and debouching into the Euxine west of Amastris; *Aldescus*: otherwise unknown.

2 *Peitho* (Persuasion); *Admete* (Unmarried); *Ianthe* (Violet); *Electra* (Shining); *Doris* (Gift); *Prymno* (Root); *Ourania* (Celestial); *Hippo* (Horse); *Clymene* (Fame); *Rhodeia* (Rose); *Callirhoe* (Beautifully Flowing); *Zeuxis* (Yoke); *Clytie* (Lovely); *Iduia* (Skilfull); *Pasithoe* (All-Divine); *Plexaure* (Whipping Wind); *Galaxaure* (Charmer); *Dione* (Divine); *Melobosis* (Sheep-Feeder); *Thoe* (Swift); *Polydore* (Much Gifted); *Plouto* (Wealthy); *Xanthe* (Blond); *Petraie* (Rocky); *Menestho* (Steadfast); *Europa* (Far-Seeing); *Metis* (Mindful); *Eurunome* (Broad-Flowing); *Telesto* (Fulfilled); *Chryseis* (Golden); *Calypso* (Concealer); *Eudore* (Good Gift); *Tyche* (Luck); *Amphiro* (Surrounding River); *Ochyrhoe* (Swift-Flowing); *Styx* (Hate).

3 Daughters of Ocean.

B. *Seeking help from Aphrodite/Venus, goddess of sex, Hera/Juno, queen of the Olympian gods, claims that she intends to help Okeanos and his wife, Tethys, reconcile after some quarrel (Hera's real intention is to seduce her husband in order to distract his attention from the Trojan War and give the Achaeans an advantage over the Trojans in battle).*

> Give me now your affection and yearning with which you overpower all deathless and dying human folk. For I am going to see the ends of the bountiful earth, Ocean, the source of the gods, and mother Tethys, who nurtured and reared me in their halls, receiving me from Rhea,[4] when Zeus placed wide-eyed Kronos beneath the unharvested sea. I am going to see them, and I will loosen their continuous quarrels. For too long a time they have kept away from each other and their bed and lovemaking since bitterness has fallen on their hearts. If, with words, I could prevail upon their dear hearts to seat themselves at their bed to unite in lovemaking, I would always be called dear by them and revered.
>
> *(Homer,* Iliad *14.198–210)*

C. *Okeanos is a wise and sympathetic advisor to Prometheus, punished for gifting humankind with fire (and thus providing them with the means to develop technology, overcome the capricious forces of nature, and lessen the power gap between humans and gods: Irby-Massie 2008). Here Okeanos expresses his sympathy for Prometheus' plight (bound to a crag in the remote Caucasus Mountains where his liver is pecked out nightly but regrows daily).*

> "Reaching the end of a long path, Prometheus, I have come to you, guiding this swift-winged bird by means of a thought, without a bridle-bit or rein. Know this, in your misfortunes I share in your suffering. For our kinship,[5] so I think, thus compels. And apart from kinship, there is not anyone to whom I would show greater respect than you. You will know this as true, nor is it in me to speak just to flatter. Come now, indicate what is necessary to assist you. For you will never say that you have a more steadfast friend than Okeanos."
>
> *(Aeschylus,* Prometheus Bound *284–297)*

D. *Okeanos appears on this black-figure dinos (wine-bowl, painted by Sophilos, c. 580 BCE), as part of the procession of guests attending the wedding of Peleus and Thetis. Wearing a crab-clawed hat and with a fishy-tail, Okeanos holds an eel in his left hand and a fish in his right.*

4 Rhea and Kronos/Saturn are the parents of Hera and the other first generation Olympians.

5 Okeanos was a Titan, brother of Iapetus, and thus Prometheus' uncle.

FIGURE 3.1D Ocean: British Museum 13159001: drawing by Georgia L. Irby.

3.1.2 Triton

Triton is the conch-playing merman son of Poseidon/Neptune and Amphitrite, here helping quell the floodwaters of a cataclysmic storm sent to destroy a race of humans who refused to worship the gods (see #1.9.11A).

Nor does the sea's anger remain, when the ocean's ruler caresses the waters with his three-pronged spear, and he calls dark-blue Triton to the surface, standing above the deep sea and covered with murex growing over his shoulder, and Neptune orders his son to blow into his resounding conch and call back the floods and waves by giving a sign. His hollow trumpet is taken up, which grows coiling from the lowest spiral into a wide one, the trumpet which—when it takes in air in the middle of the sea—then reaches the shores lying under each sun, rising and setting, with its voice. Then also when the shell has touched the moist mouth of the god with his dripping beard and, blown into, plays the commanded retreat, its sound is heard by all the waters of land and sea, and it restrains all those waters by which it is heard. Now the sea has a shore, a riverbed holds its full rivers, waves subside, and hills are seen emerging, the dry land rises, places grow from shrinking waves, and, after a long day, the forests show their bare tops and hold mud left behind in their foliage.

(Ovid, Metamorphoses *1.330–347; cf. Hesiod,* Theogony *930–933; Nonnus,* Dionysiaka *1.59)*

3.1.3 Glaucus

*Glaucus was once a human fisherman who was turned into a merman. After the metamorphosis, Glaucus would regularly wash away his mortality with running river water (*Glaucus of the Sea *fragment 26Radt), and he was worshipped as a prophetic "Old Man of the Sea" in Spain (Scholiast, Apollonius,* Argonautica *2.767). Flowing seamlessly from Galatea's account of the Cyclops Polyphemus trying to woo her (unsuccessfully), Glaucus falls in love with and recounts his own misadventure to Scylla before her horrible transformation.*

898. Then Galatea stops speaking, and the Nereids, their meeting ended, depart and swim in calm waves. But Scylla returns to shore (for she does not dare trust herself to the middle of the deep sea) and either she wanders along the thirsty sands without her clothes or, when she is tired, happening upon remote recesses of a pool, she refreshes her limbs in the enclosed water. Behold, plying the strait, a new resident of the deep sea, his limbs recently changed at Anthedon (Euboea), Glaucus is at hand, and he clings with desire at the sight of the girl and says whatever words he thinks will be able to delay her as she flees. She scampers away, nonetheless, and because of her fear she swiftly reaches the summit of a mountain positioned near the shores. The mountain is huge, in front of the strait, gathered into one point, its highest peak vaulted under the trees onto the long level seas. This is where she stops, safe in the place and not knowing whether he is a monster or a god, and she wonders at his color and the hair covering his shoulders and his back underneath at his lowest half which took on the groin of a coiling fish.

916. He sees her and, leaning on a mole which was standing nearby, he says, "Virgin, I am not a monster or a wild beast, but a god of the water. And Proteus does not have greater authority in the water than I, nor Triton and Palaemon, son of Athamas.[6] I was nonetheless mortal, but, to be sure, given to the deep waters, I was kept very busy in the waters back then. For, I was now leading in the nets. Drawing in fish, now sitting on a mole, I guided a line on a pole.[7] There are shores bordered by a green meadow, one part of which is fringed by waves, the other by grass, which neither the horn-bearing cow has damaged with a bite, nor have gentle sheep or hairy she-goats plucked it. Nor has a bee carried off flowers with their seed gathered from there. Nor have festal wreathes been given

6 Palaemon/Melicertes: see #3.11.5D introduction.

7 For fishing methods: #6.3.2A.

to a head, nor ever have sickle-bearing hands reaped there. I first settled on that turf, while I dried my dripping lines and set them out so that I might count my captive fish in order, which either chance drove into the nets, or their own credulity drove onto my curved hooks. It resembles a fiction: but what benefit do I have in making this up? Once they touched the grass, my prey began to move and turn over and make their way on land as in the sea. And while I delayed and marveled at the same time, the whole crowd fled into their waves, and they left behind their new master and the shore. I was stupefied and for a long time uncertain. And I sought the reason, whether some god did this or the sap of the grass. Nonetheless I asked, 'What grass has these powers?' And with my hand I plucked the grasses. And what I had plucked I chewed with my tooth. I had scarcely swallowed down the unknown juices in my throat when suddenly I perceived my midriff trembling within and my chest seized by the love of another nature. Nor was I able to resist for any length of time, and I said, 'Farewell, land to which I will never be returned.' And my body was dipped under the waters.

949. "The gods of the sea deemed me, accepted into their companionship, worthy of honor, and they asked Oceanus and Tethys to remove whatever mortality I still bore. With a song chanted nine times that purged the mortal wickedness from me, I was purified by them and ordered to place my chest in 100 rivers. There was no delay. Rivers slipping from different parts turned all their waters over my head. Up to this point I was able to report all the deeds that I recall. Up to this point, I remember these things, but my mind does not discern the rest. After my memory returned, I was different over my whole body than I had recently been, nor did I recover the same mind. Then, for the first time, I saw this beard, green with sea-gray gloom, and my hair, which I sweep through the long waters, and huge shoulders and blue arms and shins curved very recently with a fin-bearing fish. What is this type, nonetheless, and how is it pleasing to the marine gods? How is it gratifying to be a god if you are not touched by these things?"

966. Scylla left him speaking such things and about to say more. He was angry and, enraged by the unnatural rejection, he sought the halls of Circe, daughter of a Titan (Helios, the Sun).

(Ovid, Metamorphoses *13.898–968)*

3.1.4 Proteus

While most gods are metamorphic to some degree, transformation was the hallmark of water gods, and Proteus, a prescient, cranky Old Man of the Sea, employed his metamorphic gift to guard this knowledge from mortals. Helen's husband, Menelaus, must overpower the ever-changing god to acquire knowledge that will help him return to Sparta, his kingdom, after the Trojan War (see also #2.2.10A).

So I (Menelaus) spoke and the shining goddess (Proteus' daughter, Eidothea) straightaway answered. "Accordingly, stranger, I will declare these things very accurately. When the sun has reached the middle sky, thereupon the unerring Old Man of the Sea emerges from the salt-sea under the breeze of the west wind, hidden by a dark ripple. And coming out he lies down under the hollow grottos. Around him the seals, the children of a lovely sea-born goddess,[8] sleep in a heap, rising from the gray salt-water and breathing the bitter stench of the very deep salt-sea. Then, leading you there at dawn to the place revealed, I myself will lay you down in order. You should select three companions, who are the best in your well-benched ships. And I will tell you all the pernicious tricks of the old man. First, he will count the seals and go over them. But when he has scrutinized them by fives, he will lie down in their midst like a shepherd with his flocks of sheep. When you first see him lying down, then may you have a care for your courage and strength, and straightaway hold him eagerly desiring and struggling to escape. He will attempt to become all things,[9] whichever four-footed beast is on the earth, and water, and even divinely kindled fire. Relentlessly hold him and squeeze him. When he himself questions you with words, allowing you to see him such as when he went to rest, at that time stop from your force and release the old man, Hero, and ask which of the gods is enraged and, regarding your homecoming, how you can return over the fishy sea."

(Homer, Odyssey *4.398–424; cf. Ovid,* Art of Love *3.760–764)*

3.1.5 Nereus

A. *Nereus, the son of Gaia (Earth) and Pontus (Sea), and his wife, Doris, were also the parents of 50 sea nymphs, collectively called Nereids (daughters of Nereus), including Thetis, mother of Achilles, and Amphitrite, wife of Poseidon.*

Pontus begat Nereus truthful and without deceit, the oldest of his children. But they call him "Old Man," owing to his infallibility and kindness, nor does he forget what is established by law. But he knows customs and gentle counsels.

(Hesiod, Theogony *233–236)*

B. *Like Proteus, Nereus also employed his transformative gift to protect his prophetic knowledge. In a doublet of the Menelaus story, Herakles must wrestle Nereus. Practically nothing is known about Apollodorus (1st/2nd century CE), who penned a survey of Greek myth.*

Walking through Illyria and hurrying to the Eridanus River,[10] Herakles came upon nymphs, the daughters of Zeus and Themis. They disclosed Nereus to him. Seizing Nereus as he slept—although turning himself into all shapes—Herakles fettered him and did not release him before learning from him where

8 #2.2.3A.

9 Proteus comes into English as the adjective "protean."

10 *Illyria* is on the Eastern coast of the Adriatic Sea. The *Eridanus* might be the Po, Rhone, or Rhine.

the apples and the Hesperides[11] happened to be. Learning this, Herakles went through Libya.

(*Apollodorus,* Library *2.5.11)*

3.1.6 Thetis

A. *Nereus' daughter Thetis was also metamorphic, a skill she employed to try to avoid an unwelcome fiancé owing to her unusual fate.*

Peleus married Thetis, daughter of Nereus: Zeus and Poseidon had quarreled over marrying her. But when Themis[12] sang in a prophetic strain that a child born from Thetis would be stronger than the father, they withdrew. But some say that, when Zeus was stirred up over being with her, Prometheus declared that her child would hold power over heaven. Others say that Thetis did not want to hook up with Zeus, since she was brought up by Hera, and that Zeus, because he was furious, wanted to make her live with a mortal. When Chiron[13] advised Peleus to seize her and hold her tightly as she changed shape, Peleus, keeping a look-out, seized her as she became now fire, now water, now a wild beast, nor did he release her before he saw that she had resumed her former shape. He married her on Pelion,[14] and there, feasting sumptuously, the gods celebrated the marriage. Chiron gave Peleus a spear of ash-wood, Poseidon gave him horses, Balius ("Dappled") and Xanthus ("Golden"), and these horses were immortal.

(*Apollodorus,* Library *3.13.4)*

B. *The marriage was not a happy one, and Thetis, a watery goddess of the sea, soon abandoned Peleus to rejoin her Nereid sisters. Nonetheless, she was a doting mother, as in this poignant episode after Achilles was publicly humiliated by Agamemnon, the commander-in-chief of the allied Achaean forces at Troy.*

So spoke Achilles, weeping, and his divine mother heard him as she was sitting in the depths of the salt-sea beside her father, the old man. Swiftly she came to the surface of the grey salt-sea, like a mist, and she sat in front of him weeping tears. With her hand she caressed him, and she called him by name, "Child, why are you weeping? What grief has come to your heart? Speak out, do not hide it in your mind, in order that we both might know."

(*Homer,* Iliad *1.358–363)*

11 Containing a grove of golden apples that only the gods can pluck, one episode in Herakles' quest for immortality.

12 A Titan daughter of Gaia and Uranus, Themis was the personification of justice, divine order, law, and custom.

13 An immortal and wise centaur (half-man, half-horse) who taught many Greek heroes, including Achilles, Thetis' son.

14 A mountain in Thessaly, northern Greece.

C. *The image of Nereus' daughters riding sea creatures, often tacked, was common in Greek art. Here, seated side-saddle, Thetis travels on a Triton to deliver a new set of Hephaestus-made armor to her son Achilles. Thetis holds the new sword while the Triton has the shield. In the upper corners are symmetrical sea-cats with ventral fins and coiling piscine tails. After the Greek commander-in-chief had publicly insulted him, Achilles withdrew from battle but allowed Patroclus, his close friend and companion, to fight, wielding Achilles' armor. Hector, the Trojan hero, killed Patroclus and took Achilles' armor as spoils of war. Patroclus' death so enraged Achilles that he returned to battle after receiving new armor from his mother.*

FIGURE 3.1.6C Thetis with Triton: first quarter of 2nd century CE, Met 1993.11.2 (public domain).

3.2 Metamorphoses

A. *Like water, marine gods and mythical animals are fluid, able to change from one shape into another, owing both to the optical refraction that characterizes objects in water and the natural inclination to find watery analogues to terrestrial fauna and flora: Pliny declared, "whatever is born in any part of nature exists also in the sea, and many things in addition that do not exist elsewhere" (NH 9.2). These early examples (mid-7th century BCE) show three feline heads in a vertical row.*

FIGURE 3.2A Early composite sea creatures: Archaic, Proto-Attic vase, BMFA 6.67; Archaic Proto-Corinthian, Francavilla, South Italy, M. Stoop, *Atti e Mem. Soc. Magna Grecia* 11/12 (1970/71) 57, figure 4, pl. 23: drawing by Georgia L. Irby.

B. *According to one tradition, Tyrrhenian pirates had tried to kidnap Dionysus, god of wine, theater, and the male principle of fertility. Dionysus, however, is a god who prefers to transform rather than destroy. Here we have a stunning description of Dionysus' transformation of the pirates and their boat. As dolphins, the erstwhile pirates regretted their life of crime and were consequently friendly to human beings, especially those in danger at sea (#2.2.11E–I).*

> O Child, a Tyrrhenian band[15] captured you, and Nereus lulls the swollen sea: he alters the dark-blue straits with meadows. Here the plane-tree is vigorous with green foliage, as is the laurel grove dear to Phoebus Apollo. A chirping bird sings loudly in the branches. The oar holds vivacious ivy-vines. A grapevine binds the highest masthead. On the prow roars an Idaean lion, a tiger from the Ganges crouches at the stern. Then each fearful pirate swims in the strait, and a

15 Etruscan pirates: #6.2F.

new appearance holds the submerged men. First the arms fall from the robbers. The stricken chest joins to the belly; a tiny hand hangs at the side; each one dives below the waves with a curved back and cuts the sea with a lunate tail, and now an arched dolphin follows the fleeing sails.

(Seneca, Oedipus *449–466; cf.* Homeric Hymn 7 to Dionysus*; Nonnus,* Dionysiaca *45.105–168)*

C. *This Greek vase, imported to Vulci (Etruria, Italy), shows the pirates at the moment of transformation. The vase was repatriated to the Palazzo Barberini from Toledo, Ohio in 2012.*

FIGURE 3.2C Pirates transformed into dolphins: Etruscan black-figure *hydria* (water jug) by the Micali painter (510–500 BCE), repatriated to the Palazzo Barberini: photo by Carole Raddatto (Wikimedia Commons).

D. *An etiological myth for the Nerites shellfish.*

There is a spiral shellfish of the sea, small in size, but very beautiful to look at. And it is born in the purest sea and on rocks under the salt-waters and on those things that are called sunken rocks (reefs). Its name is nerites, and a two-fold account about this creature flows out, and both tales have reached me. To share short tales within a lengthy history is, moreover, nothing more than allowing the ear to rest and sweeten the tale. Hesiod, whom we hear always telling true and not false accounts, sings that Doris, daughter of Okeanos, bore 50 daughters to Nereus of the sea (*Theogony* 233). Homer also remembered them in his verses (*Iliad* 18.38). But they do not say that among all those daughters one son was also born. But mariners' tales celebrate this son: they say that he was called Nerites and that he was the most beautiful of men and gods. Aphrodite delighted in keeping company in the sea with Nerites, and she loved him. When the fated-time arrived, when it was necessary to be registered among the Olympians, and father Zeus commanded her to do so, I hear that as she ascended she wanted to bring her companion and playmate. But the story is that Nerites gave answer regarding that he preferred life with his sisters and parents over Olympus. He was then allowed to grow wings, and this, I think, was a gift bestowed by Aphrodite. But Nerites considered this gift a worthless trifle. The child of Zeus became very angry, and she turned his shape into a shell, and she chose instead as her attendant and companion Eros, young and lovely like Nerites, and she gave Nerites' wings to Eros.

(Aelian, NA *14.28)*

E. *A legend from the Erythraean Sea about a Nereid who turned men into fish.*

While they were sailing along the territory of the Ichthyphagoi,[16] they heard a tale about some island which lies about 100 *stadia* from this mainland and is desolate of inhabitants. The locals said that it was sacred to Helios[17] and was called Nosola, and that no men wanted to make landfall at that island. Whoever brought a ship there in ignorance disappeared. But Nearchus[18] says that one of his light *kerkouros* ships[19] with an Egyptian crew disappeared not far from that island and that, concerning this, the pilots believed that the crew disappeared because they touched the island in ignorance. Nearchus sent a triaconter (with 30 oars) in a circle around the island, ordering them not to land at the island, but for the men to shout as if attacking, sailing close by and calling by name the helmsman and any other unseen crewman. But no one answered. Then Nearchus himself sailed to the island and landed, and he forced his sailors as well, although they were unwilling. He himself disembarked and debunked the empty story about the island.

They heard another story told about the island, that one of the Nereids inhabited the island, but the Nereid's name is not reported. Whoever sailed to her island, she would have sex with him, and, after turning him into a fish, she would toss him into the deep sea. Angry at the Nereid, Helios ordered her to leave the island. She agreed to leave her home but asked to have the suffering stopped. Helios allowed it, and whichever men she had turned from men into fish, in his compassion, he made them people again from fish. The race

16 #2.2.12C and note.
17 #3.4.1.
18 #2.1.2B.
19 A long merchant ship powered by both oars and sails.

of the Ichthyphagoi came from these men-fish-men down to Alexander's day. Nearchus refutes these things as false, but I do not applaud him for this learned discussion and cleverness: it is not very difficult to refute such things, and it is distressful to tell old tales and then refute them as false.

(Arrian, Indika *31)*

F. *Just as Dionysus could transform pirates into dolphins, water gods could furthermore transmute not only themselves but also others. After the suicide of Queen Dido, Aeneas' ill-fated Carthaginian lover (see #3.6B), her sister Anna sought asylum in Latium, but Aeneas' jealous wife, Lavinia, became wrathful. The Latian River Numicus rescued Anna by changing her into the nymph Anna Perenna ("the perpetual year"), the patroness of one of Rome's most popular festivals, when, on the Ides of March on the banks of the Tiber, revelers would imbibe as many cups of wine as years they hoped yet to live (Ovid,* Fasti *3.531–532). In 44 BCE, Caesar's enemies may have deliberately chosen that day, March 15, to execute the dictator, when so many of his supporters would have been intoxicated on the banks of the Tiber.*

543. Nonetheless regarding what this goddess (Anna Perenna) is, since she flits about in rumors, no tale must be covered over by my design. Miserable Dido burned with fire for Aeneas; she also burned on pyres constructed for her own fate. Her ashes were collected, and this short epigram was on the marble of her tomb: "Aeneas offered both the cause and sword of her death. Dido herself fell, using her own hand."

551. The neighboring Numidians immediately invaded the realm, now without a protector, and Mauretanian Juba[20] took possession of the captured place, and, mindful that he had been spurned, he says, "Nonetheless I enjoy the bridal bed of Elissa (Dido), I whom she so often drove away." The Tyrians fled to where their wandering drove each one, just like wavering bees wander when their king has once been lost. Anna was driven from her home. And, crying, she left her sister's city walls. She paid rites to her own full-blooded sister before leaving: soft ashes drank ointments of tears and accepted hair clipped from Anna's head. And three times she said, "Goodbye." Three times she pressed ashes brought to her face, and her sister seemed to be near the ashes.

565. After obtaining a ship and companions for her flight, she glided with a smooth wind, looking back at the walls, the sweet work of her sister.

567. There is Melite (Malta), a fertile island near barren Cosyra (Pantelleria), which the billowing sea of the Libyican sea thrashes. Anna sought this island, trusting in the ancient hospitality of the king. Rich with wealth, Battus was king there. After he learned the misfortunes of each sister, he said, "This land,

20 The traditional name of the royal family of Mauretania, this one referring to a distant mythological ancestor of Juba II (#1.5.1B and note).

however small it is, is yours." Nonetheless, he would have delivered the duties of hospitality through to the end, but he feared Pygmalion's great strength.[21]

575. Twice the sun counted its signs, a third year passed, and a new land must be prepared for the exiled woman. Anna's brother was at hand and sought her in war. King Battus, hating weapons, said, "We are unwarlike. Flee safely." So ordered, Anna fled and linked her ship to winds and waves. Crueler than any sea was her brother.

581. Near the fish-filled rivers of stony Crathis is a small field: the local crowd calls it Camere. To there was her course, and she was no further away from there than how far a sling can send a stone nine times. The sails first luffed and were aback from wavering breezes. The mariner said, "cleave the waters with an oar." And while they made ready to furl the sails with a twisted line, the curved stern was struck by a swift south wind and born into the open sea, as the helmsman fought in vain, and the land that was in sight fled from their eyes. Waves dashed up, and the sea was overturned from the lowest depth, and the hollow ship drank in white waters. Their skill was conquered by the wind, nor did their helmsman use the steering-oars, but he also sought help with prayers. The Phoenician exile[22] was tossed about over swelling waves, and Anna covered her moist eyes with her clothing. Then, for the first time, Dido was called lucky by her sister, as is any woman who has pressed some ground with her body. The ship was led to the Laurentine shore with a huge blast, and, drawn down, she perished, but all hands disembarked.

601. Now, dutiful Aeneas was enhanced with the kingdom and daughter of Latinus,[23] and he mingled the two peoples. Accompanied only by Achates on the dotal shore, while he plucked off a hidden path with a bare foot, he beheld Anna, wandering, nor could he endure believing that it was she. Why would she come to Latian fields? While Aeneas was thinking to himself, Achates exclaimed, "It's Anna!" She lifted her face to her name. Alas, what should she do? Should she flee? Should she seek a gape in the earth? In front of her eyes were the fates of her miserable sister. The Cytherean hero[24] perceived and spoke to an alarmed Anna: he offered asylum . . . She trusted him speaking such things—for no other hope remained—and she related her own wanderings, and when she entered his home, dressed in a Tyrian outfit, Aeneas began to speak, while the rest of the crowd kept quiet. "Lavinia, my wife, there is a dutiful reason why I entrust this

21 Pygmalion, the brother of Dido and Anna, killed Dido's husband, and drove his sisters from Tyre, the Phoenician capital (Vergil, *Aeneid* 1.343–368).

22 Carthage was settled from Tyre. Anna was thus Phoenician.

23 King of Latium, the region where Rome would be founded. His daughter was Lavinia, whom Aeneas married after defeating Latinus' allies (Vergil, *Aeneid* 7.314).

24 Aeneas was the son of Venus whose sacred places included Cythera, an island off the southern Peloponnese.

woman to you. When I was shipwrecked, I ate her wealth. She comes from Tyre, she possesses a realm on Libyan shores. I pray that you love her like a sister."

633. Lavinia promised everything, and she also grasped a false wound, and in her silence she disguised fears. Although she saw in front of her eyes that many gifts were brought to Anna, nonetheless she secretly thought that more were also sent secretly. Lavinia did not have a precise plan of what she would do. But she hated Anna like a Fury[25] and prepared plots and desired to die avenged.

639. It was night. In front of her sister's bed Dido seemed to stand, her hair stiff with dried blood. "Flee, don't hesitate, flee this gloomy home" she said. Under Dido's word, a breeze struck the querulous doors. Anna left and quickly, bold in abundance (for fear itself made her bold), she hurled herself on the ground through a window. And when she was seized by fear, dressed in a loose tunic, she ran like a doe frightened by wolves she has heard. The horned River Numicus was believed to have snatched her in his desirous waves and to have hidden her in his pools. Meanwhile, the Sidonian[26] lady was sought with great clamor through the fields. Signs and vestiges of her feet were visible. Then they came to the banks. Her tracks were on the banks. The accomplice river held back his quiet waves. She herself was seen to say, "I am the nymph of peaceful Numicus. Hiding in this perennial river, I am called Anna Perenna."

(Ovid, Fasti *3.543–611, 625–654)*

3.3 Scylla

A. *Scylla was once a beautiful girl whose suitors included Poseidon and Glaucus (#3.1.3). According to one version, Amphitrite was responsible for Scylla's horrible transformation (scholia Tzetzes* on Lycophron *650 and Servius* ad Aeneid *3.420). Here we have another version: that Circe, Helios' daughter and skilled in the magic arts, caused the metamorphosis after Glaucus rejected her. Circe then wreaked her awful vengeance on an innocent Scylla.*

To Circe attempting such things, Glaucus said, "leafy trees will grow in the water and seaweed will grow on the highest mountains before my passions are changed from Scylla, as long as she is safe."

The goddess was offended and insofar as she could not harm Glaucus (nor did she want to, loving him), she became enraged at Scylla, who was preferred to her. Injured by the rejection of her love, straightaway she pounded unspeakable fodder with dreadful juices, and she mixed Hekate's[27] chants with her

25 Ovid here has invoked Vergil's Alecto, the fury who spurs the Latins and their allies into war with Aeneas, even after brokering peace with King Latinus (Vergil, *Aeneid* 7.323–510).

26 Sidon, another Phoenician city, north of Tyre.

27 Another daughter of Helios who, like her sister, was adept at magic: Hekate is the witch who protects crossroads and liminal spaces.

compounded cocktail. Then, she was dressed in blue robes, and she proceeded through a battle line of fawning wild animals[28] from the middle of her courtyard. And, seeking Rhegium opposite the rocks of Zancle,[29] she advanced through waves roiling in the sea-swells in which she set her tracks just as on solid earth. And she skimmed over the highest waves with dry feet.

There was a small stream, bent into curving arcs. The quiet there was pleasing to Scylla. There she took herself from the heat of the sea and sky when the sun was highest in the sky's middle orb and made the shortest shadows at his zenith. The goddess corrupted this stream and polluted it with unnatural poisons. Here Circe sprinkled fluids pressed with a noxious root and thrice times nine she muttered an obscure circumlocuting chant of strange words with her magical mouth.

Scylla came and descended into the stream up to her belly. When she saw that her groin was defiled with barking monsters, at first not believing that they were part of her own body, she fled and pushed them away and feared the violent faces of the dogs. But those whom she fled, she dragged them with her. Examining her body for thighs and shins and feet, she found gaping Cerberus-like[30] maws instead. And she stands on the frenzy of dogs and confines the backsides of subjected wild animals in her disfigured loins and protruding belly. Her lover Glaucus wept and fled the embrace of Circe who excessively and hostilely employed the power of herbs.

(Ovid, Metamorphoses *14.37–69)*

B. *Dwelling at the Straits of Messina, Scylla torments sailors who must choose between the certain death in Charybdis (for whirlpools: #1.3.9) or the loss of six sailors, one for each of her dog-fish sharks. Homer's Calypso vividly describes Scylla-the-dog-fish monster for Odysseus.*

"There are two promontories, one extends to the broad sky in a sharp peak and a dark cloud encircles it. The cloud does not ever flow away, nor does a bright sky hold the peak of this cliff, neither in summer nor in winter. Nor could a mortal human scale it, nor could he climb it, not even if he had 20 hands and feet. For the rock is smooth, like something highly polished. In the middle of the cliff is a misty grotto, turned towards the west to Erebus,[31] by which you should steer your hollow ship straight, radiant Odysseus. A strong man shooting an arrow from a hollow ship could not even hit the hollow cave.

28 Circe gave her male visitors a potion that turned them into animals, swine in the case of Odysseus' crew: Homer, *Odyssey* 10.233–243.

29 The sickle-shaped harbor of Syracuse.

30 A child of Typhoeus (#3.4.4 note) and Echidna, Cerberus was the three-headed dog who guarded the entrance of the Underworld to ensure that the dead did not escape (Hesiod, *Theogony* 310).

31 The darkness of Tartarus.

"Therein dwells Scylla, yelping fearfully. Her voice is as of a newborn puppy, but she is an evil monster. Nor would anyone rejoice to see her, not even if a god met her face to face. She has 12 legs, all intertwining, and six very long necks, on each of which is a fearful head, and teeth in three rows,[32] solid and closely packed, full of black death. Her mid-section plunges in the hollow cave, but she projects her heads over the terrible gulf, and there she fishes, hunting in the rock, she grasps dolphins and dogfishes and any larger sea monster that happens to be there, numberless creatures that loud-wailing Amphitrite tends.[33] Never at any time could sailors profess to escape past her unharmed with their ship: for with each head she carries off a man snatched from his dark-prowed ship."

(Homer, Odyssey *12.73–100; cf. Vergil,* Aeneid *3.424–432)*

C. *Scylla was eventually slain by Hercules and restored by her father Phorkys ("Seal"). Lycophron of Chalcis in Euboea (b. c. 330 BCE) composed and commented on tragedies, and wrote on grammar. His* Alexandra *recounts the post-war history of Troy as prophetically recounted by Cassandra, daughter of king Priam and whose unerring revelations were not believed.*

Herakles also slayed the savage dog (Scylla) watching over the narrow recesses of the Ausonian Sea[34] as she fished from her grotto, the bull-devouring lioness whom straightaway her father restored to life, treating her flesh with torches, she who did not fear Lemtysis (Persephone), goddess of the Underworld.

(Lycophron, Alexandra *44–49)*

D. *Scylla is among the beasts at the entrance to the Underworld.*

Moreover, many monsters of various forms are stabled at the doors of the Underworld: the shades of the Centaur and double-formed Scylla and the hundred-twinned Briareos[35] and the beast of Lerna[36] buzzing horribly, and the Chimera[37] armed with flames, and Gorgons and Harpies[38] and the body of three-shaped Geryon.[39]

(Vergil, Aeneid *6.285–294; cf. Statius,* Silvae *5.3.275–287)*

32 *Sharks*: #2.2.9. *Whales* with deadly rows of teeth in three rows: #2.2.12F§316 and note.

33 #2.2.3A.

34 The body of water west of Italy, as called by the Greeks. To the Romans, it was the Tyrrhenian Sea.

35 *Briareos*: one of the three hyper-powerful 100-armed Hecatoncheires, sons of Uranus (Sky) and Gaia (Earth) and among the Olympians' allies against the Titans: Homer, *Iliad*, 1.396–404; Hesiod, *Theogony* 147–153. *Triton*: #3.1.2; *Proteus*: #3.1.4.

36 The hydra, with poisonous blood, whom Hercules slew as his canonical first labor.

37 The lion-headed monster, with a fire-breathing goat-head at the midriff and dragon hind-part, slain by Bellerophon.

38 Harpies: half woman, half bird "snatchers" who personify storm winds, and pester mythological heroes, including Aeneas (Vergil, *Aeneid* 3.244–258).

39 Medusa's grandchild (son of Chrysaor), depicted with four wings and three conjoined human bodies (Apollodorus, *Library* 2.106–109).

E. *Scylla with dogfish sharks and steering-oar.*

FIGURE 3.3E Scylla: The Met 1998.210.1, .2 (public domain).

3.4 Mythical Marine Creatures

3.4.1 Introduction

Greek and Roman art overflows with lively images of sea gods and imaginative sea beasts. A pastiche of marine deities is etched onto the gold and bronze doors of Helios' palace.

> The palace of the Sun was lofty on high columns, bright with flickering gold and bronze imitating flames, whose highest pediments polished ivory was capping. The double doors shone with silver light, and the work outstripped the material. For Mulciber[40] engraved there the waters girding the lands in the middle and the circle of the lands and the sky which hangs over the world. The billowing sea holds dark blue gods, tuneful Triton and changeful Proteus and Aegaeon[41] squeezing the huge backs of baleen whales with his own arms, and Doris and her daughters (Nereids), some seen swimming, some sitting on a mole drying their green locks, certain ones even riding on a fish. There is not a single face for all, but nonetheless not entirely disparate, as is suitable for sisters. The land

40 An alternate name for Vulcan who beats on metals (*mulco*: I cudgel).
41 The name by which mortals addressed Briareus: #3.3D note.

bears men and cities and forests and wild beasts and rivers and nymphs and other divinities of the countryside. Above these is placed an image of the shining sky and six signs of the zodiac on the right-hand door and the same number on the left-hand door.

(Ovid, Metamorphoses *2.1–18)*

3.4.2 Hippocamps

A. *Swimming abundantly in Greco-Roman visual arts, but rarely treated in literature is the hippocamp/seahorse. Here we have a charming (and rare) literary description of hippocamps as depicted on a painting of Poseidon pursuing the Danaid Amymone. The* Images *of Philostratus the Elder of Lemnos (c. 190–230 CE) is a lively and artistically sensitive interpretation of paintings in a private collection in Naples.*

You have come upon Poseidon travelling over the sea, I think, in Homer (*Iliad* 13.23–31), when the god prepares to set out from Aegae to the Achaeans.[42] And the calm sea drives him escorted by those horses and those sea monsters. For there in Homer they follow and fawn over Poseidon as here. There I think you might perceive them as land horses: for Homer's hippocamps are noble with bronze-hoofs and swift wings and struck with whips. But here the hippocamps draw the chariot, moist in their hooves (webbed?), good swimmers and grey-eyed and, by Zeus, like dolphins.

(Philostratus the Elder, Images *1.8)*

B. *This fresco from Campania (c. 50–79) shows a symmetrical brace of Homer's winged hippocamps with coiling fish tails and moist feet.*

FIGURE 3.4.2B Two winged hippocamps, the J. Paul Getty Museum 72.AG.78.3 (public domain).

42 I.e., from Macedon to the northwestern Peloponnese.

3.4.3 Triton and Nereid Sightings

A. *It is unclear what aquatic biological creatures were identified as nereids or tritons, but there were occasional sightings, including at Olisippo (Lisbon).*

When Tiberius was *princeps* ("emperor," r. 14–37 CE), an embassy from Olisippo, sent out for this reason, announced that a triton was seen and heard playing his conch shell in a certain cave, and he was recognized from his appearance. The account of the nereids is also not false: its body bristles with scales even where it has a human appearance. For this nereid was seen on that same shore, whose doleful song of death locals heard from some distance, and the governor of Gaul wrote to the divine Augustus (r. 27 BCE–14 CE) that several lifeless nereids appeared on the shore. I also have illustrious authorities in the equestrian order saying that the Old Man of the Sea had been seen by them in the Gaditanean Ocean,[43] completely similar to a human over his entire body: during the night, the old man would climb onto ships and he would immediately weigh down the parts where he sat and, if he remained for some time, the boat would even dip in the water.

(Pliny, NH *9.9–10; cf. Aelian,* NA *13.21)*

B. *A detailed first-hand description of a biological triton on display.*

I saw another triton among the marvels of the Romans, smaller in size than those among the Tanagrans.[44] Tritons have this form: on their heads they have hair like marsh-frogs, both in color and because of not being able to separate one hair from the others; the rest of their body is rough with fine scales along their fishy hide; under their ears they have fins and a human nose, the mouth is broader and full of beastly teeth. To me the eyes seem grey and they have hands and fingers and nails resembling the spiral shells of murex purples.[45] Under the chest and belly they have tails like dolphins instead of feet.

(Pausanias, Description of Greece *9.21.1)*

3.4.4 Capricorn

The good-natured Pan (the composite aegipan, goat-man), friend of all wild things and protector of shepherds and their flocks, turned himself into the capricorn (goat-horned-fish) before jumping into the Nile to hide from Typhon.[46] *Pan*

43 The sea near Gades, southern Iberia.

44 In Boeotia, north of Athens.

45 #6.5.1.

46 Typhoeus, a flame-breathing, serpentine monster with 100 snaky, flaming heads emerging from his shoulders and a threat to Olympian rule but vanquished by Zeus and buried under Mt. Aetna, fueling the volcano: Hesiod, *Theogony* 875–876; Apollodorus, *Library* 1.6; Nonnus, *Dionysiaca* 2.364–564; #1.3.9A.

morphed from one hybrid creature into another, retaining his goatliness, the shared characteristic of the terrestrial and aquatic Pans. The composite, amphibious capricorn was especially popular in Roman art where the hybrid evokes Augustus, whose moon sign was the capricorn (see Dwyer 1973). Like the capricorn, who preserved Olympian rule by a watery act, Augustus presented himself as preserving the Roman state in the decisive naval battle at Actium (#7.4.3D). Augustus' capricorn held sway over the sea and came to represent the maritime victory at Actium as emphasized on coins and in public art. Pseudo-Hyginus (c. 27 BCE–14 CE) (Gaius Julius Hyginus, the overseer of Augustus' Palatine library?) composed a short Astronomy, *relating the mythic back stories of 47 constellations.*

> Capricorn: The image of the capricorn is similar to the Aegipan, whom Jupiter—because he was nurtured with him—wanted to be among the stars, just like his goat nurse, about whom we spoke above (2.13.5). When Jupiter was assaulting the Titans, Pan is also said to have cast on the enemy a fear which is called *panikos* ("panic") as Eratosthenes[47] says. For this reason it is said that the lower part of his body is with the shape of a fish because he lobbed the enemy with murex shells instead of stones.
>
> The Egyptian priests, moreover, and some poets say that, when many gods assembled in Egypt, at the same time Typhon suddenly arrived, a very sharp earth-born monster and an especial enemy of the gods. Agitated by fear they changed themselves into other forms: Mercury became an ibis, Apollo moreover a bird which is called "Thracian," Diana a cat. For these reasons, they declare that the Egyptians do not allow these animals to be violated because they are said to be images of the gods. At the same time, they say that Pan threw himself into the river and made the lower part of his body the image of a fish, the other part, the image of a goat, and in this way he escaped Typhon. Admiring his cleverness, Jupiter fastened Pan's image among the stars.
>
> *(Pseudo-Hyginus,* Astronomy *2.28)*

3.5 Sea Monsters

While the classic ketos *("sea monster") was serpentine, hybrid, huge, and terrifying (see #2.2.8–9, 12 [cephalopods, sharks, whales], #2.3.13C [crocodiles], and #6.3.7 [eels] for the biological creatures that inspired the mythical sea monster), Greco-Roman art also features miniature varieties, as on the Portland Vase (BM* 251730001)*, where Thetis cuddles a little one.*

A. *Vanquishing these monsters of the salt-deep, real or mythical, symbolized the human conquest of nature and was cast in heroic terms: #2.2.8, #2.2.12C-D. In the*

47 Pseudo-Eratosthenes, author of *Catasterisms*, including a description and mythological account of each constellation.

mythscape, sea monsters were sent to punish the hubris (extreme arrogance) of mortals against the gods. When king Laomedon of Troy refused to pay Apollo and Poseidon for building the impenetrable walls of his city, Poseidon sent a sea monster who caused floodtides. The beast could be atoned only by a virgin's blood. Laomedon was thus forced to save his people by sacrificing his daughter to the ketos. *Hercules, however, battled and vanquished this monster. Valerius Flaccus (45–before 96 CE) composed a version of Jason's quest in Latin (*Argonautica, *in eight books), dedicated to Vespasian (r. 69–79) and referring to the eruption of Vesuvius in 79 (*Argonautica *3.207–208). The text survives partially and in a corrupt state.*

> Meanwhile, Neptune gives a sign from a distance, and at the same time the monster-bearing bays bellow and the Sigean pestilence rolls the strait in a heap. The monster's flickering eyes quake under a gray cloud, and the din of lightning brandishes its maw curved in a three-forked row, and its tail reaches back over the traversed sea, and the towering neck snatches its supporting folds. The sea follows the monster pressing through a thousand coils, lapping the monster's flank. Its own storm drives the monster rushing to the agitated shores . . . At the same time the monster advances its dreadful mass and rock-encrusted back. And with a huge shadow it draws near. Mt. Ida trembles and is dashed to pieces, and the turrets, cast down, rise again. The descendant of Alceus[48] seizes his bow and bears down with the entire cloud of his quiver. No more than the great Mt. Eryx (western Sicily) is the monster moved from its seat when rains want to carry the mountain down its valleys. Now the air between them is short and useless for a flying arrow. Then, truly, there are rumblings and the frenzy of that futile undertaking and quiet modesty. And again the girl (Laomedon's daughter) turns pale. Hercules casts weapons with his hand, he looks back at the crags and nearby rocks, and he cuts them off, shaking them from the foundation of the deep sea, as much as old age aided by the winds or the clash of the sea strikes against them. Now the sea monster is at hand with its entire battle line, and now very close it gapes at its miserable prey. Uplifted in the midst of the waters, Alcides receives the rushing monster and overwhelms its rising coils with the previously gathered stones. Hercules redoubles the monstrous blows of his knotty oak club. The beast is carried into the deep waves, now its coils are loosened along all the shoals, and the Idaean mother[49] and her chorus and the rivers from her lofty summits shriek.
>
> *(Valerius Flaccus,* Argonautica *2.497–505, 518–537)*

B. *In a doublet of the Hercules story, Perseus fights another* ketos *sent by Neptune to punish Cassiopeia, queen of Aethiopia, who had claimed that she was more beautiful than the Nereids. Again, the payment is the virgin princess, Andromeda,*

48 Alceus, prince of Mycenae, a son of Perseus and Andromeda and grandfather of Hercules' mother Alcmene. Thus Hercules, Alceus' great-grandson, is also called Alcides, "descendant of Alceus."

49 Cybele, whose orgiastic cult was observed on Mt. Ida near Troy.

who was chained to a cliff on the coast. Just returning from slaying Medusa, Perseus falls in love with the beautiful girl and slays the monster in exchange for her hand in marriage.

> Look! Just as a swift ship with its prow fastened at the front plies the waters, driven by the sweaty arms of young men, so does this wild beast hasten as the waves are cleft asunder by the attack of its chest. Perseus is as far from the rocky cliffs as a Balearic sling[50] is able to send a twisted ball of lead through the middle of the sky, when suddenly the young man, uplifted on the clouds, departs from the earth which is shoved back by his feet. When the man's shadow is seen on the level sea, the beast rages against the shadow that it has seen, just as Jove's rapidly flying bird, when it sees a serpent offering its livid-blue belly to the shining sun in an empty field, seizes it from behind. Lest the serpent twist back its savage maw, the eagle fixes eager talons in the scale-bearing back. So too does Perseus, sent headlong through the empty air in a quick flight, press down the snorting monster's back. And Inachides[51] buries his iron sword up to its curved hook in the monster's right shoulder. Injured with a severe wound, now the monster lifts itself, rearing into the breezes. Now it plunges within the waters. Now it whirls over like a fierce boar when a pack of dogs—resounding all around—terrify the boar. Perseus evades the greedy snapping teeth with his swift winged sandals. And with his scythe he scourges where the beast lies exposed, now the back, planted above with empty conch shells, now the ribs of the sides, now where the slenderest tail tapers into a fish. The beast spews out waves mixed with purple blood. The wings drip heavily with spray. Nor daring to trust further his drenched winged sandals, Perseus sees that the crag, which projects with its high summit from the waters, is standing still but is hidden by the sea's motion. Leaning on this crag and holding the first yoke of the cliff with his left hand, three and four times Perseus thrusts his iron sword through the ribs, stricken again and again. Shouts and applause fill the shores and the gods' lofty homes. Cassiopeia and Cepheus, Andromeda's father, rejoice and greet their son-in-law and acknowledge him as the support and savior of the house. The girl, loosened from her chains, steps forth, the prize and cause of the labor.
>
> *(Ovid,* Metamorphoses *4.706–739)*

C. *Perseus and Andromeda, red-figure loutrophoros (water jug), c. 340 BCE (southern Italy). This monster is a winged serpentine creature with a long saw-toothed snout, spiky crest down its neck, and dorsal fin. Scales are rendered with white dots, and the coiling, serpentine tail ends in a bifurcated caudal fin.*

50 Balearic slingers from the Balearic Islands east of the Iberian Peninsula were highly skilled and served in many foreign armies as lightly armed infantry, including Hannibal's (Livy, *From the Foundation of the City* 27.2) and Caesar's (*BG* 2.7).

51 Son of Inachus, a king of Argos and Perseus' distant ancestor.

FIGURE 3.5C Perseus and Andromeda. Repatriated. With kind permission of the National Archaeological Museum, Taranto, inv 194764.

D. A *third* ketos *is invoked as punishment for a disrespectful child. In short, Theseus' son Hippolytus is punished by Venus/Aphrodite because the young man had refused to worship her actively (i.e., he refused to have sex). Venus makes Theseus' bride Phaedra (a princess of Crete and sister of his first wide Ariadne) fall in love with her stepson. Hippolytus rejects Phaedra, and Phaedra seeks revenge for her wounded vanity by accusing Hippolytus of lewd behavior. To punish his seemingly disrespectful son, Theseus demands terminal vengeance, and Theseus' father, Neptune/Poseidon, complies with a sea bull that emerges from the surf and terrifies Hippolytus' horses, sending the innocent son to his death. The gruesome event occurs off-stage in Seneca's play, described by a messenger.*

> When Hippolytus left the city in flight with a disturbed gait, unrolling a speedy course with hasty steps, he drove thunder-footed horses swiftly under the high yoke, and he bound the horses' mouths subdued with restricting bridles. Then saying much to himself and deprecating his paternal soil, he called often upon his father, and sharply, with loosened reigns, he shook his whip, when suddenly from the deep, the vast sea thundered and grew up to the stars. No wind was blowing on the salt-sea, no part of the calm sky rumbled, and a storm

of its own making drove the placid sea. Not so violently does the South Wind throw the Sicilian Strait into disorder, nor so fiercely does the Ionian Gulf surge when the Northwest Wind prevails, when rocks quiver in the waves and white foam strikes Leucate's[52] summit. The huge sea surges into a vast mound, and the swelling deep rushes the monster towards land. Nor is so great a scourge piled up for ships. It threatens the lands. By no means is the flood rolled forth in a light course, but—pregnant in some overloaded fold or other—the billowing sea carries the beast. What land will show this new head to the stars? Is a new Cycladic island arising?[53] The creature hides the crags celebrated with the divine power of the Epidaurean god[54] and the Scironean rocks, notorious for Sciron's crime and a land pressed in by two straits.[55]

While stunned, we wonder at these things. Behold, the entire sea bellows, and the cliffs all around resound in reply. The highest summit drips with expelled salt-water. The monster foams and ejects water in alternating turns just like a physeter-whale, capacious in its mouth, pouring out its ingested flood through the deep straits of Ocean. The stricken ball of water bristles and unbinds itself and conveys itself to the shore, an evil greater than fear. The deep sea rushes onto the land and follows its own *ketos*. The quivering shakes its mouth. What an appearance its huge body makes! Loftily carrying its blue neck, a bull raises its high crest up on its green brow. Shaggy ears stand, the eyes' color is variable, both which the overlord of a wild flock and a creature from under the waves might have. Here the eyes spew out flame. Here they blaze remarkably with a dark-blue stamp. The fleshy neck lifts up strapping muscles, and the broad nostrils snort with gaping breaths. The chest and dewlap are green with clinging moss. The long flank is sprinkled with red seaweed. Behind the back, the utmost appearance comes together into a monster. And the huge beast drags an immense scaly appendage, such as a *ketos* in the farthest sea that might swallow down or smash boats as they are urged on.

The earth trembles, the frightened flock flee in all directions through the field, nor does the shepherd remember to follow his own flock. Every wild beast flees from the woodland, every hunter shudders, bloodless with icy fear. Alone free from fear, Hippolytus holds his horses with tight reins, and, with the encouragement of a familiar voice, he urges them on, fearful. There is a steep road along broken crags towards Argos, touching the nearby tracts of the sea below. Here that mass of the *ketos* sharpens and prepares its anger. When it readies its intentions and, testing itself sufficiently, it rolls itself out on a steep path,

52 Lefkada, just off the western shore of north-central Greece, so-called for its white limestone cliffs.

53 Perhaps referring to Thia which emerged in 46 CE (Mela, *On the Circuit of the World* 2.111; Pliny, *NH* 5.70).

54 Asclepius, son of Apollo and a god of healing who oversaw a significant healing shrine at Epidaurus on the eastern coast of the Peloponnese.

55 #2.2.7A.

touching the top of the ground with a hurried step, and menacingly it stands fast in front of the agitated chariot team.

1064. In response, rising up with a brutal mien, threateningly, Hippolytus does not change his expression and he thunders a loud warning, "By no means does this empty terror break my spirit, for it is my paternally inherited labor to vanquish bulls."[56] Straightaway the horses, not yielding to the reins, snatch the chariot away and swerve along the highway, and—wherever panic-stricken rage conveys the frenzied horses—here they proceed to go and drive themselves through the rocks. But, like a helmsman in a roiling sea holds his ship fast, lest it bear its side obliquely, and he cheats the wave with his skill, by no means otherwise does Hippolytus guide his chariot.[57] Now he draws the horses' mouths to be bound with tight reigns, now he curbs their backs repeatedly with a twisting whip. His constant companion follows, now plucking equal spaces. Now the sea-bull flits face to face with the team, bringing terror from every side. Nor is it permitted to flee further. For the dreadful, horn-bearing beast of the deep sea rushes at them with its entire mouth. Then the thunder-footed horses, frightened in their quaking mind, reject the commands and struggle to snatch themselves out from their yoke, and upright, rearing on their hind legs, they flee and cast off their burden. Poured headlong on his face, Hippolytus catches his body falling in a noose, and, the more he fights, the more he tightens the winding knots.

(Seneca, Phaedra *1000–1087)*

E. *In the delightfully satirical and exaggerated* True Story *by Lucian, we have a fanciful encounter between a ship's passengers, just returned from the moon, and a pod of sea monsters, one of whom swallows the ship, passengers and all, an episode evoking Odysseus' adventures. The inmates eventually escape by building a bonfire and escaping through the monster's gaping mouth.*

30. On the third day after this, we saw Ocean clearly, but land not at all, except for the regions in the air. And they appeared fiery and exceedingly bright. On the fourth day, around noon, as the wind abated and fell off, we were set down on the sea. When we touched water, we rejoiced marvelously and we were very happy and we made merry. And alighting into the sea, we went swimming. And the sea happened to be calm and steady.

31. It seems that a change for the better is often the beginning of greater evils. After sailing for only two days in fair weather, the third day showing itself to the rising sun, we suddenly saw wild animals and many sea monsters and other creatures: among these the largest was 1500 *stadia* long. He came at us,

56 Hippolytus' father, Theseus, killed both the bull of Marathon and that bull's son, the Minotaur, a man-bull hybrid.

57 The simile draws on Neptune's dual role as god of the sea and horses: see #3.11.1.

gaping, stirring up the sea far in advance, washed all around with foam. And he revealed his teeth larger than the *phalloi* of Dionysus[58] in our country, all sharp like thorns and white like ivory. Bidding each other final goodbyes and embracing, we therefore waited. The monster was at hand, and gulping he swallowed us with our ship. To be sure, he came close to dashing us to pieces with his teeth. But the ship slipped inside through the crevices. When we were inside the belly, first it was dark, and we saw nothing. Later, when his mouth gaped, we saw a great hollow, flat and high on all sides, and large enough for a city of 10,000 inhabitants to dwell in. In the middle were fish, great and tiny, and many other mangled wild creatures, masts and anchors of ships, and the bones of people and cargo, and in the middle, so it seemed to me, the sediment of mud which the monster had gulped down. Then from the slime grew woods and every sort of tree and vegetables sprouted, and everything seemed to exist from cultivation. The perimeter of the land was 240 *stadia*. It was possible to see sea-birds—cormorants and kingfishers—nesting there on the trees.

32. Then therefore, we wept for a long time. Later, rousing my companions, we shored up the ship, and rubbing sticks together and lighting a fire, we made dinner from what was at hand. For there was plentiful meat of fishes of all sorts nearby, and we still had water from the Morning Star.[59] Then, getting up the next day, whenever the *ketos* gaped widely, we saw mountains here, only sky here, and even ships quite frequently. And we understood that the beast was conveyed sharply to every part of the sea. When we became accustomed to spending time this way, taking seven of my companions, we set out to the forest, wanting to examine everything. Traversing not quite five full *stadia* we found a temple of Poseidon, as the inscription revealed, and not far away many graves and funeral steles on them near a spring of clear water. We also heard a dog barking, and smoke appeared from afar and something like a farmhouse.

(Lucian, True Story *1.30–32)*

3.6 Ritual Purity and Miasma

A. *Water was a powerful tool of purification on both small and large scales (#1.9.11A). Before ritual acts or entering sacred places, worshippers would bathe or sprinkle themselves with water, as Aeneas does before entering the Underworld.*

Aeneas occupies the entrance and sprinkles his entire body with water, and he binds the (golden) branch[60] on the threshold.

(Vergil, Aeneid *6.635–636)*

58 An erect male genital, a symbol of Dionysus worship.
59 The expedition had previously visited the "Morning Star," the planet Venus.
60 See #3.10C.

B. *After the Trojan War, Aeneas and his followers were taken in by Dido, queen of Carthage, and Aeneas and Dido became lovers. He then abandoned her to establish his own kingdom in Italy. Here, a distraught and angry Dido curses Aeneas ("may there be no love or treaties between our peoples!"), and she prepares to commit suicide: her funerary preparations require ritual purity.*

> My dear nurse, place my sister, Anna, here. Tell her to hurry to sprinkle herself with clear river water and bring the sacrificial cattle with her and the indicated propitiatory sacrifices. Thus, may she come, and you yourself bind your temples with a dutiful ribbon. My mind is set on accomplishing sacred rites to Stygian Jove,[61] which I have prepared, duly begun, and putting an end to my troubles and entrusting the pyre of that Dardanian[62] man to flame.
>
> *(Vergil,* Aeneid *4.634–640)*

C. *The Parilia was an ancient festival intended to purify shepherds and their flocks, overseen by Pales, an obscure rural deity. As Rome transitioned from an agricultural society, the* Parilia *was aligned with Rome's birthday celebration (April 21, legendarily founded in 753 BCE) at which time Romans were purified annually with smoke and water.*

> Night has gone, and Aurora (Dawn) rises. I am requested to sing about the *Parilia.* I am not asked in vain if nurturing Pales favors me. Cherishing Pales, show favor to me as I sing your pastoral rites, if I attend your festive rites dutifully. Certainly I have brought ash from a calf and bean stems with a full hand, chaste offerings for purification. I have certainly leapt three times across flames positioned in a row, and the moist laurel branch has sprinkled dewy waters on me. The goddess is moved, and she favors my work. My sailing skiff leaves. My sails now have their own fair winds.
>
> *(Ovid,* Fasti *4.721–730)*

D. *Bodies were purified with smoke and water before burial, as when the corpse of Aeneas' trumpeter Misenus washed ashore after the Trojan fugitives reached Italy (Misenus had challenged the gods to a musical competition, and Triton caused the Trojan to drown: Vergil,* Aeneid *6.170–74). Misenus was written into the Italian landscape as Cape Miseno.*

> No less, meanwhile, the Trojans weep for Misenus on the beach and they carry out last rites for thankless ash. At first they build a huge pyre, rich with pitch-pines and cut oak, whose sides they weave with black fronds, and in front

61 The god of the Underworld, Jupiter's (Zeus') brother Dis Pater/Hades, the Jupiter of the River Styx.
62 Dardanus founded a kingdom at the foot of Mt. Ida near Troy. His son, Ilus, founded the city of Troy.

they situate funereal cypresses, and they embellish it above with gleaming weapons. Some fetch warm water and bronze cauldrons surging with flames, and they wash and anoint icy Misenus' corpse. There is a groan. Then they place the wept-over limbs on the couch, and they place over him purple garments, the customary coverings. Part of the mourners come under the huge bier, a sad duty, and, in the custom of their ancestors, turned away, they hold the torch beneath the bier. Collected gifts are consumed by the fire: frankincense, a funeral feast, bowls with pouring oil. After the ashes sink and the flame rests, they bathe the remains and thirsty embers with wine, and Corynaeus[63] covers the gathered bones in a bronze urn. That same man purifies his companions three times, sprinkling them with light dew. And with the branch of a lucky olive he lustrates them and speaks last words.

(Vergil, Aeneid *6.212–231)*

E. *Those who had committed crimes might also be purified with water. When the Trojan War ended, the Greek commander-in-chief, Agamemnon, was murdered by his wife, Clytemnestra (Agamemnon had sacrificed one of their daughters to appease the anger of Artemis, whom he insulted after a hunting expedition: for the story, see Aeschylus,* Agamemnon*). Agamemnon's ghost then sought vengeance and enjoined his son Orestes to kill Clytemnestra (Aeschylus,* Libation Bearers*). After that murder, Orestes sought expiation at Troezen (southwest of Athens), where he was purified by water from the Hippocrene ("Horse spring"), created by Pegasus.*

In front of the temple of Apollo is a structure called the "tent of Orestes." Before he was cleansed of his mother's blood, no one from Troezen wanted to receive him at their homes. Situating and feasting him there at the tent, they lustrated him until they had purified him. Even now, the descendants of those, who had expiated Orestes, feast there on particular days. A little way from the tent, they say that the cleansing implements were buried, and from them grew a bay laurel which stands in front of Orestes' tent even to our day.

They say that they purified Orestes with cleansing implements and other things and with water from the Hippocrene. For among the Troezens there is also a spring called "Horse," and the story about it does not differ from the Boeotian legend. For the people of Troezen say that the earth sent up water to the horse Pegasus, touching the ground with his hoof.

(Pausanias, Description of Greece *2.31.8–9)*

F. *Imprecisely understood as "ritual pollution" and often resulting from hubris, miasma includes transgressions against institutional laws, ethics, and the inappropriate shedding of bodily fluids (blood, menses, urine) on sacred ground or*

63 A minor character among of Aeneas' followers.

waters. Apollonides of Smyrna (1st century CE*) imagines a spring bemoaning its victimization by an act of miasma.*

Pure—for the Nymphs have gifted that name to my spring, pre-eminent over all dripping things—when a pirate had killed some men reclining nearby and washed his bloody hands in my hallowed waters, having reversed my sweet flow, I no longer bubble up for travelers. For, who will still call me "Pure?"
(Apollonides of Smyrna, Greek Anthology *9.257)*

G. *The epigrammatic poet Antiphanes of Megalopolis recounts a similar lament.*

Having streamed once upon a time with well-watered flows, I am now deprived of all my nymphs, even to the droplets. Defiling me with gore, a man-killer washed his hands in my streams. From that time my maidens have fled the sunlight, saying, "we are nymphs who mingle only with Bacchus, and not with Ares."[64]
(Antiphanes of Megalopolis, Greek Anthology *9.258)*

3.7 Divination by Water

Greeks and Romans employed many methods to ascertain the will of the gods, including scrutinizing the flight patterns of birds (auspices) and spots on entrails (haruspicy), interpreting breezes rustling through Zeus' sacred oak tree at Dodona, and consulting oracles. Some of these methods involved water: #7.4.3A.

A. *A well at Patrae (western Peloponnese) provides medical prognostication.*

In front of the sanctuary of Demeter is a spring. On the side towards the temple, a stone wall rises up, on the other side there is a path down to the spring. Here there is an oracle without deceit, not for every issue, but only for the ill. Tying a mirror to a cord of fine thread, they send it down, measuring out the distance so that the mirror does not come down to the bottom of the spring, but so far as it lightly touches the surface of the water with the circular edge of the mirror. And then, praying to the goddess and burning incense, they look at the mirror: it shows them whether the sick person is living or deceased.
(Pausanias, Description of Greece *7.21.12)*

B. *Another spring in Lycia (southern Turkey, northwest of Cyprus) is more generous with its predictions.*

Very close to Cyanae in the direction of Lycia is an oracle of Apollo Thyrxeus.[65] The water near Cyanae offers anyone looking into it all the things he wants to see.
(Pausanias, Description of Greece *7.21.13)*

64 *Bacchus*: metonymy for wine; *Ares*, god of war, here, metonymy for blood.
65 An obscure epithet of uncertain meaning.

C. *Also in Lycia, people sought messages from Apollo through sacred fish at a particular whirlpool. Athenaeus did not explain how the omens were interpreted.*

> Nor will I be silent about the fish-prognosticating people in Lycia, into whom Polycharmus inquired in his second Lycian book (*FGrH* 770 F 1): when they go towards the sea, where there is a grove of Apollo near the beach, in which there is a whirlpool on the dunes. Those seeking divinations there come to the side of the whirlpool, holding two skewers with roasted meat on each one, ten pieces in number. The priest is seated in silence at the grove, and the one seeking the prophecy tosses the skewers into the whirlpool and observes what happens. After tossing in the skewers, the whirlpool is filled with seawater, and such a great number of fish are at hand that the unusual sight inspires astonishment. And bystanders are cautious because of the size of the fish. Then the interpreter announces the nature of the fishes: thus does someone seeking a prophecy obtain a response from the priest concerning the matters he is praying over. Sea perch, grey fish, sometimes even whales and sawfish appear, and many unusual fishes and strange to see. Artemidoros[66] in the tenth book of his *Geographies* said that, according to the locals, a spring of sweet water emerges from which a whirlpool appears. And there are large fish in this whirling place. Those sacrificing to these fishes plunge offerings on wooden spits piercing them through with meat, boiled and roasted, and barley-cakes. The harbor is thus called *Dinon* ("Whirlpool") as is the place.
>
> *(Athenaeus,* Learned Banqueters *8.333d–f)*

D. *One prophetic spring at Taenaron in the southern Peloponnese lost its divinatory powers to an act of pollution.*

> On Taenaron there is a spring, but it now offers nothing of wonder. Before, so they say, it offered those looking into its water the ability to see harbors and ships. Some woman stopped the water from showing these maritime things when she washed her dirty clothes in the spring.
>
> *(Pausanias,* Description of Greece *3.25.8)*

E. *Lecanomancy, divination by means of a dish of water, was also practiced. One historical example is recorded by the philosopher and novelist Apuleius of Madaurus, Numidia (c. 124 CE–c. 170 CE), who was himself accused of using magic. Apuleius published his defense speech, the* Apology, *thus preserving a trove of knowledge about ancient magic.*

> When the people of Tralles[67] were consulting with magical deliberation concerning the outcome of the Mithridatic War (88–63 BCE), seeing an image of Mercury in water, a boy prophesied what would happen in 160 verses.
>
> *(Apuleius,* Apology *42.6)*

66 Artemidoros of Ephesus, a 1st century BCE Greek geographer extracted by Strabo and others.

67 Near the Meander River in Turkey.

F. *A lengthy collection of chants and incantations, dating from 100s BCE to 400s CE, survives on papyrus rolls from Egypt, including spells for lecanomancy.*

Inquiry of bowl divination and necromancy: whenever you want to inquire about matters, take a bronze vessel, either a bowl or a saucer of whatever kind you wish. Pour water: rainwater if you are calling upon heavenly gods, seawater if gods of the earth, river water if Osiris or Serapis, spring-water if the dead. Holding the vessel on your knees, pour out green olive oil, bend over the vessel and speak the prescribed spell. And address whatever god you want and ask about whatever you wish, and he will reply to you and tell you about anything. If he has spoken, dismiss him with the spell of dismissal, and you who have used this spell will be amazed.

The spell spoken over the vessel is: AMOUN AUANTAU / LAIMOUTAU RIPTOU MANTAUI IMANTOU LANTOU LAPTOUMI ANCHOMACH ARAMOUMI, hither to me, O NN god; appear to me this very hour and do not frighten my eyes. Hither to me, O NN god, be attentive to me because he wishes and commands this. ACHCHOR ACHCHOR ACHACHACH PTOUMI CHACHCHO CHARACHOCH CHAPTOUME CHORACHARACHOCH APTOUMI MECHOCHAITOU CHAKACHPTOU CHACHCHO CHARACHO PTENACHOCHEU . . .

*(*Greek Magical Papyri *PGM 4.222–242; trans. E.N. O'Neil; cf.* Greek Magical Papyri.*5.1–53)*

3.8 Sacred Fish/Tame Fish

A. *Sacred fish were widely cultivated: at Stephanopolis in Epirus (northwestern Greece), Sicily, and at Zeus' shrine in Labraunda in Caria (southwestern Turkey) where a clear spring was populated with bejewelled fishes. See #6.3.7E§4.*

Some fishes, accustomed to human hands and answering to a call and gladly receiving treats, exist in many places, and they are cultivated, just as in Epirus, in a town long ago called Stephanopolis ("Crown-city"), in the temple of Tyche ("Luck"), in the tanks at each side of the approaches, and in Helorus in Sicily, which was once a Syracusan citadel, and in the sanctuary of Zeus Labrandeus in a spring of clear, flowing water. And the fish there have golden necklaces and earrings. To be sure these are also gold.

(Aelian, NA *12.30; cf. Pliny,* NH *32.16)*

B. *Fish in Venus' pond at Hierapolis in Syria were also bedecked with gold and seemed to enjoy human contact.*

For at Myris in Lycia, in the spring of Apollo which they call Curia, fish—summoned three times by a pipe—come to provide augury: it is a joyful thing for those consulting the fish when the creatures snatch up meat tossed at them, but it is dreadful when they bat the morsels away with their tails. At Hierapolis in Syria in a lake of Venus, the fish obey the voices of the groundskeepers: when called they come, decked out in gold, eager to be tickled, and they offer their gaping mouths to those offering their hands.

(Pliny, NH *32.17)*

C. *Fish dwelling in the Arethusa Spring (#1.6C–D) are sacred to Artemis, as recounted by Diodorus Siculus (fl. c. 60–30 BCE), from Agyrium in Sicily, who composed a universal history in Greek, from the Trojan War to his own day. Of the 40 books, 1–5 and 11–20 survive plus fragments. The work was organized geographically and ethnographically, and Diodorus' research took him throughout Asia and Europe. While often dismissed as a mere compiler, much information not recorded elsewhere is preserved in Diodorus.*

From the gods Artemis took the island at Syracuse, the one named Ortygia after her both by the oracles and people. Likewise, these nymphs, to please Artemis, sent up on this island a great spring named Arethusa. Not only in ancient times did this spring have large and many fish, and even in our own times these fish continue to tarry there, sacred and untouched by people. Very often when folk eat them in wartime, the deity has indicated something contrary to expectation, and she has inflicted those daring to consume her fishes with terrible misfortunes.

(Diodorus Siculus, Library of History *5.3.5–6)*

3.9 Magical Effects of Sea Creatures

A. *Some water creatures were also thought to have sympathetic effects, as for example the very beautiful moonfish whose powers seem to align with lunar phases.*

Demostratus,[68] a man knowledgeable about fishing wisdom and, by Zeus, effective in interpreting it, says that there is some fish, beautiful in form, and it is called Selene ("Moon"), short in size, dark blue in appearance, broad in shape. Demostratus also says that the moonfish has fins on the back and that it raises these up, but the fins are soft and neither resistant nor rough. And when this moonfish swims under water, the fins open up and display half a circle, and to look at them they are the shape of a half-moon. The Cypriote fishermen say these things. But this is Demostratus' reckoning: if caught under a full moon the moonfish itself is also full, and it makes trees full if, bringing it close, you might attach it to trees. Under a waning moon, the fish wastes away and suffers. And, fastened to plants, these also dry up. When wells are being dug, if under

68 Demostratus, whose book on fishing informed Aelian, is otherwise unknown.

a waxing moon someone might throw this moonfish back into the water which you have found, there will be ever-flowing water, and the well will never fail. If under a waning moon, the water will stop. To be sure, if you toss this fish into a rising spring, you will hence have it either very full or empty.

(Aelian, NA *15.4–5)*

B. *Stingrays were also thought to have the ability to kill trees. See also #2.2.4A.*

The turtledove of the sea has the sharpest sting and is more dangerous than all other animals. As proof, if you fix a marine turtledove to a tree, thriving and especially tall, the tree dries up, down to its foundation, not at some later time, but now. And if you scratch any living thing with a marine turtledove, you kill it.

(Aelian, NA *2.36, cf.* NA *8.26)*

3.10 Water and Death

A. *In Near Eastern and Indo-European traditions, waterways separate the worlds of the living and the dead. Those who cross between these regions could also mediate between humans and gods, between life and death, between the ritual world and the "real" world. Gilgamesh crosses the sea to learn the secret of immortality (tablet 10). Egyptian souls cross the Lily Lake to reach the Field of Reeds where they would enjoy eternal life. Odysseus could only reach Hades, the Greek realm of the dead, after sailing north through Ocean, as Circe instructs here.*

"Divinely born son of Laertes, much-contriving Odysseus, may your desire for a pilot for your ship not worry you, but, after stepping your mast and spreading your white sails, sit and let Boreas' blast carry the ship northward. But when you have driven through Ocean in your ship, there is a headland and grove of Persephone: tall black poplars and fruit-shedding willows. Beach your ships by deep-eddying Ocean. But you yourself go to the dank house of Hades. There into the Acheron flow the Pyriphlegethon River and the Cocytus, which is an efflux of the Styx, the confluence of two resounding rivers."[69]

(Homer, Odyssey *10.504–15)*

B. *While the Underworld was reserved for the dead, some mythical characters (including Hercules) traveled to Hades and safely returned to the world of the living, symbolizing human conquest over death. Aeneas, founder of the Roman race, also traveled to the Underworld to see his deceased father and learn about his legacy. Accompanied by Apollo's priestess, the Sibyl of Cumae (near Naples),*

69 Rivers of the Underworld: #1.3.3E.

Aeneas must therefore cross the River Styx, which prevented both the living and the unburied dead from entering Hades. The Sibyl is speaking.

> "Born from Anchises, most resolute offspring of the gods, you see the deep marshes of the Cocytus and the Stygian swamp, on whose divine authority the gods fear to swear and deceive. This whole crowd, which you see, is resourceless and unburied. That ferryman is Charon. Those whom the stream conveys are buried. Nor is Charon allowed to transport them across the bristling shores and rough waters before their bones have been at rest in their burial places. The unburied wander a hundred years, and they flit around these shores. Then, admitted at length, they see again the hoped-for swamps."
>
> *(Vergil,* Aeneid *6.322–330)*

C. *Charon is reluctant to allow the living Aeneas passage across the Styx, until the Sibyl shows him a golden bough, a gift for Persephone and the token assuring that Aeneas' visit to the Underworld is sanctioned by the gods. See also #5.2.4E.*

> Therefore, the Sibyl and Aeneas carry on with their journey begun, and they approach the river Styx. When, from the Stygian water, the boatman sees them come through the quiet grove and turn a foot to the bank, he approaches first and upbraids them further with words, "Whoever you are, armed, you who aim at our rivers, come now, tell me why you arrive, now check your step there. This is a place of shadows, of sleep, and of drowsy night. It is not in accord with divine will to convey living bodies in the Stygian boat . . ."
>
> Admiring the venerable gift, the decreed branch (golden bough) seen after a long time, Charon directs his dark-blue ferry and nears the shore. Then he drives out the other souls who were sitting on the long beams, and he clears the gangways. At the same time, he accepts huge Aeneas in his hollow ferry. The sewn-together skiff groans under the weight and, full of chinks, it takes on much swamp-water.[70] At length, across the water, Charon sets both priestess and man safely on the shapeless mud and gray swamp-grass.
>
> *(Vergil,* Aeneid *6.384–391, 408–416)*

D. *The Hyperboreans, a mythical people dwelling "beyond Boreas" (the chilly North Wind), at the northern extreme of the world, were thought to be just, wise, and hospitable, and they were widely celebrated as carefree, living in a perfect climate and in harmony with the gods. When they have their fill of living, they seek death in the Ocean.*

> The Hyperboreans inhabit groves and forests, and when satiety of living—more so than weariness—has seized them, joyfully crowned with garlands, they hurl

70 The flimsy ferry is accustomed to conveying weightless souls, and thus reacts to Aeneas' fulsome weight.

themselves headlong into the sea from a certain crag.[71] For them, this is an exceptional funeral.

(Mela, On the Circuit of the World *3.37; cf. Pliny,* NH *4.89)*

E. *In the 4th century CE, Quintus Smyrnaeus, presumably from Smyrna (Turkey), composed a 14-book* Posthomerica, *recounting the post-Iliadic events of the Trojan War. Here water deities and beasts mourn the death of Achilles.*

Then the daughters of Nereus, who hold the great depth, give ear to rising laments. On the hearts of all there falls a grievous pain. They lament pitiably. The Hellespont is also distressed. Covered in dark-blue robes, the Nereids hasten hurriedly to where the Achaean fleet floats, with all speed through the deep blue swell. And the sea parts for them as they go. They are borne along with a din, like cranes foreboding a great storm. Sea monsters mourn banefully with weeping. The Nereids arrive there, wailing terribly for the dauntless child of their sister.

(Quintus Smyrnaeus, Posthomerica *3.582–594; cf. Homer,* Odyssey *24.47–62)*

3.11 Sailor Cults

3.11.1 Poseidon

A. Poseidon/Neptune was recognized as the primary Olympian god of the sea, and his abundance of sanctuaries at harbors, such as at Sounion, on Attica's southern tip, 60 meters (200 feet) above the water, were important beacons, serving sailors at sea and standing as a testament to the precariousness of seafaring. While Poseidon was often spiteful and angry, causing storms and earthquakes, he was also propitiated as a "savior of ships."

About Poseidon, the great god, I begin to sing, shaker of the earth and master of the unharvested sea, who also holds Helicon and broad Aegae. To you, Earthshaker, the gods have divided a two-fold honor: to be a tamer of horses and savior of ships. Greetings, earth-moving Poseidon, dark-blue-haired, and, Blessed One, having a well-disposed heart, aid those who travel by sea.

*(*Homeric Hymn *22* to Poseidon*)*

B. *In 480 BCE during the Persian Wars, a storm at sea destroyed a number of Persian ships but abated after Greek sailors offered prayers and sacrifices to Poseidon.*

Then on the fourth day the storm stopped. For the day-scouts, running down from the Euboean summits on the second day after the storm first began,

71 Voluntary suicide among the elderly is attested among some remote peoples (Massagetes: Herodotus, *Histories* 1.216.2; Iazyges: Valerius Flaccus, *Argonautica* 6.122).

described everything that happened regarding the shipwreck. When they learned this, praying to Poseidon the savior and pouring out libations, they went back to Artemisium,[72] hoping that there would be just a few ships opposing them.

(Herodotus, Histories *7.192)*

C. *Alpheius of Mitylene on Lesbos (late 1st century BCE) has invoked Poseidon for safe passage.*

You who have power over swift-ships, master of horses, and the great lookout-spot hanging over Euboea, give a fair sailing up to Ares' city[73] to those praying and loosing their dock-lines from Syria.

(Alpheius of Mitylene, Greek Anthology *9.90)*

D. *At Argos in the eastern Peloponnese, Poseidon received horses sacrificed by drowning.*

The water from Zeus (rain), flowing down from the mountains into the "Untilled Plain" renders the plain unplowable, and nothing hinders the field from becoming a lake, except that the water is buried in a chasm of the earth. The water disappears and comes up again as *Dine* ("Whirlpool"). *Dine* is sweet water emerging from the sea along what is called *Genethlium* in Argolis. Long ago, into *Dine* the Argives tossed horses arrayed in their tack for Poseidon.

(Pausanias, Description of Greece *8.7.1–2; cf. Homer,* Iliad *21.122–132)*

E. *In 74 BCE, Mithridates VI Eupator (r. 120–63 BCE) offered sacrifices to Poseidon to protect his troops before engaging Roman combatants in Paphlagonia, a region along the southern coast of the Pontus.*

At the beginning of the spring, Mithridates tested his navy. He made the usual sacrifice to Zeus Stratius ("of the army") and plunged into the sea a chariot with four white horses to Poseidon.

(Appian, Mithridatic Wars *70)*

F. *Pompey's youngest son, Sextus, fighting against Octavian and Antony in the 30s BCE, cultivated Neptune (Dio Cassius,* Roman History *48.48.5; Appian,* Civil War *5.100.416; see #7.4.3A–C) and sacrificed a live horse by drowning as a thank-offering. Lucius Annaeus Florus (c. 74–130 CE) was an African-born Roman historian.*

On account of so many successful campaigns, Sextus sacrificed 100 bulls with golden horns at Pelorum,[74] and he also sent breathing horses into the strait, as

72 On Euboea's northern coast.

73 Rome, founded by Romulus, a son of Ares/Mars, the Roman god of war.

74 The cape near Messina on Sicily's northeastern point. The bulls' horns had been gilded to enhance their sacrificial value.

gifts for Neptune, so that the ruler of the sea might allow him, Sextus, to rule in Neptune's own sea.

(Florus, Epitome of Roman History *2.18.3)*

G. *Tuna were a popular delicacy and big business (see #6.3.6C, #6.3.10B–C), and the hunt was safeguarded with prayers and offerings to Poseidon the Averter of Evil.*

After tuna have been caught in a hunt in the Pontus: I would also say off Sicily. For intending what else did Sophron write his delightful *Tuna-hunter*? There are tuna-hunts everywhere and elsewhere. After they are already entwined in the fishing-net, all the fishermen at this time pray to Poseidon *Alexikakos* ("Averter of Evil"). I deem it worthy to explain why this is the god's epithet, wanting to inquire about it for my own part, and I agree that this is the reason: they seek from the powerful god of the sea, brother of Zeus, that neither a swordfish will arrive as fellow-traveler for the tuna-school nor a dolphin. At any rate, the noble swordfish very often cuts through the net and sends the herd of captive fishes to break away free. The dolphin is also an animal plotting against the net. For they are clever at gnawing through the nets.[75]

(Aelian, NA *15.6)*

H. *In Corcyra (Corfu), a "tuna-lookout"-bull (*thunnoskopos*) would announce the appearance of schools of tuna off the shore.*

For someone entering the *temenos*,[76] there is a bronze bull, the handiwork of Theopropus of Aegina, a votive offering of the Corcyraeans. It is said that a bull in Corcyra, leaving behind the other cattle and descending to the shore, would moo. When this same thing happened everyday, the cowherd came down to the sea, and he saw a crowd of tuna-fish, uncountable in number. He clarified this matter to the Corcyraeans in the city: they had sent envoys to Delphi, since they met with distress in attempting to catch tuna. And, thus, they sacrificed that bull to Poseidon and, straightaway after the sacrifice, they caught the fish, and their dedication of thanksgiving both at Olympia and Delphi was a tenth of the catch.

(Pausanias, Description of Greece *10.9.3–4)*

I. *In the 2nd century CE, Neptune received a dedicatory inscription of thanksgiving, perhaps for safe passage to Rome.*

Sacred to Augustan Neptune and the Nymphs, Titus Aelius Olympas, a freedman of Augustus,[77] a procurator, paid his vow willingly and deservedly.

*(*CIL *6.536)*

75 #2.2.11I.

76 #2.2.13B.i note.

77 Our procurator was probably in service to Hadrian (r. 117–138: Publius Aelius Traianus Hadrianus Augustus) or his heir, Lucius Aelius Caesar.

3.11.2 Zeus

Poseidon's brother Zeus/Jupiter also protected sailors at sea and was recognized as the patron of the Pharos lighthouse at Alexandria, erected for the "safety of sailors" (Strabo, Geography *17.1.6) and topped with a statue of Zeus (Diodorus Siculus 18.14.1) or Poseidon (*Greek Anthology *9.674; see #5.3.7B–G). Poseidippus of Pella was an epigrammatic poet among the courtiers of Ptolemy II Philadelphus in Alexandria (r. 284–246 BCE). The engineer and architect Sostratus of Cnidus is credited with designing the Pharos lighthouse at Alexandria. Note the reference to celestial navigation.*

O Lord Proteus, Sostratus of Knidos, son of Dexiphanes, established this savior of the Greeks, guardian of the Pharos. For in Egypt there are no hills for beacons as on the islands, but a sea-ground breakwater stretches out, affording a safe anchorage. For the sake of this, a straight and upright tower now cuts through the aether and shines by day from an unapproachable distance. All night long a sailor, hastening on the waves, will see the great flame blazing from the summit. Even if they were to run towards Taurus' Horn,[78] navigators would not miss the mark[79] of Zeus the Savior, Proteus, sailing by this guide.

(Posidippus, Epigram *115)*

3.11.3 Apollo

A. *As a god of settlement, Apollo was a significant maritime deity (Greek settlements were invariably established by emigrees traveling on water), and Delphinius ("dolphin") is among Apollo's epithets. As a dolphin, Apollo guided Cretan sailors to Delphi to serve as his priests there.*

Then Phoebus Apollo thought in his heart: what men should he bring in as his priests, who might serve him in rocky Pytho?[80] Turning these things over, he noticed a swift ship on the wine-dark sea: in it were many men, and excellent ones, Cretans from Minoan Knossos,[81] they who perform sacrifices for the god and announce the oracular responses of Phoebus Apollo with the golden-sword, whatever prophecy he speaks from the laurel under the vales of Parnassus. In their black ship, for business and profit, they were sailing to sandy Pylos and its men.

But Phoebus Apollo fell in with them. In shape like a dolphin in the deep sea, the god sprang onto the swift ship, and there he lay, a great and terrible monster. And none of them contrived in their hearts to understand. But they wanted to cast the dolphin off. But he kept jolting the black ship in all directions, and he shook the ship's planks. Silent in the ship they sat, afraid. Nor did

78 I.e., employing the zodiac constellation Taurus, prominent in the winter sky, as a navigational beacon and thus sailing away from Alexandria.

79 #2.2.9A note.

80 Referring to Delphi, where Apollo slew a giant snake (Pytho).

81 King Minos' capital city, thus Minoan.

they loose the lines through the hollow, dark ship. Nor did they furl the sails of the dark-prowed ship. But as first they trimmed the ox-hide ropes, so they sailed. A quick Notos (South Wind) pressed the nimble ship from behind. First, they passed Malea, and then along the Laconian land they came to a sea-girt citadel and Taenaron,[82] the land of Helios who gladdens the heart, where lord Helios' thick-fleeced sheep always graze and occupy a delightful landscape.[83] The Cretan sailors wanted to stop their ship there, disembarking to consider the great marvel and to see with their eyes if the monster would stay on the decks of the hollow ship or dart back into the swelling salt-sea, abounding in fish. But the well-built ship did not obey the steering-oars. But it went holding the roads outside the rich Peloponnese. Thus, Lord Apollo who works from afar easily kept it straight with his breezy breath.

(Homeric Hymn *3* To Apollo *388–421)*

B. *As the Argonauts set off to obtain the Golden Fleece in Colchis on the Pontic Sea, Jason prayed to Apollo* Aktios *("of shores") and* Embasios *("of embarkation"). Apollo was also* Ekbasios *("of landings":* Argonautica *1.966, 1186) and* Neosoos *("protector of ships:* Argonautica *2.927). Here Jason prays.*

"Hear me, Lord, you who hold Pagasae and the city of the Ausonians named for my father, you who indicated fulfillment and an end of the path for me seeking your proclamation at Pytho, that you were the companion of my contests. Now you yourself lead the ship with my companions safe and sound to that place and back again to Hellas (Greece), and we will lay out on your altar as many splendid sacrifices of bulls as many of us as return. At Pytho and Ortygia[84] I will attend to countless gifts. Therefore, come now, Far-Shooter, and accept this sacrifice from us, the very first that we set before you as a good-faith offering on behalf of our ship. May I, Lord, loose the docking lines for a fate free from harm owing to your counsel. May your breeze breathe gently, by which we may sail enjoying fair weather on the sea."

(Apollonius, Argonautica *1.411–424; cf. 1.359–362)*

3.11.4 Aphrodite

A. *Born from the sea, Aphrodite/Venus naturally had robust maritime associations, including* akrostolia *(fitted to ships' prows) which often took the shape of a swan or goose, waterbirds that were sacred to Aphrodite (see #3.11.10, #6.1.1G). Here,*

82 Cape Maleas in the southeastern Peloponnese; Taenaron: Cape Matapan, west of Malea.

83 Helios, the sun god (#3.4.1), famous for seven herds of cattle (50 head each) and as many sheep. See #6.3.10A.

84 *Pytho*: Delphi; *Ortygia*: the site of Apollo's sister's birth.

Hesiod's version of Aphrodite's birth story. Sky/Ouranos was an elemental god who suppressed his children to avoid losing power.

First cutting Ouranos' genitals with unbreakable adamant, Kronos threw them from the land into the much-storming deep sea. As the genitalia were carried along the sea for a long time, around them arose white foam from the deathless skin, and within was nourished a maiden. First she drew near to Cythera,[85] very divine, then she went to Cyprus surrounded with water. From there she stepped, a lovely, compassionate deity, and grass grew up around her slender feet. Gods call her Aphrodite, as do human-folk, the foam-born goddess and beautifully garlanded Cytherea, owing to the fact that she was nurtured in *aphros* ("sea-foam"), but they also call her Cytherea because she arrived at Cythera, and also Cyprogenes ("Cyprus-born"), because she was born in stormy Cyprus, and laughter-loving because she was brought to light from Ouranos' genitals. Eros ("Love") accompanies her and the lovely Himeros ("Desire") follows her, when—just born—she first went to the tribe of gods. From the beginning she has this honor, obtained by lot as her share among human-folk and the deathless gods: the gossip of girls and their smiles and tricks and sweet affections and gentleness.

(Hesiod, Theogony *188–206)*

B. *Solon (640–560 BCE) was an Athenian statesman and constitutional reformer, one of the "Seven Sages" and champion of his people. Even Solon invoked Aphrodite's favor before setting out from Cyprus, an island sacred to Aphrodite.*

May purple-crowned Cypris send me from your renowned island in my swift ship. May she attend grace on this settlement and glory and a kindly return to my own fatherland.

(Solon F 19)

C. *Anyte of Tegea in Arcadia (c. 300 BCE) was so highly acclaimed in antiquity that she was nicknamed* Stephanos *("Garland"). Twenty-four of her elegant Greek epigrams survive, including this sensitive account of an Aphrodite statue that may have been a sailor's votive.*

Cyprian is this place: since it is always lovely for her to see the bright deep sea from land in order that she might make sailing pleasant for sailors. The sea is all around fearful, viewing clearly her brightly oiled wooden statue.

(Anyte of Tegea, Greek Anthology *9.144)*

85 A small island southeast of the Peloponnese.

D. *In this anonymous Greek epigram, Aphrodite protects navigation. For maritime trade: #6.1.*

Aeximenes set up this uncommonly beautiful wooden statue of Aphrodite, who keeps watch over all seamanship. Hail, O Lady of Cyprus, giving profit, accrued wealth, you will know the ship because it is in partnership with you.

(Anonymous, Greek Anthology *9.601)*

E. *Philodemus of Gadara in Jordan (110–40/35 BCE) was an Epicurean philosopher and epigrammatic poet who wrote on ethics, music, rhetoric, and theology, influencing Horace's* Art of Poetry. *Much of Philodemus' work is preserved in charred papyrus rolls from the Villa of the Papyri at Herculaneum on which the delicate work of unrolling and deciphering continues. Here, Aphrodite is* Galenaia *("the one who calms the sea").*

Cypris Galenaia, bridegroom lover, Cypris, ally of those who observe custom, Cypris, mother of storm-footed longing, Cypris, save me, half-pulled from the saffron-colored bridal chamber, frosted over my soul with Celtic snow, Cypris, save me, restful, babbling trivialities to no one, me, washed over by your purple sea, Cypris, you who love to bring ships to harbor, you who love passionate rites, Cypris, save me, Mistress, already at the harbors of the Naiads.[86]

(Philodemus, Greek Anthology *10.21)*

F. *In 688–685 BCE, assisting a shipload of severely seasick passengers and crew, Aphrodite granted a miracle at sea, providing an etiology for Naukratian garlands. For an Aphrodite ship-board sanctuary: #5.1.15D§207e.*

During the 23rd Olympiad,[87] our fellow citizen Herostratos, engaged in trade and sailing to many a place, once coming to port at Paphos on Cyprus, purchasing a small statue of Aphrodite, ancient in workmanship, he went carrying it to Naukratis.[88] As he was conveyed near Egypt, a sudden storm fell upon them, and it was not possible to see where the land was. All fled to the Aphrodite statue, entreating her to protect them. The goddess, for she was friendly to the Naukratians, suddenly filled all the vessels laid before her with green myrtle, and she filled the ship with a very sweet scent, although the passengers had abandoned the thought of safety on account of much seasickness and vomiting. When the sun shone, looking down at the harbor, they arrived at Naukratis. Herostratos disembarked from the ship with the little statue, also holding the green myrtle

86 Female spirits presiding over bodies of fresh water.

87 The first quadrennial Olympic Games were held in 776 BCE, according to tradition, and provided a standard method of reckoning time in four-year increments.

88 On the Canopic branch of the Nile Delta.

that suddenly appeared, and he consecrated those things in an Aphrodite shrine, making a sacrifice to the goddess and dedicating the Aphrodite statuette. Summoning his relatives and householders to a feast in the sanctuary, he gave each a myrtle garland, which he then called "Naukratian."

(Athenaeus, Learned Banqueters *15.675f–676c)*

3.11.5 Nereids and Other Goddesses of the Sea

A. *As the daughters of Nereus, the Old Man of the Sea, the 50 Nereids, collectively and individually, invited invocation for protection at sea. Sappho of Eresus or Mytilene on Lesbos (c. 630–570 BCE) was esteemed as the "tenth Muse," but her work survives, sadly, only in fragments. Here she has invoked the Nereids together with Aphrodite for her brother's safe passage by sea.*

Cypris and Nereids, grant that my brother arrive here safe and that everything he wishes for in his heart be fulfilled, and that whatever mistakes he previously committed, may they all be atoned and may he be a joy to his friends and troublesome to his enemies, and may no one be a cause of grief. . .

(Sappho F 5)

B. *According to one version of the Trojan War story arc, Helen never went to Troy but was instead sent to Egypt, where she remained faithful to her husband, Menelaus. Here, as Menelaus prepares to leave Egypt with Helen, he prays to the Nereids for a safe journey. Euripides (480–c. 406 BCE) was an innovative dramatist whose popularity endured (from a corpus of over 90 plays, 18 complete tragedies and fragments of others are extant). Prayers were legalistic and contractual, and Menelaus is here careful to specify the extent of his journey by sea.*

O Poseidon dwelling in the salt-sea and chaste daughters of Nereus, keep me and my wife safe from this land up to the Nauplion promontories.[89]

(Euripides, Helen *1584–1587)*

C. *Many gods were invoked for safety at sea, including Thalassa ("Sea")/Tethys, as here. Ocean could be the "friendly boundary of the earth" (*Orphic Hymn *83.7), or a terrifying source of sea monsters and storms. Nonetheless, the waterways of the ancient Mediterranean basin were also the useful (and sometimes benevolently peaceful) arena that was to be conquered for human use (Parts V-VII). The* Orphic Hymns *are a collection of 87 invocations to various deities, in dactylic hexameters, composed probably in the 2nd and 3rd centuries CE in Asia Minor and representing*

89 Nauplion (Naflio) is in the northeastern Peloponnese on the northern coast of the Argolican Bay, a point of disembarkation for those sailing from Egypt to the Peloponnese and making their way to landlocked Sparta where Menelaus was king.

the Orphic belief system, which included a distinct creation story and belief in the duality of human nature (human and divine). Those who followed the Orphic system aimed to free themselves from the cycle of reincarnation and engaged in a ritual of initiation as did worshippers of the Samothracian gods (#3.11.8).

> I call upon owl-eyed Tethys, bride of Ocean, dark-cloaked queen, rising in the quick surges, with sweet-smelling breezes treading around the earth. Her dark waves clash against the rocky strand, calmed in well-rolled soft swells, glorified by ships, nourisher of beasts, moistly pathed, mother of Cypris (Venus), mother of gloomy clouds and of every source teeming with the springs of the nymphs. Hear me, O venerable Lady, and may you approach well-disposed, sending a following breeze to straight-running ships.
>
> (Orphic Hymn *21* to Thalassa/Tethys)

D. *Dionysus' aunt Ino (who would become Leucothea) incurred Hera's wrath for caring for Dionysus, her sister's son and an illegitimate child of Zeus, Hera's husband. Hera drove Ino insane, and Ino leapt from a cliff into the sea with her own son, Melicertes. Dionysus then saved them both, transforming Ino into Leucothea ("White Goddess"), the shearwater who protects sailors from storms at sea (e.g., Homer,* Odyssey *5.333–353), and Melicertes into the divine Palaemon who also watches over sailors: #2.2.7A.*

> I call Leukothea, daughter of Cadmus,[90] solemn deity, powerful, well-garlanded nurse of Dionysus. Listen, Goddess, guardian of the deep-hearted sea, delighting in the billowing waves, great savior of mortals. For in you there is great eagerness for the sailing of ships. You alone redeem the pitiable fate of mortals in the salt-sea, to whom you come rushing as a friendly savior. But, Lady Goddess, may you come as a saving companion for well-benched ships with cheerful intention, driving a fair, ship-speeding wind for initiates.
>
> (Orphic Hymn *74* to Leukothea*; cf. Hyginus,* Fables *2; Ovid,* Metamorphoses *4.531–542)*

E. *Ino and others are invoked here to ensure a safe trip by sea to Athens.*

> O Melicertes, son of Ino, and Leucothea, the gray-blue guardian of the sea, deity who averts evil, and you chorus of Nereids, and you waves, and you, Poseidon, and you, Thracian Zephyr (West Wind), gentlest of breezes, be gracious and convey me, fleeing through a broad swell, safely to the sweet bank of the Piraeus.[91]
>
> *(Philodemus of Gadara,* Greek Anthology *6.349)*

90 The mythic founder of Thebes whose daughters included Ino (Leucothea) and Semele, the mother of Dionysus.

91 Port of Athens: #5.3.3F.

3.11.6 Achilles

Thetis' son, Achilles, was also honored with a sailor cult at a goat-inhabited island in the Pontus (cleansed daily by seabirds). Appearing to his pilgrims in distress, the hero would reveal the island's best moorage in dreams, occasionally alighting on sails or prows, like the Dioscuri. For Achilles' Pontic cult: Hedreen 1991; Rusyaeva 2003. While Thetis is often invoked in inscriptions with her son (e.g. IosPE *I² 142 to Achilles Pontarchus and Thetis), epigraphic evidence does not attest a maritime cult.*

21. Straight along the mouth, just in front for someone sailing the deep sea with a northerly wind, lies an island which some call the island of Achilles,[92] others the Racecourse of Achilles, still others call it *Leuce* ("White") for its color. Thetis is said to have created this island for her child, and Achilles inhabited the island. On it there is a temple of Achilles and a wooden statue of ancient workmanship. The island is desolate of people, and it is allotted to goats, but not many. And these goats are said to be dedicated to Achilles by whoever puts in there. Many offerings are also laid up in the temple: bowls and rings and costly gems, and all these offerings are dedicated to Achilles. Epigrams, those in the Roman language and the Greek, in one and another meter, are moreover made as panegyrics of Achilles. Some who wish to oblige Achilles honor Patroclus[93] with Achilles. Many birds dwell in the island: gulls and shearwaters and sea-crows whose number in the sea is unmeasured. These birds tend Achilles' temple. In the morning, for as many days as there are, they fly down to the sea. Then, moistening their feathers in the sea, they fly with haste back to the temple, and they sprinkle the temple. When they have done this well, they sweep the floor clean with their feathers.

22. Some folk inquire into these things. Those sailing to the island purposefully carry sacrificial victims in their ships: offering part of them, alive, to the island, the other part they kill as offerings to Achilles. Some sailors are forced to put in from under a storm, and they ask for a sacrificial victim from the god himself, consulting the god about the sacrifices: if it is agreeable and better for them, on their own judgment, to sacrifice by burning whatever animal they select grazing there; at the same time, they leave the value that seems to them worth as much as the sacrificed animal. But if the oracular response forbids it—for there is an oracle on the island—the sailors then add more to their valuation. And if this is rejected, they offer still more. When the oracle agrees, the visitors know that the valuation is sufficient. The sacrificial animal stands there

92 Modern Zmiinyi/Snake Island near the Danube Delta in the Black Sea, about 17 nautical miles from the Ukrainian coast.

93 See #3.1.6D.

of its own accord and does not flee: this explains why a great deal of silver is dedicated to the hero as payment for the sacrificial victims.

It is said that Achilles appears in dreams to those putting in at the island, and to those sailing, when they are not far away from the island. Achilles, furthermore, tells them where it is better to put in at the island and where to moor. Some say that Achilles also appears to them awake, on a mast or the tip of the *akrostolion*,[94] just like the Dioscuri.[95] They say that Achilles is second to the Dioscuri only in this regard: the Dioscuri appear visibly as often to those sailing everywhere and they are signs of safety; but Achilles appears only to those sailing to his island. Some say that Patroclus also appears to sailors in their sleep. I have written out what I have heard about the island of Achilles either from those approaching the island or making their own inquiries. To me these accounts seem not untrustworthy. For I am persuaded that Achilles was a hero, if anyone really was, for his nobility of birth and his physical beauty and the strength of his soul and also for his excessively early departure from humankind and Homer's poem about him and love and friendship such that he would even want to die for beloved friends.

(Arrian, Periplus *21–23; cf. Dionysius Periegetes,* Description of the Known World *5.541–548; Pausanias,* Description of Greece *3.19.12; Ammianus Marcellinus,* Res Gestae *22.8.35; cf. Philostratus the Younger,* Heroicus *54.6)*

3.11.7 Dioscuri

A. *Sons of Leda, the Dioscuri were half-brothers: Pollux' father was Zeus, and Castor's was Leda's mortal husband, Tyndareus. The brothers participated in the* Argo's *quest for the Golden Fleece (Apollonius,* Argonautica *1.146–150), as well as the Calydonian Boar hunt (Ovid,* Metamorphoses *8.298–316; Pausanias,* Description of Greece *8.44.6; Hyginus,* Fables *173). When Castor died, Pollux, Zeus' semi-divine son, was offered the choice of joining the Olympians or sharing his divinity with his brother. Pollux chose the latter, and the brothers traveled between Olympus and Hades, either together (Ovid,* Fasti *5.715–720) or alternately (Pseudo-Hyginus,* Astronomy *2.22.1). Like other heroes who returned from the Underworld, the Dioscuri were the focus of wide-spread worship (Pindar,* Nemean *10.51–52; Pausanias,* Description of Greece *3.16.3), and, like Poseidon, they were associated with horses and the sea, coming to help travelers, especially sailors in distress.*

Quick-glancing Muses, tell me about the sons of Zeus and Tyndareus, the splendid children of beautifully-ankled Leda: Castor, the horse-tamer, and blameless

94 A decorative finial fitted to the stern.
95 #3.11.7.

> Polydeuces (Pollux), whom—when, under the great summit of Mt. Taygetus,[96] she mingled in love with dark-clouded Zeus—she bore as savior-children of human-folk on the earth and of swift-moving ships when stormy winds hasten over the implacable sea. Those praying from the ship summon the sons of great Zeus with white lambs, stepping up to the prow. But, when a great wind and the waves of the sea have pushed the ship under water, suddenly the Dioscuri appear glancing through the air on nimble wings. Straightaway, they check the vexing winds and silence the white salt waves in the seas. Beautiful signs, they have cast toil asunder. Seeing the brothers, sailors rejoice, and they abate from their miserable labor. Greetings, sons of Tyndareus, riders of swift horses. Now I will remember you in another song.
>
> *(*Homeric Hymn *33* To the Dioscuri *11–17; cf. Plato,* Euthydemus *293a)*

B. *Sailors interpreted the mystical phenomenon known as St. Elmo's fire as the apotheosis of Castor and Pollux: a faint blue or purple glow, sometimes accompanied by a buzzing or hissing sound, caused by the ionization of air molecules along the masts of ships or other poles (including the noses of aircraft). This electrical reaction occurs on sails during bad weather, as well as on animals and trees (Seneca,* NQ *1.1). Caesar observed the sign on spear-points in Africa (Aulus Hirtius [?],* African War *47). Cf. Valerius Flaccus,* Argonautica *1.561–573.*

> These stars (Castor and Pollux) occur both at sea and on land. During night watches of soldiers in the field, I have seen them, lightning-like in appearance, cling to javelins in front of the entrenchments. They also tread on the yardarms and other parts of ships under sail with a certain tuneful sound, like birds darting about. When they occur singly, they are oppressive, and they sink vessels. If they fall on the lowest part of the keel, they set the ship on fire. But if they appear as twins, they are beneficial and presage a favorable voyage, by whose advent that dire and threatening star, called Helena,[97] is put to flight. On account of this, sailors assign the names of Castor and Pollux to the phenomenon. They invoke those gods at sea.
>
> *(Pliny,* NH *2.101; cf. Xenophanes,* TEGP *73)*

C. *The Dioscuri were also depicted as the constellation Gemini (the twins), a valuable navigational tool. The Roman poet Marcus Manilius (fl. 10–30 CE), from Syria, authored a comprehensive five-book* Astronomy, *in hexameters, the earliest complete account of Greco-Roman astronomy and astrology, including a discussion*

96 In the southern Peloponnese, overlooking Sparta.

97 The Dioscuri's sister, Helen, "destroyer of ships" (Aeschylus, *Agamemnon* 689), whose star was thought to endanger maritime traffic: "(Oebelian brothers) put your Ilian sister's cloudy stars to flight far away and shut them out from the entire sky" (Statius, *Silvae* 3.2.11–12).

of the zodiac and other constellations, linking human life with the movement of constellations.

> From the Gemini, zeal is softer and the season is milder, through various diverse songs and expressions that are modulated with voices and slender reed-pipes and lyrics that are grafted to strings and engender singing. Labor itself is even a pleasure. The Gemini want arms to be at a distance as well as war trumpets and sad old age; and they spend their time affectionately in leisure and in eternal youthfulness. The twins also find the paths to the stars, and they survey the world with numbers and measurements, and they leave the stars behind. Nature is inferior and serves them in all things. So many accomplishments of the productive Gemini are proclaimed.
>
> *(Manilius,* Astronomy *4.152–161)*

D. *The Dioscuri were popularly represented on coins. This denarius of Manlius Fonteius (108–107 BCE), a Roman moneyer, shows the brothers on the obverse with stars (their constellation) above their heads. The reverse shows a warship under oar, commemorating Metellus Numidicus' victory over Jugurtha at the Muthul River in Numidia in 109 BCE (Sallust,* Jugurtha *48.3–4).*

FIGURE 3.11.7D Dioscuri. With kind permission of wildwinds.com, ex Freeman & Sear, October 2005.

3.11.8 Great Gods of Samothrace

*Samothrace was a natural hub between Asia and Europe: Ovid changed ships there on his way to Tomis (*Tristia *1.10.19–22), and Paul stopped there on his way to Macedonia from the Troad (*Acts *16.11). From at least the 6th century BCE, Samothrace was the focus of a maritime pilgrim-mystery cult, about which little is known: neither the number, gender, or names of the gods are certain, though they were probably a triad of male deities (the Kabeiroi). Those seeking initiation into mystery rites, like Demeter's cult at Eleusis, underwent a common experience or learned some shared (secret) knowledge that perhaps entitled them to prosperity in life or special* *treatment after death (for the space and possible reconstructions at Samothrace: Cole 1984; Lehmann and McCredie 1998; Dimitrova 2008; Blakely 2012).*

A. *The penalty for revealing the secrets of the Eleusinian mysteries (in honor of Demeter and Persephone) was likely death, and similar proscriptions may have been in place for the Samothracian mysteries whose initiates vigorously guarded their proprietary knowledge (hence "mystery"). Herodotus was himself an initiate.*

> Whoever has been initiated into the secret rites of the Kabeiroi, which the Samothracians oversee after they received them from the Pelasgians,[98] this person knows what I say.
>
> *(Herodotus,* Histories *2.51.2)*

B. *The Argonauts were also initiated as they sailed eastward towards Colchis to retrieve the Golden Fleece. Here we learn something of the benefits of initiation.*

> In the evening, on Orpheus'[99] command, they put in at the island of Elektra (Samothrace), daughter of Atlas,[100] in order that—by learning the unspoken rites in gentle initiations—they could sail more safely across the icy cold sea. I will say no more on these matters. But the island herself rejoices as do the deities who have by lot obtained these mysteries of which it is not right for me to sing.
>
> *(Apollonius,* Argonautica *1.915–921)*

C. *Initiation could also yield moral benefits.*

> The epiphanies of these gods and their miraculous assistance to those in danger are proclaimed to those summoned for initiation. They also say that those who have been initiated become more dutiful and more just and better in every regard. Consequently, the most notable of the ancient heroes and demigods eagerly sought to have a share in this rite: for Jason and the Dioscuri and even Herakles and Orpheus, as initiates, hit the mark[101] in all their campaigns because of the gods appearing to them.
>
> *(Diodorus Siculus,* Library of History *5.49.5–6; cf. Livy,* From the Foundation of the City *45.5.4)*

D. *According to documentary and literary evidence, the Samothracian mysteries attracted pilgrims from across the Mediterranean, representing about 70 cities*

98 Referring generally to the inhabitants of the Greek peninsula before it was "Greek," speaking a "barbarian" (non-Greek) language (Herodotus, *Histories* 1.57.3).

99 An acclaimed lyre player from Thrace whose music was so powerfully beautiful that it charmed the gods of the dead (Orpheus ventured to Hades to recover his dead wife Eurydice unsuccessfully) and even stones (see Ovid, *Metamorphoses* 10.1–85, 11.1–66).

100 One of the Titans who opposed Zeus' rule and was sent to the world's western edge to support the vault of the sky (Hesiod, *Theogony* 507–520).

101 #2.2.9A note.

(mostly but not exclusively in the Aegean) and foreign dynasts, including Philip II of Macedon (r. 359–336 BCE) who met his bride there.

> Having met Olympias in Samothrace, himself still a lad and she an orphan daughter, Philip is said to have fallen in love with her and to have arranged their marriage, after persuading her brother, Arymbas.
>
> *(Plutarch,* Alexander *2.2)*

E. *In 18* CE, *traveling from Lesbos to Thrace, Tiberius' nephew and heir, Germanicus (#1.9.1D introduction), had hoped to be initiated.*

> Adverse north winds drove Germanicus away, aiming to see the rites at Samothrace on his return.
>
> *(Tacitus,* Annals *2.54)*

F. *Most of the dedications at Samothrace are fragmentary lists of initiates, including captains (Dimitrova 2008: #58) and entire crews (Dimitrova 2008: #49). But one epitaph suggests proof of the moral and material excellence that initiates might enjoy, including attaining old age without pain or trouble.*

> Isidoros, Nikostratou of Athens, farewell. This light earth has covered an Athenian citizen, who frequently tilled at the Bacchic altars, recounting merry speech as a mime in the third part, delighting with his natural Muse-flowing graces. He was loved by his friends, a just man, truthful to all, with reverent renown for the virtue in his soul. As an initiate, great-hearted, he saw the doubly sacred light of Kabeiros in Samothrace and the pure rites of Demeter in Eleusis. Because of this, bearing his old age well, Isidoros completed 80 years without pain or trouble. But you, gloomy Hades, extremely powerful bastion of necessity, lead this man to the Region of the Reverent and place him there.
>
> *(Dimitrova 2008: #29; trans. Dimitrova)*

G. *The cult was popular with mariners, and sailors would pray to the Samothracian gods during storms, as they prayed to the Dioscuri. Sailors would thank the Samothracian gods for deliverance. Worshippers may have believed that the Samothracian gods were more likely to save their own initiates than non-initiates, or even protect them from shipwreck altogether (Lewis 1958: #229g, 158; Mowery 2011: 117). This epigram may have been composed by the satirist from Samosata who is clearly casting his net widely in offering thanksgiving on Lucillius' behalf.*

> To Glaukus and Nereus and Melikertes, Ino's son, and the son of Kronos, lord of the deep (Poseidon), and the Samothracian gods, I, Lucillius, saved from the deep sea, clip these hairs from my head. For I have nothing else.
>
> *(Lucian,* Greek Anthology *6.164)*

3.11.9 Gallizenae

Off the Atlantic coast of Gaul an otherwise unattested pilgrim center was overseen by nine maritime priestesses whose powers included healing, controlling water, and proprietary knowledge which they shared with their pilgrims, thus inviting comparison with the Great Gods at Samothrace, the Dioscuri, and other divine protectors of sailors at sea (see Irby forthcoming-a*).*

> In the Britannic Sea, facing the coasts of the Ossismici, the (island of) Sena is remarkable for an oracle of a Gallic divinity, whose priestesses—sanctified because of their perpetual virginity—are said to be nine in number. The people call them "Gallizenae," and they think that the priestesses, gifted with unique talents, rouse the seas and winds with chants, and that they turn themselves into whatever animals they wish, they heal whatever is incurable among other peoples, they know what will come, and they predict these things, revealed to sailors and only to those who have set out in order to consult them.
>
> *(Mela,* On the Circuit of the World *3.48)*

3.11.10 Ploiaphesia

A. *Sailing communities even now open the sailing season with annual rites, including blessing the fishing fleets.* Ploiaphesia *("sailing rites") were celebrated widely at port towns throughout the Mediterranean well into late antiquity, e.g., Eretria and Ephesus (John Lydus,* On the Mind *4.45), Rome (*CIL *6.32503 [*ILS *8745]), and Lugdunum (Lyon) in honor of Venus (*Navigium/Vene/ris*: CAIG-69–02, p. 366). The* Navigium Isidis *("Sailing of Isis"), observed on March 5, was recognized as the "birthday of sailing" (Vegetius,* Epitome of Military Science *4.39), a celebration that launched the sailing season. The elaborate ritual at Cenchreae (on the isthmus between Attica and the Peloponnese) featured a richly decorated ship that was launched while the waves received milk libations and grain, a first fruits offering for the mercantile season. Apuleius'* Metamorphoses *follows Lucius' misadventures and eventual restoration to human form—the main character, Lucius, had accidently transformed himself into a donkey while attempting to become a bird—by the goddess Isis, a Hellenized version of the Egyptian divine queen and mother of the pharaohs.*

> Between these things and the bustle of festal vows, progressing now little by little to the sea's bank, we approached and arrived at that very place where on the previous day my donkey self had stabled. There, once the images of the gods were properly arranged, the high priest dedicated a ship, very skillfully crafted, adorned all around with marvelous Egyptian paintings; with a shining torch and an egg and sulfur. Uttering in advance the most solemn prayers from his chaste mouth, the priest pronounced the ship purified as purely as possible

and dedicated it to the goddess Isis. The glistening sail of this lucky hollow hull displayed letters woven with gold. These letters refreshed the annual vow about propitious sailing concerning travel in the New Year.[102] Now rose the mast, a round pine trunk, sublime with its splendor, distinguished with its remarkable masthead; and the stern, twisted about with a gosling, was shining, clothed in goldleaf, and the entire hull was blooming, thoroughly polished on its clear citron wood. Then all the people, both the scrupulous and the sightseers, emulously heaped up winnowing baskets burdened with aromatics and offerings of this kind, and they poured libations—un-milled grain prepared with milk—over the waves, until the ship was filled with plentiful gifts and well-omened offerings. Set free from its anchor lines, the ship was returned to the sea with its own calm breeze. After the ship became indistinct for us to see because of the extent of its course, the bearers of the sacred implements took up again what each one brought down. Briskly they made their return to the shrine in an arrangement similar to an elegant parade.

(Apuleius, Metamorphoses *11.16)*

B. *Other deities were also honored with ship processions, including Athena (for the Panathenaic ship, see #7.2.4) and Dionysus. Philostratus of Athens provides the only textual reference to the Dionysus festival.*

In the month Anthesterion (February/March), a trireme is sent, raised up, to the *agora*,[103] which the priest of Dionysus guides from the sea like a helmsman, loosing its cables.

(Philostratus of Athens, Lives of the Sophists *1.25.1)*

3.11.11 Superstition and Rituals for Safety at Sea

A. *Sailing was and is dangerous, and those who traveled on water often sought divine protection by means of rituals. Here Telemachus'*[104] *ship was made ready to leave Ithaca.*

Then, binding the gear along the swift, black ship, they set mixing vessels full of wine and poured libations to the deathless, everlasting gods, especially Athena, the gleaming-eyed daughter of Zeus. All night long and through the dawn, the ship pierced through her path.

(Homer, Odyssey *2.430–434)*

102 The Roman New Year began in March.
103 A central public space in most ancient Greek cities.
104 The son of Odysseus who searched for news of his father, delayed at sea for ten years after the end of the Trojan War.

B. *A launch might be delayed by inauspicious signs, including sneezing while going up the gangplank, cawing crows, magpies in the rigging, sighting wreckage on shore, or dreams (of goats, boars, or owls presaged storms or pirate attack). It was, consequently, important to interpret these signs correctly. Here the Athenian fleet makes ready to embark for Sicily in 415 BCE.*

> When the ships were full and all things were put on board which they intended to carry, then silence was signaled by the salpinx,[105] and prayers, customary for setting out, were made by a herald, not by each ship individually, but altogether. The soldiers and officers throughout the entire army then made drink-offerings as they mixed wine in golden and silver beakers. From the shore, the entire crowd of citizens, and anyone well-disposed to the Athenians, join in prayer. Chanting paeans and completing the libations, they set off.
>
> *(Thucydides,* Peloponnesian War *6.32.1–2)*

C. *Prayers were often uttered at the outset of a voyage, evolving into the stylized* propemptikon *in Greco-Roman literature where authors expressed their wishes for safe voyages for friends traveling on water. The most famous is Horace's* propemptikon *for Vergil on his return homeward from Attica, where the poet recognizes that humankind simply should not trespass into some realms. Quintus Horatius Flaccus (65–8 BCE) was a widely admired lyric poet, crafting graceful, autobiographical verses and gentle satire.*

> Thus may the powerful goddess of Cyprus (Venus), thus may the brothers of Helen (the Dioscuri), bright stars, and the father of the winds guide you,—all winds except the Iapyx[106] confined—O, Ship, who protects Vergil, entrusted to you. I beg you, may you return him safe from the borders of Attica, and may you protect him, the other half of my soul. Oak and three-ply bronze were around his heart, he who first dispatched a fragile vessel to the ferocious deep sea, nor did he fear the headlong Notus (South) Wind contending with the Aquilo (North Wind) nor the sorrowful Hyades[107] nor the Notus' rage: there is no greater arbiter of the Adriatic, whether he wants to lift up or settle the straits. What degree of death frightens him who with dry eyes sees swimming monsters, who sees a roiling sea and the high-thundering Acroceraunian Promontory,[108] those notorious cliffs? To no avail did a prudent deity hew off the lands from the dividing Ocean, if nonetheless, irreverent skiffs spring over the depths that should not be touched. The human race, boldly enduring everything, rushes through what is forbidden according to divine law. With an evil trick, the bold race of Iapetus

105 #2.2.12C.
106 The northwest wind, blowing from Greece to Brundisium.
107 A cluster of stars representing the rain-bringing nymphs.
108 A mountain range jutting into the eastern Adriatic Sea.

> brought fire to people.[109] After fire was wrested from its aethereal home, poverty and a new cohort of fevers oppressed the lands, and the slow necessity of remote death hastened its step. Daedalus[110] made an attempt with wings on empty air not allotted to people; Herculean labor broke through Acheron.[111] There is nothing difficult for mortals. We seek the very sky in our foolishness. Nor do we allow Jove to set aside his irascible thunderbolts for the sake of our crime.
>
> *(Horace,* Odes *1.3; cf. Theocritus,* Idyll *7; Propertius,* Elegy *1.8; Ovid,* Art of Love *1.177–228; Ovid,* Amores *2.11; Statius,* Silvae *3.2)*

D. *Before setting sail, the skipper would look for auspicious and inauspicious signs, such as the swallows that nested in Cleopatra's flagship in 31 BCE before the battle of Actium.*

> After others spoke other opinions, Cleopatra prevailed, advising that they entrust the most opportune positions to the guards and that the rest depart with herself and Antony to Egypt. She came to this opinion since she was troubled by signs. For swallows built their nests around her tent and on the flagship in which she sailed, and milk and blood were flowing from the wax. At the theater, thunderbolts dashed to pieces their images (of Cleopatra and Antony), which the Athenians placed in the acropolis, with the forms of the gods. Therefore, from these portents and the lack of spirit and morale for the expedition, Cleopatra herself became anxious, and she frightened Antony.
>
> *(Dio Cassius,* Roman History *50.15.1–3)*

E. *Some stones were thought to be able to protect sailors at sea or guarantee survival. Their powers are generally linked to color: transparent, green, or blue stones evoke water; red stones evoke storms. Here we have the short* Nautical Lapidary, *a Greek text of Byzantine date (after 395 CE), preserved in* Paris Graecus *2424, folio 190 (cf. Yébenes 2010).*

> These are the stones that calm typhoons and the waves of the sea.
>
> 1. Anthrax and chalcedony, worn from childhood, prevent going under when shipwrecked.
>
> 2. The diamond, especially the type called "blue green" found in Macedonia near Mt. Pangaeus, which resembles hail, averts danger against the biggest waves and typhoons. A stone found in India, which appears fiery and silvery: stronger and iron-like.

109 Iapetus' sons included Prometheus who gifted humanity with fire.

110 The skilled Athenian craftsman responsible for creating labyrinth that contained the Minotaur and wings to escape Crete, among other marvels.

111 One of the rivers in the Underworld: #1.3.3E, #3.10A.

3. Beryl is transparent and bright, sea colored. Let Poseidon in his two-horse chariot be carved on it steadfastly and, for those travelling by sea, let them be without care in the sea's uproar.

4. The dryops stone, having a white spot in the middle, is itself also suitable for fair sailing.

5. Coral, with the hide of a seal fitted to the ship's masthead, counteracts winds and waves and confusions of all sorts of waters.

6. The snake-belly stone, born in the mountains of Egypt, having on it scales girt round like a snake's belly: if someone has this stone, he will be altogether guarded without danger in the sea's surge.

7. The obsidian stone, not very black but greenish yellow, found in Phrygia and Galatia, which is also called "pitch" because when rubbed it produces an odor of pitch: it is useful when worn by those making a journey by sea and rivers.

(Anonymous, Nautical Lapidary*)*

3.11.12 Piscine Sacrifices

A. *Fish were also, naturally, sacrificed to nautical and land gods for many reasons, including as thank-offerings for good catches. Unlike some other fishes, tuna bleed and thus may have been considered suitable sacrifices (Lefèvre-Novaro 2010: note 18).*

Nor is it necessary to be amazed if they offer eels as burnt sacrifices, when, in his *On Style*, Antigonus of Carystus[112] says that the people of Halae prescribe a burnt sacrifice to Poseidon during the tuna season when they have good hunting: they sacrifice to the god the first tuna they catch and this sacrifice is called a "thynnaion."

(Athenaeus, Learned Banqueters *7.297e; cf. Polyaenus,* Stratagemata *6.24)*

B. Trigle *(red mullet) was sacred to Hekate (#3.3A note).*

To Hekate is assigned the *trigle* on account of the commonality of their names. For she is Trioditis ("goddess of the crossroads") and Triglenus ("three-eyed"?), and, on the 30th day, worshippers bring her a meal (of *trigle*).

(Athenaeus, Learned Banqueters *7.325a; cf. Aelian,* NA *9.51)*

C. *Artemis, protector of the fishing nets, also received* trigle *offerings.*

I, Menis the net fisherman, bestow on you, Artemis of the Harbor, seaweed-dwelling *trigle* from the coals, and a cup of pure, mixed wine, level

112 Third century BCE; his *Succession of Philosophers* is generously quoted by Athenaeus and Diogenes of Laertius. Carystus is in southern Euboea.

with the brim, and a dry morsel of bread broken into the wine, a paltry sacrifice. In exchange for this, grant that my nets always be full of fish. For all flaxen fishing-nets are given to you, Blessed One.

(*Apollonides of Smyrna,* Greek Anthology *6.105)*

3.11.13 Pompilos, the Guide-Fish

A. *The "guide-fish" accompanied ships into port and was thus considered sacred (#2.2.12F§62).*

They say that the *pompilos* fish is sacred not only to Poseidon, but is even beloved by the gods in Samothrace. At any rate, some fisherman in ancient times suffered retribution from this fish. And the name of the fisherman, according to the story, was Epopeus ("the watcher"): he was from the island Icarus,[113] and he had a son. Once therefore, when there happened to be a lack of fish, Epopeus led up his net, catching only pilot-fish which therefore Epopeus set out as dinner for his child. But not long afterwards, avenging justice came to him. For a sea monster, coming upon his fishing boat, gulped Epopeus down in front of his son's eyes.

They also say that dolphins are enemies of pilot-fish, nor do they escape well when they have tasted the pilot-fish. For the dolphins struggle on the spot and are driven insane and are unable to stop trembling. They are carried out on the shores and, once cast ashore from the swelling sea, they are a meal for sea crows (Homer, *Odyssey* 5. 66) and sea gulls.

Apollonius of Rhodes or Naukratis says that the pilot-fish was once a man, and he ferried a boat. Apollo fell in love with a young woman, and he tried to have sex with her. But, escaping, she came to Miletus and begged a certain Pompilos, a fisherman, to ferry her across the strait. He complied. But Apollo, appearing, seized the girl, turned the ship to stone, and the god changed Pompilos into this fish.

(*Aelian,* NA *15.23; cf. Athenaeus,* Learned Banqueters *7.283d)*

B. *Further background and anecdotes.*

The pilot-fish is an amorous creature, as one might think since it came from the blood of Ouranos at the same time as Aphrodite was born.[114] Nicander[115] in the second book of his *Oetean Tales* (F 16) says, "Pilot-fish, which reveals paths to anguished sailors in love and aiding them although without speech." Alexander the

113 Ikaria, in the Aegean southwest of Samos.

114 #3.11.4A. Hesiod, however, did not mention the birth of the pilot-fish: *Theogony* 188–198.

115 Nicander of Colophon (2nd century BCE), a physician, grammarian, and poet. His *Theriaca,* is a versified account of poisonous animals and their effects; his *Alexipharmaca,* also in hexameters, gives antidotes.

Aetolian[116] in Crica (F 2), if the poem is legitimate, says "a pompilos behind the tip of a steering-oar guides the vessel from behind, a fishy escort from a goddess."

And Erinna,[117] or whoever wrote the poem attributed to her, writes, "Pompilos, sending a fair voyage to sailors, from the stern, may you escort my dear companion" (*SH* 404).

(Athenaeus, Learned Banqueters *7.282f–283a, 283d)*

116 An author of tragedies and epics who flourished under Ptolemy II Philadelphus (r. 284–246 BCE). Only scant fragments survive.

117 A Greek poetess known for the *Distaff*, surviving only in fragments, in honor of a childhood friend who died shortly after marriage. A distaff is a spindle for spinning wool, and wool-working was the primary occupation of well-married elite Greek women.

PART IV
Water and Society

Here we consider how water management and infrastructure enhance human life within and between communities. We start with access to water and legislative regulation of that access (#4.1). Also of concern is water quality (#4.2) as well as how to find reliable sources (#4.3). Water access and quality (e.g., swampy) were also factors in where to establish or avoid building a city (#4.4), and these settlements were enhanced with a variety of waterworks for the use, convenience, and enjoyment of the inhabitants, from spring houses to aqueducts to public and private baths to latrines and sewers for removing gray and black water (#4.5). Devices that used water were both practical (water clocks) and entertaining (water organs) (#4.6), while other machines were developed to move water for human convenience, including irrigating fields and milling grain (#4.7). Water was removed from marshland to reclaim land for agriculture (#4.8) and was employed violently in mining (#4.9).

4.1 Water Rights and Access

4.1.1 Introduction

Access to potable water is a perennial concern for travelers, including armies on the march. Generals, moreover, aimed to ensure a supply for their own troops while hindering the enemy from water and other resources.

A. *After giving birth to the divine twins Apollo and Artemis/Diana, Latona/Leto wanted to refresh herself with a drink of water in Lycia (Turkey), but the locals*

DOI: 10.4324/9781003437741-5

tried to drive her away. Leto delivered a vitriolic rant on water rights and then turned the sullen Lycians into amphibious frogs (for frogs: #2.2.13B).

Why do you prohibit me from the water? The use of the waters is shared. Nature has made neither the ground, nor the air, nor the delicate waves its own: I came to public works, and yet I ask, however, as a suppliant, that you offer them to me. I was not preparing to wash my joints and tired limbs here, but to relieve my thirst. My mouth lacks the moisture for speaking, and my throat is dry, and scarcely is there a path for my voice. A drink of water will be nectar for me, and I will confess to receiving life at the same time: you will give life from the water.

(Ovid, Metamorphoses *6.349–357; compare #3.7D)*

B. *In 479 BCE, the Persian general Mardonios taunted the Spartans, accusing them of avoiding battle and then challenging them to a duel-like competition, equal numbers on each side. The Spartans did not respond to the challenge, and Mardonios took his vengeance on the spring at Gargaphia (Plataea, south of Thebes) and the nearby Asopos River. Herodotus did not explain how the spring was destroyed.*

After saying these things (the Persian taunts and challenges) and waiting for some time, not a single one of them gave any answer at all. The herald departed back. And returning he explained to Mardonios what had happened. Exceedingly glad and raised up at this cold victory, Mardonios sent the cavalry to the Hellenes. The horsemen rode out against the Greeks and injured the entire Greek army by throwing javelins and shooting arrows: for the Persians were mounted archers and were hard to deal with. The Persians agitated and demolished the Gargaphian spring from which the whole Greek army was watered. Only Lacedaemonian troops were posted near the spring, and the spring was at a distance from the other Hellenes, where each unit happened to be stationed. But the Asopos River was nearby. The Greeks were restrained from the Asopos, and thus they went back and forth to the spring. For they could not draw water from the river because of the cavalry and arrows.

(Herodotus, Histories *9.49)*

C. *The Athenian general and military reformer Iphicrates (418–353 BCE) engaged in a mercenary operation in Egypt (Cornelius Nepos,* Iphicrates *2.4), a resource-poor region that required extra diligence to keep an army supplied. From Bithynia in Asia Minor, trained as a rhetorician and dedicating his eight-book* Stratagems *to Marcus Aurelius (r. 161–180) and Lucius Verus (r. 161–169), Polyaenus described 900 strategic maneuvers of accomplished military leaders, including Greeks, Romans, and even women (833* Stratagems *survive).*

When Iphicrates was about to march along a waterless road for two days, he ordered his troops, after they dined, to fill their casks with water. And when the sun set he forced them to march through the night. When it was day, he made camp and ordered the troops to make bread, enjoy their water, and sleep during the day and take their evening meal and pack up their baggage and travel again through the night. So that instead of two days, they traveled for two nights, cooling themselves. And the collected water was sufficient for them for one day.

(Polyaenus, Stratagems *3.9.47)*

D. *Being cornered into waterless territory at Motya in western Sicily (398/397 BCE) was sufficient cause for the Carthaginians to sue for peace with Dionysius the Greek tyrant of Syracuse (d. 367 BCE), at least until their demand was granted and access to resources improved.*

When the Carthaginians were confined at a waterless spot by Dionysius, they sent a herald to sue for peace. Dionysius commanded them to evacuate Sicily altogether and give back the expenses which he incurred in the recent war. The Carthaginian representatives agreed to do these things. But they rejoined that they did not have the authority to confirm the agreement without their admiral. They asked to move their camp to where the admiral was. Dionysius agreed, although his advisor, Leptines, advised against it. After changing camp, the Carthaginians sent the useless heralds back to Dionysius.

(Polyaenus, Stratagems *6.16.1)*

E. *After the death of Alexander of Macedon, the Diadochi (his successor generals) carved the empire among themselves but continued to squabble over territory and influence. In 316/315 BCE, Antigonus I Monophthalmos ("one-eyed": r. 306–301) battled Eumenes of Cardia (Thracian Chersonese). While Eumenes won a decisive victory at Gabiene (west central Asia), he lost his life, and Antigonus rose to prominence. Antigonus made careful preparations in advance of battle, including seeing to the water supply.*

Antigonus was wintering at Gadamarta, a city of Media. Eumenes overtook the road with a cordon of troops spreading continuously up to 1,000 *stadia*. The road was along a mountain slope. Below was a level plain, unwatered, undwelled in: it had neither pasturage nor forest nor vegetation, but it was full of asphalt and salt-mines. The plain was fordable neither by living creatures nor people. Antigonus cut through the middle, sidestepping the garrisons of the generals along the road. He ordered 1,000 leather bags to be stitched and filled with water and provisions for ten days and barley for the horses and sufficient fodder. These things were prepared. He led his army through the uninhabited region, not allowing his troops to light fires by night, lest they become conspicuous to those guarding the foot of the mountains. Up to the end, the troops would have escaped enemy notice if they had obeyed Antigonus' command. But a few of them, on a chilly night, burnt a fire, such that after seeing the flames, the enemy perceived and attacked them as they withdrew from the plain at the rear and killed some of the rearmost men. All, unharmed, would have been safe under Antigonus' strategy, had they obeyed.

(*Polyaenus,* Stratagems *4.6.11*)

F. *In 168 BCE, the Romans dealt a military blow to the Macedonian empire at the battle of Pydna in central Macedonia, resulting eventually in their surrender to Roman authority. Before the battle, the Roman general, Lucius Aemilius Paullus, scouted for water (our passage continues with a lengthy philosophical digression on liquefaction).*

The men were especially irked over the lack of potable water: for very little water gushed and poured out from the seaside springs, and what did was wicked. But since Aemilius saw the great Mt. Olympus, vaulted with trees, laying near and—because of the greenness of the wood—he surmised that it had sources of running water flowing through its depths, he dug vents for his men and many wells along the foot. Straightaway these wells were filled with pure streams, rushing out together because of the weight and motion of being squeezed towards emptiness.

(*Plutarch,* Aemilius Paullus *14.1*)

G. *In 49 BCE at Ilerda in Spain, Pompey's generals fortified a water source for the troops against attacks from Caesar's forces, revealing Caesar's ultimate strategy to win the conflict against Pompey's Spanish forces without battle.*

On the following day, disturbed that they had given up all hope of provisions and the Hiberus River (Ebro), the enemy leaders discussed the remaining matters. There was one road if they wanted to return to Ilerda, another if they aimed for Tarraco. It was announced to them, as they deliberated over these matters, that their water-detail was being pressed hard by our cavalry (Caesar's). When they learned this, the Pompeians stationed closely packed units of cavalry and allies, and they scattered legionary troops between the allied cohorts, and they began to extend an earthwork wall from the camp to the water supply so that they could obtain water within their fortification and without fear and without outposts. The work was shared between Petreius and Afranius,[1] and they themselves proceeded some distance from camp for the sake of completing the work.

(*Caesar,* BC *1.73*)

1 Marcus Petreius and Lucius Afranius (both died in 46 BCE) administered the Spanish provinces for Pompey as legates from 55 BCE.

H. *In 49 BCE, Caesar's lieutenant Curio (84–49 BCE) campaigned against Pompey's ally Juba I of Numidia (r. 60–46 BCE), and he obtained the perfect campsite for an extended engagement.*

> The camp was especially suitable for a protracted war by nature and fortification and proximity to the sea and abundance of water and salt, of which there was a great supply heaped up from nearby salt-mines. Building material could not run short because of the abundance of trees, or grain, with which the fields were quite full, and so, with the consensus of all, Curio prepared the remaining forces to wait and prolong the war.
>
> *(Caesar,* BC *2.37.5–6)*

I. *In some remote, dry places, water was collected, presumably for the use of travelers.*

> On the Red Sea after Meroe the entire tract of land is preferred by the Trogodytes.[2] From Napata to the Red Sea the shore is reached by a journey of three days. In many places, in a very fertile region which is important for gold, rainwater is stored for enjoyment.
>
> *(Pliny,* NH *6.189)*

J. *Elsewhere, especially in the arid, water-poor areas of the provinces of Africa and Egypt, water was sold. Justinian (r. 527–565 CE) aimed for a true codification of Roman law by excising redundant laws and resolving conflicting ones, and curated Roman law in three collections: the* Codex Iustinianus, *presenting 5,000 laws; the* Institutions, *an elementary textbook in four books; and the* Digest, *a compendium in 50 books intended for advanced students. Ulpian of Tyre (assassinated 228 CE) was recognized as one of the greatest Roman legal minds, and his opinions provide about a third of the* Digest's *content.*

> A certain fellow left his freedmen both food and water through a trust. I was consulted about the trust. Since in that region of Africa, or perchance Egypt,[3] where water was for sale, a question was proposed for consideration, I therefore said that the advantage of the trust depended on whether the man who left the bequest had cisterns or not, and if how much water the beneficiary might have to purchase for himself was in the trust. Nor did the trust seem invalid. . .
>
> *(Ulpian,* Digest *34.1.14.3)*

2 #1.7D§18 note.

3 The Roman province of Africa was just a strip of land in the northern Sahara, slightly overlapping modern Algeria, Tunisia, and Libya. Egypt was the area of land along the Nile.

K. *At Palmyra in Turkey, visitors (private individuals or entire merchant caravans?) were charged for access to water.*

> The tax law of the exchange of Hadriana Tadmor and of the water sources of Aelius Caesar[4] . . . For the use of the two water sources, each year 800 *denarii.*
>
> *(*Corpus Inscriptionum Semiticarum *2.3 #3913.88)*

L. *In the Alpine territory of the Salassians, farmers and goldminers were in contention over water rights. When the Romans gained authority in the area, they expelled both local miners and farmers, but residents maintained control of the mountains and, consequently, access to the water which they sold to Roman mining contractors.*

> The territory of the Salassi has gold which, when they were powerful, they kept possession of previously, just as they were masters of the mountain passes. The Dourias River (Douro) was especially useful to them in their mining operations for washing the gold. Consequently, diverting the river to many places, they emptied the common water, flowing into sluices. This was beneficial to them in hunting for gold, but it vexed the farmers who were deprived of irrigation along the plains underneath. For the river was robust enough to water the land on account of its flow lying on higher ground. For this reason, warfare between the neighboring tribes was constant. When the Romans took power, the Salassi were thrown out of their goldworks and their territory. But, occupying the mountains, the Salassi still sold their water to the tax farmers who contracted it to work the gold mines, and they were always at odds with the tax-farmers because of their greed.
>
> *(Strabo,* Geography *4.6.7)*

4.1.2 Water Law: Greece

A. *Elected archon of Athens in 594 BCE, Solon was a legendary statesman responsible for reforming the Athenian political system: he enacted legislation against economic and political corruption and laid the groundwork for Athenian democracy. One of his laws, recorded by Plutarch in the 2nd century CE, concerned water access.*

> Since, as to water, it is sufficient for the place neither in free-flowing rivers or lakes or generous springs, but most folk use constructed wells, Solon wrote a law that where there was a public well within a *hippicon*, the people should use it. But where a well was further away, they should seek their own water. If they

4 Lucius Aelius Caesar was adopted by Hadrian in 136 CE but died before ascending to the throne.

did not find water, after digging to a depth of ten *orguiae*, then they could take 20 *hydrias* twice each day from their neighbor. For he thought it necessary to furnish resources against lack, but not to supply money for idleness.

(Plutarch, Solon *23.5; cf. Plato,* Laws *844a–c)*

B. *In 493 BCE, Themistocles served as* hydaton epistates *("supervisor of the waters") at Athens, overseeing the use and distribution of the city water supply and supervising guards who kept watch over public fountains and wells (Aristotle,* Constitution of Athens *43.1). As* hydaton epistates, *Themistocles imposed fines for the misuse of the public water supply.*

When Themistocles came to Sardis[5] and, spending some leisure time, he saw the state of the temples there and the quantity of votive offerings. In the temple of the Mother Goddess he caught sight of the so-called Water-Carrier, a *kore*[6] in bronze, two *pecheis* high, which, when he was *hydaton epistates* of Athens, he commissioned with the fines, after arresting those purloining and diverting the water supply. Whether suffering something from the capture of the offering or wanting to show the Athenians how much authority he had in the affairs of the Lydian king, Themistocles had a word with the Lydian satrap,[7] asking that he restore the *kore* to Athens. But the Barbarian became angry and said he would write a letter to the king. Alarmed, Themistocles fled to the women's quarters and, conciliating the concubines with money, he mitigated the satrap's anger, and he presented himself more discreetly, fearing the reproaches of the Barbarians.[8]

(Plutarch, Themistocles *31.1)*

C. *Waters, especially those that supplied temples, were to remain unpolluted, as at Ceos (one of the Cyclades islands) in an early 3rd century BCE decree protecting the waters supplying the sanctuary of Demeter. See also Chiai 2017: 61–82, for a thoughtful assessment of the intersections between clean water and sacred law where environmental pollution is viewed as violence against the gods and a city's aesthetic appeal (see #3.6).*

If anyone cleans himself or washes anything in the fountain, the *epimeletes* (water superintendent) shall have the authority to impose a penalty of ten *drachmas* on a free man and on the children of free men and to whip the slaves.

*(*IG *12 (5) 569, trans. Arnaoutoglou 1998: #88)*

5 The capital of the Lydian Empire and a regional Persian capital by Themistocles' day.
6 A free-standing statue usually of a young woman.
7 Persian provincial governor.
8 #5.3.5D and note.

D. *The tanning industry was notorious for its stench, and an early-5th-century-BCE decree at Athens aimed to mitigate environmental damage.*

> It is not permitted to allow hides to rot in the Ilissos River above the temple of Herakles; nobody is permitted to tan hides or to throw litter into the river.
>
> (IG *I*[3] *257, trans. Arnaoutoglou 1998: #87)*

E. *Plato proposed legislation to protect private water supplies.*

> Let this, then, be the law concerning the protection of private water: if anyone willingly destroys the water of another person, if in a spring or collected in a well, by means of poisons or digging or theft, let the injured party bring legal action in front of the city magistrates, registering the value of the damage. And if anyone is condemned with using poisons, in addition to a fine let him clean the springs or water-basins according to how the advisors' laws deem it necessary that the cleaning occur each time with respect to each plaintiff.
>
> *(Plato,* Laws *845e)*

4.1.3 Water Law: Rome

A. *By the late 4th century BCE, Rome began to build aqueducts and was thus supplied with a constant flow of water to public cisterns, intended to fill practical needs in accord with the legendary frugality and self-reliance of Rome's forebears, a popular trope in early Roman imperial literature (late 1st century BCE–early 1st century CE). In 97 CE, Sextus Julius Frontinus was appointed* curator aquarum *(supervisor of the water supply) at Rome by Nerva (r. 96–98). In this capacity, Frontinus compiled a handbook,* On the Aqueducts, *synthesizing information from technical reports, official plans, and senatorial decrees. A model of Roman efficiency and practicality, the treatise explores the history of the Roman aqueduct system and its administration and maintenance. Here, the challenges faced by Frontinus as* curator aquarum, *especially regarding the tensions between practical uses of water and luxury installations.*

> It follows that we indicate the law regarding conveying and safeguarding the water supply, one of which, conveying water, concerns curbing private individuals regarding the measure of procured services, the other, safeguarding, pertains to the maintenance of the very pipes. While I inquire more deeply into the laws enacted about individual aqueducts, among the ancients I have found certain points of law observed otherwise than is our modern practice. Among the ancients, every water source was expended for public utility, and the precaution was thus: "A private individual may not conduct water other than that which happens to be on the ground from a reservoir"—for these are the words of the law—that is to say, what overflows from the cistern: we call this "fallen" water. This "fallen" water was not granted for any other use than of the baths or

fullers, and it was subject to taxation, and a fee was set which was paid to the public treasury. Some water was also conveyed into the homes of the foremost citizenry at the consent of the others.

To which magistracy pertains the right of granting or selling water, this fluctuates in those ancient laws. I find the right is sometimes permitted by the aediles, sometimes by the censors.[9] It is clear that as often as there were censors in office, permission was principally sought from them. When there were no censors, then water-rights came under the authority of the aediles. From this it is clear by how much more our ancestors were concerned with the general good than private luxury, since even the very water that private individuals were drawing pertained to the public use.

(Frontinus, Aqueducts *2.94–95)*

B. *Private individuals who wanted running water in their homes had to obtain government-issued permits. For the slaves and ex-slaves employed to maintain the water supply: #4.5.31.*

Whoever wants to convey water for private enjoyment must obtain a permit and bring a letter from the emperor to the *curator aquarum*. The *curator* then must make haste to fulfill Caesar's[10] favor, and straightaway he ascribes one of Caesar's freedmen as the manager of this duty.

(Frontinus, Aqueducts *2.105)*

C. *Fees were assessed for access to the water supply at Rome.*

The heir of a bequeathed estate is compelled to pay past taxes or tributes either on a sundial or sewer or for conveying water.

(Ulpian, Digest *30.39.5)*

D. *But some folks were illegally diverting public waters from the aqueducts for private use. The conservative and stringent statesman, Cato the Elder, as censor in 184 BCE, aimed to stop the theft with austerity measures that were partly in retaliation against his senatorial detractors.*

Taking not the least thought for his accusers, Cato became all the stricter: he cut off the water-pipes by which folks were diverting public flowing water to their own houses and gardens.

(Plutarch, Cato the Elder *19.1; cf. Livy,* From the Foundation of the City *39.44.4–5)*

9 Aediles were annually elected (or appointed) magistrates who oversaw public buildings and the city's grain supply. Censors were appointed every five years, serving a term of 18 months, reviewing citizen rolls and senatorial membership, and generally supervising moral behavior.

10 #2.2.12D§15 note.

E. *Hacking was an inevitable problem, much to Frontinus' annoyance.*

> There are many lengthy and diverse spaces through which hidden pipes meander under the paving stones in the city. I have discovered that the pipes, damaged by punctures, were conveying water to all the businessmen in their path by means of private branch pipes, resulting in scant measures of water for public use. How much water has been stolen in this way I estimate by means of the fact that a certain amount of lead has been retrieved[11] owing to the removal of this kind of branch pipe.
>
> *(Frontinus,* Aqueducts *2.115; cf.* Aqueducts *2.76)*

F. *Frontinus recorded steep fines (10,000* sesterces*) for the willful pollution or sabotage of the public water supply (*Aqueducts *2.97.5–6; cf.* Digest *47.11.10), and action could be taken against those who corrupted private water sources, including wells or cisterns, the contamination of which was equated with theft. Marcus Antistius Labeo (d. c. 10 CE) was an important source for common law.*

> Regarding someone who has poured anything into a neighbor's well so that he might contaminate the water by this action, Labeo says that he is liable by the interdict against force or stealth: for living ("sweet") water is seen as part of the property.
>
> *(Ulpian,* Digest *43.24.11preface)*

G. *The deliberate pollution of the water supply ("injuries against good practices") would result in serious but unspecified punishment. Ulpian's contemporary, Julius Paulus served as a jurist under Septimius Severus (r. 193–211 CE) and Caracalla (r. 198–217), and as praetorian prefect (overseeing the emperor's elite bodyguard) under Alexander Severus (r. 222–235). Paulus wrote prolifically on many legal issues, and his legal opinions were highly admired.*

> An injury committed against good practices, as if someone might smear someone with decayed excrement or plaster him with filth or mud, or defile the waters or waterpipes or reservoirs, or pollute anything else for the purpose of injuring the public, it is customary to punish them most severely.
>
> *(Paulus,* Digest *47.11.1.1)*

11 Presumably from scavengers.

4.2 Water Quality

4.2.1 Introduction

A. *The source of water affects its quality.*

> Regarding natural waters, that from thunderous aither is suitable, that from storms is bad.
>
> (*Hippocratic* Epidemics *6.4.17*)

B. *The Hippocratic author of* Airs, Waters, Places *includes a lengthy discussion of water sources and their effects on the salubrity of water.*

> 7. I want to explain about the remaining waters, which are disease-inducing, and which are the healthiest and however many evil things occur from water and however many good things. For water contributes a great deal to health. Whichever waters are marshy and standing and swampy, in the summer these must be warm and thick and having a stench when they are not flowing out. But when rainwater is always freshly added and heated by the sun, these marshy waters are necessarily without good color, and they are wicked and bilious. In the winter they are frosty and icy and turbid under the snow and ice, so that they induce phlegm and sore throats. For those drinking such waters, their spleens are always large and knotted, and their bellies become hard and even thin and warm, their shoulders and collar bones and faces become thin and emaciated. For the flesh dissolves into the spleen. Consequently, they are withered. Such people are hungry and thirsty. And they have dry hollow cavities, both the upper one and lower one (intestines), so that they need stronger medicants (laxatives). This illness occurs for them in both summer and winter. In addition, their edemas are numerous and very deadly. For in the summer many dysenteries occur as well as diarrheas and lengthy fevers. These illnesses, if stretched out, bring constitutions of such a kind to the point of dropsy and death. These illnesses occur for them in summer. In winter, pneumonia and delirium occur in younger people; in older folks, fevers occur because of hardness of their bellies. In women swellings and white phlegm occur, and they rarely become pregnant, and they give birth with difficulty, and their young ones are large and swollen. Then, during nursing, the little ones become emaciated and grievous. The after-birth cleansing is not successful for the mother. For the babies, burning sensations especially occur. For the men, there are varicose veins and wounds on the lower legs so that people with such constitutions are not long-lived, but they age before a suitable time. Even more, women seem to be pregnant, and, when there should be a birth, the fullness of the belly disappears when the uterus is full of water. Such waters I think are distressful for every situation. Next, of all the waters that might be distressful are whatever water-springs come from

rocks—for these waters are necessarily hard—or from the earth where waters are hot or where there is iron or copper or silver or gold or sulfur or alum or asphalt or nitron (sodium carbonate). For all these things are born from the force of heat. Accordingly, from such earth good waters are not born, but those waters are hard and burning and difficult to pass and they hinder evacuation. The best waters flow from high places and earthy hills: these are sweet and white and such that they need only a little wine. These waters become warm in winter, icy in summer. For thus they emerge from the deepest sources. I especially approve those sources whose waters flow towards the rising sun and even more towards the summer rising sun. They are necessarily brighter and fragrant and light. As many as are salty and full of minerals and hard, these are not good to drink. But there are some physiques and diseases for which drinking such water is suitable, about which I will speak straightaway. But concerning such waters here is more. Whichever sources are towards the rising suns, these are absolutely the very best. Next are those between the summer risings and settings, especially those towards the risings. Third are those between the summer and winter settings. Worst are those towards the south between the winter rising and setting: these are especially bad with the south winds, but better with the north winds.

It is fitting to employ such waters thusly. Whoever are healthy and strong do not need to distinguish between waters, but they can drink whatever is nearby. But whoever wants to drink the most suitable waters on account of disease, they would thusly especially happen upon health. For those whose hollows are hard and inflamed, the sweetest and lightest and brightest waters are beneficial. For those whose hollows are soft and watery and phlegmatic, the hardest and most-mineral infused and brackish waters are beneficial: for thus they would become especially dried out. Whichever waters that are the best for seething and melting, these are likely to loosen the hollow especially and soften it. Whatever waters are mineral-rich and hard and the least good for seething, these especially contract and dry out the hollows. For, because of inexperience and because they think that salty waters are laxatives, folks are in error about salty waters. But salty waters are the opposite of laxatives, being full of minerals and unsuitable for boiling, so that they contract the hollows instead of melting them. Such are the facts about spring waters.

8. I will now discuss the facts about waters from rain and snow. Rainwaters are the lightest and sweetest and most delicate and brightest. To begin, the sun lifts these waters up and carries up the lightest and most delicate waters. Salt makes the process clear: for the salty part is left behind because of its thickness and weight, and it becomes salt, but the sun snatches up the lightest water because of its lightness. The sun draws this up not only from marshes but also from the sea and from all things in which there is some moisture: there is moisture in everything. The sun draws up the lightest and finest particles of moisture even from people. The most persuasive proof: when a person wearing a cloak walks or sits in the sun, whatever part of the skin the sun does not see, this

will not seem to sweat. For the sun snatches away whatever sweat appears. Whatever is covered under the cloak or by anything else, the sweat is held back and constrained from the sun and preserved by the covering, so that it is not removed by the sun. But when someone comes into the shade, the entire body sweats similarly: for the sun is not shining there. On account of these things, of all waters rainwater becomes putrid the most quickly and it has a difficult odor, because it is brought together and mixed from many sources, so that it quickly becomes putrid. Still more, when rainwater is snatched up and raised up mid-air, carried about and mixed about into the air, its turbidity and darkness is separated out and expelled, and it becomes mist and fog. Its brightest and lightest portion is left behind and becomes sweetened, cooked by the sun and boiled. All other boiled things always become sweet. Provided that the moisture is spread about and not yet balled together, it is conveyed mid-air. But, when it is gathered together and condenses somewhere to itself suddenly under winds setting against each other, at that time the rain breaks out where it happens to be the most twisted together. This is more likely to occur when, because of the winds, the clouds have become consistent and are set in motion and suddenly make way, mutually resisting opposite winds and other clouds. Then the first cloud is twisted together, and clouds are added later and they thus become thick and black and twisted together in one place. The clouds are broken because of their weight, and rain occurs. These are the best waters according to convenience. They do not need to be boiled off and purified from putrefaction. If not, they have a toilsome color and bring on sore throats and coughs and hoarseness in those drinking these waters.

Waters from snow and ice are all wicked. Once it is frozen, water is never restored to its previous nature. But its bright, airy, and sweet quality is expelled and destroyed. The muddiest and heaviest part is left. You will find it diminished in quantity. This is proof that the healthiest and lightest part has been removed and consumed by congealment: for the heaviest and thickest part would not be able to behave in this manner. Therefore, I think that waters from snow and ice and those following such waters are the most grievous for all purposes. Concerning rainwaters and those from snow and ice, it is such.

9. People suffer especially from kidney stones, and they are overcome by kidney disease and difficulty urinating and numbness in the legs. Tumors occur where they drink waters compounded of all sorts of stuff both from large rivers, into which other rivers flow, and also from marshes into which many and varied streams arrive. Tumors also occur in anyone who uses imported waters conveyed from a long distance and not from a short distance. For one water is not like another, but some are sweet, some are salty and astringent, some flow from warm sources. Mixing together, these quarrel against each other, and the strongest one always wins. But the same one does not always prevail, sometimes one, sometimes another, according to the winds: for the Boreas (North Wind) offers strength to this one, the Notos (South Wind) invigorates that one,

and the rest according to the same reasoning. Such waters necessarily deposit mud and sand in vessels, and the above-mentioned diseases occur when these waters are drunk.

(*Hippocratic* Airs, Waters, Places *7–9)*

C. *Pliny's further insights into the medicinal qualities of various waters. Note, however, that water actually expands when frozen.*

31. What kinds are the most useful waters is queried among physicians. They rightly condemn stagnant and slow-running waters, and they consider more useful those waters which flow. By its course, consequently, and the very agitation, water is rarefied and becomes more effective. For this reason, I marvel that cistern-waters are especially approved by some physicians. But they propose a reason: since the lightest water is rainwater which is able to rise and hang in the air.

32. Subsequently they also prefer snow and even ice over snow as if condensed in thinness to an infinite degree. These, snow and ice, are therefore lighter than water, and ice is lighter by much. It is a concern of living healthily that the opinion of these physicians be refuted. In the first place, the lightness of water can scarcely be ascertained otherwise than by sense-perception, as these waters differ between themselves with nearly no change of weight. Nor is the fact that water rises into the sky proof of the lightness of rainwater, since even stones appear to rise and, falling, they are tinged with the earth's vapor. For this reason, it happens that a lot of dirt is perceived to be contained in rainwater, and rainwater, consequently, becomes warm very quickly.

33. Indeed I wonder that snow and ice seem to be the most delicate substance when the proof of hailstones[12] is at hand, a drink from which—it is agreed—is extremely noxious. Not a few physicians proclaim among themselves to the contrary, that a drink from snow and ice is very unhealthy, since that which is the finest part has been removed. To be sure, it is understood that every liquid becomes diminished by freezing and a rash occurs with too much dew, and splotching occurs with hoarfrost, and similar effects occur with snow.

34. Indeed, it is agreed that rainwaters putrefy very quickly[13] and are the least suitable for enduring a voyage by sea. Epigenes,[14] however, says that water which has putrefied seven times will no longer become fetid. But even physicians confess that cistern water is injurious to bellies and throats because of its hardness, and in other waters there is not more mud or animals which make it disgusting.

12 #1.9.8.
13 I.e., they quickly lose their freshness.
14 Of Rhodes (2nd century BCE), an agricultural writer consulted by Pliny and Varro.

35. They likewise maintain that these same physicians must confess that river waters are not steadfastly the most beneficial, nor likewise the waters of any other source of roiling waters, and very many lakes are healthy. What then and of what kind are the best waters? One type in one place and another type elsewhere. Kings of Parthia drink only from the Choaspes and Eulaeus Rivers:[15] these waters accompany the kings even on distant trips. But it is apparent that the waters of these rivers are pleasing not because they are rivers, since the Parthian kings do not drink from the Tigris or Euphrates, nor do they drink from many other rivers.

(Pliny, NH *31.31–35)*

D. *Despite the caveats, Dioscorides praises the general healthfulness of water.*

Generally speaking, it is difficult to assess water due to its peculiarities and specific nature of its provenience, the winds, and several other factors; but on the whole, water is excellent if it is clean and sweet, free of any quality whatsoever, tarrying in the abdomen not even for the shortest period of time, and passing through painlessly and easily, causing neither flatulence nor becoming spoiled.

(Dioscorides, Medical Material *5.10, trans. Beck)*

4.2.2 Drinking Water

Did the ancients drink water straight? Hodge (2000: 98) observes that drinking unmixed water was likely rare if the sources mentioned it at all (André 1961: 163, who devotes a single page to water in his lengthy study of Roman cuisine), and the usual drink, even for children, was wine diluted with water (even a small quantity of alcohol would render water safer to drink by killing contaminants: the usual ratio was one part wine to three parts water). But there is evidence for drinking plain water. For mixed wine: #2.1.5A note.

A. *Unmixed water is prescribed for those engaged in strenuous occupations.*

Earlier I said that wine is very beneficial for those with dry and cold constitutions. Whether wine is not suitable for all folks with warm constitutions, or if a drink of water is better for them, as is written in the *Epidemics* (6.4.13), must be considered next. Perhaps it seems entirely strange to someone that a young man—a soldier or athlete or one of the diggers or reapers or those who plow the fields or any of those who perform strenuous work—might live on water alone. In this regard, concerning warm mixtures, Hippocrates was deceptive in declaring that they need a drink of water. It seems to me that Hippocrates was not

15 *Choaspes*: Karkheh in Afghanistan; *Eulaeus*: Dez in Iran.

saying this simply, but rather he was thinking about a very warm constitution, clearly so, poorly mixed, and not because the fellow has too much innate heat which Hippocrates says increases by the daily practice of athletes.

(Galen, On Preserving Health *5.12 [6.376 Kühn])*

B. *Andreas, personal physician to Ptolemy IV Philopator ("Father-Loving," r. 221–204 BCE), implies that some folk drink only water.*

Andreas assures that laser,[16] abundantly consumed, does not cause flatulence and is useful to the digestion for the elderly and women. Likewise, it is more useful in winter than in summer, and also for those drinking water.

(Pliny, NH *22.102)*

C. *Water was the preferred beverage for the notoriously austere Cato the Elder.*

Cato drank water on campaigns, except if burningly thirsty he would demand vinegar or, his strength failing, he would take a little wine.

(Plutarch, Cato the Elder *1.7)*

D. *In exile at Tomis on the Pontus, Ovid simply had no access to good wine and was compelled to drink water.*

You know that I drink nearly only water, nor am I oppressed by banqueting. Even if I were touched by a desire for such things, there is nonetheless no opportunity in Getic lands.

(Ovid, Letters from Pontus *1.10.30–32)*

E. *The waters of the Borysthenes (Dneiper), Hister (eastern Danube), and Padus (Po) Rivers are good for drinking (#1.5.5).*

i. While other rivers are agitated, the Borysthenes River flows down most serenely, gentler than the rest and very pleasant for drinking.

(Mela, On the Circuit of the World *2.6)*

ii. The Padus then leaps forth so quickly that, in scattered waves, for a long time it drives the flood such as it sent out, and it even protects its own riverbed in

16 Laser, distilled from silphium—which cannot be precisely identified—was widely used in antiquity for seasoning food and medicines (for silphium's digestive properties: Hippocratic *Regimen in Acute Diseases* 37; Theophrastus, *Enquiry into Plants* 6.4.6; Columella 12.4; Strabo, *Geography* 15.2.10). Growing along the coast of Cyrenaica (Herodotus, *Histories* 4.169; Theophrastus, *Causes of Plants* 1.5.1; Strabo 17.3.22–23), the plant was featured on local coinage (Tameanko 1992*: 26–28; Koerper and Kolls 1999: 133–143),* but the sheep had grazed it to extinction, and the emperor Nero received as a gift the last stalk that had been found within living memory (Pliny, *NH* 19.39).

the sea until from Histria on the opposite shore, flowing forth with the same force, the river Hister catches up with the Padus. For this reason, for those navigating through these places, where the rivers go on each side, there is a draught of sweet water between the sea waters.

(Mela, On the Circuit of the World *2.63; cf. Pliny 3.127–128)*

F. *The waters extracted from trees on the "Rainy" island in the Atlantic off the coast of northern Africa (one of the legendary Isles of the Blessed, the Canaries).*

The first island is called *Ombrios*, with no traces of buildings. It has a pond in the mountains and trees similar to giant fennel from which water is extracted: bitter water from the black trees, water sweet for drinking from the white trees.

(Pliny, NH *6.203)*

G. *Frequent changes of camp prevent soldiers from contracting water-borne diseases.*

If a crowd of soldiers stays too long in the same place in autumn or summer, then the most pernicious disease arises from the contagion of those waters and repulsiveness of their very odor because of contaminated drinking water and corrupted air. This is not able to be averted otherwise unless by a frequent change of camp.

(Vegetius, Epitome of Military Science *3.2.22–27)*

H. *Drinking water can alleviate belching.*

Whoever belches undigested food without any suffering of the chest ("heart-burn") should drink cold water at intervals and nonetheless restrain himself.

(Celsus, On Medicine *1.2.2)*

4.2.3 Flavors of Water and "Purifying" Water

Some waters were more palatable than others, and rainwater was particularly praised. But unpalatable particulates and pathogens often seep into rainwater. The most common methods of "purification" include masking unpleasant odors with something more appetizing, boiling, and mechanical procedures that remove particulates by straining (as recommended by Aristotle: #1.3.5A) or allowing particulates to settle to the bottom.

A. *Why the flavors of water vary.*

But why is the taste of water variable? For four reasons. The first is through which soil it is conveyed. The second according to the same reason, if the water is produced from a transmutation of the soil. The third comes from the air which is transformed into water. The fourth arises from the pollution which impure waters often receive through an injurious substance. These causes give waters their variable tastes. These causes bestow medicinal properties to waters. These causes effect the oppressiveness of the vapors and their pestilential stench. These causes are responsible for lightness and heaviness, or heat or too much coldness. It makes a difference whether the waters pass through places full of sulfur or nitron or bitumen. With danger to their lives people drink waters polluted in this way. Accordingly then Ovid says about a river which "the Cicones[17] have a drink of which renders the entrails stony and introduces marble to everything it touches" (*Metamorphoses* 5.313–15).

(Seneca, NQ *3.20.1–3; cf. Pliny,* NH *2.226)*

B. *Diophanes of Nicaea in Bithynia (1st century BCE) summarized a lengthy translation of an agricultural manual in Punic by Mago (before 146 BCE) whose 28-book study recorded North African agricultural practices. While Diophanes' abridgement was popular in antiquity, like Mago's original and Cassius Dionysius' translation, Diophanes' work survives only in extracts in later agricultural writers who mined the* Geoponika *for their own purposes. Diophanes recommended laurel to freshen up stale water.*

And you are to collect pure water in reservoirs through wooden pipes. African laurel macerated in water renders it healthy. We are to cure bad water in this way: let the water be poured in vessels, and let it remain in the open air until it has settled, and let it be gently removed into other containers without the sediment at the bottom.

(Diophanes, Geoponika *2.7.2–4)*

C. *Sweetening undrinkable water.*

i. Cooked parsley makes waters sweeter to drink.

(Pliny, NH *20.115)*

ii. If unhealthy waters must be drunk, muddled pennyroyal is sprinkled in.

(Pliny, NH *20.154)*

iii. For, within two hours, the locals—those who are seeking the Red Sea in the deserts—make nitron-rich and salty-sour waters serviceable by adding pearl barley, and then they eat that very barley.

(Pliny, NH *31.36)*

17 In southern Thrace, whom Odysseus encountered first on his return from Troy and whose flocks he and his men plundered (Homer, *Odyssey* 9.39–61).

D. *How to treat water to obtain the best results.*

38. Certain folk make a judgment about the healthiness of water with a balance. Elusive scrupulousness! Since it is extremely rare that one water would be lighter than another. Among equal things, a more certain understanding is that water, which rather quickly becomes warm and then again cold, is better.[18] To be sure, they affirm that the better water (lest they weigh it by hand), drawn from receptacles that are conveyed and placed on the ground, becomes warm. From what source is agreeable water especially likely to derive? To be sure from wells, as I see constantly in towns. But in those wells the logic of agitating the water by frequent drawing off meets with approval together with its slenderness owing to filtering the water through earth.

39. This is sufficient for health. For coldness, shadiness is necessary, and that the wells see sky.[19] Above all things, one observance—and this pertains to continuous flow—is that well-water should spring out from the bottom, not from the sides. For it happens that coolness to the touch is possible even by artifice, if water, pressed high or cast down from a height, grasps the beaten air. In swimming, the same water is perceived as colder by those holding their breath.

40. It was the discovery of the emperor Nero (r. 54–68 CE) to boil water and then chill it in glass by lowering it into the snow. Thus, the pleasantness of cold occurs without the damaging effects of snow. It is agreed that all water is more useful boiled. Likewise, heated water is more able to be cooled. A very clever discovery. This is a remedy for polluted water, if it is boiled down to half. Cold water, ingested, puts a stop to bleeding. If someone holds water in the mouth, it prevents bathers from becoming overheated in the baths. Waters which are very cold to drink are not equally cold to the touch—this good quality alternates—as many conclude from personal example.

(Pliny, NH *31.38–40)*

E. *Basil of Caesarea (330–379 CE) was a bishop of Cappadocia in Asia Minor who supported the Nicene Creed, advocated for the poor, and was an influential framer of communal monasticism. Among his writings was the* Hexaemeron, *meditations on the six days of creation. Here he reflects on God's view of the sea as good, reporting a method of desalinating seawater that may have been developed by the Arab mariners who repeated the process four or five times to produce potable water (Hales 1739; Haarhoff 2009: 237).*

Sailors, too, even boil seawater, and collect the vapor in sponges, to quench their thirst in pressing need.

(Basil of Caesarea, Homily *4.7:* Upon the Gathering Together of the Water*)*

18 For the Mpemba effect, where hot water seems to freeze more quickly than cold water: Aristotle, *Meteorology* 348b5–6.

19 I.e., be in open air.

4.2.4 Lead Poisoning

While ceramic pipes were recommended and used (Vitruvius, here; Columella, On Agriculture *1.5.2; Pliny,* NH *31.57), water was routinely conveyed through lead pipes (Frontinus,* Aqueducts *25.2), and lead poisoning is a very real threat when water remains stagnant in the pipes. The Roman aqueduct system, however, was designed for constant flow, and because of this, water did not remain in the pipes long enough for the lead to contaminate the supply. Sintering (the accretion of crystallized calcium carbonate) provided a further layer of protection that separated flowing water from the lead in the pipes.*

The advantages of earthenware pipes and the symptoms of lead poisoning.

> The conveyance of water by terracotta pipes has these advantages. First if any defect occurs in the work, anyone you like is able to repair it. Besides, water from terracotta pipes is healthier by far than water conveyed by lead pipes since the supply conveyed through lead seems to be harmful therefore because white lead is produced by it. This white lead, moreover, seems injurious to human bodies. Thus, what is produced from it, if it is harmful, is not itself doubted to be unhealthy.
>
> We are able to take an example, moreover, from those who work with lead, because their bodily colors (their complexions) are overtaken by paleness. For when, during casting, the lead is blown upon, the vapor from it, settling in the joints and from there destroying them, snatches the excellent characteristics of the workmen's blood from their limbs. Thus, it seems that water should not at all be conveyed in lead pipes if we want to have healthy water. Our daily diet can indicate that the flavor of water conveyed through terracotta pipes is better because everyone, even when they have their tables piled with silver tableware,[20] nonetheless use terracotta for the sake of preserving the water's flavor.
>
> *(Vitruvius,* On Architecture *8.6.10–11)*

4.2.5 Sabotaging the Water Supply

Water supplies were weaponized: at Athens some suspected that Spartan spies had sabotaged the wells, thus causing the epidemic in 430 BCE (see #2.1.4).

A. *After the* polis *of Kirrha, which controlled the road between the Corinthian Gulf and Delphi (Apollo's important oracular sanctuary), appropriated sacred lands, the Amphictyonic League ("of neighbors," including Athens) was formed, sparking the First Sacred War (c. 590 BCE). League members poisoned Kirrha's water supply with hellebore, a commonly prescribed emetic that causes diarrhea when taken in large doses. The weakened Kirrhans were easily defeated.*

20 Silver is generally found in combination with lead or copper mineralization.

The plain from Kirrha is entirely open, and the Kirrhans do not want to plant trees either because of some curse or because they know that the ground is useless for nurturing trees . . . and they say that the name for the place in our times comes from Kirrha. But in the *Iliad* (2.520) and likewise in the *Hymn to Apollo* (2.269, 282, 438), Homer calls the city by its ancient name, Krisa. At a later time those in Kirrha committed sacrilege against Apollo and they cut away some of the god's land. Therefore, it seemed best to the Amphictyons to wage war against the Kirrhans, and they appointed Cleisthenes, tyrant of Sicyon, as their military leader, and they brought Solon from Athens to advise them. The Pythia[21] proclaimed to them as they asked about victory, "you will not take it before you tear down this city's tower, not before dark-eyed Amphitrite's wave washes over my *temenos*,[22] crashing from the wine-dark sea."

Solon thus persuaded them to dedicate Kirrhan land to the god, in order that the sea might border on Apollo's *temenos*. Solon discovered another sly trick against the Kirrhans: he diverted the water of the Pleistos River, flowing along a channel to the city, in another direction. And, since they were drinking water from wells and from the sky (rain), the Kirrhans were still holding out against their besiegers. Then, throwing hellebore roots into the Pleistos, when he perceived that the water had sufficient poison, Solon diverted the river back to its channel, and the Kirrhans filled themselves with river-water without restraint. Those on guard-duty on the walls deserted their posts because of unceasing diarrhea. The Amphictyons took the city, and they exacted justice for the god from Kirrha, and Kirrha is now the seaport of Delphi.

(Pausanias, Description of Greece *10.37.5–8; cf. Hippocratic* Embassy *4; Frontinus,* Stratagems *3.7.6; Polyaenus,* Stratagems *6.13)*

B. *In 48 BCE, Caesar aimed to mediate the succession dispute between Ptolemy XIII and Cleopatra VII in Alexandria. The account of the Alexandrian War was probably written by Aulus Hirtius (90–43 BCE), a Roman statesman who served with Caesar from 58 onwards. Here, elaborate efforts to contaminate Caesar's water supply.*

6. After this plan was approved, Ganymedes[23] undertakes this great and difficult work. When the channels were blocked and all parts of the city which were occupied by himself were shut off, he then hurried to press out a great quantity of water from the sea by wheels and engines:[24] he did not cease from pouring this salt-water from elevated places into Caesar's section. For this reason, water,

21 The priestess of Apollo who communicated directly with the god and whose enthusiastic (that is to say, she was possessed by the god, "god within") proclamations were refined into elegant but cryptic dactylic hexameter lines. Thus, the male priesthood exercised ultimate control.

22 Amphitrite: #2.2.3A note; *temenos*: #2.2.13B.i note.

23 The eunuch tutor of Arsinoe IV, younger sister of Ptolemy and Cleopatra. Escaping Caesar's custody, Arsinoe joined the Egyptian army, was proclaimed queen, and, with her tutor, assumed military command.

24 #4.7.

a little saltier than normal, was drawn from the closest buildings and caused the men great astonishment regarding why this had happened. Nor did they themselves sufficiently believe it when those lower down the line said that their water was of the same character and taste as they had previously been accustomed to. And they were discussing the matter among themselves publicly, and they learned how much the waters differed by tasting them. To be sure, in a short span of time, the water closer to the contamination was altogether undrinkable, the water down the line was now found to be more contaminated and saltier.

7. After doubt was removed because of this, such great fear assaulted the men that they all seemed to be drawn down to the extreme misfortune of danger, and some said that Caesar delayed ordering them to embark onto the ships. Others were very seriously afraid that the Alexandrians could not be kept in ignorance while the Romans made their evacuation preparations since they were separated from the enemy by only a small distance. Nor was any retreat to the ships allowed while the enemy threatened and pursued. In Caesar's section there was, moreover, a great crowd of townspeople whom he had not moved from their homes because they openly feigned that they were loyal to our troops and seemed to have defected from their own people. But for my part, if the Alexandrians were to be protected as neither treacherous nor reckless, a long speech would be wasted in vain: when truly at a single time both their nation and nature are understood, no one can doubt that this race of people is most apt for betrayal.

8. Caesar lessened their fear with encouragement and reason. For he affirmed that sweet water could be found in wells and ditches, and that all the shores naturally had veins of sweet water. But if the nature of the Egyptian seashore was different from all the rest, nonetheless, because they securely held the sea, nor did the enemy have a fleet, they, the Roman troops, could not be prevented from seeking water daily in their ships either from the left at Paraetonium or from the right at the island:[25] these voyages in opposite directions would never be precluded at the same time by adverse winds. There was no consideration of flight not only for those who possessed rank in particular but not even for those who thought about nothing except their own lives. With great trouble they would endure enemy attacks from their fortifications. Once these were abandoned, they would be equal to the task neither in position nor number. Moreover, embarking onto the ships, especially from skiffs, would involve great delay and difficulty. To the contrary, the Alexandrians had the greatest speed and knowledge of the places and buildings. These men, especially insolent in victory, would rush ahead and occupy the higher places and buildings, and thus they would prevent our men from retreat and from our ships. Consequently, they should forget this plan and consider that there must be victory at every reckoning.

25 Paraetonium is over 160 kilometers (100 miles) west of Alexandria: the author may have intended the Nile Delta or an unknown island (Pharos would not have been on their right).

9. When this speech among the men was concluded and the minds of all were stirred, Caesar gives the centurions a task: that—all their other duties left off—they were to turn their minds to digging wells and not cease doing so for any part of the night. Because this business was undertaken and the minds of all were inspired for the labor, on that one night a great amount of sweet water was found. Thus, with effort not lasting a long time, they undid the painstaking war-engines and extreme efforts of the Alexandrians.

(Aulus Hirtius [?], Alexandrian War *6–9)*

4.3 Water Divining

A. *Water divining is a valuable skill, but literary evidence is scant. Here we have Vitruvius' thoughtful observations that derive from theory and experience, as "magical" as the process might seem.*

1. Consequently, water is especially necessary for life and pleasures and for daily use. It will be more abundant if the sources are open and flowing. But if they are not flowing forth, then sources must be sought and collected underground. These sources must be tested thusly: a water diviner lies forward onto his teeth before the sun rises, in places where the water is to be sought, and, with your chin placed on the ground and propped up, these regions are to be looked over. For your vision will not wander higher than it ought to when the chin is immobilized but will trace out a level even with a determined height in those regions. Then, where moisture is seen curling and rising in the air, there you should dig: for this sign is not able to occur on dry ground.

2. Likewise, those searching for water must notice what characteristics the places have. For there are places in which water arises. In clay the supply is thin and meager and not deep, and it will not have the best flavor. Likewise, in loose sand the supply is scant, but water will be found in lower places, and it will be muddy and unpleasant. Moreover, in black earth moisture and slender drops will be found which, gathered from winter storms, settle in hard, solid places: these waters have the best flavor. In gravel, truly, moderate but not fixed veins are discovered. These are also of excellent sweetness. Likewise, in vigorous coarse gravel and sand and red sand, the supply is more certain and stable, and these are of good flavor. Waters from red rock are abundant and good, if they do not flow through the interstices and melt. Under the roots of mountains and in flinty rocks waters flow plentifully and amply; and these waters are rather icy and healthy. From springs in level fields flow waters that are salty, heavy, tepid, not sweet; unless trickling underground they break out from mountains into the middle of the fields and there, covered by the shadows of trees, they excel over the sweetness of mountain springs.

3. Moreover, these growing things will be discovered as signs according to which the characteristics of the soil described above is written: a delicate rush, wandering (i.e., wild) willow, alder tree, chaste-tree, reeds, ivy, and other things

which are of this type that cannot grow without moisture. These same plants are accustomed to grow in pools which, settling below the rest of the soil, receive moisture from rains and fields through the winter, and on account of their capacity they retain moisture for a longer time. Such places must not be trusted, but signs are born in regions and soils, not pools, where plants are generated of themselves, not sown, and water must be sought there.

4. If these discoveries are indicated in such places, they must be tested thusly. The place ought to be dug in every direction no less than three paces wide and five paces deep, and in it, around sunset, either a bronze ewer or lead basin should be placed. What has been prepared from these should be smeared on the inside with oil and placed upside down, and the top of the pit should be covered with reeds or a frond, and earth should be sprinkled over the top. Then on the next day the pit should be opened and, if there are drops of moisture in the vessel, this place will have water.

5. Likewise, if a vessel made from clay—but not fired—covered in the same way, will be placed in a pit, if this place has water, when it is opened the vessel will be moist and dissolved by the moisture. Or if a fleece of wool will be placed in the pit and on the following day water will be squeezed out, this will show that the place has an abundance of water. Nonetheless, if a trimmed lamp, full of oil and lit, will be placed covered in that spot and on the next day it will not be burnt out but will have traces of oil and its wick and itself will be moist, this will indicate that the place has water, consequently because warmth draws moisture to itself. Likewise, if a fire is lit in that place and the soil, warmed and burnt, produces a cloudy vapor from itself, this place will have water.

6. Waters, moreover, should especially be sought in mountains and northern regions because in those regions waters are found to be both sweeter and healthier and more abundant. For these regions are turned away from the sun's course, and in these places trees are thick and woody, and the mountains themselves have blocking shadows, and the sun's rays do not directly reach towards the earth, nor are moist things able to dry out.

7. Mountain valleys especially receive rain. And on account of the thickness of the woods snowfalls are retained there for a long time because of the shadows of trees and mountains. Then, melted, snows filter through the earth's veins and thus reach the lowest roots of the mountains, from which the flowing fruits of the springs break forth. Moreover, to the contrary, folk are not able to obtain water supplies in level plains. Whatever waters are there are unable to have healthful properties, because the sun's furious attack—boiling on account of no resistance from shade—snatches up the moisture from the flatness of the fields. If any waters come into sight, from these the air scatters that which is the lightest and thinnest and with delicate wholesomeness, calling those waters away into the sky's assault. Whichever parts are very heavy and hard and unpleasant, these are left in the springs on the plains.

(Vitruvius, On Architecture *8.1; cf. Pliny,* NH *31.43–49)*

B. *King Theodoric's letter of recommendation for a water diviner from Africa. The Roman statesman Cassiodorus (c. 485–585 CE) was a scholar of antiquity and senior advisor and administrator under Theodoric, king of the Ostrogoths (r. 475–526 CE) and Athalaric (r. 526–534 CE). After retiring from public life, Cassiodorus founded the Christian* Vivarium *monastery in southern Italy. Cassiodorus' writings are a valuable source of information on Ostrogothic and Byzantine Italy.*

> King Theodoric to Apronianus, a distinguished man and count of private estates. From a referral of your magnitude we have discovered that a water-diviner has come to Rome from African regions, where the art of water-divining is always cultivated with great enthusiasm owing to the dryness of the lands, a diviner who can bring waters to dry places so that by his service he renders habitable places that were dry because of too much barrenness. . . .
>
> Therefore, if his testimonial aligns with your wisdom and reading of books and usage of things described above, you will lighten his travels and his poverty: he will accept wages when he has demonstrated the gifts of his art. For although the Roman state abounds with irrigated waters and rejoices in its fountains and is very rich with a flood of beautiful installations, nonetheless there are found many suburban places which seem to lack this practical skill, deservedly retained and known to be partly urgent. Nonetheless this engineer must be altogether enjoined so that he can elevate the waters which he has discovered and make them rise by his skill, a thing which does not prevail to rise naturally. Therefore, let this man be considered among the masters of other skills, lest it be thought that there was anything desirable which the Roman state could not retain under our authority.
>
> *(Cassiodorus,* Various Histories *3.53.1, 5–6)*

4.4 Urban Planning

A. *Some places were simply more suitable for human habitation than others. Here, drawing on the four-element theory, Vitruvius' description of the ideal situation for a city and the drawbacks of other conditions, including the threat of property damage owing to bad climate.*

> 1. In the case of walls these will truly be the guiding principles. First, the choice of the healthiest location. Moreover, this will be elevated and not cloudy, nor frosty, and looking towards regions of the sky neither burning nor chilly but temperate. Then thus a marshy neighborhood will be avoided. For when morning breezes come to the town with the rising sun and when the mists that spring forth are joined to them, and when they sprinkle the venomous breaths of swampy creatures[26] mixed with mist into the bodies of the inhabitants with their

26 #2.1.1E and note; #2.1.3E.

breath, they render the place unwholesome. Likewise, if the walls will be along the sea and look towards the south or west, they will not be healthy, because through the summer the noon-time sky (south) grows warm with the rising sun and burns at midday. Likewise, that which looks to the setting sun grows warm with the rising sun, is hot at midday, and is blazing hot in the evening.

2. Therefore because of changes of heat and cold, bodies which are in these places are injured. Moreover, it is permitted to notice this also from those things which are not animals. For, in covered wine cellars, no one takes light from the south nor from the west, but from the north because this region at no time receives changes but is continuously enduring and immutable. Consequently, granaries which look towards the sun's course quickly exchange their excellent quality, and fish-sauces[27] and fruits which are not stored in that part of the sky are not preserved for very long.

3. For always, when heat cooks out the vigor from the airs and snatches out their natural virtues by sucking them out with warm vapors, heat dissolves them and renders them weak, growing soft with warmth. As we also notice with iron, which—although hard by nature—thus softens in furnaces, warmed by the fire's vapor, so that it is forged easily into every type of shape. Likewise, when soft and glowing hot, it is cooled, dipped in cold water; it hardens again and is restored to its earlier quality.

4. It is also permitted to consider that these conditions are so from the fact that in summer not only in pestilential places but even in healthy locations, all bodies become weak because of the heat. Through the winter even those regions which are pestilential become healthy, consequently because they are frozen by the cold conditions. No less also are bodies, brought from icy regions into warm areas, able to harden, but they are dissolved. Moreover, when they are brought over to frigid northern regions, bodies from hot locales not only do not labor because of the change of location, but they are even strengthened with respect to their health.

5. It therefore seems that caution must be taken in establishing walls in those regions which are able to sprinkle warm blasts over human bodies. For all bodies are composed from the principles which the Greeks call *stoicheia* ("elements"), that is to say from heat and moistness, from earth and air, and so with these mixtures, owing to natural proportions, the qualities of all animals in the world are shaped by type.

6. Therefore when heat in these bodies surpasses the preferred ratio, then heat kills and melts the rest with violent hotness. Moreover, a burning sky from certain quarters brings about these faults, since heat settles into open veins more than the body allows owing to the natural proportion from the mixtures. Likewise, if moistness takes hold of the bodies' veins and renders them unequal,

27 #6.4.3.

other principles ("elements")—when destroyed by liquid—are washed away, and their virtues are dissolved from their compositions. Likewise, these faults are poured back into bodies by the chilling of moisture of winds and breezes. No less does the natural composition of air and the earthy element weaken the other principles by augmenting or diminishing them: the earthy by the abundance of food, the airy by the weight of the sky.

(Vitruvius, On Architecture *1.4.1–6; cf. Hippocratic* Regimen *2.37; #2.1.1E, #2.1.3E)*

B. *Some marshy areas, nonetheless, were successfully inhabited, including Ravenna (in northern Italy, on the Adriatic coast) where the air was, surprisingly, "harmless" (see Borca 2000: 57–60). Despite the challenges, marshland also offered numerous advantages, such as access to abundant flora and fauna.*

The largest city in the swampland is Ravenna, entirely built of wood and intersected by streams, and travelled by means of bridges and ferries. Ravenna receives not a small portion of sea during the flood tides, so that—all filthy debris washed away by the tides and rivers—the foulness of the air is altogether cured. Thus at any rate the place is closely scrutinized as healthy to such an extent that the leaders proclaimed the site good for nurturing athletes who fight in single combat (gladiators) and for training them there. There is indeed this marvel of the situation there: that the airs in the marsh are harmless, accordingly as in Alexandria, the one next to Egypt, during the summer: Lake Mareotis loses its wicked quality on account of the river Nile's[28] flooding and disappearance of standing marshes. But the condition of the grapevine is also worthy to admire: for the marsh produces it and makes it bear fruit quickly, and a great deal of it, but the vine dies within four or five years.

(Strabo, Geography *5.1.7)*

C. *Sometimes marshland was irredeemable, and a city might be moved, as was Salpia in southeastern Italy, c. 200 BCE. The place flourished until the expanding marsh forced the population to abandon the site in the 16th century (Gabba 1983: 514–516; Borca 2000: 58). See #2.1.1E.*

Likewise, in Apulia the town Old Salpia—which, returning from the Trojan War, Diomedes[29] established, or, as some have written, Elpias of Rhodes—was located in places of this kind (swampy). Because of this, the inhabitants, suffering from being sick every year, at some point came to Marcus Hostilius, and

28 #1.5.1.

29 Diomedes was one of several Greek heroes of the Trojan War who returned home after the war but were driven away for some offence that insulted the gods: these heroes sought refuge in southern Italy where they founded settlements, died, and were worshipped with hero cults.

publicly entreating they succeeded, convincing Hostilius to seek and select a place suitable for transferring the walls of Salpia. Hostilius did not delay, but—with all considerations investigated in a very learned fashion—he immediately purchased a holding along the sea in a healthy place, and he asked the Roman senate and people that they allow the town to transfer. Hostilius established walls and divided the areas and gave individual townspeople plots for the right of ownership for one *sesterce* each. These things done, he opened up the lake into the sea and created a port for the municipality from the lake. So the Salpians now dwell four miles from the old town in a healthy site.

(Vitruvius, On Architecture *1.4.12)*

4.5 Civic Hydraulic Engineering

4.5.1 Fountains and Spring Houses

A. *While rainwater was collected in cisterns, public fountains that linked into nearby water supplies were constructed in many cities, providing a source of fresh drinking water and a center of socialization for the women who collected it (usually lower class and enslaved women), as shown on many Archaic Greek vases (540–460 BCE), as we see here. Water jar (hydria) with women at the fountains by the Priam Painter (c. 520 BCE).*

FIGURE 4.5.1A Women at a fountain-house, Museum of Fine Arts, Boston: 61.195.

B. *There were two springs in Scherie, the capital of the mythical Phaeacians, a people renowned for their hospitality and whose king, Alcinoos, helped Odysseus return home after wandering the Mediterranean for ten years. One of Alcinoos' springs was private; the other, like many public springs, was a gift of imperial (or, as here, divine) beneficence.*

> In the orchard are two springs: one sprinkles water through the whole orchard; the other, on the other side, flows under the courtyard's entrance towards the lofty home, from which the citizens draw water. For these are the splendid gifts from the gods in the kingdom of Alcinoos.
>
> *(Homer,* Odyssey *7.129–132)*

C. *Travelers found respite at public fountain houses.*

> Hermes, I stand by a windy row of trees in the crossroads, near a grey shore, offering rest to toiling folk on the road, and a spring answers back with pure cold water.
>
> *(Anyte,* Greek Anthology *9.314)*

D. *Fountains might be erected as memorials to the deceased. This one seems to have included a bench. Nicias of Miletus was a physician and epigrammatic poet whose literary circle included Theocritus (*Idyll *11.1, 13.1, 28.7).*

> Traveler, sit here under the poplar trees since you are tired, and—coming closer—drink from my spring. Far away remember this spring which Simos set up beside Gillos, his deceased child.
>
> *(Nicias of Miletus,* Greek Anthology *9.315)*

E. *Fountain houses also incorporated images of water gods, including nymphs, or they might be dedicated to the nymphs, as at Corinth (Kopestonsky 2016). Hermocreon is known only from this epigram.*

> Nymphs of the water, to whom Hermocreon has set up these gifts, after chancing upon your beautifully flowing fountain, greetings! Full of clear water, may you dance with your lovely feet in your watery home.
>
> *(Hermocreon,* Greek Anthology *9.327)*

F. *Over time, fountain houses became increasingly elaborate, incorporating artwork and porticoes. (For the fountain house at Mégara: Hellner 2006; Longfellow 2011; for the fountains at Athens: Christaki and Nastos 2018. Actium: #7.4.3D). Here we have a rare literary reference to the fountain house at Mégara, commissioned by the tyrant Theagenes (7th century BCE) to curry popular favor.*

> In the city of Mégara is a spring which Theagenes built for them: earlier I mentioned that he joined his daughter in marriage to Cylon of Athens. As tyrant,[30]

30 #2.2.11H note.

this Theagenes constructed the spring, worthy of a glance on account of its size and beauty and for the number of its pillars. Water, called "of the Sithnid nymphs," flows into it. The Mégarians say that the Sithnid nymphs are from that territory, and that Zeus mingled in sex with one of them. Mégarus, the child of Zeus and this nymph, escaped during the flood in Deucalion's time, he fled to the peaks of Gerania, a mountain not yet having this name but on account of this was later called Gerania: for, while cranes (*gernaoi*) were flying, Mégarus was swimming towards the trumpeting of those birds.

(Pausanias, Description of Greece *1.40.1; for the flood: #1.9.11A)*

4.5.2 Greek Aqueducts

From the Bronze Age on, water was conveyed into settlements from further afield, including at Knossos in Crete (see Angelakis et al. 2006, 2007). The Assyrians also developed rudimentary aqueduct technology: e.g., Assurnarsipal II (884–859 BCE) commissioned a canal from the upper Zab River to supply the city of Nimrud with water and to irrigate its fields (Wilson 2008: 290).

A. *Wishing to gain popular support, the tyrant Polycrates of Samos (c. 550–522 BCE) authorized an aqueduct extending 2.5 kilometers (1.5 miles) through a 1 kilometer (0.6-mile) rock-hewn tunnel (a remarkable feat of engineering), known eponymously after its engineer Eupalinos of Mégara.*

I have expounded at length about the Samians because the three greatest engineering feats of all the Greeks are theirs. The first is the doubled-mouthed trench from below a lofty mountain about 150 *orguiae* high. The length of the channel is seven *stadia*, the height and width are eight Greek feet each. Another trench, 20 *pecheis* deep and three Greek feet wide, was dug through its entirety. Through this trench, water arrives at the city, conveyed through channels, drawn off from a great spring. The architect of this channel was Eupalinos son of Naustrophos, a Mégaran. This is one of the three works. The second is a breakwater around the harbor in the sea, 20 *orguiae* deep. The mole is more than two *stadia* long. As for the third, they engineered the largest temple of all those that I have seen.[31] Its first architect was Rhoikos son of Philes, a local man. Regarding these construction works I have expounded at greater length on the Samians.

(Herodotus, Histories *3.60)*

B. *An anonymous epigram promoting tourism to Assos on the Aegean coast in Asia Minor: water-poor Assos now has an aqueduct! Axiochus (the eponymous Assios) is the river that was diverted into the city.*

31 Temple of Hera. The first temple dates to the eighth century BCE. Herodotus saw the third temple, which was also erected under Polycrates. Only one column remains standing.

The whole city prays to Axiochus, passing by like a god, he has healed the city's misery. He sent out water flowing from above a spring on Assos, cutting through the hard faces of many rocks. Travelers, all of you, flee no longer, running away at a distance: I overflow with Axiochus' chilly waters.

(Anonymous, Greek Anthology *9.679)*

4.5.3 Roman Aqueducts

A. *The Romans were rightly proud of their aqueducts, which they considered a uniquely Roman accomplishment, owing in part to Roman hydraulic concrete (#5.3.1).*

May you compare the clearly idle pyramids or other works of the Greeks—sluggish but celebrated with repute—with these numerous and indispensable monuments of so much water.

(Frontinus, Aqueducts *1.16)*

B. *Rome's first aqueduct, the* Aqua Appia, *was commissioned in 312 BCE. Here we have the political backstory and the aqueduct's course.*

When Marcus Valerius Maximus and Publius Decius Mus were consuls (312 BCE), in the 30th year after the beginning of the Samnite War,[32] the *Aqua Appia* was led into the city by Appius Claudius Crassus the censor,[33] whose cognomen was later Caecus.[34] Appius was the one who took care that the *Via Appia* was built from the *Porta Capena* all the way to the city of Capua.[35] Appius had a colleague, Caius Plautius, whose cognomen was given as *Venox* on account of seeking for *venae* ("veins") of water. But because Plautius withdrew himself as censor within a year and six months—misled that his colleague would do the same—the name of the aqueduct extended as an honor to Appius alone who, while many were hanging back from the work, is said to have extended his censorship until he could complete both the road and his aqueduct. The *Aqua Appia* is drawn in on the Lucullan estate along the *Via Praenestina* between the seventh and eighth milestones on a side-branch leftward at 780 paces. Its channel, from its head all the way to the *Saliane* ("salty") spring, which is at the *Porta Trigemina*,[36] has a length of 11,190 paces. The subterranean flow of this span is 11,130 paces; above ground the substructure and arched work nearest

32 The Romans fought three wars against the Samnites, their neighbors to the southeast (343–341 BCE, 326–304 BCE, and 298–290 BCE). Among Rome's chief competitors for control over central Italy, the Samnites were courageous, fierce, predatory warriors who preferred to occupy cities built by other peoples than build their own. Frontinus refers here to the first Samnite War.

33 #4.1.3A note.

34 "Blind," from age-related macular degeneration.

35 The *Porta Capena* was a gate of the southeastern section of the early-4th-century-BCE Servian Wall. Capua is an inland city in Campania north of Naples.

36 "Old Hope": another gate in the Servian Wall, between the Aventine Hill and the Tiber.

the *Porta Capena* conveys water for 60 paces. At the *Spes Vetus*[37] within the border of the Torquatian and Epaphroditean Gardens,[38] a branch of the *Aqua Augusta*, added by Augustus as a supplement, is joined to the *Aqua Appia*. [. . .] This branch receives its source on the *Via Praenestina* at the sixth milestone, side-branch, 980 paces leftward, near the *Via Collatina*. Its channel completes 6,380 paces all the way to the "Twins"[39] in a subterranean stream. The waters of the *Aqua Appia* begin to be distributed at the base of the Publican Hill at the *Porta Trigena*, which is called *Salinae*.

(Frontinus, Aqueducts *1.5)*

C. *A brief history of Rome's aqueducts.*

121. But let the marvels, invincible in true estimation, now be described. Quintus Marcius Rex, ordered by the senate to restore the channels of the *Aquae Appia, Anio* and *Tepula* led out a new channel, called after his own name, with underground passages driven through the mountains within the time of his praetorship (144 BCE). In addition, after the *Aqua Virgo* was added and the other streams were repaired, Agrippa,[40] during his aedileship, made 70 basins, 500 fountains in addition, 130 distribution-reservoirs: many were even embellished with care. On those works he placed 300 bronze or marble statues, 400 columns of marble,[41] and all these within the span of a year. Agrippa himself adds that, during the commemoration of his aedileship, games were sponsored for 59 days, and 170 public baths—which have now increased at Rome to a boundless number—were opened up for free.

122. But the newest expense of an installation—begun by Caius Caesar ("Caligula": r. 37–41 CE) and completed by Claudius (r. 41–54 CE)—overcame the preceding aqueducts, insofar as from the 40th milestone to this elevation, the Curtian and Caerulean springs and the new *Aqua Anio* flowed together, so that all the hills of the city would be watered, with 350,000,000 *sesterces* appropriated for this work.

123. But if anyone were to consider more diligently the abundance of waters in the public supply, bathing establishments, pools, channels, homes, gardens, suburban villas, the extent of waters coming in, the built-up arches, hills cut through, valleys leveled, one would confess that nothing was to be more admired in the whole world.

(Pliny, NH *36.121–123; cf. Strabo 5.3.8; Dio Cassius,* Roman History *49.43)*

37 A temple in the eastern quarter of the city outside the Servian Wall.

38 Torquatian Garden on the Esquiline of unknown ownership and mentioned only once. Nero's wealthy freedman, who failed to prevent the emperor's suicide (Suetonius, *Nero* 49, *Domitian* 14), owned the eponymous Epaphroditean Villa Garden on the Esquiline.

39 So-called because two aqueducts join at this spot.

40 Marcus Vipsanius Agrippa (63–12 BCE), Augustus' friend and agent, assumed oversight of hydraulic infrastructure in 33 BCE, serving informally as the city's first water commissioner and taking steps to increase the overall supply and distribution as equitably as possible between public works, private homes, and businesses.

41 *Cippi*, low pillars, often inscribed, to mark graves or, as here, the course of the aqueduct.

D. *In his autobiography, Augustus made note of his own aqueduct initiatives.*

I repaired streams of the aqueducts falling from age in several places, and I lengthened the aqueduct which is called *Marcia* with a new spring sent into its stream.

(Augustus, Res Gestae *20)*

E. *In 52 CE, Claudius expanded the aqueduct system, as proclaimed on this monumental inscription displayed on Rome's eastern gate (the* Porta Praenestina*).*

Tiberius Claudius Caesar Augustus Germanicus, son of Drusus, Pontifex Maximus,[42] 12 times with tribunician authority, five times consul, 27 times general, father of the state, at his own expense took care that from its springs, which were called Caerulean and Curtian, the *Aqua Claudia* be brought into the city from the 45th milestone, likewise, the new Anio from the 62nd milestone.

*(*CIL *6.1256)*

F. *The aqueducts did leak and would thus require regular maintenance. Here Juvenal (#2.2.13B.vi) imagines an unnamed Roman preparing to leave to escape the anxieties of life in the big city. The protagonist stops for a moment under the* Aqua Capena, *once majestic, now leaky and decrepit.*

But while his entire house is brought together in one vehicle, he stopped at the old arches and the wet (i.e., dripping) *Aqua Capena.*

(Juvenal, Satire *3.10–11)*

G. *Pipes were regulated and standardized. Cf. Frontinus,* Aqueducts *1.38–63 for all pipe adjutages.*

But every tube is gauged either by its diameter or by its circumference or by the measure of its area, from which also the capacity becomes evident. So that we may distinguish more easily the difference of the inch adjutage, squared digit, and rounded digit, and the *quinaria* (five-quarter digit) itself, one must employ the nature of the *quinaria*, the adjutage that is both most certain and especially well-known. Therefore, the inch-adjutage has a diameter of one and a third digits. It takes in more than one *quinaria* and an eighth of a *quinaria*: that is 1.5/12 of a *quinaria* and 3/288 and 2/3 of 1/288. The square digit, reduced to a round slope, has a diameter of one digit and 1 ½ twelfths of digit and 1/72 in diameter. It takes in 10/12 of a *quinaria*. The round digit has a diameter of one digit; it takes in 7/12 and 0.5/12 and 1/72 of a *quinaria*.

(Frontinus, Aqueducts *1.26)*

42 #1.9.12G note.

H. *Adjutages were regulated according to use (thus controlling the flow) and these regulations were abused. Stamps authenticated the adjutage, and their lack would indicate deliberate tampering.*

> Since the issues which pertain to the regulation of the private use of waters have been explained, it is not far removed from this topic, by reason of example, to touch on certain matters by which we can discover that those very healthful ordinances are being circumvented. I have found certain pipes, larger than granted, placed in many reservoirs, and some of those not even stamped. Moreover, as often as a stamped pipe exceeds the legitimate measure, the desire of the agent who stamped it is revealed. But when the pipe is not even stamped, the evident blame of everyone is recognized, especially of the one receiving the pipe, then also of the overseer. In some reservoirs, when pipes of the legitimate measure are stamped, pipes of a larger measure have been immediately substituted. Thence it happens that the water is not controlled for a legitimate span (50 feet). But, squeezed out through short narrow pipes, it easily fills the larger pipe next to it. Consequently, as often as a pipe is stamped, this step of diligence should still be added: that the pipes closest in space—which I have said have been prescribed by a decree of the senate—should also be stamped. Thus finally, when he will know that he should not place stamped pipes otherwise, the overseer will lack every excuse.
>
> *(Frontinus,* Aqueducts *2.112)*

I. *Rome had two groups of slaves responsible for maintaining the aqueducts.*

> 116. The maintenance of the channels remains to be considered. Before I begin to speak about maintenance, a few things must be explained about the slave group that has been prepared for this reason. There are two groups, one is public, the other belongs to Caesar.[43] The public group is older, which we have said (*Aqueducts* 2.98) was left to Augustus (r. 27 BCE—14 CE) by Agrippa and by him made public property. This group has about 240 men. The number of Caesar's group is 460, which Claudius (r. 41–54 CE) established when he led his aqueduct into the city.
>
> 117. Each group, moreover, is divided into several classes of workers: overseers, reservoir keepers, inspectors, flint workers, plasterers, and other workmen. It is necessary that some of these be outside the city for those tasks which do not seem to be of great laboriousness but nonetheless seem to demand speedy help. In the city around their stations at the reservoirs and public-works (i.e., fountains) workmen ply hard on all the works, especially those relating to sudden emergencies, so that the help of abundant waters is able to be turned from several regions into the one over which necessity lays. I decided to return thus

43 2.2.12D§15 note.

to some degree of discipline and public service—such a great number of each group were accustomed to preferential treatment or were pulled away into private works because of the negligence of their overseers—so that on the previous day I would dictate what each group was to do and also so that whatever it had done on the day was recorded.

118. The wages of the public group are paid from the state treasury, an expense that is discharged by the return of taxes pertaining to water rights. These rights depend on places and buildings near the channels and reservoirs or public works or basins. The Divine Nerva's (r. 96–98 CE) dedication to justice restored to the people nearly 250,000 *sesterces*, lost or misplaced, returned in recent times to Domitian's (r. 81–96 CE) accounts. Our painstaking attention has rendered the funds to a state of settled regulation so that it was agreed which places pertained to this tax. The group belonging to Caesar accepts its wages from the imperial treasury from which are drawn all expenses pertaining to all the lead for the channels and reservoirs and basins.

(Frontinus, Aqueducts 2.116–18)

J. *Damage, maintenance, and repairs.*

119. Since I have explained the matters that seem to pertain to the slave groups, as I had promised, I now turn towards the maintenance of the channels, a thing worthy of rather eager concern since it is a particular indication of the greatness of the Roman empire. For many and extensive works constantly fall into disrepair which ought to be attended to before they begin to need extensive help. Generally, nonetheless, their care ought to be sustained with wise moderation, because those eager either to build or enlarge a work cannot always be trusted. Consequently, the supervisor of the water supply ought to be trained not only with the knowledge of skilled professionals but even with his own experience. He should employ not only the architects of his own office, but he also ought to summon the trustworthiness, no less than the detailed knowledge, of additional experts so that he might assess what must be done immediately, what can be deferred, and again what ought to be done through contractors, what should be done by his own artisans.

120. Repair work arises from these causes: something is damaged either by the owner's immoderate behavior or by age or the force of storms or the defect of faulty construction, which has happened often in recent works.

121. Generally, those parts of the channels which are sustained on arches—especially those on arches which are conveyed over a river—or situated close to the sides of mountains, are troubled either by age or the force of storms. Consequently, these repairs must be set forth with care and haste. The subterranean portions, exposed to neither frost nor heat, come to less damage. The faults, moreover, are of this kind: with the result that help comes to them, without interrupting the flow, or if they are not able to be repaired unless the flow is diverted, just as the repair which necessarily happens in the trench itself.

122. These repairs become necessary from a two-fold cause: because the path of the water is narrowed, either when silt accretes, which sometimes hardens into a crust, or because the plaster coverings are ruined, from which leaks occur, for which the sides of the channels and substructures are necessarily damaged. The pillars themselves, built from tufa,[44] also slip under so great a weight. Damage around the trenches of the flows ought not be repaired during the summer, lest the use of water is interrupted at a time when it is especially desired, but instead they should be repaired in spring or autumn and with the greatest haste so that—all things certainly prepared in advance—the flows cease for as few days as possible. It escapes no one that this must be done for individual channels—one at a time—lest, if all the channels were diverted equally, water would be lacking for the whole state.

123. The repairs which ought to be accomplished—not disturbing the water-flow—consist especially in masonry work which fittingly happens at the right times and faithfully. The suitable time for masonry work is from the Kalends of April (April 1)[45] to the Kalends of November in such a way that it is best to interrupt the work for the part of the summer that grows warm with too much heat, because there is a need for a temperate sky so that masonry work can suitably absorb and harden into a solid mass. No less than frost, moreover, does a rather piercing sun destroy building material. Nor does any work demand more diligent care than that which stands against water, and so trustworthiness must be demanded in each detail according to the law known by all, but observed by few.

124. I would believe that no one doubts that the closest trenches—that is, the ones of squared stone which stand at the seventh milestone—should be especially safeguarded, both since they are of the largest work and individually support more waters. If it would be necessary to interrupt these waters, a greater part of the city would be deprived of water. There are, nonetheless, remedies for this challenge: a temporary installation should be raised to the level of the failing infrastructure, the trench of the lead channels is extended again through the span of the interrupted channel. Further, since nearly all conduits were directed through the fields of private individuals and the allocation of future expense seemed difficult, unless bolstered by some legal decree, and at the same time lest the contractors for repairing the flows be prohibited from access, a decree of the senate, which I append below, was passed:

125. "The consuls Quintus Aelius Tubero and Paulus Fabius Maximus (11 BCE) have made this report concerning the repair of the streams, conduits,

44 A porous variety of limestone.

45 In the Roman calendar, dates were recorded as so many days (counting inclusively) before the Kalends (the first day of the Roman month, originally the day of the new moon), the Nones (the day of the half-moon, the fifth or seventh of the month; the ninth day before the Ides), and the Ides (the day of the full moon, the 13th or 15th of the month).

arches of the *Aquae Julia, Marcia, Appia, Tepula, Anio*, regarding what would be pleasing to happen in this regard concerning which the senate has decreed: that when those streams, conduits, arches—which Augustus Caesar promised would be restored by the senate at their expense—should be repaired, the earth, mud, stones, clay shards, sand, wood, and the rest of the materials, which are needed for this work, whence as each of these things is able to be removed, obtained, carried from close by without injury of private individuals, their value should be estimated by the judgment of a good man, removed, obtained, carried out. For all these materials to be exported for the sake of restoring infrastructure, as much work as there is, without injury to the property owners, let pathways be given, let rights-of-way extend through the fields of private individuals."

126. However, damages often arise from the immoderate behavior of owners who undermine the flow in many ways. For, in the first place, they fill the spaces around the aqueducts—which ought to remain open—either with buildings or trees. Trees do more harm by whose roots the vaulted roofs and the sides are weakened. Then, private property owners arrange local and rustic roads through the very infrastructures. Finally, they block the approach for repairs. All these things have been foreseen according to the senatorial decree which I append below:

127. "The consuls Quintus Aelius Tubero and Paulus Fabius Maximus (11 BCE) have made this report that the paths of waters which come into the city are occupied with tombstones and buildings and are planted with trees, regarding what would be pleasing to happen in this regard concerning which the senate has decreed: when repairing flows and conduits by which public works are damaged, it is pleasing that 15 paces should extend on each side around springs and arches and walls, and around the channels which are under ground and the conduits within the city and the building adjacent to the city, on each side five paces should be left so that in these places it is permitted to place neither a tomb nor a building nor to plant trees after this time. If there are now any trees within this space, they should be cut out except if there are estates containing them and they are confined within the buildings. If anyone will act against these mandates, for individual instances there will be a penalty of 10,000 *sesterces*, of which half will be given to the accuser as a reward by whose effort there has been a conviction of the person who acted against this senatorial decree. Moreover, the other half will be returned to the public treasury. Concerning this matter the water overseers will judge and examine."

128. This decree of the senate seems especially fair, even if these terms were claimed only for the public advantage. However, with all the more admirable equity, our ancestors did not even take by force from private individuals what pertained to public rule. But when they led waterworks through, if an owner was rather obstinate to sell a portion of his land, the state advanced money for the whole field and after defining the necessary places they again

sold the field so that public and private interests would have an individual right within their own boundaries. Many, however, not content to occupy their own boundaries, have applied their hands to the aqueducts themselves by piercing the sides of the water course everywhere, not only those who have the right to obtain the water, but also those who squander the opportunity of a trifling favor to assault the streams. What more can be done, if all these crimes were not prohibited by the most scrupulous law, and an immoderate punishment were threatened against the miscreants? Therefore, I write the words of the law below:

129. "Titus Quintus Crispinus, consul (9 BCE), rightly asked the people, and the people voted in the forum in front of the rostrum of the temple of the Divine Julius[46] on the day before the Kalends of July (June 30). The Sergian tribe was first. On behalf of the Sergians, Sextus Varro, son of Lucius, voted first. After this law has been introduced, whoever knowingly with evil treachery shall have bored through the streams, conduits, arches, pipes, tubes, reservoirs, basins of the public waters which are led through the city, or who has broken them or taken care that they were to be pierced or broken or has done even worse things, whereby, that these waters or any part of them are not able to come into the city, to fall, flow, arrive, or be led, whereby that the waters are not in the city of Rome in these places, buildings, and those places and buildings which are next to the city or will be, and not in the gardens, farms, places, of which gardens, farms, places water has either been granted or allotted to the owners or occupiers or will be, let that water leap, be distributed, divided, sent into reservoirs, basins. May anyone who compromises such waters pay a penalty of 10,000 *sesterces* to the Roman people, and whoever with evil treachery will have done any of these things shall be made to restore everything, repair, reconstitute, rebuild, position, and to demolish his damages quickly without evil treachery and all such things so that whoever is the supervisor of the waters, or will be, if no one will be the supervisor of the waters, then the praetor who administers justice among foreigners,[47] may compel by securities, or restrain them. Let this fall to the water supervisor or—if there is no water supervisor—then to the praetor: the right and authority of compelling, restraining, of attaching a penalty or binding a security. But if a slave will have done anything of this kind, his owner will be condemned to pay 100,000 *sesterces* to the Roman people. If any place around the streams, conduits, arches, pipes, tubes, reservoirs, basins of public waters, that are led into the city of Rome or will be, has been enclosed or will be, after

46 Decreed in Julius Caesar's honor in 42 BCE by Octavian, Antony, and Lepidus, but not completed and dedicated until 29 BCE, surviving in ruins on the east side of the Roman Forum.

47 By the end of the third century BCE, a *praetor peregrinus* (the praetor who administers justice among foreigners) was added to the roster of city magistrates. The duties of the *praetor peregrinus* included settling disputes between Roman citizens and foreigners.

this law is passed, may no one put anything in the way, construct, enclose, transfix, establish, place, locate, plow, sow in this place, nor may he admit anything into the place beyond those things for the sake of making and restoring the infrastructures, which is permitted by this law and is fitting. Anyone who has done anything against these mandates, let the same law, right, and procedure of all details be applied to him, and just as it is or ought to be, whoever has ruptured or punctured a channel or conduit against this law. Nothing in this law questions that in this place it is permitted to pasture herds, cut grass or hay, gather briars. Let the supervisors of the waters, who are now in office or will be, bring it about that in this place, which is enclosed around springs and arches and walls and channels and conduits, the trees, vines, briars, thorn-bushes, banks, fences, willows, reeds, may be lifted out, cut out, dug out, be brought to justice, insofar as they want it to be done rightly. By this authority, let them have the right to seize a security, inflict a penalty, and restrain, and let the right and authority to do this be permitted to them without deceit. Nonetheless, let these things remain: the vines, trees which are enclosed within estates, buildings, or fences, and the fences on which names of those water supervisors who gave permission are inscribed or engraved, fences which the supervisors of the waters have permitted owners not to demolish after the situation was reviewed. Nothing in this law questions this. Nothing in this law questions that they have permitted those to whom the water-supervisors have granted permission, to take, draw water from the springs, streams, conduits, arches. Moreover, a water wheel is allowed, as is hydraulic machinery,[48] provided there is no new well or hole."

130. I would not deny that those who despise these laws are worthy of the punishment which is extended. But it is fitting that those who have deceived the state by neglect of a lengthy timespan be recalled. So I have labored painstakingly, as has been our practice, that those who have erred remain unknown. For those who, admonished, have come upon the emperor's forgiveness, I am able to seem to have been the cause of a kindness procured. In future I hope that enforcement of the law will not be necessary, since it will be better to uphold the trust of my office, even if it gives some offense.

(Frontinus, Aqueducts *2.119–130)*

K. *Private individuals did complain about the encroachment of public works on their property, and they were occasionally compensated for their inconvenience.*

And so (in 15 CE) Pius Aurelius, a senator, having complained that because of the construction of a public road and aqueduct, his own buildings were tottering, invoked help of the senate. While the treasury praetors resisted, Tiberius

48 #4.7.

Caesar (r. 14–37 CE) came to Aurelius' assistance and bestowed the price of the buildings, desiring to pay out the money honorably. He retained this virtue (of generosity) for a long time although he doffed off the other virtues.

(Tacitus, Annals *1.75.2)*

4.5.4 Provincial Aqueducts

Wherever the Romans went, their infrastructure followed, and aqueducts were constructed as tokens of imperial or private benefaction and to support veteran settlements outside Rome (Caesar's aqueduct at Antioch-on-the-Orontes [near Antakya, Turkey] seems to be the first Roman hydraulic structure outside Italy: Lassus 1983: 211). These impressive installations, even in their fragmentary state, are indelible monuments to Rome's footprint across its sprawling empire. Among the most stunning are the (1st century CE?) double-arched aqueduct at Segovia in Spain and the Pont du Gard at Nîmes (c. 40–60 CE), which towers 55 meters (180 feet) above the river—the tallest surviving Roman aqueduct—and features an additional top tier of smaller arches. As with the aqueducts at Rome, provincial aqueducts receive little more than passing mention in the literary record (e.g., the aqueduct of Laodicea-on-the-Sea: Josephus, Jewish War *1.21.11).*

A. *As governor of Bithynia-Pontus, Pliny brought to Trajan's attention Sinope's dire need for a reliable water source (on the middle-southern coast of the Pontus).*

Pliny to Trajan: Your Majesty, the Sinopeans lack water, but it seems to me that water, both good and abundant, can be conveyed from sixteen miles away. Nonetheless, straightaway at the source the terrain is uncertain and soft (swampy) for a little more than a mile. But I have ordered that the place be examined at moderate expense, whether it can receive and support the infrastructure. Money, set aside owing to my oversight, is not lacking, if you, majesty, will concede this type of work both for the health and delight of a very thirsty settlement.

Trajan to Pliny: When you begin, dearest Secundus,[49] investigate diligently whether that place, which you are considering for the installation, can support the weight of an aqueduct. I think that it must not be doubted but that water must be brought to the Sinopean settlement, but only if it can be procured by their own resources, since it will confer a great deal to health and pleasure.

(Pliny the Younger, Epistles *10.90–91)*

49 Pliny's full name was Gaius Plinius Caecilius Secundus, and Trajan is addressing his governor by the *agnomen* or nickname, "Secundus," that the younger Pliny acquired from his famous uncle's *cognomen* (third name: Gaius Plinius *Secundus*): the *cognomen* was meant to distinguish individual families within a larger clan.

B. *Monumental inscriptions record the building and restoration of aqueducts across the empire. Here a private individual at Bir Halima in Africa Proconsularis underwrote improvements to the local system (214–217 CE).*

> For Cnaeus Apertius Gaetulicus, son of Lucius, a *Duovir*,[50] a *Cerialis*[51] man of the most splendid colony of Karthage, a very refined man of goodness and singular integrity, who, for individual citizens and for his fatherland beyond, most generously bestowed that which was enough for the construction of a public aqueduct. He joined another water source, discovered with his own money—his particular infrastructure built on an earlier aqueduct—for sending the public water into the aqueduct stream, he also built a bridge of squared work with a lot of money. In addition to all these things, from his own money, he also made a pool for the use of each water source and the ornamentation of the state, and he embellished it with marble and muse-like work for which, on account of so much generosity and bountifulness, the *Ordo*[52] decreed that, for the purpose of giving thanks for Gaetulicus' services, from the money-tips of his own clients,[53] a statue should be made which would stand in the forum in a place which he himself chose. The place was given by a decree of the *Decurio*.
>
> (AE *1992: 1800)*

C. *Aqueduct restoration was often a gift of imperial munificence to reward or win loyalty. Here Trajan (r. 98–117) commissioned an aqueduct at Zadar, Dalmatia.*

> The emperor Nerva Trajan, Pontifex Maximus, with tribunician power,[54] completed an aqueduct with his own money for the locals, to which they had previously invested by the order of the most sacred emperor.
>
> (CIL *3.2909)*

D. *The following inscription records the restoration of the aqueduct (198 and 209 CE) at Segontium (Caernarfon), a Roman military camp in northern Wales.*

> The emperors Caesar Lucius Septimius Severus Pius Pertinax Augustus and Marcus Aurelius Antoninus Pius Augustus and Publius Septimius Geta, the very

50 One of two men serving as magistrates or judges.

51 Responsible for the grain supply? After Ceres, the Roman goddess of grain.

52 The town council, also called *Decurio*.

53 Wealthy Roman families rewarded the loyalty and services (often including voting for the patron's preferred political candidates) of their dependent clients with food, money, and even land.

54 #1.9.12G note.

celebrated Caesar,[55] restored the streams of the aqueduct, collapsed from age. The first cohort of Sunicians[56] . . .

(CIL *7.142 [*RIB *430])*

E. *Severus Alexander (r. 222–235) restored an aqueduct at Dyrrachium (Durrës, Albania), one of Hadrian's (r. 117–138) many public works.*

The emperor Caesar Marcus Aurelius Severus Alexander Pius Felix Augustus restored the aqueduct of his divine parent Hadrian,[57] made at Dyrrachium from his own generosity and vexed in many places from age, and also a road from the colony through 4,000 paces . . .

(CIL *3.709)*

F. *The aqueduct at Lambaesis in Numidia, restored under Diocletian and Maximianus (r. 286–305), clearly suffered from years of neglect.*

An aqueduct of the third legion Augusta of Diocletian and Maximianus, our Augusti, falling into decay from the carelessness of many people and neglected over a long series of years. After Aurelius Maximianus, a very excellent man, governor of the province of Numidia, made arrangements, along with Clodius Honoratus, a distinguished man, commander of the same legion, the most invincible emperors and restorers and enlargers of the world, Diocletian[58] and Maximianus, Augusti, restored the aqueduct, refurbished for the better and for stability.

(CIL *8.2572)*

4.5.5 Private Aqueducts

A. *In 54 BCE, in a chatty letter to his brother Quintus, Cicero reported on the water yield of private aqueduct neighboring his property at Arcanum (Tuscany).*

55 By this time, "Augustus" is the title for a sitting emperor, while "Caesar" denotes an heir. Septimius Severus appointed his son Caracalla as co-emperor in 198. Geta became co-emperor in 209.

56 A 500-man strong troop of allied infantry soldiers originally recruited from Germany in the early third century.

57 Nerva (r. 96–98 CE) was childless and thus adopted as his heir and successor the childless Trajan (r. 98–117), who adopted Hadrian (r. 117–138), whose successor and adopted heir was Marcus Aurelius (r. 161–180). To legitimize his own rule, taking the throne after civil war, Septimius Severus declared himself the adopted son of Marcus Aurelius and thus "traced" his lineage back to Nerva. Septimius Severus' grand-nephew, Severus Alexander, also wrote himself into the family tradition of high-profile, imperial adoptions.

58 Diocletian was responsible for reorganizing and stabilizing the empire after nearly a century of conflict, civil war, and foreign invasion, when 22 legitimate emperors held office (235–284 BCE), of which only two died of natural causes ("plague," lightning strike). Diocletian divided the sprawling empire into eastern and western portions, each with two capitals. Each half was administered by an Augustus and a Caesar (Augustus-in-training).

I was in Arcanum on the fourth day before the Ides of September (September 10).[59] There I saw Mescidius with Philoxenus and the water—which they were conveying not far from the house—flowing beautifully to be sure, especially in this severe drought. And they were saying that in time they would collect water even more abundantly.

(Cicero, To Quintus *#21 [3.1.1])*

B. *At Pont d'Ael, Aymavilles (northwstern Italy) in 23 BCE, a property owner inscribed his aqueduct bridge to establish ownership and warn against encroachment.*

Caesar Augustus, consul-designate for the 13th time, Gaius Avillus Caimus Patavinus. PRIVATE.

*(*CIL *5.6899)*

C. *A lengthy inscription records the private ownership of an aqueduct at Viterbo in Etruria, granted according to a senatorial decree. The owner, Mummius Niger Valerius Vegetus (suffect consul, April to July 112 CE[60]), purchased rights to a spring from which he routed water via a private aqueduct that extended about 16 kilometers (6 miles) across 11 private estates as well as public roads and rights-of-way. Specifying the precise course of the aqueduct and emphasizing senatorial sanction of the owner's authority, the inscription is a visible, public record of the installation's ownership.*

Mummius Niger Valerius Vegetus, consularis, led his own Vegetian water which rises in the estate of Antonianus the Elder, son of Publius Tullius Varro, to the place where the spring was made subservient[61] through 5,850 paces into that very villa of Calvisius which is next to the Passerian waters, along places and routes common and subservient. Away from the owners of each above-mentioned estate the water was conveyed in pipes by structures ten-paces in width, six-paces wide, through the estates of Antonianus the Elder and Antonianus the Younger, son of Publius Tullius Varro, and Baebianus and Philinianus Avileus Commodus and Petronianus, son of Publius Tullius Varro, and Volsonianus, son of Herennus Polybius and Fundianianus, son of Caetennus Proculus, and Cuttolonianus, son of Cornelius Latinus, and Serranus the Lesser, son of Quintinus Verecundus, and

59 Roman calendar: #4.5.2J§123 note.

60 Ordinary consuls assumed their offices at the beginning of the Roman year, and the year would be named for them (e.g., 59 BCE was the year in which Julius Caesar and Marcus Bibulus were co-consuls). Under Augustus, the consulship was revised, allowing for the election of more than two consuls each year. Under the Julio-Claudians, the ordinary consuls vacated office mid-year, replaced by suffect consuls. From 69 CE, it was common for the ordinary consuls to resign after four months, allowing for two sets of suffect consuls. Ordinary consul was the more prestigious title.

61 E.g., the water source fell under the category of a servitude: the legal right to use waters owned by someone else.

Capitonianus, son of Pisibanus Celsus, and through the left-hand bank of the public road of Ferentiens and Scirpianus Pisibania, son of Lepida, and through the Cassian road to the Calvisianan estate, and likewise through the public roads and paths with the permission of a senatorial decree . . . and through the Cassian road to the Calvisianan villa likewise through roads and public rights-of-way by permission of a senatorial decree.

(CIL *11.3003 [*ILS *5771])*

4.5.6 Wells and Cisterns

While private and public cisterns for collecting and storing rainwater were ubiquitous, they are best attested in the archaeological record. Taking many shapes and forms, from simple to multi-chambered, cisterns were often covered to mitigate contamination and evaporation, and they were lined with hydraulic plaster to prevent loss of water and preserve its freshness as much as possible.

A. How and where to dig wells. Here we also have an early reference to the "canary in a coal mine" to avoid noxious fumes.

12. But if there are no springs where we lead out our aqueducts, it is necessary to dig wells. In the digging of wells, calculation must not be despised, but the natural logic of things must be considered with shrewdness and great cleverness, because the land has in itself many and varied types of things. For, like other things, soil is composed of four principles. The first is the earthy principle, and it has springs from the moistness of water. Likewise, there is warmth from which sulfur, alum, and bitumen arise, and there are huge blasts of air which, when heavy, come through intervening hollows of ground to the digging point of the well and there they strike against the digging men, and block their airy breaths in their noses with the natural force of the vapor: thus those who do not escape die there rather quickly.

13. This situation must be avoided with these methods: thus, it must be done. Let a lighted lamp be lowered: if it remains burning, then one can descend without danger. But if the light is snuffed out by the force of the vapor, then, next, shafts should be dug out along the well to the right and left. Thus, in this way, the breath through the nostrils will be scattered from the shafts. When these things will have been settled and water arrived at, then the well should be enclosed by a structure lest the veins be blocked.

14. But if, moreover, the locales are stony or the veins of water too deep, then the supply must be collected from plastered cisterns on roofs or higher places. Regarding plastered cisterns, these things must be done: when first the purest and roughest sand is at hand, let flinty stone be fractured (no heavier than a pound), let limestone as strong as possible be mixed in the mortar, thus so that five parts of sand answer to two parts of limestone. To the level of the depth which the well is to be, let the trench be trampled with iron-tipped wooden poles.

15. After the walls are plastered, let the soil in the middle be emptied to the lowest level of the walls. When this has been levelled out, let the base be trampled to a thickness which will have been determined. If the cisterns will be doubled or tripled, so that they can be shifted by straining, they will render the use of this water far healthier and sweeter. For when mire has a place where it can settle, the water will become cleaner and will preserve its flavor without an odor. But if not, it will be necessary that salt be added and that the water be made thin.

(Vitruvius, On Architecture *8.6.12–15)*

B. *Twin cisterns are better.*

Cisterns ought to be constructed with five parts pure, coarse sand, and two parts limestone as strong as possible, with fragments of flint not exceeding a pound. The base and walls alike should be trampled with iron bars. Twin cisterns are more useful, so that particulates may settle in the first one and pure water may cross through the strainer into the next one.

(Pliny, NH *36.173)*

4.5.7 Baths

A. *Bathing tubs are attested archaeologically as far back as Minoan Crete (Queen's Megaron [1700–1400 BCE]) and Mycenaean Pylos (1300 BCE). This archaic vase (now lost) shows nude women in a shower.*

FIGURE 4.5.7A Archaic shower: *Bilder antiken lebens* (Berlin): 9, 18 (public domain).

B. *From about the 6th century BCE, athletic compounds incorporated basins for washing, as also shown on vases. This lost vase (5th century BCE?) shows athletes around a wash basin inscribed ΔΗΜΟΣΙΑ (PUBLIC).*

FIGURE 4.5.7B Wash basin: W. Hamilton. (1791), *Collection of Engravings from Ancient Vases Mostly of Pure Greek Workmanship Discovered in Sepulchres in the Kingdom of the Two Sicilies but Chiefly in the Neighbourhood of Naples During the Course of the Years MDCCLXXXIX and MDCCLXXXX, now in the Possession of Sir Wm. Hamilton. with Remarks on Each Vase by the Collector (Naples)*: 1. plate 58 (public domain).

C. *The ideal bathhouse, designed as a tour de force of Roman efficiency.*

1. First, a place must be chosen, as warm as possible, that is to say away from the seven stars (Ursa Major) and the Boreas (North Wind). Moreover, let the hot and warm baths themselves have light from the west in the winter. But if the nature of the place obstructs this, at any rate let the light come from the south, because the time for bathing is generally fixed from midday to evening. Likewise, it must be considered that the hot bathing rooms for women and men are joined and located in the same areas. For thus it will happen that the furnace be common for each of those hot bathing rooms with respect to their equipment. Above the furnace, three bronze tanks should be arranged: one for the *caldarium* (hot bath), a second for the *tepidarium* (warm bath), a third for the *frigidarium* (cold bath), and they should be placed so that as much hot water that exits from the *tepidarium* into the *caldarium* should flow from the *frigidarium* into the warm bath in the same measure. The overlays of the basins should be heated from the common furnace.

2. The hypocausts (suspended floors) of the *caldaria* ought to be made thusly: first the ground should be strewn with tiles a-pace-and-half long, angled

towards the furnace so that when a ball is tossed in, it is not able to remain there but must return again to the anteroom by itself. Thus, the flame will more easily extend under the hypocaust. Even more, pillars of small bricks are strewn, situated so that tiles, two-paces square, can be arranged above. Let the pillars have a height of two paces. These pillars are arranged with clay worked up with hair, and let the tiles of two paces, which can support the floor, be placed above the pillars.

3. The vaulted roofs will be more useful if they are made from concrete. But if they are joisted, moreover, terracotta should be situated under the work. But it should be done in this way: let iron bars or arches be made, and let these things be suspended with iron hooks at the joists as thickly as possible. These bars or arches should be distributed such that the tiles are able to sit without raised edges and be conveyed by them in twos. Thus let the entire vaulted roofs be completed, balanced on iron. Of these vaulted roofs, let the upper joins be smeared with clay worked up with hair; the lower part, moreover, which looks at the floor, let it be plastered with limestone tile; then let it be polished with white stucco or plaster. These vaulted roofs, if they are made double in the *caldaria*, will have better durability: for the moisture from the vapor will not be able to ruin the material but it will spread between two vaults.

4. Moreover, the sizes of the baths seem best to be according to the crowd of people. Let them be arranged thusly: how long it is with a third removed, let that be the width, except for an apse for the basin and bathing tub. It seems best that the basin be made underneath the light, lest those standing around obscure the light with their shadows. It is fitting that the apses for the basins be spacious to such a degree that, when the first comers have occupied the places around, the remaining watchers are able to stand properly. Moreover, let the extent of the basin between the wall and screen be no less than six paces so that the lower step and the raised bath take up two paces.

5. The *laconicum* (dry sweat chamber) and *sudationes* (sweating rooms) are to be joined to the *tepidarium*. Let them have as much height as they are wide at the lowest curve of a hemisphere. Let a light be left in the hemisphere in the middle, and let a bronze tray hang from it by chains. By raising and lowering the tray, let the regulation of the sweating be accomplished. It seems best that the tray itself be circular so that the force of the flame and vapor wanders equally from the middle through the circumference of the curved space.

(Vitruvius, On Architecture *5.10)*

D. *Roman-style bathhouses rose in popularity throughout the Mediterranean in the 1st century CE, and they served as community centers where people could socialize, bathe, read, exercise, or engage in games of chance. In the picaresque novel,* Satyricon *(composed by Gaius Petronius Arbiter, one of Nero's courtiers [r. 54–68 CE]), we meet Trimalchio, a gauche and ridiculously wealthy freedman, playing a ball game at a bathhouse just before an elaborate dinner party that he is hosting.*

Trimalchio's dinner party is in part a lampoon of the super-wealthy ex-slaves who advanced to positions as imperial advisors. The homoerotic tone is blunt.

Therefore, forgetting all our misfortunes, we dressed diligently and ordered Giton, most agreeably seeing to servile attendance, to follow us all the way to the baths.

Meanwhile, dressed, we begin to wander, or rather to joke a little more, and to approach folks in groups, when suddenly we see an old bald man, dressed in a red tunic and playing a ball among long-haired boys. The boys didn't so much entice us to watch, although it was worth the reward of the effort, but the *pater familias*,[62] slippered, was exercising with a green ball.[63] He did not retrieve any ball that hit the ground, but a slave had a full bag and supplied balls to the players.[64] We also noted new features: two eunuchs were standing in a different part of the circle: one was holding a silver chamber pot, another was counting balls, to be sure not those which the players were launching between their hands—the game expelled those balls—but those which fell onto the ground. While we wonder at this splendor, Menelaus runs up and says, "This is the man at whose house you'll place your elbows,[65] and indeed you are already seeing the beginning of the banquet."

(Petronius, Satyricon *26–27)*

E. *At Rome moralizers criticized the bathing habit as endemic of an overly indulgent lifestyle, born out by the extravagant installations in Nero's* Domus Aurea *("Golden House").*

1. In no other thing was Nero more prodigal than in building. He made a house extending from the Palatine Hill all the way to the Esquiline, which at first he named *Transitoria* ("Passage-Way") then, consumed by fire and immediately rebuilt, named *Aurea.* Concerning its size and appearance, it suffices to say these things. There was a vestibule in which a colossus, 120 paces tall, in the image of Nero himself, could stand, and the spaciousness was so great that it had triple colonnades, 1,000 paces long. Likewise, there was a pool in the image of the sea, surrounded by buildings in the appearance of a city. In addition, there were plots of land, various with cultivated tracts and vineyards and pasturage and forests, together with a crowd of every type of flock and wild animal.

2. In other parts, everything was plastered with gold and adorned with gems and mother-of-pearl. The dining rooms were paneled with tiles fretted with ivory so that flowers were sprinkled from above and also unguents from pipes.

62 Head of a Roman household who exercised absolute control over family and staff, including the right to make judgements regarding marriage, divorce, life and death.

63 In a short treatise, *On Exercise with a Small Ball,* Galen promotes such exercise as the single best physical regimen: the ball-workout trains the entire body vigorously and delights the soul.

64 The unlimited supply of exercise balls is one of many examples of Trimalchio's indescribable wealth and conspicuous consumption. The game may be *lusus trigo*, involving three players tossing a ball back and forth in a triangle.

65 Wealthy Romans dined reclining, three to a couch, and thus propped up on their elbows.

Particular was the roundness of the dining room—in the image of the world—which was perpetually driven around, days and nights.[66] Baths were flowing with marine and white waters.[67] When Nero dedicated his house of this style after it was completed, thus far he acknowledged that he would say that he finally began to live like a human being.

3. Moreover, he laid the foundation for a fishpond from Misenum to Lake Avernus,[68] covered and enclosed with porticoes, where some of the hot waters at Baiae[69] were to be redirected. He also laid the foundation for a canal from Avernus all the way to Ostia so that one could make the trip by ship, but not nonetheless by sea, over one 160 miles in length and of a breadth by which quinqueremes,[70] sailing in opposite directions, could pass each other. For the sake of completing these projects, Nero gave an advance order to the watch-station that convicts should be deported from everywhere to Italy, even those guilty of a very wicked crime, to be condemned to do no other work.

(Suetonius, Nero *31.1–3)*

F. *Seneca was one of those moralizing Romans who ironically lived a very comfortable life. Here, Seneca recounts his pilgrimage to the villa of Publius Cornelius Scipio Africanus (d. 183 BCE), renowned for his military deftness and defeating Hannibal, the Carthaginian military genius, at Zama in 202 BCE. Scipio was also a proponent of Greek culture, writing his own memoirs in Greek. Scipio's villa, like many elite estates, included private bathing facilities: Seneca staunchly preferred the dark old-fashioned baths to the cheerier modern type.*

4. I have seen the whole house built up on squared stone, a wall surrounding a forest, towers also rising up on each side at the villa's rampart, a cistern placed within the buildings and shrubbery which is able to suffice for personal use or even an army's, a narrow bathhouse, dark according to the ancient custom: for a hot bath did not seem suitable to our ancestors unless shadowy.

5. Great pleasure comes to me contemplating Scipio's habits and our own. In this corner that "Bane of Carthage"—to whom Rome owes a debt because she, Rome, was captured only once[71]—washed his body fatigued from rustic work. For he exercised himself with work, and he subjugated his land himself, as was the ancient custom. Underneath this dirty roof he stood; this floor, so common, supported him.

66 More likely the ceiling rotated, not the room.
67 Marine waters: salt versus fresh ("white"). See Suetonius, *Augustus* 82.2.
68 On the coast west of Naples, about 9 kilometers (5.5 miles).
69 A resort town near Naples, popular with the wealthy and renowned for its hot springs, whose thermal baths survive. Mineral springs: #2.1.6.
70 A warship with five banks of oars or five rowers operating two oars in two banks.
71 After an unexpected victory over Roman forces in 390 BCE at Allia, Gallic forces marched to Rome, occupied and sacked the city: Livy, *From the Foundation of the City* 5.34–49.

6. But now who is there who would put up with being bathed in this way? Someone seems to himself a pauper and vulgar unless the walls glitter with great and precious spheres, unless our Alexandrian marbles are adorned with Numidian mosaics, unless the overlay everywhere is covered by variable and wrought work in the manner of a painting, unless the vaulted ceiling is concealed in glass, unless Thasian stone—once rare and seen only in some temple—surrounds our pools, into which we immerse our bodies, drained of sweat, unless silver faucets pour out the water.[72]

7. Thus far I speak about the plebeian[73] waterpipes. What should I say when I come to the bath houses of the freedmen? How many statues, how many columns supporting nothing, but placed for decoration just for the sake of spending! How much water slipping over the steps with a crash! We have come to such a point of luxuriousness that we cannot walk unless on gems.

8. In Scipio's bathhouse there are small clefts—rather than windows—cut from the stone wall, so that they admit light without damage to the building. But now days, they call bathhouses suitable only for moths if they have not been fitted in such a way that they take in the sun through the most spacious windows all day long, and unless folks can bathe and at the same time be tanned, and unless they can look out over lands and seas from their seats. Thus are those bathing establishments which receive rushing crowds and admiration when they are dedicated and shunned and driven back to the rank of "antiquated" when some new luxury is devised, by which it ruins itself.

9. But, once upon a time, there were few bathhouses nor were they decorated with any bling. For why should installations costing a *quadrans*—developed for practical use but not personal delight—be embellished? Water was not poured over a bather, nor did it always run fresh as if from a warm spring, nor did those old bathers believe that it mattered how clear the water was into which they deposited their dirt.

10. But—good gods!—how does it delight to enter those bathing installations, dark and covered with common plasterwork, which you know that your Cato, as aedile, or Fabius Maximus or even one of the Corneliuses warmed with his own hand?[74] For the most noble aediles also performed this service: they

72 *Alexandrian marble*: malachite, lapis lazuli, and porphyry, among the quarried exports of Egypt; *Numidian mosaics*: featuring *giallo antico*, a North African marble ranging from light yellow to reddish brown; *Thasian stone*: from Thasos, off Thrace, a white variety.

73 Referring to free citizens who were neither patricians (those who could trace their ancestry to the 100 families that founded Rome, according to legend) nor equites (with a certain fixed amount of wealth that varied by era [but at least enough to support a horse] and serving in the early cavalry). Plebeians were largely working-class folk, including farmers, craftsmen, and builders.

74 Quintus Fabius Maximus Verrucosus (c. 280–203 BCE) was a Roman statesman who employed guerilla-like tactics against the Carthaginians during the second Punic War, attacking supply lines and forcing military engagements of small units on favorable ground. The Corneliuses included many prominent Romans, among them a branch of the Scipio family to which our Africanus belonged.

entered these places, which received the people, and they decided that cleanliness and utility and healthfulness were regulated not to a temperature similar to fire, recently fashionable, to such a degree that a slave convicted of some crime ought to be bathed alive. To me it seems that there is not any more difference whether the bath is blazing hot or warm.

11. How some folk now condemn Scipio of rusticity because he did not admit daylight into his *caldarium* through broad glasses, or because he was not cooked down in a lot of light and waited to burn thoroughly in his bath! O miserable man! He didn't know how to live. He was not bathed in filtered water but often in murky water and, when it rained a great deal, in very muddy water. But it did not much matter whether Scipio was bathed in this way: he came there to wash off the sweat not to be perfumed.

12. What do you believe the future comments of certain folk might be? "I do not envy Scipio; truly he, who was washed in this way, lived in exile." Even more, if you might understand, he was not washed every day. For, as they say, those who hand down the ancient ways of the city, the ancients washed their arms and shins daily, the body parts which certainly gathered dirt from work, but they were entirely washed once every nine days. In this place, someone might say, "back then they seem to have been exceedingly unclean. How do you think they smelled?" Of soldiery, work, manliness.

(Seneca, Letter *86.4–12)*

G. *Marcus Aurelius, emperor of Rome (r. 161–180), renowned for his love of Greek culture and study of Stoic philosophy, disagreed with Seneca's nostalgia for the dirty bathing facilities of the hoary past (as, no doubt, would modern readers). Besides, the baths were hardly clean. While water was more or less constantly fed from aqueducts into the baths (cf. Chatr Aryamontri 2009), we do not know how often or if the facilities were scrubbed down. Even in channels with running water, bacteria in excrement that inevitably leached into the bath water would remain warm and continue to grow (Fagan 1999: 176–188, 2000; Knapp 2011: 45–46; Rogers 2018: 44).*

Such as bathing seems to you—oil, sweat, dirt, slimy water, all vile things. Such is every part of life and everything encountered.

(Marcus Aurelius, Meditations *8.24)*

H. *Artemidoros of Daldis in Lydia (2nd century CE), who traveled widely through Asia, Greece, and Italy penned a five-book* Interpretation of Dreams *in Greek where dream analysis depends on the "juxtaposition of similarities." Dreams of excreting in a public bath are among the worst possible signs.*

For least of all would anyone spend time in polluted places. For the most dangerous and fear-inducing of all dreams is defecating in the temple of a god or in the marketplace or in a street or in a bathhouse. For it bespeaks to anger of the gods and great deformity and loss, not accidentally, and with regard to secrets it betrays them, and very often hatred is even brought about for someone observing.

(Artemidoros, Interpretation of Dreams *2.26)*

4.5.8 Latrines

Chamber pots and latrines are casually mentioned in Greek and Roman sources. Public latrines were usually marble or limestone communal benches with defecation holes, accommodating tens of users at a time (Antoniou and Angelakis 2015: 61–65). Many public latrines also featured small channels with continuously flowing water, perhaps for cleaning the sponges that served as toilet paper (Antoniou 2007: 155). At Rome, there were nearly 150 unisex, stall-less, public latrines, constantly flushed with wastewater from the baths. Latrines were also featured in private houses, but not usually attached to the sewer system, thus increasing the potential for the spread of disease. One of the best preserved is the latrine at Housesteads Fort in northern Britain.

FIGURE 4.5.8 Housesteads Latrine: photo by Steven Fruitsmaak: *The Latrines at Housesteads Roman Fort along Hadrian's Wall* (Wikimedia Commons).

4.5.9 Sewers

The constant influx of water demands drainage, and initiatives to control drainage date back to the Bronze Age: Mesopotamian pit-toilets were fitted with drainage tubes (McMahon 2015: 22–23), and at Knossos a complex system of limestone and earthenware pipes drained black water from the palace latrines into a sewer system (Antoniou and Angelakis 2015: 46–48).

A. *While the evidence is almost exclusively archaeological, in Pliny we have a rare description of Rome's elaborate sewer system and reference to Marcus Agrippa's sewer tour by boat. While sewers were designed to drain and dry out the city, during floods they flowed back into the city.*

> 104. But at that time older men still admired the vast extent of the rampart—the Servian Wall from the Colline to Esquiline Gates—the substructures of the Capitoline Hill. And, moreover, the sewers—the greatest work of all worth mentioning—the hills tunneled through and, as we said before, the city hanging above and sailed from underneath during the aedileship of Marcus Agrippa[75] after his consulship.
>
> 105. Seven rivers flowing together pass through the city. And in a headlong course they are compelled to snatch and carry away everything like torrents. And, agitated up by a mass of rain above, the subterranean waters shake the bottoms and sides. Sometimes the Tiber is received, poured back into the sewers, and the opposing assaults of the waters fight within their channels. Nonetheless, the sewer's durability stands strong, pressing against the fighting waters.
>
> 106. Such great loads are dragged above. While the hollow works don't yield, falling debris hammers down or is dashed down by fires, the ground is trembled by movements of the earth (earthquakes). But nonetheless, for 700 years, from the time of Tarquinius Priscus (r. 615–578 BCE),[76] the sewers endure nearly unconquerable . . .
>
> 108. Tarquin is said to have made the breadth of the sewer tunnels such that it could convey a cartload abundantly heaped up with hay.
>
> *(Pliny,* NH *36.104–106, 108)*

B. *The sewers were flushed out with "lapsed waters" that had overflowed from reservoirs or leaked from aqueduct pipes, according to this ordinance.*

> I desire that no one should draw lapsed water unless they have permission of my favor or earlier leaders. For it is necessary that some part of the water flows from the reservoirs, for which this pertains not only to the health of the city but even to the advantage of washing out the sewers.
>
> *(Frontinus,* Aqueducts *2.111)*

4.6 Machines That Use Water

4.6.1 Water Clocks

A. *In antiquity the length of an hour was determined by the length of the day; thus, nighttime hours in the winter were longer than in the summer. Aeneas Tacticus (4th century BCE), an early author on military science (only his* How to Survive

75 #4.5.3C note.

76 #1.9.12B.

Under Siege *is extant), has a simple but clever fix to calibrate* clepsydras *(water clocks) to ensure that watch stations remain fair across seasons. Water clocks were also employed to measure the length of speeches in courts of law.*

> When nights grow longer or shorter, the watch stations become equal for all in this way. It is thus necessary to keep watch stations by a *clepsydra*, and this should be recalibrated every ten days. But it is better to wax the receptacle from within, and remove some wax as the nights become longer, so that it might contain more water, and increase the wax as the nights become shorter so that the receptacle takes in less water. Concerning the equality of watch-stations this seems sufficiently clear to me.
>
> *(Aeneas Tacticus,* How to Survive under Siege *F 48 = 22.24–25)*

B. *Vitruvius credited the mathematician and engineer Ctesibius of Alexandria (285–222 BCE) with developing the inflow* clepsydra *with overflow and float in the reservoir.*

> 2. Likewise, the designs of water-clocks were sought by these same writers, and first of all by Ctesibius the Alexandrian, who also discovered the force of natural breath (i.e., wind) and pneumatical principals. It is a worthy endeavor for the studious to recognize how these inquiries were made. For Ctesibius was born at Alexandria, and his father was a barber. Excelling beyond the rest in character and industry, Ctesibius was said to delight himself with skillful, mechanical things. For when he wished to hang a mirror in his father's shop in such a way that, when it was pulled down and then back up, a concealed cord led the weight down, he thus arranged this pneumatic mechanism . . .
>
> 4. Therefore, when Ctesibius noticed that breath and voices arose from the drawing the air and pressing it, using these principles, he was the first to set up hydraulic machines. Likewise, he explained water-powered and self-propelling machines and many types of delights, among these also the preparation of water-clocks. First, he set up a hollow tube made of gold or a pierced gem: for these materials are neither eroded by the striking of water, nor do they acquire dirt, so they are not clogged.
>
> 5. For the water, flowing smoothly through this pipe, raises an inverted bowl which is called a cork or a drum by the craftsmen. In this a rod is placed with respect to a moving drum. The drums are made with equal teeth which, propelling one into another, create the measured movements and the motions. Likewise, other rods and other drums, toothed in this same way, driven by a single motion, create the effects and variety of the motions by rotating. Little figurines are moved within, cones are turned, pebbles or eggs are cast down, horns sing out, and other extras.
>
> 6. On these water-clocks, hours are marked on a column or pillar: a small image rising from the lowest part indicates the hours with a small rod

through the entire day. The addition or removal of wedges compels achieving the shortening and lengthening of these rods on individual days and months. Stopcocks are thus situated for regulating the waters. Two cones—one solid, one hollow—are consequently made on a lathe so that one is able to enter and fit within the other. The same rod, as it loosens or constricts the cones, produces an eager or gentle course of water as it flows into the receptacles. Thus, by these procedures and engineering from water, constructions of timepieces are arranged for winter use.

7. But, moreover, with the addition or removal of wedges, the shortening of days or their growth will not be ascertained from wedges because the wedges very often introduce faults. Thus the solution is to be explained. On the column let the hours be marked transversely according to analemmas,[77] and let the monthly lines be marked on the column. Let this column be made to rotate, so that by turning towards the figurine and rod (with which rod the figurine, moving away, shows the hours) the column continually renders the shortenings and lengthenings of the hours each in their own months.

(Vitruvius, On Architecture *9.8.2, 4–7)*

C. *A 3rd-century-CE mathematical treatise provides technical (and obscure) instructions for constructing a water clock shaped like a flowerpot with an arithmetical progression of diminishing lines. Grenfell and Hunt surmised that the apparatus was filled with water and that time was calculated as water dripped through a small hole in the base (1903: 142).*

The calculation of the construction of timepieces is thus given: make a *olmiskos* (frustrum of a right cone) with an upper line of 24 dactyls, a base of 12 dactyls, and a depth of 18 dactyls. If we add the 24 dactyls to the 12 dactyls of the base the result will be 36 dactyls; 1/2 of this is 18. Multiplying, on account of the round surface, by 3 we obtain 54. 1/3 of this is 18. 1/4 is 13 ½. 18 multiplied by 13 1/2 makes 243. The first line is therefore 24 dactyls in length. Twice this number is 48. Subtract 2/3. The remainder is 47 1/3. Half of this is 23 2/3. This multiplied by 3 makes 71. 1/3 of this is 23 2/3. And 1/4 is 17 ¾. Total 420 1/12. The second figure consists of 23 1/3 dactyls. Twice this makes 46 2/3. Subtract 2/3 for the contraction. The remainder is 46. 1/2 is 23. 3 times this is 69. 1/3 of this is 23. 1/4 is 17 ¼. This multiplied by 23 makes 396 ¾. Subtract 1/16. The remainder is 396 11/16 . . . The sixth (*gramme*) is 20 2/3 (dactyls), which become 40 2/3 when the 2/3 has been subtracted.

*(*POxy *470.31–85; trans. Grenfell and Hunt)*

77 A figure-8 graph showing sun's position at a given time of day (such as noon) at one specific place throughout the year.

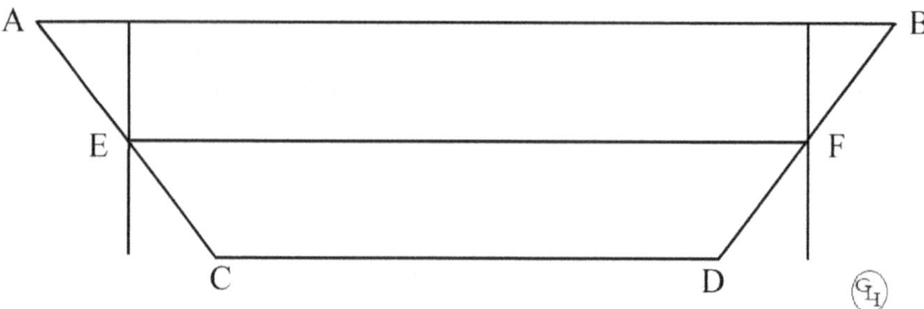

FIGURE 4.6.1C "Flowerpot" clepsydra (drawn by Georgia L. Irby).

4.6.2 Water Organ

The hydraulic organ is powered by a water pump that creates pneumatic pressure to produce the sounds. This complex machine was created by Ctesibius.

1. Concerning water organs, moreover, as briefly and precisely as possible, I will next be able to touch on what principles they have, and pursue these writings, and I will not omit it. Concerning the material of the base joined together (i.e., a frame), a box made of bronze should be placed on it. Above the base, rods are erected, joined to the right and left in the shape of a ladder, in which are fitted bronze cylinders, with pistons, worked delicately on a lathe, moving about, having iron blocks (piston rods) fixed in the middle attached to the joints with levers, and wrapped up with hides and wool. Likewise, on the highest flat surface, let there be openings about three fingers around. In these apertures bronze dolphins, placed next along the joints, have cymbals hanging by chains dropped from their mouths below the cylinders' openings.

2. Within the box, where water is sustained, there is a *pnigeus* (conical regulator throttle), like an inverted funnel. Set underneath this funnel, small dies, about three fingers high, keep the lowest space—between the lips of the *pnigeus* and the base of the box—in balance. Moreover, a small box, fixed above the neck, which is called *canon musicus* in Greek, supports the head of the machine. Along its length are four pipes, if the instrument is a tetrachord. If it is a hexachord, six pipes. If it is an octachord, eight pipes.[78]

3. In the individual pipes individual stopcocks are enclosed, arranged with iron handles. These handles, when they are turned, reveal apertures from the box into the pipes. From the pipes, moreover, the *canon* has openings arranged transversely and answering the apertures which are in the highest plank, which is called *pinax* in Greek. Between the *pinax* and *canon*, rods are inserted, corresponding at the same measure and worked with oil, so that they are easily

78 The tetrachord is a musical scale of four notes, bounded by the interval of a perfect fourth. The hexachord has six notes with a half step between the third and fourth. The octachord is any eight-note musical scale.

stricken and restored back again. Those things which close these apertures are called *plinthides*. The coming and returning of these *plinthides* closes some apertures and opens others.

4. These bars have iron gears fixed and joined with keys. Touching these keys creates the continuous motion of the bars. Above the panel are the apertures, which restrict the egress of air from the pipes. Rings are fastened by which the tongues (reeds) of all organs are enclosed. From the cylinders, moreover, extending along the funnels from the necks to the openings, joined tubes in a small box are adjacent. On these apertures are valves, worked on a lathe and placed there. When the box receives the air, the valves do not allow that air, closing the apertures, to return.

5. Thus, when the levers are raised, the piston rods draw the pistons down towards the bottom of the cylinders, and the dolphins, enclosed along the joints, working the cymbals, fill the space in the cylinders with air. The piston rods, lifting the pistons within the cylinders with a vigorous quickness of the thrust and closing the apertures above the cymbals, drive the air, which is enclosed there, forced by pressure into the pipes through which it runs into the *pnigei* and through its necks into the box. By means of the levers' rather strong motion, a repeated, compressed blast flows in the apertures of the valves and fills the pipes with air.

6. Thus, when the keys, touched by hands, propel and lead the rods back continuously by closing and opening the apertures by turns, these motions will cause resounding voices with changeable varieties of measures from musical skill. Insofar as I have been able to try, I have aimed that a poorly understood thing might be clearly divulged through my writing. But this reckoning is neither easy nor expedient for all to understand, beyond those who have training in these kinds of things. But if anyone will have understood too little from my writings, when they recognize the very thing, they will straightaway discover, attentively and acutely, all aspects of the design that has been laid out.

(Vitruvius, On Architecture *10.8; cf. Hero,* Pneumatics *1.42)*

4.6.3 A Marvelous Water-Powered Machine

Among the many marvelous water-powered curiosities described by Hero of Alexandria is this device by which flowing water causes a model bird to sing or be quiet. The Greek mathematician and engineer, Hero (1st/2nd century CE), published a collection of remarkable, experimental machines (automata), powered by air or steam: hydraulic whistling birds, self-trimming lamps, self-filling wine goblets, and steam engines, and also his Automatic Theater *for an elaborate mechanism that plays out a sacrifice and celebration for Dionysus. Hero was likely inspired by Philo of Byzantium's* Pneumatics, *surviving only in Arabic and Latin translation of the mostly lost* Mechanike Syntaxis *(see Rance 2013: 5266–5268).*

The construction is after this manner. Let A be a stream perpetually running. Place underneath an air-tight vessel, B C D E, provided with an enclosed siphon or bent siphon F G, and having inserted in it a funnel, H K, between the extremity of the tube of which and the bottom of the vessel a passage is left for the water. Let the funnel be provided with several smaller pipes, described before, at L. It will be found that, while B C D E is being filled with water, the air that is driven out will produce the notes of birds; and as the water is being drawn off through the siphon F G after the vessel is filled, the birds will be mute.

We are now to describe the contrivance by which the owl is enabled to turn herself towards, or away from, the birds, as we have said. Let a rod N X turned in a lathe rest on any support M: round this rod let a tube O P be fitted, so as to move freely about it, and having attached to it the kettle-drum top R S, on which the owl is to be securely fixed. Round the tube O P let a chain pass, the two extremities of which, T U, Q W, wind off in opposite directions, and are attached, by means of two pullies, the one, T U, to a weight suspended at Y, and Q W to an empty vessel Z, which lies beneath the siphon or enclosed siphon F G. It will be found that while the vessel B C D E is being emptied, the liquid being carried into the vessel Z causes the tube O P to revolve, and the owl with it, so as to face the birds: but when B C D E is exhausted, the vessel Z becomes empty likewise by means of an enclosed or bent siphon contained within it; and then the weight Y, again preponderating, causes the owl to turn away just at the time when the vessel B C D E is being filled again and the notes once more issue from the birds.

(Hero of Alexandria, Pneumatics *1.15; trans. Woodcroft)*

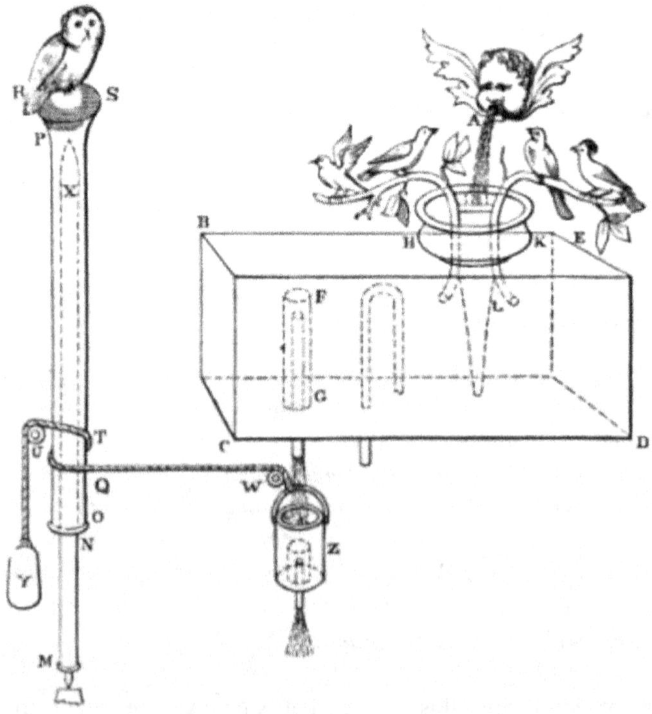

FIGURE 4.6.3 Hero's singing bird: Woodcroft 1851: 31 (public domain).

4.7 Machines for Moving Water

4.7.1 Water Wheels and Mills

A. *By the mid-1st century BCE, water-driven wheels were in use, and the first documented water wheel was constructed during the reign of Mithridates VI Eupator (r. 120–63 BCE) at Kabeira in northern Pontus, taking advantage of powerful, local rivers. The technology seems to have originated in Asia Minor, but Mithridates' water wheel may not have been the first (see Roos 1996; Roller 2020: 121–122 and n67).*

> At Kabeira, the palace of Mithridates was built, as well as the *hydrelate* (water-mill), and the animal parks and the hunting grounds were close and the quarries.
>
> *(Strabo,* Geography *12.3.30)*

B. *The underlying mechanics.*

> *Hydrelatae* (water mills) are turned on the same principle as the other water wheels, except that on one edge of the axle there is fixed a toothed drum. This, moreover, placed on the perpendicular plane, turns onto its teeth at the same time as the wheel. A second, larger drum, likewise, toothed, is placed horizontally. The teeth of the drum on the axle force a revolution of the millstone by driving the flat drum. In this machine, a suspended hopper supplies the grain to the millstone and flour is yielded as it turns.
>
> *(Vitruvius,* On Architecture *10.5.2; cf. Philo,* Pneumatics *65)*

C. *Bucket wheels, operable in restricted spaces, were likely powered by animals, as at Susa (#1.7E), where the cows apparently knew how to count.*

> For there the cows irrigate the king's park with buckets raised on waterwheels, of which the number is set. For each heifer raises up 100 buckets each day. It is not possible to exact or force more, even if you want to. The wranglers often try to increase the quota, but the cows stop and do not move after they have delivered the pre-arranged quantity. She thus has accurately calculated and memorized the count by heart, as Ctesias of Cnidus relates.
>
> *(Plutarch,* On Whether Land or Sea Animals Are Cleverer *974e)*

4.7.2 Water Pumps

A. *To supplement their rainwater, the people at Arados in Syria siphoned water from a fresh-water spring at the bottom of the sea.*

> Arados lies in front of some surf-filled and harborless place by the sea, more or less between its seaport and Marathus, about 20 *stadia* from the mainland. It is a rock, washed by the sea, a circle of about seven *stadia*, full of settlements.

Owing to being so-well-peopled, up to now it is proclaimed that the Aradeans dwell in many-storied homes. Fugitives from Sidon,[79] so they say, founded the place. They have some of their water from rain and water-cisterns and some from the mainland. In wartime, they fetch water from a channel, having a spring of bountiful water a small distance in front of the city. Into the spring, sent down from a water-fetching skiff, a container made of lead is turned upside down, wide-mouthed, attenuated to a narrow bottom having a moderate aperture. To the bottom is fastened a leather pipe—or it may be necessary to call it a bellows—receiving the water that is forced up from the spring through the container. But the first water forced up is seawater. Waiting for the flow of clear, potable water, the Aradeans collect whatever is needed in prepared containers, and they carry it back to the city.

(Strabo, Geography *16.2.13; cf. Pliny,* NH *5.128)*

B. *A force-pump invented by Ctesibius of Alexandria (3rd century BCE). A one-way valve ensures that water travels in the desired direction.*

1. Now it follows to tell about the Ctesibian machine, which lifts water to a height. Let it be made of bronze. Let there be twin cylinders a little apart, having pipes close by, similar in shape to a fork, running together in the middle of the vessel. In the vessel, let there be valves placed in the upper openings with an accurate joining. Closing off the apertures of the pipes, the valves do not allow what has been sent into the vessel by breath (air) to return (i.e., exit the vessel).

2. Above the vessel, a hooded cover, like an inverted funnel, ought to be adjusted and held back through the fastening with a wedge pierced in the vessel, lest the force of the inflowing water force the cover to become raised. Above the cover, the pipe, which is called a *tuba*, is made conjoined with it and upright in height. The cylinders, moreover, have valves, below the lower apertures of the pipes, interspersed above their apertures which are on the bottom.

3. Thus from above, the "male" pistons, smoothed on a lathe and whetted with oil and enclosed in the cylinder, are worked with rods and levers. The apertures force out what air was there with the water when the valves close. Owing to the swelling from the pressure, they push the water into the vessel through the apertures of the pipes. Receiving the water from the vessel, the cover forces the water out with breath through the pipe to a height, and thus water is furnished for springing up from a lower place fitted with a reservoir.

4. Nor, nonetheless, is this the only Ctesibian device said to be remarkable. But even more and of various kinds, forced by pressures from this liquid, breath may be exhibited to generate effects borrowed from nature, just like the voices of blackbirds and walking devices and other figurines, drinking

79 Saida, Lebanon.

and moving themselves, which flatter the amusement of the eyes and ears by the use of the senses.[80]

5. From these things I have collected the ones which I have judged especially useful and necessary. In the previous volume I thought that something must be said about *horologia*;[81] in this volume something about the forcing out of water. As for the rest, not for necessity but instead for enjoyment of pleasure, those more desirous of this cleverness will be able to find them in the commentaries of Ctesibius himself.

(Vitruvius, On Architecture *10.7; cf. Philo,* Pneumatics *app.1 chapter 2)*

C. *Such pumps could deliver jets of water and were thus effective as fire extinguishers in fire-prone Rome, which had a standing fire-brigade, the* Vigiles *("wakeful folk"), whose standard-issue equipment included carts with water reservoirs and, likely, also force-pumps with nozzles.*[82]

The siphons used in conflagrations are made as follows: take two bronze vessels, ABCD, EFGH, with its inner surface bored in a lathe to fit a piston (like the barrels of water-organs), KL, MN are the pistons fitted to the boxes. Let the cylinders communicate with each other through the tube XODF, and be provided with valves P, R as explained above, within the tube XODF and opening outwards from the cylinders. In the base of the cylinders pierce circular apertures, S, T, covered with polished hemispherical cups, V, Q, W, Y through which insert spindles soldered to, or in some way connected with, the bases of the cylinders and provided with shoulders at the extremities so that the cups might not be forced off the spindles. Attach the vertical rods SE, SE to the center of the pistons, and attach the beam A′ A′, working, at its center, around the stationary pin D, and around the pins B, C, at the rods SE, SE. Let the vertical tube S′ E′ link with the tube XODF, branching into two arms at S′, and provided with small pipes through which to force up water, such as explained above in the description of the machine for producing a waterjet with compressed air (1.9). Now, if the cylinders, provided with these additions, be plunged into a vessel containing water, IJUZ, and the beam A′ A′ be made to work at its extremities A′, A′, which move alternately around the pin D, the pistons, as they descend, will drive out the water through the tube E′S′ and the revolving mouth M′. For when the piston MN ascends it opens the aperture T, as the cup WY rises, and shuts the valve R. But when it descends it shuts T and opens R, through which the water is driven and forced upwards. The action of the other piston KL is the same. Now the small pipe M′, which waves back and forth, ejects the water to the required height but

80 See #4.6.3 introduction.

81 #4.6.1.

82 By the seventh century CE, force-pumps were employed for cleaning vaulted ceilings: Isidore of Seville, *Origins* 20.6.9; cf. *Oleson 1984: 56.*

in the required direction, unless the entire machine is turned around: on urgent occasions this is a tedious and difficult process. Therefore, in order that the water may be ejected to the required area, let the tube E′S′ consist of two tubes, closely fitted together lengthwise. One of these must be attached to the tube XODF, the other to the part where the arms branch off at S′. Thus, if the upper tube is turned around, by the inclination of the mouthpiece M′, the stream of water can be forced to any spot we like. The upper joint of the double tube must be secured to the lower, to prevent its being forced from the machine by the violence of the water. This may be brought about by holdfasts in the shape of a letter L, soldered to the upper tube, and sliding on a ring encircling the lower tube.

(Hero of Alexandria, Pneumatics *1.27; trans. Woodcroft)*

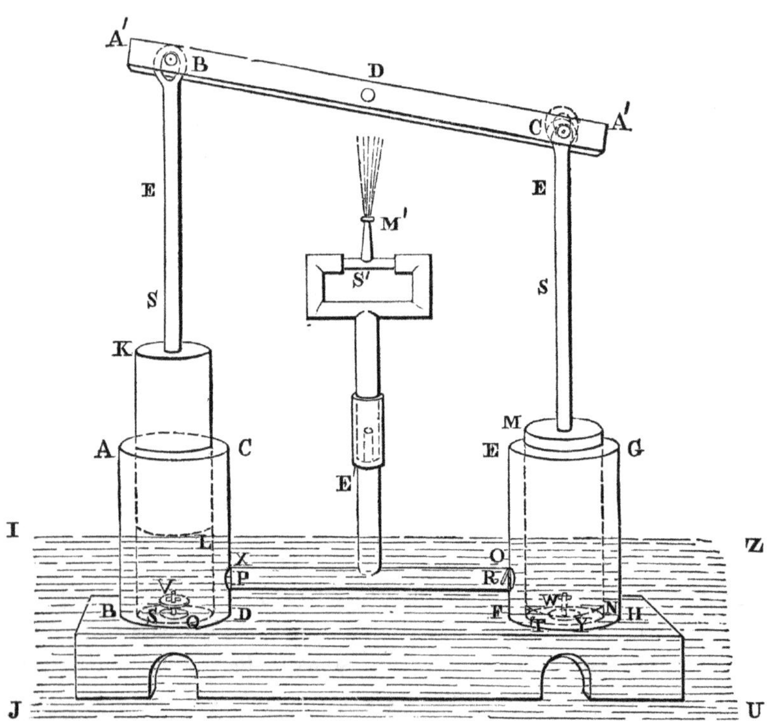

FIGURE 4.7.2C Fire pump: Woodcroft 1851: 44 (public domain).

D. *The force-pump fire extinguishers were operated by specialized* siphonatores, *one of whom was memorialized with an epitaph at Rome (2nd century CE).*

To the spirits of the departed, Titus Avidius, a Roman soldier of the 7th cohort of *Vigiles*, a *siponarius* in Laetorius' century. Avidia Romana, his mother (set this up) for her most dutiful son.

*(*CIL *6.2994; cf. 6.1057–1058, 6.31075)*

4.8 Wetland Reclamation

A. *One of the earliest projects of wetland reclamation occurred during the Bronze Age at the Kopais Basin in central Boeotia (central Greece). The Mycenaean system included a central 25-meter-long, stone-lined canal and several dykes to drain excess water (Simpson 2006). By Alexander's day, the system was failing, and Krates was commissioned to re-drain the Kopais (c. 330 BCE).*

> The Kephissos River, filled with the Kopais Lake, makes this water drainage especially clear. For when the lake increases so that the *polis* Kopae risks being swallowed—Kopae, "oars" as the poet thus named the place (Homer, *Iliad* 2.502), and from its lake it takes its eponymous name—a chasm, arising near the lake near Kopae, opened up a stream under the earth, about 30 *stadia* long, and it received the river. Then the river broke through to the surface near Larymna, the upper Larymna. For there is another Larymna which I have recalled (9.2.13), the Boeoetian Larymna by the sea, to which the Romans joined the Upper Larymna. The place is called Anchoe ("Outflow"). There is a homonymous lake. From there the Kephissos leads out to the sea. Then therefore, when the flooding stopped, there was little danger for those dwelling nearby, except for the cities already swallowed down. The pathways flooded over again, the metallurgist Krates, a man of Chalkideus, stopped clearing out the barriers, while the Boeotians were quarreling, even as he himself says in a letter to Alexander, many places were already drained. Some people understood that among these places was the ancient dwelling of Orchomenos, others, Eleusis and Athens along the Triton River. It is said that Cecrops,[83] when he ruled over Boeotia—called Ogygia at that time—founded them, but that later, covered over, these were flooded. They also say that there was a chasm near Orchomenos and it received the Melas River flowing through Haliartus and making the marsh which produces the aulos-reed.[84] But this river has disappeared entirely: either the chasm scattered it towards unseen channels, or the marsh meadows around Haliartus used up the lake water, after which the poet calls the place grassy, saying "also grassy Haliartus" (Homer, *Iliad* 2.593).
>
> *(Strabo,* Geography *9.2.18)*

B. *The* polis *of Eretria in Euboea hired the engineer Chaerephanes to drain the local marshy lake, for which work a contract was drawn up and inscribed on a now damaged stele that was publicly displayed (cf. Foxhall 2007: 69–71).*

> According to these things, Chaerephanes announces to the Eretrians that he will make the land dry and drive out the lake in Ptechae. Chaerephanes himself will supply the expenses for the drainage project, but not lay out the duties to the

83 An earth-born, serpent-hybrid king and legendary founder of Athens.
84 #2.3.4.

city for whatever is imported and exported for the sake of the work. And he will be exempt from taxes for importing stone and wood, whichever is necessary for the work, accordingly as is written for contracts of public works. When he will have drained the lake, paying 30 *talents*, he will enjoy the fruits of the land for ten years, paying the rent to the city monthly. Chaerephanes will drain the lake within four years at most. The time of the agreement will begin when Hippokydes and his colleague are fellow archons over the local council and the span of four years will begin at that time. Chaerephanes will not lay out duties, if he sells the produce in Eretria and does not export it.

The citizens agree and bind themselves in oath to Apollo Daphnephoros ("Laurel-wearing") to allow Chaerephanes to enjoy the fruits of the land for ten years for 30 *talents*, when he has drained the lake. This contract will be inscribed on a stone slab. And the contract and oath and all other matters will be inscribed and placed in the temple of Apollo Daphnephoros. If some war hinders Chaerephanes from draining the lake to make the place dry, as it is written, then, when it is possible if there is peace, time will be conceded equal to the war which obstructed Chaerephanes. If another war occurs and it is not possible to enjoy the produce of the land . . . time will be conceded equal to the war which impeded his work, whenever it is possible.

It will be possible for Chaerephanes to make underground conduits in individual properties, but he shall not dig through any place, not before he has paid out the worth. Along the lake, if he needs land, calculating at the rate of one *drachma* per foot. Chaerephanes will pay this when he is draining the lake. If he leads the marsh out in channels, he will lead those away from worked fields through untilled places, in order that cultivated lands are not damaged. And let him make a cistern for the channels not larger than two *stadia*. When Chaerephanes is enjoying the profits of the land, he shall maintain the underground system and the channels, and he shall take pains over them, and he will do this well and for the entire time. And he will make fences around the cistern. And there, where the water falls out into the underground conduit, he shall construct a door (sluice gate) in order that if there is a desire of water, the farmers who need it can close the outflow and use the water. If Chaerephanes suffers something (i.e., dies) before draining the marsh, this contract conveys to all those accomplishing the work after Chaerephanes (i.e., his heirs). If anyone, either an archon or a private individual, desires to annul these agreements, in writing or by a vote, or compels Chaerephanes and his partners to break these contracts, by any pretext or argument whatsoever, he will be despised and his property will be sanctified to Artemis, and he himself and his family will be of themselves: what they have suffered, they will suffer without compensation.

Charephanes will pay the promised sureties when he has drained the marsh and the marsh will be dry as promised . . . and he will offer a security of 30 *talents* to enjoy the profits. The city-councilors have spoken. This seems good to the council and the people. It will be inscribed regarding the contract that Chaerephanes . . .

(IG *12.9.191.1–35)*

C. *Marshlands could be rendered habitable by human enhancements.*

Likewise, if walls are to be established in swamplands which are along the sea, and if they look towards the north or between the north and east, and if the swamps are higher than the seacoast, such walls will seem to be reasonably laid down. For if ditches are cut, there is an outlet of waters at the shore. When the sea is raised by storms, the overflow in the swamps, roused by the motions and mixtures of the sea, does not allow types of marshy beasts to be born there. Those which arrive close to the shore by swimming from more elevated locales are killed because of the unaccustomed salinity.[85] An example of this occurrence, moreover, can be found in Gallic swamps, those swamps which gird Altinum, Ravenna, Aquileia,[86] and other municipalities in places of this kind that are very close to the marshes because, by means of these reasons, they have extraordinary healthfulness. However, those places in which there are standing marshes and which do not have flowing discharges—neither rivers nor through ditches, as at Pomptina[87]—by standing they putrefy and emit heavy and pestilential moistures in those places.

(Vitruvius, On Architecture *1.4.11–12)*

D. *Both Julius Caesar and Augustus considered draining the Fucine Lake near Rome (Augustus demurred over the expense, despite local entreaties: Suetonius,* Claudius *33.1). The project was inaugurated in 52 CE, taking 11 years and the labor of 30,000 men. Hadrian later widened and deepened the tunnel (Dio Cassius,* Roman History *61.33.5), but the basin was not completely drained until 1877.*

Among the especially noteworthy achievements of that same emperor Claudius, although abandoned by the enmity of his successor (Nero), I should recount that the mountain was dug through for the purpose of draining the Fucine Lake, at indescribable expense and a crowd of day-laborers over many years, since either the confluence of the waters, where the mountain was earthy, was to be discharged to the summit by machines, or the flint was to be cut. Much of this happened within the shadows as works which are not able to be understood in the mind or described in human speech except by those who saw them.

(Pliny, NH *36.124; cf. Suetonius,* Claudius *20.1–2;*
Dio Cassius, Roman History *60.11.5)*

85 Seawater's salinity helps to control the populations of harmful fenland creatures (cf. Strazzulla 1989).

86 *Altinum*: northeast of Venice in northeastern Italy; *Ravenna*: #4.4B; *Aquileia*: on the northeastern corner of Italy's Adriatic coastline.

87 Marshes southeast of Rome between the Volscian mountains and Tyrrhenic Sea (cf. Pliny, *NH* 3.59).

4.9 Creating Artificial Waters

In a disastrous vanity project, Ariarathes (V?) of Cappadocia (2nd century BCE, central Turkey) attempted to create an artificial pleasure-sea by manipulating the Melas River.

> There is a river in the plain in front of the city, called Melas, about 40 *stadia* away from the city, and having its sources in a low-lying district of the city. For this reason it is useless to them, not having its flow on higher ground but scattering towards the marshes and pools. It distresses the air around the city during the summer and makes the stone-quarry hard to work, although it is easy to work: for there are flat ledges from which they are able to collect plentiful stone for the Mazakenian building projects.[88] But hidden by the waters, the ledges act in conflict, and these marshes are everywhere volcanic. The Melas River has some narrow outlet into the Euphrates,[89] and Ariarathes the king, blocking it, created this sea-like pool near the plain. Receiving therein some islands, like the Cyclades, in this artificial lake, and spending his time on them, Ariarathes made these youthful diversions. But the barrier snapped all at once, the water washed back out. The Euphrates, filled up again, carried away much of the land of the Cappadocians and concealed many dwellings and planted fields and despoiled no small part of the region of the Galatians, those holding Phrygia. In exchange for the damage, the Melians, turning the decision over to the Romans, exacted a penalty of 300 *talents*. The same thing happened around Herpa.[90] For there, Ariarathes blocked the Karmalas River. Then, the river-mouth breaking open and utterly destroying some districts of Cilicia around Mallos, the king paid a penalty to those who had been wronged.
>
> *(Strabo,* Geography *12.2.8)*

4.10 Hydraulic Mining

Pliny the Elder served as procurator of Hispania Tarraconensis in 74 CE, *where he observed the complex, expensive, dangerous, and destructive method of mining for gold at Las Médulas by hushing, the process whereby water is brought forcefully to the ore by diverting surface streams, which in turn wash the rocks towards settling tanks. The description is a technical and rhetorical tour de force, and Pliny's disapproval of the destruction of the landscape, for the sake of greed and vanity, is palpable. Labor-intensive but very profitable, hydraulic mining is probably the starkest example of human use of water to conquer (and destroy) the natural world.*

> 74. There is another equally work-intensive method and of greater expense: to convey rivers away from the yokes of mountains, generally from the 100th milestone

88 Mazaka was the ancient name of Caesarea in Cilicia (Kayseri, Turkey).
89 Strabo, or his source, means the Halys River (Kızılırmak), not the Euphrates.
90 Another Cappadocian city, east of Melas.

away for the purpose of washing this debris. They call these water-conduits *corrugi*, from *conrivatio*, the "drawing together of water-streams," I believe. This process also involves a thousand steps: there must be a descent straight down, so that the water rushes out rather than flows. Thus, water is conveyed from the highest parts. Ravines and valleys are joined by channels built from below. Elsewhere, roadless rocks are cut away and forced to offer a foundation for the hollowed-out beams.

75. He who cuts the rock hangs from cords so that—to those watching from a distance—there is the appearance not of wild animals but of birds. For the most part those men hanging from the cords balance themselves and lead out the lines for the journey, and where there is no place for a man's steps to tread, rivers are diverted by a man. There is imperfection in washing the ore if the flowing river carries mud in they call this kind of earth *urium*. Therefore, they lead the water through flint and pebbles and avoid *urium*. At the head of the falling water on the brows of the mountains, fishponds are hollowed out, 200 paces towards each direction and ten paces deep. In these ponds drains are left in, three each nearly five paces squared, so that, when the reservoir is full and the stopping barriers are shaken away, the flood breaks through with such force that it tumbles the gold-bearing rocks forward.

76. There is yet another task on the flat ground. The ditches through which the water flows are hollowed out: they (the Greeks) call these ditches *agogai*, "leaders." These ditches are gradually strewn along the ulex-gorse: this shrub is similar to "sea-dew" (rosemary), rough and holding back the gold. The sides are shut in with planks, and the channels are suspended through the snapped off mountains. Thus, flowing along, the earth slips into the sea, and the ruptured mountain is washed away. For these reasons, Hispania has already moved a great deal of land into the sea.

77. The gold which is emptied out by the prior type of mining at immeasurable labor is moistened in this way so that it does not enter the shafts. Gold acquired in an *arrugia*[91] is not cooked (smelted) but is itself immediately. Thus, nuggets are also found in shafts and exceeding ten pounds in weight. Some call these lumps *palagae*, others call them *palacurnae*, and the same folk call the gold, which is found in very small pieces, *balux* ("gold dust"). The shrub is dried, burnt, and its ash is washed on grassy turf laid out underneath so that the gold settles on it.

78. They say that, in this way every single year, Asturia and Callaecia and Lusitania[92] produce 20,000 pounds of gold (thus Asturia itself produces the most). Nor in any other part of the world over so many generations does this level of abundance persist. We have said that by an old interdiction of the senatorial fathers Italy is spared. No land would otherwise also be richer in metals.

(Pliny, NH *33.74–78)*

91 Gold shaft or pit mine.

92 *Asturia*: northern Spain; *Callaecia*: Gallaeca, northwest Spain; *Lusitania*: Portugal.

PART V

Humans on the Water

The Mediterranean is sprinkled with islands and shaped by coastlines. Here we consider the phenomenon of people on the water, and our passages explore the history of sailing in the Mediterranean (#5.1.1), long-distance sails beyond the Pillars of Herakles and attempts to circumnavigate Africa (#5.1.2), as well as technical aspects of sailing and navigating, including deck officers (#5.1.3), launching and anchoring (#5.1.4–5), divers (#5.1.6), and the military sailing season (#5.1.7). Essential to a navigator's success is a knowledge of the winds, the stars, and marine "topography" (#5.1.9–12). Navigators were also aided by professional pilots who guided visiting ships safely to harbor (#5.1.13). But did the ancients have maritime charts (#5.1.14)? We also look at some particularly famous and remarkable ships and a ship race (#5.1.15–16). And we hear the voices of some who sailed (#5.1.17). Moreover, we consider short- and long-haul travel on water (#5.2). Finally, waterways were enhanced for comfort and safety: harbors were constructed and dredged, canals shortened the distance of journeys, bridges allowed traffic across rivers, and lighthouses served as beacons for navigators (#5.3).

5.1 Sailing and Navigating

5.1.1 History of Navigation

Artistic and archaeological evidence attests that peoples were actively sailing the Mediterranean from the Neolithic Age onward, and the Minoans of Crete may have been the first to make open-water voyages across the sea-roads. An inscription in Amenhotep III's tomb (c. 1800 BCE) cites Aegean toponyms, possibly recording an eastern Mediterranean voyage from Egypt (Wachsmann 1998: 297).

DOI: 10.4324/9781003437741-6

A. *A brief history of sailing and boat designs.*

206. Danaus[1] first came to Greece from Egypt in a ship. Before that, there was navigating with rafts—discovered by King Erythras—in the Red Sea between islands. There are found those who think that Mysians and Trojans devised earlier boats in the Hellespont when they crossed over to Thrace. Even now in the Britannic Ocean woven boats (coracles) are made, stitched with a skin. In the Nile boats are made from papyrus and bulrush and reed.

207. Philostephanus[2] is the authority that Jason was the first to have sailed in a long boat,[3] that Hegesias sailed to Parhalus,[4] that Ctesias[5] sailed to Samiramis, that Archemachus sailed to Aegaeo.[6] Damastes is the authority that the Erythraeans made the bireme;[7] Thucydides that the Corinthian Ameinocles made the trireme; Aristotle that the Carthaginians created the quadrireme.[8]

208. Mnesigiton[9] is the authority that the Salaminii[10] made the quinquereme; Xenagoras[11] that the Syracusians made a ship of six banks of oars; Mnesigiton that Alexander the Great designed from it a ship up to ten banks; Philostephanos that Ptolemy Soter ("savior," r. 305/4–282 BCE) made a ship up to 12 banks, and that Demetrius son of Antigonus made a ship up to 15 banks,[12] that Ptolemy Philadelphus commissioned a ship of up to 30 banks,[13] and that Ptolemy Philopator who is nicknamed Tryphon ("the luxurious") made a ship

1 Danaus' brother, King Aegyptus (of Egypt), proposed a marriage alliance between his 50 sons and Danaus' 50 daughters. Danaus refused and fled to Argos. But the cousin-fiancés pursued, demanding the marriages. Danaus pretended to consent, giving each girl a dagger with instructions to kill her groom on their wedding night. One husband, Lynceus, spared the virginity of Hypermnestra, his cousin-bride, and she spared her husband's life. But, for their crimes, the other 49 Danaids are punished in Hades by trying to fill a cauldron using leaky jars to carry the water from a spring. All the water seeps out before they reach the cauldron, and the task is impossible and unending. See Apollodorus, *Library* 2.1.5; Ovid, *Heroides* 14.

2 Of Cyrene, third century BCE, Philostephanus studied under Callimachus and wrote a history of Cyprus.

3 During the quest for the Golden Fleece: see Apollonius, *Argonautica.*

4 The philosopher Hegesias of Cyrene, fl. 290 BCE; Parhalus is in Phoenicia.

5 *Ctesias*: #2.3.4C introduction. *Samiramis*/Semiramis was a legendary Assyrian queen who stabilized the Middle east and Levant in the ninth century BCE.

6 Of Euboea, third century BCE, Archemachus wrote a history of his native island.

7 Fourth century BCE? Cited by Strabo (1.3.3) and others. Ancient ships were designated according to how many banks of oars or how many rowers manned each oar. The Erythraeans inhabited the coasts along the Erythraean Sea: Red Sea, Persian Gulf, Indian Ocean.

8 Neither passage survives.

9 Mnesigiton: fourth century BCE.

10 *Salamanii*: inhabiting Salamis in the Saronic Gulf east of the Peloponnese. The *quinquereme* has five banks of oars.

11 An historian from Heraclea Pontica, before the late first century BCE.

12 Demetrius I Poliorcetes, "besieger of cities," ruled Macedonia 294–288 BCE.

13 Ptolemy II Philadelphus ("Sibling-Loving," for his marriage to his full sister, Arsinoe II) among Alexander's generals and successors, ruled Egypt 284–246 BCE.

up to 40 banks.[14] Hippias the Tyrian discovered the cargo ship. The Cyrenians developed the *lembus* (a small fast-sailing boat), the Phoenicians the *cumba* (a skiff), the Rhodians the *celes* (fast yacht), the Cyprians the *cercyrus* (a fast light vessel).

209. The Phoenicians discovered the observation of the stars in sailing; the people of Kopae ("Oars") created the oar;[15] the folk of Plataea established its width (oar blade). Icarus developed sails. Daedalus invented the mast and yard-arm.[16] The Samians or Pericles of Athens[17] developed the horse-transport boat; the Thasians, long decked ships: beforehand there was fighting only from the prow and stern. Pisaeus son of Tyrrenus added the curved bow (beak); Aupalamus added the anchor.[18] Anarcharsis added the same, but double-pronged.[19] Pericles of Athens added grappling hooks and fists. Tiphys[20] added the support for guiding the ship (tiller). Minos[21] was the first to fight with a fleet.

(Pliny, NH *7.206–209)*

B. *The development of sailing among the Greeks.*

As Hellas became more powerful and acquired even more wealth than before, tyrannies[22] were established in the *poleis*, and income became greater: beforehand there were hereditary kingships based on old conditions. Hellas began to prepare fleets and lay claim to the sea. The Corinthians are said to be the first to manage nautical matters very close to how we do now, and triremes were built in Hellas first in Corinth. The Corinthian shipwright Ameinocles[23] made four ships for the Samians. It was also about 300 years before the end of this war[24] that Ameinocles came to the Samians (704 BCE). The most ancient sea-battle, of which we know, occurred with the Corinthians against the Corcyraeans, and this was 260 years from the same date (664 BCE). For, inhabiting a city on the isthmus, the Corinthians have always had an emporium at that place—long ago the Hellenes, both those within the Peloponnese and those without, dealt with each other on land more so than by the sea through Corinth—and they were powerful with money, as is made clear by the ancient poets: they called the place "wealthy" (Homer, *Iliad* 2.570;

14 Ptolemy IV Philopator, "Father-Loving," r. 221–204 BCE.
15 See #4.8A.
16 #3.11.11C.
17 Athenian statesman (495–429 BCE) responsible for the monumental rebuilding of the acropolis after the Persian Wars and orchestrating the Delian League into an Athenian empire.
18 Pisaeus and Aupalamus, otherwise unknown.
19 An inventor also credited with the potter's wheel (Strabo, *Geography* 7.3.9).
20 The *Argo*'s helmsman.
21 A son of Zeus and legendary king of Crete, for whom the "Minoan" era was named.
22 Tyranny: #2.2.11H note.
23 Otherwise unknown. Cf. Dionysius of Halicarnassus, *Ancient Orators: Thucydides* 5.19, repeating the same information.
24 Peloponnesian War: 431–405 BCE.

Pindar, *Olympian* 13.4). When the Hellenes sailed more on the sea, the Corinthians, acquiring ships, took down piratical enclaves, and, furnishing an emporium, they had a city powerful with the income of property. For the Ionians there was later a fleet in the time of Cyrus (r. 559–530 BCE), the first king of the Persians, and Cambyses, his son (r. 530–522 BCE). Fighting against Cyrus, for some time the Ionians were powerful over the sea along their lands. Polycrates (r. 540s–522 BCE), tyrant of Samos at the time of Cambyses, strong with his fleet, subjected some of the islands and, taking Rhenea, he dedicated it to Delian Apollo. The Phocaeans, settling Massalia,[25] fighting in ships, conquered the Carthaginians.

(*Thucydides,* Peloponnesian War *1.13*)

5.1.2 Long-Distance Sails

Early voyages were generally short day-hauls (when visibility is optimal), keeping within sight of land, and the Phoenicians established settlements along Africa's Mediterranean coast every 25 to 30 nautical miles (46.3–55.5 kilometers [29–34.5 miles])—the average length of a day's sail—usually in conjunction with natural harbors (Aubet 1993: 140). But there were, in addition, ambitious journeys beyond the Pillars of Herakles, as well as attempts to circumnavigate Africa.

A. *After attempting a canal of the Nile (#5.3.5D), Necho II (c. 600 BCE) sponsored a voyage around Libya (i.e., the African continent), perhaps hoping to prove that Libya was fully circumnavigable, as long suspected. Herodotus used the event to criticize contemporary cartographical theory of three roughly equal continents. For the sailing season: #5.1.7, #5.2.3.*

I am amazed at those distinguishing and dividing Libya and Asia and Europe. For their differences are not small. Europe comes alongside both in length, and it seems to me to be as broad by no comparison. For Libya is clearly surrounded by water, except where it borders Asia. We know that Necho, the king of the Egyptians, first discovered this. When he had made an end of digging the canal leading from the Nile to the Arabian Bay, he sent Phoenician men in ships, enjoining them to sail on the return trip through the Pillars of Herakles towards the northern sea and thus to arrive at Egypt. Setting out from the Erythraean Sea, the Phoenicians sailed the southern sea. When autumn occurred, putting in, they would sow the land, wherever in Libya they arrived sailing, and they would await the harvest. Then reaping the grain, they would sail so that—two years passing, rounding the Pillars of Herakles in the third year—they arrived at Egypt, and they said, something not credible as far as I'm concerned, that while sailing around Libya they had the sun to their right.[26]

(*Herodotus,* Histories *4.42*)

25 Marseille, founded in 600 BCE.

26 As the Phoenician crew rounded the Cape of Good Hope, the sun seemed to shift its position owing to the geometry of a spherical earth: in the Northern Hemisphere, in the morning, the sun appears to the left for those facing south. See also Kahanov 1999: 155–160; Roller 2006: 23–26.

B. *C. 500 BCE, the Carthaginian "suffete" (or "king" [*basileus*]) Hanno led a Carthaginian expedition through the Pillars of Herakles down the western coast of Africa, turning back when supplies ran out. An account of the voyage was recorded on a Punic inscription in a Carthaginian temple of Kronos/Saturn, eventually translated into Greek (preserved in* Codex Palatinus Graecus *398*; 9th century CE). *The voyage was known to Aristotle (*On Marvelous Things Heard *833a11–15), Mela (*Circuit of the World *3.90), Pliny (*NH *6.200), and Arrian (*Indika *43.11). Here we have Hanno's account.*

The *Periplus* ("sailing around") of Hanno the Carchedonian (Carthaginian) King, to the Libyan portions of land beyond the Pillars of Herakles, which he placed in the *temenos*[27] of Kronos, explaining these things:

1. It seemed good to the Carthaginians that Hanno sail beyond the Pillars of Herakles and establish *poleis* of Libyphoenicians,[28] and he sailed out leading 60 penteconters, and a crowd of men and women to the number of 30,000 and grain and other equipment.

2. Setting sail, we left the Pillars behind and sailed out for a journey of two days. We founded the first city which we called Thymiaterion ("Incense Burner"): below, there was a great plain.

3. And then, sailing to the west to Solois, we came to a Libyan promontory shaggy with trees.

4. Establishing a temple of Poseidon there, we embarked again towards the sun (east) for half a day until we arrived at a marsh lying not far from the sea, full of many and large reeds. And elephants and very many other wild animals were grazing there.

5. And, passing a day's sail along the lagoon, we established cities at the sea, calling them Karikon Teichos ("Walls of Karikon") and Gytta and Akra ("Lofty") and Melitta ("Sweet") and Arambys.

6. Putting to sea, from there we came to the great River Lixos (Loukkos), flowing from Libya. The wandering folk, the Lixitans, were grazing their flocks by it. We stayed with them for some time since they were friendly.

7. Above them dwelt the inhospitable Aethiopians,[29] inhabiting a land full of wild beasts and pressed by large mountains, from which they say the Lixos River flows. Around the mountains live strangely formed people, the Troglodytes,[30] whom the Lixitans say are swifter than horses in races.

27 #2.2.13B.i note.

28 The Phoenicians who had settled "Libya" (the Greek designation for the African continent: Herodotus, *Histories* 4.41) and now live there. See Diodorus Siculus, *Library of History* 17.113; Strabo, *Geography* 17.3.19.

29 The less wealthy western Aithiopians, distinct from the wealthier, eastern Aithiopians south of Egypt.

30 Cave dwellers, distinct from the "nibblers" in eastern Africa: #1.7D§18.

8. Taking interpreters from them, we sailed southward past a desert for two days. And, turning back from there to the sun for a one-day run, we found there, in a nook of some bay, a small island, five *stadia* around, which we settled, calling it Kerne. From our *periplus*, we judged that it lay opposite Carthage. For the sail from Carthage to the Pillars seemed the same as from the Pillars to Kerne.

9. From then on we arrived at a lake, sailing through some great river whose name is Chretes. Chretes has three islands larger than Kerne. Completing a day sail from there, we arrived at the corner of the lake, above which stretches a very large mountain, filled with savage folk wearing wild animal skins, who struck us with the stones that they were throwing, preventing us from disembarking.

10. Sailing from there, we came to another river, large and broad, full of crocodiles and river horses (hippopotami). Turning back from there, we returned to Kerne.

11. From there, we sailed to the south for 12 days, plucking along the land, all of which the Aethiopians, fleeing from us and not tarrying, inhabited. They spoke words senseless to the Lixitans with us.

12. But on the last day we came to anchor at great mountains shaggy with copses. The wood of the trees was sweet-smelling and dappled.

13. Sailing around these mountains for two days, we came upon an immeasurable gulf in the sea, on each side of which was a plain towards the land, from which, at night, we saw fire rising up from all sides in the distance, some greater, some less.

14. Watering there, we sailed along the headlands for five days, until we arrived at a great bay which our interpreters said was called *Hesperu Keras* ("Horn of the West"). In it there was a large island, and in the island there was a lagoon like the sea. In this there was another island. Disembarking on this island we saw nothing but woods during the day. But at night we saw many fires burning, and we heard the sound of flutes and cymbals and the clash of drums and countless din. Fear seized us, and the diviners commanded us to leave the island.

15. Sailing away quickly, we passed by a fiery land, full of incense. From it, very large, fiery, rushing streams tumbled down to the sea.[31] The land was impassable because of the heat.

16. And therefore hurriedly from there we away sailed hastily in fear. Carried along for four days, we saw the land full of flame at night. In the middle was a steep fire, greater than the rest, which seemed to fasten onto the stars. By day this appeared to be a very high mountain, called *Theon Ochema* ("Chariot of the Gods").

31 The eruption, perhaps, of Mt. Cameroon, still an active volcano.

17. From there, sailing for three days alongside the fiery streams, we arrived at a bay called *Notos Keras* ("Horn of the South").

18. In a nook was an island, similar to the previous one, having a lagoon and in it another island, full of savage folk. There were women there, more by far, shaggy over their bodies: our interpreters called them "Gorillae." Chasing the males, we were unable to collect them. Indeed, they all fled by climbing steep precipices and defending themselves with rocks. But killing three females, who did not want to follow us—they bit and scratched their leaders—we flayed them and brought their hides back to Carthage.[32] But we did not sail any further, our grain failing us.

(Hanno, Periplus*)*

C. *Pytheas of Massalia was, it seems, the first Greek explorer to travel to Britain and beyond (late 4th century BCE), perhaps reaching as far as the Orkneys or Iceland. Recording his account in* On Ocean *(lost but extracted by later geographical writers), Pytheas thus increased Greek knowledge of the west and contributed to a deeper understanding of latitude and its ramifications for a spherical earth (Irby 2021b: 72; cf. Roller 2006: 57–91). To Polybius and Strabo, Pytheas' claim to have traveled so far seemed too fantastical to believe.*

Concerning the chorography[33] of Europe, Polybius says that he omits the ancient writers but examines those refuting them, Dichaearchus[34] and Eratosthenes,[35] the most recent one writing about geography, and Pytheas, by whom many have been led astray. Asserting that he came to Brettanike (Britain), all of it on foot, Pytheas reported that the perimeter of the island was more than 40,000 *stadia*, observing in addition these things about Thule[36] and those places in which neither land exists along it nor sea nor air, but some mixture, similar to a sea-lung,[37] in which he says

32 The hides were displayed in the temple of Tanit in Carthage until the Romans destroyed the city (Pliny, *NH* 6.200).

33 Chorography is a fraught term, referring to "descriptions of the world" (Strabo, *Geography* 14.5.22) or detailed (but non-mathematical) topographical accounts of smaller and larger tracts (Ptolemy, *Geography* prologue 1, 1.1). See also Irby forthcoming-b: introduction.

34 Among Aristotle's students, Dichaearchus of Messana (c. 370/350 to after 323 BCE) was a philosopher and geographer who, among other things, wrote a geographical description of the earth (*Circuit of the Earth*), establishing a prime latitude and attempting to calculate distances.

35 #1.3.7C.

36 Thule's precise location is disputed: the Shetlands, Orkney, or perhaps Iceland, where the juxtaposition of ice and volcanic activity is particularly noticeable.

37 Perhaps some combination of exotic north Atlantic sea creatures, the behavior of coastal ice, or seemingly contradictory geothermal hot springs in an icy environment (Roseman 1994: 127–131; Romm 1992: 22–23; Roller 2006: 85–86). The Vikings referred to these waters as a "sea of worms" (*madkasjo*), where, according to the Saga of Erik the Red, the Icelander's ship *Bjarni* was destroyed by marine worms (Kunz 1997: 18).

that earth and sea and all things are lifted up together,[38] and this is a junction of the whole, neither possible to pass through or sail over. Pytheas himself says that he saw something similar to a sea-lung, but the rest is from hearsay. These are the things about Pytheas, and consequently, returning from there he travelled the entire ocean-coast of Europe from Gadeira (Cadiz) to the Tanais River (Don).

Polybius says that this is incredulous, how such distances could be sailed and trod by a private individual and a poor man, and that he was at a loss if he could trust such accounts. Notwithstanding, Eratosthenes believed the story about Brettanike and those about Gadeira and Iberia. But Eratosthenes says that it is better by far to trust the Messenian[39] than this source, Pytheas.

(Strabo, Geography *2.4.1–2)*

D. *The Greek historian Polybius (c. 200–118 BCE) also traveled beyond the Pillars of Hercules, leading an expedition of exploration sponsored by Scipio Aemilianus (185–129 BCE), the Roman general responsible for the final destruction of Carthage after the Third Punic War (149 BCE). Polybius' account is lost but extracted and summarized by later writers.*

While Scipio Aemilianus was managing affairs in Africa,[40] after accepting a fleet from Scipio, Polybius, the founder of annalistic history, sailing about for the sake of examining that region, reported that beyond that mountain (Atlas) to the west there were jungles full of the wild animals which Africa produces.

(Pliny, NH *5.9)*

5.1.3 Watch Stations

A. *Here we have a summary of the hierarchy of sailors' duties aboard ship, with the possibility of advancement from the menial (but essential) job of rowing to captaining a ship. Ancient warships were powered both by oars and sails, depending on the winds.*

. . .Before being a rudder-man, it was necessary to be a rower, then to serve as lookout, and then to examine the winds, and only then to govern the boat.

(Aristophanes, Knights *542–544)*

B. *The highest-ranking officer was the helmsman:* kubernetes *in Greek ("steerer": κυβερνήτης),* gubernator *in Latin (whence "governor"), so-called for his ability to lead a crew, rather than simply for his skill in navigating a ship.*

38 Eliciting a primeval environment where the landscape was not yet formed (cf. Plato, *Phaedo* 111e–112e; Irby 2021a: 37).

39 Euhemerus of Messenia, Sicily, 3rd century BCE, a mythographer whose fragmentary *Sacred History* recounts a fictionalized travelogue.

40 #4.1.1J note.

What is the *kubernetes*? Is the *kubernetes* rightly the leader of the sailors or a sailor?

The leader of the sailors.

I think that this should not be taken into account at all, that he sails in a ship, nor should he be called a sailor. For not according to sailing is he called *kubernetes* but according to his skill and leadership of the sailors.

(Plato, Republic *1.341c–d)*

C. *The term* kubernetes *refers both to the helmsman, per se, and to the captain, whose prerogatives include taking the steering-oar. Odysseus, for example, was at the helm when he left Aeolus' island (*Odyssey *10.32–33). Aeneas' helmsman, Palinurus, was a master of the sailing arts, including celestial navigation and reading the winds. Here Palinurus makes ready to set sail for Italy when the conditions are favorable.*

Not yet over the middle course, night was at hand, driven by the hours.[41] By no means sluggishly does Palinurus rise from his blankets and studies all the winds and catches the breezes with his ears. He notes all the stars slipping in the silent sky: Arcturus and the rainy Hyades and the twin bears. And he looks around at Orion, armed with gold. After he sees that everything accords with a serene sky, he gives a clear signal from the stern. We strike camp and test the sea-road and spread the wings of our sails.

(Vergil, Aeneid *3.512–520)*

D. *In Lucan, Telo, the Gallic helmsman (perhaps from Gallia Narbonensis), is equally skilled, guiding Pompey's fleet against Caesar. Marcus Annaeus Lucan of Corduba (39–65 CE), nephew of Seneca, was educated by his uncle and is acclaimed for his epic poem, recounting the civil war between Caesar and Pompey, the anti-Neronian, pro-Republican* Pharsalia, *in ten books.*

The right-hand of lamentable Telo also guides the stern here. In an agitated sea, keels listen to no hand better than his. Nor is tomorrow's light better known to anyone, whether he sees Phoebus (the sun) or the horns of the moon. Telo always sets his sails to the coming winds.

(Lucan, Pharsalia *3.592–596)*

E. *Sailing requires skillful and disciplined cooperation from the crew, from the captain down, and we see here a crew taking meticulous precautions to run before a storm sent by the gods to destroy Ceyx for his* hubris *(boastfully calling his wife "Juno." In answer Alcyone called Ceyx "Jupiter").*

41 Like Helios the sun, Night (moon/Selene or Artemis/Diana) was envisioned as driving a chariot across the sky.

> The captain shouts: "Lower the yards, already, and close-reef the whole sail."[42] He commands, but hostile winds ensnare his orders, nor does the din of the waves allow any voice to be heard. On their own initiative, however, some crewmen hurry to remove the oars, some protect the hull, some deny the sails to the winds. This one bails the water into the waves, that one snatches up the spars.
>
> *(Ovid,* Metamorphoses *11.482–487)*

F. *Sometimes weather conditions are so bad that even the most experienced crew are unable to keep the ship straight.*

> When the hold was half-full with the flood, and the masts were already unsteady while the waves splashed over the other side of the stern, when experience offered no help, the white-capped helmsman began to strike a deal with the winds.
>
> *(Juvenal,* Satire *12.30–34)*

G. *"The one who orders," the* keleustes *(κελευστής;* pausarius *in Latin, from the verb* pauso*: "I halt/cease"), gives the beat to the oarsmen, "in a piercing voice" (Seneca,* Epistle *56.5; see* ILS *2867). Since it was essential for the rowers to work in unison, the* keleustes' *job was vital. Here the crew practice on land.*

> They made the men sit on rower's benches on dry land, having the same arrangements as they would on voyages. Making the *keleustes* stand in the middle to teach them all to drive their striving arms back at the same time and then to stoop their thrusting arms forward, they became accustomed to begin and stop their motions at the calls of the *keleustes*.
>
> *(Polybius,* Histories *1.21.2; cf. Propertius,* Elegy *3.21.12)*

H. *During a violent storm off Patrae (Peloponnese) in 429 BCE (early in the Peloponnesian War), weather and cramped conditions made it impossible for the rowers to follow the* keleustes' *beat.*

> When the wind came up and the ships, already in a narrow space, were stirred both by the wind and at the same time also by the nearby ships, and ship was dashed against ship and the men were pushing away with poles, using shouts and warnings to each other and reproaches, they heard neither those who were commanding nor giving the beats, and the unskilled men, unable to lift their oars in the waves, caused the ships to be more disobedient to the *kubernetes*. Then, at the proper time, Phormio[43] gave a signal, and the Athenians, falling upon the

42 To reduce the sail's surface area and render the ship more controllable in high winds.
43 An acclaimed Athenian admiral, orchestrating Athenian victories in 429 BCE.

Peloponnesians first, sank one of the admirals' ships, and then they destroyed the others where they advanced. They brought the Peloponnesians down to such a state that none of them turned towards defense from the disorder, but they fled to Patrae and Dyme, *poleis* of Achaea.

(Thucydides, Peloponnesian War *2.84.3; cf.* Peloponnesian War *7.70.6)*

I. *In contrast, some situations called for non-verbal communication, as when the Spartan general Gorgopas orchestrated a surprise attack on the Athenian navy, under the command of Eunomos, as it returned to the Piraeus (#5.3.3F) in 388 BCE during the Corinthian War.*

When night came, Eunomos led the way, having a light, as was customary, so that the ships following him might not wander off course. Gorgopas then, embarking straightaway, followed behind the lantern, staying behind so that he would not be visible, nor would he offer any notice. The *keleustai* used the clinking of stones—instead of their voices—and a sliding motion of the oars.[44]

(Xenophon, Hellenika *5.1.8)*

J. *To lighten their work, rowers might accompany themselves by singing as in #2.2.12F§236 (after the whale hunt). Longus (2nd century CE), possibly from Lesbos, is known only for his pastoral romantic novel,* Daphnis and Chloe, *whose eponymous protagonists were abandoned by their families at birth, grew up together, and fell in love. Longus spins out their misadventures, including Chloe's other suitors, Daphnis' abduction by pirates, their eventual reunion with their parents, and their happy ending.*

While they were eating and loving on each other more than they ate, a fishing boat was seen sailing alongside. There was not any wind, the sea was calm, and it seemed best to row, and the fishermen were rowing formidably: they were pressing on to the city to keep newly caught fish fresh for some rich guy. As sailors are accustomed, to take their minds off their work, they lifted their oars doing this: as their *keleustes* whistled songs, the rest, in one voice like a chorus, shouted along at the thrum of his voice.

(Longus, Daphnis and Chloe *3.21.1–2)*

K. *Also essential to a well-functioning boat is the* prorates *(lookout officer:* πρῳράτης: *"who observes from the ship's bow," Latinized as* proreta*). The prorates looks out for hazards, including debris in the water, shallows, smaller craft, enemy*

44 I.e., the rowers did not splash the water.

ships, swordfish for sport fishing (Polybius, Histories *34.3.3), and even monsters, such as Scylla (#3.3), here. Odysseus is speaking.*

> "And at that time I forgot Circe grievously commanding, ordering me that I should not arm myself at all. But, after donning my renowned gear and grasping my two long spears in my hands, I went to the prow's deck. From there I expected Scylla's rock to appear first, she who would bring calamity to myself and my companions. But I was not able to observe her anywhere, and my eyes labored as I glanced searchingly in every direction towards the misty rock."
>
> *(Homer,* Odyssey *12.226–233)*

5.1.4 Moving the Boat

A. *Many ancient ships were small enough to beach, but launching a vessel, especially a large one, could be labor-intensive, as vividly described here when the* Argo *first sets sail on the quest for the Golden Fleece.*

> Jason spoke, and he was the first to turn to the work. Of their own will the others stood and piled their woven garments on a smooth surface which the sea did not strike with its waves. But long ago the stormy brine washed it off. On the advice of their helmsman, Argos, the Argonauts first of all successfully girt the ship with rope, well-twisted within, stretching it at each end, so that the planks would be well-fitted together with pegs and have strength to receive the dashing waves. They quickly dug a trench as wide as the beam of the ship and as long as from the prow to the salt-sea that the ship was about to traverse, dragged by their hands. Advancing, they were continuously digging low to the ground below the keel. In the trench they spread out hewn logs, and on the first logs they sloped the ship downward, so that, slipping she would be guided down of her own accord. Then on this side and that, turning the oars aloft, they bound them, projecting the length of a *pechus*, around the thole holes. Then they stood at both sides alternately at the oars, and they pressed their chests and at the same time also their hands into the work. Then Tiphys embarked to stir the young men to pull the ship at the right time. Urging them on, he shouted exceedingly loudly. Immediately applying their weight, with one thrust they struck the ship from its resting-place and moved her forward, bracing with their feet. Then the Pelian[45] *Argo* followed very swiftly, and on each side the men cheered as they rushed. The logs groaned, grazed under the stout keel, and around them dark smoke bubbled up from the weight. The ship slipped down to the salt-sea. Drawing her back from there, they checked her as the ship advanced forward. Then they fitted the oars to the thole holes, and they loaded the mast, well-wrought sails, and supplies.
>
> *(Apollonius,* Argonautica *1.363–393)*

45 So-called because she was constructed of wood largely from Mt. Pelion.

B. *Oar handles are levers, and the rowers amidships exert the greatest impact: there is simply more oar blade amidships than fore and aft. It is unclear if the peripatetic author of* Mechanical Problems *assumed oars all of the same length or longer oars amidships.*

> Therefore, the ship is moved while the oar blade is supported against the sea, owing to the oar's handle, within the ship, moving forward. And the ship, attached to the tholepin, advances where the oar's handle goes. For where the oar blade cleaves through the greatest quantity of sea, there the ship is mostly thrust forward by necessity, and it plies the most water where there is the greatest portion from the oar's tholepin. Because of this, the rowers in the middle move the ship the most. For amidships, there is the greatest length from the oar's tholepin within the ship.
>
> *(Aristotelian* Mechanical Problems *4 [850b21–29])*

C. *Until the 16th century ships were steered either with steering-oars or tillers attached directly to the rudder.*[46] *Like an oar, the tiller is a lever providing torque to turn the rudder. The rudder's fulcrum is where it attaches to the ship, working on a horizontal plane and taking the sea obliquely. The Peripatetic author recognizes that the tiller's length and the force required to move it are proportional to the vessel's size.*

> For the fulcrum is turned to an opposite direction, the sea to the inside, the fulcrum to the outside. The ship follows the fulcrum because it is attached. Therefore, the flat oar-paddle pushes the weight and, pushed in the opposite direction by it, it drives the ship straight. But the rudder, since it is positioned obliquely, causes an oblique movement, either this way or that.
>
> *(Aristotelian* Mechanical Problems *5 [850b31–851a2])*

D. *Men would draw lots in pairs for their turns at the oars. Propertius (50/45–15 BCE) was an elegiac poet, friendly with Vergil and Augustus. Many of his elegies, in four books, treat a literary love affair with his poetically constructed Cynthia. Here, the only cure for a lover's quarrel is travel.*

> There will be one support. With lands changed, love will be as far from my mind as Cynthia from my eyes. Come now, my friends, drive a ship into the waters; lead out pairs of oars by lots in turn, and hoist lucky sails to the top of the mast. The breeze now favors a serene journey for sailors. May you fare well, towers of Rome, and you, my friends, and goodbye to you, Girl, however you have behaved towards me.
>
> *(Propertius,* Elegy *3.21.9–16)*

46 The ship's wheel was a late-17th-century Dutch invention, improving on the 16th-century whip-staff.

E. *Here a ship is vividly propelled by oar.*

On one side Caesar's ships are exalted, on the other a fleet with many a Greek oarsman; oar-stricken hulls quiver, and repeated strikes set the lofty ships in motion.

(Lucan, Pharsalia *3.525–528)*

5.1.5 Anchoring

If adequate beaches were not available, or as security demanded, ships would anchor out (#1.3.6F).

A. *Aeneas drops anchor off western Greece where a temple of Apollo is a beacon for sailors.*

Anchises then orders the Trojans to snatch the mooring cable hurriedly from the shore and loosen the rigging. The Notos Wind (South) stretches the sails. We flee on foaming waves wherever the course and the wind and the helmsman are calling. Now in the middle of the waves appears grove-filled Zacynthus and Dulichium and Same and Neritus lofty with crags. We escape the crags of Ithaca, Laertian kingdoms,[47] and we curse that land, the nurse of savage Ulixes. Soon the cloudy peaks of Mt. Leucate[48] appear and Apollo, fearful to sailors.[49] Tired, we seek this place, and we approach a small town. The anchor is tossed from the prow; the sterns stand on the shore.

(Vergil, Aeneid *3.266–277)*

B. *Two anchors, naturally, are better.*

For two hawsers better defend a ship.

(Propertius, Elegy *2.22a.41)*

C. *Sailors took many clues from nature, including sea urchins.*

Of the same type are sea-urchins that have spines instead of feet. For them to advance is to roll into a sphere, and they are often found with their spines rubbed off. Those whose spurs are the longest are called *echinometrae*, the smallest are *calyces* ("cups"). Nor do they all have the same glassy color. Around Torone[50]

47 Odysseus, king of Ithaca during the Trojan War, was the son of Laertes and thus the leader of "Laertian kingdoms." As a Greek leader he was the Aeneas' enemy. Cf. Homer, *Odyssey* 9.19–24.

48 #3.5D§1000 note.

49 That is to say, Apollo's temple, the god in metonymy for his shrine.

50 In northwestern Greece.

they are born white, with a small spine. All their eggs are bitter, laid in number by fives. Their mouths are in the middle of their bodies, turned towards the ground. They say that urchins presage savageness of the sea and, steadying themselves with weight from clutched stones, they wait out a storm: for they are unwilling to wear off their spines by rolling. When sailors see this, they immediately restrain their ships with more anchors.

(Pliny, NH *9.100)*

D. *In 212 BCE (Second Punic War), the Carthaginian general Bomilcar, in charge of Hannibal's supplies, was able to secure reinforcements while a violent storm prevented the Roman fleet from lying at anchor in open water.*

All attention was averted to the tumult in part of the captured city,[51] meeting with a night on which the Roman fleet could not stand at anchor in the salt-sea on account of the force of a storm. Setting out with 35 ships from the Syracusan port in free water, Bomilcar set sail in the deep water: 55 ships were left for Epicydes[52] and the Syracusans. When the Carthaginians were informed how much danger the Syracusan situation was in, Bomilcar returned after a few days with 100 ships, and also with many gifts from Epicydes from Hieron's[53] treasury, so the rumor goes.

(Livy, From the Foundation of the City *25.25.11–13)*

E. *Anchors were usually secured by ropes, but anchor-chains were also used, as by Alexander protecting his ships from sabotage at Tyre (Lebanon) in 322 BCE.*

When many engineers from Cyprus and all of Phoenicia had already been collected by Alexander, many machines were constructed: some on the breakwater; some on the horse-transports which Alexander had conveyed with him from Sidon; some on the triremes, however many of them were not fast-sailing. When these were fitted out all at once, they brought the machines down from the newly constructed mole, and the ships anchored here and there alongside the wall where they made a test of the wall.

The Tyrians placed wooden turrets for defending those troops facing the mole, so that on battlements along the mole, and—wherever the machines were moved—the Tyrians defended themselves with missiles, and they struck the ships with fiery arrows so that they might produce fear in the Macedonians who drew near the wall. The height of the walls facing the mole was about 150 feet and of a similar breadth, constructed with large stones laid in mortar. It was not easy for the Macedonian horse-transports and triremes—which were bringing

51 Acgradina, near Syracuse.

52 A Carthaginian ally and general of the Sicilian army.

53 Tyrant of Syracuse, r. 478–467 BCE; see #2.2.11H note.

the engines to the wall—to approach the city because many stones, thrown into the sea, prevented a close assault.

Alexander then intended to drag those stones from the sea. But this work progressed with difficulty since it was occurring from the ships and not on firm ground. The Tyrians, otherwise fortifying their ships, came alongside the triremes' anchors, cutting the anchor-lines and making anchoring difficult for the enemy ships.

Fortifying many of his triaconters in the same way, Alexander set them athwart in front of the anchors, so that an attack of the Tyrian ships against their own might be repulsed. But divers cut the anchor-ropes under the sea. Using chains instead of ropes for their anchors, the Macedonians let them fall so that there would be no more success for the Tyrian divers. Fastening slings around the stones, dragging them out of the sea from the mole, then raising them up with their engines, the Macedonians dropped them into the deep, so that, tossed out, they would no longer harm their ships. Where the wall was cleared of obstructions, the ships already put in without difficulty.

(Arrian, Anabasis *2.21.1–7; cf. #5.1.6B)*

5.1.6 Divers Attached to the Navy

We have already met Tharsys, who died gruesomely (#2.2.9D), and Arrian (#5.1.5E) has just referred to divers who sabotage enemy fleets.

A. *Scyllis of Scione (on Pellene in northeastern Greece) was a legendary diver who, together with his daughter, Hydna, helped sabotage Xerxes' fleet in 480 BCE: they were consequently honored with a statue in Sardinia.*

Next to a portrait of Gorgias is a votive offering from the Amphictyons[54] depicting Scionian Scyllis, who has the reputation of diving to the deepest parts of the entire sea, and he taught his daughter Hydna to dive. When a violent storm fell upon Xerxes' fleet near Mt. Pelion,[55] they, Scyllis and Hydna, accomplished the fleet's destruction, dragging the anchors and fortifications from the triremes. In return for this service, the Amphictyons dedicated a statue of Scyllis himself and his girl.

(Pausanias, Description of Greece *10.19.1–2)*

B. *In 413 BCE, Athenian divers shaved down pilings installed as a defense for the Syracusan harbor, thus facilitating enemy access to the harbor.*

A skirmish occurred around the pilings in the harbor which the Syracusans drove down in the sea in front of the ancient docks, so that their ships might lie

54 #4.2.5A.
55 #3.1.6A note.

at anchor within the harbor and the Athenians, sailing in, might not damage the Syracusan ships while trying to attack them.

Against these pilings the Athenians led a ship with a 10,000-*talent* burden, with wooden turrets and bulwarks. From small boats they hauled up to the pilings, binding them, and diving they broke them off and sawed them down. The Syracusans were attacking them from the dockyards, but the Athenians were returning fire from their merchant ship, and they destroyed many of the pilings.

But the most difficult part of the stockade was the hidden aspect. For some of the pilings which they had driven down in the sea did not rise up so that it was dangerous to sail in, lest anyone not looking out might wreck his ship on a pillar. But divers plunging down sawed these off, as well, for pay. All the same, the Syracusans drove pilings in again. They devised many and other such tactics against each other, such as is likely for armies in proximity and opposing each other, and they employed skirmishes and all sorts of trials.

(Thucydides, Peloponnesian War *7.25.5–8)*

C. *The Greeks were excellent swimmers. And in 325 BCE, Alexander's general Nearchus (see #2.1.2B) employed them strategically in an underwater phalanx against hostile locals along the Tomerus River (between the Indus and Arabis Rivers in Pakistan).*

Setting out from there they sailed with a strong wind and, traversing about 500 *stadia*, they anchored at a swollen river. The river's name was Tomerus, and there was a lagoon at the river's outlet, and, at the shallows near the shore, men were living in stifling huts. When they saw us sailing towards them, they shuddered and, stretching themselves along the beach, they marshalled themselves in battle formation to fight us as we disembarked. They were carrying stout spears, about six *pecheis* long. The tips were not iron, but hardening the tips in fire made them sharp. Their number was about 600. Nearchus observed them standing firm and drawn-up in battle order. He then commanded the ships to ride at anchor within missile range so that the Macedonian arrows might reach land from the ships. For the Barbarians'[56] thick spears seemed good for hand-to-hand combat, but they caused no fear in a javelin fight.

Nearchus himself commanded the troops—as many as were very nimble and very lightly-armed and very experienced in swimming—to swim out on a signal. Their instructions were, as soon as any swimmer stood in water, to wait for the one who would stand next to him, and not to attack the Barbarians before they drew up a phalanx of three men deep. Then they should go at a run, raising a battle cry. At the same time, those arrayed in battle formation cast themselves from the ships into the sea, and they swam quickly, and they stood in order, and

56 #5.3.5D and note.

they made a phalanx from themselves as they ran, raising a battle cry to Enyalios.[57] Those from the ships rejoined in the war cry, and arrows and missiles were shot at the Barbarians from the machines.

But, alarmed at the flash of our weapons and the swiftness of the attack and pelted by arrows and other missiles, the half-naked men gave way, not at all turning to defend themselves. Fleeing, some died; others were captured; some escaped to the hills.

(Arrian, Indika *24.1–8)*

D. *The sad fate of the exceptional diver Phoceus ("Seal" man).*

In that battle, Phoceus was alone remarkable at preserving his breath underwater and examining the narrow sea (strait) in case anything had sunk within the sands, or dislodging the bites of an anchor too firmly stuck, as often as he perceived that a line would not be led up with its anchor. Here, when he had just deeply pulled down an enemy in his grasp, Phoceus was returning to the highest waters, victorious and alive. But, while he trusted that he was rising through empty waves, he struck the stern and at length remained dead under the water.

(Lucan, Pharsalia *3.696–704)*

5.1.7 The (Military) Sailing Season

While sailing, especially commercial voyages, did occur in the winter, the best conditions were generally from late May to mid-September with longer days and better visibility, and the ancients preferred not to sail during the stormy winter.

A. *The "lubberly" farmer Hesiod restricted sailing to the 50 days following the summer solstice.*

For 50 days after the turning of the sun (solstice), the toilsome warm season coming to its end, sailing is suitable for dying folk (i.e., "mortals"). Neither would you wreck your boat, nor would the sea destroy men, if kindly Poseidon the Earth-Shaker or Zeus king of the deathless gods does not wish to destroy them. For in these gods, nevertheless, is the fulfillment of good things and bad. At that time, breezes are well-ordered, and the sea is without pain. Then, free from care, entrusting your swift ship to the breezes, drag it to the sea, place all your cargo in it, but hurry to return back homeward as quickly as possible, nor wait for the new wine and early autumn rain and approaching winter and terrible gales of the Notos (South Wind) which rouse the sea together with Zeus' rain and renders the sea difficult.

Springtime is another sailing season for human-folk: at which time—when it seems to a man that a crow, as she treads, makes a track as large as a leaf

57 An epithet for Ares, god of war, and also the name of one of his sons with Enyo, goddess of war.

on the top of a fig tree—the sea is then first able to be sailed. This sailing is springtime. But I won't praise it. For it is not agreeable to my heart. Snatched away, you would escape its evil with difficulty. But people do it from ignorance of the mind. For mercantilism is the life for vile folk. It is terrible to die in the waves. I enjoin you to consider all these things in your heart, as I announce them publicly: do not place your entire life in hollow ships, but leave more behind, load up less. For it is terrible to meet suffering in the sea's waves.

(Hesiod, Works and Days *663–691)*

B. *The sailing season was, however, complex and localized. Seeking the best waters and conditions according to the season, Xenocrates of Acragas (Sicily), victor of the chariot race at the Isthmian games (490 BCE?), enjoyed sailing year-round, from the Phasis (#1.5.5) to the Nile (#1.5.1).*

Nor ever once did a swelling fair wind make him furl his sail around his friendly table, but he crossed towards Phasis in the summer, and in the winter he was sailing towards the headland of the Nile.

(Pindar, Isthmian *2.39–43)*

C. *The distastefulness of winter sailing. The Attic orator Andocides (c. 440–370 BCE) was implicated (together with Alcibiades) in revealing the mysteries of Demeter in 415 BCE.*

For what greater danger is there for people than sailing the sea in winter?

(Andocides, On the Mysteries *1.137)*

D. *Sources often refer to when the seas again become "navigable," as here when Antiochus III (r. 223–187 BCE) anticipated campaigning against invading Romans in 192 BCE.*

For as soon as the time of year offered a navigable sea, Antiochus would fill all Greece with weapons, men, horses, the entire maritime coast with ships, he would spare neither expense nor labor nor danger until—once Roman authority was finally thrust from their necks—he made Greece and the Aetolian leaders in it truly free.

(Livy, From the Foundation of the City *35.44.5–6)*

E. *Ovid welcomed the beginning of the sailing season in the inhospitable Pontus (Black Sea) of his exile.*

But I feel the snow melting in the springtime sun, and water is no longer dug out hard from the lake. The sea does not freeze with ice, nor, as before, do the Sauromatian herdsmen drive their creaking carts over the Hister. Some ships, nonetheless, will begin to sail here, and there will be a foreign boat on the Pontus' shore. I will zealously meet the sailor, and, after a greeting is spoken, I will ask why he comes or who he is or from what places. Indeed, it will be wonderful if he is not from a nearby region and not one who has safely plied neighboring waters. It is also right that, from the mouth of the strait and the waves of the far-away Propontis, someone has thus far given sail with a reliable Notos (South Wind). For a rare mariner crosses so great a sea from Italy, a rare seaman comes to these shores bereft of harbors.

(Ovid, Tristia *3.12.27–38)*

F. *Sources also foregrounded the sailing season that was observed by ancient navies, in parallel with the infantry's military calendar that extended roughly from March to October, taking advantage of more predictable conditions on land and sea.*

The treatment of months and days follows. For the force and bitterness of the sea do not allow sailing through the whole year, but certain months are very suitable, certain ones are variable, the rest are intractable for ships owing to the law of nature. When "Pachon" has run its course—that is after the rise of the Pleiades, from the sixth day before the Kalends of June (May 27) all the way to the setting of Arcturus,[58] that is on the 18th day before the Kalends of October (September 14)—sailing is believed to be safe because the bitterness of the winds is mitigated by the benefit of heat. After this time, all the way to third day before the Ides of November (November 11), navigation is variable and verging on danger for this reason, because Arcturus rises after the Ides of September (September 13), a very violent star, and on the eighth day before the Kalends of October (September 24) an embittered equinoctial storm occurs. Around the Nones of October (October 7) the rainy Hyades rise, and on the fifth day before the Ides of the same month (October 11) Taurus rises. From the month of November, moreover, the wintry setting of the Vergiliae (Pleiades) confuses ships with closely packed storms. Therefore, from the third day before the Ides of November (November 11) all the way to the sixth day before the Ides of March (March 10) the seas are closed. For minimal light and the extensive night, density of clouds, obscurity of the air, showers of winds or ferocity doubled with snow drive not only ships from the sea but even travelers from a land journey. But truly after the birthday of navigation, as they say, which is celebrated with a ceremonial contest and a public show in many cities,[59] because of the many stars and the time itself, all the way to the Ides of May (May 15), the seas are tested with danger, not that the business of trade ceases, but because

58 Arcturus was thought to forebode bad weather since its risings and settings coincided with the change from summer to fall and winter to spring. Roman calendar: #4.5.2J§123 note.

59 See #3.11.10.

greater precaution should be employed when an army navigates with (light, fast) *liburna* than when the recklessness of private merchants hurries along.

(Vegetius, Epitome of Military Science *4.39)*

5.1.8 Measuring Distance at Sea

While it is possible to calibrate a wheel's diameter to a unit of distance and thus estimate distance traveled, it is less intuitive to measure distance traveled by sea. Here is one method.

5. With a few things changed, distances are similarly estimated for voyages by sea with the same procedure. For, over the sides of the hull there is fixed an axle A, having heads jutting beyond the ship. Enclosed in these axles are wheels B with a diameter of four and half paces having paddles fixed around the edges, touching the water. Likewise, the middle of the axle in the middle of the ship has a solid disc C with a single tooth D projecting beyond its own circumference. At this point is placed a compartment E having fixed to itself a drum with 400 equal teeth corresponding to the tooth of the disc, which is fixed to the axle. Moreover, another tooth F extending beyond the circumference is fixed to the same side.

6. Above, in another compartment fixed with it, a flat (horizontal) drum G is enclosed, toothed in the same way. To these teeth there corresponds a little tooth which is fixed on the vertical drum to the side, which is located on the point like those teeth which are on the flat drum, so that this tooth turns the flat drum in a circle by driving individual teeth in individual turnings. Moreover, openings should be made on the flat drum. Round stones are placed in these openings H. In the box of this disc, or if it is a compartment, one opening should be scooped out and have a small channel I where a pebble moves freely from obstruction when it falls into a bronze dish and makes a sound.

7. Thus, when a ship receives a goad either from oars or the breeze of the winds, the paddles, which are on the wheels touching the water, compelled by a violent back-turning force, turn the wheels. These, moreover, drive the axle by rolling themselves. The axle moves the drum whose tooth—driven around by striking the individual teeth of the second drum with individual turnings—causes the revolutions. Thus, when the wheels have been turned by the paddles 400 times, at the same time the drum, driven around, strikes a tooth of the flat drum with the tooth fixed to its side. Therefore, as often as a revolution of the flat drum guides pebbles to the opening, it will expel them through the little channel. Thus, by their sound and number, this contrivance indicates the miles and intervals of a sea-voyage. I have completed these things to be prepared for utility and delight in calm times and without fear as they ought to be made.

(Vitruvius, On Architecture *10.9.5–7; cf. #4.7.1B)*

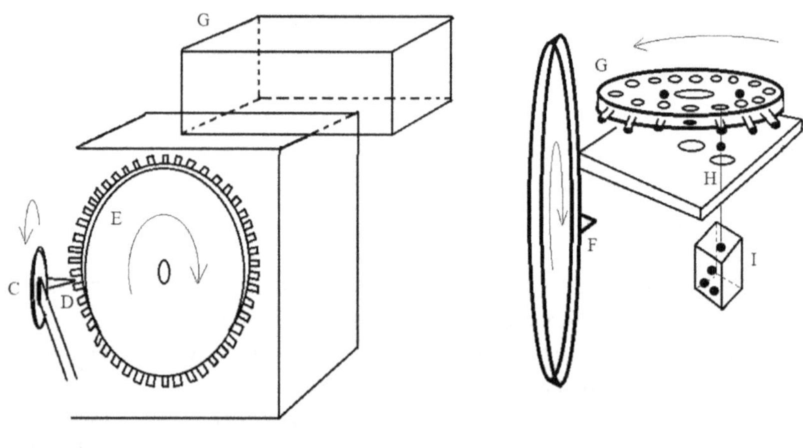

FIGURE 5.1.8 Measuring distance at sea: drawn by Georgia L. Irby (with Angélique Lemarchand).

5.1.9 Winds

Since wind was one of the two primary means of propulsion, it was essential for sailors to observe and understand them. In the Mediterranean, prevailing summer winds are northerly (i.e., blowing from the north), expediting travel to the south, but many factors affected conditions: currents, topography, weather, and meandering coastlines. See #1.5.1 for winds causing the Nile's flooding.

A. *Aeolus, king of the winds, gifted Odysseus with a bag of winds to facilitate the sail to Ithaca. Later, while Odysseus naps as the ships are within sight of Ithaca, the crew, thinking the bag is full of gold and silver, greedily open it, release all the winds, rouse a storm, and are sent back to Aeolus' island (*Odyssey *10.28–55; see also #1.8A).*

> He gave me the stripped hide of a nine-year old ox, and therein he bound the paths of the blustering winds. For Kronion[60] had made him the steward of the winds, and he could check or rouse whichever wind he wanted. In the hollow ship he bound it with a radiant silvery cord, so that not even a local breeze would escape. But for me he sent the Zephyr's blast to blow ahead, in order that it might carry the ships and the men. But it was not to come to fulfillment, for we were destroyed by our thoughtlessness.
>
> *(Homer,* Odyssey *10.19–27)*

B. *Winds prevent Odysseus and his crew from leaving Helios' island. They need to travel southwest.*

> For an entire month the Notos blew unceasingly. Nor was there any other wind but the Euros and Notos.
>
> *(Homer,* Odyssey *12.325–326)*

C. *Epic poems invariably opened with an invocation to the appropriate Muse or deity to seek divine favor and inspiration for the work. Many ancient epic poets included, in addition, a second invocation, as here, Apollonius' second invocation, emphasizing the maritime importance of the winds for Jason and his crew seeking to return to Iolchus (eastern Greece) by ship.*

> But, goddesses, how is it that beyond the salt-sea, around the Ausonian land and Ligustidan islands, which are called Stoechades, countless signs of the *Argo* ship clearly survive? What necessity and desire conveyed them so far away? What winds drove them?
>
> *(Apollonius,* Argonautica *4.552–556)*

60 Zeus/Jupiter, son of Kronos.

D. *A fair wind would blow from the stern, as when Aeneas' crew left Sicily and headed, at last, for Italy.*

A wind rising from the stern followed them as they went.

(Vergil, Aeneid *3.130 = 5.777)*

E. *Ovid prays for favorable winds to shorten his unpleasant sea voyage to his exile at Tomis on the Black Sea.*

I hope for easy winds—who could believe it?—because it is the Sarmatian land which is what my sails seek. I am obliged to touch the wild shores of the unfavorable Pontus, and I protest that my exile from my fatherland is so slow.

(Ovid, Tristia *1.2.81–84)*

F. *Some natural anchorages might be protected from winds blowing from certain quarters.*

4. For there is in the Euxine Pontus a place so-called, and there is a Greek temple there of Athena, whence it seems to me that this is the name of the place, and there is also a neglected fort. There is an anchorage, such as can receive not many ships during the summertime, and it can offer protection to them from the Notos Wind and even from the Euros. The anchorage can even save ships from the Boreas but not the Aparkios nor even the Wind called Thrasican in the Pontus, nor from the Skiron Wind from Hellas. In the night there was rough thunder and lightning, and the wind was not the same, but it changed to the south, and in a little while the wind came from the south to the southwest, and the anchorage was no longer safe for the ships. Before the sea became altogether savage, we hauled onto the beach, however, as many as that place, Athenae, was able to receive, except for a trireme. Hooking under some rock, the trireme road there safely at anchor.

5. It seemed best to send many ships towards the neighboring strands to be hauled onto land, and the men beached the ships such that all endured unimpaired except one which—moored near the beach before the proper time, turned sideways—a wave, seizing up, carried off to the shore and crashed. Everything to be sure was saved, not only the sails and nautical equipment, but also the men and even the nails, and the wax was scraped off, so that nothing was lacking for repairs other than the wood, which, as you know, is very much abundant along the Pontus. This storm continued for two days, and it was necessary to stay there. It was thus incumbent that we not sail past Athenae in the Pontus like some deserted and nameless anchorage.

(Arrian, Periplus *4–5)*

G. *Aristotle's Windrose.*

Concerning the situation of the winds, it is necessary to envision with a diagram together with words. Therefore, to have some clarity, the circle of the horizon is drawn. Consequently, the diagram is round. And it is necessary to understand that this is the section inhabited by us. For it is possible to divide that other section in the same way. First, let it be established that the opposite places are most distant in space, just as opposite things are most distant in shape according to shape. Things lying opposite each other along a diameter are most distant in space.

Let A therefore be the equinoctial sunset, opposite this point, let B be the equinoctial sunrise. Another diameter cutting this at a right angle, let H on this line be north. Opposite this diametrically, on this line, let Θ be south. On this, let Z be the summer sunrise, E the summer sunset, Δ the winter sunrise, Γ the winter sunset. From Z let the diameter be drawn to Γ, and from Δ to E. Since therefore they are most distant in space which are opposite one another, and points along the diameter are most distant, necessarily those winds are opposite each other which are opposite on a diameter.

According to the situation of their places the winds are so-called thusly: Zephyr from A: this is the equinoctial sunset. Opposite this, Apeliotes from B, the equinoctial sunrise. Boreas or Aparctias from H, here is the north. Opposite this, Notos from Θ, for it is the south from which it blows. And Θ is opposite H along the diameter. From Z, the Caecias. For this is the summer sunrise. Its opposite blowing not from E, but from Γ, the Lips. This is from the winter sunset, opposite this (for it lies on the diameter). From Δ, Eurus. For this blows from the winter sunrise, neighboring Notos. Accordingly, the Euronotoi are often said to blow. Opposite this is not from Γ, the Lips, but from E, which some call Argestes, others call Olympias, others call Sciron. For thus from the summer sunset it blows, and it alone lies opposite the Eurus along the diameter.

These therefore are the winds lying along the diameter and which they are opposite. But there are others against which there are no opposite winds. From I, which they call Thrascias: for this is midway between Argestes and Aparctias. From K, which they call Meses: for this is midway between Caecias and Aparctias. The diameter IK prefers to be along the always appearing circle,[61] but not quite. Opposite these winds there are none. Nor to the Meses, for some wind would blow from it to M: for this is its opposite. Nor I to it, the Thrascias: for it would blow from N. This is the opposite, unless some winds blows from it and from a local breeze, which those dwelling around that place call Phoenicias.

(Aristotle, Meteorology *363a27–364a4; cf. Seneca,* NQ *5.16)*

61 The circumpolar stars (*On the Heavens* 297b30–298a7)? Or the Arctic circle?

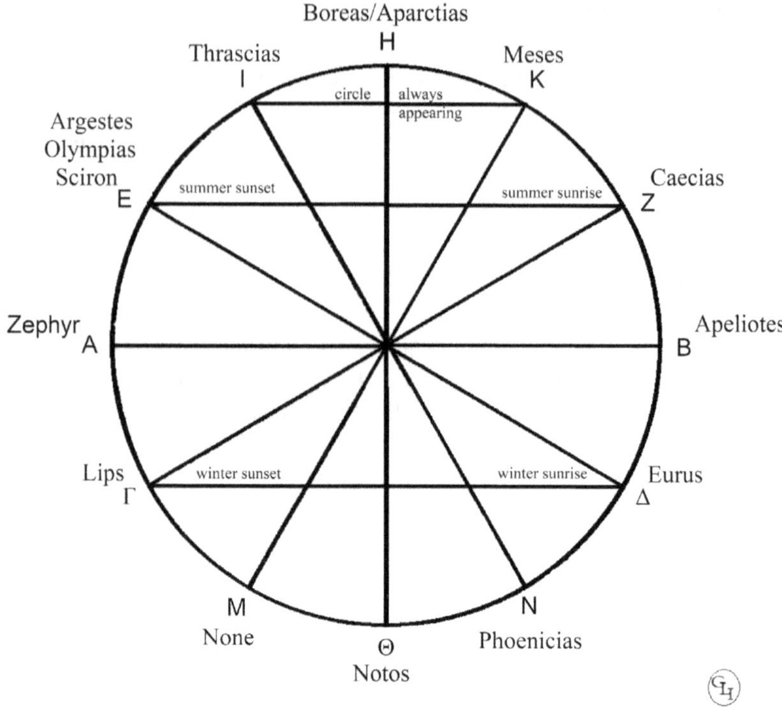

FIGURE 5.1.9G Aristotle's Windrose: drawn by Georgia L. Irby.

H. *The winds and their quarters.*

Whoever is conveyed in armed ships with an army ought to understand in advance the signs of storms. For *liburnae* have perished more often from gales and waves than from the force of the enemy. In this regard all the cleverness of natural philosophy ought to be applied because the nature of winds and storms is learned from celestial study. Regarding the bitterness of the sea, as caution protects the forethoughtful, so carelessness destroys the neglectful. Therefore, the art of navigation ought to consider first the number of the winds and their names.

The ancients believed, moreover, that according to the position of the pole only four principal winds blew from individual parts of the sky, but the experience of a later time includes 12. We offer their names not only in Greek but also in Latin to remove uncertainty. Thus, when the principal winds have been declared, we will also proclaim those which are placed next to them on the right and left. So, from the vernal equinox, that is from the eastern cardinal point, we will take up our beginning, from which rises the *Apheliotes*, that is the *Subsolanus*. Next to this one on the right is *Caecias* or *Euroborus*, to the left is *Eurus* or *Vulturnus*. Moreover, the *Notus*, that is to say the *Auster*, possesses the southern cardinal point. The *Leuconotus*, this is the *White Notus*, is joined next to this one on the right. At the left is the *Libo Notus*, this is *Corus*. *Zephyr* truly holds the western cardinal point, that is the *Subuespertinus* ("under the Evening"). To the right the *Lips* or *Africus* is joined. At the left is the *Iapyx* or *Favonius*. The *Aparctias* or *Septentrio* truly obtain the northern cardinal point, to which the *Thrascias* or *Circius* clings on the right, the *Boreas* to the left, that is the *Aquilo*.

These winds are often accustomed to blow singly, sometimes by twos, but, moreover, in great storms even by threes equally. Because of their fury, seas which are calm and quiet of their own accord bluster with the seething waves. By their blowing, according to the nature of the times or places, favorable weather is returned from the gales and calm conditions are again changed into tumultuous seas. For a ship finds its hoped-for ports with a favorable breeze, but it is compelled to stand at anchor or return or endure the crisis with an adverse wind. Therefore, with difficulty does he, who has diligently studied the science of the winds, endure shipwreck.

(Vegetius, Epitome of Military Science *4.38)*

I. *Winds are caused by dry exhalations.*

There is in the earth a great deal of fire and a great deal of heat, and the sun not only draws up the earth's watery sediment, but it also dries out the earth itself, heating it up. A double exhalation, as we have said, is created: one is steamy, the other is smoky, both happen by necessity. Of these, the exhalation having more moisture is the origin of rain, just as we said earlier (340b14–32), but the dry exhalation of the winds is the origin and nature of all things. It is necessary that these things happen according to this way. And this is clear from these facts. For necessarily there is a difference in the exhalations, and it is not only possible but also necessary that the sun and the earth's heat make these windy exhalations.

(Aristotle, Meteorology *360a7–18)*

J. *Agreeing with his teacher on the formation of winds, Theophrastus here muses on the effects of topography and latitude on winds.*

Wind carried through a narrow place is vehemently colder, while wind carried over a distance is rather warmed up and relaxed. Consequently, the Notos is colder there, in northern climes, than among us, as some say, even more so than the Boreas.

(Theophrastus, On Winds *3)*

K. *The Boreas (North) and Notos (South) Winds.*

It is necessary to attribute that the Boreas blows against the Notos, the Notos does not blow against the Boreas, for this reason, each according to their places.

For this happens among us and altogether to those dwelling towards the north. But for those dwelling towards the south, it is opposite. The reason is the same for both. For the Boreas is near the former, the Notos near the latter, so that, at the beginning, they blow immediately with whichever sensation, but they reach a distance more slowly.

Since the Boreas and Notos are the most frequent winds, as has been said, there is an order according to logic at which times each blows especially. For the Boreas, this time is in winter and summer and up to the end of autumn. For the Notos, it is through the winter and beginning of spring and end of autumn. For the sun's turnings do not work with both winds, and reciprocity occurs just as air flows back: what has been thrust back throughout the winter—for the Boreas blows more at that time—and again before the summer by the Etesians and by those winds that follow the Etesians, those winds are given back again to the same places in the spring, when autumn ends, and around the setting of the Pleiades proportionately.

(Theophrastus, On Winds *9–10)*

L. *The effects of the moon on winds.*

The moon does these things also, except not similarly, since it is a weak sun. Consequently more terrible at night [. . .] and the meetings of the months (i.e., "new moons") are stormier. It therefore happens that, as the sun rises, winds are raised up, and they stop. Similarly for the sun's setting. Sometimes it stops them, sometimes accordingly it releases them. It must be scrutinized if these things happen according to coincidence, as for the risings and settings of the stars.

(Theophrastus, On Winds *17)*

5.1.10 Bearings and Navigation

Sailors use landmarks and topography to determine where they are, including headlands and mountains (see #3.10A).

A. *Mt. Athos is the highest peak in the northeastern Aegean, casting a long shadow and situated 340 kilometers (over 200 miles) from Lemnos: see Pearson 1917: 3.26–27.*

Mt. Athos overshadows the backs of a Lemnian cow.

(Sophocles F 776Pearson)

B. *The Pontic route taken by the Argonauts. Cf. #5.1.5A.*

From there they rowed along the depths of the Black Sea, going along the Thracians' land, they kept Imbros beyond to the north. The sun just setting, they reached Chersonesus at its promontory. From there, a brisk Notos blew them onward. Bending on their sails to the wind, they entered the precipitous flows of Athamas' daughter.[62] They left one open sea behind them at dawn, but during the night they passed within the headlands of Rhoeteum, keeping the Idaean[63] land to their right. Leaving behind Dardania, they set course towards Abydos, they passed Perkote and after that the sandy coastline of Abarnis and very holy Pitueia. Indeed, while the ship was tacking by night, they crossed the Hellespont roiling with eddies.

(Apollonius, Argonautica *1.922–935)*

C. *In 325 BCE, Alexander enjoined his fleet captains in India to investigate waterways and coasts. For Onesicritus: #2.2.13C.iii note. For Nearchus: #2.1.2B.*

And those knowing these regions said that the jutting headland was of Arabia and that it was called Maceta. From there cinnamon trees and other things were brought to the Assyrians. From this beach, where the fleet rode at anchor, and from the headland which they saw straight down jutting out into the sea, the bay—so it seems to myself and Nearchus—runs back to the interior, which seems to be the Red Sea. When they looked down at this promontory, Onesicritus commanded them to sail for it, so that they would not endure rowing along the bay. Nearchus replied that Onesicritus was being childish if he failed to understand why the expedition was fitted out by Alexander. For it was not because he was at a loss to bring his entire army safely through on foot that he then sent the ships here. But he wanted to investigate the beaches along the route and the anchorages and the small islands, and they should sail around whatever bay stretched out along the course and the cities whichever were lying along the sea, and if any land was fruitful or any was barren. It was necessary that, already near the end of their labors, they not suppress the work, they who otherwise yet encountered no difficulties of necessities in their *periplus*. Nearchus feared that, because the headland stretched to the south, they would find the land barren and unwatered and fiery hot. These views prevailed, and it seems to me that Nearchus clearly saved the expedition by this plan. For the story goes that this promontory and the land near it are entirely barren and are lacking in water.

(Arrian, Indika *32.7–13)*

D. *While longitude could not be determined with any precision until the development of accurate chronometers in the 18th century (see Sobel 2007), latitude was understood by the late 4th century BCE. Pytheas of Massalia (Marseille),*

62 Athamas was a king of Boeotia whose wife, the goddess Nephele ("Cloudy"), abandoned him, leaving him with their two children. The king remarried, and his new wife, Ino, Dionysus' aunt, was a jealous stepmother, aiming to kill Nephele's children. But their mother saved them, sending a flying ram with a golden fleece. The girl, Helle, fell off the ram as he flew over the strait that bears her name: Hellespont, "Helle's Sea." See Apollodorus, *Library* 1.9.1.

63 Mt. Ida, near Troy.

traveling the northern Atlantic, noticed that hours of daylight increased as he sailed further north during the summer months, and he surmised that latitude was connected to the duration of a place's solstitial day. For Hipparchus: #1.3.7C note.

Hipparchus at any rate says that, along the Borysthenes and the Celtic land[64] through entire nights in the summer, the light of the sun appears to linger from its setting to its rising, and that during the winter solstice the sun rises at most to nine *pecheis*. Among those folk dwelling 6,300 *stadia* distant from Massalia—whom Hipparchus takes as Celts, but I (Strabo) think are Brettanians (Britons), 2,500 *stadia* further north of the Celtic land—this happens to a greater extent. On winter days the sun rises to a height of six *pecheis*, and only four *pecheis* among those 9,100 *stadia* distant from Massalia, less than three *pecheis* among those beyond, who, according to my argument, would be further north than Ierne (Ireland).

But, trusting Pytheas (T 5), this Hipparchus puts this inhabited place further south, and he says that the longest day there has 19 equinoctial hours, but 18 where the winter sun rises four *pecheis*: he says that these people are 9,100 *stadia* distant from Massalia. Inasmuch as the most southerly of the Brettanians are more to the north than the Massalians. Therefore, they are on the same parallel as the Bactrians on the Caucasus or some nearby parallel. For it is said that, according to those following Deimachos,[65] there is agreement that those Bactrians along the Caucasus are 3,800 *stadia* further north than Ierne. These *stadia*, added to those from Massalia to Ierne, are 12,500. Therefore, who has made records in the places there—I say those around Bactra—of the length of the longest days or the rising of the sun at the winter solstices? All these things are apparent even to a private individual and do not require mathematical observation, so that many could have recorded these data, both those ancient writers of Persian history and the later ones down to our own time. How could the above-mentioned fortunes of these places correspond to such phenomena?

(Strabo, Geography *2.1.18; cf. Strabo,* Geography *2.5.42)*

E. *In 55 BCE, with data from water clocks (#4.6.1), Caesar confirmed that summertime days were longer at northern latitudes.*

In the middle course is an island which is called Mona (Anglesey). Many smaller islands, moreover, are thought to lie nearby. Concerning these islands some have written that the night is continuous for 30 days in winter. We learned nothing about this from inquiries, except, from precise measurements by water, we saw that the nights are shorter here in Britain than they are on the continent.

(Caesar, BG *5.13)*

64 For this extreme northern coast, Strabo, *Geography* 7.2.11–27.

65 Served as ambassador to the Mauryan court of Bindusara (r. 297–273 BCE) in Pataliputra, India.

5.1.11 *Celestial Navigation*

*While much early sailing was within sight of land, and landmarks remain important guides for travel, navigators observed the paths of the sun and other stars as guides (#5.1.1A§209), making it possible to sail at night and out of sight of land (McGrail 2001: 17). For Aristotle, celestial navigation is "nautical astronomy" (*nautike astrologia*:* Posterior Analytics *78b34–79a6; see also Manilius,* Astronomy *5.279–280). For Lucan, Cynosura (Ursa Minor) provides "a very certain guide" for Pompey's eastern allies as they rally to his cause (*Pharsalia *3.218–19).*

A. *Leaving Ogygia, sailing a raft fitted with sails and a steering-oar, Odysseus carefully watches the stars and constellations as instructed by Calypso.*

> Joyfully, godlike Odysseus spread his sails wide to the wind. Sitting, he skillfully kept his raft straight with a steering-oar. Nor did sleep fall on his eyelashes as he observed the Pleiades and Boötes setting late and Arctos (the Bear), whom they call, in addition, the "Wagon" and who seems to turn around Orion and is alone without a share in Ocean's bath.[66] For Calypso, shining goddess, had enjoined Odysseus to hold the Bear on his left hand as he sailed over the sea.
>
> *(Homer,* Odyssey *5.269–277)*

B. *While sailing back to his Latian camp at night, Aeneas explains the course of the stars to his young friend and new Arcadian ally, Pallas. The elder Pallas had emigrated from Arcadia in Greece to Italy, where he established a kingdom (Vergil,* Aeneid *7.41). His grandson, Evander, entered into an alliance with Aeneas, partly because of their* xenia *bond ("guest-host": Evander had once hosted Anchises) and partly because of their shared ancestry from Atlas' daughters Electra and Maia (*Aeneid *8.127–174).*

> Here great Aeneas sits, and he considers with himself the various outcomes of war, and Pallas, clinging to his left side asks now about the stars, the journey through shady dark night, and now what Aeneas had suffered on land and sea.
>
> *(Vergil,* Aeneid *10.159–162)*

C. *Lucan's Pompey inquires about celestial navigation, and his helmsman replies in detail.*

> 161. Now the Titan (Helios the sun) lowered himself in the sea to his middle fires, and not entirely, neither to those from whom he concealed his orb nor if there were any to whom he uncovered it. The wakeful cares in Pompey's chest

66 I.e., Arctos never sets: cf. Ovid, *Metamorphoses* 2.171–173, where the Bear attempts, for the first time (*primum*), to plunge into the Ocean to escape the heat of the sun, as Phaethon, son of Helios, tried and failed to drive his father's chariot, and the horses ran amok, leaving a wake of destruction.

now came to the allied cities of the Roman federation and the varying minds of kings, now to the pathless fields of the world lying beyond the excessively hot suns and southward. Often the gloomy labor of his concerns and the enmity of the future cast off the weary agitation of his uncertain spirit, and he asks his helmsman about all the stars: from what does he make note of land; what is the measure in the sky of cutting the sea; by what star does he make for Syria; or what starry fire in the Wagon guides them well to Libya.

171. The learned observer of silent Olympus speaks to these things: "Whichever stars flow slipping in the sign-bearing sky, deceiving wretched sailors because the pole is never stationary, we do not follow those stars. That star, the north pole, which is not submerged in the waves, guides ships. Since this one will always rise to the zenith and Ursa Minor will always rise over the yardarm, then we face the Bosporus and the Pontus rounding the shores of Scythia. When Boötes descends from the highest yardarm and Cynosura is borne closer to the sea, the ship makes for Syrian ports. Then follows Canopus, a star content to wander in the southern sky, fearing the Boreas: with that one on your left, proceed past Pharos;[67] the ship will reach Syrtes in mid-ocean. But where do you order the sails to be given? Where do you command the flaxen sails to be stretched at the foot?"

(Lucan, Pharsalia *8.161–186)*

5.1.12 Navigability

Literary and technical accounts are rich with details regarding where it is safe (or unsafe) to sail owing to hydrology, topography, shoals, currents, and many other factors. Here we have a sample, arranged chronologically by author.

A. *The Ister (Danube), which does* not *have a mouth that debouches into the Adriatic (see Pliny,* NH *3.128).*

They say that the Ister splits, flowing from the forests called Hercynian:[68] one part flows to the Pontus, the other debouches into the Adriatic. We have seen proof not only in the present day but all the more even in ancient times that the river is un-sailable there. For they say that Jason made his voyage in through the Cyanean Rocks, but they sailed out of the Pontus through the Ister. They bring to bear other proofs and not a small number, and they point out altars along that region dedicated by Jason, and on one of the islands of the Adriatic, a temple of Artemis established by Medea.

(Aristotle, On Marvelous Things Heard *839b10–19)*

67 #5.3.7B-G.

68 Orcynian Forest (Eratosthenes F 150), "a nine-day march across for someone traveling lightly" (Caesar, *BG* 6.24.2). Variously positioned near the Pyrenees (scholium ad Dionysius Periegetes 286; n2.74), the northern ocean (Diodorus Siculus, *Library of History* 5.21.1), or the sources of the Istros and Rhenos (Strabo 7.1.3).

B. *Greater and Lesser Syrtes (Libya).*

i. The land of Pelops had just become visible, when a deadly squall of the Boreas snatched them up violently in mid-course and bore them towards the Libyan sea for nine entire nights and as many days until they arrived further within the Syrtes where return back home is no longer possible for ships, when they are pressed to arrive at that gulf. For everywhere there is a shallow, everywhere a seaweedy thicket in the deep; and the silent water's foam washes over them. Misty sand stretches along. Nor does anything creep here, nor does any winged thing alight here. Here a floodtide—for the tide often withdraws from the mainland, and then rushes out, boisterously attacking the headland—quickly thrusts them on the shore, only a little bit of the keel was left in the waters.

(Apollonius, Argonautica *4.1231–1244)*

ii. But the town, Leptis, is situated between the two Syrtes whose name is applied from their situation. For there are two bays nearly at the edge of Africa, unequal in size, equal in nature. The waters closest to land are very deep, but as chance bears some waters that are deep, others that are shoaly in stormy weather. For when the sea begins to swell and rage with the winds, the waves churn mud and sand and huge rocks. Thus the configuration of the places is at the same time changed with the winds. The Syrtes are so-called from the churning.

(Sallust, Jugurtha *78.2–3)*

iii. The Great Syrtes has a circle of about 3,930 *stadia* and a diameter at its innermost part of 1,500 *stadia*, and the width of its mouth of about 1,500 *stadia.* The difficulty of both this Syrtis and the Small Syrtis is that in many places the shoaly water is deep. And by the ebbtides and rising tides, it happens to some sailing in that they sit in the shallows and it is rare that a ship be saved. Consequently, sailors make a *periplus* from a distance, keeping guard lest they fall into these gulfs, grasped by the winds. To be sure, the risk-taking of all folks compels them to make a trial of it, and especially of *periploi* along the coast.

(Strabo, Geography *17.3.20)*

C. *The coast of Arabia.*

This *periplus* of the Arabic mainland is thus on the whole dangerous. The place is harborless and with bad anchorages and dirty with breakers and inaccessible because of crags and fearful in all ways. Consequently, as we sail, we keep to the middle course, and we spur ourselves on quickly to the Arabian region up to the Burnt Island, after which forthwith are territories of gentle peoples and wandering cattle and camels.

(Anonymous, Erythraean Sea *20)*

D. *The Nile at various points. See #1.5.1.*

From there (the junction of the Nile), partly fierce, partly enduring ships, the Nile arrives into an enormous lake, passing beyond with a headlong force and embracing Tachempso, another island, all the way to Elephantine, an Egyptian city, still fierce and raging. Then, at last rather calm and now well navigable, first, next to the town Cercasorus, the Nile begins to be threefold. Then, again and again divided at Delta and at Melyn, the Nile goes through Egypt, wandering and scattered, cutting itself into seven mouths; it is nonetheless unrolled large in individual courses.

(Mela, On the Circuit of the World *1.51)*

E. *The Clitumnus River in Umbria, central Italy, which can support two-way boat traffic.*

Have you at any time seen the source of the Clitumnus? If not yet—and I think not yet: for you would have otherwise told me—see it, which I saw recently: I regret my sluggishness. A moderate hill rises up, woody and shady with an ancient cypress grove. Beneath it, the source comes out and is squeezed out in many but unequal veins, and forcing out the swirl which it makes, it lies open in a broad bay, clean and glassy, so that you can count the coins that were tossed in and the shining pebbles. Then not by the slope of the place but by its very abundance and, as if because of its weight, it is urged on, still a spring and now a very ample river, and it even supports boats. The Clitumnus dispatches them across and carries them through even face to face as they stretch in a contrary motion in different directions. The current is robust to the point that, wherever it hurries itself along, although through level ground, it is helped along without oars. But the same upstream current is overcome with great difficulty by means of oars and punting poles. It is pleasant for those floating along for sport and diversion to change up exertion for ease and ease for exertion as they turn their course.

(Pliny the Younger, Epistle *8.8.1–4)*

F. *One example from the Black Sea.*

Setting out from Apsarus we passed the Acampsis River in the night, 15 *stadia* from Apsarus. The river Bathys ("Deep") is 75 *stadia* from there (Acampsis). Acinasis is 90 *stadia* from the Bathys. The river Isis is also 90 *stadia* from Acinasis. The Acampsis and Isis are navigable, and they send out strong breezes early in the morning. From the Isis, we sailed past the Mogrus. There are 90 *stadia* between the Mogrus and the Isis, and this river, the Mogrus, also navigable.

(Arrian, Periplus *7.4–5)*

5.1.13 Pilots

Pilots would guide merchant ships through unfamiliar waters, especially the large rivers of western Europe and reefy shoals near coastlines. The art of piloting was so important to maritime communities that the Egyptians considered it one of the seven primary occupations (Herodotus, Histories *2.164). See also #1.9.11D.*

A. *Poseidon's son, the merman Triton, aided the* Argo *winding through reef-filled waters near Cyrene, a sea-road unfamiliar to the* Argo's *helmsman, Tiphys.*

And the beaches and hidden reefs near Taucheira[69] mourn the others, cast out at Atlas' lonely dwelling,[70] shuddering at the casings of the wreckage, where the seamen solemnly buried Mopsos,[71] the Titaeronian, after he died, and they set up on his tomb on its foundation a plank broken from the *Argo*, a relic of the deceased, where the moistening Cinypheian stream anoints the Ausida with its stream, where the Colchian woman[72] gave a broad mixing vessel worked with gold as a gift to Triton, descended from Nereus, showing them a broad path by which Tiphys pressed the ship unharmed through narrow reefs.

(Lycophron, Alexandra *877–890)*

B. *Pilots are essential to commerce in the Erythraean Sea.*

On account of this, around this entrance, royal fishermen, locals with crews in long-boats which are called *trappaga* and *kotumba*, go to meeting stations as far as Syrastrane, from which they guide boats as far as Barygaza. They bend them straight from the mouth of the bay through the narrows with their crews, and they tow these same ships to stations already arranged, taking them from the beginning of the floodtide, and bringing them to anchor along some anchorages and basins. These basins are deeper than the river as far as Barygaza. Barygaza lies about 300 *stadia* up the river from the mouth.

(Anonymous, Erythraean Sea *44)*

C. *One pilot of the Erythraean Sea, Hippalus, was accomplished enough to be remembered by name.*

They would traverse this entire *periplus*, as described, from Cane and Eudaemon ("Fortunate") Arabia, sailing around in rather small boats. Observing the siting of emporia and the behavior of the water, the helmsman Hippalus first discovered the sea-road through this sea. Through which sea-road and locally from the Ocean at the same time as the Etesians blow among us, in the Indian

69 Near Cyrene.

70 At the Pillars of Herakles where the Titan was condemned to support the vault of heaven for opposing Olympian rule (Hesiod, *Theogony* 507–509).

71 The *Argo's* diviner, from Thessaly, who died from a snakebite in Libya (Apollonius, *Argonautica* 4.1518–1525).

72 Medea, from Colchis on the eastern Euxine, a granddaughter of Helios, who, like her aunts (Hekate and Circe) was adept at magic (e.g., Ovid, *Metamorphoses* 7.179–233).

> Sea the Libonotos appears, called the Hippalus after the name of the one first discovering the passage.
>
> *(Anonymous,* Erythraean Sea *57)*

D. *Animals also guided ships, as here a dove guides an expedition c. 750 BCE. See also #3.11.13. Velleius Paterculus (c. 19 BCE to c. CE 31) wrote a history of Rome from the Trojan War to Augustus' day. As a soldier he saw action on the Euphrates under Augustus' grandson Gaius Caesar and served in Germany under Tiberius.*

> The Athenians occupied Chalcida and Eretria in Euboea with settlements, the Lacedaemonians took Magnesia. Not much later, the Chalcidians, sprung from the Attican people, as I have already said, founded Cumae in Italy, with Hippocles and Megasthenes as leaders. Some say that the course of this expedition was guided by the flight of a dove. Others say that it was guided by the nocturnal sound of the air, such as is accustomed to be raised in the rites of Ceres.[73]
>
> *(Velleius Paterculus,* History of Rome *1.4.1–2)*

E. *A swan guides settlers to an otherwise unattested site in the eastern Euxine. Swans are particularly welcome signs for sailors because they reputedly never dip below the waves (Servius,* ad Aeneid *1.397).*

> But in the first bend of the now-curved shore is a town which Greek merchants established, and because—when they were driven about in a blind storm, unaware of where the land was—the voice of a swan gave a sign. They are said to have called the place *Cycnus* ("Swan").
>
> *(Mela,* On the Circuit of the World *1.110)*

5.1.14 Maritime Charts

There is little evidence of nautical charts in the modern sense, and some scholars argue that they did not exist in antiquity (Casson 1995: 246; Arnaud 2005: 46–50) or that they simply did not survive (Dunsch 2012: 270–283). Some routes date as far back as the Bronze Age, and most maps in antiquity were either narrative or monumental (Irby 2019). There is nonetheless an intriguing passage in Apollonius' Argonautica *that suggests a monumental nautical chart on display in Aeëtes' Colchian palace, reflecting perhaps monumental charts that might have been displayed in the Hellenistic courts of Apollonius' day.*

> They preserve the writings of their fathers on pillars on which are all the roads and paths of both the wet and the dry for those who travel around.
>
> *(Apollonius,* Argonautica *4.279–281)*

73 Mystery rites: #3.11.8.

5.1.15 Ships

There were many ship designs, serving various functions, from a variety of warships (#5.1.1A) to Odysseus' raft equipped with sails and a rudder (#5.1.11A) to coracles used locally (#5.1.1A§206). Here we have a selection of ships that were remarkable enough to merit description.

A. *Magical self-steering Phaeacian ships returned Odysseus to Ithaca after ten years of wandering the Mediterranean.*

> Speak about your land, and your district, and your *polis*, I order that our ships, made ready, might convey you according to your heart. For there are not helmsmen among the Phaeacians, nor are there steering-oars, which other ships have. But our ships know the thoughts and hearts of folk, and they also know human *poleis* and fertile fields of humans. And, quick, they pierce over the depth of the salt-sea, hidden in air and cloud, nor is there ever alarm of destruction or ruin. But once, hearing this story from my father, Nausithos, who told it, saying that Poseidon would bear a grudge against us whenever we were kindly conductors of all people. Nausithos said that when at some time well-built ships of the Phaeacian folk would go out to sea in a convoy in the misty ocean, Poseidon would shatter them and enfold a mountain over our *polis*. So the old man, my father, spoke. The god might either bring these things to pass, or they might remain unfulfilled, as might be pleasing to his heart.
>
> *(Homer,* Odyssey *8.555–571)*

B. *The ships of the Veneti (Brittany), carefully designed and purpose-built to withstand the rough waters of the English Channel.*

> Now their ships were made and armed in this way: the keels are to some degree more flat than those of our ships, by which they are more easily able to take on the shoals and ebb-tides. Their prows are raised up to the proper measure, and their sterns are likewise fitted for the magnitude of the waves and storms. The ships are made entirely from oak to endure force and abuse as much as possible. The crossbeams are made from timbers a pace in width, fastened with iron pins with the thickness of a thumb-finger. The anchors are bound with iron chains instead of ropes. Instead of flax sails, there are skins and thinly prepared soft leather: whether owing to a scarcity of flax and ignorance of its use, or—what is probably closer to the truth—because they think that such great storms of Ocean and such great assaults of the winds could not be endured and the great burden of their ships could not be sufficiently guided with flax sails. There was an encounter of our fleet with these ships, such that ours excelled in speed and striking oars. Regarding the rest, they were more suited and adaptable than our ships for the nature of the place and force of the storms. For our ships could not harm them with our beak—so great was their durability—nor on account of

their height was a missile easily hurled against them. For the same reason they were less successfully held by grapnel-hooks. It also happened that—when the wind began to rage and they gave themselves to the wind—they more easily endured the storm and stood safely in the shallows. And, abandoned by the tide, they feared nothing with regard to rocks and crags. The calamity of all these things was to be dreaded by our ships.

(Caesar, BG *3.13)*

C. *Demetrius I Poliorcetes ("Besieger of Cities") of Macedon (r. 294–288 BCE) built a fleet of megaships.*

At the same time, he laid down the keels for 500 ships, some in the Piraeus, some in Corinth, some in Chalcis, some around Pella. Demetrius himself went to each port and gave instructions as to what was necessary and helpful. All were amazed not only at the great number of ships but also at the size of the works. For no human being had seen a ship of 15 banks of oars before, nor of 16 banks.

But later Ptolemy Philopator (IV: r. 221–204 BCE) would build ships of 40 banks. With a length of 280 *pecheis* and a height, up to her *akrostolion*[74] of 48 *pecheis*. She was manned by 400 sailors, apart from the rowers, and by 4,000 rowers, apart from them, she took on about 3,000 hoplites on her gangways and decks. But the ship only offered a spectacle, differing little from stationary structures, to be seen as an exhibit not a necessity, moved precariously and with difficulty.

The beauty of Demetrius' ships was not contested, nor were these ships despoiled of utility by their extraordinary fittings, but they had speed and workmanship well worth seeing more than their size.

(Plutarch, Demetrius *43.3–5)*

D. *Here we have Moschion's detailed description of the three-decked mega-yacht* Syrakousia/Alexandris, *whose construction was supervised by Archimedes of Syracuse for Hieron II of Syracuse (r. 270–215 BCE: Moschion is otherwise unknown). A mathematician and engineer, Archimedes devised a method of naming extremely large numbers to estimate the number of grains of sand that would fill the universe* (The Sand Reckoner)*, designed many war machines for Hieron, and was famously killed by a Roman soldier during the siege of Syracuse (231–212 BCE: Livy,* from the Foundation of the City *24.21–39, 25.23–31). The ship, whose embellishments included an Aphrodite shrine, was sent on a tour to the east but was too large for most of the harbors on its intended route. The ship eventually made it to Alexandria*

74 The ornamental finial on a ship's stern.

and was gifted to Ptolemy III Euergertes (r. 246–222 BCE): its cargo was no doubt much-welcomed relief during a grain shortage.

206d. Concerning the ship commissioned by Hieron of Syracuse, over which Archimedes, the geometer, was the overseer, I do not judge it worthwhile to be silent since a certain Moschion produced a treatise which I, incidentally, happened upon recently. This Moschion wrote thusly (*FGrHist* 575 F 1): Diocles of Abdera is admired for the city-destroying device brought to the walls of the *polis* of Rhodes by Demetrius (305/4 BCE); Timaeus (*FGrH* 566 F 112) for the fire fitted out for Dionysius the tyrant of Syracuse (Dionysius I, d. 367 BCE); and Hieronymus (*FGrH* 154 F 2) for creating a wagon which was suitable for conveying Alexander's body (323 BCE); Polycleitus (*FGrH* 128 F 4) for a lamp prepared for the Persian.

King Hieron of Syracuse, always a friend to the Romans, attended eagerly to the preparations of temples and exercise facilities. But, underwriting grain ships, he also loved the honor of shipbuilding. I will recall the construction of one of these ships. For the wood for building the ships, he had collected from Mt. Aetna a quantity sufficient for building the hulls of 60-banked ships. He prepared bolts and belly planks and ribs and the material for other necessities, some from Italy, some from Sicily, and white esparto from Iberia for the ropes, hemp and pitch from the Rhodanus River and all other things as needful from many places. He also brought together shipwrights and other craftsmen: of all of them he appointed Archias the Corinthian as the master builder. Archimedes ordered them to attack the work eagerly. He himself devoted six days.

207a. Half of the entire ship was brought to completion in six months, and the shipbuilding crew always enclosed each portion with tiles made of lead since 300 artisans, apart from their assistants, were working on the ships.

Demetrius therefore enjoined that this part be dragged to the sea in order to seize upon the remaining preparations there. After much inquiry concerning its launching to the sea, Archimedes, the engineer, moved it by himself with only a few men. Preparing a very large screw windlass, he moved the hull to the sea. Archimedes first discovered how to build a screw windlass. The remaining parts of the ship were prepared in another six months, and the whole structure was bound together with bronze pins, of which many were ten-*minae* heavy,[75] and the others were half that weight. These pins were fitted in with augurs, holding the ribs together, and they were made watertight with lead tiles on the wood, linen with pitch (oakum) placed underneath. When therefore he made the exterior watertight, he began the construction of the interior.

75 An ancient Near Eastern unit of weight for silver or gold, approximately 0.57 kilograms (c. 1.25 pounds).

c. The ship was equipped like a 20, but with three gangways. The lowest having (†)[76] to the cargo hold, down to which there was a descent through several ladders. The second gangway was constructed for those wishing to enter the cabins. After this the last cabin was for those arrayed in battle gear. From the middle gangway there were 30 cabins for the men, along each side of the hull, spacious enough for four couches. The captain's cabin had 15 couches, three rooms had three couches. The one at the stern was a roasting room (galley). All these had a floor laid down in mosaics from all sorts of stones, in which the whole story of the *Iliad* was marvelously arranged. As for the furniture and ceilings and doorways, all these were prepared as such: along the upper gangway were an exercise room and promenade deck having a measurement constructed to the size of the ship, on which were gardens of all sorts where plants marvelously spilled over, watered through enclosed lead plates, and there were screens of white ivy and grapevines, whose roots took their nourishment in jars filled with soil, and these took their watering just like the gardens. But the screens shaded the walkways.

e. Next, an Aphrodite temple with three couches, having a floor of agate-stone and other very elegant stones which were found on the island of Sicily. It had walls and a ceiling made of cypress wood, and doors of ivory and citron wood, and it was furnished with paintings and statuettes and with exceedingly wrought drinking cups.

After this was a study with five couches, fitted with walls and doors of boxwood. It had a library in it, and in the ceiling was a sundial copying the sundial in Achradine.[77] Also, the three-couched bathing room had three bronze cauldrons and a washing-basin, many colored with Tauromenion marble, receiving five measures of water. More rooms were furnished for the marines and those guarding the hold. Aside from these things, there were ten horse-stalls on each side of the hull. The fodder for the horses lay in these same stalls and also equipment for the riders and grooms, and a cistern lay near the prow, receiving 2,000 measures of water, constructed from timbers and pitch and linen.

208a. Next to the cistern was constructed an enclosed fishpond of lead and timbers. This was full of seawater in which many fish were cultivated. On each side of the hull there were projecting beams at symmetrical intervals. On them were prepared wooden bins and covered terracotta pots and ovens and mills and many other service instruments. Atlases, six *pecheis* high, ran around the exterior of the ship, supporting the mass of the upper decks and the triglyph,[78] all placed at symmetrical intervals. The entire ship was wrought with suitable paintings.

76 The text is corrupt and unrestorable.

77 A neighborhood of Syracuse. The sundial was commissioned by Dionysius I.

78 *Atlases*: statues of the Titan who supported the vault of heaven (see #5.1.13A note). *Triglyphs* are decorative, horizontal triple channels in Doric architecture: ||| ||| |||

There were eight turrets on it, symmetrical in height to the ship's size. Two were at the stern, an equal number at the prow, the remaining ones along midship. To each of these were fitted two projecting beams, on which projecting platforms were furnished, from which stones were discharged against those enemies sailing against them. Four young men climbed up on each of the towers, fully armed, and two archers. The interiors of the towers were full of stones and missiles. The ship had a defensive wall and decks equipped throughout on trestles, on which Demetrius placed a stone-thrower from which a three-*talent* stone or 12-*pecheis* missile could be shot. Archimedes built that machine: it threw each type of projectile a *stadion*. After these things, curtains of thick leather were contrived, hanging on bronze chains.

c. Two stone-throwers hung on each of three masts, from which hooks and bricks of lead were hurled against attackers. There was also a spiked iron palisade in a circle around the ship as a protection against those trying to board, as well as iron ravens ("hooks") which, when shot by machines, overpowered the enemy's hulls and dragged them towards a strike.

At each side of the ship, 60 young men, in full armor, stood, and a number equal to them stood around the masts and the platforms for stone-throwers. Along the masts in the tops, made of bronze, three men were on the first mast, then the remaining masts had two, then one. Stones and also missiles in woven baskets were supplied to them to the masthead by enslaved men with windlasses. There were four wooden anchors, and eight iron anchors. The logs for the second and third masts were found easily, but the 1st mast was located by a swineherd with difficulty in the mountains of Bruttium.[79] Phileas the Tauromenian, an engineer, drew it down to the sea. The hull, although having an excessive depth, was drained by a single man with a screw-pump: Archimedes invented it. The ship's name was *Syrakousia*. But when Hieron sent her off, he changed her name to *Alexandris*.

As for the small boats, first behind her was a *kerkouros* (small boat), accepting 3,000 *talents* burden, powerful, this one was entirely furnished with oars. After this, barks with 1,500 *talent* burden and many more skiffs. The fleet of ships was not less than †. In addition to those already mentioned, there were 600 others by the prow, looking out for orders.

209a. For any crimes committed in the ship, the captain, helmsman, and lookout officer sat as the court of justice, on which they administered justice according to Syracusan law. On the ship were loaded 6,000 measures of wheat, 1,000 jars of Sicilian salted fish, 2,000 *talents* of wool, and 2,000 *talents* of other freight. Apart from these things, there was provisioning for all sailing aboard.

While Hieron heard about all the harbors—some were not able to receive the ship, some were dangerous—he had it in mind to send it to Alexandria as a gift

79 Calabria, southern Italy.

for Ptolemy the king. For there was a scarcity of grain in Egypt, and Demetrius did this, and the ship was led down to the Alexandrian harbor, and there it was hauled on land.

(*Athenaeus*, Learned Banqueters *5.206d–209b)*

E. *In the mid-2nd century CE, the mega-freighter* Isis *came from Egypt to the Piraeus in Athens (#5.3.3F), eliciting a crowd of onlookers. Casson (1991: 209) estimates that the ship was 55 meters long (180 feet), with a beam of over 14 meters (45 feet), and a hull depth also 14 meters, with the capacity to carry 1,200–1,300 tons of grain.*[80]

What a ship! 120 *pecheis*-long, the shipwright said, and the beam over a fourth of it, and from the deck to keel, 29 *pecheis* through the deepest part of the bilge. How big a mast, and what a yardarm it supports, and with what a forestay it is furnished and held together! How the curved stern crests up gently, sweeping towards its golden goose-head finial, and on the opposite end the prow rises up proportionately, and having on each side the running nameplate of this nautical temple, *Isis*. As to further ornamentation, the illustrations and the fiery bright topsail sailcloth, and more than these, the anchors and the rigging and the windlasses and the deckhouses on the stern seemed to me entirely marvelous.

The crowd of sailors could be likened to an army camp, and it was said that she was carrying as much grain as would suffice for food for everyone in Attica for a year. Finally, some tiny little old manling kept all these things safe, whirling around the rudder by means of a delicate vine-pole tiller.

(Lucian, Navigium *5–6)*

F. On Warlike Things *(*de Rebus Bellicis: *mid 4th to 5th century CE) is a compilation of fantastical war engines, intended to mitigate contemporary military and economic challenges. One of the devices is an ox-powered warship.*

A *liburnean* ship suitable for naval matters, which, on account of its size, human weakness prohibits from being managed by human hands in any way. Wherever utility might call in the direction for the ease of the course, strength drives it on, relying on the aid of human ingenuity. In the hull or hold, oxen, yoked by twos, roll the wheels attached to the ship's sides. As those same wheels rush along, projecting beyond the edge or roundness (rim) of the wheels and striking the water with exertion in the manner of oars, spokes toil with some marvelous outcome of skill, as their striking produces movement. This same warship, nonetheless, because of its mass and the engines performing within it, engages

80 While Zheng He traveled the Pacific in the early 15th CE in mammoth nine-masted, four-decked ships, ships of such a size would not be built in the west until the 18th century.

in battle with such a great rush of strength that, with an easy grinding, it shatters all enemy *liburnae* coming at it.

(Anonymous, On Warlike Things *17)*

FIGURE 5.1.15F Ox-powered paddle wheel boat (after 15th century ms: Bodleian Library, Oxford. Shelfmark: MS. Canon. Misc. 378). Published in *Notitia vtraqve cvm Orientis tvm Occidentis vltra Arcadii Honoriiqve Cæsarvm tempora . . .* (*Notitia dignitatum*). Basileae. [Apvd H. Frobenivm et Episcopivm], 1552. Re-published in Leonard C. Bruno, 1995. The *tradition of technology: Landmarks of Western technology . . .* Washington, DC, Library of Congress, 1995, p. 20 (public domain). Enhanced by Georgia L. Irby.

G. *Until the 19th century, most ships were constructed of wood. Even with careful maintenance, the average lifespan of a wooden boat is 20 to 30 years. Some ships, however, were worthy of preservation, like Sir Francis Drake's* Golden Hind *(London, UK, launched 1577), Horatio Nelson's HMS* Victory *(Portsmouth, UK, launched 1765), the USS* Constitution *(Boston, MA, launched 1797), and the USS* Constellation *(Baltimore, MD, launched 1854), to name a few, and the ship that conveyed Theseus to and from Crete (see also #5.3.3F note). In order to preserve these ships, rot was replaced with fresh wood, raising a Socratic question about what is real. How much of the original vessel remains?*

> The Athenians maintained the ship in which Theseus sailed with the young Athenians and was kept in safety, a triaconter, until the time of Demetrius of Phalerum (d. 280 BCE). They removed the old bits of wood, installing and thus constructing strong planks so that the ship was a model with respect to the indecisive account of augmentation for the philosophers: some argued that it was the same ship, others argued that the original ship did not remain.
>
> *(Plutarch,* Theseus *23.1)*

H. *We conclude our selection of individual ships with Catullus' encomium to an aging skiff, once-great but still noble, the bean-pod-shaped* phaselus. *Gaius Valerius Catullus (c. 84–c. 54 BCE) was a Roman poet deeply influenced by Greek models (including Sappho of Lesbos [#3.11.5A]). Catullus was among the* neoteric *poets who rejected heroic topics, instead focusing on private matters, including his affair with his literary* femme fatale, *Lesbia, in verse that is often sexually explicit.*

> That *phaselus*, which you see, friends, says that he was once the fastest of ships, nor could the force of any floating beam pass him by, whether there was a need to fly with oars or with sail. And, he says, the shore of the threatening Hadriatic does not deny this or the Cyclades islands and celebrated Rhodes and the rough Thracian Propontis or the grim Pontic Bay, where that *phaselus*, as later, was beforehand a leafy forest. For on the Cytorian yoke, he often uttered a whistle with a speaking leaf.[81] O, Pontic Amastris and boxwood-bearing Cytorus, the *phaselus* says that these things have been and are well-known to you: from his first beginning, he says that he stood on your peaks, that he dipped blades in your waters, and from there through violent straits (Hellespont) he bore his master, whether a right-hand breeze called or a left-hand breeze, whether a following Jupiter fell at the foot of the sail at the same time. Nor were any vows made to the shore gods on his behalf when he came at last from the sea all the way to this limpid lake. But these things have been so. Now he grows old with retired quietude, and he dedicates himself to you, twin Castor and twin brother of Castor.[82]
>
> *(Catullus,* Poem *4)*

5.1.16 Ship Races

Some religious celebrations featured ship races, including possibly the Panathenaia and the Isthmian Games at Corinth. Here we have the ship race that was

81 Evoking the sanctuary of Dodonan Zeus, from whose sacred oak tree priests interpreted oracular proclamations.

82 #3.11.7.

among the events at the funeral games for Aeneas' father, Anchises, capturing the excitement (and danger) of the live event.

114. For the first contest, four equal ships chosen from the entire fleet enter with heavy oars. Mnestheus captains the swift *Pristis* ("Sawfish") with a sharp crew of rowers, soon to be Mnestheus the Italian,[83] from whom is a family, Memmi by name. Next, Gyas captains the *Chimera*, huge with a great bulk, the work of a city, which Dardanian[84] young men drive on in a triple row; their oars rise in sequence by threes. Then Sergestus, from whom the Sergian house has its name, is conveyed on the great *Centaur*; and Cloanthus in the dark-blue *Scylla*, whence your family, Roman Cluentius.

124. From a distance in the sea, facing the frothy coasts, is a rock which, submerged at one time, is beaten by swelling waves when wintry *Cori* (northwest winds) hide the stars. In a calm, its level flatness is silent, and it is lifted up from an unmoved wave, and it is a very pleasing perch for sun-loving diving birds. Here, father Aeneas establishes a green *meta* (rounding mark) for the race from an oak frond as a sign for the sailors whence they might know to return and where to bend back their long course. Then the men choose their places by lot, and on the sterns the captains themselves gleam from a distance with gold and purple finery. The young men are wreathed with poplar fronds, and they shine, steeped with oil over their nude shoulders. The men settle on the rowing benches, and their shoulders stretch over the oars. Eagerly they await the sign, and hammering anxiety and excited desire for praise drain their thumping hearts. Then, when the shrill war trumpet gives a sound, all leap up from their starting places with no delay. The nautical shout strikes the sky. Turned over with flexed arms, the straits foam. Equally the men cleave furrows, and the entire sea gapes, battered by oars and three-pronged beaks.[85] Chariots in a two-yoked contest do not rush so fast to snatch up the field, poured out from their stalls. Nor in such a way do charioteers hang onto their whips, prone to shake waving reigns over their teams of horses who have been let loose. Then the entire grove resounds with the men's applause and shouting and the zeal of those supporting one ship or another, and the sheltered coastline twists the sound, and the hills, stricken with the shouting, echo it back.

150. Gyas flies in front of the others and glides in the first waves between the crowd and din. Cloanthus follows him, better with the oars, but his slow pine boat checks him with its weight. After them, at an equal distance, the *Pristis* and *Centaur* strive to win first place. Now the *Pristis* has it, now the huge *Centaur* surpasses the *Pristis*, now they are both conveyed together—their prows harnessed side by side—and they ply the salt channel with a long keel. Now they

83 These Trojan exiles are thus linked with important Roman families.
84 #3.6B note.
85 Rams fitted to the prow.

approach the rock and hold the *meta* when Gyas, first and victor in the middle of the gulf, taunts Menoetes, his ship's helmsman, with a call, "To what end do you go so far to the right? Straighten her course; hug the shore and let her graze the cliffs on the left without oarage. Let the others hold the deep." Gyas says. But Menoetes, fearing hidden rocks, twists the prow to the deep sea's waves. "To what end are you turned off course? Head for the rocks, Menoetes!" Gyas calls back again. Behold, he sees Cloanthus pressing at his back and holding the nearer course. Between Gyas' ship and the resounding rocks, Cloanthus grazes his journey closer to the left, and he suddenly passes the former ship and holds safe, deep waters, the *meta* behind him. Then, truly, a great anguish burns in the young man's bones, nor are his cheeks lacking tears. Forgetful of his own dignity and his crew's safety, from the lofty stern he throws timid Menoetes overboard, headlong into the sea. He himself as captain moves up to the helm, he himself as helmsman urges on the men and twists the rudder to the shores. But, when Menoetes returns at length from the sea's bottom, already old, and dripping heavily in drenched clothing,[86] he seeks the top of the rock, and he sinks down onto the dry cliff. The Teucrians laughed at him slipping and swimming, and they laugh at him now vomiting out the salty waves from his chest.

183. Here a happy hope is kindled for the two at the back, Sergestus and Mnestheus, to overcome Gyas as he delays. Sergestus takes the lead and approaches the rock, but he is not first by a keel's length, but first by a part. But the rival *Pristis* squeezes by a little with her beak. Strolling amidships through his crew, Mnestheus urges them on, "now, now, rise up on your oars, companions of Hector,[87] you whom I chose as my companions on Troy's last day. Now exert your strength, now your courage, which you employed in the Gaetulian Syrtes,[88] and the Ionian Sea, and the waves following Malea. Certainly I, Mnestheus, no longer seek to win first place. O, notwithstanding! But let those conquer to whom you, Neptune, have granted victory. Let it be shameful to return last. Win this contest, Citizens,[89] and prevent an outcome not in accord with divine will." With the greatest struggle, they lean forward on their oars. The bronze stern trembles with their prodigious strokes, and the seafloor is drawn away from underneath. Then thick panting shakes their limbs and dry mouths. Sweat flows everywhere in streams. Chance itself brings hoped-for honor to the men. For while Sergestus, raging in his heart, urges his prow close to the rocks and enters the unfavorable space on the inside course, unluckily he strikes against jutting rocks. The crags are stricken, and the oars—pressed on the sharp murex-stone—crack, and the

86 #5.2F; #6.5.2E§105.

87 A son of King Priam of Troy, the greatest Trojan warrior, killed in a duel by Achilles: *Iliad* 22.247–366.

88 #5.1.12B.

89 The *Aeneid* is a Roman epic, and its heroes are the founders of Rome's elite families and cherished traditions, including its Republican government.

prow hangs where it crashed. The sailors spring up and delay with a great shout and fetch the iron boathooks and poles with sharp points, and they collect their broken oars in the raging abyss. But, cheered and more energetic with his success, with a swift sweep of oars, and the winds called upon, Mnestheus seeks the seas bent towards land, and he runs from the open water, just as a dove—suddenly agitated from her cave, whose home and sweet nestlings are in a hidden rock—is conveyed flying to the fields and, frightened, she gives a huge strike with her wings away from her home. Soon, gliding in the quiet air, she skims her smooth journey and does not move her quick wings. Thus Mnestheus, thus the *Pristis* herself plies the last waters in her flight, thus the very momentum bears her along, flying. Mnestheus first leaves Sergestus behind struggling on the lofty rock and calling for help in vain from the shoals and learning to run with broken oars. Then Mnestheus overtakes Gyas and the *Chimera* herself with her huge bulk. The *Chimera* yields since she is stripped of her helmsman.

227. And Cloanthus alone remains in the end, whom Mnestheus seeks, and he bears close, pressing the greatest strengths. Then the shouting is repeated and all goad Mnestheus on as he zealously follows after Cloanthus, and the sky resonates with the din. These men deem their glory and their acquired honor unworthy unless they keep it, and they are willing to contract out their life for the praise. Success sustains them. They are strong because they seem to be. By chance they have seized rewards with equaled beaks, except Cloanthus, stretching both palms over the sea, pours out prayers and calls the gods towards his vows, "Gods, whose authority is over the sea, over whose water I run, I will gladly set up a shining bull on the shore in front of your altars, a witness of my vow, and I will toss entrails into the salty waves, and I will pour out clear wine."[90] Cloanthus speaks, and from under the deep waves, the entire chorus of Nereids and Phorcus ("Seal"), and the virginal Panopea (a Nereid), and Portunus,[91] the father himself, Neptune, with his great hand, pushes Cloanthus' ship running along. Swifter than a flying arrow, the *Scylla* flies to land and conceals herself in the deep port. Then—all called according to custom with the loud voice of a public crier—the son of Anchises declares Cloanthus the victor.

(Vergil, Aeneid *5.114–246)*

5.1.17 Sailors Speak

While a rich body of literary and archaeological evidence attests sailing traditions in the ancient Mediterranean, those ships were captained and manned by living sailors. Here we have a selection of inscriptions left by professional sailors.

90 Cloanthus' prayer underscores many aspects of Roman religion, including its contractual nature ("I give so that you might give": *do ut des*) and focus on *pietas* (devotion to family, state, and the gods who protect Rome). The gods reward Cloanthus for his *pietas* and his humble respect.

91 The god of harbors (Latin, *portus*).

A. *An undatable damaged stone from Olisippo (Lisbon), Lusitania, attesting a gift in recompense for protection: it is unclear if the dedicants were grateful for a successful fishing operation, naval battle, or expedition of exploration.*

> Sacred to the gods of the sea, the ocean sailors and rowers offered this in the temple of Thetis on behalf of protecting. They gave their gift well.
>
> (CIL *2.24)*

B. *Romans (and their auxiliary troops) made countless dedications to secure the goodwill of local deities, as at Fectio (Vechten, Lower Germany) on the Rhine, where the citizens of the Tungri joined with the Roman sailors to honor the local goddess, 151–250 CE.*

> To the goddess Viradecdis, the Tungrian citizens and the sailors who stopped at Fectio fulfilled their vow willingly and deservedly.
>
> (CIL *13.6324)*

C. *Sailors honored the emperor in a declaration of uncertain date (2nd century CE) on stone from Lausonne, Upper Germany, a common expression of loyalty, especially among allied, auxiliary troops and sailors.*

> For the *numina* (divine spirits) of the emperors, at Lake Lemannus sailors who stopped at Leusonna. This place was given by a decree of the administrator.
>
> (AE *1939: 102)*

D. *A votive for the health of the emperor and the protective spirit of the sailors, Marbach am Neckar in Upper Germany, 151–250 CE.*

> For the health of the emperor and the *genius* (protective spirit) of sailors, Gaius Iulius Urbicus gave a gift and fulfilled a vow freely, happily, deservedly.
>
> (CIL *13.6450)*

E. *An inscription on stone that seems to commemorate a gift at Lugdunum (Lyon) by a man who sailed the Rhone. A bonus? A funerary bequest?*

> Gaius Iulius Sabinianus, a Rhodianian sailor, in honor of the Rhodianian sailors, gave this. The spot was given by a decree of the Rhodianian sailors. By way of a dedication, I gave three *denarii* to each of the sailors.
>
> (CIL *13.2002)*

F. *A diploma (formal military discharge) on bronze, dating to 71 CE, granting citizenship and the right of marriage to the nautical command staff (thus their children would have full citizen rights). The Ravenna Fleet, supporting Vespasian's bid for the emperorship in 69 CE, was stationed in the Adriatic and may have been responsible for patrolling the Eastern Mediterranean. These officers were presumably settled in Pannonia, northeast of Italy, and would have been allied, auxiliary soldiers.*

The emperor Caesar Vespasian Augustus—Pontifex Maximus,[92] with tribunician power for two years, emperor, father of his country, consul for the 3rd time, consul designate for the 4th time—granted citizenship to the ships' captains and triremes' captains and rowers who fought in the Ravenna fleet under Sextus Lucilius Bassus and were previously awarded stipends because they conducted themselves bravely and diligently in the campaign of battle and because they have been dismissed from service and led into Pannonia, whose names are written below. Vespasian also grants citizenship to their children and descendants, and legal recognition of marriage with their spouses whom they had with them when citizenship was granted or, if they were unmarried, then with the spouses they married afterwards, one wife only for each man, on the Nones of April (April 9)[93] when Caesar Domitian, son of Augustus, and Cnaeus Pedius Cascus were consuls.

*(*AE *2004: 1282 =* AE *2007: 1232; see* CIL *16.24 where the discharged officers and men are cited by name)*

G. *From Meschenich, north of Köln, 89–150 CE. A funerary monument?*

Verus, a *velarius*[94] of the German fleet *Pia Fidelis* ("Dutiful and Faithful"), a friend, took care that (this monument) be made.

*(*CIL *13.8160)*

H. *An inscription on stone from Köln, 89–150 CE.*

Cassius, a *velarius* of the German fleet *Pia Fidelis* fulfilling 28 years of military service, 50 years, and his wife Comita took care from a will that this monument be made.

*(*CIL *13.8321)*

I. *An epitaph for a* velarius duplicarius *from Misenum, 2nd century CE.* Duplicarius *is a fraught term but seems to refer to a position of distinction or leadership within a squadron of 30 men: Pseudo-Hyginus,* Astronomy *16.*

To the spirits of the departed, Valerius, an Alexandrian by birth, fought for 26 years as a *velarius duplicarius*. He lived 56 years, four months, 12 days.

92 #1.9.12G note.
93 Roman calendar: #4.5.2J§123 note.
94 Who worked the sails, *vela* (sails).

Lucius Valerius Justus and Varenia Helena, his heirs, made this monument well and deservingly.

(CIL *10.3500)*

J. *The sailors' guild at Peschiera del Garda/Arilica, northeast Italy, saw to burial rights, presumably for the family of one of their members, 161–230 CE.*

Likewise, the guild of sailors at Arilica gave 12 coin *sesterces* so that from the return on the sum the Rosalia and Parentalia[95] might be administered for Justus, the son, and Justa the wife, and for himself perpetually for all the years. And Pontia Justa added the same amount, in memory of Fortuna, her freedwoman, for the same reason, and so that the monument might be safeguarded.

(CIL *5.4016)*

K. *An undatable epitaph for a sailor at Lugdunum (Lyon). Lucius Hilarianus Cinna may have operated a barge that conveyed goods along the Rhone.*

To the spirits of the departed, Lucius Hilarianus Cinna, a Lugdunensian citizen, a Rhodianian sailor, navigator, guardian, tradesmen of the same body, Quintus Maspetius Severianus, his father-in-law, and Claudius Severianus, his friend, took care that this gravesite be established for his heirs and they dedicated it *sub ascia.*[96]

(CIL *13.1996)*

5.2 Transporting People by Water

5.2.1 Ferries

People were transported across water, and ferries (πορθμεῖα: porthmeia *in Greek;* traiectus *in Latin) that made quick runs between short distances were fairly common. The most famous mythical ferry was Charon's, transporting souls of the dead across the river Styx (#3.10B–C; see #5.2.4E; Lucian,* Charon*).*

A. *Another ferry service in the Greco-Roman mythscape was provided by the centaur Nessus who conveyed passengers across the Evenos River (western Greece). Soon after his wedding to Deianira, Herakles hired Nessus to ferry his new bride across the river, but the centaur tried to rape her mid-stream. Herakles shot Nessus with his*

95 *Rosalia*: occurring in May, featured public prayers, processions, and decorating the military emblems with roses. *Parentalia* (Feralia): an annual nine-day observance in February, observed in honor of family ancestors: Ovid, *Fasti* 2.533–616.

96 The formula *sub ascia* suggests that the tomb is new and solemnly dedicated while the stonemason, who first shaped the block with his adze, was completing the monument.

*hydra-poisoned arrows, killing the beast, who, as he died, advised Deianira to collect some of his poisoned blood as a love-charm. Years later, Deianira unwittingly used the centaur blood to kill Herakles in a very painful way. Sophocles of Colonus (a suburb of Athens: 497/6–406/5 BCE) was an acclaimed tragedian. Seven of his plays survive complete, including three that treat the Oedipus saga (*Oedipus the King, Oedipus at Colonus, Antigone*). Here Deianira recalls her centaur-ferry-ride.*

> Long ago, as a girl, I once had an ancient gift, hidden in a bronze jar, taken as a love charm from a beast, shaggy-chested Nessus, from his blood as he died. For hire, he used to convey mortal folk over the deep-flowing Evenos River in his forepaws, not with guiding oars nor by a ship's sails. While I followed as wife with Herakles, on account of my father sending me off,[97] Nessus, carrying me on his shoulders, while I was mid-passage, grasped me with wicked hands, and I screamed out. Turning straightaway, the son of Zeus shot a feathered arrow from his hands. Into the lungs of Nessus' chest, the arrow whooshed. Dying the beast said . . .
>
> *(Sophocles,* Women of Trachis *555–569)*

Here we have a selection of historical ferries arranged chronologically by author.

B. *The Cimmerian Strait (Kerch Strait) in Scythia between the Euxine Sea and Lake Maeotis (Sea of Azov).*

> And now in Scythia there is the Cimmerian walls, there is a Cimmerian ferry, there is also a Cimmerian region, and there is the Bosporus ("Ox-crossing") called Cimmerian.
>
> *(Herodotus,* Histories *4.12.1; cf. 4.45.2)*

C. *There was a modest fee for taking the ferry across the Tiber. Gaius Lucilius (d. c. 103 BCE) was an acclaimed Roman satirist, admired by Horace and others. Only fragments survive.*

> *Velabrum* comes from "conveying." Those who do this for profit are even now said to practice *velatura*. The fee for this conveyance for those who crossed on rafts was a *quadrans*. Lucilius wrote about this: a *quadrans* for the raft.
>
> *(Varro,* Latin Language *5.44 = Lucilius 1,162)*

D. *Here Decius Jubellius, appointed commander of the garrison at Rhegium in 280 BCE, instead plundered the city, killing the men and seizing their property. For this he received divine punishment (loss of his eyesight), and his vengeful*

97 Deianira, daughter of Oeneus, king of Calydon, was courted by the River Achelous, whom Hercules defeated, taking Deianira as his prize (Apollodorus, *Library* 2.7.5, see also Sophocles, *Women of Trachis*).

ophthalmologist sought a quick getaway by ferry to Messana after the "cure." Dionysius of Halicarnassus (c. 60 to after 7 BCE) was a rhetorician and historian who moved to Rome in the 20s BCE, studied Latin, and composed a 20-book history of Rome in Greek.

> Anticipating the arrival of the Romans, divine foresight took vengeance on Decius, the leader of the garrison for his unholy deeds with respect to the supreme portion of his living body: inflicting on the eyes a disease that brought on terrible, excruciating pain. Eager to heal, a man sent a physician from Messana, Dexicrates by name, learning that he was the best among the healers of his time, but not knowing that he was Rhegian by birth. Arriving at Rhegium, Dexicrates anointed Decius' eyes with a corrosive poison and instructed him to endure the pains until he should return. Dexicrates then went down to the sea and embarked on a ferry that was made ready, and he sailed back to Messana before anyone knew what had happened.
>
> *(Dionysius of Halicarnassus,* Roman Antiquities *20.5.2; cf. Diodorus Siculus,* Library of History *22.1.2–3; Appian,* Samnite Wars *9.3)*

E. *Across the Rhone to Caballio (Cavaillon, southeastern France).*

> For those beginning at Massalia and making their way to the spot between the Alps and the Rhodanus, up to the Drouentia River, the Sallyes inhabit a span of 500 *stadia*. But for those making the crossing by ferry to the *polis* Kaballio, all the adjacent land belongs to the Caovari up to the confluence of the Isar with the Rhodanus. The length of the trip to here from Drouentia is 700 *stadia*.
>
> *(Strabo,* Geography *4.1.11)*

F. *Across the Nile to Philae.*

> We crossed over to the island in a *pacton*. A *pacton* is a small boat fitted together from willows so that it looks like wickerwork. Standing in the water and seated on small boards, we were carried across easily, fearing without reason. For the journey is free of danger unless someone overpacks the ferry boat.
>
> *(Strabo,* Geography *17.1.50)*

G. *From Tanagra across the Asopos River in Boeotia. For biological tritons: #3.4.3.*

> One of those administering the *boule* (council), chosen by lot and entrusted to administer Hellas for a year, touching a triton and querying the nature of what he saw, detaching a little bit of skin, burnt it in the fire. The grievous stench of the burnt scrap thrown into the fire attacked the noses of the bystanders. But he says that they did not agree whether the creature was of the dry land or the sea nor what nature it had. But the experiment of trying to catch a triton did not reward

him. For not long afterwards he lost his life, crossing a small and narrow strait, in a short, six-oared ferry boat.

(Aelian, NA *13.21)*

H. *A regular ferry likely conveyed passengers across the Hellespont. Paulus Silentarius was courtier of Justinian at Constantinople (r. 526–562 CE).*

From the other side, Paulus Silentarius sends a note copied in duplicate to his friend Agathon: Love, violently fighting, does not know law, nor does any other business deprive a man from mad love. If the work of legal cares does not restrain you, then there is no furious love in your breast. What sort of thing is love when a small salt-strait knows how to divide your flesh far away from your girl? By swimming, and not heeding the waves at night, Leander demonstrated what sort of power Love has. But for you, my friend, there are towing ferries. But you are constantly engaged with Athena, thrusting Cypris away.[98] Pallas Athena has the law, Paphian Aphrodite has desire. Tell me, what man can serve both the Palladian and Paphian goddess at one time?

(Paulus Silentarius, Greek Anthology *5.293)*

5.2.2 Long-Haul Passenger and Cargo Ships for Hire

Cargo ships and war vessels were familiar, and long-distance travel by sea, especially from the 1st century onward, was not altogether uncommon.

A. *In an argument against Kallipos, seeking to recover a sum of money that he claims was wrongfully paid out, an orator makes a casual reference to a fee for passage in an argument spuriously ascribed to Demosthenes (see #6.1.1A).*

Come now, gentlemen of the jury, I will demonstrate that Lykon did not meet with Kallipos at all. Thus, I think that this will be proof against the false pretension of this affirmation that this money was given to him (Kallipos) as a gift by Lykon. Lykon had given out 40 *minae* as a loan to Megacleides of Eleusis and his brother Thrasyllus for a trip to Ace.[99] They changed their minds not to sail there nor to risk the danger. Then, Lykon, bringing a charge about the interest,

98 *Cypris*: Aphrodite/Venus: #3.11.4. Hero and Leander were lovers who lived on opposite sides of the Hellespont: every evening Leander would swim across the strait from Abydos, guided by Hero's lamp at Sestos, until the autumn storms surged, and visibility failed. He drowned in the turbulent waters. Hero committed suicide by jumping off her balcony (Ovid, *Heroides* 18–19). In May 1810, the then-unknown 21-year-old Lord Byron was determined to swim the Hellespont, succeeding on his second attempt ("After Swimming the Hellespont"). Since 1986, the Turkish government has formally sponsored an annual swim across the Hellespont on "Victory Day" (August 30): 4.5 kilometers (about 2.7 miles) between Europe and Asia, in currents and choppy, open water (cf. Minchin 2016).

99 *Minae*: #5.1.15D. *Ace*: on the island of Kepallonia, in the Ionian Sea, northwest of the Peloponnese.

believing that, deceived, his interests were at stake, he prosecuted Megacleides for the loan to be repaid.

(Pseudo-Demosthenes, Against Kallipos *52.20)*

B. *While there were dedicated ferries for short-haul transits across straits or rivers, civilians usually made* ad hoc *arrangements for longer voyages. Waterfront heralds would announce when ships were making ready, confirmed by the shouts of the crew weighing anchor, as when Apollonios of Tyana in Cappadocia (c. 15–c. 100 CE) attempted to escape Nero's wrath (Apollonios had disregarded imperial bans on philosophers from entering Rome and was accused of using magic and performing human sacrifice).*

Apollonios said, "Neither will he, the emperor, nor anyone else chase after me, and my sail is headed for Greece." Demos replied, "It's a dangerous and very open country. Nor could you escape by hiding. How could you dodge his notice in the open?" "I don't need to evade him," Apollonios replied, "for if, as you think, the whole world is the tyrant's, then those dying in the open are better off than those living in hiding." And then he said to Damis, "Do you know of a ship heading to Sicily?" Damis said, "I do know, and we are staying near the sea, and the herald is near the door, and a ship is now making ready. I understand from sailors' shouting and their preparations about weighing anchor that they are about to set sail." "Damis, let's embark on this ship about to sail to Sicily and from there to the Peloponnese." "This seems good to me," Damis replied, "let's sail."

(Philostratus, Apollonios of Tyana *8.14)*

C. *Libanius (314–392/3 CE) inquired about vessels sailing for Athens from Constantinople's great harbor. Libanius was a rhetorician and philosopher from Antioch, Coele-Syria, who studied at Athens, taught at Constantinople, and corresponded with the emperor Julian (r. 361–363 CE).*

All things had been accomplished for Crispinus,[100] concerning which he had taken me to Constantinople, as I was preparing to return back to the *polis* (Athens), I went down to the great harbor at Constantinople and inquired regarding whoever was sailing to Athens.

(Libanius, Oration *1.31)*

D. *After arriving at Berytus (Beirut), the star-crossed lovers Leukippe and Klitophon take the first ship they see, just casting loose. Achilles Tatius of Alexandria (early 2nd century CE) is best known for* The Adventures of Leukippe and Klitophon, *an eight-book romantic novel following the travels and amorous travails*

100 Libanius' close friend and co-eval (*Oration* 1.27).

of his protagonists through the eastern Mediterranean until they finally marry at Byzantium and return to their home-town of Sidon where, presumably, they live happily ever after.

> Asking nothing about where she was sailing, we changed our outlook from land to sea, and it was the moment before dawn. She was sailing to Alexandria, the great city of the Nile.
>
> *(Achilles Tatius,* Leukippe and Klitophon *2.31)*

E. *We then get a glimpse of what Leukippe, Klitophon, and their entourage experience as they travel by ship. Satyrus is their servant.*

> Some young man happened to pitch his tent near us, and at breakfast time, in a very polite way, welcoming us to take breakfast with him. Satyrus then served us so that placing what we have in the middle, we shared our food, and then conversation. I (Klitophon) speak first, "Young man, where are you from and what is it necessary to call you?" "I'm Menelaus," he says, "Egyptian by birth. What about you?" "I'm Klitophon, this one is Klinias, Phoenicians both." "What's your reason for going away?" Klitophon replies, "First tell us yours, and then hear ours from us."
>
> *(Achilles Tatius,* Leukippe and Klitophon *2.33)*

F. *In 407* CE, *Synesius, future bishop of Ptolemais, was probably sailing on a small ship on a coastal run between Ptolemais and Cyrene. As a storm approached, the skipper put out to sea, a common precaution against a threatening storm, but the passengers complained, demanding that the ship make for land.*

> Then a vigorous southerly wind arose by which we were quickly obscured from the sight of land. We were sailing quickly alongside merchantmen—fitted with double sails[101]—that did not have the same need of Libya—and safety—as we had; but they were sailing another road. While we moaned and in this timid way made our lament of being forced from land, Amarantos, our Iapetus,[102] standing at the stern, histrionically exclaimed murderous curses: "Indeed we won't fly," he said. "How can anyone assist you who are suspicious of both land and sea?"
>
> *(Synesius,* Epistle *4.7)*

101 Synesius' smaller ship was fitted with a single sail.

102 A Titan, brother of Kronos and Rhea, father of Atlas, Menoetius, Epimetheus, and Prometheus (who gifted humanity with fire and technology: cf. Irby-Massie 2008). Iapetus and his brothers attacked their oppressive father (Sky, who resisted progress), enabling Kronos to castrate their father and take power for himself. Iapetus also represents the western pillar of the world, separating Sky and Earth (mother of the Titans). The Titans later battled and lost to the Olympians (under Zeus' leadership) for authority.

5.2.3 Official Transport

Those on governmental business often traveled in military ships.

A. *Cicero took several types of ships for his two-week journey from Athens to assume his governorship of Cilicia (western Asia Minor) in 51 BCE.*

> On the day before the Nones of Quintilis (July 6),[103] I send this letter as I depart Athens: I was there for ten days. Pomptinus came together with Cnaeus Volusius. The quaestor arrived. Your friend Tullius alone is absent. I had some undecked, unarmored Rhodian *aphracts* and two-banked Mytilenian *dicrota* and some boats under oar. There was silence about the Parthians. May the gods help us with what will happen!
>
> *(Cicero,* To Atticus *#104 [5.11.4])*

B. *In 70* CE, *while Titus besieged Jerusalem, his father, Emperor Vespasian (r. 69–79), voyaged from Alexandria to Italy also on a variety of ships. Flavius Josephus (c. 37–c. 100 CE) of Jerusalem was a Jewish historian who wrote accounts of Jewish history and the war with Rome. Josephus defected to the Roman side, becoming friends with the imperial family and receiving Roman citizenship. The Jewish War reached its climax in 69/70 CE after a bloody year of contentious civil war among the Romans.*

> At the time when Titus Caesar (r. 79–81) was besieging Jerusalem, Vespasian, embarking on a merchant ship, travelled from Alexandria to Rhodes. From there he sailed in triremes and stopped along his *periplus* at all the *poleis* which received him with prayers. He travelled from Ionia to Hellas, and from there from Kerkyros (Corcyra) to the Iapygian promontory (Italy's "heel"). There he made his journey to Rome by land.
>
> *(Josephus,* Jewish Wars *7.21–22)*

C. *For his governorship of Bithynia-Pontus, Pliny the Younger was conveyed partly by ships.*

> Gaius Pliny to the Emperor Trajan: Because I trust, Majesty, that it extends to your concern, I report to you that I have sailed around Cape Malea[104] to Ephesus with all my staff, although we were held back by contrary winds. I now intend to head for my province partly in oared ships, partly in carriages. For intense heat opposes a land journey, and the northwesterly Etesians resist a journey altogether by sea.

103 Roman calendar: #4.5.2J§123 note.
104 Southern Peloponnese.

Trajan to Pliny: you have correctly reported back, my very dear Secundus.[105] It does reach out to my heart to know by what journey you attain your province. Moreover, you wisely decide to use ships sometimes, sometimes carriages, as the local conditions have persuaded.

(Pliny the Younger, Epistle *10.15–16)*

D. *Roman law outlines the responsibilities of captains or ship owners to their paying passengers. Little is known about Gaius (c. 130–c. 180 CE), not even his full name. With an interest in ancient Roman law, Gaius wrote explications of the* Twelve Tables *(Rome's earliest code of law) and the* Lex Papia Poppaea *(#6.1.3C note) and an introductory textbook on Roman law,* Institutes.

i. A ship's captain and an innkeeper and a stable master accept pay not for safe keeping, but the captain so that he conveys passengers. . .

(Gaius, On the Provincial Edict *5 [Digest 4.9.7.5])*

ii. An owner ought to be responsible for the behavior of all his sailors, whether free or enslaved. Nor without cause does he oversee their behavior since he himself hired them at his own risk. But he is not responsible for matters other than if some damage has been done on the ship itself. But the captain will not be responsible although it was committed by the sailors off the ship. Likewise, if he announces in advance that each of the passengers watch their own property and that he will not pay damages and the passengers agree, then the captain will not be sued.

(Ulpian, On the Edict *18 [*Digest *4.9.7.7])*

5.2.4 Seasickness

Seasickness is cited casually in literary sources, especially in the context of sudden storms at sea.

A. *The etymology explained by Plutarch.*

Nausea is so-called for those unloosing their throats on a ship (*naus*: "ship"). The custom now prevails that this is the name of the ailment for those suffering in any way whatsoever.

(Plutarch, Table Talk *6.8 694b)*

B. *Why people become seasick.*

But neither of these causes, smell or fear, aggravates those sailing by river: for the scent of fresh water is customary to everyone, and the sailing is without

105 #4.5.4A note.

danger. But at sea, folks are unable to endure the scent because of its strangeness, and, not trusting present circumstances or those things about to happen, they are afraid. There is no help in the stillness of the sea; but the soul, fearing and imagining the pitch and roll, is stirred up and fills the body with confusion.

(Plutarch, Causes of Natural Phenomena *914e–f)*

C. *A remedy. See also #3.11.4F.*

The fellow who sails and is pressed by nausea, if he has vomited out a lot of bile, he ought to abstain from food or take just a little something. If he has spewed out sour phlegm, he should take food, but lighter than his usual custom. If there will have been nausea without vomit, either he should abstain or vomit after food.

(Celsus, On Medicine *1.3.11)*

D. *Larger ships are not necessarily more comfortable for those prone to seasickness.*

But just like those who are cowardly and suffering from seasickness on a sail, and think they will sail more easily if they switch from a light boat to a merchantman and again if they transfer to a trireme, they accomplish nothing, bringing their cholic and cowardice with them. Thus, interchanging lifestyles does not remove grief and troubles from the soul.

(Plutarch, On the Tranquility of the Mind *466c)*

E. *In this dialogue of three deceased Cynic philosophers, Diogenes (#1.1.2§2) reports to Crates and Antisthenes about the dead becoming seasick as they cross the river Styx.*

And when I came down, I did not at all mix with the others, but I left them wailing and ran ahead to the ferry to seize a place in advance so that I might sail comfortably. Throughout the crossing, they cried and were nauseous, but I was delighted by them.

(Lucian, Dialogues of the Dead *27 (22).6)*

F. *A vivid account of one poor seasick passenger who falls overboard. Lucian's* Toxaris *explores the Scythian veneration of Agamemnon's son Orestes.*

Up to Sicily they sailed with following seas, said Simylos. When they were sailing in the Ionic Sea itself after passing through the narrows, a great storm fell upon them. But why should someone tell these many things: the triple swells and twisting winds and hail and whatever other evils there are of a storm? But when they were already along Zacynthus[106] in the Ionian Sea, they were sailing

106 #5.1.5A.

with their yard stripped of its sails, and they were dragging twisted lines in the water to handle the rush of their forward movement. Around midnight in such a great buffeting of the ship, a seasick Damon vomited, leaning out to the sea. Then, I think, since the ship was rolling rather violently to the part over which he was leaning and swells were contributing to the ship's listing, Damon fell into the sea head-first, nor was the poor guy nude so that he could swim more easily.[107] Straightaway, therefore, he shouted. Choking and with difficulty he kept himself above the waves.

(Lucian, Toxaris or Friendship *19)*

G. *An episode of seasickness on Marius' ship heading for Africa where Marius spent his exile after losing to Sulla in civil war (88 BCE). Marius (c. 157–86 BCE) was a Roman statesman and general, known for professionalizing the Roman army, which had, up until then, been a military force of citizens under obligatory service.*

When the elder Marius put out to sea, carried by a following wind along Italy, he feared a certain Geminus, one of the powerful men of Terracina and his enemy. He instructed his sailors to keep away from Terracina. They were willing to oblige him. But the wind changed towards the shore and drove the waves a great deal. Nor did it seem likely that the boat would hold up against the surge: Marius fell ill and was in a bad state from nausea. So, with difficulty, they took the coast around Circeium.[108]

(Plutarch, Marius *36.1)*

5.3 Marine Hydraulic Engineering

5.3.1 Hydraulic Concrete

A. *Many ancient hydraulic installations have endured in large part because of the remarkably durable and innovative hydraulic concrete made from pozzolana, volcanic ash collected at Puteoli. Here, why Roman concrete was so water-tight. See also Mogetta 2021.*

There is also a type of dust which naturally brings about things to be admired. It is formed in the regions around Baiae in the fields of the townships which are around Mt. Vesuvius. When this is mixed with limestone and rubble, not only does it furnish strength to buildings but even when moles are constructed in the sea, they solidify under water, which moreover seems to happen for this reason: because under the mountains there are both boiling lands and abundant springs which would not exist if, in the deep, they did not have very large fires burning from either sulfur or alum or asphalt. Therefore, the fire within and the steam of

107 #5.1.16§150; #6.5.2E§105

108 Cape Circeio: on central Italy's western coast, just south of Rome.

the flame remaining and burning between the veins renders the earth light. And the emerging tufa, which is produced there, is without moisture. Therefore, when three things formed by the force of fire in a similar way arrive together into one mixture—liquid suddenly admitted—they adhere together and, hardened, are quickly firmed up. Nor is a wave or any force of water able to dissolve these things.

(Vitruvius, On Architecture *2.6.1; cf. #5.3.3B§2)*

B. *Ironically, something as strong as Roman concrete is made from such an insubstantial material as volcanic dust.*

Who could sufficiently wonder that the least part of the earth and consequently that so-called dust which is deposited in the Puteolean hills, straightaway plunged in the sea's swells would become a single, inexpugnable rock in the waves and even become stronger every day, especially if mixed with Cumaean quarry-fragments?

(Pliny, NH *35.166; cf. Seneca,* NQ *3.20.3)*

5.3.2 Naval Craftsmen

A. *Roman hydraulic engineering is without contention a marvel, and it is easy to lose sight of the living men who built these structures. Here we have a 2nd century CE epitaph dedicated by a naval craftsman from Pisa.*

To the spirits of the departed, Venuleia Pelagia lies here at rest. Her son, Marcus Naevius Galeria Restitutus, son of Marcus, a soldier of the 10th praetorian cohort,[109] lies at rest here, he who left as a testament to the very ancient and very dutiful guild of naval craftsmen at the outpost of Pisa 4,000 coin *sesterces* from whose revenue they should observe the Parentalia and Rosaria[110] annually and honor his sepulcher. If this should not be done by the guild, then by this same contract, the beam-working craftsmen of Pisa themselves ought to fulfill these observations, the 4,000 coin *sesterces* accepted from the naval guild as a penalty.

(CIL *11.1436)*

B. *From Arles, Gallia Narbonensis, unknown date.*

Gaius Iulius Pot[], an associate of the naval craftsmen of the guild at Arelates, the overseer of this same guild, and Severa, his wife, placed and dedicated this tomb for themselves while alive, *sub ascia.*[111]

(CIL *12.730)*

109 #2.2.12D§15 note.
110 #5.1.17J note: The epigrapher probably means the Rosalia.
111 #5.1.17K note.

C. *Caecilius Niger, another naval craftsman from Arlete, is honored by his colleagues with an artfully poetic epitaph.*

For Caecilius Niger, a naval craftsman, may you, whoever is passing by, read these verses of ours which will give you the true names of a deceased man. I seek indulgence for these unpolished elegies lest you dread to read them through. And may you say that I have a poem, well-spoken. Caecilius Niger is buried here where you see an inscription stand. Now, for you, we few naval craftsmen pay the last vows, an offering for this deceased body. We hope that the bones rest sweetly in your cinerary urn, and may the vexing earth be light on your limbs. We craftsmen give to Niger, a craftsman, our companion, these prayers which our good wish, now discharged, fulfils.

*(*CIL *12.5811)*

5.3.3 Harbors

A. *A lovely natural harbor in Sicily. Odysseus is speaking.*

"And in Sicily there is a harbor with good mooring, where a ship's cable is not needed. Nor is it necessary to toss an anchor stone nor to make them fast with stern lines. But one can stay the beached ships for a time for the sailors' heart to be stirred on and the breezes to blow. Nevertheless, shining water flows at the head of the harbor. There is a spring from a grotto, and black poplars grow all around. There we sailed, and some god led us through a murky night. Nor was there light to see, but around the ship there was a thick mist. Nor did the moon shine from the sky: it was held back by clouds. From there no one looked at the island with eyes, nor did we see the large waves rolling on the beach until we ran our well-benched ships ashore. And we lowered all the sails from the beached ships, and we ourselves stepped on the sea's strand. Disembarking from there we awaited the shining dawn."

(Homer, Odyssey *9.136–151; cf. Vergil,* Aeneid *1.159–169)*

B. *Emphasizing the virtues of working with nature and topography, Vitruvius offered a tantalizing glimpse into ancient harbor construction. The harbor-works at Massalia (Marseille) seem to reflect Vitruvius' model: Vitruvius had served under Julius Caesar during the Civil War and may have been present at the siege of Massalia in 49 BCE (*On Architecture *2.1.5, 10.16.11; see Hesnard 2004; #5.3.1*).

1. The fitness of harbors, moreover, must not be overlooked, but it remains for me to explain by which methods ships can be protected from storms in harbors. If, furthermore, harbors are well-positioned and have headlands or promontories running out into the sea, by which the bays are curved within or shaped by the

nature of the place, these naturally seem to have the greatest utility. For shipyards should be made either around the colonnades or approaches to the markets from the colonnades, and towers should be located at each side, by which chains can be drawn by machines.[112]

2. But if we would not have a natural place nor one suitable for protecting ships from storms, it thus seems best that one should be made in this way: if no river impedes but there is an anchorage on one side, then, on the other side a pier should be prepared from built-structures or embankments, and thus the enclosures of the harbor are to be shaped. These built-structures, moreover, which will be in the water, thus seem to be best made in this way: that ash be brought from the regions which are continuous from Cumae to the promontory of Minerva (Punta Campanella), and this ash is to be mixed as two parts correspond to one part (of lime) in the mortar.[113]

3. Then in that place which is marked out, boxes[114] of oaken trunks shut in by chains must be let down into the water and firmly made fast. Then between these, the lower part must be levelled and cleaned, and it must be constructed there with the concrete from the mortar with the stuff mixed in, as described above, until the span of the structure, which would be between the boxes, is filled. These places, described above, moreover, have this natural advantage. But if, on account of breaking waves or the assault of the open sea, the supports are not able to contain the boxes, then from the very land or the masonry base let the platform be arranged as firmly as possible, and let this platform be arranged as a flat surface, less than half its width. Let the rest which is towards the shore have a side sloping down.

4. Then towards the very water and the sides of the platform, let borders be arranged, about a pace and a half long, perfectly level with the flat surface, described above. Then let the slope be filled with sand and made level with the border and the platform's flat surface. Then above this level surface let there be a pillar as large as agreed, let it be built there. When it is constructed, let it be left alone no less than two months so that it might dry. Then, moreover, let the border which supports the sand be cut away: thus the sand, washed away by the sea, will bring about the fall of the pillar into the sea. In this way, as often as necessary, the pier will be able to extend into the water.

5. In these places, moreover, where ash does not arise, it will be done in these ways, so that double boxes, bound together with planks and chains, are situated in this place which will be marked out. Between the supports, clay is pressed in baskets made from swamp sedge. When it will be well-pressed and as densely as possible, then the place which is marked out by this wall will be emptied and dried by the water screws, wheels, and drums that are arranged there, and there between the walls let the foundations be dug. If the foundations will be earthy, all the way

112 Defense mechanisms, employed at *Cyzicus* in 365 CE (Ammianus Marcellinus, *Deeds* 26.8.8).

113 See #5.3.1.

114 Cofferdams: more or less watertight enclosures that facilitate work below the water line.

to the solid sea-base, let them be thicker than the wall above, let them be emptied and dried, and then let the structure be filled with concrete of limestone and sand.

6. But if the place is soft, moreover, let the foundations be fastened together with charred alder or olive trees and filled with coal, in the way prescribed for the foundations of theaters and city walls (*On Architecture* 1.5). Then let the wall be raised on a squared stone with joins as long as possible, so that the middle stones may especially be bound together by the joins. Then, for the place that is within the wall, let it be filled with rubble or masonry. Thus, it is possible to build a tower above it.[115]

7. These things completed, this will be the method of shipyards, that they be established looking especially to the north. For, on account of their warmth, the southern regions generate rot, woodworms, moths, and other types of harmful beasts, and southern regions preserve these beasts by feeding them. Such buildings, harbor-works, are not at all to be built from wood because of fire. Concerning their sizes, moreover, there ought to be no limit, but they should be made to accommodate the largest model of ships so that, even if larger ships can be beached, they will have there a mooring with room.

(*Vitruvius,* On Architecture *5.12)*

C. *As further protection against the elements, many harbors were fitted with ship-sheds. The narrow, roofed sheds at the Piraeus, opening towards the water, had inclined slipways to facilitate launching and pulling ships out of the water (see Lovén and Schaldemose 2011). Strabo here makes reference to the capacious ship-sheds at Cyzicus on the southern coast of the Propontis (Sea of Marmara).*

Cyzicus is an island in the Propontis, linked by two bridges to the mainland, excellent in its quality. But in size it has a perimeter of about 500 *stadia.* It has an homophonous city towards the bridges and two harbors that can be closed and more than 200 ship-sheds.

(*Strabo,* Geography *12.8.11)*

D. *Many important market towns along the Erythraean Sea lacked harbors.*

i. And from here the Arabian Bay stretches to the east and at Avalites it is especially narrowed. After about 4,000 *stadia,* for those sailing along the same mainland to the east, there are other barbarian markets, called "far-side" markets, lying in order in anchorages and swells, having anchorages suitable in fair weather. The first is called Avalites, to which the shortest sailing from Arabia is along the far coast. Along this place is Avalites, a small emporium: visitors reach it on rafts and small boats. The imports into this market are glassworks, assorted stones and Diospolitan juice of unripe grapes and barbarian cloth,

115 I.e., a lighthouse: #5.3.7.

assorted, pressed, and grain and wine and a little tin. Exports from the same place, sometimes even by Barbarians[116] crossing over in rafts to Okelis and Mouza on the opposite side, include aromatics and a little ivory and tortoise-shell and a very little bit of myrrh, different from other myrrh, and the Barbarians dwelling around the place are very undisciplined.

(Anonymous, Erythraean Sea *7)*

ii. The emporium Mouza is harborless but with a good roadstead on account of a sandy anchorage around it.

(Anonymous, Erythraean Sea *24)*

E. *Mytilene on Lesbos was one of many coastal towns that had multiple harbors.*

Mytilene has two harbors. Of these, the southern one can be closed for 50 ships with triple banks of oars. The northern harbor is large and deep, protected by a mole.

(Strabo, Geography *13.2.2)*

F. *A brief history of the harbors at Athens.*

The Piraeus was a district in ancient times, but it was not a seaport before Themistocles the Athenian became leader (493 BCE). But Phaleron—for the sea is the least distant from the city at this place—was their sea-port, and they say that from that very spot Menestheus set out to Troy (*Iliad* 2.552), and before him, Theseus set out to administer justice on Minos for the death of Androgeos.[117] When Themistocles became the city leader, he made this (the Piraeus) the sea-port for the Athenians: for the Piraeus seemed to be situated more suitably for sailors and had three harbors instead of the one at Phaleron. Recently, even up to my day, there were docks, and near the largest harbor is the grave of Themistocles.

(Pausanias, Description of Greece *1.1.2)*

G. *Because of siltation from the Tiber, Ostia, Rome's link to the sea (35 kilometers [c. 22 miles] downstream from the Tiber's estuary), was harborless until Claudius commissioned the infrastructure.*

Claudius constructed the port at Ostia with an "arm" (breakwater) curved around on the right and left and at the entrance a mole interposed in the now deep water: to fix the mole all the more steadily, he sunk the ship on which the

116 #5.3.5D and note.

117 A son of King Minos of Crete, Androgeos was killed in Athens. Minos exacted an annual penalty of fourteen Athenian youths (seven young men, seven young women) as fodder for the dangerous Minotaur under his care. Theseus went to Crete, killed the Minotaur, and ended the annual tribute (Pseudo-Apollodorus, *Epitome* 1.1).

great obelisk had been conveyed from Egypt,[118] and, mortar-piles heaped up, he superimposed the highest tower on the model of the Alexandrian Pharos, so that ships could direct their course to its nocturnal fires.

(Suetonius, Claudius *20.3; cf. Strabo,* Geography *5.3.5; Dio Cassius,* Roman History *60.11; Tuck 2019: 441)*

H. *This Neronian coin shows the busy harbor in aerial view: four boats are under sail, three are rowed. In the upper register, Neptune stands atop a lighthouse, wielding a scepter. A reclining Tiber in the lower register holds a rudder and a dolphin. Along the left edge the crescent-shaped pier is depicted as a portico with 14 pillars, balanced by a crescent of 14 slips to the right.*

FIGURE 5.3.3H Harbor at Ostia: ART346189, photo credit: © The Trustees of the British Museum/Art Resource, NY.

I. *Some "improvements" just made matters worse, as when Attalus [II] Philadelphus (159–138 BCE) installed a mole at Ephesus.*

The city of Ephesus has both a shipyard and a harbor. The architects made the harbor's mouth shorter, being deceived, along with the king ordering the work. This was Attalus Philadelphus. For thus he thought that the approach would be deep enough for large ships that were towed in, as would the harbor itself, formerly shoaly owing to siltation from the Cayster River, completely wide, if

118 The obelisk had been transported from Heliopolis under Caligula (*CIL* 6.882; Pliny, *NH* 16.201; 26.74); see #6.1.2.

a mole were added at the mouth. Attalus therefore ordered that there should be a mole. But the opposite happened. For the silt shut within made the harbor, up to the mouth, altogether shoaly. Beforehand, the risings of the sea and its back-flow removed the silt and drew it to the outside. Such therefore is the harbor.

(Strabo, Geography *14.1.24)*

J. *Locals would gather at the well-sheltered natural port at Puteoli to watch for ships arriving from Alexandria.*

Suddenly ships from Alexandria appeared, which are accustomed to be sent ahead and announce the arrival of a following fleet. They call them "mail boats." It is a pleasing sight in Campania: the whole crowd stands on the piers of Puteoli and from the very type of sails—although in a great throng of vessels—the crowd recognizes the ships as Alexandrian. For it is allowed to them alone to stretch their topsail which all other ships make use of only in the deep. For nothing likewise aids a ship more than the highest part of the sail: from there the ship is especially spurred on. And so, as often as the wind becomes stronger and more intense than is expedient, the yardarm is lowered: for the snorting breeze has less strength at a lower level.[119] When they have made Capreae and the promontory where lofty Pallas observes from a stormy summit, other ships are ordered to be satisfied with the mainsail. The topsail of the Alexandrian ships is conspicuous. During this running about of everyone hurrying to the shore, I feel great pleasure in my own indolence because, even though I am about to receive letters from my friends, I did not hustle to know what was the status of my affairs, or what news the letters might convey.

(Seneca the Younger, Letter *77.1–3)*

5.3.4 Dredging

#5.3.31 demonstrates the need for regular maintenance, and there is some scant archaeological evidence for dredging at Massalia and Neapolis (dredging boats and fossilized dredging scoops: Pomey 1995; Pomey and Rieth 2005: 47–53; for chrono-stratigraphic evidence: Morhange and Marriner 2010 2008; Morhange et al. 2016). Common methods of regulating the accumulation of silt included constructing small channels in harbor walls to ensure that detritus could flow freely out of a basin, or positioning breakwaters within the harbors to create currents that would wash away siltation (as at Ephesus before Attalus' "improvements").

A. *Julius Caesar, at least, recognized the hazards of debris accumulating in waterways and planned to clear out such threats in the Tiber River (cf. #1.9.12D).*

He also planned to bend the Tiber in a deep trench straight below from the city and towards the Circeium to empty it at the sea near Terracina, thus devising a

119 Cf. Aristotle, *Mechanical Problems* 851a39–b6.

precaution and convenience for those travelling back and forth towards Rome on account of commerce. In addition to these things, diverting the marsh-meadows around Pomentinum and Setia, he intended to create an agriculturally productive field for many thousands of men, and to provide moles with earthen banks at the sea nearest to Rome, and to clear out the blind spots and bad anchorages of the Ostian shoreline, and to build safe anchorages suitable for such a great fleet. And these things were in preparation.

(Plutarch, Julius Caesar *58.4–5)*

B. *While the literary record is largely mute, dredging is implied at Ephesus.*

During his proconsulship of Asia (66 CE), Ostorius Sabinus, a Roman *eques*, increased the emperor's displeasure with his energy and sense of justice, and because he expended care by "opening up" (*aperiendo*) the port of Ephesus and because he omitted applying force against the Pergamean city, unpunished, prohibiting Acratus, Caesar's freedman, from carrying out statues and pictures.

(Tacitus, Annals *16.23.1)*

5.3.5 Canals

A. *Waterways were manipulated for many reasons, including controlling flooding (see #1.9.12E) and irrigating crops. While most of the evidence is archaeological (and legal), in Vergil we have a lovely description of the happy effects of irrigation on parched fields.*

And when the scalded field boils with dying crops, behold, does the farmer entice water from the brow of the sloping channel? He stirs a hoarse murmur, falling across polished stones, and he tempers waterless fields with gushes of water.

(Vergil, Georgics *1.107–110)*

B. *Strategically situated channels serve many purposes, from national defense to flood control to irrigation.*

First in such a manner that the place will be as well-fenced as possible against enemies, the citizens should make and be cut off by ditches wherever there is a need, and, with respect to their ability, they should build cross-walls for shutting out those attempting in any way to work evil against the place and its property. They should use yoked draught animals and slaves in each place for these things, breeding those (the draught animals), supervising these (the slaves), choosing especially slaves who are free from their own work. They should make all paths impassable for the enemy, but, as for friends, they should make roads especially passable for people and draught animals and pastured flocks. They should manage the roads thus that each one becomes as smooth as possible. As for the waters from Zeus (rain), in order that they not do evil to the place, but rather help, flowing from high places to those valleys in the mountains, as many as are hollow. The citizens should enclose their outflows with ditches and infrastructure, so that the infrastructure can receive and drink in waters from Zeus and make streams and springs in the low-lying fields and all places and even render parched areas much-watered and well-watered. Regarding spring-waters, if there is some river or a spring, arranging these waters with landscaping and buildings and leading all the springs together with excavated tunnels, they should make them plentiful with water pipes according to each season, if anywhere there is a sacred grove or *temenos*[120] at hand around these things, they should put these places in order by sending flowing waters to these same holy districts of the gods. Everywhere in these places it is necessary that the young men equip gymnasia[121] for themselves and also prepare warm baths for the elderly, furnishing kindling wood—and dry wood at that—abundantly, graciously receiving those bodies distressed by illness or agricultural labor, a reception better than that of a physician not altogether skillful by far.

(Plato, Laws *6.760e–761b)*

C. *The Mesopotamian canal system.*

The place is flowed through by more rivers, the greatest of them are the Tigris and Euphrates. After the Indian rivers, these rivers are said to be second among the southern parts of Asia. They offer inland sailing: the Tigris to Opis and modern-day Seleucia: the village Opis is a market-town of those places around it. And the Euphrates to Babylon, more than 3,000 *stadia* away. The Persians therefore, cunningly wanting to prevent sailing out of fear of attacks from outside, constructed cataracts (canals) made by hand. Alexander, attacking the Mesopotamians, demolished as many artificial canals as he could, especially those towards Opis. He also paid attention to the canals. For the Euphrates overflows at the beginning of the summer, rising in the spring when the snows from Armenia melt, so that it necessarily forms pools and overflows the ploughed lands unless the spilling over of the river and the surface water is channeled by ditches and conduits, just as in the case of the Nile in Egypt. Hence, the trenches were made. But there is a need of much maintenance: for the soil is deep and soft and readily yielding so that it is easily drawn out by the flowing waters and the plains are bare. The canals are full, and the silt handily blocks their mouths. Thus, it happens again that the overflow of waters falling out towards the plains by the sea forms pools and marsh-meadows and reed-beds from which reed-vessels of all kinds are woven. Some, with asphalt smeared over them, are

120 #2.2.13B.i note.

121 In Greek antiquity, young men would socialize and train, physically and mentally, in gymnasia, so-called because wrestling, the preferred sport for elite men, was practiced in the nude (*gymnos*).

fit for water. As for others, they are used bare, and they make reed-sails, similar to rush-mats or wickerwork.

It is therefore equally not possible to prevent such flooding in all places, but it is within the power of good leaders to offer help. This is the aid: to prevent the majority of overflow by means of dams, and to prevent the filling up again, which the silt does, by clearing out the canals and opening the mouths. The clearing away is therefore easy, but a dam requires many hands. For the earth is easily yielding and soft and does not stand firm under the silt piled on top, but yielding and drawing it along, the soil makes the mouth hard to dam. For there is also a need that the canals be shut quickly and that all the water does not spill out from them. For parched in the summer, they even dry out the river. Lowered, the river is not able to supply the sluices in a timely fashion when the land, hot and scorched, has the most need during the summer. It does not make a difference if crops are deluged by an abundance of waters or utterly destroyed by a water-lacking thirst. At the same time, inland sailings, having much advantage, were always ruined by both these above-mentioned eventualities. Nor was it possible to restore the situation unless the mouths of the canals were opened quickly, and also closed quickly, and the workmen always maintained the canals so that the water in them was neither excessive nor fell short.

(Strabo, Geography *16.1.9–10)*

D. *Around 600 BCE, Necho II (r. 610–595 BCE), pharaoh of Egypt, began construction of a canal that connected the Nile to the Erythraean Sea, with a grim human price.*

Necho was the son of Psammetichus and he ruled Egypt. Necho was the first who put his hand to the canal leading to the Erythraean Sea, which Darius (r. 522–486 BCE) the Persian later dug through. The length of the sail is four days. The canal was dug wide enough so that two triremes under oar could sail through together, side by side. Water from the Nile is led towards it. It is carried a little above Boubastis beside the Arab city Patumus. It pours into the Erythraean Sea. The digging was first done in the Egyptian plain near Arabia. The mountain range, in which there are stone quarries, stretching along to Memphis, extends above the plain. Along the foot of this range the canal leads from the west in a long span to the east, and then it stretches towards gorges, bearing along from the mountain range to the south and the Notos Wind towards the Arabian Bay. The shortest and most abridged passage to travel from the northern sea to the southern sea and the same so-called Erythraean Sea is from the Casian Mountain, dividing Egypt and Syria. From this place there are altogether 1,000 *stadia* to the Arabian Bay. This is the shortest passage, but the canal is longer by much, by as much as it is curved. In Necho's kingship, 20,000 Egyptian diggers died. But Necho stopped the digging in the middle when an oracle came to his feet of such a kind: that he was working in advance for a Barbarian. For the Egyptians call "Barbarians" all people not speaking the same language as themselves.[122]

(Herodotus, Histories *2.158; cf. Diodorus Siculus,* Library of History *1.33.9–12)*

E. *Darius I (r. 522–486 BCE) commemorated his restoration of the canal with an inscription in Persian.*

I (Darius) commanded to dig this canal from the Nile . . . to the sea which goes from Persia; afterwards this canal (was dug) thus as I commanded, and (ships) passed from Egypt by this canal to Persia as was my (will)

(Chalouf Stele: trans. Gray and Cary 1926: 200)

F. *In 483–480 BCE at Mt. Athos, Xerxes cut a canal as a display of power and memorial to himself. The canal was constructed in sections, each with its own work crew, including one of Phoenicians. The other work crews had excavated their trenches as deep as they were wide, and the steep sides, naturally, collapsed. But working on their own section, the Phoenicians took a more effective approach.*

22. Since first suffering shipwrecks while sailing around Athos, Xerxes made preparations in advance for three years especially regarding the conditions around Athos. For the triremes were moored at Elaios ("Olive City") of the Chersonese. From there, urged on by whips, all sorts of soldiery dug the canal, back and forth in turns, and also those dwelling around Athos dug. Boubares son of Megabazos and Artachaies son of Artaios, Persian men, supervised the work. Athos is a mountain, large and notable, reaching the sea, inhabited by people. At the end, towards the mainland, the mountain is peninsular and an isthmus, and this is about 12 *stadia*, and there are hills, not large, from the sea by Acanthus to the sea over against Torone. On this isthmus, Athos is at the end. The Greek town Sane is inhabited. Beyond Sane, inland of Athos, towns are inhabited whose citizens the Persians at that time started to make into islanders instead of mainlanders: Dion, Olophyxos, Acrothoum, Thyssos, Cleonae.

23. These cities are distributed on Athos. And the Barbarians,[123] dividing the space among themselves, were digging according to peoples. Making a measuring line along the *polis* Sane, when the canal became deep, some standing at the bottom continued to dig, some always handed over the dirt that had been dug out to others standing from above on the stepped ground, those in turn taking the dirt away from the others, until they arrived at those topmost workers. These men carried the dirt away and threw it out. For all of them, except the Phoenicians,

122 Referring generally to the inhabitants of the Greek peninsula before it was "Greek," speaking a "Barbarian" (non-Greek) language (Herodotus, *Histories* 1.57.3).

123 #5.3.5D and note.

the overhanging banks of the trenches, breaking down, resulted in doubled toil. Just as the opening above and below were made at the same measurement, this same thing was destined to occur. But the Phoenicians displayed their skill as in their other works and even in this one. Obtaining the portion which fell to them, they dug out the upper part of the trench, making it double the required width of the channel, and reducing the width as they progressed. At the bottom their work was equal to the rest. At that place is a meadow, where there was a meeting place and a market. And much milled grain came to them there from Asia.

24. As for me conjecturing to discover this, on account of his arrogance Xerxes commanded the digging, wanting to make his power known and leave behind a memorial. Dragging their ships across the isthmus they would take on no toil. But he commanded them to dig a canal from the sea broad enough so that two triremes being pushed on could sail together side by side. For, in addition to the canal, these same men were also posted to bridge the Strymon River,[124] yoking it.

(Herodotus, Histories *7.22–24)*

G. *Perhaps the best-known ancient canal project was intended to cut across the narrow isthmus at Corinth, as first envisioned by Periander in the 7th century BCE but not begun until 67 CE on Nero's order (Suetonius,* Nero *19; cf. Pliny,* NH *4.9–11) and quickly abandoned (work on the modern canal began in 1881). Instead, smaller ships were dispatched by means of an overland track, the* Diolkos, *which was weaponized in 428 BCE during the Peloponnesian War.*

When the Lacedaemonians and their allies heard these things, receiving these words favorably, they made the Lesbians their allies, and the Spartans advised their allies who were present to go to the isthmus as quickly as possible with two parts (two thirds) of their troops to prepare for their invasion of Attica. They themselves arrived first and began to fit the hauling machines out on the isthmus to convey ships from Corinth to sea near Athens to attack both by ships and on foot.

(Thucydides, Peloponnesian War *3.15)*

H. *Romans also aimed to canalize rivers in Gaul and Germany to save shipping lanes from the treacherous North Sea passage.*

Up to this time (55 CE), things had been quiet in Germany, owing to the temperament of the leaders who—the triumphal insignia broadcasted to the people—were hoping for all the more honor if they could prolong the peace. Paulinus Pompeius and Lucius Vetus were in charge of the army at this time. Lest they keep the soldiery sluggish, Pompeius completed the dam for

124 Struma, northeastern Greece and Bulgaria.

confining the Rhenus, a project begun by Drusus 63 years ago; Vetus prepared to link the Mosella and Arar with a canal dug between them, so that supplies could run up by sea, then be conveyed over the Rhodanus and Arar Rivers through this canal, then from the Mosella into the Rhenus, and then into the Ocean, and—the difficulties of the journey removed—the shores of the Western and Northern Seas could become navigable between themselves. Aelius Gracilis, the governor of Gallia Belgica, was prejudiced against this work, and deterred Vetus lest he (Vetus) bring in the legions of another province and advance his own ambitions over the Gauls, saying again and again that this action (digging the canal) would be terrible for the emperor, by which honorable initiatives are averted.

(Tacitus, Annals *13.53)*

I. *Along the Appian Way, mules towed boats through a canal over the marshes near Terracina, just as "mules" continue to tow ships through the locks of the old Panama Canal (constructed 1904–1914).*

Near Tarracina for someone walking towards Rome, next to the Appian Road is a canal filled in at many places with marshy and river waters. It is sailed especially at night, so that those embarking in the evening can disembark early in the morning and walk the rest of the journey by road, and during the day vessels are towed by a mule.

(Strabo, Geography *5.3.6; cf. Horace,* Satires *1.5.9–23)*

5.3.6 Bridges

A. *In 480 BCE, Xerxes ordered the construction of a seven-*stadia *pontoon bridge to "yoke" the Hellespont, a flagrant act of* hubris *(Aeschylus,* Persians *432–434; Herodotus,* Histories *7.33–36). The newly constructed bridge was quickly destroyed by a storm, to Xerxes' extreme consternation. For a theoretical reconstruction of the engineering required to construct the bridge: Hammond and Roseman 1996.*

33. After these things, Xerxes prepared to travel to Abydos. At the time, they were bridging the Hellespont from Asia to Europe. On the Chersonese side of the Hellespont, between the city Sestus and Madytus, is a massive promontory extending to the sea along Abydos . . .

34. Urged on, the men built a bridge to be situated to this promontory from Abydos. The Phoenicians built a work of white flax, the Egyptians built another of papyrus. From Abydos to the opposite shore are seven *stadia*. But when the strait was bridged, a great storm shattered all those works and destroyed them.

35. When Xerxes learned this, raging, he ordered the Hellespont to be hit with whips with 300 blows and a brace of shackles to be dropped into the sea.

I have heard that at the same time he also sent tattooers[125] to mark the Hellespont. He then commanded that, as they cudgeled the water, they say these foreign and wicked words: "O bitter water, our master imposes this judgment on you because you wronged him, he who committed no injustice against you, and our king Xerxes will strut across you, whether you are willing or not. In accord with justice, no man will make sacrifices to you since you are a turbid and briny river." Xerxes thus enjoined them to punish the sea and to cut off the heads of those overseeing the bridge over the Hellespont.

(Herodotus, Histories *7.33–35)*

B. *The engineering and swift construction of Caesar's first bridge over the Rhine, built in 55 BCE.*

17. For these reasons which I have mentioned above, Caesar had decided to cross the Rhenus. But he neither considered it sufficiently safe to cross in boats nor did he think it worthy of his own status or the dignity of the Roman people. So, although the greatest difficulty of building a bridge was posed on account of the breadth, swiftness, and depth of the river, nonetheless he thought that he must make the effort or otherwise not lead his army across. He established this plan for the bridge. He joined tree-trunks by twos—a pace and half long—sharpened a little at the bottom, measured for the depth of the river, at an interval of two paces between them. He fixed them, lowered into the river with machines, and drove them in with mallets, not straight up in the manner of a pile on the perpendicular, but angled and sloped, so that they inclined according to the nature of the river (i.e., its current). Likewise, opposite these, he set up two breakwaters joined in the same fashion at an interval of 40 paces from the lower part, turned against the force and attack of the river (i.e., against the current). With two-pace-long beams set on top, each of these breakwaters was separated by buckles by twos at each end, as far apart as the connection of the tree-trunks. When these were separated and bound fast to the opposite part, the strength of the work and the nature of the construction were so great that the greater the force of water that struck the bridge, the more tightly the bindings held. These trestles were woven with material laid in and covered with poles and wickerwork. Furthermore, the piles were obliquely driven to the lower part of the river, which—placed underneath like a ram and joined with the whole work—relieved the force of the river, and others were likewise driven at a moderate space above the bridge, so that, if tree-trunks or ships were sent for the sake of knocking down

125 The Greeks and Romans adopted the Persian practice of tattooing criminals and runaway slaves as a physical mark of punishment: e.g., Aristophanes, *Frogs* 1508.

the infrastructure, the force of those things would not threaten these defenses or harm the bridge.

18. In ten days, from when the material was begun to be brought together, the entire work was completed, and the army was led across. After a strong garrison was left at each side, Caesar set out for the territory of the Sugambri.

(Caesar, BG *4.17–18.1)*

C. *Trajan's Column (dedicated 113 CE) celebrates Trajan's campaigns in Dacia. The first spiral shows the army crossing the Danube (represented as a large, bearded man) over a pontoon bridge comprised of small boats, linked together and supporting a wooden superstructure over which soldiers and animals marched.*

FIGURE 5.3.6C Bridge over the Danube: Trajan's Column (VI/III–VII/IV): AR9163057, photo credit: HIP/Art Resource, NY.

5.3.7 Lighthouses

A. *The gleam of Achilles' new, Hephaestus-made shield is compared to a mountain-top light beacon for sailors.*

But then Achilles grasped the shield, great and sturdy, from which came a brightness like the moon from afar, just as when from the deep sea a flame appears to sailors: a fire burning, which is kindled aloft on mountains in a lonely station. But winds carry them unwilling over the fishy sea far from their friends. Thus did the brightness of Achilles' lovely, cunningly wrought shield reach heaven.

(Homer, Iliad *19.373–380)*

B. *Among the seven wonders of the ancient world was the Pharos lighthouse-tower at Alexandria where the need for a navigational guide was great.*

Since Alexandria and the area around it are the largest part of this task and the most powerful, one must begin from there. Accordingly from Pelusium, for those sailing westward as far as the Canopic mouth, the coast is about 1,300 *stadia*, the "base" of the delta as I have said. From there to Pharos Island, another 150 *stadia*. Pharos Island is oblong, adjoining the mainland, making a double-mouthed harbor. For the shore is a bay, propelling two promontories towards the sea. Between these is settled an island shutting in the bay, for it lies beside the shore along its length (i.e., parallel). Of the extremities of Pharos Island, the eastern side is rather closer to the mainland and to the promontory facing it—this promontory is called Lochias—and it makes the harbor narrow towards the mouth. And there are rocks in the middle of the passage—some are under the salt-water, some are jutting out—at every hour making the crashing waves, rough from the sea. This promontory of the island is also a rock washed around by the sea, having on it a marvelously equipped tower, many-storied, of white stone, having the same name as the island, Pharos. Sostratus of Cnidus, a friend of kings, dedicated it "for the sake of safety of sailors," as the inscription says. For, since the coast is harborless and low on each side, having reefs and also some shoals, it seemed best to have an elevated and bright sign for those sailing in from the deep sea so that they might hit the mark of the harbor's port of entry.

(Strabo, Geography *17.1.6; cf. Josephus,* Jewish Wars *4.614; #3.11.2)*

C. *The Pharos tower was widely praised in antiquity for both its beauty and practicality: "the greatest and most beautiful of all works, that a flame might blaze from it for sailors over much of the sea" (Lucian,* How to Write History *62), whose light "rivaled" the moon's (Statius,* Silvae *3.5.101). Here the structure is compared to a mountain.*

It was a mountain lying in mid-sea, touching the clouds themselves. Water flowed underneath the structure, which stood as if suspended on the sea. At the acropolis of this mountain rose up the pilot of the ships, another sun.

(Achilles Tatius, Leukippe and Klitophon *5.6.3)*

D. *This anonymous epigrammist imagines the tower proudly proclaiming its utility after restoration.*

In the *Pharos* of Alexandria: I am the tower aiding wandering sailors, offering Poseidon's joyful flame. At his own toil Ammonius, who is the father of our emperor,[126] stood me back up, as I was about to fall from the loud-thundering

126 A patrician by class.

windblasts. To that man, then, sailors lift up their hands just like to the renowned Earthshaker.[127]

(Anonymous, Greek Anthology *9.674)*

E. *Ibn Jubayr traveled through Alexandria to Mecca in 1183, linking the lighthouse to the glory of Allah.*

One of the greatest wonders that we saw in this city was the lighthouse which Great and Glorious God had erected by the hands of those who were forced to such labor as "a sign to those who take warning from examining the fate of others" (Quran 15:75) and as a guide to voyagers, for without it they could not find the true course to Alexandria. It can be seen for more than 70 miles, and is of great antiquity. It is most strongly built in all directions and competes with the skies in height. Description of it falls short, the eyes fail to comprehend it, and words are inadequate, so vast is the spectacle.

We measured one of its four sides and found it to be more than 50 arms' lengths. It is said that in height it is more than 150 *qamah* [one *qamah* = a man's height]. Its interior is an awe-inspiring sight in its amplitude, with stairways and entrances and numerous apartments, so that he who penetrates and wanders through its passages may be lost. In short, words fail to give a conception of it.

(Ibn Jubayr, The Travels of Ibn Jubayr, *trans. Broadhurst 1952: 32–33)*

F. *At roughly the same time, the Chinese historian Zhao Rukuo (Chau Ju-kua: 1170–1231 CE), described the world as known to the Chinese Song Dynasty, including a section on Alexandria and its famous lighthouse.*

The country of O-kön-t'o belongs to Wu-ssï-li (Egypt). According to tradition, in olden times a stranger, Tsu-ko-ni by name, built on the shore of the sea a great tower under which the earth was dug out and two rooms were made, well connected and very well secreted. In one vault was grain, in the other were arms. The tower was 200 *chang* high. Four horses abreast could ascend to two-thirds of its height. In the center of the building was a great well connecting with the big river.

To protect it from surprise by troops of other lands, the whole country guarded this tower that warded off the foes. In the upper and lower parts of it 20,000 men could readily be stationed to guard, or to sally forth to fight. On the summit there was a wondrous great mirror; if warships of other countries made a sudden attack, the mirror detected them beforehand, and the troops were ready in time for duty.

127 Poseidon, a god of storms who caused earthquakes with his trident.

In recent years there came to O-kön-t'o a foreigner, who asked to be given work in the guard-house of the tower; he was employed to sprinkle and sweep. For years no one entertained any suspicion of him, when suddenly one day he found an opportunity to steal the mirror and throw it into the sea, after which he made off.

(Chau Ju-kua, On the Chinese and Arab Trade *#37, trans. Hirth and Rockhill 1911)*

G. *This coin of Antoninus Pius (observe) shows on the reverse the Pharos lighthouse topped by a statue of Zeus or Poseidon surrounded by Tritons at each corner.*

FIGURE 5.3.7G Antonius Pius and the Pharos: ric/antoninus_pius/koln_1408. With kind permission of wildwinds.com, ex CNG, June 2005.

PART VI
Mercantile Waters

Here we consider the importance of water to ancient industry and trade. Some ports were mercantile hubs, and some trade routes were proprietary (#6.1.1). Guilds at Rome and elsewhere oversaw some industries (#6.3.9). While military sailing was largely restricted to the summer months (#5.1.7), mercantile trade was necessarily more flexible (#6.1.3), and, wherever goods were conveyed over water, pirates opportunistically pillaged unarmed merchant ships (#6.2). Seas and rivers are, moreover, sources of food (fishes and seafood: #6.3), preservatives (salt: #6.4), sponges (#6.3.1), and luxury goods (purple, pearls, coral: #6.5).

6.1 Transporting Goods by Water

6.1.1 Trade Routes and Entrepots

Long-distance trade routes are in evidence in the Mediterranean from the at least the 3rd millennium BCE when Egyptian ships ventured into the Erythraean Sea (Red Sea, Persian Gulf, Indian Ocean), and from there to the eastern coast of central Africa for trading in exotic goods (McGrail 2001: 17). By the mid-2nd millennium BCE, the Phoenicians had established extensive trade routes that linked markets between Phoenicia and Israel (1 Kings 5:8–9, 10:11), Egypt (Herodotus, Histories *2.9.2), Greeks* poleis *(Herodotus,* Histories *3.107, 111), and others, especially along the northern coast of Africa (McGrail 2001: 129). Mycenaean Greeks were dealing with goods traded from as far west as Sicily, as evidenced by the Uluburun wreck, late 14th century BCE (Pulak 2005, 2010; Tartaron 2013: 26). And in the early 10th century BCE, King Solomon of Israel seems to have derived his own immense wealth from Hiram, king of Tyre, who sent ships laden with precious metals (gold, silver, ivory, tin) from Tarshish (Tartessos) every three years (2 Chronicles 9:21;*

DOI: 10.4324/9781003437741-7

Ezekiel 27; Isaiah 23). Water was the cheapest, most efficient, quickest, and most comfortable method (storms aside) of transporting goods and people.

A. *In 355/4 BCE at Athens, Demosthenes argued to veto a law proposed by Leptines which would deny exemptions from tariffs. Leptines' law, so Demosthenes contended, would have negative repercussions for the grain imports that fed Athens, much of which came from the Black Sea. Demosthenes (384–322 BCE) was an Athenian orator whose court arguments provide a valuable glimpse of contemporary politics, culture, and life.*

> Perhaps you know this, that, of all peoples, we consume the most grain imported from beyond. Accordingly, the grain arriving to us from the Pontus is the same as all that from other emporia sailing it out. Reasonably so. For not only does this occur on account of this region having the most grain, but also owing to Leukon—having authority over this trade—giving exceptions to public taxes to those merchants bringing grain to Athens. Leukon announces that your ships will be filled with cargo first. That man, having this exemption for himself and his children, has granted the same exemption to all of you. Consider how much this exemption is. Leukon exacts a tariff of 1/30th on those exporting grain from this place (the Pontus). There are about 400,000 measurements of grain arriving here from there, and you can know this from the written accounts of the grain inspectors. Therefore from 300,000 measures, Leukon gives us 10,000, for the 10,000, about 3,000.
>
> He is, therefore, far from defrauding the *polis* of this gift, having opened another emporium at Theodosia,[1] which our sailors say is not inferior whatsoever to the Bosporus market. Here also he has given us an exemption. But I am silent about the other things, although I have many things to say regarding how much this man, both himself and his ancestors, has bestowed on you. But two years ago, when there was a grain shortage among all people, not only did he send sufficient grain to you but such that there was an additional coverage of 15 *talents* of silver which Callisthenes managed.
>
> *(Demosthenes 20,* Against Leptines *31–33)*

B. *An early Romano-Carthaginian treaty (509/508 BCE) established Carthaginian military and commercial jurisdiction over local waters.*

> The friendship between the Romans and the Roman allies and Carthage and the Carthaginian allies will be according to these conditions: neither the Romans nor their allies may sail beyond the Lovely Promontory unless they are compelled to do so by a storm or by enemies. If someone is driven beyond the promontory by force, it is not allowed to purchase in the marketplace or to take

1 On the Black Sea's northwestern coast.

away anything except what materials are necessary for the repair of the ship or for sacrifices. And he must depart within five days. As for those at hand for the purpose of commerce, there may be no transaction except in the presence of a herald or registrar.

(Polybius, Histories *3.22.4–8)*

C. *Well into the 2nd century BCE, the Phoenicians, whose settlements included Carthage, considered their trade routes proprietary.*

Earlier, only the Phoenicians engaged in this trade from Gades, concealing their sailing route from everyone. When the Romans followed some merchant-ship closely so that they themselves might know the markets, out of spite the captain purposely drove his ship off course to the shoals, leading those following him to the same destruction. He himself was saved by a piece of wreckage, and he took from the public treasury the value of the freight that he had lost.

(Strabo, Geography *3.5.11)*

D. *Here we have a lively account of the busy emporium at Muza.*

After these places in the very last bay on the left-hand side of the sea is a lawful emporium by the sea, Muza, about 12,000 *stadia* distant from Berenice for those sailing south. The whole market is crowded with Arab ship-owning folk and sailors and is bustling with trading-matters. For they have dealings with far-side trade and Barygaza with their own equipped ships.

(Anonymous, Erythraean Sea *21)*

E. *By the early 1st century CE, trade between Rome and India increased, with a hub at Alexandria.*

Before this, not 20 ships would be bold enough to cross over the Arabian Bay, as to peep through the narrows. But now large ships make ready as far as India and the Aethiopian edges, from which the most highly valued freight is brought to Egypt, and from there it is sent to other places, so that double tariffs are collected, on both imports and exports, and the tariff is steep on expensive wares. And indeed Egypt has a monopoly. Alexandria alone is the entrepot of such things for the most part and furnishes goods to those beyond.

(Strabo, Geography *17.1.13)*

F. *Some harbors, with their adjacent warehouses, were dedicated to the import of specific wares. Here we have an epitaph of a man who worked at the wine port.*

A money collector from the wine port lived [. . .] and he made (this monument) for his wife Calpia Quartilla who lived 70 years—when Nero, for the 5th time, and Trachalus were consuls (58 CE), you who have arrived at this obligation, don't refuse the Underworld.

(CIL *6.9190; cf.* CIL *6.9189)*

G. *The Torlonia Relief shows a busy harbor scene, dominated by a larger-than-life Neptune/Poseidon with his trident. Above Neptune, a nude Venus/Aphrodite holds a wreath over a lighthouse fire. A ship comes into port under sails decorated with Venus' descendants Romulus and Remus as they suckle the she-wolf. The two upper corners feature other deities: Liber (Dionysus) and Ceres (Demeter), both especially important to maritime commerce as the deities of wine and grain, respectively. In the upper right corner, Liber pours a wine libation, holding his thyrsus, accompanied by his panther. To his right, an elephant-drawn cart—a statue group atop a building—evokes Liber's exotic, eastern origin. Between Neptune and Liber, a large apotropaic eye appears under the yard arm of a moored ship with a furled sail. In the relief's upper left corner is Ceres with her cornucopia. Jupiter's eagle flutters in front. The sails of the ship putting in are inscribed VL ("a vow to Liber": in fulfillment of a promise for some unrecorded divine favor, from the temple of Liber near the port).*

FIGURE 6.1.1G The busy Port at Ostia: *Museo Torlonia #430; Drawn by Giovanni Montiroli 1866.* Delle due navi romane scolpite sul bassorilievo portuense del principe Torlonia dissertazione. *Roma: Tip. delle belle arti* (public domain).

H. *This 2nd-/3rd-century fragmentary Romano-Gallic bas-relief shows a river-boat, laden with freight, rowed by one man and hauled upstream by a brace of men.*

FIGURE 6.1.1H Bas-relief: Gallic River Boat: Cabrières d'Aigues (Vaucluse). With kind permission of Avignon, Musée Calvet Inv. 16273, Legs Marc Deydier à l'Institut Calvet, 1919.

I. *And here we have the remains of a flat-bottomed river barge from Arles (66–70 CE), discovered in 2004: 31 meters/102 feet long; about 10 feet across the beam (3 meters), with a capacity of about 21 tons (Marlier 2014: 66–71; Marlier et al. 2017).*

FIGURE 6.1.1I Remains of Gallic River Barge: AR6178751, photo credit: Manuel Cohen/Art Resource, NY.

6.1.2 Importing an Obelisk

Both Augustus (r. 27 BCE–14 CE) and Caligula (r. 37–41 CE) ordered special barges to convey obelisks from Egypt to Rome, ballasted by 120 bushels of lentils and with a capacity of 1,450 tons (Pomey and Tchernia 1978: 246, 249; Swetnam-Burland 2010). Augustus' obelisk (23.7 meters = 78 feet), brought to Rome in 10 BCE, formed the gnomon (casting the shadow) of a sundial in the Circus Maximus. Caligula imported another obelisk from Heliopolis in 37 CE, displayed in the Circus of Caligula.

> Above all things was the difficulty of conveying obelisks to Rome by sea, in ships gawked at to full measure. The divine Augustus dedicated the ship which conveyed the first obelisk in the permanent shipyards at Puteoli for the sake of a marvel; this one was consumed by fire. After a number of years, the divine Claudius preserved the ship on which Caligula imported his obelisk, more extraordinary than all the things which have ever been seen at sea. Since the turrets on it were made from Puteolean ash[2], Claudius sank the ship which was brought to Ostia for the sake of the harbor. Regarding this there was another concern about the ships which would convey the obelisk up the Tiber, by which trial it was clear that the Tiber was no less deep than in the Nile.
>
> *(Pliny,* NH *36.70; cf.* NH *16.201–202)*

6.1.3 The Mercantile Sailing Season

A. *This argument spuriously ascribed to Demosthenes, but delivered after his death (322 BCE), recounts the private action in an Athenian court brought by the businessman Dareios. With his partner Pamphilus, Dareios had made a loan to the merchants Dionysodoros and Parmeniscos for a trading voyage between Egypt and Athens. Dareios brought this action against Dionysodoros for breach of contract: Dionysodoros had made an unauthorized stop at Rhodes. Here we learn that ships and their crews were under contract for mercantile sails, and they were restricted by local regulations. For more on maritime loans: Carey and Reid 1985: 195–197.*

> Thus, from Egypt the brokers loaned silver to those men sailing to Athens when they arrived at Rhodes and they put their ship to port there. I think that they suffered nothing from remitting the interest and receiving their loan in Rhodes and then preparing to conduct business in Egypt. But this profited them much more than sailing to the second port (Athens). For sailing from there, Rhodes, is always seasonable, and they took the initiative to put this money to work two or three times. But staying at home, in Athens, it is necessary to winter here and

2 Roman concrete: #5.3.1, 5.3.3B.

to await the sailing season. Those loan brokers have thus made a profit and they laid out nothing more to these merchant mariners. For us, however, it is not a matter of profit but if we will be able to take back the principle.

(Demosthenenic Corpus 56 Dareios against Dionysodoros in the Matter of a Loan *29–30)*

B. *As noted elsewhere (#5.1.7B), the sailing season was complex and localized, but regulations were in place. In 380 CE, the emperors issued an edit restricting mercantile sea traffic: Gratian's prohibition likely applied only to state-controlled cargo from North Africa because of the great liability to the grain shipments (Beresford 2013: 23).*

The emperors Gratian, Valentinian, and Theodosius, Augusti send a greeting to the African ship-owners . . . It pleases us that in the month of November navigation will be ended and resumed for trade in the month of April, which is the month closest to the summer season. The necessity of this acceptance from the Kalends of April to the Kalends of October shall remain in effect.[3] But navigation will be extended to the Ides of those same months.

*(*Theodosian Codex *13.9.3)*

C. *Roman authors, nonetheless, implied that shipments came to Rome year-round. The grain fleet was at Ostia in February of 62* CE, *either wintering there or waiting to be unloaded (Tacitus,* Annals *15.18.2; Tuck 2019: 447). Here we see that Claudius (r. 41–54 CE) authorized wintertime grain shipments in response to the famine of 51 CE, enticing cautious merchants with perks and averting the crisis within two weeks (intimating that "that numerous grain freighters remained in a state of readiness throughout the winter months": Beresford 2013: 34; cf. Rickman 1980: 127).*

Very solicitously Claudius always gave care to the city's grain supply. When the Aemelianian[4] suburb burned unyieldingly, Claudius remained in the Diribitorium[5] for two nights. Since the crowd of imperial soldiers and personal slaves was deficient for rendering aid, through the magistrates he called people together from all the neighborhoods. And, after baskets of money were placed in front of him, he urged the people to help, displaying a worthy reward to each one for their effort. Moreover, during a grain shortage owing to drawn-out droughts, Claudius was once detained by a crowd in the middle of the Forum and attacked with outcries and at the same time with chunks of bread to such a degree that

3 Roman calendar: #4.5.2J§123 note.

4 A suburb north of Rome, outside the 4th century BCE Servian Wall.

5 The large structure—the largest under a single roof (Dio Cassius, *Roman History* 55.5)—in the Campus Martius where votes were cast, counted, and stored.

he prevailed to escape onto the Palatine with difficulty and only through a back door. Claudius then contrived every means for importing provisions even during the winter. He consequently proposed guaranteed profits to the businessmen, undertaking any losses upon himself if anything should happen to them from storms. And to those folk building ships for the purpose of trade, he offered great opportunities in order according to the terms of each rank: exemption from the *Lex Papia Poppaea* to a citizen,[6] the right of citizenship to a Latin ally,[7] to women the right of four children.[8] All these are preserved as granted to this day.

(Suetonius, Claudius *18–19)*

D. *Imperial prerogative was abused, and Domitian (r. 81–96 CE) received a gift of roses imported from Egypt during a famine. Martial would have preferred food crops. Marcus Valerius Martialis (c. 38/41–c. 102/104 CE) came to Rome from Bilbilis in southern Iberia. His extensive corpus includes 16 books of colorful epigrams, rich with keen observations of daily life in the city of Rome.*

Caesar, the Nilotic land, eager to please, had sent you roses as fresh gifts. The sailor from Pharos laughed at the Pharian gardens when he entered the first thresholds of your city. So great was the honor of spring and the grace of fragrant Flora (goddess of flowers), and so great was the glory of the Paestan countryside. Thus, wherever he bore his wandering steps and eyes, every path blushed with shorn wreaths. But you, Nile, ordered to yield to a Roman winter, send your crops, take back your roses.

(Martial, Epigram *6.80)*

E. *For Pliny, luxury imports from India were a sign of declining morality and increasing hedonism at Rome.*

This is a matter worthy of attention: in no year does India drain less than 50 million *sesterces* of the empire and send back merchandise which they sell with us at a 100% markup.

(Pliny, NH *6.101)*

F. *Publius Aelius Aristides Theodoros of Mysia (117–181 CE) was a Greek orator and devotee of Asklepios owing to frequent illnesses (including smallpox in 165 CE). His extant writings include over 50 orations and the* Sacred Tales *recording Asklepios' revelations to Aelius in dreams. This Oration,* To Rome, *is Aristides' most famous, delivered in Rome in 154/55 CE, detailing Rome's civil and military*

6 With provisions against celibacy and adultery, the *Lex Papia Poppaea* aimed to encourage marriage and the birth of legitimate citizen children. Such exemptions could be lucrative: Field 1945.

7 Including the right to vote, marry a freeborn person, and practice commerce.

8 Thus, no longer requiring a male guardian to conduct her financial (and social) affairs.

achievements and emphasizing Rome as a mirror of the perfect, ordered cosmos. See also Harris 2008. Here we have a lively description of Rome's eternally busy port that connects the entire world and all its goods to Rome.

> Around this sea continents slope great "over a vast space" (Homer, *Iliad* 16.776), always making your ports full with something from there. From every land and sea there has brought here whatever the seasons bring forth and what all the lands produce, as well as the rivers and marshes and the handicrafts of the Hellenes and Barbarians,[9] so that if anyone wanted to see all these things, it would be necessary to see them thus by visiting every inhabited land, or to be in this city. It is not possible that whatever is grown and manufactured among each peoples would not always abound here. So many provisioning ships under tow arriving here from all places at all times, at every turn of season, convey goods so that the city is like some common workshop of the earth. It is possible to see so many cargos from India, if you like, and Arabia Eudaimon,[10] that you might imagine that the trees remaining there are left bare and that it is necessary for the inhabitants to come here, begging for their own resources if they need something. In turn, clothing from the Babylonians and fashion accessories from the barbarian land beyond come in much greater quantities and more easily than if it were necessary that a freighter, conveying goods, put in at Athens from Naxos or Cynthos (in the Cyclades) there. Your farmlands are Egypt, Sicily, Libya, however much is tamed.[11] The arrivals and departures never leave off, so that it is possible to marvel not only at the harbor but also at the sea because it suffices for ships under tow: just as Hesiod said simply about the limits of Ocean, that it is a place where all things are connected within a channel into one beginning and to the same end (*Theogony* 736–741). And all things fall together here: commerce, seafaring, husbandry, the excavation of quarries, whatever skills exist and have existed, all things that are produced and grown. Whatever one does not see here, it is either not among things that ever existed or does not exist now.
>
> *(Aelius Aristides,* Oration *26:* Regarding Rome *11–13)*

6.2 Piracy

As long as there has been trade on the sea, there have been profiteers and sea robbers taking advantage of unarmed (or lightly armed) merchantmen across the Mediterranean and into the Erythraean Sea. See Casson 1991; de Souza 1999; Beresford 2013: 237–264.

9 #3.5.5D and note.

10 Arabia Eudaimon (Felix: "fertile, fruitful, fortunate, of good omens"), so-called because it seemed a prosperous "paradise on earth" (Diodorus Siculus, *Library of History* 2.49.1; Pliny, *NH* 5.65).

11 Libya (northern Africa), the Greek designation for the African continent: Herodotus, *Histories* 4.41.

A. *The Cyclops Polyphemus here distinguishes between trade and "piracy" as a career choice for energetic, adventurous men. In Homeric epic, piracy was the less disgraceful occupation, since traders were generally regarded as liars and cheats and pirates at least were transparent in their intentions.*

> Strangers, who are you? From where did you sail over the watery paths? Is it for business, or do you roam about recklessly over the salt-sea like pirates, who wander hazarding their souls and bringing evil to foreigners?
>
> *(Homer,* Odyssey *9.252–255; cf. 15.415)*

B. *Sea raiders took opportunistic advantage of bad sailing conditions and treacherous seabed topography.*

> Here (at Salmudessus), of the ships sailing to the Pontus, many run aground and are wrecked. For the shallows extend over much of the seabed. The Thracians living along these places—each group delimiting tracts with stones—loot the ships that fall within their own span.
>
> *(Xenophon,* Anabasis *7.5.12–13)*

C. *Coastal settlements were especially vulnerable to pirates, as at Aigiale on Amorgos in the Cyclades in the 3rd century BCE.*

> It was decided by the council and by the deme.[12] When the son of Soteres, Pheidos of Kosyllis, was presiding, the son of Philothemios, Philoxenos of Alsis, spoke. Since, attacking our territory at night and seizing young girls and even married women and other people, both free and enslaved—altogether more than 30—pirates laid waste to the ships in the harbor, and they took the ship of Doreios in which they left, having the bodies and other stuff which they took. When this happened, Hegesippos and Antipappos, sons of Hegesistratos, among those captured, joined in persuading Sokleidas, the leader of pirates, sailing with them, to release the free people and some of the freed-people and slaves. Hegesippos and Antipappos offered themselves as hostages to the pirates, indicating every desire that none of the free female citizens or male citizens be taken as plunder nor sold[13] nor suffer from violence and distress. Nor did any free citizen disagree, but, owing to Hegesippos and Antipappos, each captive was saved to a person, unharmed.
>
> Therefore, it seems good to the deme that Hegesippos and Antipappos each be crowned with a wreath of olive, on account of their deliberate actions and love of honor which they happened to perform towards those of the citizens who

12 A small district or village, organized as an administrative unit, distinct from the larger *polis.*
13 For piracy and the slave trade: de Souza 1999: 60–65; *IG* 11.4.1054A.

were captured. We will proclaim this decree at the Dionysia[14] during the contest of tragedians. Let the herald announce that the deme will crown Hegesippos and Antipappos on account of their excellence and love of honor towards those captured with them. This decree will be inscribed on a stele and stand in the temple of Athena Polias ("of the city state"). Hegesistratos, their father, will see to the inscribing.

(IG *12.7 386; cf.* IG *12.8 53)*

D. *In the early 2nd century BCE at Arkesine, also on Amorgos, Timessa, a wealthy woman citizen, paid a ransom to rescue her fellow citizens. This is one of the earliest decrees to honor the eugertism of a woman (such public recognition became more common in the 1st century BCE), and, unusually, her father's name is omitted.*

This seems good to the council and deme. Epigonos, son of Epigonos, spoke. Nikion, son of Philokrates, was presiding. When those of the citizens who arrived announced that Timessa, one of our female citizens, is well-minded to our *polis*, and that she does a good deed for any of the citizens who meet her because she is able, and in public she acts beneficently in the interest of the *polis* according to whatever good she can. After a misfortune occurred against our city, she made all haste for saving all the citizens who had been seized, as much as she was able.

Therefore, concerning these things, it seemed good to the council and the deme to commend Timessa and to crown her with an olive wreath for her deliberate action towards our deme, and that she will have preeminence in the assembly of the Itonia[15] and in all other citizen assemblies. We will announce her crown in the Itonia assembly together with other crowns. . .

(IG *12.7.36)*

E. *Rhodes was an important commercial and naval hub, and Demetrius Poliorcetes ("Besieger of Cities," r. 294–288 BCE) sought an alliance with Rhodes against Ptolemy I Soter ("Savior": r. 323–282 BCE). Rhodes rejected the alliance as well as Demetrius' demand to use the island's harbors. Demetrius then blockaded the city, and some of Demetrius' allied mercenary troops (including pirates: Diodorus*

14 Dionysus was a god of transformations (#3.2B–C) and theater. Throughout the Greek world, he was honored with annual festivals, *Dionysiae*, where tragedians produced sets of plays: three tragedies (not necessarily treating the same story arc but linked thematically) and a Satyr play, mimicking the structure of tragedy but presenting a tale with a lighter, comic, or even ribald touch, to relieve the intensity of tragedies performed one after the other.

15 Athena Itonia (who protects the *polis* of Itonos), attested especially in Thessaly. The cult was chthonic, connecting the goddess with Hades and the Underworld (Strabo, *Geography* 9.5.14; Pausanias, *Description of Greece* 1.13.2).

Siculus, Library of History *20.82.4) opportunistically tried to raid this rich but vulnerable* polis *under siege.*

> The Rhodians sent out three of their ships sailing best against the enemy ships and the fleet of merchantmen carrying supplies. These ships, appearing out of the blue, sank many of the merchantmen sailing for the sake of plundering local spoils. Dragging not a few ships onto the beach, they burnt them, and they escorted those of the prisoners able to pay a ransom to the *polis*: for the Rhodians agreed with Demetrius that they should give each other a ransom of 1,000 *drachmas* for a free person, 500 for a slave.
>
> *(Diodorus Siculus,* Library of History *20.84.6)*

F. *Greek sources described the Etruscans (inhabiting central to southern Italy) as pirates marauding the western Mediterranean.*

> Among the Romans, the Tyrrhenians are called Etruscans and Tuscans. But the Hellenes thus named them after Tyrrhenus, a son of Atys who furnished, so they say, settlers from Lydia here. During a famine and a barren stretch, Atys, one of those born from Herakles and Omphale,[16] since he had only two children, kept Lydus back by lot, and, collecting a crowd, he sent them out with his son Tyrrhenus. When Tyrrhenus arrived at the place, he called it Tyrrhenia after himself, and he peopled 12 cities, making Tarcon an *oikistes* ("colony founder")—after whom the *polis* Tarcynia is called—who, they say, because of his intelligence, was born with grey hair from childhood. At that time, therefore, marshalled under one leader, they had great strength. But in later times, their organized government was dispersed and broken up into *poleis* by the force of their neighbors submitting. For, leaving behind a fortunate land, they would not otherwise have put to the sea to follow a life of piracy, some turning to one and other seas. But whenever they worked together, they were sufficient not only in warding off those who laid hands on them but also in making counterattacks and accomplishing long voyages.
>
> *(Strabo,* Geography *5.2.2)*

G. *A naval station was erected at Rhegium (in Italy's "toe") as a watch-station against piracy.*

> Next there follows Scyllaion, a lofty rock forming a peninsula. Its isthmus is low and accessible on both sides. Anaxilaus (d. 476 BCE), the tyrant[17] of Rhe-

16 A mythic queen of Lydia who placed a winning bid on Herakles when he was sentenced to a year of slavery to pay a blood debt. The year was spent amorously (Apollodorus, *Library* 2.6.3; Diodorus Siculus, *Library of History* 4.31.5).

17 Tyrants: #2.2.11H note.

gium, fortified the place against the Tyrrhenians. Establishing a naval station there, he stripped the pirates of their passage through the strait.

(Strabo, Geography *6.1.5)*

H. *In 75 BCE, crossing to Rhodes, Julius Caesar was famously kidnapped by pirates off Pharmakousa in the Aegean Sea.*

But after the civil dissension had been settled, Caesar charged Cornelius Dolabella,[18] an ex-consul and triumphal general, with extortion. Dolabella was acquitted, and Caesar decided to retire to Rhodes both to avoid Dolabella's enmity and that he, Caesar, with rest and leisure, might give some attention to Apollonios Molo, at that time a very famous teacher of oratory. While Caesar crossed during the winter months, around the island Pharmakousa he was seized by pirates and, with only his physician and two body-servants, he remained with the pirates without any disdain for about 40 days. For, at first, he immediately sent his companions and the rest of the slaves to procure money with which he might be ransomed. Then, after 50 *talents* were counted out, Caesar was set on shore, and, once his fleet turned around from its course, he did not delay in pursuing the pirates as they went their way and were brought back to their place of power. But he weakened them with the punishment which he had often threatened as a joke.[19]

(Suetonius, Caesar *4)*

I. *Despite several initiatives to quell piracy in the east, it endured, especially in the 60s BCE off the coast of Cilicia. At first the locals may have had legitimate grievances as they responded to political instability and foreign incursions into their waters. But they were uniformly presented as vicious and exploitive (Appian,* Mithridates *92; Dio Cassius,* Roman History *36.20–23; Plutarch,* Pompey *24). They attacked ships opportunistically, raided islands and coastal cities, and engaged heavily in the slave trade (#6.2C). They had also devised an early form of "walking the plank" for any captive who, like the apostle Paul (Acts 22.25–28), tried to appeal on the strength of Roman citizenship. The Cilician pirates were eventually quelled by Pompey, who received a special senatorial commission.*

Piratical power was stirred up first in Cilicia, having its beginning as foolhardy and unseen. But during the Mithridatic War,[20] it acquired spirit and courage, sup-

18 Consul in 81 BCE, allied with Sulla during the civil war, and was thus Caesar's political rival (Caesar supported Marius). Dolabella received a triumph in 77 for his campaigns over the Thracians. Civil dissension: Marius' loss to Sulla in the civil war of 88 BCE; see #5.2.4G introduction.

19 Humanely, Caesar first slit their throats and then crucified them (Suetonius, *Caesar* 74.1). Crucifixion was a slow, lingering method of execution.

20 The third Mithridatic War (73–63 BCE) under Mithridates VI Eupator ("from a noble father"), king of Pontus (r. 135–63 BCE).

plying themselves to the royal rowers. Then, while the Romans dashed against each other in civil war around the gates of Rome,[21] the sea, bereft of a watch-guard, drew the Cilician pirates in little by little and persuaded them no longer to attack only sailors but also to devastate the islands and *poleis* by the sea. Those men, already powerful because of their wealth and illustrious owing to their birth and deeming it worthy to apply their prudence, embarked and participated on piratical ships since the work brought some reputation and distinction.

In many places there were even piratical anchorages and beacon-towers built-up. And, for their particular work, fleets put in here, adorned not only with the abundance of the crews filling out the ships' complements, but also with the skill or dexterity of the helmsmen and the swiftness and lightness of ships. But even more than terror, their invidiousness and arrogance were vexing: with golden masts and purple sails and silver oar blades, as if reveling and showing off in their evil-doing. Their flutes and seven-stringed citharas and drunkenness along every headland and their seizures of people in authority and ransoming of cities taken by the spear, all these things were a source of reproach to the Roman leadership. For there were over 1,000 pirate ships, more than 400 cities taken by the spear.

Moreover, they devastated holy places,[22] inviolate and not to be trodden, attacking the Clarion sanctuary, Didymaion, Samothracian, the temple of Chthonian Earth at Hermione, of Asklepios at Epidaurus, of Poseidon at Isthmus and Taenarum and Calauria, of Apollo at Actium and Leucas, of Hera at Samos, Argos, and at Lacinium. They also offered their own strange burnt offerings at Olympus and they observed some forbidden liturgies, of which the rites of Mithras are maintained up to now, discovered first by them.[23]

21 See #5.2.4G.

22 This catalogue includes the most sacred sites of the Greek gods, and the Cilician treatment of them is an act of *hubris* (arrogance against the gods): the eventual downfall of the Cilician pirates could consequently be construed as divine justice. *Clarion*: an oracular sanctuary to Apollo at Claros on the Ionian coast. *Didymaion*: an oracular sanctuary of Apollo near Miletus. *Samothracian*: #3.11.8. *Chthonian Earth*: Demeter as a goddess of the soil (or death) at Hermione, on the southeastern corner of the easternmost Peloponnesian peninsula. *Asklepios at Epidaurus*: #2.2.4D note. *Poseidon at Isthmus*: where he was honored with quadrennial Panathenaic games that may have included ship races. *Taenarum*: at the southern end of the middle Peloponnesian peninsula where Poseidon was honored with a cave cult (caves were considered to be entrances to the Underworld). *Calauria*: an island between Epidaurus and Hermione with an ancient temple of Poseidon; *Actium and Leucate*: #7.4.3D; *Samos*: an island in the eastern Aegean, an ancient cult site of Hera established by the 8th century BCE (Strabo, *Geography* 14.1.14; Pausanias, *Description of Greece* 7.4). *Argos*: in the eastern Peloponnese with a Hera sanctuary, and where she reputedly renewed her virginity annually (scholiast on Homer *Iliad* 1.609; Pausanias, *Description of Greece* 2.38.2). *Lacinium*: in southern Italy at the "ball" of the foot, where Hera was worshipped as the eponymous Lacinia with a splendid temple cult.

23 *Forbidden*: "secret/mystery," see #3.11.8 introduction. Mithras was imported to Rome from Persia, where the cult was popular in the 2nd and 3rd centuries CE, especially with soldiers and traders and other traveling professionals. *Mithras'* origins are in Persian Zoroastrianism, which promotes a cosmology of good and evil, where good ultimately triumphs, overseen by the benevolent Ahura Mazda, a god of wisdom.

But, most of all, insulting the Romans, coming up from the sea, they even plundered the roads and sacked nearby country houses. Once they also seized two generals, Sextilius and Bellinus,[24] in their purple-edged togas, and carried them away and at the same time those they had with them, their subordinates and lictor-bearers.[25] Also captured was the daughter of Antonius, a triumphal man, as she traveled to the country and was ransomed for a great deal of money.[26]

But this was the most outrageous: whenever some prisoner of war shouted that he was Roman and declared his name, the pirates, feigning amazement and fear, would beat their thighs, and supplicate him as they entreated their captive to show leniency; and the Roman would be persuaded, seeing them humbled and begging. Then some pirates would put Roman boots on their prisoner's feet, and others would throw a cloak round him, so that indeed there would be no further misunderstanding. After railing thus and making sport of the man for a long time, finally they tossed over a rigs-ladder in mid-ocean, and they cheerfully commanded him to alight and disembark. And, pushing him off, they would dunk him under the water. This piratical power encroached our entire sea at once so that it became un-sailable and inaccessible to all trade.

(Plutarch, Pompey *24–25.1)*

J. *Under Roman law, ships' captains were not liable for losses from shipwrecks or piracy. After the defeat of senatorial forces at Philippi, Marcus Antistius Labeo (c. 54 BCE–10/11 CE) withdrew from political life and devoted himself to jurisprudence. His staunch republicanism was admired by Tacitus (*Annals *3.75.2).*

Labeo writes that if anything is destroyed by shipwreck or the force of pirates, it is not unfair that an exception (of liability) be given to the captain.

(Ulpian, On the Edict *66 [*Digest *4.9.3.1])*

6.3 Harvesting the Sea

The sea is a source of wealth, from fish and other seafoods to sponges used medicinally and luxury goods including pearls, harvested by diving, fishing, and cultivation.

24 Publius Sextilius, praetor in 92 BCE. As governor of Africa (88 BCE), he denied asylum to Marius after his defeat by Sulla (Plutarch, *Marius* 40.3–4; Appian, *Civil War* 1.62). Bellinus, a shadowy character, cited only here.

25 Carrying fasces, lictors preceded high-ranking Roman magistrates on official business, serving as personal bodyguards and an emblem of importance. Fasces are bundles of sticks bound with an axe, symbolizing the authority of life and death over fellow Roman citizens held by praetors, consuls, censors, and provincial governors while in office.

26 Marcus Antonius (143–87 BCE; consul, 99 BCE) was governor of Cilicia in 102 BCE where he campaigned against piracy and won a triumph (hence, he was "triumphal"). In retaliation, the pirates kidnapped his daughter Antonia from a family estate near Misenum (Cicero, *For the Manilian Law about the authority of Gnaeus Pompey* 33).

6.3.1 Sponge Cutters

Diving was a valuable skill. For military divers: #5.1.6. Here we have Oppian's detailed account of diving for sponges. This passage aligns closely with #2.2.12F in tone and theme.

612. I say that there is not any toil worse nor work more woeful for human folk than sponge cutting. Truly, first of all, when they are armed for their struggles, they take an interest in food and rather weak drinks, and they are ameliorated by sleep that is not appropriate for fishermen. As when a man prepares himself for a sweet-sounding contest, playing a tune well on the phorminx,[27] delivering a prayer for Apollo, he gives a thought to every detail, in every way he keeps watch, enriching the strain of his clear-voiced song. So steadfastly do the sponge cutters pay cheerful attention that their breath may be unscathed when they descend to the depth and that they might recover from their earlier exertion. But when they struggle to complete this great toil, praying to the blessed gods, guardians of the deep salt-water, beseeching that they, the gods, defend them, the sponge cutters, from calamity against sea monsters, and that might not meet with any ruin in the sea. If they gaze on a "beautiful fish," then great courage comes to them. For the beautiful fish does not swim in those pasturages where there is an unapproachable sea monster nor a dangerous beast nor where any nautical calamity appears. But the beautiful fish always delights in clean and wholesome paths. And, so, they call it the "holy fish."[28]

634. Rejoicing in this beautiful fish, the sponge cutters lay into their labors. A man is girt at his waist with a long cable. In both palms he grasps a mass of lead, taking hold of it. In his right hand, he stretches out a well-pointed hook, and in the jaws within his mouth he carries white oil. Standing at the prow, he examines the sea's swells, turning over in his mind his weighty task and the indescribable expanse of water. Encouraging him, his companions urge him on to his toil with daring words, as when a man has taken his stand, skilled in racing around the turning post, swift of foot. But when he has taken courage in his heart, the sponge cutter leaps into the eddying waves. The hurling onrush of the weighted mass of gray lead drags him down.

646. When arriving at the seabed, he spits out the oil, and it glitters greatly, and its gleam mixes with the water, as when a beacon flame shines its eye in the dusky darkness. Coming near the rocks, the diver sees the sponges which grow on the bottommost flat ledges, clinging on the sea rocks. Convention says

27 An ancient instrument with two to seven strings over a crescent-shaped sound box, common in Homer day's but falling out of favor. Oppian may here mean a kithara, a seven-stringed, sophisticated version of the lyre.

28 #3.11.13.

that there is breath in the sponges,[29] such as also in other things that grow on the far-sounding sea rocks.

653. Straightaway rushing at the sponges, with the stout hook in his hand, just like some reaping man, the sponge cutter cuts the sponges' frames. Nor is he about to tarry. He shakes the cable swiftly, as signs for his companions to draw him up quickly. For hateful blood is immediately trickled from the sponges and twists around the diver. With its rank breath it chokes the man, holding its heavy sap in the sponge cutter's nostrils. Therefore, the diver emerges to the top of the water, dragged up as swift as thought. Someone seeing him flying up to the surface of the sea would rejoice and at the same time mourn, pitying him. Thus, relaxing in his frame, his limbs are loosened with fear and heart-grieving toil. Very often coming upon his hated and ungentle prey, leaping into the depth of the sea, no longer does the sponge cutter emerge, ill-fated, meeting an ugly, monstrous wild beast face-to-face. Often shaking the cable for his companions, he commands them to draw him up. But the strength of the sea monster and the accompanying men tug at the sponge cutter's body—pitiable to see—still longing for the ship and his companions. Grieving, they nimbly leave behind that passageway and their baneful toil, and they return to dry land, weeping over the remains of their unfortunate companion.

(Oppian, Fishing *5.612–674)*

6.3.2 Fishing Gear

A. *Greco-Roman commercial and sport fishermen employed four methods of fishing, each with its own moral currency.*

There are four methods, they say, of hunting beasts in water: nets and pole-fishing and with creels and additionally with a hook. Net-fishing is wealth-producing and similar to taking a camp and seizing prisoners of war. It requires various equipment such as esparto and linen, white and black, and galingale and cork-oak and lead and pine and leather straps and sumac and stone and papyrus and horns (yardarms) and a ship with six oars and an axle (windlass) and bars and a *cottane*[30] and a drum and iron and wood and pitch. Differing types of fish and a herd, variegated and many, fall into the net.

Pole-fishing is the manliest of these different methods, and it requires a hunter strong of body. It is necessary that he have a straight pole of fir-wood and esparto cord and firesticks of oily pine, and he needs a small boat and rowers, eager and good with their arms.

29 Aristotle had suggested that sponges have reasoning ability: *HA* 487b9; cf. Pliny, *NH* 9.148, Plutarch, *Whether Land or Sea Animals are Cleverer* 980c.

30 A mechanical device?

Creel-fishing is the most deceitful and frightfully treacherous, and it seems the least distinguished for free men. It requires club-rushes, unsoaked, and twigs and a large pebble and a nest and seaweed and rush and cypress foliage and cork-oak and bait and a small boat.

Hook-fishing is the most skilled, most suitable for free men. It requires horsehair, colored white and black and fiery red and half-gray. Of dyed hair, they select sea gray and sea purple. The rest, they say, are bad. They also use the straight bristles of wild pigs and terebinth and a great deal of bronze and lead and esparto and feathers, especially white and black and dappled. Salt-fishermen use crimson wool and purple sea-wool and cork-oak and wood. There is a need of iron and other things, among which are reeds, straight and unsoaked, and dipped club-rushes and fennel and a pole of cherry wood and the horns and hide of a goat. Some fish are caught in one way and others in other ways.

(Aelian, NA *12.43; cf. Agatharchides,* On the Erythraean Sea *5.32–33; Strabo,* Geography *15.1.2; Anonymous,* Erythraean Sea *2; Marzano 2013: 57–58)*

B. *Fishermen used baited creels to lure cuttlefish. See also #6.5.1B§132.*

Fishermen also trick cuttlefish with creels in the springtime. Covering the creels over with saplings of tamarisk or foliage of sprouting strawberry plants or some soft wool, they situate them on a very sandy seashore. Desiring a family and intercourse, the cuttlefish hurry to the creel and they settle within the foliage, and they bring their desire to an end. They also bring their miserable life to an end, drawn up by the clever fishermen.

(Oppian, Fishing *4.164–171)*

C. *At the Menuthias Islands in the Erythraean Sea, fishermen used baskets or wicker traps instead of nets to catch turtles and fish.*

In this same place there are stitched boats and boats from a single log (i.e., a dug-out canoe), which they use for fishing and hunting turtles, and, on this same island, they hunt turtles in a particular way with wicker baskets, instead of nets, placing them along the narrows of the breakers.

(Anonymous, Erythraean Sea *15)*

6.3.3 Luring and Catching Fish

A. *Fishermen took advantage of many conditions to improve their catch, such as fishing in low light.*

Female fish are larger than males. Among a certain type there are no males at all, such as the red tuna and sea perch: for they are all caught heavy with eggs.

The scaly ones of this kind wander in flocks. They are caught before the sun's rising. At that time the fishes' vision especially fails. At night they rest, but on clear nights they see as well as by day. They also say that, if the seabed is ground up, it makes a difference to the catch, and so more are caught in the second hauling than the first. Fish especially rejoice in the taste of oil, then also by moderate rainfalls, and they are nourished by these things. To be sure, although generated in a swamp, reeds grow without rain, and fishes, constantly in the same water, die if the water does not flow out.

(Pliny, NH *9.56; cf. Aristotle,* HA *8.19.602a)*

B. *Fishermen employ patience and tricks to lure* anthias *fish in the Swallow Islands, off southern Asia Minor.*

180. Nor is it fitting to be silent about the *anthias* fish with respect to things that, I observe, many people have believed. We have talked about the Chelidoniae ("Swallow") Islands, of Asia's rocky sea, situated in front of a promontory of Mt. Taurus. Here the fish is constant and quickly caught by one method. In a small boat and in the same color clothing as the boat at the same hour for several continuous days, the fisherman sails out to a certain distance and tosses out bait. Whatever might be changed in this routine is suspected as deceit by the prey, and the fish is cautious because it is afraid.

181. When this is often done, one *anthias*, finally lured by the familiarity of the routine, attacks the bait. This one is marked with careful effort as the author and promoter of hope for the haul. Nor is it difficult since for several days this one alone dares to approach. At length, the first *anthias* even finds others, and, attended by a few more, little by little the leader-fish finally leads a countless flock. Now, the oldest ones are accustomed to recognize the fisherman and take food from his hand. Then, throwing a hook fixed on the bait a little beyond his fingers, the fisherman rushes at individual ones rather than capturing them, snatching them up from the shadow of the boat with a quick try lest the others perceive what's happening, while someone else in the boat picks up the catch in rags lest any agitation or sound drives the rest off.

182. It is profitable to know your decoy-fish for this reason, that he may not be caught as the school is about to flee. They say that a quarrelling fisherman, lying in wait for a very well-known leader-fish, caught it with nefarious desire. Mucianus adds that the leader-fish was recognized in the market by the fisherman for whom the loss of the fish was an injury, and that a contract of losses was drawn up and that the first fisherman was condemned in a trial, after which charges were estimated. Likewise, when *anthias* fish see that one of their own is held with a hook, they are said to cut the line with spines that they have on their serrated backs: the captured fish stretches out the line so that it is able to be cut.

(Pliny, NH *9.180–182)*

C. *Bright lights (and gleaming gems) scare the fish away.*

On this island (Cyprus) on a tomb of prince Hermias next to the sea-farms, they say that emerald eyes, inserted in a marble lion, were shining so brightly even into the deep that the tuna fled in terror. For a long time, the fishermen wondered at this strangeness until they changed the gems in the eyes.

(Pliny, NH *37.66)*

D. *Fishing for* galeotes *(swordfish) in the strait of Messina between Italy and Sicily.*

Saying these things, Polybius explains hunting for *galeotai*, an activity that is organized around Scylla's Rock. Thus, a lookout takes point, common for the many fishermen who bob about in two-oared skiffs, two men to each skiff. One man sets the boat in motion and the other stands at the prow holding a spear when the lookout indicates the appearance of the *galeotes*. The creature is seen with a third part of its body above water. When the skiff makes an approach, one man strikes it close and then pulls the spear out of the body, up to the pointed tip. For it is purposely hooked and fitted loosely to the spear, and it has a long cord fastened on it. Then they loosen this line from the wounded fish until he is weary from his struggles and trying to escape. Then the fishermen drag the *galeotes* to land or receive him into the skiff, if his body is not entirely large. But if the spear falls into the sea, it is not lost: it is built from oak and silver-fir, so that, when the oak sinks on account of its weight, the rest is on the surface and easy to recover.[31] Sometimes the rower in the skiff is wounded on account of the size of the *galeotai's* swords and because the animal's sharp point and style of hunting is like a wild boar's.

(Strabo, Geography *1.2.16 = Polybius,* Histories *34.2)*

E. *Some fishermen employed several methods simultaneously to improve their success, as in this vivid description of a painting of a busy scene that shows tuna both as they migrate from the Black Sea and as fishermen are hunting the tuna (cf. Marzano 2013: 71–72). For Philostratus and his* Images *see #3.4.2A.*

"Why then do you not go to another painting? This one about the Bosporus has been sufficiently explained for me." What do you say? It remains for me to talk about the fishermen, as I said I would at the beginning. So that we not relate the small points, but instead those worthy to discuss, let us set aside discussion with

31 Compare the "balloons" employed by whalers: #2.2.12F§176 and note.

respect to those hunting with a rod or employing creels or if anyone drew up a net or dashed a trident—for you will hear a little about these things and they will seem to you to be rather embellishments of the painting itself—let's see those men putting their hand to catching the tuna. Those fishermen are worthy of discussion because of the scale of the hunt. The tuna travel back and forth from the outer sea from the Pontus, having their birth in it and there grazing on fishes and slime and other juices, which the Ister and Maeotis bring to it, because of which the Pontus is sweeter and more drinkable than any other sea, and they swim like a phalanx of soldiers, in eights and sixteens and twice as many, they surge beneath each other, one swimming over another such that their depth is the same as their breadth.

The methods, therefore, by which they are caught are infinite. For iron is sharpened against them and drugs are sprinkled on them, and a small net suffices for whomever some small portion of the school is sufficient.

Indeed, the best hunting is this: someone looks out from a lofty tree, a man quick at counting, capable with respect to vision. He must fix his eyes on the sea, as far as they can reach, and if he sees fish approaching, he must shout loudly towards those in the light boats, and he declares their number and countlessness. The fishermen, corralling the fish with a deep net that can be closed, receive a radiant catch by which even the leader of the hunt is ready to assist.

Look now at these very duties. The lookout watches over the sea, sending his eyes in all directions for a reckoning of their number. In the grey foam of the sea, these are the colors of the fish: those above seem black, those that follow are less so. After them, the tuna deceive the sight, now shadowy, now watery. For, descending to the water, vision is blunted at examining objects in it, and the group of fishermen is charming, and they are tanned in color from being sunburnt. One yokes an oar, another rows with bulging arms, another urges on the fisherman nearby, another punches a guy not rowing. The fish are already falling at the net, the fishermen's shouts are raised up. Some fish they have caught, some they are catching. At a loss over what they will do with such a quantity, they open the net and allow some to flee and escape. They revel at such a great hunt in their hearts.

(Philostratus the Elder, Images *1.13; cf. Oppian,* Fishing *3.637–644)*

F. *The Villa of the Nile Mosaic shows a variety of fishing techniques. From left to right: men in boats spear fish with tridents and harpoons; men drag a net with a heavy haul; men in the water set a net; a man crouching on shore holds a portable "butterfly" net to help land the fish he has just caught with his rod; an older fisherman sits on a rock as he prepares his rod.*

FIGURE 6.3.3F Fishing mosaic: villa of the Nile Mosaic Archeological Museum of Tripoli: ART416190, photo credit: © Gilles Mermet/Art Resource, NY.

6.3.4 Sport Fishing

A. *According to Plato, fishing is a lazy and morally inferior sport that does not befit gentlemen.*

> After these prefatory remarks, there will be moderate approval and censure of hunting in order, approving whichever produces better souls in our youth, censuring the opposite. Let us then say after this, addressing the youth with a wish: my friends, may neither any yearning nor love of hunting in the sea take hold of you, nor of pole-fishing, nor of hunting altogether animals living in water, nor with creels (for you) laboring at lazy hunting whether you are energetic or asleep. Nor, in turn, may desire of piracy or hunting people in the sea, coming upon you, make you crude and lawless. Nor may theft, in the country and city, come to your furthest mind. Nor in turn may the wily love of hunting birds, excessively unsuitable for free people, seize any of our youth. For our athletes, the only remaining hunting is indeed hunting on foot.
>
> (*Plato,* Laws *7.823d–824a*)

B. *Marc Antony enjoyed fishing for pleasure, but he also cheated to show off.*

> To describe many of the boyish games played by Antony would be very silly. Once going fishing and having bad luck, he was annoyed since Cleopatra was there. He then ordered his fishermen, diving down, to fasten some fish from the earlier catch to his hook, drawing out two or three. But this did not deceive the Egyptian woman. Pretending to marvel, she described the episode to her friends, and she summoned them to see it the next day. After many embarked into fishing boats and Antony let his fishing-line fall, Cleopatra commanded one of her own entourage, hurrying off and swimming to Antony's hook, to pierce a Pontic *tarichos* (salted codfish?) to it. Persuaded that he had something, Antony drew it up. Since there was laughter, as is natural, Cleopatra said, "Autocrat, hand your rod to us, the fishermen of Pharos and Canopus. Your hunt is for cities and kingdoms and lands."
>
> (*Plutarch,* Antony *29.3–4*)

C. *Pliny the Younger makes a casual reference to recreational fishing on Lake Como in Cisalpine Gaul.*

> Gaius Plinius to his friend Caninius, greetings: are you studying or fishing or hunting or all at the same time? All three pursuits are able to be done at the same time at our Larium estate. For the lake supplies fish, the woods by which the lake is surrounded supply beasts, and that very noble retreat of yours furnishes abundant places for study.
>
> (*Pliny the Younger,* Epistle *2.8.1*)

D. *Antoninus Pius (r. 138–161 CE) was also fond of fishing. For the* SHA *see #2.1.6K introduction.*

Antoninus Pius loved the theatrical arts, he entertained himself with fishing and hunting a great deal, and with walking with friends and conversation. He spent the grape-harvest time with his friends like a private citizen.

(SHA, Antoninus Pius *11.2)*

6.3.5 Invasive Species

Parrotfish were introduced to Italian waters and protected to ensure that their numbers thrived, raising a question about their environmental effects. Most parrotfish are herbivores.

Preference is now given to the parrotfish, which alone of the fishes is said to ruminate and feed on grasses and not on other fishes. It is especially common in the Carpathian Sea (southern Aegean). It never willingly crosses the Lecton promontory in the Troad. When Tiberius Claudius was emperor (r. 14–37 CE), Optatus, one of his freedmen and overseer of the fleet, sprinkled the parrotfish between Ostia and the coast of Campania after they had been imported from the Carpathian Sea. Care was taken that, for a five-year period, they would be returned to the sea if caught. Afterwards they are found so frequently on the coast of Italy, not caught there before this time. Thus, gluttony has supplied flavors for itself with sown fishes and has bestowed a new resident in the sea, lest anyone also marvel that foreign birds are present in Rome.

(Pliny, NH *9.63)*

6.3.6 Fish Migrations

A. *Fishermen studied and took advantage of natural migratory patterns.*

"Fluid" is the name of a sea creature wise at knowing the passage of the seasons. At any rate when winter begins, escaping the icy cold, these fish take their rest, and happily they warm themselves in an equal, brotherly fashion. Then in the spring, they begin to swim out along longer spans and they graze on food, not only what they come upon but also what they track and then catch.

(Aelian, NA *9.46)*

B. *Mackerels migrated into the Black Sea after wintering in the Sea of Marmara.*

Pontic mackerel imitate the king of the Persians, wintering at Susa and summering in Ecbatana in the Zagros mountains.[32] For these fish winter in the sea called Propontis. For that land is still warm. But they spend the warm months near Aegialus (in Paphlagonia): the formerly mentioned sea offers them gentle winter breezes.

(Aelian, NA *10.6)*

32 Running southeast to northwest from Iran to Turkey. Susa: #1.7.E.

C. *Tuna migrations.*

Types of tuna are made in Ocean with broad ways, and they migrate to the tillage of our sea when they are goaded by the rage of mating in springtime. First, long-haired Iberian men hunt them within the Iberian salt-sea. Then, by the mouth of the Rhodanus River, Celtic hunters, long ago said to be inhabitants of Phocaea, and third whoever dwell on the Trinakrian island and by the waves of the Tyrsenian Sea.[33] There in the boundless depths, they migrate to one place or another and they sail over the entire sea.

(Oppian, Fishing *3.620–630)*

6.3.7 Fish Farms and Fishponds

A. *Fish were broadly cultivated commercially and privately.*

Stranger: I know that you have not happened upon fish placed in the Nile and in royal lakes. But perhaps you have observed those in fountain houses.

Young Socrates: Certainly. I have gazed at these, and I've heard many things about those foreign preserves.

(Plato, Statesman *264c)*

B. *A culinary delicacy, eels were cultivated in tanks.*

Regarding eels, in some places they are nourished on mud and grain if someone tosses it in. Nevertheless, most eels are nourished on potable water, and eel-cultivators take care of this in order that it be especially clean, always flowing away and flowing over flat surfaces. Or the eel-cultivators plaster the tanks. Eels thus quickly suffocate if the water is not clean: for they have small gills. Consequently, when men hunt eels, they agitate the water. In the Strymon River,[34] eels are caught around the rising of the Pleiades.[35] For at that time the water and mud are stirred up by the winds coming from the opposite direction. Otherwise, it is expedient to have quiet.

(Aristotle, HA *592a1–11; cf. Pliny,* NH *9.75)*

C. *A large fishpond at Acragas, Sicily.*

The Acragantini also equipped an extravagant swimming bath, with a perimeter of seven *stadia*, a depth of 20 *pecheis*. After river and spring waters were brought into it, it became a fishpond offering many fishes for eating and enjoying. Since

33 *Phocaea*: Western Turkey, settling Massalia (Marseille; Pliny, *NH* 3.5). *Trinakrian* ("three-pointed"): Sicily. *Tyrsenian Sea*: Tyrrhenian.

34 #5.3.5f§24.

35 Between October and April.

many swans flew down to it, there was agreement that its appearance was delightful. But, neglected in later times, it became clogged. And after a long time, it was destroyed. But the locals made the whole place, being good, a vineyard and thick with trees of every type, so that they took a great deal of profit from it.

(Diodorus Siculus, Library of History *11.25.4–5; cf. Athenaeus,* Learned Banqueters *12.541f)*

D. *Enclosures for different types of fishes.*

16.7. After purchasing islands or maritime lands, if someone will not be able to harvest fruits of the land on account of the soil's poorness as is generally the case near the coast, let him establish an economic return from the sea. The beginning of this enterprise, as it were, is to examine the nature of the place where you have decided to make your *piscinae* (fishponds): for not every type of fish is able to be kept on all shores. A muddy spot produces a flat-fish, like sole, turbot, sparrow-fish. The same condition is especially suitable for shellfish: purple-murexes, then mussels, oysters, small scallops, sea-mussels, or spring-oysters. Sandy swirls are not altogether the worst for flat fishes, but they are better for cultivating deep-sea fishes, like the golden fish and toothed fish, and also the Punic and indigenous shadow-fish. But sandy swirling waters are less suitable for shellfish. Further, a rocky sea best nurtures fish of its own name, which, to be sure, because they stable themselves among the rocks (*saxa*), are called *saxatiles*, such as sea-carp and thrush-fishes and nonetheless the black-tailed fish.

16.9. And it is fitting to know the differences between shores and straits, lest foreign fishes deceive us. For not every fish can exist in every sea: like the sturgeon which is fed in no other place than in the Pamphilian depth;[36] or like the dory in the Atlantic, which is counted among the most noble fishes in our municipality of Gades[37] and which we call "Zeus" according to an old practice; like the parrotfish which leaves the shores of all of Asia and Greece as far as Sicily but has never swum into the Ligustican Sea,[38] nor through Gallic waters to the Iberian Sea. So, even if, captured, they were conveyed to our fish-preserves, they would be unable to be kept there for any length of time. Although from the Tartessian and Carpathian Seas,[39] which are very distant, alone of the valuable fishes, the murena endures a foreign sea in whatever water it is a guest.

17.1. But now we must talk about situating *piscinae*. We consider the exceptionally best *piscina* to be the one that is positioned so that the water following the sea removes the earlier water (i.e., tides), nor does it allow old debris to remain within the enclosure. For that type is most like the sea, which, agitated by the winds, is constantly renewed, nor is it able to grow hot,

36 A southerly coastal region of central Turkey.
37 Columella was from southern Iberia: see #2.1.3E.
38 North of Corsica.
39 *Tartessian*: the gulf off southwestern Iberia. *Carpathian*: southern Aegean.

because a cold wave rolls up from the deep into the higher part. This pool, moreover, is cut out from rock—this happens very rarely—or it is built on the shore from plastered work. But, however it is constructed, if it is always cold because of an inflowing swirl, it ought to have a cavity near the bottom: some of these should be simple and straight where the scaley flocks can withdraw, others twisted into a spiral, not too spacious, in which the murena might hide themselves. Although it is not pleasing to some cultivators to mix these with fishes of other markings because, if they are vexed by madness—a thing which is accustomed to happen to this type of creature as to dogs[40]—they very often chase after the scaly fish and consume many of them by chewing on them. If the nature of the place permits, it is fitting that pathways be given along each side of the *piscina*: for the old water is moved out more easily when an outlet spreads open on the opposite side from where a wave is pressing on. Moreover, we believe that these passages should be made at the deepest part of the enclosure, if the situation of the place is suitable, so that when a water-plummet is placed at the bottom of the pond, it shows that it is seven paces higher than the surface of the sea. For such a measurement of the swirling water to this height is ample for the fish of the pond. There is no doubt but that the deeper the sea from which the water comes, the colder it is, a thing which is very suitable for the fish.

17.4. Moreover, if the place where we decide to establish the fish-preserve is equal with the level of the sea, the *piscina* should be dug out to nine paces, and the streams should be led along channels about two paces from the highest part, and care must be taken that the waters come abundantly, since the water lying beneath the level of the sea is only pressed out as a greater force of freshwater advances in. Many think that, in ponds of this kind, long recesses and hollows full of twists ought to be fabricated on the sides for the fish so there might be shadier hiding places from the heat. But if fresh seawater does not continually pass through the pond, to do this is counter productive. For a reservoir of this type does not easily admit waters, and it ejects old waters with difficulty. And putrid water causes more harm than shade provides benefits. Nonetheless, something similar to cells ought to be cut out from the walls which can protect the fishes fleeing the sun's heat and no less easily send back the water which they have taken in. But it is fitting to remember that bronze railings with small openings ought to be fixed on the streams through which the *piscina* flows out, by which the fishes' escape might be hindered. But if space allows, it will not be strange to arrange rocks—which are especially clothed with seaweed—from the shore along the spans of the pond, as much as the cleverness of a person prevails to devise to represent the appearance of the sea, so the enclosed fish feel their constraint as little as possible.

17.7. With the stabling set out on this principle, let us introduce our aquatic flock. May it be of prime importance in our riverine business to remember what

40 Rabies: #2.1.5.

is taught about business on land: what each region might produce. Nor, if we want to, as we have sometimes seen in the sea, can we pasture a crowd of red mullets since it is a very delicate race and very resentful of servitude. Rarely do one or two from many thousands suffer confinement. But to the contrary we frequently notice deep sea-flocks within enclosures: the idle mullet and the ravenous wolf-fish. Therefore, as I have proposed, let us contemplate the quality of the shore. And if we see it rocky, let us commend it. Let us shut in many types of thrush-fish and sea-carp and greedy weasel-fish, then also spotted wolf-fish—for they are varied—likewise the flat fishes which are especially esteemed, the murenas, if there are any other marked *saxatiles*, whose prices are high. For it is not even fitting to catch the cheap fish nor even to nurture them. These same types are also able to be kept in the ponds of a shady shore. For those which are smeared with mud and dirt, as I have said before, are more suitable for shellfish and animals lying at the bottom. Nor is there the same layout for a lake which receives reclining fish. Nor is the same food offered to prostrate and upright fishes. For soles and turbots and similar animals, the *piscina* should be pressed down two paces on that part of the shore which is never destitute of a deep recess of water.

17.10. Then, enclosed lattices are fixed on the edges, which always extend above the water, even when the sea's tide swells. Then moles are cast in a circle in such a way that they embrace the pond in its fold and nonetheless exceed the pool's level. For thus the sea's ferocity is broken by the intervention of a masonry block, and remaining in tranquil water the fish are not disturbed in their own seats, nor is the fish-preserve itself filled with seaweed which the violence of the deep sea vomits out in storms. It will be fitting in some places, moreover, that a mole be cut in the fashion of the Meander River[41] with small and narrow courses, which send the sea across without a wake no matter the savagery of a storm.

(Columella, On Agriculture *8.16.7–17.11)*

E. *Expenses, diligence, and sometimes even the affection with which wealthy Romans tended the fishes in their* piscinae.

2. There are two types of *piscinae*, sweet and salt, one is for the common people and is not without profit, where Nymphs supply water for our villa fish.[42] The salt-water *piscinae* of the nobles, however, for which Neptune supplies both the water and the fishes, pertain more to the eyes than to the wallet, and they drain the owner's pouch rather than fill it. First of all, they are built at great expense, secondly, they are filled at great expense, thirdly, they are maintained at great expense.

41 #3.1.1A note.

42 The distinction is between the fresh-waters of the Nymphs and salt-sea of Neptune's realm.

3. Hirrius[43] used to take 12,000 *sesterces* from the buildings around the *piscinae*, but he consumed all the profit for the food which he gave to the fish. No wonder. Once I recall that he gave Caesar 2,000 murenas by weight, and then he sold the villa for four million *sesterces* owing to the multitude of fishes. Our inland and common *piscina* is rightly called "sweet" and that other one "bitter." For who of us is not content with a single such pond? Who, on the contrary, does not have more seawater *piscinae* connected from individual *piscinae*?

4. For just as Pausias and other painters of the same type have large, compartmentalized boxes, where there are wax pigments of different colors, thus these folk have compartmentalized fish-ponds, where they keep different fishes separated, as if they were sacred and more inviolate than those in Lydia,[44] which, Varro, as you were making sacrifices, you were accustomed to say would come up in flocks to the tibia (flute) player at the edge of the shore and altar because no one would dare seize them: at the same time you had seen the dancing islands of the Lydians. Thus, no cook dares to summon these fish to gravy.

5. Our friend Quintus Hortensius has *piscinae* built at great expense at Bauli:[45] I have often been with him at his villa; so, I know that he was always accustomed to send to Puteoli to buy fish for dinner.

6. Nor was it enough that he was fed from his *piscinae*, unless he fed the fish himself. All the more, he took greater care that his mullets did not go hungry than I have that my donkeys at Rosea not go hungry. Even more, with both food and drink, he supplies their food not less sumptuously than I. For I maintain my expensive donkeys with one little stable-boy, not much barley, local water. Hortensius first had several fishermen who attended to the fish, and they were constantly heaping up tiny fishes which were consumed by the larger ones.

7. Moreover, Hortensius cast purchased salt-fish to these fishes when the sea was agitated during a storm and the fish market did not offer provisions. Nor—with a net—could they draw live food, the fish of a common dinner, onto the shore. With Hortensius' consent, you could more quickly lead out the carriage mules from the stable than a barbed mullet from his *piscina*.

8. He also said that he had no less concern over his ailing fish than his ailing slaves, and he took fewer pains lest a sick slave should drink cold water[46] than his fish should drink fresh water. He also used to say that Lucius Lucullus[47] worked carelessly and he, Hortensius, disdained Lucullus' *piscinae* because they did not

43 Gaius Hirrius was the first to have *piscinae* dedicated to eels, supplying 6,000 for Julius Caesar's triumphal banquets in 46 BCE (Pliny, *NH* 9.171).

44 Cf. Labraunda: #3.8A.

45 Quintus Hortensius Hortalus (115–50 BCE) was the famous orator who allegedly wept when his favorite murena eel died (Pliny, *NH* 9.172). Bauli: in Campania, west of Naples.

46 Cold water was believed to be therapeutic: e.g., Hippocratic *Uses of Liquids*; Celsus 4.12.8–9; Galen, *Method of Medicine* 7.9 (10.508 Kühn).

47 Lucullus (118–56 BCE) kept either 40,000 eels (Macrobius, *Saturnalia* 3.15.9) or 400,000 (Columella, *On Agriculture*, 8.16.5).

have suitable agitations and consequently his fishes dwelt in motionless water in such unhealthy conditions.

9. On the other hand, after he dug through a mountain near Naples and sent a maritime river into his *piscinae*, which flowed back and forth,[48] Lucullus did not yield to Neptune concerning fishing. It happened that, on account of the heat, he seemed to have led his beloved fish into colder places, just as Apulian shepherds are accustomed to do, leading their flocks through the hills into the Sabine mountains. Moreover, while building in Baiae, Lucullus blazed with such great concern that he permitted the architect to spend money, provided that he lead a hollow channel from the *piscinae* into the sea with an intervening mole.

(Varro, On Agriculture *3.17.2–9)*

F. *Vedius Pollio (1st century BCE) would feed any slave who had incurred his wrath to his eels.*

Who does not hate Vedius Pollio worse than his own enslaved men because he would fatten his murenas with human blood and he ordered those who offended him in any way to be thrown into his fish-preserve, or what other than (a preserve of) serpents? A man worthy of a thousand deaths, whether he cast in slaves to be devoured to the eels, which he would later eat, or if he maintained the eels for this reason that he would feed them in this way.

(Seneca, On Clemency *1.18.2; cf. Pliny,* NH *9.39; Dio Cassius,* Roman History *54.23.2)*

6.3.8 Bivalves

A. *Oysters were thought to generate spontaneously.*

The fact that all shellfish are created spontaneously is clear from the following: because they occur on boats when foaming mud decays. In many places where this has not happened earlier, after a place becomes muddy because of a lack of water, those things called lake-oysters are produced, a type of shellfish, such as when a naval expedition cast anchor around Rhodes and ceramic shards were thrown into the sea, with the passage of time and mud accreting around them, oysters were found in them.

(Aristotle, GA *763a25–34)*

B. *Types, sources, and medicinal effects of oysters.*

59. Oysters withstand the same poisons (discussed earlier: *NH* 9.96), nor is it possible to seem to have said enough about them, since the palm of victory of

48 I.e., the river was tidal.

the tables has for a long time been attributed to them. Oysters rejoice in sweet waters and where many rivers flow in. Consequently, sea-oysters are small and rare. They are nonetheless also grown in places rocky and lacking the approach of sweet water, as around Grynium and Myrina.[49] They increase in size, indeed, especially by the method of the stars,[50] as we have said regarding the nature of aquatic animals, but aside from that, oysters are pregnant with much milkiness around the beginning of summer and when the sun passes into the shoals.

60. This seems to be why smaller oysters are found in the deep. Opacity restrains their growth, and because of sadness they go after less food. Oysters vary in color: red in Spain; dusky in Illyricum;[51] black in both flesh and shell in Circeium. Closely packed oysters, not slippery with their own saliva, are especially regarded in any country, to be valued because of their thickness rather than breadth, seized not in muddy nor sandy conditions, but from a solid seabed, with a short spondylus[52] and not fleshy, nor jagged with filaments and entirely in the hollow of the shell.

61. Those who are more expert add a mark: a purple hair surrounding the filaments. On this proof, they explain that these oysters are noble, calling them "beautifully eye-lidded." Oysters rejoice in travel and being transferred to unknown waters. Thus, Brundisian oysters pastured in Lake Avernus are believed to retain their own juice and to acquire the juice from Lake Lucrine.[53]

62. These things are said about the body. We will now also talk about their birthplaces, lest their shores be cheated of glory. But we will discuss this with someone else's tongue, a man whose voice was the most knowledgeable of this appraisal in our time. These are the words of Mucianus[54] which I will set out below. "Cyzican oysters are larger than Lucrine oysters, sweeter than British oysters, more agreeable than Medullan oysters, sharper than Ephesian ones, plumper than Illiciensian oysters, drier than Coryphantian oysters, more delicate than Histrician ones, whiter than Circeiensian oysters.[55] But it is discovered that other oysters are neither sweeter nor more delicate than these."

63. In the Indian Sea, authors of the deeds of Alexander hand down that foot-long oysters are found, and among us Romans, a cheapskate has given the name *tridacna*, desiring that the name be understood for an oyster of such a size that it must be bitten three times.[56]

49 Both on Asia Minor's Aegean coast.

50 I.e., oyster growth was thought to align with the phases of the moon.

51 On the Adriatic's eastern coast.

52 The animal inside the shell.

53 *Brundisium*: on Italy's "heel." *Avernus*: in Campania near Cumae. *Lucrine*: near Naples.

54 #1.7D note.

55 *Cyzicus*: on the southern shore of the Propontis (Sea of Marmara). *Medulla*: a river in northern Gaul? *Iliensis*: a region in Sardinia. *Coryphaeus*: mountains north of Syria. *Histria*: the eastern extent of the Danube. *Cerceiensis*: from Circeium.

56 *Dakno* (I bite) plus *tris* (three).

64. In this place, their entire medicinal quality will be described. They uniquely settle the belly, cure disdain of food, and extravagance adds chilliness when they are buried in snow, mixing the heights of mountains and depths of the sea. They gently soften the belly. Cooked with honey-wine, they cure constipation, if it is without irritation. They also purge sores of the bladder. Cooked in their own shells, when they are found closed, they are wonderfully useful for runny noses.

65. Oyster-shell ash settles the uterus and tonsils, when honey is mixed in. In the same way, the ash treats ear tumors, abscesses and hardness of the breasts. With water, the ash smooths head sores and women's skin. It is also sprinkled on burns, and is pleasing as a toothpaste. With vinegar, it heals itching and also discharges phlegm.

(Pliny, NH *32.59–65; cf. Strabo,* Geography *3.3.1 [Tagus], 4.1.8 [Massalia], 5.4.6 [Lucrine])*

C. *In his fourth* Satire, *Juvenal recounts the deliberations of the emperor's counsel regarding an impressively large fish that has presumably escaped from imperial waters, and is thus the emperor's personal property. Among the advisors are foodies, one of whom, Montanus, has particular expertise regarding oysters. See #6.3.9D.*

In my time, the skill of eating was greater for no one: whether the oysters were born in Circeium or near Lake Lucrine or were emitted from the Rutupian seabed.[57] He knew how to recognize the oyster at the first bite.

(Juvenal, Satire *4.139–142)*

D. *Coastal Tourdetania in southern Iberia was a particularly rich source of excellent oysters and mussels.*

Although the inland region in Tourdetania is such (i.e., fruitful), one would find the region along the coast a match in good things from the sea. For all of its oyster types and kinds of mussels excel in both number and size on the whole along the entire outer sea (Atlantic). They differ here, just as the rising and ebbing here is increased, which is a reasonable cause of their number and size on account of exercise.

(Strabo, Geography *3.2.7)*

E. *Depending on social status, some dinner guests might receive better quality food, including shellfish, at banquets, inspiring Martial's complaint here. At Rome there was a recurring distribution of money,* sportula, *as financial relief for the poor (Martial, Epigrams 3.7, 4.68). The lack of a financial benefit should at least merit an equitable at dinner parties.*

57 Richborough, Kent, England.

Since I am no longer invited to dinner for financial relief as before,[58] why isn't the same dinner given to me as to you? You are eating oysters glutted in the Lucrine Lake; I am sucking on a *mytilus*-mussel, while my mouth is cut. For you there are mushrooms, I'm eating the funguses fed to pigs. Dinner for you is a turbot, for me a bream. A golden turtle dove fills you with its disproportionate butt, a magpie dead in its cage is set before me. Why, Ponticus, do I dine without you when I am dining with you? Let the *sportula* which no longer exists be beneficial, let's eat the same stuff.

(*Martial,* Epigram *3.60)*

6.3.9 Fishing Guilds

Inscriptional evidence attests fishing guilds with various benefits throughout the empire, including the Chelidoniae islands, Cyzicus, and Parius (I.Parion 5; SEG 14.638; Marzano 2013: 42–47).

A. *The fishermen of Liguria in Cisalpine Gaul, honored Neptune with a sculpted stone in the early 1st century CE. The stone shows the god standing on a boat, leaning on his trident. Some names are damaged, but several men listed here probably belonged to the same families.*

Sacred to Neptune, Maximus Teurius, the deputy, Metela Danius Carb[], the fishermen Vibius Velagenius Peda, Parra Enicius, Miranius Carb[], Silvanus Velagenius Ebelin[], Lasser Metela Edanius Car[], Maximus Minatius Carb[], and Secundus Enicius Parrae, son of Barg[] dedicated this freely and deservedly.

(CIL *5.7850 [*ILS *3287])*

B. *At Rome fishermen and divers were also organized into guilds, according to this inscription of 206 CE. This guild enjoyed exclusive rights to debris on the Tiber's bed. For lictors: #6.21 note. For the Roman calendar: #4.5.2J§123 note.*

For Tiberius Claudius Severus on the Esquiline, a member of the board-of-ten jury, a lictor, and patron of the guild of fishermen and divers, quinquennial patron of this same body for the 3rd time, owing to his services, that here, at his own expense, he has placed two statues, one of our emperor Antoninus Augustus (Septimius Severus, r. 193–211 CE), the other of Julia Augusta our empress, together with his son Claudius Pontianus, a Roman eques, and he has donated 10,000 *sesterces* so that, from their interest, every year on his birthday, the 17th day before the Kalends of February (January 14), *sportulae* might be

58 At Rome there was a recurring distribution of money as financial relief for the poor: Martial, *Epigrams* 3.7, 4.68. Martial is observing that the lack of a financial benefit should at least merit a quality dinner.

divided man by man, especially since the sailing of skiffs was acquired by his diligence and confirmed by a decree, according to which, by a senatorial decree, that it be permitted to the guild of fishermen and divers to collect debris from the entire Tiber riverbed. With their own money they placed this monument, dedicated on the 16th day before the Kalends of September (August 17) when Nummius Albinus and Fulvius Aemilianus were consuls, and when Juventius Cornelianus and Julius Felicissimus, quinquennial patrons, were in attendance, as well as Claudius Quintianus and Plutius Aquilinus, managers, Aelius Augustale and Antonius Vitalis and Claudius Crispus.

*(*CIL *6.1872 [*ILS *7266]; cf.* CIL *6.29700, 29702)*

C. *This leader of a fishermen's guild (*princeps piscator*) dedicated a funerary inscription for a woman, possibly his wife (date unknown).*

Mummia Fortunata, a freed woman, Quintus Calmaeus, first-fisherman, freedman of Curtius Publius Nica, lived 20 years.

*(*CIL *6.9799)*

D. *Domitian's huge fish is caught (see #6.3.8C).*

When the last Flavian[59] was already mangling a half-dead world and Rome was enslaved to bald Nero, there came to light—in front of the house of Venus which Doric Ancon[60] holds up—a wonderful expanse of an Adriatic turbot, and it filled the fold of the fishing net. Nor did it lie there smaller than those fish which Maeotic ice covers, when, at length broken by the sun's rays, it pours out torrents, slow and fat with long-standing cold, to the idle mouths of the Pontus. The master of the skiff and fishing net designates this monster for the Pontifex Maximus.[61] For who would dare to display or purchase such a fish when even the seashores were full of many an informer? Straightaway scattered seaweed-inspectors would be dealing with the nude oarsman. Nor hesitating, would they say that the fish was a fugitive and was pasturing for some time in Caesar's fish-preserves, and thence that it ought to be returned to its old home since it slipped away. If we trust Palfurius or Armillatus with regard to anything, whatever is remarkable and beautiful in the entire deep is a matter of the imperial treasury, wherever it swims. Therefore, let it be given as a gift, so that it not be wasted.

(Juvenal, Satire *4.37–56)*

59 Titus Flavius Vespasianus (r. 69–79), who rose to power in 69 CE, ending a year of chaos and bloody civil war after Nero's suicide in 68.

60 "Elbow," a town settled in the 4th century BCE from Syracuse (a Dorian city) on the gentle bend on Italy's northerly eastern coast. Ancon's patron deity was Venus/Aphrodite, goddess of sexual desire, a subtle jab at Domitian, who aimed to eradicate sexual immorality in his subjects while indulging himself: Ferguson 1979: 163n40.

61 #1.9.12G note.

6.3.10 Consuming Fish

A. *While fish was a significant part of the Mediterranean diet, sometimes it could be too much so, as when Odysseus and his men landed at Thrinakia (the island of the Sun God) and were warned not to touch Helios' splendid herd of cattle. After being stuck on the island for a month, the temptation got the better of the men (they sacrificed and consumed some of the cows), all of whom would perish for their act of* hubris. *By convention, while the gods enjoyed the scent of roasting meat, they could not eat it, and blood sacrifices were convenient opportunities for worshippers to eat meat. Here Odysseus recounts his crew's frustration over their piscine diet and their intentions to eat some beef instead.*

> "As long as they had grain and red wine, they kept away from the cows, longing for their lives. But when all the ship's provisions had been consumed, and out of necessity they roamed and labored with bent hooks at hunting fish, birds, whatever pleasing thing might come to their hands: for hunger distressed their bellies. I (Odysseus) went up the island to pray to the gods, if someone might show me the road to be travelled. But when, going through the island, I escaped my companions, washing my hands where there was shelter from the wind, I prayed to all the gods who hold Olympus. But the gods poured sweet sleep over my eyelids. My companion Eurylochus then initiated an evil counsel to our companions: 'Listen to my words, my friends who are suffering evils. All deaths are hated by miserable mortal folk, but most pitiable is it to die from hunger and fall upon fate. But come now, driving off the best of Helios' cows, we will make a sacrifice to the deathless gods who hold the broad sky. If we ever reach Ithaca, our paternal land, we will quickly build a rich temple to Helios Hyperion,[62] and in it we will place many and excellent ornaments. If Helios is at all angry over his straight-horned cows and might want to destroy our ship, and the other gods follow, I prefer to make an end of it once and for all, gaping at a wave, rather than grieve thenceforth on a barren island.'"
>
> *(Homer,* Odyssey *12.327–351)*

B. *On the other hand, Archestratus traveled far and wide for the best tuna. Archestratus of Gela or Syracuse (mid-4th century BCE), "the Daedalus of tasty dishes," composed a* Hedypatheia ("Life of Luxury")*, in hexameter verses, excerpted by Athenaeus.*

> Archestratus (F 15), *periplusing* the inhabited world for the sake of his belly and the parts under his belly says: "a cut of Sicilian tuna . . . sliced when about to be placed in jars.
>
> *(Athenaeus,* Learned Banqueters *3.116f)*

62 Helios (the Titan god of the sun) was often conflated with his father, the Titan Hyperion, who also personified the sun.

C. *The best season for fresh tuna is early summer. Ananius was a Greek lyric poet (c. 540 BCE) often quoted by Athenaeus.*

> There also, tuna from the sea is not bad eating, and it excels all fishes in garlic paste.
>
> *(Ananius* F *5 West = Athenaeus,* Learned Banqueters *7.282b)*

6.4 The Salt Industry

6.4.1 *Salt*

Another important product from the sea was salt, the root of the term "salary" and widely used in preparing foods and drugs. Salt was collected as seawater evaporated from shallow basins and was then cleaned by carefully raking salt from pans and filtering it through fresh water, or by leaching it with rainwater and then drying it on the beach.

A. *The best salts for medicinal applications.*

> The most effective salt is that which is mined and of this kind, in general, that which is white, free of stones, translucent, dense, smooth in its formation, particularly the Ammonian in origin,[63] that can be split and has straight cracks. But you must select sea salt that is dense, white, and smooth. Excellent is the salt produced in Cyprus, especially in Salamis of Cyprus, and in Mégara, then that produced in Sicily and Libya, and among the above-mentioned, salt from marshlands is preferable. Of this type, the Phrygian, which is called *Tattaion*, is very strong.
>
> *(Dioscorides,* Medical Material *5.109.1, trans. Beck)*

B. *Preparation, flavors, uses, and cultural importance of salt.*

> 83. In a certain part of Spain, they draw salt-water from wells, calling it *muria*. Some also think that the wood makes a difference to the *muria*. Oak is best, since of itself it returns the force of salt with its ash. Elsewhere hazel is praised. Even wood is turned into salt when salty liquid is poured over it. Whichever salt is prepared with wood, that salt is black. I discover in Theophrastus that the Umbrians[64] were accustomed to cook the ash of reeds and rushes in water, until a scant amount of liquid remained. To be sure, the liquid of salted foods from *muria* is recooked and again, the liquid evaporated, returns to its own salty nature. According to popular opinion, the most pleasing is from *menae* (sardines?).

63 Mined near the temple of Jupiter Ammon in Libya.

64 Central Italy. The Theophrastean passage cited by Pliny has not survived.

84. Of sea salt, Cyprian salt from Salamis is especially praised, as is Tarentine salt from the lakes and Phrygian salt which is called "Tattaeus." These two are good for the eyes. Salt from Cappadocia, imported in small bricks, is said to produce a shine on the skin. Nonetheless this salt—which we have called Clitian—better smooths the skin, and thus they smear it on the belly with melanthium[65] after childbirth.

85. The saltiest salt, which is the driest, most pleasing of all, and the whitest, is Tarentinan salt. But concerning the rest, salt, which is especially white, is brittle. Rain showers sweeten all salts; dew nonetheless makes it even sweeter, but a blast of the North Wind makes it abundant. Salt is not formed under the South Wind. Flower of salt[66] is not made unless by the North Wind. Neither Tragaesaean nor Acanthian salt, called after a town, neither crackles nor leaps in a fire, nor does the froth of any salt or its shavings or its powder. Enduring fire, Agrigentinan salt leaps out from water.

86. They are also different in color. Salt at Memphis is blushing ruddy, tawny around Oxus, purple at Centuripae, around Gela, in the same Sicily, salt is of such a great sheen that it reflects an image. In Cappadocia, saffron-colored salt is quarried, very clear and very sweet-smelling. For the use of medicine, the ancients especially praised Taurentine salt, after that, whatever came from sea-salt, and from that, especially foamy salt. But for the eyes of draught animals and cows, the ancients praised Tragaeaean and Baetican salt.[67]

87. Rather useful as a relish and for food is whichever salt easily liquifies and is likewise rather moist: for they have less bitterness, like Attican and Euboean salt. For preserving meats, more suitable is pungent and dry salt, such as Mégarian. Salt is given zest with added fragrances, and it completes relishes of foods, stirring and summoning eagerness for all foods so that, among countless condiments, discernment of salt is singular and is likewise sought after while eating garum.

88. Moreover, both sheep and cattle and draught animals are especially tempted to pasture by salt, providing more abundant milk and even more pleasingly delightful cheese. Therefore, by Hercules, civilized life is not possible without salt, and this substance is so indispensable that its meaning crosses over to remarkable delights of the mind: they are called salty ("witty"). And every charm of life and the greatest cheerfulness and rest from labor corresponds more with no other word. Salt is also inserted for honors and military service, from which salaries ("salt-money") are called.

89. With great authority among the ancients, as is apparent from the name of the Salarian Road, because it happened that salt was carried to the Sabines along it. Ancus Marcius (r. 642–617 BCE) gave 6,000 measures of salt as largesse to the people, and he first instituted salt works. Varro is also the authority that the

65 Black false hellebore, a perennial flowering plant. Cappadocia: on the southern coast of the Pontus.

66 A softer, red variety with an unpleasant garum-like odor (Pliny, *NH* 31.90).

67 *Memphis*: just south of the Nile delta. *Oxus River*: eastern Asia Minor. *Centuripae*: eastern Sicily. *Tragea* on Naxos in the Cyclades. *Baetica*: southern Iberia.

ancients employed salt as a relish, and the fact that they ate salt with bread is clear from a proverb. Nonetheless persuasion of this is understood especially in ritual sacrifices, since no sacrifices are done without *mola salsa* ("salted meal").

(Pliny, NH *31.83–89)*

C. *Salt was quarried widely, including in the Caucasus (Strabo,* Geography *11.5.6), and at Arabia and Aethiopia (*Geography *17.2.2). Here we have a snapshot of the importance of salt to the local economy at Tourdetania in Iberia.*

There are salt quarries among the Tourdetanians and not a few streams of salt rivers. The fish-salting is also not trivial not only from there, but also along the other seacoasts beyond the Pillars of Herakles, not worse than Pontic salted fish.

(Strabo, Geography *3.2.6)*

D. *Salt as an aphrodisiac. For Aphrodite's birth: 3.11.4A.*

Ships carrying salt produce an immense crowd of mice, because, as some say, the females conceive without intercourse when they lick salt. It is more likely that saltiness creates urges in the sex organs and encourages living creatures to join together. Likely on account of this, female loveliness, neither glistening nor unlikely, but mingled and moved with charm, they call it "salty" and "sharp." I think that the poets called Aphrodite "salt-born," and they consequently transferred the story told about her, how she had her birth in the sea, speaking in riddles with regard to the fruitful nature of salt.

(Plutarch, Table Talk *5.10.4 685d–e9)*

E. *The people of Gerrha on the coast of Arabia built their houses from super-abundant salt.*

For those sailing along Arabia for 2,400 *stadia*, the city of Gerrha lies in a deep bay. Chaldeans, fugitives from Babylon, inhabit a salt-rich land and have salt-houses, which—since bits of salt constantly flake and fall off on account of the sun's burning—the locals, sprinkling the walls with water, keep the houses compacted.

(Strabo, Geography *16.3.3)*

6.4.2 Salt-Fish

*Without refrigeration, fish and other meats spoiled quickly unless otherwise preserved. Fish were thus dried, smoked, salted, and marketed widely across the Mediterranean world (Bekker-Nielsen 2005; Nonnis and Ricci 2007; Lowe 2017). Fish-salting factories (*taricheiai/cetaria*) were established in coastal areas near tuna fishing waters where salt could be collected in large quantities, such as at Malaca and Baelo Claudia in Hispania Baetica (Strabo,* Geography *3.1.8, 4.2), Cotta and*

Lixus in Morocco, Troia in Lusitania, and Porto Palo in southern Sicily. The lake at the eponymous Taricheai ("salting factory") also produced "nice fish for salting" (Geography *16.2.45). Strabo's references to these installations are merely in passing.*

A. *The same facilities and methods were often utilized for salting various proteins according to season (pork was especially popular). We have a detailed description of salting pork in Columella. Fish, of course, would be salted in the summer months during the fishing season, utilizing largely the same methodology.*

> Now concerning the salting of pigs. It is fitting that every flock animal, especially the pig, is prohibited from drink on the day before it is killed, so that its flesh might be drier. For if it drinks, the salted meat will have more moisture in it. Therefore, when you kill a thirsty pig, take out the bones: for this process renders the salted meat less fatty and more enduring. Then, when you have removed the bones, salt it down with roasted salt, not too fine, but carefully broken up in a hanging mill. And especially fill plentiful salt into those parts in which the bones are left. After the backsides and morsels have been arranged over a board, place great weights on them so that they are drained of blood. On the third day remove the weights, and with your hands carefully rub the salted meat. When you want to put it back, sprinkle it with fine and crushed salt, and thus put the meat back. May you also not stop rubbing the salted meat daily until it is ready. But if there will be favorable conditions on those days on which the meat is rubbed, you will allow it to rest for nine days, sprinkled with salt. But if there is a cloud or rain, it is fitting for the salted meat to be brought down to the pond on the 11th or 12th day, and first for the salt to be shaken off, then for the meat to be washed carefully in fresh water, lest the salt cling to the meat, and for the meat, a little bit dried out, to be hung in a meat rack where a little smoke can reach it, which, if any amount of moisture is held back, is able to dry out the meat. The salting will happen especially when the moon is waning at mid-winter, but suitably even in the month of February before the Ides. There is another salting method, which can be employed at any time even in hot places. When the pigs have been prohibited from water the day before, on the next day they are slaughtered, and they are exfoliated either with boiling water or with flame from slender twigs—for bristles are removed by each method—and the flesh is cut into pound-sized pieces. Then roasted salt is spread out underneath in a large jar, but broken up moderately, as we said above. Next the little pieces of meat are packed together tightly, and salt is sprinkled between the layers. But when the stacking comes to the jar's throat, the remaining part is filled with salt, and is pressed down into the jar, with weights put on top. This meat is always preserved and, like saltfish, remains in its own brine.
>
> *(Columella,* On Agriculture *12.55)*

B. *The initial cleaning of fish for salting usually occurred on the beach, both according to material evidence (Morales Muñiz 1993; González et al. 2004: 82) and this poetic account that also describes the process of harvesting salt from the sea: the industries were symbiotic.*

> On the left, under the last portions of the Fishes, the stars of the Whale rise, following Andromeda in the sea as well as in the sky.[68] This beast draws its offspring of scaly flock to the slaughter and wounds of the sea. Those born under this constellation strain to snare the deep with nets, and they rage to compress the sea with chains. They will enclose seals, as if safe in the spacious water, in scattered prisons, and with a fetter they will bind and drag tuna, off their guard in meshed nets. Nor is it enough to have captured the fishes. Their bodies struggle against the knots, and they receive new battle lines, and they are killed with iron. The sea, mixed with its own blood, is thus dyed. Then also, when the prey lie on the shore, another slaughter is made on the first. The tuna are wrested into narrow bits. From one body, a varied use is assigned. This part is better when its juices are given out, another part when the juices are retained. Here, the valuable fluid flows and vomits out a flower of blood: it makes a relish for the mouth from the mixed-in salt. That entire heap of the rotting crowd is blended together, and it mixes its own shapes into mutual loss of distinguishing characteristics and supplies a common use and relish for food. Or, when a cloud of scaly creatures, very similar to the blue sea, takes a stand, and the crowd clings motionless, it is removed, surrounded by a vast seine-net, and they fill huge tanks and Bacchic jars,[69] and they vomit out liquids and shared gifts mutually, and the fish, loosened in their marrow, flow into liquid putrefaction. But more, men born under this constellation will be able to fill large saltpans and cook the sea and separate out the sea's venom (salt), when they have stretched out a solid field with an edge and invoke the wave that has been led out from its own water and deny it an outlet by shutting it with a sluice. Thus, the area supports the waters and begins to shine when moisture is swallowed by the sun. The dry sea is heaped up. And the hoary grayness of the sea, stripped off for tables, makes huge mounds of solid foam, the poison of the sea by which the enjoyment of water is destroyed, tainted by bitter sap. They exchange this for life-giving salt and return something salubrious.
>
> *(Manilius,* Astronomy *5.656–592)*

C. *The shelf-life of the final product depends on the species of fish and time allotted for salting. Methods of processing also varied: some fish were preserved fully or partially, some were salted with or without scales, and some were cut according to specific shapes (see Curtis 2008: 385–386).*

i. The Bosporus, full of salt-fish, delights as do those who cut the underbellies to craft squared salt-fish.

   (Athenaeus, Learned Banqueters 3.116b)

68 Pisces, a zodiac constellation (those straddling the sun's apparent orbit around the earth), followed by Cetus (the Whale), the sea monster slain by Perseus (#3.5B).

69 The amphora used for transporting wine and other liquids.

ii. Conveying them along the Ionian waves from Gades or from good Tarentum, a Brettian or Campanian will bring triangles of *orkus*-tuna, which, placed in terracotta jars, they dine alternately on in the first course.

(Athenaeus, Learned Banqueters 3.116c)

iii. The cubed saltfish was three *obols*.

(Athenaeus, Learned Banqueters 3.118a)

6.4.3 Garum

*Garum (similar to Vietnamese nuoc cham), along with liquamen and allec, were by-products of the fish-salting process and the standard sauces for seasoning food in the ancient Mediterranean: an early recipe is recorded on a 17th century-BCE Babylonian clay tablet (Bottéro 1995: 253). While the best-documented production site was at Pompeii (Curtis 1979, 1984), garum and other fish sauces were big business throughout the Mediterranean. The sauces were produced from several types of fishes, mixed with salt in particular ratios, covered, occasionally stirred, and fermented for up to three months. The solids dissolved, leaving two layers in the vat: the top liquid layer (garum) and the undissolved sediment (allec: Curtis 1991: 15–26, 191–192). The sauces were decanted into amphorae and shipped throughout the Mediterranean. The process was a redolent one: Seneca called garum the "the costly extract of toxic fish" (*Letters *95.25), and Artemidoros described it as "putrefaction" (*On the Interpretation of Dreams *1.66; cf. Lowe 2017: 309).*

A. *The process, varieties, and uses of garum.*

93. There is another kind of fluid to be investigated, which they call garum, from the intestines of fishes and other things, which must be cast off, steeped in salt, so that garum is the pus of decaying things. Once upon a time this was made from a fish which the Greeks were calling *garos*, showing that—its head flavored from burning—inferior parts were drawn out.

94. Now, the most highly praised garum is from the scomber fish from fishponds of Carthage Spartaria—this is called the garum of the allies—1,000 *sesterces* exchanged for about two *congii*. Nor has nearly any other fluid except perfume come to be of such a greater price, and even a source of renown for the peoples who make it. In Mauretania and Baetica and Carteia, they also catch scomber entering from the ocean, useful for nothing else. Clazomenae is also praised for its garum and Pompeii and Leptis, just like Antipolis and Thurii are valued for their *muria*, as also Dalmatia is now.[70]

70 *Carthage Spartaria*: southeastern Iberia. *Mauretania*: north central Africa. *Baetica* and *Carteia*: southern Iberia. *Clazomenae*: western Asia Minor, a little north of the parallel of Athens. *Leptis Magna*: a Punic settlement on the African coast southeast of Carthage. *Antipolis*: on the Mediterranean coast in southeastern Gallia Narbonensis. *Thurii*: on the instep of Italy's "boot." *Dalmatia*: a province on the eastern Adriatic.

95. The defect of this is allec, dregs unfinished and unstrained. Nonetheless it is beginning to be made privately from tiny fishes, useless and very small. We call it *apua* ("small"), the Greeks call it *aphye* ("small fry") because this tiny fish is born from rain. People at Forum Julii[71] call the fish from which they make garum "wolf." Allec then crosses into luxury, and the varieties have grown to an infinite number, just as garum is mixed to the color of old honey-wine to such a sweetness that it can be drunk. But another kind of garum is consecrated for the fanaticism of chastity and Jewish rites,[72] and is made from fishes lacking scales. Allec thus is made from oysters, sea-urchins, sea-nettles, mullet livers, and in countless types it is melted to the taste of the palate's flavor.

96. These things should be pointed out in passing for the pleasures of life. And the same product itself, nonetheless, is by some means an advantage in healing. For, itching of the skin is healed with allec poured over incised skin, and it is useful against bites of a dog or sea-dragon. It is applied, moreover, on linen strips.

97. Fresh burns are also healed with garum, if someone pours it on but does not call it garum. It is also beneficial against the bites of dogs and especially crocodiles and for sores which creep or are filthy. Also for sores or pains of the mouth and ears, garum is marvelously beneficial. *Muria* also, or that briny salsugo, thickens, bites, diminishes, dries. It is useful for dysentery, even if a sore might take hold of the intestines. *Muria* is also poured on for hip-pains and old stomach complaints. Also among inland peoples it takes the place of sea-water for warming.

(Pliny, NH *31.93–97)*

B. *Scomber-garum from New Carthage in southern Iberia is the best.*

Then, very near (New) Carthage is the island of Herakles, which they call Scombraria after the scomber fish caught there, from which the best garum is prepared.

(Strabo, Geography *3.4.6; cf. Athenaeaus,* Learned Banqueters *3.121b)*

6.5 Luxury Goods from the Sea

6.5.1 Murex Purple Dye

*Tyrian purple is attested in Akkadian and Ugaritic texts from the 14th century BCE, and it was produced especially at Tyre in Phoenicia and in Crete, where the mollusks were harvested. The cloth became such a successful export that the toponym (Phoenicia) was thought to derive from the color (*phoinos *["dark red"]).*

71 Forum Julii: in Gallia Narbonensis.

72 Possibly a snide reference to Jewish dietary restrictions (Leviticus 11:13–19; *Deuteronomy* 14:12–18).

A. *According to myth, purple murex dye was discovered by Melqart's (Hercules') dog whose snout turned "purple" after eating the mollusk. Hercules' mistress, Tyros, liked the color so much that she asked for a garment of the same hue, and the industry was born. Hercules had long been assimilated with Melqart, Tyre's patron deity (Herodotus, Histories 2.44; see Daniels 2021). Julius Pollox (2nd century CE) was a scholar and rhetorician from Naukratis in Egypt whose* Onomasticon *is an encylcopedia of Greek terms in ten books, each with a dedication to Commodus (r. 177–192 CE; sole emperor after 180).*

> The Tyrians say that Hercules loved a local nymph. Tyros was the name of the young woman. They say that Hercules had a dog, according to ancient legend. Know that dogs accompanied heroes as far as the assembly. Further, Hercules' dog, having seen something purple creeping on a rock—its flesh jutting out—biting it he made it a snack. But then the gore, having bloodied the dog's lips (snout), turned purple. When the hero then arrived at the nymph's home, she, having seen the dog's lips blooming with the unusual dye, she did not say that Hercules would conjecture the future unless he brought her a garment more beautiful than the dog's lips. And so Hercules found the creature and he collected the gore and he bestowed a gift on the nymph, being the first inventor of the Phoenician dye according to Tyrian report.
>
> *(Julius Pollox,* Onomasticon *1.45–47; cf. Irby 2021b: 151 and n85)*

B. *The end-color varies according to the mollusk's origin.*

> I will now begin to say something about *ostrum*-purple, which has the most costly and distinguished charm of appearance beyond those colors. It is, moreover, removed from a marine murex shell from which purple is made. For those contemplating the nature of things, the wonderment of murex purple is no less than of other things because it does not have the color of a single type in all places where it is born, but it is naturally tempered by the course of the sun. So, what is gathered in the Pontus and Gaul, because these regions are closest to the north, is black. For those proceeding between the north and west, slate-colored dye is found. What is collected at the equinoctial east and west is found with a violet color. But what is received from the southern regions is created with a ruddy power. This dye, therefore, is also created on the island of Rhodes and in other regions of this kind which are closest to the course of the sun. When they are collected, the shells, are cut into pieces with iron tools. From the shells the purple pus shoots out, like a flowing tear, shaken out, and collected in troughs by rubbing. Because it is extracted from seashells, it is consequently called *ostrum* ("shell"). Moreover, because of its saltiness it quickly becomes parched unless it has honey poured around.
>
> *(Vitruvius,* On Architecture *7.13)*

C. *The murex and purple mollusks, the process of preparing the dye, and the dye's social and historical ramifications.*

124. And nonetheless, a pearl is nearly an eternal possession, it follows to an heir, it comes up for sale like some estate. But every hour rubs away murex shells and purples for which the same Mother Luxury has made nearly as valuable as pearls.

125. Purples live about seven years at the most. Like murex snails they lie hidden for 30 days around the rising of the Dog-Star.[73] In the springtime they flock together, and owing to mutual grinding they salivate a certain sticky wax. Murexes behave in a similar fashion, but they have that flower of purple, desired for dying cloth, in the middle of their throats.

126. Here there is a white vein of very little fluid whence that expensive fluid is drained, glimmering with the color of a black rose. The rest of the body is unprofitable. They strive to capture the mollusks alive because the creatures vomit out their juice with their lives. Indeed, from larger purples they remove the juice with the shell stripped off. They break the smaller ones alive with their shells, thus eventually spitting out the juice.

127. Especially fine is the dye at Tyre in Asia, at Meninx in Africa, and on the Gaetulian coast of the ocean, in Laconia in Europe. The Roman fasces and axes make a path for the dye, and the same dye is used for the dignity of boyhood.[74] It distinguishes the senate from the equites.[75] It is summoned for placating the gods. It brightens every garment. In a triumph it is mixed with gold. Therefore, the madness for purple might be justified. But where does the price of purple dyes come from? Which dyes have a heavy odor in the dying process? And which have a color sour in its grayness and similar to an angry sea?

128. The purple's tongue is the length of a finger, by which it feeds by perforating other shellfish, so hard is its spike. They die in sweet water and anywhere a river is discharged. Otherwise caught, they live for 50 days on their own saliva. All shellfish grow very quickly, especially the purples. They fill out their size in a year.[76]

129. But if our account were to hasten up to this point, straightaway luxury would believe itself cheated and discredit us for negligence. For this reason, let us even follow up on its manufacture so that—just as the principle of fruits is learned in food—thus all who delight in these things will have an understanding in this prize of lifestyle.

130. The shellfish of the mollusks for purple colors are of two kinds (the material is the same but the proportional blending differs): the *bucinum* (trumpet

73 #2.1.5D.

74 *Fasces*: #6.21 note. *Dignity*: elite boys, some priests, and some magistrates wore the *toga praetexta* with a broad purple stripe. The color was restricted to those of the senatorial class.

75 #4.5.7F§7 note.

76 That is to say, within a year they reach their mature size.

whelk), a smaller shell similar to that from which the sound of a trumpet is emitted, whence the reason of the name, cut on the edge because of the roundness of its mouth. The other is called "purple" with a grooved beak running out and a grooved tubular side within, from where the tongue is brought forth. Moreover, it is studded towards a whirling shape all the way into a ring with about seven spikes which are not on the *bucinum*, but for each spike there are as many rings as they have years. The *bucinum* clings only to rocks and is collected around crags.

131. Purples are called by another name, *pelagiae* ("of the sea"). There are many kinds of them, different according to food and ground. The mud-purple is nourished on decaying mud, and the seaweed purple on seaweed, each is very cheap. Better is the reef-purple collected in reeds of the sea, this is also nonetheless still lighter and more pale. The pebble-purple is so-called from the pebble in the sea, remarkably suitable for purple dyes. By far the best is the mud-dwelling purple: this one feeding on a various type of soil.

132. Purples are, moreover, caught in small creels, delicate as if woven, tossed into the deep. In the creels there is bait: cockle shells that snap, just as we see mussels snap. The purples go after these cockles, half-dead but returned to the sea and reviving with a greedy gaping, and they harass the cockles with extended tongues. But the cockles, goaded with a stinger, shut themselves and clinch at those biting them. The purples are then lifted up, hanging to the creel because of their own greed.

133. After the rising of the Dog-Star[77] or before springtime is the most advantageous time for purples to be caught since, when they have spawned a waxy slime, they have flowing sap. But the workshops of the dyers do not know this, although the highest importance hinges on this. Afterwards, the white vein which we mentioned is extracted, to which it is necessary that salt be added, about a *sextarius* for every hundred pounds. It is proper for the veins to be steeped for a three-day period—to be sure the fresher the salt, the greater the strength—it is fitting to heat it in a lead container, 50 pounds of dye for individual amphoras of water roasted at a uniform and moderate heat with a pipe brought in from a distant furnace. Thus, the flesh that was necessarily clinging to the veins is thereupon skimmed off, the cauldron is strained after about the tenth day, a fleece, washed clean, is dipped as an experiment and the liquid is heated until there is sufficient hope: a reddish color is inferior to black.

134. The wool drinks the dye for five hours and is again dipped after it is carded, until it drinks up all the sap. The *bucinum* of itself is condemned since it returns the dye.[78] To a moderate degree it is bound with sea-purple, and to its very dark blackness it yields the somberness and a sheen of scarlet which is sought after. Thus, with the strengths mixed together, one hue is raised or restricted by the other.

77 #2.1.5D.
78 It is not colorfast but bleeds.

135. The sum total of dye for 1,000 pounds of fleece is 200 pounds of *bucinum* and 111 pounds of sea-purple. Thus is that exceptional color of amethyst made. Tyrian purple is sated first with sea-purple in an unripe and green cauldron, soon it is thoroughly transformed by the *bucinum* mollusk. The highest praise is for that dye with the color of clotted blood, growing black at a glance and likewise gleaming in esteem, whence blood is called "purple" by Homer (*Iliad* 5.82–83).

136. I see that there has always been the use of purple at Rome, but Romulus (r. 753–716 BCE) restricted it for his own cloak. For it is sufficiently agreed that Tullus Hostilius (r. 672–641 BCE) was the first of the kings to use it in a *toga praetexta* with rather broad stripe, after the Etruscans were defeated.

137. Nepos Cornelius,[79] who died during Augustus' principate, said, "when I was young, violet-purple was popular, a pound of which sold at 100 *denarii* a pound." Not much later it was ruddy purple from Tarentum. Twice-dyed purple from Tyre came next, which was not able to be bought at 1,000 *denarii* per pound. Publius Lentulus Spinther, a curule aedile, using this on a *toga praetexta* was condemned, "who does not now make *triclinia* with this purple?"[80] he said. Spinther was aedile in the 641st year of the founding of the city when Cicero was consul (63 BCE). That which was dyed twice was then called *dibapha* ("twice dipped") as if at extraordinary expense, but now nearly all purples are dyed in this way.

(Pliny, NH *9.124–137)*

D. *The most famous factories were at the Phoenician cities of Sidon and Tyre.*

The city of Tyre had the misfortune to be taken by a siege under Alexander (332 BCE), but from such disasters it set itself up as stronger and it restored itself with seamanship—according to which, of all peoples, the Phoenicians are in general always better—and also with purple. For Tyrian purple is approved as the loveliest of all by far; and the creatures are near the coast and the various supplies for the dye are convenient to obtain, and the great number of dyers make the city unpleasant to live in, but wealthy because of such manliness.

(Strabo, Geography *16.2.23)*

79 Cornelius Nepos (c. 110–c. 25 BCE) of Hostilia in Cisalpine Gaul, near Verona (Vergil's birthplace), was a Roman biographer and historian. Surviving are 20 biographies: on illustrious Greek military commanders, as well as biographies of the Carthaginians Hamilcar and Hannibal, and the Romans Cato and Atticus. Lost are 16 books of parallel lives and his epitome of world history (three short books), among others.

80 From a patrician family and thus eligible for the curule aedileship, open to both classes of Roman statesmen. *Aediles* had authority over economic regulation and oversaw festivals. A *triclinium* was one of three (*tri*) couches surrounding a dining table on which three banqueters reclined (for a total of nine banqueters): see #4.5.7D note.

E. *If manufactured properly, the dye could retain its color for centuries.*

> After Alexander became master of Susa, he seized 40,000 *talents* in coin in the royal treasury and furniture in addition and indescribable sumptuousness. They say that somewhere purple from Hermione[81] was also found, 5,000 *talents*, lying there for 200 years less ten, retaining its freshness and still youthful bloom. The reason for this, they say, is that the dye became this way because of the honey in the purple dyes and the white olive oil in the white dyes, and for equal time these dyes seem to keep their pure splendor and glitter.
>
> *(Plutarch,* Alexander *36.1–2)*

F. *Under Nero (r. 54–68 CE), purple dye was subject to sumptuary laws, and the emperor aimed to reserve the best colors, Tyrian red and amethyst, for his exclusive use.*

> When he had prohibited the use of amethyst and the Tyrian purple color and had sent out an agent to sell a few ounces on a market day, he then closed all the dealers. It is, moreover, said that he pointed out to his deputies a matron, noticed among the spectators at his recital, dressed in the forbidden purple, and they undressed her on the spot, not only of her clothing but also of her property.
>
> *(Suetonius,* Nero *32.3–4)*

G. *By the late 4th century CE, the purple-dye industry came under the strict control of the state, with a penalty of death for illegal dye production.*

> The emperors Gratian, Valentinian, Theodosius, Arcadius (383 CE). No private individual may have the opportunity to dye and sell purples, either in silk or in wool, which are called *blatta* or *oxyblatta* and also hyacinth. Moreover, if anyone sells the wool dyed with the aforementioned murex purple, may he know that he might undergo a crisis of his fortunes and even of his head.
>
> *(Justinian,* Codex *4.40.1)*

6.5.2 Pearls

A. *Pearls from the Erythraean Sea (see Schneider 2019).*

> i. Around the remote edge of the head of the islands of Calai is a mountain range called Calon. Following that, not far from the mouth of the Persian Bay, there is also a great deal of diving for the pearl mussel.
>
> *(Anonymous,* Erythraean Sea *35)*

81 Southeastern corner of the easternmost Peloponnesian peninsula.

ii. From Comari, stretching out to the north up to Colchi, there is a diving region for pearls, and it is worked by convicts. It is under the authority of King Pandion. After Colchi, another region follows, a coastal area lying on a bay, having an inland area called Argalos. And there in this place (†)[82] near the same island of Epiodoros, the pearl is also collected.

(Anonymous, Erythraean Sea *59)*

B. *Pearl-diving from rafts.*

The Persians and Medes and all Asians are much more eager for pearls than stuff made of gold. In his *Handbook of Parthia* (*FGrH* 781 F 1), Isidoros of Charax[83] says that in the Persian (Erythraean) Sea there is an island where the most pearls are found. Consequently reed-rafts are all around the island, from which they dive into the sea down to a depth of 20 *orguiae* to bring up the double-folded shellfish (bivalves). They say that when the thunder there is constant and there is also a downpour of rain, at that time the pinna conceives, and the most pearls are produced and are well-sized.

(Athenaeus, Learned Banqueters *3.93d–e)*

C. *Gathering pearls with nets.*

Megasthenes[84] says that the shellfish is hunted with nets, that many live in the sea like bees, and that there is a king or queen for pearl-oysters, as there is for bees.

(Arrian, Indika *8.11)*

D. *British pearls.*

Ocean also bears pearls, but brownish dark and lead colored. Certain people think that skill is lacking from their pearl gatherers. For in the Red Sea, pearls are torn from rocks alive and breathing, but in Britain they are collected as they are thrust out of sea. I would more easily believe that character was lacking in British pearls than greed in us.

(Tacitus, Agricola *12.6)*

E. *For Pliny, pearls served no practical function and only underscored Roman descent into vice and hedonism. Here, Pliny's detailed account of how pearls are*

82 The text is corrupt and unrestorable.

83 Fl. c. 40–41 BCE, a Greek geographer from southern Mesopotamia on the Persian Gulf, who composed *Stathmoi Pathikoi*, describing the caravan trail from Zeugma to India.

84 Megasthenes (350–290 BCE) traveled with Alexander to India in 326 BCE, and later served as ambassador for Seleukos I to King Candragupta, compiling his research and observations into an account of the geography, ethnography, philosophy, and paradoxa of India, *Indika*.

formed according to contemporary understanding (pearls are actually formed by the accretion of calcium carbonate).

104. But why do I mention these trivial things when luxury and the despoiling of character emerges from nothing greater than a type of shellfish? Indeed, from the entire nature of things, the sea is most detrimental to the belly in so many ways, with so many dishes for the table, with so many tastes of fishes, by which the prices of those catching them become a source of danger.

105. But how great is this share for those considering purples, purple dyes, pearls! To be sure it has been insufficient to hide the seas in our throats, unless they are also worn on our hands, ears, head, and the entire body by women and men alike. But what purpose does the sea have with our clothing? What purpose for waves and billows with wool? This nature of the things (the sea) does not rightly receive us unless we are naked![85] So be it, may there be so great a connection for our belly with the sea: but why for our backside? Is it insufficient unless we who feed on dangers are also clothed with them? To such an extent are souls demanded of a man to please us for the sake of pampering the entire body?

106. Pearls hold the first and therefore peak of all things in price. The Indian Ocean sends these out, especially between the beasts of such a nature and such a size which we have mentioned, coming over such a long tract of land from such great heat of the sun. Pearls are also sought for the Indians on islands, but exceedingly few. They are most abundant on Taprobane and Stoidis,[86] as we have said in our circuit of the world (*NH* 6.81, 110), likewise on India's Perimula promontory. Moreover, pearls around Arabia in the Persian Bay of the Red Sea are especially praised.

107. The origin and generation of pearl-oysters are not much different from oysters. When the generative hour of the year goads them on—they say—opening themselves up by a certain type of gaping, they are filled with a dewy conception, Heavy, they give birth afterwards, and the offspring of the shellfish are the pearls according to the quality of the dew that has been received: if pure dew flows in, radiance is conspicuous. But if the dew is cloudy, the offspring become dirty. The same offspring become pale when the sky threatens: for it is agreed that the pearl was conceived from the sky, and there is a greater connection for them with the sky than with the sea, and consequently a cloudy color is derived or a bright color in accord with early morning clarity.

108. If pearl-oysters are seasonably nourished, then their offspring also grow large. If there is lightning, the shells are folded shut, and the offspring are reduced in accord with the manner of food. If there is also thunder, the

85 Swimming is easier with tight-fitting clothing (or none): see #5.1.16§150, #5.2.4F, for men overboard hampered by their clothing.

86 Islands off the eastern coast of India. Taprobane is probably Sri Lanka. Stoidis, an island off the Indian coast, cited only by Pliny.

oysters—terrified and suddenly shut closed—create what they call *physemata* ("wind-pearls"), inflated only into an empty appearance without a substantive body. These are the miscarriages of shellfish. Indeed, healthy offspring are fixed with a many-layered skin, so that it might not inappropriately be thought a hard skin of the body. They are thus cleansed by experts.

109. I wonder that they, the pearls, delight so much in the sky itself: they grow red under the sun and lose their radiance like a human body. Therefore, sea-pearls preserve their special radiance, immersed more deeply than the rays of the sun can penetrate. Nonetheless they grow yellow and sluggish with wrinkles: not unless the pearls are youthful does the liveliness which is sought stand firm. Pearls even become fat in old age and cling to their shells, and they are unable to be plucked out except with a file. For some pearls, there is only one face and roundness at that side, but flatness on the backside: on account of this, they are called *tympania* ("drums"). We see them clinging on shells which were used for carrying perfumes because of this quality. Regarding the rest, a single large pearl is soft in water, but it hardens straightaway when it is removed.[87]

110. The shell itself, when it sees a hand, folds itself closed and buries its wealth, knowing that it is being attacked on account of its pearl. And, if the pearl-oyster anticipates the hand, it cuts that hand with its own sharp edge, a greater justice than no other punishment. And they are fortified with other tortures: to be sure a greater part are found among the rocks, but in the deep, marine dogs (sharks) also attend them. Nonetheless, they are not protected from women's ears.

111. Indeed, they say that for swarms of shellfish, like bees, there are individual pearl oysters—remarkable for their size and age—that are like leaders of extraordinary skill at taking precautions. These are sought attentively by the divers. When they are caught, the rest, scattering aimlessly, are easily imprisoned in the nets and then overwhelmed with salt in terracotta jars. After all the flesh is pecked away, certain kernels of their bodies, that is the large pearls, fall to the bottom.

112. It is not doubted that pearls are worn away by use and that color changes with negligence. Their whole quality is in their brightness, size, roundness, smoothness, weight. Because of their manifested qualities by no means does it happen that two indistinguishable pearls are obtained. Thus, Roman luxuriousness has evidently imposed the name *unio* ("one of a kind") on large pearls, for this is not a word among the Greeks, nor is there even a word among the Barbarians,[88] discoverers of the object, other than margarita.

113. Thus, there is a great difference in their brilliance. For those found in the Red Sea, the radiance is brighter. In the Indian Sea, the brilliance imitates flakes of mirror-stone (mica), excelling others in size. The greatest praise of color is to be called alum-colored. There is a sui generis grace to the longer ones. Those

87 Like coral: see #2.3.2G.

88 #5.3.5D and note.

with a tapered length ending in a rather full orb in the shape of a perfume bottle, they call them elenchoi ("tests").

114. It is the ambition of women to hang these pearls on their fingers, and by twos and threes on their ears, and foreign names are passed on to this luxury, sought accordingly by reckless extravagance. When they make these types of earrings, they call them *crotalia* ("rattles") as if they also delight in the sound and the very striking together of the pearls. Even poor folk desire them now, repeatedly declaring that a large pearl is a lictor[89] for a woman in public. But they wear pearls even on their feet, and they attach them not only to the straps of their sandals but also all over their low-heeled Greek slippers. Nor is it enough to wear pearls now unless women trample them and even walk over these *uniones*.

(Pliny, NH *9.104–114)*

F. *Some merchants (*margaritarii*) also specialized in pearls (cf. Marzano 2013: 170–171), like Julia Schole's husband in this epitaph from Rome (1st century CE).*

Julia Schole made this monument for herself and Caius Aspanius Clymenus her husband, a *margaritarius*, and Tiberius Claudius Archelaus and her freedmen and freedwomen and their children and for Aulus Cottius Eunomus. This does not convey to the heirs.

*(*CIL *6.9544)*

G. *The chatty epitaph of another* margaritarius *at Rome, 1st century CE.*

Friend, stop and take a look at the little mound of soil to your left. The bones of a good man are contained over there, a merciful lover, a poor man. I beg you, traveler, do nothing bad to this monument. Caius Ateilius Euhodus, freedman of Serranus, a *margaritarius* on the Sacred Road,[90] is buried in this monument. Farewell, Traveler. According to a testament, it is permitted that no one else be brought nor buried in this monument except for those freedmen to whom I have given and allotted in this will.

*(*CIL *6.9545)*

6.5.3 Coral

Coral was used medicinally and also prized, especially in India, but rare.

21. Coral is as valued among Indians as Indian pearls are valued by us, about which I have already spoken in its own place:[91] for value is agreed according to

89 #6.2I note.

90 The *Sacra Via*, Rome's major road, stretching from the Capitoline Hill, through the Forum to the Flavian Amphitheater, the traditional route of triumphal parades for victorious generals.

91 #6.5.2E.

the conviction of the peoples. Coral is also borne in the Red Sea, but blacker, likewise also in the Persian Sea—this is called *lace* ("lace")—the most highly praised is found in the Gallic Bay around the Stoechades Islands[92] and on Sicily around Aeolia and Drepana. Coral is also produced at Graviscae[93] and in waters near Naples in Campania. But in the Erythraean Sea it is especially red but soft, and for that reason worthless.

22. Its shape is of a shrub; its color is green. Its berries are white under water and soft, but, removed, it immediately becomes hard and grows red. In size and appearance, it is like cultivated cornel (cherries). They say that it immediately becomes stony with a touch if it is alive.[94] So it is seized and plucked from nets or cut off with a sharp iron tool. For this reason they understand that it is commonly called *curalium* (coral).[95] The most highly esteemed coral is as red and branchy as possible, not rough or stony or, on the contrary, hollow or concave.

23. The preeminence of the berries is no less valued by the men of the Indus as large Indian pearls are valued by our women. Indian haruspices[96] and prophets especially consider coral a supernatural amulet for removing danger. Thus, they delight in its beauty and sanctity. Before this was known (Indian love of coral), the Gauls embellished their swords, shields, helmets with it. But now there is such a scarcity of it, owing to the selling price, that it is very rarely seen in its own part of the world.

24. Sprouts attached to an infant child are believed to offer protection, and coral aids against complaints of colic and bladder problems and kidney stones, reduced to dust in a fire and drank with water, in a similar fashion if consumed in wine or, if there is a fever, in water it brings on sleep. For a long time, it resists fire. But they rather often say that the spleen is consumed with drink of the same remedy. Coral ash heals those throwing out or excreting blood. Coral ash is mixed with eye-remedies. It thickens and it cools, it fills up the hollows of sores, and it stretches out scars.

(Pliny, NH *32.21–24; cf. Dioscorides,*
Medical Material *5.121–122)*

92 Îles d'Hyères off southeastern France.
93 The port for the Etruscan town Tarquinia, northwest of Rome.
94 See #2.3.2G.
95 From Greek κείρω, I cut.
96 Liver readers, who ascertained the will of the gods by examining spots on the livers of sacrificial animals, a type of divination developed by the Etruscans and embraced by Romans.

PART VII
Conquering the Waters

The Inner (Mediterranean) Sea and other prominent bodies of water (e.g., the Arethusa Spring at Ortygia: #1.6B–D) profoundly shaped how Greco-Roman communities viewed and presented themselves. These waters were politicized, and maritime activities contributed to "national" identity and empire-building. (For navies, naval warfare, and individual sea battles, treated extensively elsewhere: Strauss 2004; DeSantis 2017; Bradford 2019; Rees 2019). Here we consider thalassocratic initiatives, including Athenian capitalization on ship imagery (#7.2), the emphatic links between sea gods and Hellenistic autocrats (#7.3), and the growth of Roman naval initiatives, culminating with the conquest of Ocean (#7.4).

7.1 Minoan Thalassocracy

Minos, the legendary king of Crete, was the first to establish a navy ruling over the Cyclades and reducing piratical activity (see Meyer 2018: 19; see #5.1.1A).

> Having established Minos' fleet, waters among various folk became more fit for sailing: for evil-doers were expelled from the islands by him, even when he settled many of those islands. And the people dwelt along the sea, acquiring property more steadfastly. And some put up walls since they were becoming wealthier than before. Desiring profit, the weaker folk endured subjugation by the stronger, and the stronger ones, having surplus resources, acquired the weaker ones and their lesser *poleis*.
>
> *(Thucydides,* Peloponnesian War *1.8.2–4)*

DOI: 10.4324/9781003437741-8

7.2 Hellenic Maritime Endeavors

7.2.1 Persian Wars

By 490 BCE, as the Persian Empire had expanded under King Darius and his son Xerxes, the Persians soon encroached onto the Greek mainland, fomenting war (490–479 BCE) and inspiring the Athenians to build up their navy with profits from the Laurium silver mines (Herodotus, Histories *7.144; Corvisier 2008: 132–133; #5.1.1B).*

A. *In 480 BCE, the fleet of the allied Greek* poleis *met the Persian fleet in the narrow strait between Attica and Salamis in the Saronic Gulf (too narrow for typical fleet deployment), providing the Hellenes with a stunning maritime victory over Xerxes' troops. The Athenian leader Themistocles (c. 524–c. 460 BCE) recognized that the outcome of war against Xerxes "hangs on the ships" (Herodotus,* Histories *8.62), as did Artemisia, queen of Halicarnassus, who advised the Persian king against a naval encounter (*Histories *8.67). Xerxes ignored her, losing many ships and sailors who, unlike the Greeks, did not know how to swim. For the full account, see Herodotus,* Histories *book 8. Here we have Thucydides' brief summary of Athenian contributions to the Battle of Salamis, delivered by Athenian envoys at an assembly in Sparta before the Peloponnesian War.*

> "As this happened such and as it had been made clear that the affairs of the Greeks at Salamis depended on the ships, we provided three beneficial services: the greatest number of ships and the wisest man as general and resolute enthusiasm. Our ships were 400, a little less than two parts (two thirds). The leader was Themistocles who was the one most responsible for the naval battle in the narrows, the very thing which most clearly saved our affairs, and, on account of this, you yourselves honored him, especially, a foreigner among those coming to your region, and we at least exhibited much very courageous enthusiasm when no one came to our assistance by land[1]—up to our borders everyone else was already enslaved—we deemed it best to leave our city and destroy our belongings but not to abandon the common cause of our remaining allies nor, scattering, to become useless for them, but embarking in our ships to risk danger and not be angry because you did not help us ten years before. We ourselves say that we gave no less help than we received from you. For you came to our aid from your inhabited cities and to the end for enjoying them again, when you feared for yourselves and not the rest of us: at any rate, while we were safe you did

1 Claiming that pressing religious obligations kept them at home, the Spartans did not fight in 490 BCE at the Battle of Marathon, outside Athens, where the Athenians resoundingly defeated the Persians.

not approach. But, setting out from a city that no longer existed[2] and risking danger on a slender hope on behalf of a city that did still stand, we saved you and ourselves. But if we had joined the Persian Mede earlier, fearing, like the others, for our region, or did not dare to embark on our ships later, as if we were already destroyed, in no regard would it be necessary for you, not having sufficient ships, to fight a sea-battle, but the enemy's affairs would have proceeded quietly, as he desired."

(Thucydides, Peloponnesian War *1.74)*

B. *Twenty or so* poleis *contributed a combined fleet of about 370 ships against Xerxes' 1200. The Corinthians supplied 40 ships (Herodotus,* Histories *8.43). Burying their dead near the city, they erected an epitaph.*

O foreigner, we inhabited the well-watered city of Corinth, but now Salamis, Ajax' island, holds us.[3] In this place, after seizing Phoenician and Persian and Medean ships, we plucked sacred Hellas from defeat.

(Plutarch, Malice of Herodotus *39)*

C. *The cenotaph dedicated on the isthmus explicitly credits the Corinthians with the victory at Salamis.*

For all of Hellas standing on the razor's edge, we lay dead, having plucked her out from danger with our lives.

(Plutarch, Malice of Herodotus *39)*

D. *The allies broadly claimed that the naval battle at Salamis saved Hellas from the Persians.*

i. And now Ajax' city, Salamis, could have borne witness that she was saved by sailors in Ares (battle) in Zeus' destructive storm, like hail, with the murder of countless men.

(Pindar, Isthmian *5.48–50)*

ii. It was almost impossible. But, stranger, we Cretans, at any rate, declare that the sea battle at Salamis—waged by the Hellenes against the Barbarians[4]—saved Hellas.

(Plato, Laws *4.707b)*

2 In 480/79 BCE, the Persians invaded Athens, destroying the city and the acropolis' monuments.

3 The greater Ajax, Greek hero of the Trojan War, came from the island of Salamis where he was honored with a temple, cult image, and annual festival, the *Aianteia* (Pausanias, *Description of Greece* 1.35).

4 #5.3.5D and note.

7.2.2 The "Delian League" and the Peloponnesian War

After the Hellenic victory against the Persians, in 478/7 BCE, about 150 poleis *entered into a formal agreement, the so-called "Delian League" (a modern label), secured with binding oaths "to have the same enemy and friend" (Aristotle,* Athenian Constitution *23.5; cf. Thucydides,* Peloponnesian War *1.96.2), intended to check further Persian expansion, seek financial recompense for wartime damages, and exact "simple revenge" (Pomeroy et al. 2008: 229). Athens, now on the path to thalassocracy (Corvisier 2008: 135; de Souza 2017), quickly assumed military responsibility and leadership in exchange for ships or money while ostensibly respecting the political autonomy of their allies but exercising ultimate control over the treasury, which was initially deposited on the island of Delos. Athens consolidated control of the Aegean as the allies continued to campaign against the Persians (cf. Meiggs 1972; de Souza 2017: 415–418). But stresses between Sparta and Athens escalated into war (cf. Mavrogiannis 2013–2014).*

*In making the case for war, Pericles appealed to Athenian naval prowess. Pericles (*archon*: 461–429 BCE) was a prominent statesman who spearheaded the rebuilding of the Athenian Acropolis after its destruction by the Persians and orchestrated the conversion of the "Delian League" from an anti-Persian alliance into an Athenian empire. He died from the epidemic that devastated Athens and other* poleis *early in the Peloponnesian War (#2.1.4). Here we have a brief selection from the longer speech (Thucydides,* Peloponnesian War *1.140–144).*

> 142.6. "Nor easily will knowledge of the sea come to the Spartans. Nor did you, straightaway taking thought for it after the war with the Persian Medes, master it in any way. How then could men, working the land but not the sea besides, practice seamanship, they who are not permitted to do so on account of our numerous ships always attacking them, if it were a worthy thing to do? For they might risk danger against a few attacking ships, emboldened by their paucity in their ignorance. But, blockaded by many ships, they would remain quiet. If they would witlessly not take thought in nautical matters, because of this they would become more timid. For seamanship is a skill, just like any other, and folks cannot attend to it whenever they happen upon it, taking thought for it as by-work (a "hobby"). But rather nothing else can be a by-work to seamanship.
>
> 143. "Even if, moving money from Olympia or Delphi, they try to entice those foreigners among our sailors for better pay, it would be a terrible thing if we and our metics (resident foreigners) were not closely matched on ships. But as it is now—this is our best advantage—we have citizen *kubernetes*.[5] And our ships' crews are more plentiful and better than all in the rest of Hellas. Not a single one of our foreigners would consider fleeing from his own fatherland in danger,

5 #5.1.3B–D.

and then, at the same time with a lesser hope, fight on their side for the sake of a higher wage for a few days. As far as I'm concerned, this seems to be the situation of the Peloponnesians, or approximately so. As for our own situation, we have other advantages and greater ones than those matters with which I have found fault in them. If they come against our land on foot, we'll sail against theirs: striking a portion of the Peloponnese will no longer be the same as striking all of Attica. For they will not be able to possess any other territory without fighting. But for us, there is a lot of land, some in the islands, some along the mainland. For there is great power in the sea.

(Thucydides, Peloponnesian War *1.142.6–143; cf. 2.65.7)*

7.2.3 Ship of State

At the same time, ships became a significant feature of popular culture, and nautical and hydrological metaphors were casually sprinkled in literature: e.g., "reef of justice" (Aeschylus, Eumenides *564); sea (of troubles: Sophocles,* Oedipus at Colonus *1746). The "ship of state" was an especially popular image. Alcaeus (621–550 BCE) may have been the first writer to use the image as a metaphor for the troubled political climate in his hometown of Mytilene on Lesbos (*F *208 Campbell).*

A. *At Athens, an oracle came to Solon (630–560 BCE) from Delphi, comparing the city to a ship and the citizens to oarsmen.*

Guiding straight the helmsman's work, be seated amidships. Many allies you'll have at Athens.

(Plutarch, Solon *14.4)*

B. *For Herodotus' Themistocles, the ships represented the state while the Persians occupied Athens. Eurybiades was the Spartan naval commander.*

Then Themistocles said many and evil things against that Corinthian man, Adimantus, and the other Corinthians, making it clear to them with a word that the Athenians had a city and land greater than theirs, so long as they had 200 ships filled (with men). For none of the other Greeks could ward off the Athenians coming after them. Indicating these things with a word, Themistocles walked over to Eurybiades, speaking more earnestly. "If you stay here, by staying you will be a good man, but if not, you will destroy Hellas. For our ships carry everything for us in war. But be persuaded by me. If you don't do these things, then taking our property, such as we have, we will travel to Siris in (southern) Italy, which remains ours from long ago, and the oracle says that it is necessary that that place be peopled by us. But you, apart from your allies, remember my words."

(Herodotus, Histories *8.61–62; cf. Thucydides,* Peloponnesian War *6.10.5)*

C. *Aeschylus'* Seven Against Thebes *opens by evoking the ship of state. After Oedipus' death, his sons were to share the governance of Thebes, taking the throne in alternate years. Eteocles, however, refused to yield, and Polynices collected a band of seven heroes (including himself) to besiege each of the seven gates of the city. In the end, the brothers kill each other. The play explores the psychology of the seven attackers and inspired Akira Kurosawa's* Seven Samurai *(1954) and John Sturges'* The Magnificent Seven *(1960). Cadmus was the mythic founder of Thebes. Here, Eteocles is speaking, rousing the Thebans to fight against Polynices.*

> "Citizens of Cadmus, it is necessary that whoever oversees the matters of the city on the stern, he should speak timely things while he guides the tiller."
>
> *(Aeschylus,* Seven Against Thebes *1–3)*

D. *A priest of Zeus compares Corinth, beset with a plague and famine, with a storm-tossed ship owing to Oedipus' unwitting crimes of killing his father and marrying his mother, despite deliberate attempts to avoid his bizarre fate.*

> For the city rolls and can scarcely lift its head from the depths.
>
> *(Sophocles,* Oedipus Rex *22–24)*

E. *Plato also employed the allegory of a ship with a mutinous crew in defense of his argument that states (like ships) are best captained by benevolent, omnipotent philosopher-kings who have true knowledge of the Forms. Plato's Socrates is in dialogue with Plato's brother, Adeimantus of Collytus, son of Ariston of Athens.*

> "Observe such a thing happening, whether regarding many ships or just one. In size and strength, the shipowner is above all those in the ship, but rather deaf and to some degree nearsighted, and his knowledge of seamanship is much the same. The sailors are quarreling with each other about helming the ship: each thinks that he should be helmsman, but has never learned the skill nor can he point out his teacher nor the time when he learned navigation. In addition to these things, asserting that navigation cannot be taught, but they are also ready to cut down anyone saying that it can be taught. They are always pouring around the owner himself, begging and doing everything so that he might transfer the steering-oar to them. Some don't persuade the owner, while others do. Then, killing those others or throwing them from the ship, binding the owner with intoxicating mandrake[6] or liquor or something else, the crew take control of the ship and sail off, using up everything in it, drinking and enjoying themselves as is expected of such men.
>
> "In addition to these things, they applaud and call someone who knows something about ships a *kubernetes*. And they call him a seaman who was clever enough

6 A sedative and analgesic (Dioscorides, *Medical Matters* 4.75), several varieties of mandrake are hallucinogenic.

to take the ship in such a manner as to lead either by persuading or constraining the owner. But they rebuke as useless the guy who did not do this. They do not at all give an ear to the true *kubernetes*: that it is necessary that he, the true *kubernetes*, have a concern for the seasons of the year and the sky and the stars and the winds and all things belonging to the skill. If he is to be fit for command of a ship, how he will helm the ship, even if some want to work and others don't? Nor do they, the true *kubernetai*, think that it is possible to gain this skill at the same time as they practice steering. If such things really happen, then truthfully it would not be considered a helmsman's skill but would be called stargazing and babbling and useless to them by those sailors on ships so equipped."

"Certainly," said Adeimantus.

"I do not think," I said, "that you need my allegory to be interpreted to see that it represents the disposition of city-states towards true philosophers, but you do need to learn what I say."

"Indeed," he said.

"First then teach this allegory to the person marveling that philosophers are not valued in their *poleis* and try to persuade him that it would be more marvelous if the philosophers were valued."

"I will teach it," he said.

"And that you are speaking the truth, when you say that the folks most useless to the city are those who are most capable among those practicing philosophy. However, instruct him to censure as useless those folk who do not employ philosophers, but also not to censure those who are capable. For it is not according to nature that the *kubernetes* begs his sailors to be led by him nor that wise men approach the doors of the wealthy. But the person inventing that expression lied.[7] The truth suggests that if someone, whether rich or poor, falls ill, then it is necessary to go to the doors of the physicians, and everyone needing to be governed ought to go to the doors of someone able to govern, nor should the governor beg those being governed to be governed by him, if in truth he is useful. But comparing our current city-leaders with those sailors we were just talking about would not be missing the mark,[8] as would comparing those who are called useless and stargazers with the true helmsmen."

(Plato, Republic *6.488b–489c)*

7.2.4 Panathenaic Festival

The ship of state metaphor also found expression at the mid-summer Panathenaic festival, traditionally a birthday celebration for the city to honor the patron deity, Athena, who was credited in myth with building the first ship (the Argo*), thus*

7 Plato alludes to Simonides (6th century BCE), suggesting that it was better to be rich than wise "because the wise spend their time at the doors of the rich" (Aristotle, *Rhetoric* 1391a7–12).

8 #2.2.9A note.

making the ship a cultically resonant symbol for Athens. The festival's final day featured a procession that included a ship on wheels, from whose yardarm Athena's new peplos-*dress was bent-on like a sail. When the ship was added to the parade is robustly debated (Parke 1977: 39; Norman 1983: 44; Mansfield 1985: 52–53, 68n62; Wachsmann 2012, 238 and n6): the iconographic and literary evidence is late. Philostratus provides an intriguing description of the subterranean machines commissioned by Herodes Atticus for the Panathenaia of 138/9 CE, a seemingly unique installation.*

> Regarding the Panathenaia I have heard the following: attached to the ship, the *peplos* was more tasteful than a painting, with a fold in a fair wind, and the ship ran not with draught animals driving it, but it slipped along on underground mechanisms. From the Kerameikos harbor with the force of a thousand oars it arrived at the Eleusinian harbor and circling it, it passed by the Pelasgican harbor and from there it came to the Pythian harbor where it is now moored.[9]
>
> *(Philostratus of Athens,* Lives of the Sophists *2.550; cf. Pausanias,* Description of Greece *1.29.1; Scholiast on Homer,* Iliad *5.734)*

7.3 Thalassocracy and the Hellenistic League of the Islanders

A. *Often associating themselves with marine deities, Hellenistic ruling families promoted thalassocracy. Arsinoe II (316–270 BCE), the sister-wife of Ptolemy II Philadelphus (r. 283–246 BCE) was honored with sand altars at Alexandria as Arsinoe Euploia-Zephyritis, "the fair-sailing West Wind" (Robert 1966: 192–208: Ox. 2465; Barbantani 2005), according to an epigram attached to a marvelous rhyton (drinking cup) designed by Ctesibius (see #4.6.1B, #4.7.2B). Hedylus (3rd century BCE) was an epigrammatic poet from Athens or Samos, son of Melicertus and Hedyle, and ascribed with 11 epigrams in the* Greek Anthology.

> In his *Epigrams*, Hedylus, recalling a rhyton constructed by Ctesibius, the mechanician, says: You who drink unmixed wine, see this rhyton of Arsinoe, beloved of the West Wind, in her temple, showing the Egyptian dancer Besas,[10] who trumpets a shrill sound from the spring opened to the wine's flow. Not a symbol of war, it proclaims, with its gold bell, a signal for good cheer, the sort of dear, paternal refrain that gleaming Lord Nile has devised from his waters for his initiates as they carry offerings. But revere this clever invention of Ctesibius. Come, young men, to this temple of Arsinoe.
>
> *(Athenaeus,* Learned Banqueters *11.497d)*

9 The boat made a tour of harbors near Athens until being moored at Kirrha in a nook in the northern Corinthian Gulf and serving tourist traffic to the popular oracular shrine of Apollo at Delphi.

10 Bes, widely worshipped as a goddess of music, partying, and childbirth. For (un)mixed wine: #2.1.5A note.

B. *Arsinoe was worshipped with a cult at Cape Zephyrion (near Alexandria), established by Ptolemy's admiral Kallikrates of Samos. Her association with Isis Euploia ("Fair-Sailing") aligned with the Ptolemaic Dynasty's promotion of its naval power. Poseidippus of Pella (fl. 290–240 BCE) worked in Athens, Kos, and Alexandria, and he composed epigrams on many topics, including several on the proveniences of gems and their travels through the Hellenistic world to the hands of the women for whom they were destined.*

> Poseidippus (F 119) wrote this epigram for Aphrodite honored at Zephyrion: in both sea and land, propitiate this temple of Philadelphus Cypris Arsinoe, which the admiral Kallikrates first placed to reign on the Zephyrion coast. She will grant a fair sail, and even in the middle of a storm she will make the level sea as smooth as oil for those entreating her.
>
> *(Athenaeus,* Learned Banqueters *7.318d)*

C. *Also at Zephyrion, Arsinoe Zephyritis (of the gentle, westerly wind) received an inscribed shell from a young woman who may have survived a storm at sea.*

> I am a shell, Lady Zephyritis, very old. But now, Cypris, you have me, the first offering of Selenaia, a nautilus shell[11] that sailed over the deep seas. If there is wind, I stretch the sail from the forestays where I dwell, and if there is calm, Shining Goddess, I row entirely with my own feet, as I hurry along—my name is in harmony with the work—until I fell on the strand of Iulis[12] so that I might be for you a little plaything to admire, Arsinoe. Nor in my rooms as before—for I am lifeless—will the damp halcyon lay its eggs.[13] But give grace to the daughter of Clinias; for she knows to behave bravely, and she is from Aeolian Smyrna.
>
> *(Callimachus,* Epigram *5 Pfeiffer = 14 Gow-Page)*

D. *Demetrius Poliorcetes ("Besieger of Cities"), king of Macedon (r. 294–288 BCE), was a thalassocratic ruler whose authority derived largely from naval successes and whose coinage emphasized Poseidon's alleged favor. This* tetradrachma *shows a winged* Nike *(Victory) alighting on a ship's prow and playing a salpinx (see #2.2.12C). The obverse, inscribed* ΔΗΜΗΤΡΙΟΥ ΒΑΣΙΛΕΩΣ *("of Demetrius the King"), shows a nude Poseidon wielding a trident. Demetrius' usurpation of Poseidon's imagery underscores that his military and political claim over the eastern Mediterranean is with Poseidon's favor (Holton 2014: 376–380).*

11 *Cypris*: #3.11.4B. *Nautilus*: #2.2.3A.
12 A Ptolemaic navel base at Ceos.
13 #1.9.1A note.

FIGURE 7.3D Demetrius Poliorcetes coin with Nike: AMNG 4; Bompois 874; McClean 3574; greece/macedonia/kings/demetrios_poliorcetes/AMNG_04. With kind permission of wildwinds.com, ex TimeLine Auctions, September 2015.

E. *At Athens, Demetrius was honored with an encomium that proclaimed him the son of Poseidon and Aphrodite. While some suggest that the combination of Poseidon and Aphrodite shows that Demetrius has conquered both realms (Holton 2014: 382–385), sea-born Aphrodite was also a significant maritime deity who protected sailors at sea (#3.11.4). Demochares (fl. 322 BCE–c. 275 BCE), a nephew of the orator Demosthenes (#6.1.1A), wrote an oratorical history of his own times (Cicero,* Brutus *83).*

> At any rate, Demochares wrote in his 21st book (*FGrH* 75 F 2): the Athenians received Demetrius arriving from Leucate and Kerkyra (Corfu), not only with incense and crowns and libations of wine. But processional and ithyphallic choruses[14] greeted him with dancing and singing. Standing in front of the crowds, they praised him as they danced and sang, that he alone was a true god, that the other gods were sleeping or away from home or that they did not exist at all, that he, Demetrius, was born from Poseidon and Aphrodite, that he was exceptional in beauty, and that he was the common benefactor for all people. And they approached him like suppliants, entreating him, so says Demochares, and offering prayers. Demochares has said these things about the fawning of the Athenians.
>
> *(Athenaeus,* Learned Banqueters *6.253b–d)*

7.4 Roman Watery Propaganda

7.4.1 Tiber

A. *The very identity of the city of Rome was intimately linked with the Tiber and other local rivers. Here Aeneas, the Trojan fugitive whose destiny is to found the Roman race, receives a dream of the Tiber declaring his favor for the Trojan*

14 A chorus of men carrying ceremonial erect *phalloi* (penises), a feature of rites in Dionysus' honor.

refugees and predictions of their future victory against the indigenous, hostile Latins and their allies.

It was night. And deep sleep was holding tired creatures and the race of birds and flocks through all the lands, when father Aeneas, disturbed in his heart by sad war, lay on the bank under the axis of the icy air and gave late rest to his limbs. From his pleasant stream Tiber himself, the venerable god of the place, seemed to lift himself between the poplar fronds—for delicate linen covered him in a sea-gray cloak and a shady reed covered his hair—then he spoke thus and removed Aeneas' concerns with these words: "O born from the race of gods, you who carry back our city from your enemies and keep safe the eternal Pergamum,[15] O long-awaited on Laurentine soils and Latin fields,[16] here you have a certain home, and steadfast *penates.*[17] May you not withdraw. May you not be frightened by threats of war. All the swellings and angers of the gods have withdrawn, and now, lest you think that sleep has forged empty words, a huge sow will be found lying under the oaks on the shore, having just given birth to bear 30 piglets, reclining on the ground, the piglets around her teats, all white. This will be the place of your city; this will be a true resting place from your labors. After this, the years revolving by ten times three, your son Ascanius will found a city, Alba ("White") of shining name. By no means do I prophecy uncertain things. Now I will teach in a few words how as victor you might make your way through what approaches. Pay attention. On these shores, the Arcadians, a race having set out from Pallas,[18] who as companions followed king Evander, who followed his standards, chose a place and established a city in the mountains, Pallenteum from the name of their ancestor Pallas. They constantly wage war with the Latin race. Turn to them as allies in your camp and join them in an alliance. I myself will lead you along the banks and a direct stream, so that with your oars, conveyed in the opposite direction, you might overcome the river. Rise, Goddess-born,[19] the first stars are setting. Duly offer prayers to Juno. And overcome her anger and threats with humble vows. As victor you will pay me honors. I am the one whom you see grazing the banks with a full stream and carving out rich cultivable land, blue Thybris, the river most pleasing to the sky. Here is my great home, my head withdraws from lofty cities." Tiber spoke. Then the river hid himself in his deep pool, seeking the depths.

(Vergil, Aeneid *8.26–67)*

B. *The river Tiber saved Rome's founder Romulus and his twin brother, Remus, from death by exposure as ordered by their jealous, power-hungry uncle, Amulius. As the flooding waters receded, the basket carrying the babies eventually floated ashore,*

15 The citadel of Troy.

16 Referring to Italian regions: *Laurentium* to the southwest; *Latium*, the historical home of the Latins and the region in which Rome was built.

17 Household gods who protect the *penus*, food provisions.

18 #5.1.11B introduction.

19 Aeneas was the son of Venus.

and the infants were rescued either by a shepherd or a she-wolf. When they reached adulthood, they fulfilled their destiny by ousting their uncle and founding their eponymous city (#3.2G: Anna Perenna; #3.6C: Parilia; Ovid, Fasti *5.635–662).*

Perchance by steadfast divine influence, poured out above its banks from gentle pools, the Tiber was not able to be approached at the course of its regular flow, and, although sluggish, the water was offering hope to the men bringing the babies to the riverbank that it was possible that they, the infants, be drowned. So, as if discharging the commands of the king, Amulius' agents exposed the boys at the closest overflow where the fig-tree Ruminalis is now: they say it was called "Romulan." At that time, the wildernesses in these places were vast. The rumor holds that, when the floating basket in which the boys were exposed was set down on dry earth, a thirsty wolf bent her course from the mountains to the babies' crying, and she offered her teats so gently to the babies that the keeper of the royal flock found her licking them with her tongue. They say that his name was Faustulus.

(Livy, From the Foundation of the City *1.4.4; cf. Dionysius of Halicarnassus,* Roman Antiquities *1.76.2; Plutarch,* Romulus *3–4; Campbell 2012: 13)*

C. *Tiber mourns the death of Drusus, the son of Livia, who was empress of Rome and wife of Augustus. Nero Claudius Drusus Germanicus ably campaigned for Augustus in Germany, defeating and conquering several peoples who resisted Roman encroachment. Popular with his troops (and the Roman people), he died after falling from his horse near the Elbe River in 9 BCE. While preserved in an Ovid manuscript, the authorship is disputed.*

Father Tiber himself shuddered in his golden waves and, cloudy, he lifted his head from the midst of the current. Then, with his great hand he collected his caerulean tresses, entwined with willow and moss and reed, away from his face. And he sent out rivers of tears from his abounding eyes. Scarcely does his deep bed take the watery tears poured in. And now he was determined to quench the flames of the funeral pyre by smiting the stream and raising up Drusus' corpse untouched. Tiber held back his waters and restrained their course towards the flat sea, so that he might be able to wash the pyre away with the entire river. But Mavors,[20] nearby in his temple and a neighbor of the Campus Martius, himself spoke so many words and not with dry cheeks, "Although anger is suitable for rivers, Tiber, may you nonetheless be calm. It is not granted to you, nor any others, to overcome fate. That Drusus, mine, has perished. He perished among weapons and swords and as a leader on behalf of his fatherland. The cause of his death elevates his burial rite. I have granted what I have been able to allot. Victory has been acquired. The author of the work has gone away, but the work nonetheless still stands. Once upon a time, I tested Clotho and her

20 An archaic variant of Mars, Roman god of war, often employed by the poets.

two sisters[21]—who with a true thumb draw out austere payments of fate—that Remus, son of Ilia,[22] and his brother the founder of the city might escape the boundless expanses (of death) by some path. Of the three sisters, Clotho said to me, 'Accept the allotment of the gift which is given. One of the two brothers will be the one whom you seek. This one was promised to you, each Caesar (Julius and Augustus) have been promised to Venus. Martian Rome owes these two as gods.' Thus, the goddesses of fate sang. Nor you, Tiber, oppose, nor delay the flames with useless waters, nor ruin the final rites of a young man laid down. Go now and glide away, reclining on your waters let loose." Tiber obeys and unfolds his spacious waters lengthwise and approaches his home constructed from hanging volcanic rock.

(Pseudo-Ovid, Consolation to Livia *221–252)*

D. *This Pentelic marble statue group (height: 222 centimeters; length: 317 centimeters; depth: 131 centimeters; 2nd half of 3rd century CE) shows the River Tiber personified as a virile, middle-aged, bearded, well-muscled man. He holds a cornucopia and steering-oar as he flows alongside the wolf and the babies that she suckled. Note the delicately carved waves beneath, resembling the folds of a fine cloak.*

FIGURE 7.4.1D The River Tiber: *Louvre* (MR 356; N 817; Ma 593): photo by Georgia L. Irby.

21 Clotho (who spins), Lachesis (who measures), and Atropos (who cuts) were the three sisters who oversaw the fated length of individual human lives (Hesiod, *Theogony* 217–222, 904–906).

22 Rhea Silvia, the mother of Romulus and Remus.

7.4.2 Rome and Carthage

A. *In 264 BCE, Rome and Carthage, rising superpowers, were at war, contending for control over the western Mediterranean. The Romans began to fit their warships with innovative, swiveling, spiked (grappling) gangways (*corvus*: "crow") that allowed Roman marines to board enemy ships, thus enabling them to turn sea battles into "land" battles. The Carthaginian were astonished at the new technology. And the Romans won their first Roman naval victory under the leadership of Gaius Duilius at Mylae (northern Sicily).*

As soon as he learned about the defeat which the commander of the fleet suffered, Gaius Duilius handed his infantry over to the military tribunes, and he himself crossed over to the fleet. Hearing that the enemy were ravaging the Mylaetian region of western Sicily, he sailed with the entire fleet. Seeing him, with joy and zeal, the Carthaginians launched one and thirty ships, looking down on the Romans' inexperience, and they all sailed, prow-to-prow against the enemy, not deeming the danger worthy of attack, but as if they were descending on prey that they had clearly already won. Hannibal led them—this man was the one who was sneaking his troops from the city of Agrigentum at night—in the seven-banked ship that was once King Pyrrhus'.[23] When they sailed up, seeing crows perching on the prows of each Roman ship, the Carthaginians were at a loss for a certain time, and they were astonished at the construction of the works. But notwithstanding, despising the enemy, those in the front line, sailing boldly, threw themselves against them. But, locked together, the ships were always grappled by the machines. The Romans straightaway boarded by means of the *corvi* and fought at close quarters on the decks. Some Carthaginians were slain, others surrendered themselves, panic-stricken at what was happening. For the sea-battle happened to become like the danger of a land fight. Consequently, the Carthaginians lost the 30 ships in their first battleline, men and all, engaging with the Romans: among these the general's ship was also taken by the spear. Unexpectedly and extraordinarily, Hannibal himself fled in a skiff. The remaining number of Carthaginians sailed their ships up as if for an attack. But as they drew near, seeing what happened to the ships sailing ahead, they came about and glanced off the thrust of the machines. Trusting in their fast sailing, they hoped to make attacks in safety, some sailing athwart, others along the sterns. But as the engines were swinging around and turning in every direction in all sorts of ways thus so that by necessity those drawing near were grappled, the Carthaginians, wheeling around, finally fled, astonished at the strangeness of this encounter, and they lost 50 ships.

(Polybius, Histories *1.23)*

23 *Agrigentum*: on the coast of western Sicily. *Pyrrhus* of Epirus (319/8–272 BCE) won his military battles at a great cost of men and supplies, in particular at Tarentum in southern Italy in 280–275 BCE (thus, "Pyrrhic victory," a modern phrase).

B. *To commemorate his victory, Duilius dedicated a rostral column (with ships' prows, i.e.,* rostra*) in the Roman forum, a clear message of using the sea to conquer a foreign enemy, and he distributed coins (Crawford 1974: #35) showing a prow on the reverse, eliciting his naval victory at Mylae, on the obverse, Janus protector of the Roman armory for whom he built a temple (Tacitus,* Annals *2.49).*

i. *Here we have the damaged inscription attached to the lost rostral column.*

> The consul freed the Secestani, allies of the Roman Republic, from a Carthaginian siege; and all the Carthaginian legions and their greatest magistrates fled their camps openly in the light after nine days. He seized Macela, a town to be attacked. And in that same command, as consul, he accomplished a maritime exploit in his ships, the first, and he outfitted and prepared his naval fleet. And with those ships he vanquished the entire Phoenician fleet and likewise the greatest Carthaginian troops, with their admiral Hannibal present, in the depth of the sea. And with force he seized ships with their crews, one septireme, 30 quinqueremes and triremes; he sank 13. Gold seized: 3,600 (?) pieces; silver seized with plunder: 100,000 (?). Altogether 3,200,000 *aes*, (which) he gave to the people as plunder in his naval triumph. And he led many Carthaginians marching in front of his chariot.
>
> (CIL *1.2)*

ii. *Additionally, at Naples a eulogistic inscription of uncertain date celebrates the victory.*

> Caius Duilius, son of Marcus, grandson of Marcus, first consul accomplished a naval triumph over the Carthaginian fleet, 493 years from the foundation of the city on the Kalends of an Intercalary month.[24]
>
> (AE *1927, p. 116)*

C. *In 202 BCE, the Second Punic War came to an end with the devastating Punic defeat at Zama in North Africa, the Carthaginian navy was disbanded, the ships were burnt at sea (Livy,* From the Foundation of the City *30.43.11–12), and Carthage was allowed to maintain only ten ships for defending coastal waters (Polybius,* Histories *15.18.3). Livy imagines the Carthaginian reaction after the loss of the ships that defined their identity.*

> Then it was permitted for us to weep at the moment when our weapons were seized from us, our ships burned, and we were forbidden from waging foreign wars. We perished from that wound.
>
> *(Livy,* From the Foundation of the City *30.44.7)*

24 *First consul*: probably referring to rank between the consuls whose rank alternated by month. Gaius Duilius' ancestor Caeso Duilius was listed as consul for 336 BCE. Thus, our Duilius was not a *novus homo*, or first man in the family to hold a consulship. *Intercalary*: To align the solar and lunar calendars, the Romans would insert an intercalary period of the necessary number of days.

7.4.3 Civil War

A. *By 44 BCE, Rome was once again in civil war, and Pompey's youngest son, Sextus Pompeius, took command of his father's fleet, calling himself* pius *("dutiful":* Magnus Pompeius Magni filius Pius, *"Pompeius Magnus Pius son of Magnus") as a proclamation of filial loyalty. He also "adopted" Neptune as his father to underscore that he fought under Neptune's protection (Welch 2002: 17–20; Powell 2002: 121–127). Despite his highly maneuverable ships and skilled crew, Sextus was defeated in 36 BCE at Naulochus, Sicily, by Augustus' lieutenant, Marcus Vipsanius Agrippa (Suetonius,* Augustus *16.1; Appian,* Civil War *5.116–122; see #4.5.3C note), and his defeat was presaged by a sign from the sea.*

> In this part of nature there are auguries and prognostications in fishes. During the Sicilian War, when Augustus was walking on the shore, a fish from the sea leapt at his feet, from which token the bards responded that, although Sextus Pompey was then adopting Neptune as his father—so great was the glory of his naval accomplishment—those who at that time were holding the seas (Sextus and his followers) would be under Caesar's feet.
>
> *(Pliny,* NH *9.55)*

B. *After Augustus' victory at Actium, Horace here reminisces about the war, including Sextus Pompeius' watery role. Sextus' troops included a number of slaves who sought asylum from Pompey's son.*

> When, blessed Maecenas,[25] shall I happily drink with you the Caecuban wine,[26] laid out for festive banquets in honor of a victorious Caesar, at your lofty home—thus it is pleasing to Jove—while the lyre peals a song mixed with flutes: Dorian on this instrument, "barbaric" on those?[27] As we did recently when that Neptunian leader (Sextus Pompey) fled, driven from the strait, after his ships were burned, he who threatened chains on the city which he removed from treasonous slaves as their friend.
>
> *(Horace,* Epode *9.1–10)*

C. *Sextus' coin issues featured maritime imagery. Here we have a silver* denarius, *Sicily 42–40 BCE. The obverse shows a helmeted Neptune atop a light-tower with a foot on a ship's prow (to proclaim maritime victory), holding a trident. A galley with eagle, scepter, and trident approaches the lighthouse. The reverse features Scylla brandishing a rudder like a club to demonstrate the maritime destruction of Sextus' enemies. The inscription reads:* PRAEF ORAE MARI ET CLAS S C *("By order of the Senate, Prefect of the Sea Coasts and Fleet").*

25 #2.2.11E note.

26 From Amyclae, coastal Latium. A highly acclaimed, smooth white wine that turned ruddy as it aged (Strabo, *Geography* 5.3.6; Athenaeus, *Learned Banqueters* I.27a).

27 Blending the dignified Dorian music played on the lyre with the more celebrative, exotic, and foreign Phrygian flute.

FIGURE 7.4.3C Sextus Pompey and Scylla: Crawford 511/4d; Sydenham 1349; BMCRR Sicily 20; Sear *CRI* 335b; Babelon *Pompeia* 23; Cohen 3. With kind permission of Classical Numismatic Group, LLC (http://www.cngcoins.com).

D. *Resonant in Augustan propaganda was the battle at Actium off Greece's western coast where Octavian defeated Antony and Cleopatra on September 2, 31 BCE in a sea battle. After his victory and investiture as Rome's sole, authoritarian leader, Augustus rebuilt the temple of Apollo Actius ("of the shores"), revived or instituted Actian games, and founded a Victory City (Nicopolis), peopled with residents resettled from nearby towns (Suetonius,* Augustus *18.2; Dio Cassius,* Roman History *51.1.2–3; Gurval 1995). Here, the sea battle features prominently on Aeneas' shield where the hegemony of the Roman Empire is delimited by major waterways: the Nile, Rhine, and Euphrates Rivers, and the Caspian Sea (cf. Irby 2019: 94–99).*

Between these scenes there went a golden image of the broadly swollen sea, but the dark-blue depth foamed from its white-capped wave, and dolphins all around, bright with silver, struck the level waters with their tails and plowed the spray. In the middle it was possible to pick out the bronze-fitted fleet, the Actian fight, and you could see all Leucate burn with drawn-up Mars (war) and the waves glitter with gold. Here, Augustus Caesar, leading the Italians into battle, with the Senatorial Fathers and the people, with the *penates*[28] and the great gods, standing on the lofty stern. His forehead darts out twin flames. And, on the crown of his head, the star[29] of his ancestors is revealed. On one part, with favorable winds and gods, is Agrippa, tall, driving the battle-line: his temples shine with a naval crown, a proud honor of war.[30] Here with foreign resources and varied weapons, Antony, the victor from peoples of the eastern Dawn and the ruddy coast of the Erythraean Sea, conveys Egypt with himself and the strengths of

28 #7.4.1A note.

29 A comet appeared after Caesar's assassination in 44 BCE, widely accepted as proof of his apotheosis as a Roman god: Vergil, *Eclogue* 9.47; Horace, *Odes* 1.12.47.

30 A military crown decorated with ships' prows, awarded first to Agrippa for his victory at Actium: Pliny, *NH* 16.8.

the East and distant Bactra,[31] and his Egyptian spouse[32] (unspeakable!) follows. All rush together, and the entire sea foams, shattered with sweeping oars and three-toothed prows. They seek the deep. You would think that the plucked-out Cyclades were swimming in the sea or that lofty mountains were clashing with mountains, in so great a mass did men press hard on the turreted sterns. Flaming tow is sprinkled from hands and flying iron from missiles. The Neptunian fields grow red with fresh slaughter. In the middle, the queen calls her battle lines with the ancestral sistrum:[33] not yet does she even glance back at the twin snakes.[34] Unnatural monsters of every shape and a barking Anubis[35] hold the sails against both Neptune and Venus and against Minerva. In the midst of the struggle, Mars rages, carved in iron, and Furies from the aether are gloomy, and Discord prances, rejoicing in her tattered dress, whom Bellona[36] follows with a bloody whip. Seeing these things, Actian Apollo stretches his bow from above. All Egypt and India, all Arabia, all the Sabaeans[37] turn their backs in terror. The queen herself seems to spread sails after the winds are called, and she already now seems to cast off the loosened lines.[38] Within the slaughter, the fire-powerful god (*Ignipotens* Vulcan) had made the queen pale owing to her imminent death, borne on the waves by a Iapyx wind.[39] Moreover, facing her, Vulcan had made the cerulean Nile, grieving in his great body and spreading out his folds and with his entire robe calling his conquered people into his lap and into his furtive currents. But Caesar (Augustus), carried into the Roman walls with a triple triumphal procession,[40] was dedicating an everlasting offering to the Italian gods, 300 very great shrines throughout the whole city. The streets were roaring with happiness and games and applause. There was a chorus of mothers in all the temples, altars in all the temples. Slaughtered bulls were strewn on the ground in front of the altars. Augustus himself, sitting in the snowy entrance of shining Phoebus Apollo's temple, examines the peoples' gifts, and he fits them to the proud doorposts.[41] In a long line the conquered peoples proceed, as varied in

31 *Erythraean Sea*: Red Sea, Persian Gulf, Indian Ocean. *Bactra*: central Asia, Iran.
32 Cleopatra, so despised by the Roman people (for seducing Marcus Antoninus and spurring him to civil war against his own people) that Vergil will not even mention her by name.
33 An Egyptian rattle with crossbars, associated with rituals in honor of Isis.
34 Cleopatra took her own life with a bite from an asp or a poisonous ointment: Strabo, *Geography* 17.1.10.
35 The Egyptian god of the dead, who protects graves and guides the deceased to the Underworld, depicted as a dog or as a man with a dog's head.
36 An armor-clad goddess of war who drives a four-horse chariot.
37 Inhabiting the southern Arabian peninsula.
38 After heavy fighting, Cleopatra set sail for Egypt with 60 of her ships. Antony soon followed.
39 Aeneas' armor was crafted by Vulcan at the request of his flirty wife, Venus (Aeneas' mother). Iapyx Winds: #3.11.11C.
40 In August, 29 BCE for victories in Dalmatia, Actium, and Alexandria.
41 Including laurel to symbolize his victory over Marc Antony and a civic crown for saving the lives of fellow Roman citizens: Augustus, *Deeds* 34.2.

language as in custom and clothing and armor. Here Mulciber[42] had molded the race of Nomads and the loose-girt Afri, here the Lelegae and the Carae and the arrow-bearing Geloni.[43] Now gentler with its waves, there flowed the Euphrates, the Morini, the limits of men, and the two-horned Rhenus, and the unconquered Dahae, and the Araxes River resenting its bridge.[44]

(Vergil, Aeneid *8.671–728; cf.* Aeneid *3.280, where the Trojans celebrate Ilian games on the shores of Actium, anticipating Augustus)*

7.4.4 Naumachia

Roman leaders also celebrated victories at sea with naumachia *(staged naval battles).*

A. *Julius Caesar included a* naumachia *in a purpose-made basin in one of the Tiber's bends in the Campus Martius for his quadruple triumph in 46 BCE (for victories over Gaul, Egypt, Pontus, and Numidia). Fearing disease from stagnant waters, the senate voted to fill in the basin after the games (Dio Cassius,* Roman History *45.17.8).*

For a naval battle, after a lake was dug out in the lesser Codeta, biremes and triremes and quadriremes, of both the Tyrian and Egyptian fleets, put on a staged show with a great number of fighters. So large a crowd of people flowed in from all sides for all the spectacles that many out-of-towners stayed either between the streets or between the roads where they pitched their tents, and the crowd in front was crushed and many were killed, and among these were two senators.

(Suetonius, Caesar *39.4; Dio Cassius,* Roman History *43.23.4; Appian,* Civil Wars *2.102; Plutarch,* Caesar *55.4)*

B. *Staging a re-enactment of the battle of Salamis, Augustus also sponsored a* naumachia, *whose basin was watered with a purpose-built aqueduct, the Aqua Alsietina (Frontinus,* Aqueducts *1.11) and (Dio Cassius,* Roman History *55.10.7–8).*

For the people I gave the spectacle of a naval battle across the Tiber, where the grove of the Caesars is now. The ground was excavated 1,800 paces in length and 1,200 paces in width, in which spectacle 300 beaked ships, triremes or

42 #3.4.1.

43 Peoples inhabiting lands beyond Roman hegemony. *Nomads*: wandering folk, including those tending their flocks in the dry fringes of Libya (northern Africa), Arabia, and Scythia. *Afri*: inhabiting "Africa." *Lelegae*: peoples inhabiting the Aegean regions before the arrival of the Greeks. *Carae*: inhabiting southwestern Anatolia on the eastern coast of the Ionian Sea. *Geloni*: a Scythian people dwelling on the Borysthenes River in the modern Ukraine.

44 In this passage Vergil includes four rivers that represent the four cardinal points (see Irby 2019): Nile (south), Euphrates (east), Rhine (west), and Aras (north). Alexander had built a bridge over the Araxes (#1.5.4) but destroyed it. Augustus later rebuilt the bridge to tame the disgruntled waterway: Servius, *ad loc.*

> biremes, but several of them smaller, fought amongst themselves; in these fleets, approximately 3,000 men fought, in addition to the rowers.
>
> *(Augustus,* Res Gestae *23; cf. Suetonius,* Augustus *43.1)*

C. *Claudius also sponsored a* naumachia *to celebrate his conquest over the Fucine Lake (#4.8D)—an almost Xerxes-like show of force over the water (#5.3.6A)—staging a battle (historical or fabricated?) between "Sicilian and Rhodian" fleets, according to Dio Cassius (*Roman History *61.33.3).*

> At nearly the same time, the mountain between the Fucine Lake and the river Liris was broken through. So that the magnificence of the work might be seen by many, a naval battle was prepared for in the very lake, as Augustus had once staged in a lagoon constructed across the Tiber, though he delivered it with lighter ships and a smaller force. Claudius armed triremes and quadriremes and 19,000 men. The edges were girt with rafts lest there might be roving avenues of escape. But, nonetheless, the surrounding space was sufficient for the force of rowing, the skills of the helmsmen, the onslaught of the ships, and the customary stuff of sea-battles. On the rafts stood maniples and squadrons of praetorian cohorts.[45] Defenses were stationed on the rafts from which catapults and stone throwers could be aimed. Roman marines in decked ships held the rest of the lake. A numberless crowd filled the shores and hills and elevations of the mountains in the manner of a theater, some from the closest towns and some from the city itself, out of a desire to see the spectacle or out of obligation to the emperor. Claudius himself, in a remarkable general's cloak, and Agrippina (his niece-wife), not far away in a golden cloak, presided. The fighting, although between criminals, occurred with the spirit of brave men, and, after much wounding, the men were exempted from massacre.
>
> *(Tacitus,* Annals *12.56; cf. Suetonius,* Claudius *21.6)*

D. *In 57 CE, Nero staged another re-enactment of the battle of Salamis, perhaps to "celebrate" his uncompleted canal project at Corinth (#5.3.5G) or to appropriate Augustan glory or conquer the watery realm through an engineering feat (#7.4.4C).*

> While commanding a spectacle in some theater, and then suddenly filling that theater with seawater so that fishes and sea monsters could swim in it, Nero sponsored a naval battle of some Persians and Athenians. After this he straightaway drained the water. . .
>
> *(Dio Cassius,* Roman History *61b.9.5; cf. Suetonius,* Nero *12)*

E. *In 81 CE, the Flavian Amphitheater was opened with a celebration lasting 100 days, featuring gladiatorial combats, beast "hunts" (resulting in the*

45 #2.2.12D§15 note.

slaughter of nearly 10,000 exotic animals), and several naumachiae *in the lake, one re-enacting a naval engagement between the "Syracusans and Athenians," a battle that, historically, the Athenians lost (413 BCE: Thucydides,* Peloponnesian War *7.21, 36–45), but was won by the Attic re-enactors: audiences may have enjoyed the suspense of men fighting for their lives, representing foreign navies (the Roman fleet was never featured in a* naumachia *and therefore could not be defeated). Titus'* naumachiae *represent the conquest of Ocean by his father, Vespasian (#7.4.5H–J), for which horses and bulls were trained to perform in the water (Dio Cassius,* Roman History 66.25*), as Martial hints here. Martial's* On the Spectacles *is a collection of 36 short epigrams commemorating Titus' inauguration of the Flavian Amphitheater. Here, Titus'* naumachiae *were more elaborate than Augustus' by far.*

> It had been a labor of Augustus' to engage the fleets here and agitate the straits with a naval trumpet. How much a part of this was our Caesar's? Thetis and Galatea[46] saw unknown wild animals in the waves. In the watery spray Triton saw seething chariots and he thought that his master's (Neptune's) horses had flowed past. While Nereus provided fierce battles for savage ships, he bristled to tread in the limpid waters. Whatever is seen in the Circus and in the Amphitheater, Caesar, wealth has brought this to bear in your water. May the Fucine Lake and the pool of terrible Nero be silent. May the generations know this *naumachia* alone.
>
> *(Martial,* On the Spectacles *34; cf. Suetonius,* Titus *7.3)*

F. *Some of the naval spectacles were fantasy shows or perhaps even early versions of synchronized swimming or lightshows at night.*

> A docile chorus of Nereids played over the entire water and painted the affable waters with a varied order. There was a threatening trident with its straight tooth, and a curved anchor: we might believe it to be an oar; we might believe it to be a boat. The star of the Laconian brothers,[47] pleasing to sailors, glittered. And broad sails swelled in a clear fold. Who came upon such skills in clear waters? Either Thetis taught these games, or she learned them.
>
> *(Martial,* On the Spectacles *30)*

7.4.5 Oceanus Domitus

*Ocean marked the limits of the Roman world, and travel to Britain—Horace's "most distant (island) of the earth" (*Odes *1.35.29–30) "which, abounding in monsters, roared around Britain" (*Odes *4.14.47–48)—meant overcoming Ocean.*

46 *Thetis*: #3.1.6; *Nereus*: #3.1.5. *Galatea* was another of Nereus' daughters.

47 The Dioscuri (#3.11.7) from Laconia, the region of Sparta.

A. *Caesar had semiotically battled Ocean during storms at sea and unfamiliar tidal activity (#1.3.6F). Here the conquest is presented as real.*

> Caesar is conveyed as victor to his fatherland, receiving his first triumph over Gaul: here was the Rhenus and the Rhodanus and captive Ocean rendered in gold.
>
> *(Florus,* Epitome of Roman History *2.13.88)*

B. *Augustus' great-grandson, Gaius Caligula (r. 37–41 CE), who had failed to obtain his own military victories, instead created them, waging war on Ocean twice. He first aimed to outstrip Xerxes' Hellespont Bridge (#5.3.6A) by bridging the Bay of Naples in 39 CE.*

> Gaius did not esteem that sort of triumph at all (for he did not think that it was anything great to drive a horse over dry land). But he set his heart on driving his chariot through the sea in some way, bridging the waters between Puteoli and Bauli. For this place, Bauli, is on the opposite coast from Puteoli, 26 *stadia* away. Some ships for the bridge were collected there, and others were built there. For the ships collected there in a very short time were not sufficient, even though all possible ships were gathered together. Because these ships were commandeered, there was a severe famine in Italy and especially at Rome. Not just some simple passageway was built as a bridge, but stopping places and resting places were built on it, so that these had flowing, potable water. When it was ready, Caligula donned Alexander's cuirass, so he said, and over it a purple-dyed silk cloak, with much gold and Indian stones,[48] and he hung a sword at his belt, and he took a shield, and he crowned himself with an oak garland. He then made sacrifices to Poseidon and some of the other gods and Envy, lest there be any slander against him, so he said. He entered the bridge from Bauli, leading a crowd, both horsemen and armed infantry. With haste, he burst into Puteoli as if against some enemy. Stopping there for a day, as if (resting) from battle, he was conveyed over the same bridge in a chariot, dressed in a gold cloak. Champion horses, worthy of the excellent victories, drew his chariot, and many things, as if spoils, followed him, including Darius, an Arsacid man, who was among those Parthians taken as hostages.[49] Caligula's friends and companions, wearing flowery clothing, followed in vehicles, then the army and the rest of the crowd, each adorned as they liked. In such a campaign and in such a victory, it was necessary that the emperor deliver a speech. He ascended a pedestal built on the

48 Pearls or coral?: #6.5.2–3.

49 Darius I (r. 522–486) was king during the Achaemenid (Persian) dynasty, followed by the Arsacid (Parthian) dynasty controlling much of the same territory. Here Caligula has symbolically also "conquered" the Achaemenid dynasty that had vexed the allied Greek *poleis* in the 5th century BCE. Caligula's Darius was the son of King Artabanus II (r. c. 10–38 CE: Josephus, *Antiquities* 18.4.5).

ships and near the center of the bridge. First, he glorified himself as an enterprising person of great works, then he commended the soldiers as industrious and running risks, but saying this in particular, that they crossed over the sea on foot, and he gave them money on account of these things. And, after this, he himself and those anchored in their boats feasted on the bridge, as if on some island, for the rest of the day and through the entire night. There was a great deal of light from that very place and also shining on them from the mountains. Since the place was a crescent, fires were shining from all sides, just as in some theater, so that they did not notice at all that there was darkness: Caligula wanted to turn the night into day as he had turned sea into land. Quite full and glutted with food and drink, he cast many of his companions into the sea from the bridge, and, sailing around in boats with rams, he sank many of the others, so that some might be killed. But many, although drunk, were saved. The reason is that the sea was very smooth and very still, both while the bridge was being built and while the other things were being done. Caligula was also puffed up over this, saying that even Poseidon feared him, but then he jeered at Darius and Xerxes, since he had bridged a much larger measure of sea than they had.

(Dio Cassius, Roman History *59.17; cf. Suetonius,* Gaius *19)*

C. *While "campaigning" in the Rhineland in 40 CE, Caligula set his sights on Britain but quickly abandoned that plan, declaring war and then victory over Ocean.*

Finally, as if about to complete the war, a battleline was drawn up on Ocean's shore and stone-throwers and siege-engines arranged, and no one knew or imagined what Caligula might do. He suddenly commanded them to collect seashells and fill their helmets and folds of their clothes, calling these things "the spoils of Ocean owed to the Capitoline and Palatine." As a token of the victory, he erected a very tall turret, from which fires glittered to guide the courses of ships during the nighttime, as on Pharos.[50] Then a bonus was promised to the soldiery, 100 *denarii* each, as if exceeding every example of generosity, he said, "Go away happily; go away rich."

(Suetonius, Gaius *46–47)*

D. *Like his nephew, Claudius lacked military experience and sought to acquire it without risking real danger. Britain was selected, but the "soldiers were violently irritated at campaigning beyond the inhabited world" (Dio Cassius,* Roman History *60.19). Nonetheless, in 43 CE, Claudius' agent Aulus Plautius was sent to Britain. The "conquest" was speedy, and Britain and Ocean symbolically emphasized*

50 #5.3.7B–F.

the reach of Claudius' authority. By the time Suetonius was writing, Britain had been "conquered" again, and glory for it went to the Flavians (see #7.4.5E).

Claudius undertook altogether one campaign, and a moderate one at that. When triumphal regalia was decreed by the Senate to him, he considered the empty honor trivial to his imperial dignity, and he wanted the honor of a justified triumph. Thus, he chose Britain as the place to obtain it: Britain had not been tested by anyone after the Divine Julius. And it was causing a disturbance because deserters[51] had not been returned. When Claudius sailed there from Ostia, he was nearly sunk twice by the violent Circius wind near Liguria and next to the Stoechades islands. Therefore, a journey by foot was made from Massalia all the way to Gesoriacum.[52] From there Claudius crossed over, and within a few days part of the island was received into surrender without any battle or blood. Claudius returned to Rome in the sixth month after he set out and celebrated a triumph with great preparation. He permitted not only provincial overseers to travel to the city to see the spectacle but even certain exiled folk. Among the enemy spoils, he fixed a naval crown to the gable of his Palatine house, next to his civic crown, as a sign of Ocean crossed and as if conquered.

(Suetonius, Claudius *17)*

E. *In 51 CE, a victory arch was erected in Claudius' honor. The inscription is greatly damaged. For Pontifex Maximus: #1.9.12G note.*

For Tiberius Claudius Caesar Augustus Germanicus, son of Drusus, Pontifex Maximus, with tribunician power for one year, consul for the 5th time, greeted as Father of his country 21 (?) times, the Senate and the Roman People (dedicate this arch) because Claudius accepted in surrender 11 kings of Britain (defeated) without any expense or loss and was the first to reduce barbarian peoples across Ocean to the authority of the Roman people.

(Barrett 1991: 12)

F. *A rare tragedy treating historical, rather than mythical events, the* Octavia *(attributed to Seneca but now considered apocryphal) focuses on the span of three days in 62 CE when Nero divorced his wife, Claudius' daughter Octavia, and married his mistress, Poppaea Sabina. Here, Octavia's woman-servant (*nutrix*) notes the*

51 According to Dio Cassius, *Roman History* 60.19, a certain Bericus, expelled from Britain during a revolution, persuaded Claudius to send troops.

52 *Circius*: the west-north-west wind. *Liguria*: the crescent shaped coastal region of northern Italy. The *Stoechades*: Îles d'Hyères, off the right angle where Gaul juts into the Mediterranean. *Massalia* (Marseille): on the Mediterranean coast to the northwest. *Gesoriacum* (Boulogne-sur-Mer): on the mainland coast of the Britannic Ocean.

contrast between Claudius' very real accomplishments—Ocean's obedience—and Nero's unplumbable degeneracy. Here, Octavia's nutrix *is speaking.*

> Whoever is amazed, thunderstruck, captured by the first flash and the fragile goodness of a deceptive court, behold he discerns a very powerful house just now overthrown by the sudden assault of lurking Fortune and the Claudian offspring[53] to whose authority the world was subjected. Free for a long time, Ocean obeyed him, Claudius, and unwillingly has received his ships. Behold he who first placed a yoke on the Britons, who covered unknown straits with such great fleets, and was safe between barbarous men and ferocious seas. He fell because of the crime of his wife.[54]
>
> *(Seneca?,* Octavia *34–44)*

G. *The anonymous author of this 1st century CE epigram emphasizes that, while the world may have been bounded by Ocean, Claudius'* imperium (*authority*) *was not.*

> Never outraged by Ausonian triumphs, stricken by your thunderbolt, Caesar, did the earth lie outstretched. But Ocean gazes back at your altars beyond itself, Ocean, which is the end of the world, but not the limit of your authority.
>
> *(Anonymous,* Latin Anthology *419)*

H. *During Claudius' invasion of Britain, Vespasian had served with distinction.*

> When Claudius was emperor, Vespasian was sent to Germany as a legionary commander, thanks to Narcissus,[55] and from there he was transferred to Britain where he came into conflict with the enemy 30 times. He reduced to surrender two very powerful races and more than 20 towns and the island Vectis (Wight), close to Britain, partly under the leadership of Aulius Plautius the governor and partly under Claudius himself. Therefore he, Vespasian, received triumphal regalia and two priesthoods in a short time.
>
> *(Suetonius,* Vespasian *4.1–2)*

I. *When his family came to power in 69 CE, Vespasian's participation in Claudius' British invasion was elevated, and the narrative was rewritten to credit Vespasian with the conquest of Britain and Ocean, extending all the way to the mysterious island of Thule (#5.1.2C). Tiberius Catius Asconius Silius Italicus (c. 26 CE–c. 100*

53 The Julio-Claudian dynasty traced its lineage through Gaius Julius Caesar and Tiberius Claudius Nero, the first husband of Augustus' wife, Livia, the father of Tiberius and Drusus, who was in turn Claudius' father and Nero's grandfather.

54 Agrippina, sister of Caligula and Germanicus, reputedly murdered her husband by poisoning his favorite dish, mushrooms, so that her son Nero could assume the throne (Suetonius, *Claudius* 44).

55 Tiberius Claudius Narcissus (d. 54 CE) was a freedman in Claudius' court, overseeing imperial correspondence, and one of the emperor's most trusted advisors.

CE) was a Roman senator and poet who composed a densely-packed 17-book epic on the Second Punic War, Punica.

> From here, the father will grant conquest over unknown Thule and will first draw battle lines against Caledonian groves, and he will restrain the Rhenus with riverbanks, and he will energetically rule Africans and, as an old man, he will tame palm-bearing Idyme (Judaea) with war.
>
> *(Silius Italicus,* Punica *3.597–600)*

J. *Another Flavian poet, Valerius Flaccus, declared that a now "opened" Ocean (*pelagi aperti*) enhances Vespasian's glory all the more, contrasting sharply with the less-than-successful initiatives of the Julio-Claudians.*

> You—whose fame for the sea opened-up was greater after the Caledonian Ocean, which had earlier despised the Phrygian Julii[56], conveyed your linen sails—rescue me from peoples and a cloudy land, sacred Father, and favor me singing the venerable deeds of ancient men.
>
> *(Valerius Flaccus,* Argonautica *1.7–12)*

K. *Tacitus even credited his non-royal (but noble) father-in-law Agricola with pacifying and Romanizing the Britons and with quelling Ocean (*victus Oceanus*) when he served as governor of Britain (77–85 CE). Bodotria is on the river Forth in northern Britain.*

> But during the summer, when he began his sixth year of office, having embraced the states situated across from Bodotria, because an uprising of all the tribes beyond was feared as well as journeys unsafe owing to a hostile army, Agricola inspected the harbors with a fleet, which, taken in first by Agricola as part of his forces, followed along striking a distinguished appearance. Both by land at the same time and by sea, the war was pushed on. And often in the same camps the infantry and cavalry and marine soldiery mingled with their supplies. And rejoicing, each one elevated their own deeds and their own downfalls, now the depths of the forests and heights of mountains, now the tribulations of storms and waves, here, the land and the enemy, here, Ocean conquered. Thus, would they compete with soldiery boasting.
>
> *(Tacitus,* Agricola *25)*

L. *Britain and Ocean would continue to remain remote and inaccessible in the Roman political imagination into the 4th century CE, when Constantine's son*

56 Julius Caesar traced his ancestry to the goddess Venus through the Trojan, and therefore Phrygian, Aeneas. In the *Aeneid,* Turnus (whom Aeneas fought for control of the area that would become Rome) calls Aeneas a half-man "Phrygian" in contempt for the reputed effeminacy of easterners who were, reputedly, effeminate silk-wearing and perfume-soaked instead of manly, warlike, courageous Romans (Vergil, *Aeneid* 12.99).

*Constans (r. 337–350 CE) made an unusual winter crossing, again conquering Ocean. Firmicus Maternus worked under Constantine and Constans, writing a comprehensive account of Roman astrology (*Eight Books of Mathesis [Astrology]*) and an attack of traditional religions and non-Christian mystery rites (*Error of Profane Religions*), dedicated to Constans and his brother Constantius.*

After the destruction of the temples, you have been conveyed to greater things by the excellence of God. Under your oars, you have conquered enemies, you have extended authority, and, so that greater glory might be added to your courage, with the order of the seasons changed and despised. In winter—a thing which has not ever been done nor will it happen—[57] you have trampled the swelling and twisting waves of Ocean under your oars. The wave of a sea nearly unknown to us quivered, and the Briton became terrified at the unhoped-for face of the emperor. What more do you want? The elements, overcome, have yielded to your manliness.

(Firmicus Maternus, Error of Profane Religions *28.6; Libanius,* Oration *18.82–83)*

57 But see #5.1.7B, #6.1.3.

PASSAGES

BIBLIOGRAPHY

Ammerman, A.J. 1990. "On the Origins of the Forum Romanum," *AJA* 94: 627–645.

Ammerman, A.J. 1998. "Environmental Archaeology in the Velabrum, Rome: Interim Report," *JRA* 11: 213–223.

André, J. 1961. *L'alimentation et la cuisine à Rome* (Paris: Les Belles Lettres).

Angelakis, A.N., Y.M. Savvakis, and G. Charalampakis. 2006. "Minoan Aqueducts: A Pioneering Technology," IWA 1st International Symposium on Water and Wastewater Technologies in Ancient Civilizations, Iraklio, Greece, 28–30 October 2006.

Angelakis, A.N., Y.M. Savvakis, and G. Charalampakis, 2007. "Aqueducts during the Minoan Era," *Water Supply* 7: 95–101.

Anonymous. 1876. "Tyrian Purple," *The Ladies' Repository* 4: 424–427.

Antoniou, G.P. 2007. "Lavatories in Ancient Greece," *Water Supply* 7: 155–164.

Antoniou, G.P., and A.N. Angelakis 2015. "Latrines and Wastewater Sanitation Technologies in Ancient Greece," in P.D. Mitchell (ed.), *Sanitation, Latrines and Intestinal Parasites in Past Populations* (London: Routledge): 41–68.

Arnaoutoglou, I. 1998. *Ancient Greek Laws: A Sourcebook* (London: Routledge).

Arnaud, P. 2005. *Les routes de la navigation antique: Itinéraires en méditerranée* (Paris: Errance).

Aubet, M.E. 1993. *Phoenicians and the West* (Cambridge: Cambridge University Press).

Barbantani, S. 2005. "Goddess of Love and Mistress of the Sea: Notes on a Hellenistic Hymn to Arsinoe-Aphrodite (P.Lit.Goodsp. 2, I-IV)," *Ancient Society* 35: 135–165.

Barrett, A.A. 1991. "Claudius' British Victory Arch in Rome," *Britannia* 22: 1–19.

Beaulieu, M.-C. 2016. *The Sea in the Greek Imagination* (Philadelphia, PA: University of Pennsylvania Press).

Beck, L. 2017. *Dioscorides: De Materia Medica*, 3rd ed. (Hildesheim: Olms).

Bekker-Nielsen, T. 2005. "The Technology and Productivity of Ancient Sea Fishing," in T. Bekker-Nielsen (ed.), *Ancient Fishing and Fish Processing in the Black Sea Region* (Aarhus: Aarhus Universitetsforlag): 83–96.

Beresford, J. 2013. *The Ancient Sailing Season* (Leiden: Brill).

Blakely, S. 2012. "Toward an Archaeology of Secrecy: Power, Paradox, and the Great Gods of Samothrace," *Archeological Papers of the American Anthropological Association* 21: 49–71.

Boardman, J. 1987. "Very Like a Whale. Classical Sea Monsters," in A.E. Farkas (ed.), *Monsters and Demons in the Ancient and Medieval Worlds. Papers Presented in Honor of Edith Porada* (Mainz: von Zaburn): 73–84.
Borca, F. 2000. "Towns and Marshes in the Ancient World," in Hope and Marshall 2000: 56–62.
Bottéro, J. 1995. "The Most Ancient Recipes of All," in J. Wilkins, D. Harvey, and M. Dobson (eds.), *Food in Antiquity* (Exeter: University of Exter Press): 248–255.
Bradford, A.S. 2019. *Cruel and Ancient Sea: A History of Naval Warfare in the Ancient World* (London: I.B. Tauris).
Broadhurst, R.J.C. 1952. *The Travels of Ibn Jubayr: Being the Chronicle of a Mediaeval Spanish Moor Concerning His Journey to the Egypt of Saladin, the Holy Cities of Arabia, Baghdad the City of the Caliphs, the Latin Kingdom of Jerusalem, and the Norman Kingdom of Sicily* (London: Cape).
Brock, A.L., L. Motta, and N. Terrenato. 2021. "On the Banks of the Tiber: Opportunity and Transformation in Early Rome," *The Journal of Roman Studies* 111: 1–30.
Broodbank C. 2013. *The Making of the Middle Sea A History of the Mediterranean from the Beginning to the Emergence of the Classical World* (London: Thames and Hudson).
Burstein, Stanley. 1996. "Ivory and Ptolemaic Exploration of the Red Sea. The Missing Factor," *Topoi. Orient-Occident* 6.2: 799–807.
Campbell, B. 2012. *Rivers and the Power of Ancient Rome. Studies in the History of Greece and Rome* (Chapel Hill, NC: University of North Carolina Press).
Carey, C., and R.A. Reid. 1985. *Demosthenes: Selected Private Speeches* (Cambridge: Cambridge University Press).
Casson, L. 1991. *Ancient Mariners: Seafarers and Sea Fighters of the Mediterranean in Ancient Times*, 2nd ed. (Princeton, NJ: Princeton University Press).
Casson, L. 1995. *Ships and Seamanship in the Ancient World* (Baltimore, MD: Johns Hopkins University Press).
Chatr Aryamontri, Deborah. 2009. "Running Water: Advances in Urban Water Supply during the Roman Empire," in C. Kosso and A. Scott (eds.), *The Nature and Function of Water, Baths, Bathing and Hygiene from Antiquity through the Renaissance* (Leiden: Brill): 319–336.
Chau Ju-Kua. 1911. *His Work on the Chinese and Arab Trade in the Twelfth and Thirteenth Centuries, Entitled Chu-fan-chï. Translated from the Chinese and Annotated by Friedrich Hirth and W.W. Rockhill* (St Petersburg, FL: Imperial Academy of Sciences).
Chiai, G.F. 2017. "Rivers and Waters Protection in the Ancient World: How Religion Can Protect the Environment," in Cordovana and Chiai 2017: 61–82.
Christaki, M., and P.T. Nastos 2018. "Springs, Fountains of Athens," *Hellenic Geographical Society* 1075.
Cole, S.G. 1984. *Theoi Megaloi: The Cult of the Great Gods at Samothrace* (Leiden: Brill).
Corvisier, J.-N. 2008. *Les Grecs et La Mer* (Paris: Les Belles Lettres).
Crawford, M. 1974. *Roman Republican Coinage* (Cambridge: Cambridge University Press).
Croon, J.H. 1952. *The Herdsmen of the Dead: Studies on Some Cults, Myths and Legends of the Ancient Greek Colonial Area* (Utrecht: de Vroede).
Croon, J.H. 1956. "Artemis Thermia and Apollo Thermios (With an Excursus on the Oetean Heracles-Cult)," *Mnemosyne* 9: 193–220.
Curtis, R.I. 1979. "The Garum Shop of Pompeii (I.12.2)," *Cronache Pompeiane* 5: 5–23.
Curtis, R.I. 1984. "A Personalized Floor Mosaic from Pompeii," *AJA* 88: 557–566.
Curtis, R.I. 2008. "Food Processing and Preparation," in J.P. Oleson (ed.), *Oxford Handbook of Engineering and Technology in the Classical World* (Oxford: Oxford University Press): 369–392.
Daiber, H. 1992. "The *Meteorology* of Theophrastus in Syriac and Arabic Translation," in Fortenbaugh and Gutas 1992: 166–293.

Daniels, M. 2021. "Heracles and Melqart," in D. Ogden (ed.), *The Oxford Handbook of Heracles* (Oxford: Oxford University Press): 464–488.
Davies, R.W. 1970. "The Roman Military Medical Service," *Saalburg-Jahrbuch* 27: 84–104.
de Souza, Ph. 1999. *Piracy in the Greco-Roman World* (Cambridge: Cambridge University Press).
de Souza, Ph. 2017. "The Athenian Maritime Empire of the Fifth Century BC," in de Souza and Arnaud 2017: 412–425.
DeSantis, M.G. 2017. *A Naval History of the Peloponnesian War: Ships, Men and Money in the War at Sea, 431–404* BC (South Yorkshire: Pen and Sword).
Dimitrova, N.M. 2008. *Theoroi and Initiates in Samothrace: The Epigraphical Evidence* (Athens: American School of Classical Studies at Athens).
Dittmeyer, L., ed. 1907. *Aristotelis De animalibus historia* (Leipzig: Teubner).
Drews, R. 1998. "Canaanites and Philistines," *Journal for the Study of the Old Testament* 81: 39–61.
Dunsch, B. 2012. "*Arte rates reguntur*: Nautical Handbooks in Antiquity?" *Studies in History and Philosophy of Science* 43: 270–283.
Dvorjetski, E. 2007. *Leisure, Pleasure and Healing: Spa Culture and Medicine in Ancient Eastern Mediterranean* (Leiden: Brill).
Dwyer, E. 1973. "Augustus and the Capricorn," *MDAI* 80: 59–67.
Eckenrode, T.R. 1975. "The Romans and Their Views on the Tides," *Rivista di cultura classica e medioevale* 17: 269–292.
Fagan, G.G. 1999. *Bathing in Public in the Roman World* (Ann Arbor, MI: University of Michigan Press).
Fagan, G.G. 2000. "Hygienic Conditions in Roman Public Baths," in G.C.M. Jansen (ed.), *Cura Auqarum in Sicilia. BABesch* Supplement 6 (Leiden: Brill): 281–287.
Ferguson, J. 1979. *Juvenal: The Satires* (New York, NY: St. Martin's Press).
Field, J.A. 1945. "The Purpose of the *Lex Iulia et Papia Poppaea*," *CJ* 40: 398–416.
Foxhall, Lin. 2007. *Olive Cultivation in Ancient Greece* (Oxford: Oxford University Press).
Frost, F.J. 1968. "Scyllias: Diving in Antiquity," *Greece and Rome* 2nd ser. 15: 180–185.
Gabba, E. 1983. "La rifondazione di Salapia," *Athenaeum* 61: 514–516.
Giannini, A., ed. 1966. *Paradoxographorum Graecorum reliquiae* (Milano: Istituto editoriale italiano).
González, F., L. Serrano, and J. Llompart. 2004. *El emporio fenicio precolonial de Huelva (ca. 900–770 a.C.)* (Madrid: Biblioteca Nueva).
Gray, G.B., and M. Cary. 1926. "The Reign of Darius," in J.B. Bury, S.A. Cook, and F.E. Adcock (eds.), *Cambridge Ancient History, Volume IV—The Persian Empire and the West* (Cambridge: Cambridge University Press): 173–228.
Green, P. 2007. *The Argonautika: Apollonios Rhodios* (Berkeley, CA: University of California Press).
Grenfell, Bernard P., and Arthur S. Hunt. 1903. *The Oxyrhyncus Papyri: Part III: Edited with Translations and Notes* (London: Egypt Exploration Fund).
Grmek, M.D. 1979. "Les ruses de guerre biologiques dans l'antiquité," *Revue des Études Grecques* 92: 141–163.
Gurval, R.A. 1995. *Actium and Augustus: The Politics and Emotions of Civil War* (Ann Arbor, MI: University of Michigan Press).
Haarhoff, J. 2009. "The Distillation of Seawater on Ships in the 17th and 18th Centuries," *Heat Transfer Engineering* 30: 237–250.
Hales, S. 1739. *Philosophical Experiments: Showing How Sea-Water May Be Made Fresh and Wholesome: And How Fresh-Water May Be Preserved Sweet* (London: W. Innys and R. Manby).
Hamilton, W. 1791. *Collection of Engravings from Ancient Vases Mostly of Pure Greek Workmanship Discovered in Sepulchres in the Kingdom of the Two Sicilies but Chiefly in the Neighbourhood of Naples During the Course of the Years MDCCLXXXIX and*

MDCCLXXXX Now in the Possession of Sir Wm. Hamilton. with Remarks on Each Vase by the Collector (Naples: J.H.W. Tischbein).

Hammond, N.G.L., and L.J. Roseman 1996. "The Construction of Xerxes' Bridge over the Hellespont," *JHS* 116: 88–107.

Harris, W.V. 2008. *Aelius Aristide between Greece, and Rome, and the Gods. Colombia Studies in the Classical Tradition* (Leiden: Brill).

Hedreen, Guy. 1991. "The Cult of Achilles in the Euxine," *JASCSA* 60: 313–330.

Hellner, N. 2006. "The Krene in Megara. The Analysis of a Thin Black Layer on the Floor Plaster," *Πρακτικά: 2nd Annual International Conference on Ancient Greek Technology* (Athens: Τεχνικό Επιμελητήριο Ελλάδας): 172–178.

Hesnard, A. 2004. "Vitruve, *De Architettura*, V, 12 et le port romain de Marseille," in A. Gallina Zevi and R. Turchetti (eds.), *Le strutture dei porti e degli approdi antichi, II Seminario ANSER, 16–17 aprile 2004, Roma-Ostia Antica* (Soveria Mannelli: Rubbettino): 175–204.

Hines, Harry M. 2000. *Lucius Annaeus Seneca: Natural Questions* (Chicago, IL: University of Chicago Press).

Hodge, A.T. 2000. "Wells," in Wikander 2000: 29–33.

Hohlfelder, R.L. (ed.) 2008. *The Maritime World of Ancient Rome: Proceedings of «The Maritime World of Ancient Rome» Conference Held at the American Academy in Rome 27–29 March 2003* (Ann Arbor, MI: University of Michigan Press).

Holton, J.R. 2014. "Demetrios Poliorketes, Son of Poseidon and Aphrodite: Cosmic and Memorial Significance in the Athenian Ithyphallic Hymn," *Mnemosyne*, Series 4, 67: 370–390.

Horden, P., and N. Purcell. 2000. *The Corrupting Sea: A Study of Mediterranean History* (Malden, MA: Wiley-Blackwell).

Ierodiakonou, Katerina. 2015. "Hellenistic Theories of Vision," in B. Holmes and K.-D. Fischer (eds.), *The Frontiers of Ancient Science. Essays in Honor of Heinrich von Staden* (Berlin: de Gruyter): 227–250.

Irby, G.L. 2019. "The Politics of Cartography: Foundlings, Founders, Swashbucklers, and Epic Shields," in Duane W. Roller (ed.), *New Directions in Ancient Geography: Proceedings of the Association of Ancient Historians* 14 (University Park: Penn State University Press): 80–102.

Irby, G.L. 2021a. *Conceptions of the Watery World in Greco-Roman Antiquity* (London: Bloomsbury).

Irby, G.L. 2021b. *Using and Conquering the Watery World in Greco-Roman Antiquity* (London: Bloomsbury).

Irby, G.L. forthcoming-a. "Pilgrimage, Healing, and Maritime Oracles: The Gallizenae of Sena, Achilles of Leuke, and Apollo," in Sandra Blakely and Amelia R. Brown (eds.), *Sailing with the Gods: Ancient Mediterranean Maritime Religions*. Studies in Ancient Mediterranean Religions 5 (Atlanta, GA: Lockwood Press).

Irby, G.L. forthcoming-b. *Pomponius Mela's* Geography of the World: *Translation and Commentary* (Liverpool: Liverpool University Press).

Irby-Massie, G.L. 2008. *"Prometheus Bound* and Contemporary Trends in Early Greek Natural Philosophy," *Greek Roman and Byzantine Studies* 48: 133–157.

Kahanov, Y. 1999. "Ma'agan-Michael Ship (Israel)," in P. Pomey and E. Rieth (eds.), *Construction navale maritime et fluviale Archaeonautica* 14: 155–160.

King, L.W. 1902. *The Seven Tablets of Creation* (London: Luzac & Co.).

Kingsley, P. 1995. *Ancient Philosophy, Mystery, and Magic: Empedocles and Pythagorean Tradition* (Oxford: Clarendon Press).

Knapp, R.C. 2011. *Invisible Romans* (Cambridge, MA: Harvard University Press).

Koerper, H., and A.L. Kolls. 1999. "The Silphium Motif Adorning Ancient Libyan Coinage: Marketing a Medicinal Plant," *Economic Botany* 53: 133–143.

Kopestonsky, Theodora. 2016. "The Greek Cult of The Nymphs at Corinth," *Hesperia* 85: 711–777.

Kowalski, J.-M. 2012. *Navigation et géographie dans l'antiquité gréco-romaine: La terre vue de la mer* (Paris: Éditions Picard).

Kunz, Keneva (trans.). 1997. *The Sagas of Icelanders* (Reykjavík: Leifur Eiriksson Pub)

Lassus, J. 1983. "L'eau courante à Antioch," in J.-P. Boucher (ed.), *Journées d'études sur les aqueducts romains: Tagung über römische Wasserversorgungungsanlagen, Lyons, 26–28 mai, 1977* (Paris: Les Belles Lettres): 207–229.

Lefèvre-Novaro, D. 2010. "Les sacrifices de poissons dans les sanctuaires grecs de l'Âge du Fer," *Kernos* 23.

Lehmann, K., and J.R. McCredie 1998. *Samothrace: A Guide to the Excavations and the Museum*, 6th ed. (Athens: American School of Classical Studies at Athens).

Lesky, A. 1947. *Thalatta: Der Weg der Griechen zum Meer* (Wien: Arno Press).

Lewis, N. 1958. *Samothrace: The Ancient Literary Sources* (New York, NY: Pantheon Books).

Lewis, S., and L. Llewellyn-Jones. 2018. *The Culture of Animals in Antiquity: A Sourcebook with Commentaries* (London: Routledge).

Lisé-Pronovost, A., F. Salomon, J.-P. Goiran, G. St-Onge, A.I.R. Herries, J.C. Montero-Serrano, D. Heslop, A.P. Roberts, V. Levchenko, A. Zawadzki, and H. Heijnis. 2019. "Dredging and Canal Gate Technologies in Portus, the Ancient Harbour of Rome, Reconstructed from Event Stratigraphy and Multi-proxy Sediment Analysis," *Quaternary International* 511: 78–93.

Longfellow, B. 2011. *Roman Imperialism and Civic Patronage: Form, Meaning, and Ideology in Monumental Fountain Complexes* (Cambridge: Cambridge University Press).

Lovén, Bjørn, and Mette Schaldemose. 2011. *The Ancient Harbours of the Piraeus: The Zea Shipsheds and Slipways, 2 vols. Monographs of the Danish Institute at Athens, 15.1–2* (Aarhus: Aarhus Universitetsforlag).

Lowe, B. 2017. "The Consumption of Salted Fish in the Roman Empire," in de Souza and Arnaud 2017: 307–318.

Malkin, I. 2003. *Myth and Territory in the Spartan Mediterranean* (Cambridge: Cambridge University Press).

Mansfield, J.M. 1985. *The Robe of Athena and the Panathenaic πέπλος* (Berkeley, CA: University of California Press).

Marlier, S. 2014. "La batellerie fluviale gallo-romaine: Le chaland Arles-Rhône 3," *Dossiers d'Archéologie* 364: 66–71.

Marlier, S., P. Poveda, and N. Ranchin. 2017. "The Arles-Rhône 3 Project (Arles, France). From the Excavation and Raising of a Gallo-Roman Barge to Its Documentation and 3D-modelling," in Jerzy Gawronski, André Van Holk, and Joost Schokkenbroek (eds.), *Ships and Maritime Landscapes: Proceedings of the Thirteenth International Symposium on Boat and Ship Archaelogy, Amsterdam 2012 (2011–2012)* (Eelde: Barkhuis): 383–389.

Marzano, A. 2013. *Harvesting the Sea: The Exploitation of Marine Resources in the Roman Mediterranean* (Oxford: Oxford University Press).

Mason, D.J.P. 2003. *Roman Britain and the Roman Navy* (Stroud, Gloucestershire: Tempus).

Mavrogiannis, T. 2013–2014. "Consequences of the Battle at Salamis in the Eastern Mediterranean and Cyprus from 478 to 449 B.C.: The « Hellenikos Polemos »," *Ostraka* 22–23: 129–168.

McGrail, S. 2001. *Boats of the World: From the Stone Age to Medieval Times* (Oxford: Oxford University Press).

McMahon, A. 2015. "Waste Management in Early Urban Southern Mesopotamia," in P.D. Mitchell (ed.), *Sanitation, Latrines and Intestinal Parasites in Past Populations* (London: Routledge): 19–40.

Meiggs, R. 1972. *The Athenian Empire* (Oxford: Oxford University Press).

Meyer, A. 2018. *Gods and Robots: Myths, Machines and Ancient Dreams of Technology* (Princeton, NJ: Princeton University Press).

Mogetta, M. 2021. *The Origins of Concrete Construction in Roman Architecture: Technology and Society in Republican Italy* (Cambridge: Cambridge University Press).

Morales Muñiz, A. 1993. "Where are the Tunas? Ancient Iberian Fishing Industries from an Archaeozoological Perspective," in A. Claxton (ed.), *Skeletons in her Cupboard: Festschrift for Juliet Cluton-Brock* (Oxford: Oxbow): 135–141.

Morhange, C., and N. Marriner. 2010. "Mind the (stratigraphic) Gap: Roman Dredging in Ancient Mediterranean Harbours," *Bollettino di Archeologia* online I 2010/Volume speciale B/B7/4.

Morhange, C., N. Marriner, and N. Carayon. 2016. "The Eco-history of Ancient Mediterranean Harbours," in T. Bekker-Nielsen and R. Gertwagen (eds.), *The Inland Seas: Towards an Ecohistory of the Mediterranean and the Black Sea* (Stuttgart: Franz Steiner): 85–106.

Morrison, S.J. 1968. *Greek-Oared Ships: 900–322 BC* (Cambridge: Cambridge University Press).

Mowery, R.L. 2011. "Theoroi and Initiates in Samothrace," *Biblica* 92: 112–122.

Nonnis, D., and C. Ricci. 2007. "Supplying the Roman Army. La *legio II Augusta* in *Britannica*: il contributo dei materiali iscritti," in E. Papi, and M. Bonifay (eds.), *Supplying Rome and the Empire: The Proceedings of an International Seminar Held at Siena-Certosa di Pontignano on May 2–4, 2004, on Rome, the Provinces, Production and Distribution, Journal of Roman Archaeology. Supplementary Series; no. 69*: 193–207.

Norman, N.J. 1983. "The Panathenaic Ship," *Archaeological News*, 12: 41–46.

Nutton, V. 2013. *Ancient Medicine*, 2nd ed. (London: Routledge).

Oerlemans, A.P.A., and L.E. Tacoma. 2014. "Three Great Killers: Infectious Diseases and Patterns of Mortality in Imperial Rome," *Ancient Society* 44: 213–241.

Oldach, D.W., R.E. Richard, E.N. Borza, and R.N. Benitz 1998. "A Mysterious Death," *New England Journal of Medicine* 338: 1764–1769.

Oleson, J.P. 1984. *Greek and Roman Mechanical Water-Lifting Devices: The History of a Technology* (Toronto: University of Toronto Press).

Oleson, J.P. (ed.). 2008. *The Oxford Handbook of Engineering and Technology in the Classical World* (Oxford: Oxford University Press).

Parke, H.W. 1977. *Festivals of the Athenians* (Ithaca, NY: Cornell University Press).

Pavolini, C. 1986. *Ostia Antica. Raymond Chevallier, Ostie Antique, Ville Et Port* (Paris: Les Belles Lettres).

Pearson, A.C. 1917. *The Fragments of Sophocles*, 3 vols. (Cambridge: Cambridge University Press).

Pitassi, M. 2011. *Roman Warships* (Rochester, NY: Boydell Press).

Pomeroy, S.B., S.M. Burstein, W. Donlan, and J.T. Roberts. 2008. *Ancient Greece: A Political, Social, and Cultural History* (Oxford: Oxford University Press).

Pomey, P. 1995. "Les épaves grecques et romaines de la place Jules Verne à Marseille," *Comptes Rendus de l'Académie des Inscriptions et Belles Lettres* 139: 459–484.

Pomey, P., and E. Rieth. 2005. *L'archéologie navale* (Paris: Errance).

Pomey, P., and A. Tchernia 1978. "Le tonnage maximum des navires de commerce romains," *Archaeonautica* 2: 233–252.

Pope, J.M., M.H. Weir, and J.B. Rose 2012. "History of Water and Health," in A.N. Angelakis, L.W. Mays, and D. Koutsoyiannis (eds.), *Evolution of the Water Supply through the Milennia* (London: IWA): 43–75.

Powell, A. 2002. "'An Island Amid the Flame': The Strategy and Imagery of Sextus Pompeius," in Powell and Welch 2002: 103–133.

Powell, A., and K. Welch (eds.). 2002. *Sextus Pompeius* (London: Classical Press of Wales).

Pulak, C. 2005. "Discovering a Royal Ship from the Age of King Tut: Uluburun, Turkey," in G.F. Bass (ed.), *Beneath the Seven Seas: Adventures with the Institute of Nautical Archaeology* (London: Thames and Hudson): 34–47.

Pulak, C. 2010. "Uluburun Shipwreck," in E. Cline (ed.), *The Oxford Handbook of the Bronze Age Aegean (ca. 3000–1000 BC)* (Oxford: Oxford University Press): 862–876.

Rance, P. 2013 "Philo of Byzantium," in R.S. Bagnall et al. (edd.), *The Encyclopedia of Ancient History* (Chichester/Malden, MA: Wiley-Blackwell): 5266–5268; revised 2020 in A. Erskine et al. (edd.).

Rees, O. 2019. *Great Naval Battles of the Ancient Greek World* (South Yorkshire: Pen and Sword).

Reynolds, J.M., and J.B. Ward-Perkins 1952. *The Inscriptions of Roman Tripolitania* (Rome: British School at Rome). Electronically enhanced and reissued by G. Bodard and C. Roueché, 2009: http://inslib.kcl.ac.uk/irt2009/.

Rickman, G.E. 1980. *The Corn Supply of Ancient Rome* (Oxford: Clarendon).

Robert, L. 1966. "Sur un décret d'Ilion et sur un papyrus concernant des cultes royaux," in A.E. Samuel (ed.), *Essays in Honor of C. Bradford Welles* (New Haven, CT: American Society of Papyrologists): 175–211.

Robinson, D., and A.I. Wilson. 2011. *Maritime Archaeology and Ancient Trade in the Mediterranean* (Oxford: Oxford Centre for Maritime Archaeology).

Rogers, D.K. 2018. *Water Culture in Roman Society* (Leiden: Brill).

Roller, D.W. 2003. *The World of Juba II and Kleopatra Selene: Royal Scholarship on Rome's African Frontier* (London: Routledge).

Roller, D.W. 2006. *Through the Pillars of Herakles: Greco-Roman Exploration of the Atlantic* (London: Routledge).

Roller, D.W. 2010. *Eratosthenes' Geography: Fragments Collected and Translated with Additional Material* (Princeton, NJ: Princeton University Press).

Roller, D.W. 2014. *The Geography of Strabo: An English Translation with Introduction and Notes* (Cambridge: Cambridge University Press).

Roller, D.W. 2018. *A Historical and Topographical Guide to the Geography of Strabo* (Cambridge: Cambridge University Press).

Roller, D.W. 2020. *Empire of the Black Sea: The Rise and Fall of the Mithridatic World* (Oxford: Oxford University Press).

Romm, J.S. 1992. *The Edges of the Earth in Ancient Thought: Geography, Exploration, and Fiction* (Princeton, NJ: Princeton University Press).

Roos, Pavo. 1996. "Strabo and the Water-Mill at Cabeira: Some Considerations," *Orom* 20: 99–102.

Rose, J.B., and Y. Masago 2007. "A Toast to our Health: Our Journey toward Safe Water," *Water Science and Technology: Water Supply* 7: 41–48.

Roseman, C.H. 1994. *Pytheas of Massalia: On the Ocean* (Chicago, IL: Ares).

Rusyaeva, Anna S. 2003. "The Temple of Achilles on the Island of Leuke in the Black Sea," *Ancient Civilizations from Scythia to Siberia* 9: 1–16.

Russell, F. 1955. *Man's Mastery of Malaria* (Oxford: Oxford University Press).

Sallares, R. 2002. *Malaria and Rome: A History of Malaria in Ancient Italy* (Oxford: Oxford University Press).

Sallares, R., A. Bouwman, and C. Anderung. 2004. "The Spread of Malaria to Southern Europe in Antiquity: New Approaches to Old Problems," *Medical History* 48: 311–328.

Sambursky, S. 1959. *Physics of the Stocis* (Princeton, NJ: Princeton University Press).

Sandbach, F.H. 1975. *The Stoics* (New York, NY: Chatto and Windus).

Schimpf, M. Thomas Ulmer, Hugh Hiller, and Alexander F Barbuto. 2023. "Toxicity From Blue Lotus (Nymphaea caerulea) After Ingestion or Inhalation: A Case Series," *Military Medicine* 188: 2689–2692.

Schneider, Pierre. 2019. "Erythraean Pearls in the Roman World: Features and Aspects of Luxury Consumption (Late Second Century BCE-Second Century CE)," in M. Cobb (ed.), *The Indian Ocean Trade in Antiquity. Political, Cultural and Economic Impacts* (London: Routledge): 135–156.

Sharples, R.W. 1992. "On Fish," in W.W. Fortenbaugh and D. Gutas (eds.), *Theophrastus: His Psychological, Doxographical, and Scientific Writings* (New Brunswick, NJ: Rutgers University Studies in Classical Humanities): 347–385.

Sharples, R.W., and D. Gutas. 1998. *Theophrastus of Eresus: Sources for his Life, Writings Thought and Influence: Commentary*, Vol. 3.1: *Sources on Physics* (Leiden: Brill).
Simpson, R. Hope. 2006. *Mycenaean Fortifications, Highways, Dams and Canals*. D.K. Hagel (Sävedalen: Paul Åströms Förlag).
Smid, T.C. 1970. "'Tsunamis' in Greek Literature," *Greece&Rome*, 2nd Ser. 17: 100–104.
Sobel, D. 2007. *Longitude: The True Story of a Lone Genius Who Solved the Greatest Scientific Problem of His Time* (London: Bloomsbury).
Spivey, N., and T. Rasmussen. 1988. "Dionisio e I pirati nel Toledo Museum of Art," *Perspettiva* 44: 2–8.
Strauss, B. 2004. *The Battle of Salamis: The Naval Encounter That Saved Greece—and Western Civilization* (New York, NY: Simon & Schuster).
Strazzulla, M.J. 1989. "In paludibus moenia constituta: problemi urbanistici di Aquileia in età repubblicana alla luce della documentazione archeologica e delle fonti scritte," *Antichità Altoadriatiche* 35: 187–225.
Swetnam-Burland, M. 2010. "'Aegyptus Redacta:' The Egyptian Obelisk in the Augustan Campus Martius," *The Art Bulletin* 92: 135–153.
Tameanko, M. 1992. "The Silphium Plant: Wonder Drug of the Ancient World Depicted on Coins," *Celator Journal of Ancient and Medieval Coinage* 6: 26–28.
Tartaron, T. 2013. *Maritime Networks in the Mycenaean World* (Cambridge: Cambridge University Press).
Testaguzza, O. 1970. *Portus: Illustrazione Dei Porti Di Claudio E Traiano E Della Città di Porto a Fiumicino* (Roma: American Academy in Rome).
Thonemann, P. 2015. *The Hellenistic World: Using Coins as Sources* (Cambridge: Cambridge University Press).
Tuck, S.L. 2019. "Was the *tempestas* of AD 62 at Ostia Actually a Tsunami?" *CJ* 114: 439–462.
Wachsmann, S. 1998. *Seagoing Ships and Seamanship in the Bronze Age Levant* (College Station, TX: Texas A&M University Press).
Wachsmann, S. 2012. "Panathenaic Ships: The Iconographic Evidence," *Hesperia* 81: 237–266.
Wachsmuth, D. 1967. *Pompimos Ho Daimōn: Untersuchung Zu Den Antiken Sakralhandlungen Bei Seereisen* (Berlin) Diss. Freie Universiẗat Berlin.
Welch, K. 2002. "Both Sides of the Coin: Sextus Pompeius and the so-called *Pompeiani*," in Powell and Welch 2002: 1–30.
Wikander, Ö. 2000. *Handbook of Ancient Water Technology* (Leiden: Brill).
Wilson, A.I. 2008. "Hydraulic Engineering and Water Supply," in Oleson 2008: 285–318.
Wilson, A.I. 2013. "The Mediterranean Environment in Ancient History: Perspectives and Prospects," in Harris 2013: 259–276.
Woodcroft, B. 1851. *The* Pneumatics *of Hero of Alexandria* (London: Taylor, Walton and Maberly).
Yébenes, S.P. 2010. "Magic at Sea: Amulets for Navigation," in R.L. Gordon and F.M. Simón (eds.), *Magical Practice in the Latin West: Papers from the International Conference Held at the University of Zaragoza, 30 September–1 October 2005* (Leiden: Brill): 457–486.

INDICES

Toponyms

Regions

Waterways

Islands

Towns, Cities, and Harbors

Mountains, Passes, and Other Landmarks

Ships, Boats, and Sailing (Including Navigation and Infrastructure)

Historical People

Gods and Mythical People

Animals

Plants

Stones

Fluids

Festivals

Wars and Battles

General Index

For Product Safety Concerns and Information please contact our EU
representative GPSR@taylorandfrancis.com
Taylor & Francis Verlag GmbH, Kaufingerstraße 24, 80331 München, Germany

www.ingramcontent.com/pod-product-compliance
Lightning Source LLC
Chambersburg PA
CBHW071730110726
47908CB00006B/1554

* 9 7 8 1 0 3 2 5 6 9 3 0 7 *